Information Technology and the Corporation of the 1990s

INFORMATION TECHNOLOGY AND THE CORPORATION OF THE 1990s

Research Studies

Edited by

THOMAS J. ALLEN

MICHAEL S. SCOTT MORTON

New York Oxford

OXFORD UNIVERSITY PRESS

1994

Oxford University Press

Oxford New York Toronto
Delhi Bombay Calcutta Madras Karachi
Kuala Lumpur Singapore Hong Kong Tokyo
Nairobi Dar es Salaam Cape Town
Melbourne Auckland Madrid

and associated companies in
Berlin Ibadan

Published by Oxford University Press, Inc.,
200 Madison Avenue, New York, New York 10016

Library of Congress Cataloging-in-Publication Data
Information technology and the corporation of the 1990s :
research studies / Thomas J. Allen and Michael S. Scott Morton, editors.
p. cm. "Intended to accompany and support its companion,
The corporation of the 1990s"—Pref.
Includes bibliographical references and index.
ISBN 0-19-506806-8
1. Management—Data processing. 2. Information technology—Management.
3. Organizational change. I. Allen, Thomas J. (Thomas John), 1931–
II. Scott Morton, Michael S.
HD30.2.I528 1993
658.4'038—dc20 91-46832

2 4 6 8 9 7 5 3 1
Printed in the United States of America
on acid-free paper

Preface

This volume is a report on research, the chapters produced as part of the five-year Management in the 1990s research program. The program was funded by a group of 12 industrial and governmental sponsors from the United States and Britain, and this book is intended to accompany and support its companion, *The Corporation of the 1990s*.

The research reports in themselves tell only a very small part of the story, however. To cope with the dynamic environment of the 1990s, management will have to be innovative and develop new products and services for rapidly changing markets in order to remain competitive. This process of innovation is a response to two sets of forces on the enterprise.

Innovation is a process that mediates between two streams of human activity (Figure P.1). Market and technology develop in parallel and independently, save for a linkage through innovation. Innovation, therefore, is a response to changes in one or both of these streams. As the market changes, firms are driven to innovate with new products and services, frequently having to seek out new technology in order to accomplish this. On the other side, rapidly changing technology creates new opportunities and sometimes even creates changes in market structure. As a consequence,

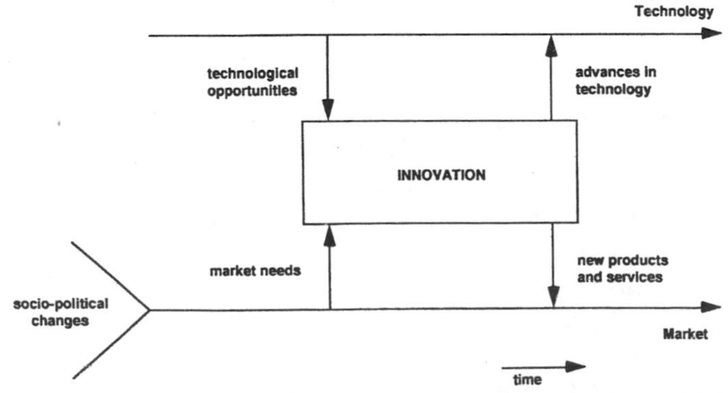

Figure P.1. Innovation as a response to changes in market and technology.

the more rapidly that either stream changes, the greater the pressure will be for firms to be innovative.

In the decade of the 1990s, it is generally agreed that both of these streams are accelerating. Markets are changing at a rate rarely before experienced. Needs and tastes are changing, and entirely new markets are opening in both established geographic areas and entirely new ones. In regard to technology, the rate of change in information technology has been estimated to be 20 to 30 percent per year. These diverse technologies, which we label *information technology,* are crucial to the organization. We are no longer talking about *data processing*, in which responsibility and impact were confined to a usually small and identifiable segment of the business. Rather, today, information technology is ubiquitous. It is integral to processes internal to the firm, to product design, to delivery of services, and to interorganizational relations. It is the lifeblood of the organization, shrinking the effects of time and distance and altering the very nature of work.

The Management in the 1990s Program, as the research program was called, was in many ways an experiment in collaboration among the university, industry, and government. We who were involved in it like to think of this program as a very successful experiment. One measure of this is the fact that several of the sponsors have decided to continue the relationship (in a somewhat different form), even though the program was designed and intended to be of limited and well-defined (five years) duration. The ultimate determinant of success will be the degree to which the ideas that were generated are found to be useful in helping organizations manage the impact of information technology. This book is intended to help in this process by directly disseminating some of these ideas, making them available to organizations for implementation but, in a more important sense, by raising issues and stimulating further thought by both academics and managers.

When we say that this was an experimental program, we mean that we tried to learn from it how to better manage collaboration and technology transfer between a university group and a set of external sponsors. Such relationships have traditionally been marked by failure and frustration. On the university side, the complaint is that the sponsors are too shortsighted and want short-term consulting rather than the longer-term, more fundamental research that the university is better able to supply. On the industry side, the complaint is that the academics are too separated from reality in their "ivory towers" and are not concerned with the real issues of implementing ideas. One of our major goals in this experiment was to address and resolve both of these issues by creating a strong joint team of researchers and sponsors to promote communication, to direct the program toward relevant, long-range issues, and to create a structure that would enable more effective implementation in at least the sponsoring organizations and, we hope, other organizations as well.

In all honesty, we must admit that at the outset we had only a very vague idea of how to do this. In fact, university–sponsor relations in the first year or two of the program were anything but smooth. Both sides needed to learn more about the other's perspective. The faculty researchers, through their direct contact with the staff of the sponsoring organizations, better understood the needs and concerns of those organizations and were able to direct their research toward addressing those needs. The sponsors (particularly the sponsor representatives) learned the ways in which universities function, in particular that universities are organized and structured in a way that is very different from the structure to which they are accustomed. The hierarchical structure of the sponsor organizations does not exist in universities. Faculty cannot be "directed." No one can order a professor to do research on a particular topic. However, a faculty member can be influenced, and to do this, one must be aware of how the academic reward system functions and the importance of external peer evaluations.

When both sides of our team recognized these issues, relationships improved substantially and an effective working team emerged. The sponsor representatives produced a major guiding document for the program, labeled the "vision document" (Alexander et al., 1985). It addressed the sponsors' concerns in both written form and by means of a two-day conference, attended by both faculty and sponsor representatives. This was followed with a more specific "request for proposals" based on the vision document. The request for proposals was sent to all interested faculty and described the research areas that the program would be interested in funding. The proposals listed the hypotheses to be tested, the research method to be used and an estimate of the required budget.

The proposals were reviewed by the sponsors and a faculty steering committee for the program. All sponsor representatives received copies of the proposals without the proposed budget. The sponsor representatives then evaluated each proposal and achieved consensus ratings by communicating through electronic mail. The faculty steering committee did the same, with the additional step of adjusting the budgets to make the total fit the amount available for the time period.

The sponsor representatives elected three of their number to meet with the faculty steering committee in what became known as the "joint steering committee." In this meeting, differences in the two sets of evaluations were discussed and usually were easily resolved. The research director for the program then matched the budget to the projects in order of their jointly ranked priority and indicated how many the budget would allow. Through mutual agreement, the director and the research director for the program were authorized to spend up to 30 percent of the budget on projects in which the sponsors did not believe but that the two directors believed would be to the sponsors' benefit. In fact, this option had to be exercised only once for a single project (much less than the 30 percent limit) during the five years of the program.

The process of joint proposal review was repeated each year during the duration of the program. But this was not the only point of contact between sponsors and researchers. Perhaps the most important contact occurred through the research and data gathering by faculty and research assistants in the sponsor organizations. In addition. there was a weekly seminar, open to the public but attended primarily by researchers and employees of the sponsor organizations, and periodic meetings organized around either a research topic or an issue of interest to one or more of the sponsors. The latter gathering was closed to the public, with the exception of invited speakers and guests from other organizations, who might provide information or knowledge bearing on the topic. Finally, there was a two-day annual meeting to review progress and make plans for the following year.

After the initial growing pains, the system worked very well. The sponsor representatives, who were from a diverse set of organizations—some industry, some government, some British, and some American—became a cohesive team and formed a strong relationship with the researchers and program managers at MIT. One indication of this was evident at the final working meeting. Before the scheduled two-day meeting with the MIT faculty, the sponsor representatives had their own meeting at which they assessed what they had gotten for their investment, what they were going to do with the research results, and how they could manage the implementation process within their respective organizations. They decided that this trading of ideas, particularly on implementation, had been an extremely valuable experience. They then presented the results of their meeting to the MIT faculty and spent the following two days discussing their strategies for implementation.

The response to the original request for proposals turned out to be far broader and more diverse than anyone had expected. Information technology is a broad set of individual technologies, and there are many ways in which these technologies affect management and organizations. Accordingly, the resulting research projects are, as we shall see, extremely diverse, in at least three ways.

First are the many subtechnologies of information technology and the many facets of management and organizational life that these technologies affect. Together these spell out a variety of research problems. Multiply this by the diversity of disciplinary backgrounds and methodological approaches to be found in a management school, and you will have a multitude of possibilities.

Our attempt, therefore, to organize the results has been difficult. Nevertheless, there has been one redeeming feature: The quality of the research is so high and the results are so interesting that they should quickly capture the attention of the concerned reader.

In accordance with the organization of the accompanying volume (Scott Morton, 1990), we grouped papers (now chapters) into three parts: Part I: The Information Technology Revolution, Part II: Strategic Options, and Part III: The Organization and Management Response. Part I deals less with the nature of the revolution in information technology and more with the real and projected implications of that revolution. Part II explores different strategies for gaining advantage through information technology, and Part III examines its impact on people and organizations and the ways in which organizations have responded to that impact.

No research program of the magnitude of the Management in the 1990s Program is possible without the combined efforts of many people. We cannot name them all, but there are a few whose special efforts must be acknowledged. First is Jack Rockart, who with Michael Scott Morton conceived of such a program and contributed to it through its five years. Then there are the sponsors, particularly those who represented their sponsor organizations. They kept us in touch with reality and steered the research toward appropriate goals. Then there is Alvin J. Silk, who as deputy dean of the Sloan School encouraged, protected, and nurtured the program in its formative period. Al deserves special mention for his patience and help. Roger Samuel and Patricia White managed the program's operation and served in that most difficult position of mediating between the sponsors and the researchers, always seeming to be able to keep both sides coordinated and reasonably happy. They also were able to stay within the budget. Roger, in particular, provided an effective counterbalance to the erratic personality of the first editor. Finally, this volume could never have come into existence without the extraordinary efforts of Pamela Spencer. She not only tolerated and covered up for the absent-minded editors, but she also put in many long hours outsmarting the information technology of the many word-processing systems in which the papers were originally embedded. To her must go a very special thank you!

Cambridge, Mass. T.J.A.
Cambridge, Mass. M.S.S.M.
March 1993

REFERENCES

Alexander, J., T. Condon, J. A. Hernon, K. H. Macdonald, J. Martens, & J. G. Sifonis (1985). Sponsors' future vision, MIT Management in the 1990s working paper no. 85-002.

Scott Morton, M. S. (Ed.) (1990). *The corporation of the 1990s: Information technology and organizational transformation*. New York: Oxford University Press.

Contents

Information Technology and the Corporation of the 1990s

PART I

THE INFORMATION TECHNOLOGY REVOLUTION

As does its companion volume, *The Corporation of the 1990s*, this book begins with an overview of the information technology revolution. In the first chapter, Charles Jonscher places these revolutionary changes into historical perspective in an intriguing economic analysis. According to Jonscher, the era into which we are now entering will see qualitative changes wrought by information technology. No longer will information technology be simply overlaid onto existing business; it will now be used to restructure the enterprise. (We made this point in the Introduction, and we will make it over and over again in this book. It is the most recurrent theme in our consideration of the impact of information technology on management.) Jonscher then argues that this restructuring is taking place between as well as within organizations. The boundary between customer and supplier is becoming difficult to define as electronic integration blurs the distinction. Within organizations, distinctions between information technology and production technology and between information workers and production workers are becoming increasingly difficult to maintain. Finally, Jonscher explains that the electronic communications system occupies the critical path. Communication by electronic means is essential to interorganizational integration and can proceed only at the pace permitted by communication technology.

Restructuring work to use the technology effectively will, in turn, lead to changes in organizational form. In the second chapter, Michael J. Piore points this out and contends that a revolution is taking place in both American managerial practice and technology. Basic structures are changing with the introduction of multiple lines of reporting, team management, parallel decision making, the integration of suppliers and vendors, and attempts to reduce in-process inventory and to introduce new forms of industrial relations. It takes little imagination to realize the role of information technology in the first four of these, beyond the so-called networked organization, to what one might call the *flexible corporation*, a new organizational form enabled by information technology. But information technology is necessary to the new industrial relations as well. We shall see this in Part III, when we examine, for example, how the interaction between the introduction of automation in plants and advances in human resource management affects worker productivity.

Information technology therefore opens up strategic options. In Chapter 3, Thomas W. Malone, JoAnne Yates, and Robert I. Benjamin look at the impact, at the industry level, of information technology on market structure and the challenges and opportunities that this presents. Such shifts in structure change competitive options, and so companies will compete on entirely new bases. The authors offer an interesting historical perspective, seeing information technology contributing in different ways to the development of both "electronic markets" and "electronic hierarchies." When information technology reduces production costs, it will favor the development of electronic hierarchies. When it reduces coordination costs, it will favor the development of electronic markets. Malone, Yates, and Benjamin believe that the second alternative will dominate, and they see the net effect of information technology as an overall shift toward the greater use of market coordination.

Chapter 4, by Gary W. Loveman, raises some fundamental and controversial issues when, operating at a macroeconomic level, he fails to find evidence of any impact of information technology on productivity. Although this may be true, a lot can be lost in an examination at this level. Any study of this scale that looks at applications of the technology must necessarily include many misapplications as well. Information technology by itself is not a magic solution to industry's problems, and the remainder of this book will be devoted to examining issues more closely and identifying the most effective strategies for applying information technology.

The identification of potentially fruitful areas for applying information technology will create an opportunity for new product development. Eric von Hippel, in Chapter 5, shows us how this can and often should involve the users of the technology, and he points to the value of identifying those customers whose needs often precede those of the general market. These *lead users*, as he labels them, are often led to innovate in order to meet their own needs, and they can therefore be a valuable source of innovative ideas for the developers of information technology. This concept goes well beyond the simplified scheme depicted in Figure P.1. There is far more than just a connection between market activities and the innovation process. In many instances, the actual locus of innovation is with the customer; in other words, the innovation process is connected to the market.

It is impossible to gain full advantage from the technological revolution unless the firm has flexibility and a culture that is open to innovation. Some organizations are just not able to change because their culture inhibits change. As Edgar H. Schein points out in Chapter 6, innovation itself can be regarded as a property of culture. He amplifies a major point that will be made in Part II and warns that if the cultural and technological conditions are not right, it will be pointless to work directly on organizational processes and structures. That is, to be truly effective, we must create a synergy between culture and the capabilities of information technology.

CHAPTER 1

An Economic Study of the Information Technology Revolution

CHARLES JONSCHER

The growing significance of information—its creation, processing, and management—in today's economies has been well documented. The sociologist Daniel Bell (1973) observed that the developed world is entering a postindustrial phase in which "what counts is not raw muscle power, or energy, but information," and economists have attempted to quantify this phenomenon.[1] Their studies show that businesses in the United States now spend more on the office-based functions of information handling than on the physical production and processing of goods, a proportion that was less than 18 percent in 1900.[2] This shift of economic resources from the traditional productive activities of industrial and agricultural workers to the information-handling functions of white-collar workers constitutes one of the major changes of this century in the structure of industrialized economies.

A related change is the adoption of information technology, which is transforming the way that business is conducted. Computers prepare invoices, issue checks, keep track of the movement of stock, and store personnel and payroll records. Word processing and personal computers are changing the patterns of office work, and the spread of information technology is affecting the efficiency and competitiveness of business, the structure of the work force, and the overall growth of economic output. This transformation in the way in which information is managed in the economy constitutes a revolution that may have economic consequences as large as those brought about by the industrial revolution (Drucker, 1968).

Many people believe that the primary driving force behind this information revolution is progress in microelectronic technology, particularly in the development of integrated circuits or "chips." Thus, the reason that computing power that used to fill a room and cost $1 million now stands on a desk and costs $5000 or that pocket calculators that used to cost $1000 now cost $10 is that society happens to have benefited from a series of spectacularly successful inventions in the field of electronics. But fewer people understand why the introduction of information technology occurred when it did or took the path that it did—why data processing came before word processing or why computers transformed the office environment before they transformed the factory environment. Because this technology-oriented view of the causes of the information revolution offers little guidance to the direction that technological developments have taken thus far, it offers little insight into the direction that they will take in the future.

ECONOMIC PRINCIPLES

An economic analysis of these technological developments must be based on a thorough understanding of the role of information in the economy. Economic theory has only recently addressed the study of information as a distinctive commodity. In 1973 Kenneth Arrow, presenting the customary lecture of the winner of the Nobel Prize in economics to the Federation of Swedish Industries, spoke on the subject of information and economic behavior. He described information as "an economically interesting category of goods which have not hitherto been afforded much attention by economic theorists" (1973, p. 8). The purpose of the address was to "indicate the importance of information as a variable affecting economic behavior and the rather diverse ways in which the economic system is affected by its scarcity and diversity" (p. 25). The theoretical literature now referred to under the heading of the "economics of information" is concerned with analyzing the consequences of imperfect or costly information in areas of economic theory in which information had previously been assumed to be perfect or costless.[3] Attention was first given to information about prices, following a seminal paper by Stiglitz (1961), and has since been extended to cover a wide range of "attributes" about which economic agents are uncertain: product quality, insurance risk and labor quality. Arrow pointed out that the phenomena of informational deficiency and diversity may have quite profound consequences for conventional economic theory (Arrow, 1973) but that a satisfactory general model of economic activity in which information needs and activities play a major part has yet to be developed.

The special characteristics of information as an economic commodity

The purpose of much of this literature is to determine how the economic attributes of information differ from those of other kinds of goods. An important attribute of information as an economic good that has been given much attention is that it cannot be depleted. This gives rise to the well-known "public good" property of information: If a piece of data is of value to many agents, then (provided that reproduction costs are low) it is in the public interest for it to be made available to all of them at a low price. But unless rights to ownership are granted that allow a higher price to be charged, there will be a loss of incentive to create knowledge. The consequences of such characteristics of knowledge as a commodity are extensively discussed in relation to the economics of research and development, copyright and patent regulations, and, more generally, the economics of intellectual property.[4]

There is, however, an additional characteristic of information that we will show to be important to understanding the changes we are seeing in the way that information is handled in the economy. This is the fact that economic information is embodied in symbols and that the value of the information is independent of the value of the symbols by which it is represented. Thus a market research study (a piece of economically valuable information), undertaken at a cost of $10,000, may be sent to its recipient in the form of a leather-bound document costing $25 or in the form of a machine-readable magnetic tape costing $5. The creation and distribution of the symbols representing the information will have certain economic characteristics (e.g., the cost of producing the document or magnetic tape, the cost of transmitting it, and the cost of storing it) which I will refer to as the *economics of symbol manipulation*. These characteristics differ greatly from medium to medium but are independent of the value of the information that the symbols represent. Thus the cost of making a hundred copies of the market research report differs greatly depending whether the chosen symbolic representation is typeface on paper or electronic encoding on tape, but it is largely unrelated to whether the cost of the market research was $10,000 or $5000.

The production of market research information has its own peculiarities, which are typical of intellectual property. We can use the term *economics of knowledge* to refer to these, to distinguish them from the economics of symbol manipulation, and the term *economics of information* to cover, somewhat ambiguously, both cases.[5]

The two features of the economics of symbol manipulation that have driven forward the information technology revolution are, first, that the variety of symbols by which economic information is represented is very small, despite the huge variety existing in the content of the information, and, second, that the physical embodiment of symbols can be changed without affecting the value of the information that they represent.

The first characteristic allows for enormous economies of scale in the production of machinery that manipulates information. A very large proportion of all economically valuable facts are created, stored, and communicated using only 26 characters and 10 digits. Therefore once a typewriter or word processor that can handle these 26 characters and 10 digits is produced, an identical machine can be used equally for recording information about a farm, an automobile factory, or a hamburger restaurant. This phenomenon has no counterpart in the economics of noninformation manipulation. For example, machinery used in farming cannot be used to manufacture automobiles or cook hamburgers. Similar economies of scale exist in handling information represented by other than alphanumeric text. For example, the human voice, an important mode of communication of business information, can be accommodated (satisfactorily) within the bandwidth of a telephone line having the internationally accepted standard bandwidth of 300 to 3400 kHz. The telecommunications networks that have been constructed across the country and the world to handle such voice messages can equally accommodate conversation on any topic from the petroleum business to clothing manufacture. Again, there is no counterpart in the realm of noninformation goods; different kinds of trucks are needed to transport petroleum and to transport clothing.

The second characteristic—the fact that the value of information is independent of the size, weight, or other physical attributes of the symbols by which it is represented—provides another dimension for exploiting economies of scale in information handling. It means that the representation of knowledge in the form of symbols is not subject to resource constraints in the conventional sense of the term *resource*, such as material, energy, and space. Provided that the economics of the creation, storage, communication, and, finally, interpretation of the symbols makes this worthwhile, the quantity of physical resources used to represent symbols can be reduced without affecting the value of the knowledge that they embody. Once more, there is no analogous phenomenon in the realm of conventional (noninformation) goods. An automobile manufactured to one-hundredth of the usual scale does not have the same value to its user as does a full-sized one, whereas market research information packed one hundred times more densely onto a magnetic tape does retain the same value.

Electronics as the technology of information processing

Electronics is almost synonymous, in today's economies, with information technology. This is what distinguishes electronics from other forms of technology, such as steam, diesel, nuclear, or electrical power machinery. In these latter systems the power levels present in the machinery are sufficiently high to enable useful physical work to be performed, work that before the Industrial Revolution would have been done manually. An electronic system is a particular case of an electrical system in which the power levels are so low that substantial physical objects cannot be manipulated—only symbols can. The power in an electronic circuit is sufficient to represent a character of information, but not to operate an elevator or turn a lathe. Insofar as it replicates human effort, electronic power performs functions requiring intellectual rather than manual labor.

A great deal could be written to clarify and perhaps qualify the statements in the preceding paragraph. There are a few cases (e.g., in the medical field) of electrical systems in which power levels are sufficiently weak to classify as electronic but are nevertheless used to have a physical effect other than the manipulation of symbols. Conversely, even an electronic—or symbol-manipulating—system may develop enough power to move a physical object such as a printer key. So long as the physical objects being manipulated have no other function than to represent symbols (as in the case of printer keys), we regard the activity as one of information handling rather than physical labor. Strictly speaking, one should regard the printer on a computer system as an electrical rather than electronic component; it is thus an item of information technology that is not electronic. Perhaps more importantly, there still exist purely symbol-manipulating systems that have no electronic or even electrical components. They are mostly either mechanical systems, in which case they are usually being replaced by electronic systems (an example is the traditional semaphore-style railroad signal) or optical systems, in which case they are still in the precommercial phase (as in the case of optical computers). In both cases they are of relatively minor economic significance. In this chapter we shall ignore all these qualifications, instead focusing on electronics as the preeminent information-processing technology of the present era.

Because of the interdependence between the cost of production and the volume of production of information technology components, an economic analysis of the information technology phenomenon must have both a demand and a supply side. The demand side must assess what it is about the development of a modern industrialized economy that has caused the information management requirements of economic agents to grow. The supply side must consider the way in which costs of information technology components vary with the volumes demanded. We shall consider these two points in the next two sections.

PHASE 1: THE GROWTH OF INFORMATION MANAGEMENT (NINETEENTH CENTURY TO CA. 1960)

The economic problem facing a society can be said to have two components: the production task, that of producing goods and services using the limited labor and material resources available, and the information-handling task, that of managing, organizing, coordinating, and developing the many individual productive activities. The information-handling activities are those of management, administration, clerical work, accounting, brokerage, advertising, banking, education, research, and other professional services. Their counterparts we term *production activities:* factory, construction, transportation, mining, and agricultural work.

Identifying the pattern of expenditures on information activities is made possible by the high degree of occupational specialization present in modern societies. We can use occupational statistics to distinguish two kinds of labor in the economy:

1. Information labor, comprising the activity of all individuals whose primary function is to create, process, and handle information.
2. Production labor, comprising the activity of all individuals whose primary function is to create, process, and handle physical goods.

The defining characteristic is the nature of the output produced by each individual (together with the capital equipment or tools associated with his or her work). If the output has value because of its information content—as in a memorandum, decision, financial document, lecture, or research report—then the activity is classified as information labor. The extent to which information is used as an input to the task is not an issue, as all tasks require some knowledge in their execution.

If a person is classified in the labor statistics as a billing clerk, we may be reasonably confident that his or her primary functions are to prepare and process bills; these are information-handling activities, and consequently the billing clerk is assigned as information labor. Conversely, if a person is classified as a sheet metal worker, his principal output is worked metal and not information; we therefore classify this as production labor. Occasionally, the billing clerk may help unload a delivery truck (production, not information handling), and the sheet metal worker may fill out time sheets (information handling, not production), but these activities are the exception rather than the rule.

A few worker types are more difficult to classify; in these cases we have to make a (sometimes rather arbitrary) choice. Foremen, for example, spend some of their time administering and some carrying out the same work as that of their subordinates. The introduction of automated factory equipment thus blurs even the conceptual distinction between information and production sector activities, and we shall address this issue later, in our discussion of Phase 3 of the information revolution. Fortunately for our purposes, the number of occupations for which classification problems of this kind arise is a small proportion of the total. The great majority, perhaps 95 percent, of the working population can be identified with confidence as fitting into a particular category.

Table 1.1 shows the historical trend in the percentage of the United States work force accounted for by information workers. In the year 1900, it was only 18 percent, but it has risen steadily throughout the century, reaching 53 percent by 1980.

This growth in the information work force constitutes what we describe as the first phase of the information revolution, namely, the transition from an economy in which most resources were expended on the production task—undertaking productive activities—to one dominated by the information-handling task—managing, coordinating, and developing these productive activities.

What do information workers do? Figure 1.1 shows a breakdown of the functions they perform. The data are based on an allocation of occupations to functions in accordance with occupational definitions published by the Bureau of Labor Statistics. The categories have been chosen to allow us to distinguish among the major functional roles performed by the information sector. A further distinction we wish to make is that between work that contributes to the long-term or capital stock of knowledge and that concerned with the coordination and management of current economic activity. Research and development, education and training, and creative professional work such as writing are the major constituents of the former category. The latter category includes such functions as management, accounting, buying, selling, and brokerage, and these cover the actions of inquiring, directing, monitoring, and recording, which accompany and organize economic production. The relative sizes of the two groups are shown on the right-hand side of Figure 1.1. It is clear that most information workers, some 80 percent, fall into the latter group, being concerned with current information management and coordination rather than contributing to the capital stock of knowledge.

Figure 1.2 provides a diagrammatic representation of the functions performed by the four-fifths of the information work force engaged in the management, coordina-

Table 1.1. Employment of production and information labor, United States, 1900–1980

Year	Number of production workers (000s)	Number of information workers (000s)	Ratio of information to production work force
1900	23,135	5,196	0.22
1910	29,170	8,121	0.25
1920	31,434	10,771	0.34
1930	34,091	14,595	0.43
1940	35,367	16,373	0.46
1950	36,970	22,029	0.60
1960	36,916	27,621	0.75
1970	41,061	38,665	0.94
1980	46,620	52,683	1.13

Source: Detailed Occupation of the Economically Active Population 1900–1970. U.S. Bureau of Census Historical Statistics Series D232–682; 1980 data from U.S. Bureau of Labor Statistics Bulletin 2175. December 1983, adjusted for consistency with definitions in 1970 data.

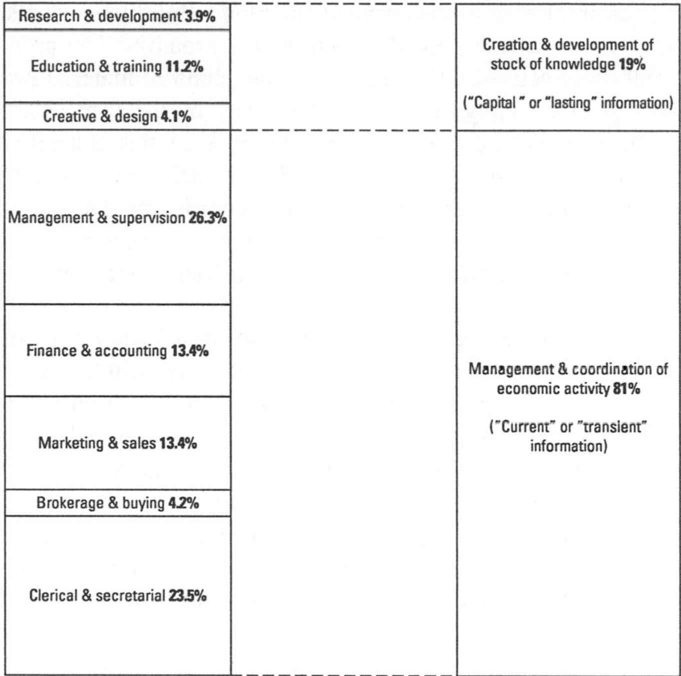

Figure 1.1. Functions performed by information workers.

tion, or organization of economic activity. The figure illustrates a chain of production involving two firms: Each firm takes as its inputs raw materials from another firm and provides outputs to the next firm in the chain. Clearly, this representation is simplified, because in reality each firm will have several major sources of input and usually more than one destination of output. Accompanying the production activity

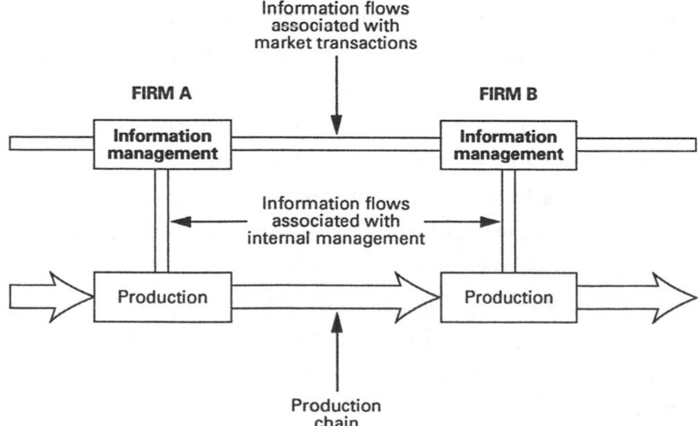

Figure 1.2. Diagrammatic representations of the information-processing activities associated with the management of the economic system. (1) For estimates of the magnitude of labor resources associated with the different elements of this diagram, see Figure 1.1 and Table 1.4. (2) This is a simplified version of a more detailed model of information management in the economy described by Jonscher (1981).

in each firm is an information management function. Both these labels, production and information management, should be interpreted broadly. The production function includes all those activities that are part of the chain of material processing and handling leading to the supply of goods and services by the firm. The information management function includes, as we have said, all activities concerned with organizing, coordinating, controlling, monitoring, or recording the production activity.

The functions of management—or organizing, coordinating, and monitoring—are by their nature information-handling functions. It is information—symbols, words, messages—that flows along the channels of communication and control in an organization. The occupations we have listed in the management sector (administrators, clerks, accountants, and the like) are primarily office based and use products and services designed for handling information: paper, pens, files, telephones, computers.

It is because some 80 percent of all information-processing activity in the economy falls into the categories represented in Figure 1.2 (as opposed to such functions as education, research, and development) that an appreciation of these information-handling requirements is fundamental to analyzing the demand for information technology. To understand why the resource needs of these organizing or managing functions are increasing, we must consider technological progress, and in particular its tendency to make the economic system more complex.

The growing complexity of economies

With the progress of technology, productive work has changed in two ways. It has tended to become, on the one hand, more specialized and, on the other, more efficient. Specialization of individual tasks, or division of labor, means that each person in a chain of production makes a smaller contribution to the creation of each of the items emerging from the chain. The tendency toward increased specialization has been apparent throughout much of history. The transition from primitive communities to the early civilizations was marked by the emergence of specialist crafts and trades. The most dramatic step in this direction took place with the coming of the Industrial Revolution. Whereas previously the division of labor had left each craftsman or tradesman still largely responsible for providing a finished product or service, the division now became minute. Adam Smith's famous description of the production of pins illustrates the extent to which specialization was being practiced in some workshops as early as the mid-eighteenth century: Some 18 individuals carried out different tasks in the chain of production. During the nineteenth and twentieth centuries, the extent of the division of labor—and hence the number of different specialized tasks performed by workers in the industrialized world—has continued to increase. The chains and networks of production have become so complex that a typical worker now makes only a tiny contribution to each of the final products with which he or she is involved.

Accompanying the increase in specialization has been an increase in efficiency. Greater efficiency can be defined as a reduction in the quantity of labor time required for the output of a good or service, including the labor time embodied in capital equipment and tools used in the production process. The reduction of this required labor time, by means of inventing more roundabout techniques of production, has been the basis of technological progress. The introduction of more roundabout and indirect techniques results in both greater specialization and increased efficiency. Productivity data confirm these efficiency trends: The quantity of real output produced by each production sector worker in the U.S. economy was 6.4 times greater in 1970 than in 1900.

If the effects of technical progress at the level of individual activities are an increase in efficiency and specialization, the consequences for the economy as a whole are an increase in output and complexity. A rise in aggregate output per worker follows, by definition, from an increase in average labor efficiency in business units. The complexity of the economic system is more difficult to measure than the output is. There is an intuitively clear sense in which the introduction of more roundabout production methods, the spread of specialization, and the greater division of labor make the economy more complex. A larger variety of inputs is required for each stage of production. The number of transactions among business units, and of internal transfers of intermediate goods and services within business units, grows. Thus this greater complexity and efficiency bring about an increase in the informational tasks of managing and coordinating the economy. As industrial technology develops, the processes of production leading to the final output of goods and services become more complex. The organizational or informational task of coordinating the diverse steps in the production chain grows as the number of transactions within and among productive units rises. Because the functions of information handling have not benefited from comparable efficiency improvements, the number of information workers must grow in response to this larger organizational task.

If this interpretation of economic progress is correct, we should observe an increase in the size of the information work force as the productivity of industrial processes rises, and this effect has indeed been observed in industrial economies.

I created a mathematical model of the interaction between productivity growth and the growth in information requirements arising from the need to coordinate or organize production. This model shows that information-handling requirements can be expected to rise with increasing productivity, but not in direct proportion to such increases. The forecast growth of information requirements is in fact equal to the square root of the growth rates in productivity—the square root law corresponding to a point midway between the extreme cases of (1) information requirements rising in direct proportion to productivity increase and (2) information requirements not responding to productivity increases at all.

Figure 1.3 illustrates the results of this modeling exercise, based on data for the United States from 1900 to 1970. The graph compares the growth of information-handling requirements, as given by the square root law, with the observed growth in the information work force. The shaded line shows the actual percentage of information labor in the work force, and the solid line measures the growth of information requirements following the productivity increases that have taken place during that period. The figure shows that the pattern of growth in the information work force, though not corresponding precisely to that implied by increasing specialization and complexity in the economy, is broadly consistent with those factors. It demonstrates that the information work force has grown in approximate proportion to the greater information requirements arising from changes in economic productivity.

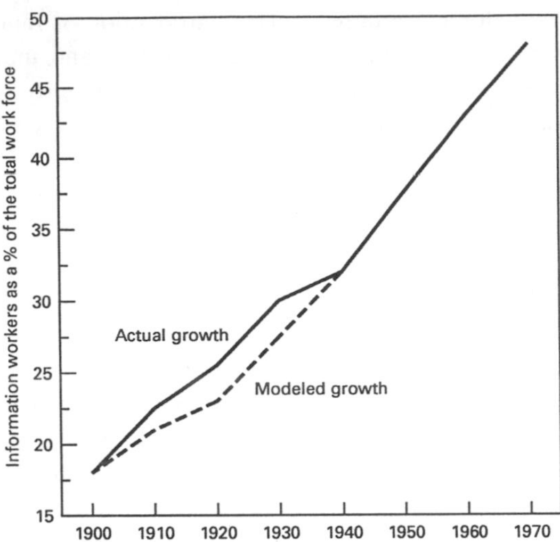

Figure 1.3. Growth of the information work force during phase 1, United States, 1900–1970.

PHASE 2: THE INTRODUCTION OF INFORMATION TECHNOLOGY (CA. 1960 TO 1990)

As the proportion of the costs of businesses accounted for by information-handling rose, so did the incentive to introduce technologies that could automate information-processing tasks. Technological developments in the production sector were having less effect on overall output as the proportions of production to information labor fell. The largest untapped opportunities for improving economic performance lay in the area of information handling. Consequently, large research and development resources began to be directed to creating technologies that process, store, transport, and manipulate information. These include computers, telecommunications systems, electronic data bases, word processors, and a wide range of other data-handling equipment.

Electronics was, as we stated earlier, the key technology adopted to achieve this automation of information-processing tasks. We cannot provide here a history of the early years of development of information-processing machines; this already has been well documented (Beniger, 1986). Among the many key milestones were the invention of the transistor in 1948 and the integrated circuit in 1959. We are concerned here, instead, with understanding not the exact timing of the initial inventions but the subsequent path of cost reduction and demand growth.

The production of electronic components is subject, like other production processes, to the experience curve effect. This is the empirically well-established fact that the unit cost of production of industrial goods tends to fall by an approximately constant factor with each doubling of the cumulative output (i.e., the output from the date when production began) of the item in question. This effect has been estimated for numerous industries, especially by the Boston Consulting Group (1968). The constant factor by which the cost of output falls with each doubling of output lies in the range of 20 to 30 percent for a wide variety of products, including those in the aerospace, automotive, chemical, and textile industries.

An excellent description of the way in which this phenomenon has affected the costs of silicon chip production is given in Noyce (1977). This shows that for a period of approximately two decades the cumulative output of integrated circuit devices increased by a factor of two in every year.[6] This remarkable growth in output—corresponding to a total increase of a thousandfold in a decade and a millionfold in the two decades studied—showed a surprising consistency, as it did not slow down appreciably in the years following this analysis. Over the same period there was a similarly steady fall in the cost per unit of performance delivered (specifically, binary memory). This drop in cost amounted to approximately 35 percent per year (compound, corrected for inflation).

Figure 1.4 shows that this 35 percent drop in annual cost can be broken down into components. On the one hand, technological progress has allowed the number of bits stored on each silicon device to be increased, from only one in 1967 to 1K (1024) in 1971 and now to 1 million or more.[7] The other source of cost decline is the conventional experience curve effect acting on the cost of producing each generation of silicon device taken separately, representing progress in the methods of manufacture.

This effect takes precedence over the importance of changing device capacity as a determinant of cost. The experience curve effect in semiconductor device manufacture accounts for about a 25 percent drop in cost per doubling of output.[8] This pattern can be confirmed by examining the slopes of the individual curves in Figure 1.4.

The contribution to the cost decline of 25 percent per doubling of output accounted for by the experience curve effect lies clearly within the range of 20 to 30 percent which categorizes most other industrial production activities. That the cost of electronic devices has fallen at the unprecedented rate of over 30 percent per annum is primarily due not to an intrinsically greater potential for cost decline but to

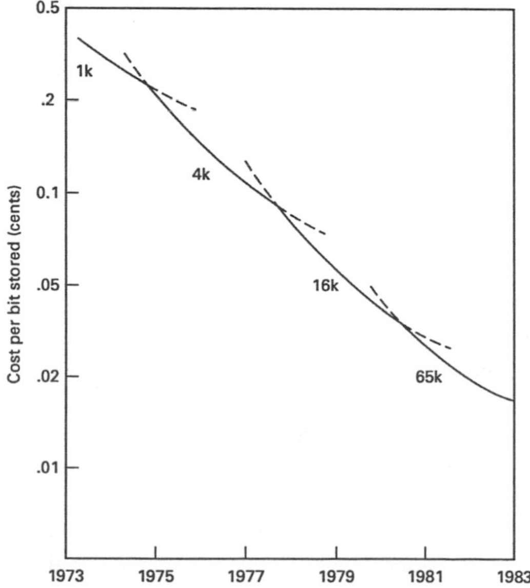

Figure 1.4. Drop in the cost of microelectronic memory devices. (Adapted from Noyce, 1977)

the very large growth in demand. The doubling of cumulative requirements each year for a period of more than two decades is unmatched in other sectors, and it is this that has driven down costs at the rates we have noted.

Expressed as an annual rate of decline, the cost curves in Figure 1.4 are much steeper than those for other industrial products. However, expressed as a fall in cost per unit of output growth, they are not appreciably different.

What, then, has caused this unprecedented growth in demand? The clue to the answer lies in our earlier analysis of the changing information-handling requirements of the economy during the period of buildup of the white-collar work force. This revealed the existence of a now very large sector of economic activity—namely, the sector of information processing—which is much more homogeneous in character than is the remainder of the economy. We noted in our earlier discussion of economic principles that information, viewed as a commodity, had certain peculiarities that made its handling unusually standardized in character. This is borne out by empirical data on information resource expenditure, which show a remarkably high degree of statistical regularity across firms, industries, and economies. After working extensively with data of this kind, one cannot help noticing how standardized are the informational activities carried out in diverse businesses. The number of billing clerks per accountant, of secretaries per administrator, of telephones per office worker—indeed, practically any measure of the pattern of expenditure on information activities—appears to be stable across industries. Office activities are information-handling activities, and there are only a few ways in which information can be handled. There are a few different ways in which it can be stored (e.g., on paper, on magnetic tape, on microfilm, or in the human memory), a few different ways by which it can be transmitted (in writing, in spoken words, in computer code), and a few different ways in which it can be processed (by hand, by electronic machines). By contrast there are countless thousands of entirely different processes carried out on noninformation goods. There is practically nothing in common between the actions of assembling furniture and mining coal; yet the office layout in the headquarters of a furniture manufacturer may be much the same as that in the headquarters of eight mining corporations.

We can think therefore of an economy as containing, at the end of Phase 1 of the three phases of development, a pool of applications ripe for automation. These applications—such as file handling, word processing, and transaction support—are relatively uniform across firms and industries, so that they offer scope for automation in huge volumes. The path of cost decline and volume growth exhibited by information-processing components in Phase 2 depends on the extent of this scope for automation.

We now turn to the second influence on cost reduction in microelectronics: the increasingly dense packing of logic elements onto individual devices. The fact that ever-larger numbers of memory cells can be accommodated on a silicon chip is a consequence of a unique characteristic of the economics of symbol manipulation noted earlier, that the physical embodiment of symbols can be reduced without affecting the value of the information they represent. Any technology developed for representing symbols, be it electronics or otherwise, can exploit this feature.

It is interesting to consider whether a technology other than electronics, if it had been adopted as an alternative basis for mechanizing information processing, could have exploited this feature as successfully. I speculate that it could. Two alternatives to electronics (electrons in wires) that have been developed as bases for symbol manipulation are optical (light in fibers) and fluidic (gas or liquid in pipes).[9] Clearly, the miniaturization of either of these on the scale achieved in integrated electronics would require the invention of very intricate mechanical production machinery. But so did and does the fabrication of microelectronic circuits. We must not underestimate the development efforts that have gone into the latter or the results that could be achieved if similar development funds and subsequent production scale were available for alternative technologies.

Why do we stress the extent to which trends in the economics of information processing can be explained by analyzing the economics of demand (by applying the principles outlined earlier) rather than by accepting that there are unique features of the technology of supply? The purpose is not to detract from the inventions that have been made in the electronics field, but to show by demystifying the role of exogenous technological inventions that relatively predictable economic forces are at play. We show now how these forces help explain the differential rates of cost decline experienced by different device categories.

We can distinguish four separate functions performed by an information technology system:

1. Processing: numerical calculations, logical operations, sorting, and related functions, almost all carried out in modern information technology systems by means of integrated circuits.
2. Memory: storage of text, data, image, or other information, usually either in integrated circuit memory or on rotating magnetic devices (disk or tape).
3. Transmission: communication of information between remote locations, using either a private telecommunications network or the services of telecommunications network operators.
4. Input/output: the interface between the information technology system and the persons (or possibly machines) using it. The most common input device is a keyboard, and the most common output is a printer or the VDU screen.

Commercial information-processing facilities such as computers, word processors, and office automation systems typically contain subsystems performing each of these functions. It is instructive to consider how the cost per unit performance of each of these functions has varied during the last two to three decades.

Figure 1.5 summarizes the results of such an analysis. We must emphasize that the data for this figure (and in the following text) are intended to be much more approximate than those presented earlier in this chapter. When referring to the typical rate of cost decline of, say, memory devices, we must bear in mind that there are numerous different memory technologies in use, each subject to different cost pressures. The same is true for each of the other functional categories under consideration. Nevertheless, I believe that the following broad generalization can be made.

Processing

Since the late 1950s, most processing in commercial computers has been carried out by semiconductor logic devices. It has been subject to declining costs partly because processing speed has increased and partly because the number of logic elements on

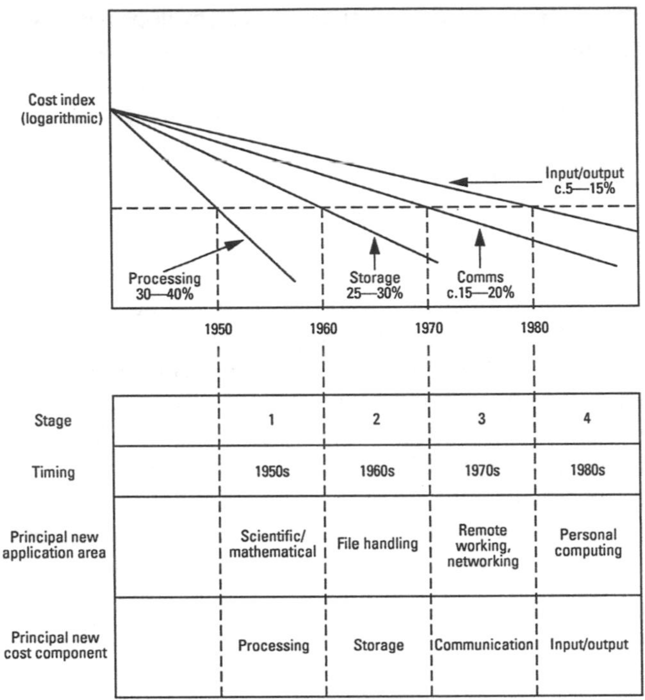

Figure 1.5. Approximate rates of cost decline for four information-handling functions and the corresponding four stages of development of information technology applications.

each device has grown. Many analyses have studied the rate of improvement in performance per-unit cost of processing components.[10] A commonly used measure that captures both these trends is one million instructions per second per dollar (MIPs/$). Estimates of the (compound) annual rate of cost decline for the period of interest in our analysis (1950–80) range from as high as 50 percent (Rudenberg, 1969) to as low as 27 percent,[11] depending on the particular commercial products used as the basis of the estimation procedure. Based on the sources we have reviewed, we conclude that a figure in the range of 30 to 40 percent per annum provides a reasonable average of the trends that have been documented in this literature.

Storage

Storage devices are, as we have noted, of two main types: semiconductor memory and magnetic memory. Semiconductor memory is embodied in integrated circuits, the cost decline characteristics of which were described in detail earlier (about 35 percent per year). The reduction of the cost per-unit performance of magnetic tape and disk devices has been slightly less sharp. Data on costs of various types of storage device have been provided by Phister (for the period 1960 to 1970), McKinsey and Company (1976 to 1986), Frost and Sullivan (1965 to 1985), and others.[12] The corresponding compound annual rates of cost decline, when adjusted to reflect constant value dollars, are 34 percent, 30 percent, and 28 percent, respectively. Adjusting slightly downward some of the figures reported to reflect overoptimistic estimates typically arising when a short time period is analyzed, we have concluded that the range of 25 percent to 30 percent represents the real rate of average cost decline reported in this category of components.

Transmission

Arriving at a representative figure for rates of cost decline in transmission systems presents even greater difficulties, owing to the wide range of communications media used. The underlying technology consists of a physical transmission medium (usually copper cable, fiber optic cable, or electromagnetic radiation), coupled with electronic devices for coding and multiplexing (interleaving) signals at each end of the link. Copper cable, still the most common transmission medium, is a relatively mature technology not exhibiting significant cost variations except in the underlying price of the metal commodity. The electronics of multiplexing, routing, and coding are subject to the same downward cost trends as are the other electronic devices we have considered. Reflecting these various changes, it has been possible for telecommunications services operators to offer data transmission services at prices that have fallen at approximately 15 to 20 percent per annum compound during the past two decades.[13] We can take this figure as representative also of the costs that private telecommunications network operators face when providing similar services internally to users within a corporation.

Input/output

The largest cost components in the category of input/output devices are printers, keyboards, and VDUs. Printers contain a combination of electromechanical and electronic devices. During the past two decades, printers have experienced a rate of cost decline estimated at approximately 10 percent per annum. The costs of keyboards, visual display units and other input/output devices have also been falling moderately during this period. The range of 5 to 15 percent is a reasonable estimate for the rates of cost decline reported in this category of devices.[14]

At the expense of repetition, we reemphasize that these cost trends, illustrated in Figure 1.5, are intended to provide only rough guides to the average cost behavior of the many different components that fall into each of the four functional categories. For our purposes the absolute magnitudes of cost decline in each of the four cases (which is clearly subject to a relatively wide margin of error) are less important than is the rank ordering of the four. On the subject of rank ordering, there would probably be little controversy. Although specialists may disagree as to whether transmission costs have been falling at, say, 15 percent or 20 percent per year on average, there is little disagreement that they have been falling more slowly than either processing or memory costs have. Similarly, it would be generally agreed that input/output devices display the slowest downward cost trend of all these functional categories.

We now consider the implications of these differential cost trends for the spread of different kinds of information technology applications in the economy. We noted earlier that there is a large body of relatively homogeneous information-handling activities taking place within the economy (relative, that is, to the heterogeneity of non-information-handling activities). These activities are potential candidates for early automation through technology.

The lower part of Figure 1.5 describes the four stages through which business applications of information systems have passed during the time since their introduction in the 1950s. We can associate each stage with one of the four decades between 1950 and 1990:

Stage 1: The 1950s. During the 1950s, computers were designed essentially for scientific and mathematical, rather than commercial, applications. They were used almost exclusively to support research, helping perform calculations that would have been cumbersome or impracticable to solve manually. The emphasis in these computers was on their processing capability, rather than on their memory, communications, and other functions that have subsequently become important. FORTRAN, ("FORmula TRANslation"), a language better suited to calculations than to file management or communications, became the most popular programming language.

Stage 2: The 1960s. The 1960s saw the introduction of computers for the purpose of automating routine information-handling functions in business organizations. They began to be used to hold payroll records, to assist in processing accounts payable and receivable, and to support stock control. We can describe this new main application of computers by the generic term *file handling*. The bulk of computer processing time was used to store, reorder, and retrieve files containing large numbers of identically structured records; the amount of processing or calculation associated with the contents of each record was generally minimal. COBOL, essentially a computer language for file handling rather than calculations, became the dominant commercial programming language.

Stage 3: The 1970s. The 1970s were the years in which remote terminal working, networking, and communications became features of business computing. In the 1960s and before, a business computer was installed both physically and electronically apart from its surrounding environment, typically in a "clean room" to which only operators (not even programmers) had access. Input and output to the machine was effected by the physical carriage of paper tapes, punch cards, magnetic tapes, disks, and computer printout into and out of this room. In the early 1970s, however, this pattern changed radically when the central computer facility became connected to numerous terminals placed throughout the business organization. Public and private data networks arose in the United States and other industrialized countries, and the electronic isolation of the mainframe computer in its clean room became a thing of the past.

Stage 4: The 1980s. The major new feature of computer use by businesses in the 1980s was clearly the personal computer. Personal computing, or the placing of processing power on the desk of each individual requiring computing services rather than in a central facility, is now such a common feature of information technology that the popular visual representation of a computer is no longer a large processing unit flanked by tape drives but, rather, a small screen and keyboard on a desk.

To what extent is there empirical evidence to support this four-stage characterization of the development of information processing and the approximate association of a new stage with each decade? A useful study seeking to test this hypothesis, following my lecture presentation of Figure 1.5, was made by Michael Epstein (1985).

Epstein analyzed the contents of issues of *Computing* magazine during the four decades under study, taking the incidence of advertisements and feature stories as the measure of the major new applications in this industry. He confirmed that each of the four major functional areas that I listed did indeed tend to dominate their respective decades. (I am grateful to Michael Epstein for this research.)

Associated with each of these major new applications is a principal new cost component in the information technology environment. These new cost components are also noted in Figure 1.5.

1. Scientific and mathematical applications (Stage l) are processing intensive; that is, they require the computer to be designed primarily to make calculations and to carry out related logical operations effectively. The earliest computers were essentially calculating devices.
2. File-handling operations (Stage 2) are storage intensive. A computer used primarily for file handling must, by definition, be equipped with extensive peripheral memory devices to store the files. In the 1960s, the purchase of bulk storage devices—tape drives, disk drives, and core memory—loomed large in commercial computer installation budgets.
3. Remote working or networking applications (Stage 3) are communications intensive. The major new cost component was communications support: The provision of networks, communications processors, and other hardware and software to facilitate remote working and interconnection.
4. With the advent of personal computing (Stage 4), the input/output devices—keyboards, screens, and printers—began to be a dominant cost of the machines. Previously, terminals had been incidental to the main cost center, namely, the computer to which the terminal was attached. Now the terminal became the computer, the necessary processing capability being added at relatively low cost.

It is interesting to observe the consistency between the major new functional areas characterizing these four stages of development, as shown in the lower half of Figure 1.5, and the four patterns of cost decline shown in the upper half. This pattern is consistent with the notion that there is in the economy a vast pool—perhaps ocean is a more appropriate analogy—of relatively homogeneous information-handling activities. These activities are potential candidates for automation through technology. With the progress of technology, the relative costs of automated versus manual execution pass a break-even level at which automation is worthwhile, at which the very rapid "virtuous circle" of growing demand and falling prices begins. We can expect the most rapidly falling cost component—namely, processing—to reach this break-even level first, followed by storage, then by communication, and finally by input/output–intensive functions. Figure 1.5 provides a diagrammatic interpretation of this process. The horizontal broken line represents the break-even level, and the falling cost curves cut across it at intervals of, roughly, one decade. I must emphasize that this feature of the diagram is intended to be purely illustrative; there is no suggestion of quantitative precision here.

We might ask why the lines in Figure 1.5 have the different relative slopes we noted. Once the threshold of cost had been reached at which automation of the corresponding function was worthwhile, why did input/output costs fall at a rate much lower than did processing costs, and the other two functions at rates intermediate between these two extremes? Following the general theme of this study, we would prefer not to have to resort to the explanation that the cost of production of input/output devices such as keyboards and monitor screens is intrinsically less susceptible to cost declines than is semiconductor logic or memory. When measured as the percentage drop in cost for each doubling of cumulative industry output, a cost decline factor in the usual range of 20 to 30 percent per doubling of output is to be expected in the case of input/output devices, too.

What makes the cost decline of keyboards or monitor screens so much less steep—say in the region of 10 percent per annum—is that neither are devices new to this phase of the information technology revolution. There was an enormous base of production experience, dating from the age of typewriters and televisions. Therefore the number of years required to achieve each doubling of cumulative industry output is much larger. The keyboards used in information systems (for terminals and personal computers) are based on electric typewriter keyboards, over 100 million of which had been produced before the advent of personal computing. The screens used in personal computers are based on cathode ray tubes in television sets, of which, again, hundreds of millions had been produced before they were required in data-processing systems. The technology of semiconductor processors is, by contrast, completely new. An increase of any given magnitude in the cumulative production output required to service data-processing requirements corresponds to an increase by the same factor in the cumulative world industry output of this technology.

Storage devices and transmission systems present intermediate cases. We noted that storage devices can be divided into two main categories. Solid-state memory (previously "magnetic core" and now semiconductor) is used for immediate access. This is technology that computing applications brought new to the world and hence, consistent with our expectations based on the experience curve concept, is subject to steep cost decreases on the order of 35 percent per annum. Rotating magnetic memory (magnetic tape and disks) are—at least in the case of tapes—based on technology that has widespread application before and outside the data-processing environment (specifically, consumer and professional audio tape machines). Correspondingly, its introduction into information technology systems has had less impact on the rate of cumulative industry output growth, and the annual cost declines observed are much lower. Magnetic tape memory is, however, only one of the major storage technologies in use; the others—disk and solid state—were newly developed for data-processing applications. Therefore storage costs, when aggregated or averaged, fall at a rate closer to that of processing than of input/output devices (see Figure 1.5).

Communications costs constitute another intermediate case, this time closer in cost decline to that of input/output devices. Communications costs in a data-processing environment are made up in large part of the costs of renting or owning communication networks. Telecommunication networks predate data-processing applications by some decades, having been built up for the purpose of voice communication. Voice communications networks were, as we shall note later, the communications infrastructure appropriate to Phase 1 of the information revolution. They were already in existence to provide a backbone, albeit not a fully satisfactory one, for network applications in information systems when the need subsequently arose during Phase 2; subsequent cost declines have therefore not been as marked as they would otherwise have been.[15]

We have not attempted to analyze quantitatively the relationship between increasing demand and falling costs of devices of the different functional categories noted in Figure 1.5, as we did in the earlier analysis of integrated circuit manufacturing. A great deal more could be done to make this discussion more precise. All we have done at this stage is to indicate that the divergent cost trends exhibited by different functions within the overall information system environment are roughly consistent with a demand-driven explanation, rather than one that falls back on the idea that there are differences in intrinsic susceptibility to cost reductions.

In summary, the pattern of cost decline in information technology devices during Phase 2 can be attributed to a combination of demand growth and price reductions: Increases in demand lead to reductions in price due to the experience curve effect, and the reduction in price then leads to further increases in demand due to the usual downward sloping demand curve. This "volume–price loop" in the economics of technology is illustrated schematically in Figure 1.6.

The arrow on the right shows the linkage from demand growth to price reduction, and the graph adjacent to that arrow illustrates the experience curve that gives rise to that linkage. The slope of a typical experience curve for information technology devices is shown on that graph. The arrow on the left represents the linkage from price reductions to demand increases, and the graph adjacent to that arrow illustrates the downward sloping demand curve that gives rise to that linkage. The slope of the curve marked on that graph corresponds to the data on overall demand for semiconductor devices quoted earlier: Price falls of 35 percent per annum have been associated, for a period of some two decades, with quantity increases of 100 percent per annum, yielding a (logarithmic) downward slope or demand elasticity in the region of 0.6 to 0.7.

We have illustrated how this volume–price loop has characterized the trends in cost and demand for information technology devices during Phase 2. In fact, the same phenomenon can be shown to have affected technological developments before the emergence of information technology (i.e., during Phase 1) and will almost certainly influence the path of technical progress in the phase to come. We conclude this study by applying the lessons learned from Phases 1 and 2 to predict some of the trends that are likely to emerge in Phase 3.

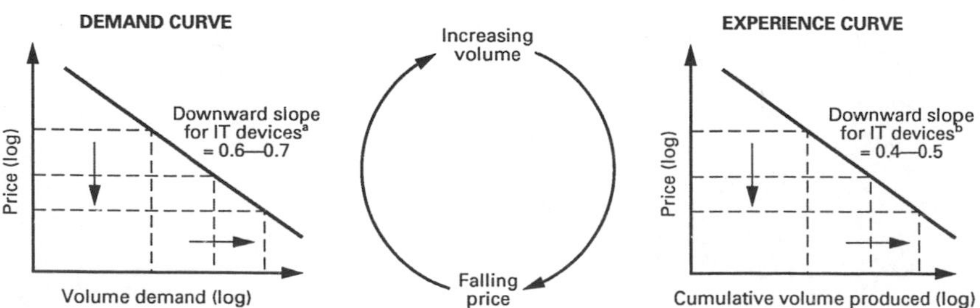

Figure 1.6. The "volume–price" loop in the adoption of information technology. *corresponds to approximately a 35 percent drop in price for each doubling of volume demanded. [b]Corresponds approximately to a 25 to 30 percent drop in price for each doubling of volume produced.

THE TRANSITION TO PHASE 3 (CA. 1990)

There is a widely felt sense that the adoption of information technology in advanced societies, though already into its third or fourth decade, is only now beginning to have genuinely revolutionary consequences. This perception is shared by writers from various disciplines (Piore & Sabel, 1984; Strassman, 1985; Toffler, 1980) and by policymakers in many industrialized countries.[16] In the 1960s and 1970s, computers and related devices were largely used to streamline operations in individual businesses. They had relatively little effect on production within firms or on competition among firms. But by the 1980s this had begun to change. Information systems were moving into areas beyond the individual business office. Telecommunications networks were linking offices to factories and customers to suppliers. Industries that were particularly dependent on information flows, such as banking and finance, began to rely on information technology for many aspects of their operation. Other industries, such as manufacturing, were starting to undergo similar changes as computer technology entered the factory. The retail sector became increasingly automated as checkout desks were linked into computerized stock control systems.

This latest set of changes represents a transition to a new phase, which we call Phase 3. It is more difficult to define and measure than the previous two phases were. Before describing it, we shall review the forces that led to the previous two phases and show how in an advanced industrial economy such as that of the United States, the preconditions for a new stage in this process are now in place. The timing of the three phases is illustrated in Figure 1.7, which may be used as a reference.

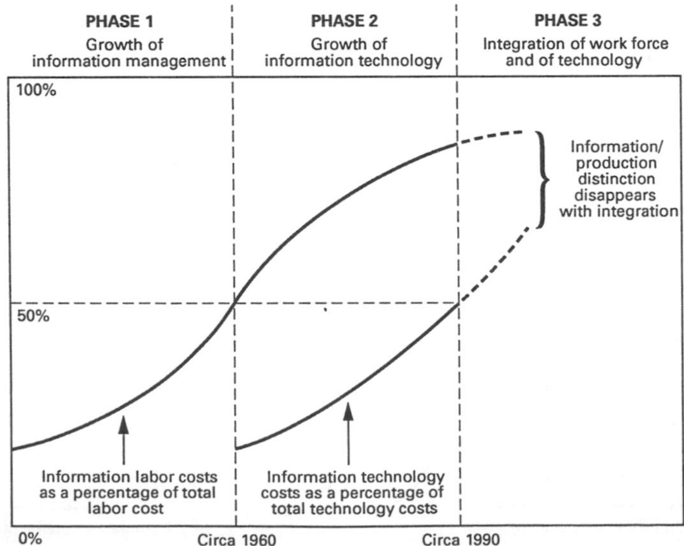

Figure 1.7. The three phases of the information revolution. For data on information labor and technology, see Tables 1.1 and 1.2. All data refers to U.S. private business enterprise.

Phase 1 was the era of development of production technologies, coupled with a buildup of information management requirements in the economy. This resulted in the employment of more information workers, as shown in Figure 1.7.

Although we defined this phase by the increasing reliance on information workers, the main technological developments in this era were in the field of production technology, not information technology. This was to be expected. Because labor costs account for the overwhelming majority of all costs in the economy (salaries and wages make up some 75 percent of the gross natural product), the rising curve in Figure 1.7 provides a good estimate of the relative magnitude of resources spent on the two aspects of the economic problem that we identified earlier: the production task and the information-handling task. The Industrial Revolution came at a time when the production task was a major one and production efficiency was the chief determinant of economic progress. Consequently, the energies of inventors and the resources of industrialists were directed toward improving the throughput of production activities. New machines in factories processed and produced goods more efficiently, and rail and road infrastructures were created to transport and deliver the goods more quickly and cheaply. Effective management, organization, and the handling of information were relatively less urgent problems.

Thus, Phase 1 saw the emergence of the "volume–price" loop illustrated in Figure 1.6: a series of virtuous circles of falling technology costs and rising technology demand. In Europe and the United States this process began in the late eighteenth and early nineteenth centuries, with the development of mass markets and the creation of the institutions of capitalism, especially the joint stock corporation, which made practical the raising of the finance necessary for large-scale production.

The virtuous circle operates as follows: In response to economic incentives created by conditions of demand, resources are devoted to developing technologies that reduce the cost of some productive activity. The products of those industries that were subject to technological innovation—initially the textile industry and then countless others—fall in price. This stimulates demands for the products and hence for the machinery to produce it. Increases in the volume of production of the technology leads to lower technology costs, because of the experience curve effect. Falling technology costs lead to cheaper products, hence greater demand, and so the cycle begins again.

As we note in Figure 1.6, this volume–price loop is driven by two analytic relationships: the downward sloping demand curve, which links falling prices and increasing demand, and the negative slope of the experience curve, which links increasing supply quantity and falling prices. Both of these have been well documented in many product markets. Although we shall not provide any quantitative analysis of either of these phenomena as they affected production technologies during Phase 1, we did note that their overall effect was to cause an increase by a factor of more than six in the labor productivity of the production sector in the United States during this century.

Our discussion of Phase 1 earlier in this chapter described how this increase in productivity gave rise to the necessary preconditions for the transition to Phase 2. Figure 1.7 illustrates that by about 1960 the information-handling burden in the United States had grown to the point that it was consuming about half of all economic resources. The curve beginning at the left end of the diagram indicates how the relative proportions of labor costs spent on information-handling versus production activities had changed during Phase 1. The position of this line can be derived from the data in Table 1.1 on the number of workers in the information and production categories, subject to an adjustment to reflect the higher average pay of information workers.[17] By 1960 the percentage of the work force represented by information labor amounted to 43 percent and the corresponding proportion of labor costs was now at least 50 percent, as shown in Table 1.1.

Thus Phase 2 began in the mid-twentieth century. It was a new cycle in the volume–price loop, and this time it was information technology that was the driving force. With mounting information labor costs providing the economic incentive, large research and development resources were redirected from creating production technologies to processing, storing, transporting, and manipulating information. These investments resulted in dramatic improvements, as described earlier, in the availability, cost, and performance of technology to support information management. As Porter and Millar observed, "The cost of computer power relative to the cost of manual information processing is at least 8,000 times less expensive than the cost 30 years ago. Between 1958 and 1980 the time for one electronic operation fell by a factor of 80 million" (Porter & Millar, 1985, p. 152).

As with the production technologies in Phase 1, declining costs created a substantial increase in demand. This consequent rise in demand for information technology by U.S. business is indicated by the second curve in Figure 1.7, which shows the rise of information technology costs as a percentage of total technology expenditures during Phase 2. (The relevant data are presented in Table 1.2.) Thus, the period since the late 1950s has seen the introduction on a massive scale of machines for processing, storing, and communicating information. These machines include computers, telecommunications systems, mechanical and electronic file-handling systems, duplicating machines, word processors, and a wide range of other office equipment.

Phase 1, beginning in the nineteenth century and lasting until just after the halfway mark of this century, was the era of mass production. The critical technology was production machinery, which greatly increased the scale of output of industrial enterprises, leading to growth in the average firm size and to the emergence of large clerical bureaucracies to handle the paperwork within these firms. Phase 2, beginning in the 1950s and lasting until approximately the end of the 1980s, saw the introduction of information technology. Mass production continued but was accompanied by computerization of the office functions in organizations. Information technology led to the mass handling of transactions, marketing, and internal organizational control. During this period the average firm size remained relatively stable. The main driving forces and manifestations of Phases 1 and 2 are summarized in Table 1.3.

The United States economy recently reached the point that expenditure on information technology exceeds that on traditional industrial or production technologies. The fact that business enterprises now spend as much on the equipment that supports the manipulation of business information as on the machinery and equipment on which it has depended for the last century and more for all aspects of industrial production is striking evidence of the central role now played by information processing in the economic system.

We may ask why Phase 2 progressed as rapidly as it did, requiring only some 30

Table 1.2. Expenditure on production technology and information technology, United States, 1965–1985

Year	Expenditure on production technology (1985 U.S. $/m)	Expenditure on information technology (1985 U.S. $/m)	Ratio of information to production technology expenditure
1965	60,355	18,795	0.31
1966	66,955	22,529	0.34
1967	66,539	23,062	0.35
1968	62,157	23,219	0.37
1969	63,808	27,340	0.43
1970	63,449	28,568	0.45
1971	58,657	27,212	0.46
1972	62,993	26,778	0.43
1973	69,741	29,953	0.43
1974	74,523	31,321	0.42
1975	68,613	27,434	0.40
1976	77,258	32,311	0.42
1977	87,858	31,241	0.42
1978	98,290	42,863	0.44
1979	100,576	47,858	0.48
1980	96,725	52,053	0.54
1981	98,333	55,720	0.57
1982	81,080	56,791	0.70
1983	77,221	61,456	0.80

Data refer to expenditure by U.S. business enterprises, adjusted by GDP price deflator.

Production technology category includes: engines and turbines; agricultural machinery except tractors; construction machinery; mining and oil field machinery; metal working machinery; special industry n.e.c: general industrial, including materials handling, equipment; service industry machines; electrical transmissions, distribution, and industrial apparatus; other electrical equipment.

Information technology category includes office computing and accounting machinery; communications equipment.

Source: Survey of Current Business, various issues.

Table 1.3. The three phases of the information revolution

Phase	Measures and timing	Driving technology	Manifestations
1. Growth of information management	Ratio of information labor to production labor costs Passed 1:1 circa 1960 (U.S.A.)	Production machinery (stand alone)	Mass production Growth of large clerical bureaucracies Growing average firm size
2. Growth of information technology	Ratio of information technology to production technology costs Passed 1:1 circa 1990 (U.S.A.)	Information systems (stand alone)	Mass production and mass marketing Automation of large clerical bureaucracies Stable firm size
3. Integration	—	Integrated networked information production systems	Programmed production Electronic markets Falling average firm size

years to reach the point at which we are now, whereas the transformation of production technologies characterizing Phase 1 took a century or more. The answer lies in our earlier description of the homogeneity of information-handling processes in the economy, which contrasts with the heterogeneity of their counterparts in the production sectors. The speed with which the virtuous economic loop acts on technology costs depends on the volume of applications to which a given technological development can be applied. Because in Phase 2 the application of information technology was restricted to office environments, rather than factories or other non-information-handling situations, a large demand for the technology was ensured. The pool of functions carried out by office workers was much larger than that awaiting automation during Phase 1.

Now that both production and information technologies have experienced, as stand-alone technologies, the benefit of this virtuous economic circle, the conditions are right for the emergence of Phase 3. We call this the phase of integration. Like the previous two phases, it is characterized by the development of new technological capabilities, to combine information technology with the production and distribution of goods and services. In Phase 3 the traditional distinction between production and information-handling tasks is reversed.

At least three factors combine to create economic incentives for integration. First, the potential for cost reduction in the office is declining as the automation of stand-alone information-handling tasks matures. Cost savings must come from new applications of the technology. Second, as the cost of information technology continues to drop, new and more complex applications requiring integration become feasible. Finally, improvements in the technology have made the bundling of information in products and services a critical strategic objective in many industries (Porter & Millar, 1985).

These incentives are encouraging the development of certain new technological capabilities in the areas of networking, standard interfaces, and telecommunications infrastructures. All of these technological developments are essential to integration.

And although they are costly to use at first, reductions in cost follow as experience increases, which further increases demand and opens up new opportunities for the use of integrating technologies. The history of technology development indicates there will be a relatively rapid drop in the cost of computers manufactured with standardized interfaces—hence the desirability of standardization initiatives such as open systems interconnection (OSI).

The process of integration has two dimensions: the integration of information technology with production technology, linking the office and the factory, and the integration of transactions internal to a business with those external to the business.

Integrating office and factory

During Phase 2, information technology was used almost exclusively to support information rather than production labor. In other words, computers and telecommunications equipment were used by office workers rather than factory workers. Why did clerical automation precede factory automation, and why are we now ready for the latter? We can gain some insights into these questions by inspecting the trends in Figure 1.7. The development of low-cost computing technology was driven by the presence of a vast untapped demand for information-processing machinery to perform homogeneous tasks common to all office environments. That is, the rise of information technology (Phase 2) would not have occurred without growth in information labor (Phase 1). Now that the huge volume of general-purpose office applications (e.g., data, word processing, and file handling) has brought the costs of information-processing devices to sufficiently low levels, these devices can be applied to the less uniform—and more heterogeneous—applications on the production side of the economy.

The 1960s and 1970s were characterized by the automation of clerical tasks. Electronic automation of the factory began in the 1980s and will be a feature of the 1990s and beyond. Figure 1.8 illustrates the changing relationship between information management and production as the technology evolved. In Phase 1, the information management functions within firms began to grow, and they became separate from production activities but were not yet subject to mediation by technology. In Phase 2, information technology permeated the information management functions within individual businesses, but they did not cross the boundary between the firm's management and production activities. In Phase 3, the integration phase, information technology will permeate the linkages between the different boxes in Figure 1.8. In his book *Manufacturing for Competitive Advantage*, Gunn summarized this situation: "Generally, we hear about the factory of the future or the office of the future as if there is a great wall between them. . . . Aren't we really talking about the business of the future? . . . The task that lies before us in manufacturing is only a small part of

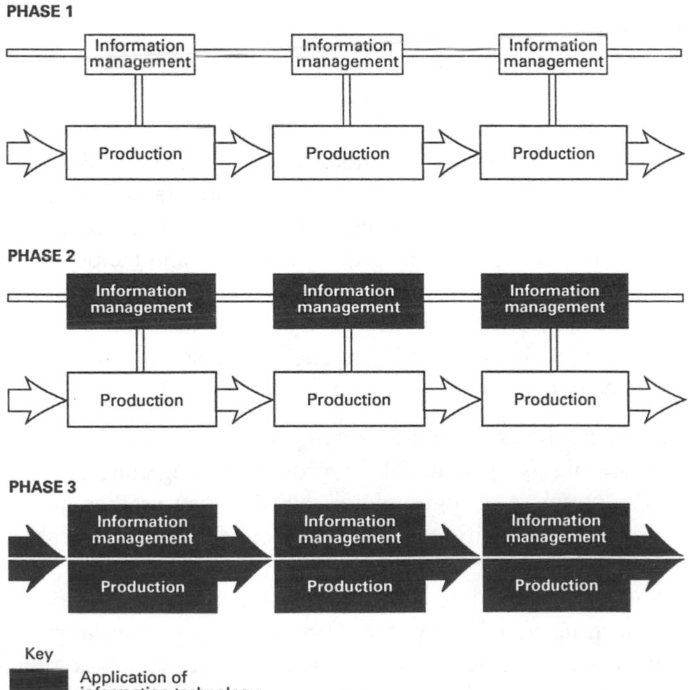

Figure 1.8. The pattern of adoption of information technology, Phases 1, 2, and 3.

the far larger evolution (or revolution!) of computer-integrated business" (Gunn, 1987, pp. 207, 213).

The integration of factory and office functions has two major strategic implications. First, it makes possible the transition from traditional mass manufacturing to what might be termed *programmed production*. Other terms that have been used to describe this phenomenon are *flexible specialization*, *customized automated production*, and *postindustrial manufacturing* (see Ferdows & Skinner, 1987; Jaikumar, 1986; Piore & Sabel, 1984; Reich, 1984; Toffler, 1980).

In this new mode of production, manufacturing continues to be highly automated, as it was under mass production techniques, but the reprogrammability of machine tools or robots allows the tailoring of product or services to individual user's requirements. Customizing an individual product or service more precisely to the needs of a given buyer presents new opportunities for achieving competitive advantage. One example of this new mode of operation can be found in the semiconductor industry, in which programmed production has emerged as an important strategic concept. In another case, BMW installed a "smart" manufacturing system that allows it to build cars, on a normal assembly line, with their own tailored gearboxes, transmission systems, and interiors (Porter & Millar, 1985, p.156).

The second strategic implication of office/factory integration is that it will become increasingly difficult in Phase 3 to distinguish between information and production technologies, and it will not be practical to distinguish between information and factory labor. This trend is suggested in Figure 1.7: Because of the nature of the integration taking place, it will no longer be meaningful to measure information technology as a proportion of total technology, or information labor as a proportion of total labor. This traditional distinction between white-collar and blue-collar workers has already begun to break down. Should an operator in a largely automated factory be classified as a computer programmer (information worker—white collar) or as a machine operator (production worker—blue collar)? Is a robot an item of information technology or production technology (see Thomas, 1987; Zuboff, 1988)?

The evolution of programmed production is inevitable because of economic forces driving technological developments and changes in the structure of business. But there already is evidence that integrating the office and factory and moving from high-volume assembly line production to lower-volume customized production will be a painful process, as different industries and countries adopt the technology at an uneven rate. Reich looked at the U.S. situation and made it clear that moving to this process will not be easy:

> Flexible system processes cannot be simply grafted onto business organizations that are highly specialized for producing long runs of standardized goods. The premises of high-volume, standardized production—the once-potent formula of scientific management—are simply inapplicable to flexible system production.
>
> . . . Some U.S. firms are adopting flexible system production, but they are very much in the minority, far short of the proportion required for any kind of truly national adjustment. . . . Flexible production is so fundamentally different from standardized production that the transition requires a basic restructuring of business, labor, and government; any reorganization of this

> magnitude threatens vested economic interests and challenges established values and is thus bound to be resisted. . . . As we shall see, the transition also requires a massive change in the skills of American labor, requiring investments in human capital beyond the capital of any individual firm. (Reich, 1984, pp. 133–34)

Gunn also noted the human obstacles in the path of such change:

> While it is literally and technically true that no one can buy or has a complete CIM [computer-integrated manufacturing] or world-class manufacturing system, it is possible to get 80 to 90 per cent of the way there with the technology available today. Yet, most companies haven't gotten even 25 per cent of the way. . . . Time and again, the major impediment to implementation . . . is people: their lack of knowledge, their resistance to change, or simply their lack of ability to quickly absorb the vast multitude of new technologies, philosophies, ideas, and practices that have come about in manufacturing over the last five to ten years. (Gunn, 1987, p. 153)

Despite these difficulties, there are clear signs of progress in the transition from automated offices to integrated automated businesses. The obstacles we noted must not be underestimated, but their effect will be to slow down rather than to block the transitions predicted here.

Integrating across organizational boundaries

In addition to the integration of office and factory technologies, the other dimension of integration that characterizes Phase 3 is the extension of information systems beyond organizational boundaries. During Phase 2, information technology was applied almost exclusively to automating activities internal to a business. Computers and telecommunications networks were used to automate the internal generation of invoices, checks, and other financial records and the internal control of inventory or stock movements. Once prepared, information records usually were transferred between a business and its suppliers and customers by traditional manual means such as the mail. Direct linkages among the computer facilities of different organizations—which allows full automation of a transaction between two parties—have been rare. Although extensive networks link the data-processing centers within large organizations, often the only electronic connection between businesses has been the telephone service.

The fastest-growing segment of interorganizational networking is in the area of electronic data interchange (EDI), the computer-to-computer exchange of formatted business documents such as purchase orders, invoices, and bills of lading. In the late 1980s, EDI became a major factor in customer–supplier relationships in the transportation, grocery, and automotive industries, and it is rapidly taking hold in other fields such as chemicals, electronics, financial services, and government (see Benjamin, De Long, & Scott Morton, 1988; Edwards, 1987).

The transportation industry was the first to adopt the EDI concept as a way of coordinating its business. Today more than 80 percent of railroad bills of lading are sent electronically. An industrywide network allows the exchange of invoices, purchase orders, freight claim information, and so forth. The system improves fleet management and scheduling by enabling companies to know the exact location of their rail cars every day.

The grocery industry has probably benefited most from interorganizational electronic links. Today about 25 percent of all transactions among manufacturers, distributors, and retailers are handled by EDI. For example, one large grocery wholesaler reduced its inventory costs by $2 million annually, using the electronic network to order products closer to when they are actually needed. The wholesaler also estimates savings of more than $100,000 a year on the processing of purchase orders (Edwards, 1987; Rochester, 1988).

Major U.S. auto manufacturers now use EDI to exchange information on production schedules and to ship notices to hundreds of suppliers. These networks help support just-in-time inventory management systems, which dramatically reduce inventory costs by closely coordinating the suppliers' deliveries with the manufacturers' production schedules. The automakers have also begun requiring—not requesting—that their suppliers accept electronic invoices. Auto manufacturers in Europe are also now establishing electronic links to suppliers, customs authorities, and transportation carriers to speed information flows and reduce the overhead of paperwork. IBM planned for EDI links to its 12,000 largest suppliers by 1991 by developing external electronic networks. One IBM vice-president commented, "Doing business without EDI will soon be like doing business without a telephone" (Keefe, 1988, p. 40).

Finally, a major force behind electronic integration of organizations will be the adoption of EDI as standard practice by government agencies. The U.S. Department of Defense (DOD), for example, currently has electronic ordering links to about 50 companies and has announced its commitment to expand these systems to other suppliers. One report concluded,

> In the procurement area, DOD handles about 30 million communications with 300,000 suppliers annually, as well as generating over 700 million internal transactions. . . . Major suppliers . . . will be under pressure to establish standardized EDI links with DOD, and the ripple effect of such a DOD policy upon the procurement operations of other governmental departments and vendors could be tremendous. (Edwards, 1987, p. 13)

In addition to the trend toward EDI, there is other empirical evidence that the economy is shifting the focus of its resource expenditures from internal information management tasks to more market-oriented external functions. Table 1.4 shows the way in which the balance of information management effort in U.S. businesses has been shifting since 1900. We can distinguish between information resources aimed mainly at supporting interaction in the marketplace and those directed toward internal management of the company. Marketing, sales, brokerage, purchasing, and many financial accounting functions are concerned with coordinating the interaction of buyers and sellers in the marketplace, and general managers, foremen, and administrators direct activity within centrally organized units. The distinction is fundamental, in that the extent to which economic management is centralized or left to the interaction of independent trading parties lies at the heart of the distinction between market and nonmarket allocation processes, and indeed between socialist and capitalist economies.

Table 1.4. Market-oriented versus internal information management effort in U.S. businesses (000's of persons 14 years and older)

	1900	1910	1920	1930	1940	1950	1960	1970
Market-oriented								
Accounting and auditors	23	39	118	192	238	390	477	713
Buyers and department heads, store	0	11	20	35	74	147	236	387
Credit men	2	2	14	22	30	34	48	60
Purchasing agents and buyers	7	8	11	29	34	65	105	164
Agents (n.e.c.)	25	25	64	102	73	128	163	
Collectors bill and account	34	36	31	43	45	24	32	53
Bookkeepers	174	336	462	553	541	746	936	1574
Cashiers	55	112	154	185	180	248	492	575
Ticket station and travel agents	27	36	37	38	47	61	73	100
Shipping and receiving clerks	23	65	132	168	233	304	295	427
Advertising agents and salesmen	12	11	25	40	41	35	35	65
Auctioneers	3	4	5	4	4	6	4	5
Demonstrators	3	4	5	5	10	14	26	40
Miscellaneous sales occupations	77	80	50	57	55	24	57	122
Insurance agents and brokers	78	88	120	257	253	312	369	461
Real estate agents and brokers	34	75	89	150	119	145	196	266
Stock and bond salesmen	4	6	11	22	18	11	29	99
Salesmen and sales clerks	1089	1454	1724	2472	2893	3485	3888	4186
Total	1673	2401	3079	4372	4888	6179	7463	9600
Internal management								
Managers, officials, and proprietors	1511	2135	2390	3113	3197	4419	4586	3756
Construction	58	183	107	199	175	296	378	397
Manufacturing	174	350	446	447	432	665	526	752
Transportation	66	82	83	98	90	151	159	164
Telecommunications, utilities, and sanitary	6	19	25	39	54	65	108	115
Wholesale trade	78	104	143	152	225	343	338	310
Retail trade	930	1119	1220	1592	1620	1977	1628	1119
Other services	199	278	446	586	601	919	1149	899
Managers and superintendents, building	0	32	43	71	72	68	54	85
Officials, lodge, society, union, etc.	0	0	12	15	26	25	34	51
Personnel and labor relations workers	2	3	5	12	26	50	99	296
Foremen	162	318	485	551	585	867	1199	1618
Total	1675	2496	2935	3762	1306	54~3	5972	5806
Ratio of market-oriented to internal management	1.00	0.96	1.05	1.17	1.25	1.14	1.25	1.65

n.e.c.: not elsewhere classified

Source: Detailed Occupation of the Economically Active Population, 1900–1970, Bureau of the Census, Historical Statistics, Series D233.682.

It is difficult to ascertain precisely the relative magnitudes of information labor effort accounted for by the market as opposed to the centralized mode of management. However, the data in Table 1.4 (bottom line) shows that the ratio of market-oriented to internal information management resources stayed within the range of 0.96 to 1.25 between 1900 and 1960 and then jumped sharply to 1.65 by 1970. A comparable analysis of data for 1980 presents some difficulties owing to a change in occupational definitions, but the ratio is continuing to rise. This suggests an ongoing trend toward a market-based coordination of transactions consistent with a reduction in average firm size.

Telecommunications networks

One of the reasons for the lack of integration during Phase 2 was the lag in providing public telecommunications facilities. Compared with the path of economic structural development mapped out in Figure 1.7, the provision of public telecommunications facilities was delayed by some decades. The public telecommunications infrastructure appropriate to Phase 1 was the voice telephone network. It is primarily information workers, not production workers, who use the telephone, and historically, they used it for voice and not data. (In most businesses, there is approximately one telephone set per white-collar worker and almost no telephones for shop-floor workers), In Phase 2, information workers had the assistance of information technology, and the corresponding telecommunications requirement began to include data transmission. Ideally, we would have seen the development of public voice telephone services in keeping with the growth of information labor in Phase 1 and of public data networks in keeping with the spread of information technology in Phase 2.

In fact, even though white-collar work became extensive beginning with the end of the nineteenth century, telephones did not become commonplace in businesses until a few decades later. Near-universal penetration of telephone service was not achieved in most industrial countries until the 1960s and 1970s, even though the information work force had become a substantial component of the economy as early as the 1930s and 1940s.

The lag in the provision of public data communications facilities in Phase 2 is equally clear. By the late 1960s, most major corporations were making substantial use of computers to automate at least some clerical functions, but an interconnection between them was practically nonexistent. Because there was a wealth of requirements for interconnecting data centers, corporations began to build private data networks linking their establishments. In the 1970s they were able to draw on the services of packet switch network providers to provide links with centers that did not justify a fully dedicated private data link. However, to date, no country's telecommunications network operators offer the general business public a switched data service that would provide a data interconnection analogous to that available for voice (except through the rudimentary procedure of sending data signals through a modem over a voice telephone link).

In view of this shortcoming in the communications infrastructure, it is not surprising that even now, most data communications take place within rather than between organizations. The only intercompany networks of any significance that existed before the 1980s were those serving the banking and airline sectors, both of which had exceptional needs for a worldwide interconnection of their data facilities. This is beginning to change, however, with the emergence during the late 1980s of some intercompany networks linking interest groups such as buyers and sellers in an industry, or retailers and banks in the case of financial transactions (Estrin, 1985).

Recognizing the large potential for further exploiting information technology once the universal data interconnection of establishments is available, the telephone companies in the United States and their counterparts in other industrialized countries are developing plans for integrated services digital networks (ISDN), which will provide widespread data connections among general business users (see Jones, 1988, p. 18; Keen, 1986, pp. 141–42).

As with previous generations of the public telecommunications infrastructure, however, we can predict that the reality of universal data networks will lag far behind the apparent market need. Technologies for external integration are appearing first as EDI, which will be an intermediate step before the development of integrated data networks. The speed at which interorganizational integration takes place will depend not only on the technology but also on the economic and competitive needs in particular industries. Just as certain industries, for example, banks and insurance, led the way in automating clerical functions in Phase 2, other industries such as transportation and auto manufacturers are proving to be early adopters of integration technologies as they become available.

Not only will the impact of intercompany integration vary from industry to industry, but individual firms will find themselves confronted with a confusing array of strategic decisions about networking technologies, as described by Keen:

> The concept of "integration" in telecommunications and computers is elusive and at times rather like an advertising slogan, "New and improved." From the perspective of the senior manager, the issue is not integrated technology but integrated customer service. What range of services can the customer get access to from a single workstation?
>
> . . . It is far cheaper and easier to design a network capability that provides specific services than one that plans ahead for full integration. It may . . . be that customers do not need integrated financial services, integrated software that combines spreadsheets, word processing and database management, or integrated terminals. Or they may. When? Why? The issue of the degree of integration that the architecture should provide for is again a business question that cannot be answered by forecasts, only by vision and the act of faith to make radical business moves. (Keen, 1986, pp. 154–55)

Strategic implications of interorganizational integration

The integration of internal and external transactions between firms will contribute to at least five strategic trends in Phase 3:

First, integration inherently means that businesses are more tightly linked to one another. For example, the onset of networking between buyers and sellers means that companies can give their customers direct access to internal data bases. Pacific Intermountain Express, a major trucking company, allows customers to access its computer files directly to check the status of their shipments, and American Hospital Supply electronically monitors the production schedules and inventory levels of its major suppliers to make sure they can meet the projected needs of the medical supply company (Keen, 1986, pp. 54, 47).

In addition, external integration makes practical these new business processes, such as just-in-time inventory control, which reduces inventory levels by an average

15 to 20 percent (Keen, 1986, p. 71). In many cases, electronic integration will lead to shorter lists of suppliers for major customers who want to establish a few close relationships. Although not entirely attributable to integration, IBM's Lexington, Kentucky, plant has lowered its number of suppliers from more than 700 to fewer than 45. Similarly, Xerox has cut its number of global suppliers from 5000 to 370. This trend represents substantial cuts in clerical overhead needed to manage all these relationships (Gunn, 1987, p. 181; Malone, Yates, & Benjamin, 1987, 1988).

The integration of information systems also causes sellers to become more service oriented, using information networks to reach and service their customers. Ford has enhanced customer service by providing a system that allows its dealers to access one another's parts inventories to locate more quickly those parts needed for repairs (Wiseman & MacMillan, 1984, p. 47). Meanwhile, a chemicals company has shifted the basis of competition from solely price to more of a service orientation by giving its customers microcomputers to access directly its mainframe. Customers use the system to decide on product mix and order frequency, as well as to order directly (Cash & Konsynski, 1985, p. 139). This trend toward increased service orientation clearly complements the emergence of programmed production mentioned earlier, as it allows an immediate and precise response by the production system to a change in the customers' needs.

Computer integration will not only provide faster, more efficient information exchange between firms, but it will also create fundamental changes in market structures. Interorganizational integration will have different effects on different industries, and in many cases it will lead to the evolution of electronic markets for buyers and sellers. There is growing theoretical and empirical evidence that the ability of information technology to reduce coordinating costs will increasingly encourage the use of markets, instead of hierarchies, to coordinate activity (Malone, 1987, pp. 1317–22; Malone et al., 1987, pp. 484–97).

Airline reservation systems are a classic example of the growth of an electronic market made possible by information technology. In another case, Western Union created an electronic market that matches freight shippers with motor freight carriers. Western Union adds value for the shipper by verifying the carrier's legal authorization and insurance coverage (Malone et al., 1987, p. 492).

The trend toward electronic markets is encouraged by two capabilities of information technology. Improved communication capabilities—the ability to access more complex information faster—makes it feasible to describe many more products to potential customers over electronic networks. In addition, programmed production technologies make it practical for firms to shift from producing one product to another in response to market demand. This type of flexible manufacturing means that customers are likely to find an increasing number of suppliers trying to respond to their needs, thus creating fewer permanent, hierarchical buyer–seller relationships (Malone et al., 1987, p. 489). Networking technologies will, in many cases, lead to a level of integration that builds economic incentives for coordination in the form of electronic marketplaces.

The emergence of global communication networks encourages the transition of worldwide firms from multinational to transnational modes of operation, extending the geographical reach of firms into new markets. Dow Jones, for example, now pursues a more global strategy by publishing Asian and European editions of the *Wall Street Journal*, which has thereby become a true national and international newspaper owing to electronic communications capabilities that allow Dow Jones to distribute editorial content to printing plants worldwide (Porter & Millar, 1985, p. 157). In another example, IBM can manufacture products on a global basis because of an electronic network that links about 55 plants and design centers around the world. As a result, any engineering change can be sent electronically in seconds to all 55 plants (Gunn, 1987, p. 205; Poynter & White, 1987; A scramble, 1988).

There are many markets in which the development of integrated data networks will influence both the market structures and the products being sold. This will be particularly evident when the product itself is information rather than a physical good. Industries ranging from publishing and broadcasting to all aspects of retail and commercial financial services will be affected. In these businesses, the much improved communications networks, which characterize Phase 3, will radically change the way that products are delivered.

One firm that has redefined its role in the information business in order to take advantage of electronic integration is Reuters, the London-based news-gathering service. Reuters developed a computerized information retrieval system that gives clients direct access to the latest prices from financial, oil, commodity, and other international markets, as well as providing instant access to financial and general business news (Wiseman & MacMillan, 1984, p. 48). Reuters' clients now have terminals in more than 24,000 locations in 160 countries.

In some cases, networking technology is dramatically reshaping industries. For example, the Publix supermarket chain in Florida turned its cash registers into point-of-sale banking machines, using its customer contact and ownership of a sophisticated telecommunications network to force major banks to cooperate in its new venture (Keen, 1986, p. 5).

Integration breaks down walls between industries. Suddenly, retailers and oil companies are moving into banking, banks into publishing, and customers into suppliers' functions. The concept of delivering multiple information-intensive services and products through the same terminal is what makes this feasible. And when time and information represent key product differentiators or open up new market opportunities, those with electronic networks have the chance to gain significant competitive advantage (Keen, 1986, p. 5).

Electronic marketplaces will evolve in many instances, with communications networks being used not only to accept orders, fulfill transactions, and so forth but also to deliver the goods themselves. The large investments currently being undertaken by financial institutions in communications and information-processing technologies is one symptom of the transformation that will alter the structure, behavior, and performance of the markets for information-intensive products.

Finally, there is growing evidence to support the theory that integration will lead to a reduction in average firm size. The hypothesis that information technology will affect market structure because of its impact on the process of coordination among firms has been subject to much theoretical study and mathematical modeling. Although the findings must still be considered tentative, Brynjolfsson and colleagues (1989) and Oniki (1987), among others, explored the relationship between the changing costs of coordination and its impact on firm size. Although the models used by these two researchers are different, their broad conclusions are the same: The adoption of information technology tends to decentralize the economy and to reduce the average firm size, even if information technology lowers both internal and external coordination costs.

We noted earlier that there will be obstacles to this transition, chiefly as a result of the understandable rigidity and inertia of human organizations. We must also expect that not all progress in the directions indicated by this prognosis will be beneficial, either to the individual businesses involved or to society as a whole. But we can predict with some confidence that the changes we have forecast in connection with the transition to Phase 3 will take place, because they depend on underlying economic forces that are difficult, in the long term, to resist. In the same way that the automation of routine computational and file-handling functions within offices became almost complete during Phase 2, despite organizational and human resistance, we can expect progress in the direction of integration (as defined in this paper) to accelerate during the early years of Phase 3.

In summary, Phase 3 of the information technology revolution will bring about changes qualitatively different from those that characterized the previous two phases. Electronic technologies will not just be adopted in larger numbers, but they will also be used to restructure businesses. The emphasis will be on improving the quality of products and services delivered, rather than on improving the efficiency of self-contained information-handling operations. This will in turn require the adoption of information technologies that integrate previously separated domains of automation—the office and the factory, and one business with the next.

The fact that we are entering a Phase 3 that is qualitatively different from Phase 2 justifies both the investments being made by corporations to upgrade their information systems in order to cope with the new phase, and the investments being made in public telecommunications infrastructure (especially digital networks) to serve the emerging requirements. Both these activities are being pursued with considerable vigor, even without the benefit of systematic economic analysis or justification. Business organizations are planning for an era in which the ability to compete by taking advantage of all the capabilities of information technology is a key criterion of success. Telecommunications and computer companies throughout the world are laying the foundations for digital networks. There is some vagueness in the minds of both parties as to just what the nature of this new competition will be, why information system networking is a critical element of it, and why it has not been so important in the past. In this study we have attempted to explain the rationale behind this new wave of investment. Why are businesses now seeing information systems as a key competitive weapon? Why are societies investing in a new generation of telecommunications infrastructure?

Clearly, this chapter is not intended to answer those questions in detail, as circumstances will differ from industry to industry and application to application. What it has tried to show is that at the macroeconomic level, the transition from Phase 2 to Phase 3 has an economic logic or rationale in the same way that the transition from Phase 1 to Phase 2 did.

NOTES

1. Machlup (1962) was the first to measure the extent of the allocation of resources to creating knowledge, as opposed to other kinds of products and services. Other analyses of this kind were carried out by Porat (1977) and again by Machlup (1980).

2. This is taken from Jonscher, 1985. Measurements of the information-handling resources of other industrialized countries were compiled by the Organization for Economic Cooperation and Development (1981). For a discussion of information labor trends in Japan and Britain, see also Ohira, 1987 and Gleave, Angell, and Woolley, 1985.

3. Fritz Machlup produced the most thorough classification to date of writings on the economics of information and knowledge, to be published posthumously by Princeton University Press as volume 3 of his planned 10-volume study: *Knowledge: Its Creation, Distribution and Economic Significance.*

4. For reviews of this area, see Arrow, 1980, and Lamberton, 1984.

5. Why do the special features of what we have described as the economics of symbol manipulation, rather than the special features of the economics of knowledge, provide the key to understanding the causes behind the information revolution? The answer is implicit in Figure 1.1. For those information activities that produce knowledge of a lasting or "capital" value, the problem of resource allocation concerns, typically, the amount of resources that should be devoted to the production of the knowledge in question, and the number of agents who should be recipients of that knowledge. These resource allocation issues arise in the case of research and development expenditures (given the tension between the desire to provide incentives for funding research and development, on the one hand, and the desire to make the results available to all who could benefit from it, on the other, what should be the period of protection granted by patent law?) and in the area of creative arts such as the production of programs for mass entertainment (where an analogous tension arises). However, Figure 1.1 indicates that the resources allocated to this kind of information creation (as measured by an occupational breakdown of the work force) accounts for only one-fifth of the information-handling expenditures in the economy. The remaining four-fifths are concerned with the routine handling of information of transient value. It is clear from inspecting the occupational descriptions of persons in these latter categories of information handling that the "public good" characteristics of knowledge as a commodity are of little concern. The people—buyers, sellers, clerks, administrators, typists—do not produce knowledge that should be patented or copyrighted and then licensed or sold to one or more other potential users. The transformation we are seeing in the role of information in the economy is due primarily to the way in which technology is transforming these routine information handling processes.

6. For example, the cumulative output was about 3 million units in 1964 and 2000 million units by 1972.

7. The current state-of-the-art size of random access memory in a single integrated circuit for commercial production is 1M (1,048,576); larger capacity devices are under development.

8. This is the estimate of the Boston Consulting Group (1968), based on data published by the Electronics Industry Association. Noyce (1977) arrived at a figure of 28 percent.

9. Optical transmission of information (through optical fibers) is now widespread, but these systems remain electro-optical in the sense that electronic components are required at each end of a link and at all amplification points. Optical processing is still in its infancy.

10. For a thorough discussion of the history of manufacturing costs of data processing systems, see Phister, 1979, pt I.4.1 (supplement). This covers not only the main functional categories of component such as processing and memory but also miscellaneous cost elements such as power supplies and mounting hardware (printed circuit boards, cabinets). Another historical source used in this study was Rudenberg, 1969.

11. Proprietary data prepared by Frost and Sullivan.

12. The original data have been adjusted as necessary to adjust for the effects of inflation.

13. However, estimates range from as high as 24 percent (Phister, 1979) to as low as 10 percent (proprietary data from the Diebold Group), depending in part on the bundle of communications services that forms the basis of the analysis.

14. See also the extensive data in Phister, 1979.

15. The case of communications costs is complicated by the fact that communications facilities are, in the main, provided as services by third-party industries rather than as products and that the industries providing them have not operated in normally competitive markets. Both these aspects of communications service provision are undergoing change (see, among several other texts, Tyler, Jonscher, & Watts, 1988).

16. During the late 1970s and early 1980s, many governments took the first steps toward establishing an information technology policy. In the United States, the National Telecommunications and Information Administration (NTIA) was established within the Department of Commerce, and it was charged with developing a broad approach to information and communications policy in that country (see, e.g., NTIA, 1981). Under the Thatcher government, the United Kingdom's Department of Industry embarked on a series of studies of the information and telecommunications industries and appointed a minister of information technology to take overall responsibility for this sector of the economy. Former President Giscard d'Estaing of France commissioned a wide ranging report entitled "The Computerization of Society" (Nora & Minc, 1977). In addition to similar initiatives in a number of its member countries, the Organization for Economic Cooperation and Development (1981) carried out a series of systematic studies of the impact of the emerging information technologies and industries on employment, productivity, investment, and growth.

17. Wage data for different occupational categories are given in the *Statistical Abstract of the United States*, Table 386, "Median Annual Earnings of Civilians, by Sex and by Occupation," various years.

REFERENCES

Arrow, K. J. (1973). *Information and economic behavior.* Stockholm: Federation of Swedish Industries.

——— (1980). The economics of information. In J. Dertouzos & J. Moses (Eds.), *The complete age.* Cambridge, MA: MIT Press.

Arrow, K. J., H. B. Chenery, B. S. Minhas, & R. M. Solow (1961). Capital-labor substitution and economic efficiency. *Review of Economics and Statistics* 63 (August): 225–317.

Bell, D. (1973). *The coming of post-industrial society.* New York: Basic Books.

Beniger, J. (1986). T*he control revolution: Technological and economic origins of the information society.* Cambridge, MA: Harvard University Press.

Benjamin, R. I., D. W. De Long, & M. S. Scott Morton (1988). *The realities of electronic data interchange: How much competitive advantage?* Working paper no. 88–042, *Management in the 1990s*, Sloan School of Management, Massachusetts Institute of Technology.

Berndt, E. R., & B. C. Field (Eds.) (1981). *Modeling and measuring natural resource substitution.* Cambridge, MA: MIT Press.

Berndt, E. R., & C. J. Morrison (1979). Income redistribution and employment effects of rising energy prices. *Resources and Energy* 2 (October): 131–50.

Boston Consulting Group (1968). *Perspectives on experience.* Boston: Boston Consulting Group.

Branscomb, L. M. (1982). Electronics and computers: An overview. *Science*, February 12.

Brynjolfsson, E., T. W. Malone, V. Gurbaxani, & A. Kambil (1989). Does information technology lead to smaller firms? MIT Center for Coordination Science technical report no. ITSF7.

Cash, J. T., Jr., & B. R. Konsynski (1985). IS redraws competitive boundaries. *Harvard Business Review*, March-April.

Chismar, W. G., & C. H. Kriebel (1985). A method of assessing the economic impact of information systems technology on organizations. GSIA working paper no. 40–84–85. Carnegie Mellon University, Graduate School of Industrial Organization.

Christensen, L. R., D. W. Jorgenson, & L. J. Lau (1971). Conjugate quality and the transcendental logarithmic production function. *Econometrics* 39 (July): 255–56.

——— (1973). Transcendental logarithmic production frontiers. *Review of Economics and Statistics* 55 (February): 28–45.

Cobb, C. W., & P. H. Douglas (1928). A theory of production. *American Economic Review*, 18 (March): 139–65.

Drucker, P. (1968). *The age of discontinuity*. New York: Harper & Row.

Edwards, D. W. (1987). Electronic data interchange: A senior management overview. ICIT briefing paper, International Center for Information Technologies, Washington, DC.

Epstein, M. (1985). Computer applications: A historical perspective. Mimeo, Sloan School of Management, Massachusetts Institute of Technology.

Estrin, De. L., (1985). Access to inter-organizational computer networks. Ph.D. diss., Massachusetts Institute of Technology.

Ferdows, K., & W. Skinner (1987). The sweeping revolution in manufacturing. *Journal of Business Strategy* 8 (Fall): 64–69.

Gleave, D., C. Angell, & K. Woolley (1985). Structural change within the information profession: A scenario for the 1990s. *Aslib Proceedings* 37 (February): 99–133.

Gunn, T. G. (1987). *Manufacturing for competitive advantage*. Cambridge, MA: Ballinger.

Jaikumar, R. (1986). Post-industrial manufacturing. *Harvard Business Review*, November-December, pp. 69–76.

Jones, R. S. (1988). Companies testing ISDN's viability as a commercial service. *InfoWorld*, February 29.

Jonscher, C. (1981). Models of economic organizations. Ph.D. diss., Harvard University.

——— (1983). Information resources and economic productivity. *Information Economics and Policy* Vol. 1.

——— (1986). Information technology and the United States economy: Modeling and measurement. In E. Noam & R. Tasley (Eds.), *The impact of information technologies on the service sector.*

Keefe, P. (1988). Can you afford to ignore EDI? *Computerworld Focus*, January 6.

Keen, P. (1986). *Competing in time: Using telecommunications for competitive advantage*. Cambridge, MA: Ballinger.

Kelley, M. E. Programmable automation and skill questions: A reinterpretation of the cross-national evidence. *Human Systems Management* 6: 223–41.

Lamberton, D. (1984). Information economics. In Martha E Williams (Ed.), *Annual Review of Information Science and Technology* 19 (Fall).

Machlup, F.(1962). *Knowledge: Its location, distribution and economic significance*. Princeton, NJ: Princeton University Press.

——— (1980). *The production and distribution of knowledge in the United States*. Princeton, NJ: Princeton University Press.

Malone, T. W. (1987). Modeling coordination in organizations and markets. *Management Science* 33 (October): 1317–32.

Malone, T. W., J. Yates, & R. I. Benjamin (1987). Electronic markets and electronic hierarchies. *Communications of the ACM* 30 (June).

——— (1988). The realities of electronic data interchange: How much competitive advantage? Working paper no. 88–042, Management in the 1990s, Sloan School of Management, Massachusetts Institute of Technology.

National Telecommunications and Information Administration (1981). U.S. Department of Commerce, *Issues in information policy*. Washington, DC: U.S. Government Printing Service.

Nora, S., & A. Minc (1977). L'Informatisation de la société. Trans. as *The computerization of society*. Paris.

Noyce, R. (1977). Microelectronics. *Scientific American* September.

Ohira Gosei (1987). Economic analysis of information activities in Japan. *KEIO Communication Review*, no. 8.

Oniki Hajime (1987). New information technology and organization of economic coordination. Paper presented at the Fifteenth Telecommunications Policy Research Conference, Airlie House, VA, September.

Organization for Economic Cooperation and Development (1981). Information activities, electronics and telecommunications, no. 6. Information Computer Communication Policy series. Paris: OECD.

Phister, M., Jr. (1979). *Data processing technology and economics*, 2nd ed. Bedford, MA: Digital Press.

Piore, M., & C. Sabel (1984). *The second industrial divide*. New York: Basic Books.

Porat, M. (1977). The information economy: Definition and measurement. OT special publication no. 77–12 (1). (U.S. Department of Commerce).

Porter, M. E., & V. E. Millar (1985). How information gives you competitive advantage. *Harvard Business Review*, July-August.

Poynter, T. A., & R. E. White (1987). Organizing for worldwide advantage. Working paper no. 1989–88, Sloan School of Management, Massachusetts Institute of Technology, November.

Reich, R. B. (1984). *The next American frontier*. New York: Penguin Books.

Rochester, J. B. (1988). There's a rosy future in EDI. *CIO Magazine*, January–February.

Rudenberg (1969). Large scale integration: Promises versus accomplishments—The dilemma of our industry. *A.F.I.P.S. Conference Proceedings* 359, November 18–20.

Samuelson, P. A. (1953). Prices of factors and goods in general equilibrium. *Review of Economic Studies* 21:1–20.

A scramble for global networks (1988). *Business Week*, March 21, pp. 140–48.

Strassman, P. A. (1985). *Information payoff: The transformation of work in the electronic age*. New York: Free Press.

Thomas, R. J. (1987). Technological choice: Obstacles and opportunities for union management consultation on new technology. Working paper no. 987–88, Sloan School of Management, Massachusetts Institute of Technology.

Toffler, A. (1980). *The Third Wave*. New York: Bantam.

Tyler, R. M., C. Jonscher, & T. Watts (1988). *The transition to competition in telecommunications: Japan, UK and the USA*. Lexington, MA: Lexington Press.

Wiseman, C., & I. C. MacMillan (1984). Creating competitive weapons from information systems. *Journal of Business Strategy*, Fall.

Zuboff, S. (1988). *In the age of the smart machine: The future of work and power*. New York: Basic Books.

CHAPTER 2

Corporate Reform in American Manufacturing and the Challenge to Economic Theory

MICHAEL J. PIORE

Modern business organization has been a subject of social science research and theory at least since the mid-nineteenth century. In recent years, however, scholars have increasingly concentrated on a particular characterization of the modern enterprise. This characterization derives from the work of the business historian Alfred Chandler, as stylized and interpreted by Oliver Williamson. It is one of a vertically integrated, hierarchical organization, as contrasted with the egalitarian relations among units in a competitive marketplace. In the last decade, this organizational form has become a major focus of research even in theoretical economics, which in the past has been concerned primarily with markets.

Paradoxically, however, at the very moment that the Chandler–Williams model came to dominate research, the structural characteristics that it highlights came under more and more criticism in the managerial community, and in the decade of the 1980s, something of a revolution occurred in American managerial practice. This chapter attempts first to characterize the reforms in progress and then to assess them in the light of various hypotheses about the direction in which economic organization is headed. It is divided into two parts. The first part, which describes the basic changes, should be of interest even to those people who are not involved in the theoretical debates on which the second part is centered and to those who come to those debates with a perspective different from mine.

The empirical material that this chapter reports—and some of the theoretical insights—was gathered through open-ended interviews with engineers and managers in several of the companies participating in MIT's Management in the 1990s Program. These companies operate in a variety of different industries, but they are clearly not a representative sample of American business enterprise. The most obvious bias of the group is the very large size of the companies and the fact that most of them have a special interest in information technology, as either producers or exceptionally large consumers thereof. But even a cursory reading of the business press suggests that the organizational reforms in which these companies are engaged are widespread, and from this point of view, the companies might in fact be quite typical of major American corporations of the type on which Williamson and Chandler concentrate, although that supposition cannot be substantiated on the basis of the interviews that constitute the basic material for this chapter.

PART I: THE REVOLUTION IN CORPORATE STRUCTURE

These interviews yielded three different types of findings. First, the companies were in the process of introducing a series of deliberate, self-conscious reforms, which they themselves viewed as fundamental changes in organizational structure and practice. Comparable reforms have also been widely reported in the business press. They may be taken as the markers of this revolution under way. Second, the interviews revealed a widespread consensus among the managers in all of these companies about the way in which the geographic dispersion of production and authority within the organization would evolve over the next 10 years. This vision has not generally been reported in other commentaries about the evolution of business practices, and it contrasts sharply in certain respects with the conventional wisdom about trends in the international division of labor; for that reason alone it is worthy of attention. It also casts the reforms in a somewhat different light than that in which they appear when the list is presented by itself. Finally, the interviews revealed a variety of tensions surrounding the reforms. These tensions are frustrating the attempt to revise the corporate structure and might ultimately lead to unintended and unanticipated outcomes. It would require much more intensive, longitudinal case studies to develop this aspect of reform process, but the interview material, nonetheless, suggests certain revisions of the initial hypothesis, which are developed in the second section of this chapter.

The markers of corporate reform

The markers of the revolution in corporate structure and managerial practice are multifold, but the essence of the changes can be captured by five items:

First, in terms of the classic corporate structure, the most startling of these reforms is the shift to matrix management. The traditional corporation was organized by business and/or function, with clear lines of authority and a strict division of labor. But in the new structures, there are overlapping responsibilities, and managers report simultaneously to several superiors. This organizational form was not completely unknown in the past, but previously it was largely used to compromise the choice between a function and a business structure, and the matrices were essentially composed for these two types of units. Now, not only is this older matrix structure becoming much more common, but firms also are introducing other two-dimensional matrix structures and, in some cases, multidimensional matrices. The effect is to increase lateral communications within the organization as subordinates try to forestall conflicts among their several supervisors by resolving problems at lower levels of the organizations themselves. Matrix structures also give more independence and authority to subordinate levels of the organization and increase their direct responsibilities. Other reforms that enhance these effects include a conscious reduction in the number of managerial levels and an effort to develop decentralized systems for monitoring and rewarding performance typified by the expansion of the number of independent profit centers within the organization and of performance-based compensation systems. There has also been an increase in internal competition among components of the organization. In most cases, especially in manufacturing, this seems to have been the result of overall excess capacity, but some companies have deliberately created organizational components with parallel capabilities and sometimes have orchestrated a competition among them with outside vendors, for company business.

A second reform is the increased use of managerial teams and of parallel, as opposed to sequential or iterative, decision-making processes. This is most apparent in engineering, in which the usual procedure is to pass a decision down an engineering hierarchy, starting with product engineering, then to process engineering where the equipment is designed, and finally to the industrial engineers who design the plant layout and the initial manning tables. In principle, the design can be passed back from the latter stages, but in practice, designs at one stage tend to be frozen before they move forward and are revised only when truly insurmountable obstacles arise further on. The new procedures involve groups of engineers working simultaneously on all aspects of the project and interacting with one another continuously so that process and industrial engineers have a say very early, long before the product design is complete. In some companies, the design teams include not only the company's own engineers but also personnel drawn from outside parts producers and from among production and maintenance workers. These new engineering procedures have been facilitated by technological developments, particularly computer-aided design, which makes it possible to keep the product design fluid until relatively late in the engineering process and to simulate alternative manufacturing approaches without actually creating and testing a physical model. Much of the pressure to adopt these new structures is also technological: The shortening of the product life cycle and the use of more flexible production equipment mean that manufacturing equipment typically outlasts any single product, which was not the case in the past when most equipment was dedicated to a particular product design. Because the equipment is not created anew each time around, however, embedded technologies are more of a constraint on the design process than they were in the past.

In one sense, these project teams (or "skunk works," as they are called) seem to work in the opposite direction from that of matrix management: They tend to centralize decision making, sometimes moving engineering capability out of the shop toward higher levels of the corporation, and to blur individual responsibility. They operate like matrix management, however, to abrogate a strict functional division of labor, to enhance lateral communication, and to replace traditional hierarchy with more egalitarian relationships.

A third set of changes are the relationship between the corporation and the outside organizations with which it does business. These include both vendors and subcontractors from which the company traditionally purchases inputs into the production process, and other businesses that the company purchases in an effort to expand its product line and/or to diversify. Traditionally, U.S. companies have had an arm's length relationship with suppliers, buying from a large number when possible and encouraging competition among them. These reforms reduce the number of suppliers and create a more permanent and collaborative relationship with those that remain. It is these new permanent partners that are asked to join the engineering design teams: Usually, they are encouraged to locate facilities close to the plants that they will supply and, as we shall see, to feed directly into the production process.

At first glance, the collaborative relationship with parts manufacturers appears to contradict the internal reforms that create competition among corporate divisions and between corporate units and outside producers. But the contradiction disappears if one sees the thrust of the reforms as an effort to displace the boundaries of the organization while at the same time changing the relationship among the organizational components within those boundaries. The boundary is being moved out to encompass within a larger community of interests some organizations that are formally independent entities, but at the same time internal units are being encouraged to assume some of the independence of outsiders. Thus, for outsiders, this seems to mean closer collaboration, and for insiders, more distance.

That this is the case is apparent when one examines the new strategies for innovation. The old strategy was to look for new products in companies outside the organization, to buy the concerns that were producing them, and to integrate the new acquisition. A new division was often created for the product that had motivated the purchase, and the other operations of the acquired company were closed down, sold off, or distributed among other divisions of the corporate purchaser. In the new strategy, outside companies are seen not so much as the source of a particular product but, rather, as a source of entrepreneurship and technological creativity that a large organization cannot maintain internally. Hence the trend is toward some form of arm's length financial participation that establishes a collaborative relationship without abrogating the separate identity and personality of the outside organization. Interchanges among the personnel of the two companies are encouraged, and the large corporation may commit itself to produce new products under license or in separate joint ventures, but one organization is not folded into another. Moreover, these forms of intimate collaboration with outsiders often are accompanied by parallel efforts to give insiders the independence required to engage in entrepreneurial activities internally. These include opportunities to create separate divisions to produce and market new products and funds that provide seed money for corporate employees to leave the company and open their own firms on the outside.

Fourth, still another series of organizational reforms are associated with the movement to reduce, and ultimately eliminate, in-process inventory in manufacturing. This began as an effort to imitate the Japanese *Kamban* system in which automobile subcontractors deliver parts just in time to go into production, thereby dispensing with the warehousing that used to be required at the assembly site. The procedure has the advantage—assuming that the parts producers do not simply maintain the inventories at their own plants—of increasing the ease with which the production facility can shift from one product to another, as it no longer first has to work off in-process inventories. But for this to work out, inventories must be eliminated not only at the entry of the production process but all along the line as well. Production without inventories, however, fundamentally changes the relationship among workstations. American manufacturing has traditionally been organized as a classic Adam Smith pin factory. Each operation was designed to be done in isolation, in accord with its own internal logic and without reference to the operations that preceded or followed it, and a premium was placed on the continuous employment of both capital equipment and labor. This approach to production encouraged—or was encouraged by—the use of highly specialized, dedicated equipment and labor. Both labor and capital were essentially useless when not engaged in their precise assigned task. It encouraged an approach to production that tried to minimize equipment downtime. Workers, when they were not needed in American shops, were simply laid off. It also created a natural hierarchy. Because each workstation functioned in isolation, only the supervisor standing outside understood the whole enough to control and coordinate it. But the approach is feasible only as long as there are large banks of in-process inventory between workstations. Only then can each workstation go on operating irrespective of what happens upstream in the production process. As soon as those inventories are eliminated, attention is focused on the relationship among workstations in an altogether new way. In order to ensure continuous production, workers are forced to relate to, and to learn to understand, adjacent operations. Once they do so, they become capable of coordinating the production process, and the supervisor no longer performs quite the same function. At the same time, because downtime is now inevitable, pressures are generated to find ways of employing idle resources in secondary tasks. This in turn creates an environment more conducive to flexible machinery and more generally trained labor and a management attuned to the problem of finding supplementary tasks, and this in turn creates a set of dispositions favorable to moving away from the traditional system of layoff and recall toward continuous employment policies. In its fundamentals, then, the impact of the elimination of in-process inventories is much like that of matrix management and engineering teams: greater lateral communication, less hierarchy, a more broad-based, generally trained labor force, and a greater capacity to respond flexibly to changing market conditions.

Fifth and finally, these changes in corporate structure and managerial practice have been accompanied by significant changes in industrial relations. These include a decentralization of collective bargaining to the plant level; a shift in the focus of collective bargaining from the negotiation and applications of rules and procedures to the negotiation of substantive outcomes; a broadening of job classifications and permissible work assignments; a movement away from layoff and recall based on seniority toward continuous employment; the introduction of quality circles and similar forms of worker participation in production planning and shop management; a movement in compensation from rates based on job assignment to personal rates based on skill level and "knowledge"; profit sharing; and worker representation on corporate boards of directors. None of these changes should be too surprising in light of the changes in work organizations associated with the elimination of in-plant inventories, although they are an independent phenomenon not in any sense confined to those operations in which inventory policies have been changed. But like that reform and the changes affecting managerial organization and structure, they have the effect of enhancing workers' independence while at the same time reducing hierarchy and increasing the capacity and the incentive to communicate laterally across work divisions.

Geographic reconfiguration

In addition to the markers of corporate reform, the interviews revealed what the informants described as a new vision of the manufacturing process. This vision could not be anticipated solely on the basis of recent reporting in the business press, yet it was very widely shared. Indeed, the way in which it was described from one company to the next was so similar that it is difficult to believe that the views being expressed were really independent. In a certain sense, however, this is irrelevant, because many of the respondents were in a position to realize this vision through their own actions and, in fact, had already moved to do so.

The central elements of that vision are as follows:

1. Productive equipment can no longer be dedicated to a single product, because the product life cycle is now so much shorter than the life of the equipment. Hence, production will depend increasingly on computer-aided manufacture (CAM): multipurpose equipment adjusted to the production of the particular product through a computer program. A corollary is that a number of different products can be run simultaneously on the same production line.
2. The cost of direct labor as a proportion to the total is falling rapidly and will soon no longer be an important factor in business decisions. This will obviate the need to locate factories in areas with low labor costs; in the next 10 years, most companies will abandon those developing areas whose low wages are their principal attraction.
3. With decreasing economies of scale in production and minimal direct labor costs, location decisions will be dominated by pressures to produce within the major national markets. These pressures are coming from what the engineers describe as an inevitable trend toward protectionism in foreign trade. As a result, most companies plan to produce in the future in the United States, Japan, the European Economic Community, and in the large developing countries. Among the latter, Brazil, Mexico, and India are generally mentioned.
4. The engineers believe that there will still be substantial economies of scale in product development and design. As a result, they plan to concentrate design facilities mostly at corporate headquarters but perhaps also in certain foreign centers with large pools of highly skilled labor power (again, North America, Western Europe, and Japan are generally mentioned). Design will be computer aided (CAD) and feed directly into CAM equipment at the dispersed facilities over long-distance telephone lines.

The most startling thing about this vision of the manufacturing process is the geographic distribution of production and power that it implies and how that distribution conflicts with conventional views of the new international division of labor. The developing world, rather than drawing production away from the industrial nations, is essentially written off. The location of production is determined by market size, not labor costs. Production is decentralized, but real power, responsibility, and control is not: The new technology is in fact used to centralize control at headquarters; power and responsibility may be slightly more dispersed but follow the distribution of engineering and design talent, not wage levels.

Conflicts and tensions

The third type of material that emerged from the interviews consisted of a series of insights into the tensions and conflicts inherent in the efforts at corporate reform. It is impossible to do justice to these findings in a format of this kind, but the tensions that seem most relevant to the analytical issues discussed in the second part of this chapter may be summarized as follows:

The central tension appearing in the interviews is between the decentralization that the reforms are generating and the organization as a single entity. The question lurking in the background is whether power and responsibility can be delegated to individual organizational components without jeopardizing the integrity of the organization as a whole. This problem had different forms in different companies, although in its generic form, it was pervasive.

It was most acute in companies that were structurally closest to the classic Chandler–Williamson corporation. Such a company has historically produced a group of clearly defined products for an identifiable set of markets, most of which it has dominated for almost a century. Those traditional markets are now, however, largely saturated; the company, moreover, faces sharp competition from several large and powerful competitors; and the old market boundaries are dissolving as computer and telecommunication technology combine to bring hard images, image reproduction, computer systems and long-distance telephone lines, and transportation and delivery all into direct competition. The company's strategy is to use the technological competencies associated with its old product lines to develop and market new products, but it does not have a clear idea what those new products probably will look like. Hence, it is decentralizing authority in an attempt to give its various components the freedom to discover new directions. It talks about refocusing its activities around its "core competencies," but it does not know what these are, and one suspects that the attempt to restructure the organization in this way may be like peeling an onion. Meanwhile, the old organizational culture survives, and middle management is continually frustrating attempts to change the traditional hierarchical structure. One of these managers most tellingly explained how he had "solved" the problem of matrix management by anticipating and removing all ambiguity in the lines of authority so that pressures for lateral communication were eliminated.

A second company, in a different industry but also confronting the competitive problem posed by the dissolution of barriers between transportation, communication, computers, imaging, and storage technologies, created a major independent research facility to bring new technological competencies into the organization. The facility was located close to the institutional centers where the new technologies were being developed, but it was far away from the company's other activities. It thus succeeded in becoming a leader in these technological developments, but without impact on the company's own products. Almost all the innovations of the research facility were brought to the market by outside organizations, some of which turned out to be the company's major competitors.

The case that is most telling, however, is the company that up to now has been most successful in creating and maintaining the decentralized organizational structure. This company manufactures a series of components that are linked together to form an operating system, like a computer network or a stereo system. The company's competitive advantage in the industry comes from the capacity of its products to network with one another in order to form systems that are peculiarly adapted to the specialized needs of individual customers. The company's operations thus divide into two major components: One of these is the production of the component parts, that is, manufacturing in the strict sense of the term. The second component is the construction of the network or system to fit the customers' needs: This component is closely tied to sales and is essentially a service activity. Manufacturing and service must nonetheless be closely linked so that the capacity of the products to network with one another as they evolve in time is maintained; so that the people who built the products into systems are aware of the products' capacities and can stretch those capabilities to the maximum to meet the customers' needs; and so that the manufacturers sense the pressure of customers' needs, which are actually experienced only by the sales people, and are led to reflect those needs in subsequent equipment design.

The organizational structure that has evolved in an attempt to meet these requirements is unstable: It has been revised several times in the last 10 years, and further revisions are under discussion. Hence the instability of the structure can almost be taken as its salient characteristic. Each of the structures that has emerged, moreover, involves apparently confused and certainly ambiguous lines of authority: The confusion and ambiguity are, of course, heightened by the continual organizational reform. There have been historically, for example, three distinct sales structures: geography, industry, and profession. Hence, in principle any given client falls within the territory of three sales representatives, creating a sense of internal competition that various organizational structures have sought to temper or resolve. In addition, the company sells much of its equipment through third parties that provide the services involved in building the equipment into networks and hence compete with the internal sales and "service" divisions.

A second major organizational issue concerns the relationship between manufacturing and sales. The company has been unable to resolve the question of which of these two functional divisions is subordinate and how to allocate profits and resources between them. The appearance of confusion and conflict is further heightened by a corporate culture in which subordinates are encouraged to be outspoken and to challenge their superiors, and by a great deal of lateral communication and lateral movement of company personnel across the various departments and divisions.

This organizational structure is the subject of continual concern within the company itself, and outsiders are often shocked at and generally critical of the company's internal operations. Nonetheless, it is clear in interviews with personnel inside the company that it does tend to create a network of people who know—and know well—both the company's markets and its products and that in the continuing effort to adapt one to the other, they know to whom to talk outside their own domain. Often they have a good idea, from having worked in other parts of the company, of exactly what needs to be done. Finally, the organizational structure not only necessitates the kind of lateral communication that networking entails, but we noted, the organization's culture encourages it as well. People are expected to take the initiative themselves and to challenge higher authority. The structure then appears to be designed to ensure that the company's physical products, as they evolve in time, are likely to be compatible with one another and that they will be stretched toward the customers' needs. The organizational structure is thus a metaphor for the company's product. Actually, it is more than a metaphor: The product is a reflection of the structure. A great deal of deliberate effort is directed at ensuring both that the company's products are capable of networking with one another and that these networks can be stretched to meet specific customer needs. But the organizational culture is such that if everybody were suddenly to be isolated from one another and left to perform his or her current functions alone, the product line would continue to evolve for some time into the future in a way that promoted the twin goals of compatibility and customization. Thus, despite the instability of the company's formal structure, the organization could be said to have reached some kind of dynamic equilibrium.

That equilibrium is now being threatened by the geographic redistribution of the company's operations in response to protectionist pressures. The question that is now being posed is how long the centralized design of a limited product line can be maintained in the face of decentralized production and sales. It seems hard to believe that the protectionist pressures—if indeed they are as a commanding as the engineers seem to believe—can be accommodated simply by decentralizing the production facilities, especially if these facilities no longer yield much employment. But in this firm, one would hardly need political pressure to produce this result. Once production takes place in physical proximity to the customer, the manufacturing end of the business will be in much closer physical contact with sales and service than with product design. The increasing flexibility of the production equipment makes it relatively cheap to change the physical product to meet the customers' needs. The organizational culture validates the pressures to do so and the kinds of organizational alliances likely to accommodate them. It may be difficult to design a totally new product at the production facilities, but marginal changes in existing designs should not be too difficult to introduce. The skills necessary for these purposes are not all that different from those required to assemble, out of standardized components, a customized network, and the internal mobility and staffing patterns of the company make it easy for a division to acquire personnel with whatever supplemental skills are required for this purpose.

Declining economies of scale in manufacturing is one of the basic hypotheses that the interviews on which this chapter is based were designed to investigate. The manufacturing engineers resisted that hypothesis adamantly, so adamantly that the resistance appeared less a response to the abstract question than to real pressures within the organization. Other respondents in the company confirmed this view and were even prepared to talk about how the integrity of the product design could be invaded, which parts could be changed easily without seriously raising production costs, and where a change would actually pose the kind of threat to cost control against which the manufacturing engineers were attempting to protect themselves. Clearly, in their image of the business, the customization of the product would not, in the long run, be limited to the configuration of a standard set of parts. What remains unclear is how pervasively the integrity of the standard product line is likely to be invaded. In the minds of all respondents, there would be decided limits to this process. But given the fact that all the technological trends and the environmental pressures are promoting a progressive reduction of economies of scale and a growing flexibility in all aspects of manufacturing, these limits will probably diminish over time.

If the organizations reviewed for this chapter were to dissolve, what would take their place? Williamson and Chandler drew a sharp dichotomy between the classic corporation and the market. This dichotomy implies that the changes now in progress are moving toward a set of isolated business units indirectly communicating with one another indirectly through price signals. This prognosis, however, seems to be largely a product of the poverty of the conceptual apparatus with which we are working. Outside the corporate sector, where small independent business units predominate, organization seems to be moving in another direction: not, to be sure, toward a single integrated business entity but toward a relatively closed community of firms variously described as industrial districts, federations, cocontractors, and networks. These communities are held together by a common industrial culture and a jargon (or language) that permits a much richer structure of communication than the impersonal price signals of the market. The development of such communities is suggested by a diverse set of case studies ranging from traditional manufacturing districts in central Italy to high-tech centers in Northern California's Silicon Valley and around Boston's Route 128. The attraction of geographically centered high-tech communities constituted the hidden pressures on the classic corporation, not visible in the interviews, but more obvious when these corporations are seen from the outside. These pressures are pulling the centralized design facilities in one case, the distant laboratories in the other, away from the corporate culture and into the culture of the local scientific and engineering community. This suggests that to capture the changes in progress, we need a much richer conceptual apparatus. We thus turn to the problems that this poses.

PART II: PRACTICE AND THEORY

The basic question is where these reforms are headed. Why was the tightly integrated, hierarchical corporation once considered an efficient organizational structure? What has occurred to render it less efficient now? Why do the particular reforms being introduced seem to increase efficiency? And where is the reform process headed? Which of the reforms is likely to prove stable in the long run? What kind of new organizational structures are likely to emerge as the end product of the reform process?

It is natural to turn to economic theory for answers to these questions and, in that context, not only to ask whether theory provides the answers, but also, to the extent that it does not, to use the management practices that give rise to the questions to point to the directions in which theory could be revised.

There are two basic theoretical approaches to understanding organizational structure in economics. The first explains structure by referring to the exigencies of production and the characteristics of the technology, the second, by referring to the problems of exchange, or transactions. The interviews on which this chapter is based were designed to explore a set of hypotheses about productive technology that I developed in collaboration with Charles Sabel in our book *The Second Industrial Divide*. Perhaps for that reason—but also, I believe, because it is more natural to the way in which the respondents themselves think about organizational problems—the views expressed in the interviews lend themselves naturally to the language of production theory (although not necessarily to the particular theory that Sabel and I developed). The first part of this section accordingly attempts to interpret the results in those terms. The new theories of industrial organization that are exiting the mainstream of the economics profession are, on the other hand, based on transactions. The second part of this section discusses what it might mean to translate the interviews into the language of transaction theory and what such an effort says about the strengths and weaknesses of that theoretical approach.

Production-based theories of industrial organization

The postulates of production-based theories of industrial organization were initially developed by Adam Smith. They are essentially twofold: (1) Productive efficiency is dependent on the division of labor, and (2) the division of labor is limited by the extent of the market.

Smith's idea of the division of labor, and the engineer's view of the theory underlying the tightly integrated, hierarchical organizational structures, was that productivity would be maximized by dividing the productive process into as many distinct tasks as possible and by developing resources that were specially adapted to the performance of each task. The prototype of this structure was, for Smith, the pin factory. The modern prototype was Henry Ford's Model T assembly. At each workstation, there is either a worker who is specially trained in the requirements of the particular tasks at hand and/or a machine that is specially designed for that purpose. The highly articulated functional divisions of the Chandler–Williamson corporate structure are simply an extension of this same logic: The division of responsibilities within the organization on the basis of product lines and functions is precisely analogous to the division of work in the pin factory into the separate jobs of "wire-puller," "wire-cutter," "pin-header," "pin pointor," and the like. The organization of productive activity in this way poses, however, certain problems.

First, the extensive division of labor creates a problem of coordination. When there is an elaborate functional division of responsibility and the people who are assigned those responsibilities are narrowly specialized, they lose sight of the larger picture, and so they no longer possess the knowledge required to coordinate their activities with those of other parts of the organizational structure. In order to make sure, then, that the parts will fit back together to form the whole, the separate elements of the productive process, or the separate divisions of the organizational structure, must be strictly subordinated to some higher authority that does possess this knowledge and the information required to coordinate the separate activities. It is this requirement that explains the tightly integrated, hierarchical structure of the old corporate organization.

Second, as Smith emphasized, the efficiency of the division of labor is limited by the extent of the market. Unless the market is large enough to absorb the increased output that the new organizational structure permits, the resources that it entails will become unemployed once the market has become saturated, and because the efficiency of these resources is achieved by specializing them for the particular tasks at hand, they will be unemployable elsewhere in the economy. By an extension of this logic, the market must also be relatively stable and predictable. Production can be maintained in the face of small, predictable fluctuations in demand by varying inventories, but if demand fluctuations are large or unpredictable, producers will be reluctant to hold inventories, and the specialized resources will be laid off. The market must be willing to absorb, moreover, a relatively standard product; otherwise it will be impossible to stabilize and define the separate work tasks. Much of the evolution of the modern corporate organization can be understood in terms of the need for markets that meet these requirements.

The dominant explanation in the interviews for the changes in organizational structure was that the business environment is no longer conducive to the production of standardized products for a stable market. Any number of different explanations were offered in the interviews as to why this was the case: increased instability and uncertainty (due to floating exchange rates, fluctuations in the price of oil, interest rate variability and the like); increased consumer demand for variety (attributable to higher incomes); a more rapid pace of technological change; and a greater flexibility in the underlying technology itself. Some of these factors are probably basic, others derivative. It may not be possible to separate out the chain of causality. In any case, it does not appear that for our purposes it is necessary to do so. The relationship to the organizational changes is clear: Instability and uncertainty essentially translate into risk, as they encourage the diversification of resources. The emergent organizational structure is an effort to diversify.

These views are congruent with the argument that Sabel and I made in *The Second Industrial Divide*. We contended further, however, that the changes in the business environment (to use the managerial term) were leading to a new technological paradigm that we called *flexible specialization*. This new paradigm brought back into play the principles of craft production as it was understood and practiced in the mid-nineteenth century. Its essential characteristic is that relative to mass production, it uses many more general resources to produce an ever-changing product. We argued that this led to a much looser organization structure but one in which, unlike the market of neoclassical theory, competition was limited by rules and procedures that forestalled wage and price cutting in such a way as to channel entrepreneurial activity into product and/or process innovations.

The interviews did not support this second part of our argument. A number of the managers and engineers who participated in the study insisted that the adjustments that they were making did not imply the end of mass production at all. Instead, they suggested that the economies of scale associated with mass production were simple shifting from investments in labor training or in the physical equipment to investments in software or in marketing. A few, like the manufacturing engineers in Company I, insisted that economies of scale would continue to be important even to production itself. Indeed, the basic proposition about flexible specialization was disputed by enough of the respondents so as to create the suspicion that the remainder had simply misunderstood the hypothesis or were too polite to attack it directly.

This conflict suggests the need for a much richer typology of the ways in which production forms are accommodated to market characteristics.

Mass production, flexible specialization, and flexible mass production

The basic logic of flexibility would seem to imply a sixfold distinction. At one extreme is the classic *mass production*: a productive system that is able to turn out only a single product. This system has in fact probably not existed in its pure form since Ford's Model T. It was replaced early in the history of the automobile industry by a second system, which might be called *mass production with cosmetic variation*. As consumers of the products of such a system, we all have an intuitive understanding of what it means: variation in the superficial aspects of the design, that is, the paint, the trim, the upholstery, and the capacity to add options such as radios, power steering, and automatic transmission. It is a little more difficult to define this alternative formally. Essentially, it seems to mean a distinction between independent and interdependent design features. Independent features—the paint, the trim, the upholstery—can be varied in isolation without complementary changes in other features of the design. The marginal costs of such variations is thus relatively low. Interdependent features such as the motor block and the chassis do require a number of complementary adjustments. In principle, one might think of design features as forming a continuum in this regard (measured, e.g., in terms of the marginal cost of adjustment). But the notion of cosmetic variation seems to imply a sharp dichotomy between design changes that are easy to make and those that are not.

The approach that the American manufacturing firms are now taking goes considerably beyond cosmetic variations. It seeks to introduce into the productive system the capacity to produce several, basically distinct designs. This became economically feasible with the introduction of computer-aided manufacture, which uses relatively general equipment specialized for a particular design by a computer program. Instead of a program that produces one design, programs are written for two, three, or four designs. It is in this sense that the scale economies shift from the equipment itself to the programming. This third alternative can be called *flexible mass production*. Formally, it is a productive system that consists of a closed set with a finite number of elements.

Flexible specialization involves still a fourth type of variation, one in which the number of designs is not predetermined. Variety in flexible specialization is thus infinite, whereas in flexible mass production it is finite.

Within systems of flexible specialization, however, one can distinguish further between closed systems and open systems. A closed system is one in which the boundaries upon variety are fixed and unalterable. An open system is one in which the boundaries themselves can be changed. The distinction coincides roughly with the distinction between the garment industry of New York City, which produces only garments and, among garments, generally only those of a recognizable "New York" style, and the Route 128 Venture Club, which generates firms producing a constantly new and different set of products.

Finally, it is useful to classify open systems in terms of the cost of moving to new designs. In any system, some moves will be incremental, and others will be large and discontinuous. As will become clear shortly, an open system for which a change is large and discontinuous is in some respect similar to a system of flexible mass production.

In sum, then, we have identified three types of mass production: classic mass production, mass production with cosmetic variation, and flexible mass production; and three types of flexible specialization: a closed system, an open system with marginal adjustment, and an open system with discontinuous adjustment.

When one rereads the interviews with the aid of this typology, it becomes clear that some of the respondents see the changes over which they are presiding as a shift from classic mass production to flexible mass production and that others see those changes as a shift to flexible specialization. The organizational reforms that we are observing are thus associated with two distinct, albeit related, organizational paradigms. Relative to classic mass production, both involve more decentralization of authority and more general resources, but the degree of decentralization and the degree of generality is different in each case.

Take first the case of flexible mass production. It is clear that it requires a change in inventory policy: Either in-process inventories must be increased to the point that there are banks of parts for each model in the repertoire, or else in-process inventories must be eliminated altogether so that they do not inhibit the shift from one design to another. All three companies appear to have chosen the latter alternative. This inevitably means much greater interdependence among workstations and hence more lateral communication within the production process. There is also more lateral communication between production and marketing, for the information from the latter is required in order for the former to know exactly what to produce. All of this appears as a decentralization of authority. Nonetheless, the product designs are still built into the system in advance, and hence the product engineers direct the whole organization. The communication between marketing and production occurs within the context of a predetermined menu of designs, as does the communication among workstations within the production process. The "despecialization" of resources is limited in a similar way: Both the equipment and the work force are, by definition, less specialized. But their real generality may still be limited to the range of products actually being produced. From the point of view of the "humanization of work," the outcome may be particularly disappointing: The workers are likely to have more variety in their jobs than in classic mass production, but production can still be taught to them as a routine or, more precisely, as a series of routines, which permit little scope for originality or improvisation, and however great the workers' responsibility is in switching from one design to another, it must still be exercised within strict limits imposed by the design engineers. (Actually, in the companies studied, it appeared that equipment in flexible mass production was becoming quite general but that worker training was not. Thus the engineers talked about equipment that would outlast any given design cycle and whose capabilities might thus constitute a constraint in design. But at the same time, they talked about workers who were still retained for each product cycle so that there was no point in seeking their participation in the design process, however useful their participation might be in the production process itself once the designs were frozen and the decision was limited to those associated with the switch from one item on the menu to another.)

With flexible specialization, the same organizational reforms have much more far-reaching effects and achieve a qualitatively different result. This is so because the menu of products is not known in advance: It is necessary to invent new items continually. In-process inventories must be eliminated. Because one no longer knows what will be produced, it becomes impossible to stockpile in advance. But the resulting lateral communication in production is no longer simply the effect of reducing the isolation of the workstations. Workers must have a genuine skill that enables them to figure out how to do new operations. Similarly, the equipment must be able to produce a whole range of products. Marketing and production are forced into a genuine collaboration, which may circumvent the product designers at the center (in fact the design process is decentralized).

We should note that all of this is true simply because the set of possible products is infinite. But if the set is also open and the changes are discontinuous, the decentralized authority and general resources associated with changes in the original set or marginal expansions in the set itself may be combined with centralized authority responsible for the decision making and investments in equipment training associated with large, discontinuous changes. This is essentially the structure one now sees in Company I.

Is flexible mass production stable?

Although it is clear in the light of the extended typology that many of the reforms discussed in the interviews were really intended to implement a system of flexible mass production and not flexible specialization, one may still wonder whether flexible mass production is likely to prove a stable technological form given the changes in the business environment to which it is meant to respond.

Two considerations suggest that it is not. First, the tendency in all of these companies is clearly toward increasing the range of basic designs that they can offer at any moment of time. Thus, over time, they are being pressured to move not toward systems capable of producing two or three basic designs but ultimately toward systems capable of producing 15 or 20 varieties. As one increases the number of varieties in this way, one must eventually cross a threshold where it seems more natural not to try to anticipate the market in advance but, rather, to build into the system the capacity for marginal innovation. The second set of factors that indicate that this is likely to happen pertain to the background conditions in which the movement toward flexible mass production is taking place. All the engineers and managers interviewed seem to share two basic assumptions. One is that the equipment will outlive any given product design and hence must be much more general than the programs that are being run on it at any moment of time. Second, the product life cycle, that is, the time between generations of products, is decreasing. The last assumption creates a lot of pressure towards continuous design, which is essentially what is involved in an open system of flexible specialization. The first factor, that is, the flexibility of the existing equipment, suggests that once people begin to build open systems, the systems will be relatively easy to implement.

Finally, one might add that in most of the industries studied, discontinuous changes in the product design may still remain important to the evolution of the industry. To the extent that this is the case, they are likely to remain a central component of the organizational structure. Nonetheless, the shift from flexible mass production to flexible specialization will require considerable decentralization over and above what is currently being contemplated.

Transaction cost analysis

How does the engineering (or technological) view of organizational structure translate into more contemporary economic approaches? The most comprehensive contemporary statement is Oliver Williamson's transaction cost economics. As we saw at the outset, in Williamson's view, the principal organizational alternatives are the corporations and the market. In the latter, transactions are governed by contract, and the essential thrust of transaction cost economics is to identify a set of factors that make it difficult to write contracts covering certain transactions and hence lead instead to the internalization of these functions in the corporate organization. The principal forces on which Williamson focuses in this endeavor are specialization, uncertainty, and small number. Specialization reduces the numbers of people performing any given operation. This reduction in numbers in turn eliminates competition that might otherwise force people to reveal the true costs of performing a given task and gives rise to uncertainty as to exactly what the cost is. Such uncertainty forestalls stable, long-term relationships, and internal organizations arise because they merge the two protagonists into a single unit, essentially overcoming this problem.

Small numbers and uncertainty are clearly critical factors in the organizational shifts that are presently occurring, but they seem to be associated with the demise of the corporation rather than with its origins. As we have just seen, the whole thrust of the progressive division of labor is to create productive components that are so specialized that any shift in the level or composition of output will render them unemployable. Hence, the division of labor is intolerant of variability, particularly variability that is unanticipated. The classic corporation that Williamson set out to explain existed in an environment in which these factors had been minimized. Indeed, one can argue that the corporation arose out of the effort to create exactly that kind of environment, by gaining control over factors that in a competitive economy tended to aggravate instability and uncertainty. In this sense, the rise of the corporation is certainly associated with uncertainty, but with the effort to change uncertainty, not to accommodate it. Nor does the division of labor associated with the corporation create a small-numbers problem in the sense that Williamson understood this problem. It is true that the number of people performing a given operation is minimized (in fact, the logic of the division of labor is that only one person performs any given operation), but by the same token, the number of times the same operation is performed over time rises (in the logic of the problem, it becomes infinite). And this increase in the number of repetitions permits a variety of monitoring devices and incentive schemes that enable the parties to learn about the capabilities of their trading partners while at the same time extending their time horizons to the point that it justifies the investment that this learning, and the subsequent negotiation of a contract, requires.

Indeed, there is considerable question as to whether the distinction between the corporation and the contract is meaningful at all. Interviews with managers leave the impression that the amount of information generated in the classical mass production operation of the past was more than sufficient to write a series of specific contracts for each of the critical internal inputs and that the fact that there was in reality only a single organization had more to do with historical accident than with the logic of the transactions involved. On the other hand, the environment in which reforms of the classic corporation are now being introduced makes difficult both contracting and tight internal integration.

A more promising approach in the transaction cost tradition was outlined by Sanford Grossman and Oliver Hart in a paper entitled "The Costs and Benefits of Ownership: A Theory of Vertical and Lateral Integration." For Grossman and Hart, the critical issue in organization theory is what they call the *rights of residual control.* These are the rights to make decisions concerning the redeployment of resources that are not anticipated in a contract between the parties cooperating in the production process. When these are held by organizational components downstream in the production process, the organization is tightly integrated. When they are held by organizational components upstream, the organization is more decentralized. The relative costs of allocating these rights in different ways depends on the relative uncertainties attached to different outcomes and the distribution of the information required to make the optimal decision for contingencies that are expensive to anticipate. Our interview material was easily assimilated into this model: The increased instability in the business environment has made very large the number of contingencies that would have to be anticipated in a written contract. At the same time, it has promoted a flexibility of productive resources, and this has in turn meant that more and more of the critical information is located upstream in the production process (or at least at lower levels of the organizational hierarchy).

The ability of this model to assimilate the recent corporate changes into a transaction cost framework is, however, more limited than it appears. The critical outcomes ultimately depend, in the model, on the location of the information required to make decisions that are expensive to anticipate, and the model itself does not reveal where that information is located. For that, one must turn to a production- (or technologically) based theory, and then it is production, and not transactions, that determine the result.

A second limitation of this model, particularly in comparison with Williamson's approach, is that in applying it to the problem of corporate reform, one loses the market as a referent. Actually, this does not happen in Grossman and Hart's own work because for them, the right of residual authority is synonymous with ownership. In corporate organizations, however, we are dealing with the distribution of decision-making authority among organizational components, none of which actually owns the assets that it controls. The theory of internal organizational structure is thus purchased at the expense of a theory that explains the boundaries between the internal organization and the outside. This is also a problem in the production-based theories discussed earlier.

The lack of a theory of the market is a serious problem for orthodox economics because of the importance of the market as a referent in the conventional analytical system. It would not necessarily be a problem in analyzing corporate reorganization if one could take the corporation as a given. But as we have seen, one cannot. The precise limits of the disintegration of the classic corporation are not at all clear. It appears that such limits do indeed exist, but in order to say what they are precisely, one would need a theory of why the market fails. And in this sense Williamson's work continues to be a model for an approach to theorizing, even if the corporate reforms seem to render the theory itself inadequate.

ACKNOWLEDGMENT

The research on which this chapter is based was supported by the Management in the 1990s Research Program of the Massachusetts Institute of Technology and by the International Institute for Labour Studies of the International Labour Organisation in Geneva, Switzerland. It was conducted in collaboration with Michael Scott Morton and Gary Loveman, both of whom made extensive comments on the initial draft of the manuscript. Although some of their suggestions had already been incorporated, the manuscript required further changes in the light of their views. I am particularly grateful to Nitin Nohria, who performed the greater part of the research on the Route 128 Venture Club. I also am grateful to my colleagues Peter Temin and Charles Sabel and to the participants at several seminars in France at which the initial draft of this chapter was discussed. I, however, remain responsible for errors of omission and interpretation.

REFERENCE

Piore, M. J., & C. F. Sabel (1984). *The second industrial divide: Possibilities for prosperity.* New York: Basic Books.

CHAPTER 3

Electronic Markets and Electronic Hierarchies

THOMAS W. MALONE, JOANNE YATES, AND ROBERT I. BENJAMIN

The innovations in information technologies of the past two decades have radically reduced the time and cost of processing and communicating information. These reductions have in turn brought many changes in the ways that tasks are accomplished in firms. Data-processing systems have transformed the ways in which accounting data are gathered and processed, for example, and CAD/CAM (computer-aided design and manufacture) has transformed the ways in which complex machinery is designed. Underlying (and often obscured by) these changes in how business tasks are performed may be more fundamental changes in how firms and markets organize the flow of goods and services through their value-added chains (e.g., see Porter & Millar, 1985). This chapter addresses this more basic issue of how advances in information technology are affecting firm and market structures and discusses the options that these changes present for corporate strategies.

In brief, our thesis is that new information technologies are allowing a closer integration of adjacent steps on the value-added chain through the development of electronic markets and electronic hierarchies. Although these mechanisms are making both markets and hierarchies more efficient, we argue that they will lead to an overall shift toward proportionately more market coordination. Some firms will be able to benefit directly from this shift by becoming "market makers" for the new electronic markets. Other firms will be able to benefit from providing the interconnections to create electronic hierarchies. All firms will be able to benefit from the wider range of options provided by these markets and by the possibilities for closer coordination provided by electronic hierarchies.

After presenting the analytic framework on which our argument is based, we shall illustrate its usefulness in explaining several major historical changes in American market structures. Then we shall use the central part of this framework to predict the consequences that changing information technologies should have for our current market structures. Because we are attempting to forecast changes that have not yet occurred on a large scale, our predictions are based on a simple conceptual analysis rather than on systematic empirical studies. A conclusive test of our model and our predictions will, therefore, require further empirical and analytical work. Nevertheless, in many cases, we have been able to identify early examples of the predicted changes that have already taken place in some industries. In the final part of the chapter, we summarize some of the implications of these predicted changes for corporate strategy.

In addition to the changes in information technology that we discuss here, there are, of course, other important forces (such as changes in stock prices, antitrust regulations, and interest rates) that might affect firm and market structures. The possible consequences of these other forces are outside the scope of this chapter. The examples we describe, however, demonstrate the importance of changes in information technology, even in cases in which other forces are involved as well.

ANALYTIC FRAMEWORK

Definitions of markets and hierarchies

Economies have two mechanisms for coordinating the flow of materials or services through adjacent steps in the value-added chain: markets and hierarchies (e.g., see Coase, 1937; Williamson, 1975). Markets coordinate the flow through supply-and-demand forces and external transactions between different individuals and firms. Market forces determine the design, price, quantity, and target delivery schedule for a given product that will serve as an input into another process. That is, the buyer of the good or service compares many possible sources of it and chooses the one with the best combination of these attributes.

Hierarchies, on the other hand, coordinate the flow of materials through adjacent steps by controlling and directing it at a higher level in the managerial hierarchy, rather than by letting market transactions coordinate it. Managerial decisions, not the interaction of market forces, determine design, price (if relevant), quantity, and delivery schedules at which products from one step on the value-added chain are procured for the next step. Thus the procurer does not select a supplier from a group of potential suppliers; it simply works with a single predetermined supplier. In many cases, the hierarchy is simply a firm, whereas in others, the hierarchy may span two legally separate firms in a close, perhaps electronically mediated, sole supplier relationship.

Variants of the two pure relationships exist, but they can usually be categorized as primarily one or the other. When a single supplier serves one or more buyers as a sole source of some good, the relationship between the supplier and each buyer is primarily hierarchical, as the buyers are each procuring their supplies from a single, predetermined supplier rather than choosing from a number of suppliers. If, on the other hand, a single buyer uses multiple suppliers serving only that buyer, the relationship between that buyer and each supplier is governed by market forces, as the buyer is choosing among a number of possible suppliers. As the number of suppliers is reduced toward one, relationships may be created that have characteristics of both types.

Factors favoring markets or hierarchies

A number of theorists (e.g., Coase, 1937; Williamson, 1975, 1979, 1981a) analyzed the relative advantages of hierarchical and market methods of organizing economic activity according to various kinds of coordination costs or transaction costs. These coordination costs take into account the costs of gathering information, negotiating contracts, and protecting against risks of "opportunistic" bargaining. Building on this and other work, Malone and Smith (1988; Malone, 1987) summarized several of the fundamental trade-offs between markets and hierarchies in terms of the costs of activities such as production and coordination. Table 3.1 shows the part of their analysis that is most relevant to our argument here.[1]

In this table, the designations L and H refer only to relative comparisons within columns, not to absolute values. Production costs include the physical or other primary processes necessary to create and distribute the goods or services being produced. Coordination costs include the transaction (or governance) costs of all the information processing necessary to coordinate the work of people and machines that perform the primary processes (e.g., see Jonscher, 1983; Miller & Vollmann, 1985; Williamson, 1975). For example, coordination costs include determining the design, price, quantity, delivery schedule, and other similar factors for products transferred between adjacent steps on a value-added chain. In markets, this means selecting suppliers, negotiating contracts, paying bills, and so forth. In hierarchies, these are the managerial decision-making, accounting, planning, and control processes. The classification of a specific task as a production or coordination task sometimes depends on the level and purpose of analysis, but at an intuitive level, the distinction is clear.

Table 3.1 is consistent with both an analysis of the simple costs of information search and load sharing (Malone, 1987) and with an analysis of costs resulting from "opportunistic" behavior by trading partners with "bounded rationality" (Williamson, 1975). As Williamson explained, "Tradeoffs between production cost economies (in which the market may be presumed to enjoy certain advantages) and governance cost economies (in which the advantages may shift to internal organization) need to be recognized" (1981a, pp. 558).

In a pure market, with many buyers and sellers, the buyer can compare many different possible suppliers of the product and select the one that provides the best combination of characteristics (such as design and price), thus presumably minimizing production costs for the desired product. One of the obvious benefits of this arrangement is that it allows the demands of numerous buyers to be pooled in order to take advantage of economies of scale and load leveling. The coordination costs associated with this wide latitude of choice, however, are relatively high, because the buyer must gather and analyze information from a variety of possible suppliers. In some cases, these market coordination costs must also include additional negotiating or risk-covering costs that arise from dealing with "opportunistic" trading partners.

Hierarchies, on the other hand, restrict the procurer's choice of suppliers to the one supplier hierarchically connected to the procurer, either within a single company or in a closely linked relationship between two companies, thus leading, in general, to

Table 3.1. Relative costs for markets and hierarchies

Organizational form	Production costs	Coordination costs
Markets	L	H
Hierarchies	H	L

higher production costs than in the market arrangement. This arrangement, however, reduces coordination costs over those incurred in a market, by eliminating the procurer's need to gather and analyze a great deal of information about various suppliers.

Various factors affect the relative importance of production and coordination costs, and thus the relative desirability of markets and hierarchies (cf. Williamson, 1975, 1979, 1981a). In this paper, we will focus on those factors that are particularly susceptible to change by the new information technologies. Clearly, at a general level, one of these factors is coordination cost. Because the essence of coordination involves communicating and processing information, the use of information technology seems likely to decrease these costs (cf. Malone, 1987). Two other, more specific, factors that can be changed by information technology are also important to determining which coordination structures are desirable: asset specificity and complexity of product description. The importance of asset specificity has been amply demonstrated by previous analyses (e.g., Williamson, 1981a), but the importance of the complexity of product descriptions has not, we believe, been satisfactorily analyzed before.

Asset specificity

An input used by a firm (or individual consumer) is highly asset specific, according to Williamson's definition (1981a), if it cannot readily be used by other firms because of site specificity, physical asset specificity, or human asset specificity. A natural resource available at a certain location and moveable only at great cost is site specific, for example. A specialized machine tool or complex computer system designed for a single purpose is physically specific. Highly specialized human skills, whether physical (e.g., a trade with very limited applicability) or mental (e.g., a consultant's knowledge of a company's processes), that cannot readily be put to work for other purposes are humanly specific. We propose yet another type of asset specificity to add to Williamson's list: time specificity. An asset is time specific if its value is highly dependent on its reaching the user within a specified, relatively limited period of time. For example, a perishable product that will spoil unless it arrives at its destination and is used (or sold) within a short time after its production is time specific. Similarly, any input to a manufacturing process that must arrive at a specific time in relation to the manufacturing process or involves great costs or losses is also time specific.

There are several reasons that a highly specific asset is more likely to be obtained through hierarchical coordination than through market coordination (Williamson, 1979, 1981a). Transactions involving asset-specific products often require a long process of development and adjustments for the provider to meet the needs of the procurer, and this process favors the continuity of relationships found in a hierarchy. Moreover, because there are, by definition, few alternative procurers or suppliers of a product high in physical or human asset specificity, both the procurer and the provider in a given transaction are vulnerable. If either one goes out of business or changes its need for (or production of) the product, the other may suffer sizable losses. Thus the greater control and closer coordination allowed by a hierarchical relationship is more desirable to both.

Complexity of product description

Complexity of product description refers to the amount of information needed to specify the attributes of a product in enough detail to allow potential buyers (whether producers acquiring production inputs or consumers acquiring goods) to make a selection. Stocks and commodities, for example, have simple, standardized descriptions, whereas business insurance policies or large and complicated computer systems have much more complex descriptions. This factor is frequently, but not always, related to asset specificity; that is, in many cases a highly specific asset, such as a specialized machine tool, will require a more complex product description than will a less specific asset. The two factors are logically independent, however, despite this frequent correlation. For example, coal produced by a coal mine located adjacent to a manufacturing plant is highly site specific, though the product description is quite simple. Conversely, an automobile is low in asset specificity, as most cars can be used by many possible consumers, but the potential car buyer requires an extensive and complex description of the car's attributes in order to make a purchasing decision.

Other things being equal, products with complex descriptions are more likely to be obtained through hierarchical than through market coordination, for reasons centering on the cost of communication about a product. We have already noted that coordination costs are higher for markets than for hierarchies, in part because market transactions require contacting more possible suppliers to gather information and negotiate contracts. Because highly complex product descriptions require more information to be exchanged, they also increase the coordination cost advantage of hierarchies over markets. Thus, buyers of products with complex descriptions are more likely to work with a single supplier in a close, hierarchical relationship (whether in house or external), and buyers of simply described products (such as stocks or graded commodities) can more easily compare many alternative suppliers in a market.

As Figure 3.1 shows, then, items that are both highly asset specific and highly complex in product description are more likely to be obtained through a hierarchical relationship, and items that are not very asset specific and are simple in product description are more likely to be obtained through a market relationship. The organiza-

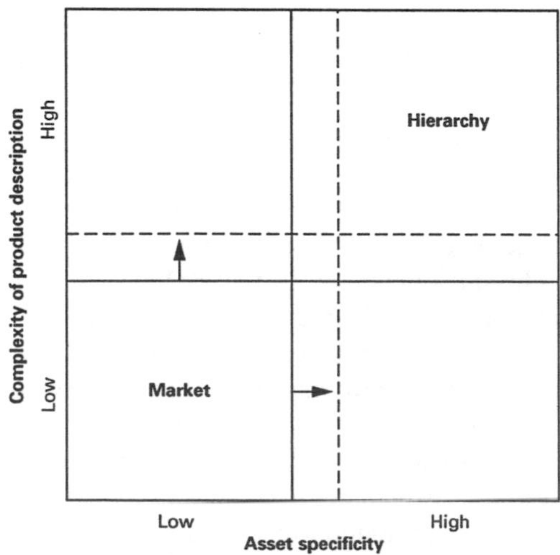

Figure 3.1. Product attributes affect forms of organization.

tional form likely for items in the other two cells of the table depends on which factor dominates.

HISTORICAL CHANGES IN MARKET STRUCTURES

To illustrate the application of our analytic framework, we shall briefly examine the historical evolution of market structures in America, paying particular attention to the effects of a key nineteenth-century information technology, the telegraph. (The analysis in this section draws on arguments by Du Boff, 1983; Malone,1987; Malone & Smith, 1988; and Williamson, 1981b. Yates, 1986, develops this application in more detail.)

Up through the mid-nineteenth century, small-scale local and regional markets, not hierarchies, coordinated adjacent stages in American industrial activity. In manufacturing, the three major functions—procurement, production, and distribution—were generally handled by different parties. By the middle of the nineteenth century, the dramatic improvements in communication and transportation provided by the telegraph and the railroads created a network for exchanging information and goods over great distances, thus effectively increasing the area over which markets or hierarchies might be established.

Our analytic framework helps explain how these developments encouraged larger and more efficient markets in some cases and larger, multifunctional hierarchies in others. On the one hand, as Table 3.1 shows, markets are more communication intensive than hierarchies are. Therefore, reducing the time and cost of communication favored markets more than hierarchies and thus encouraged the growth of markets. On the other hand, the growth in market area increased the number of economic actors that could be involved in transactions and thus increased the total amount of communication necessary for efficient markets to operate. This change favored hierarchies over markets (see Malone, 1987; Malone & Smith, 1988). The net effect of the telegraph in different industries depended in large part on the other factors from our framework.

Just as our framework would lead us to expect, nationwide markets mediated by telegraph developed for products such as stocks and commodities futures. These products were nonspecific assets with many potential buyers. In addition, they could easily be described, and consequently were susceptible to standardized designations that lowered telegraph costs further. The commodities futures market, for example, emerged on a national scale only after a uniform grading scheme that simplified product description had been adopted (Du Boff, 1983).

The detailed evolutionary path of large integrated hierarchies was more complex than that of national markets, and it involved several factors other than the telegraph. Nevertheless, our framework again proves useful in explaining which conditions led to which forms. The growth of market areas, according to Chandler (1977), encouraged producers to increase their production, frequently by developing new techniques of mass production that offered economies of scale. Such firms, however, often found that existing procurement and distribution mechanisms did not support the high volume of output necessary to realize the economies, especially when procurement or distribution for the product required specialized equipment or human expertise.

As Williamson (1981b) pointed out, the companies that Chandler identified as the first to vertically integrate procurement, production, and distribution within a hierarchy were those companies with asset-specific products, such as meat packers with perishable products requiring railroad refrigeration cars and rapid delivery, and manufacturers of complex machine tools with specialized sales and support needs. In the first case, high time specificity outweighed low complexity of product description. In the second case, the products were complex to describe, and the sales process was high in human specificity. For these firms, the telegraph provided a mechanism by which close hierarchical coordination could be maintained over great distances. Although the economies of scale were the major factor driving this integration, asset specificity and complexity of product description played a role in determining which firms were likely to integrate, using the telegraph as a mechanism of hierarchical coordination rather than as a mechanism of market communication.

Thus our analytic framework is useful in interpreting the impact of communication technology on past changes in organizational form, even when noncommunication factors also played a large role. In the next section, we apply the framework to contemporary developments.

CONTEMPORARY CHANGES IN MARKET STRUCTURES

We can now give a fuller explanation of the nature of electronic hierarchies and markets, the conditions under which each is likely to emerge, and the reasoning behind our thesis that the balance is shifting toward electronic markets.

Emergence of electronic interconnection

Let us begin by looking briefly at the technological developments that make electronic interconnection of either type possible and desirable. New information technologies have greatly reduced both the time and cost of communicating information, just as the telegraph did when it was introduced. In particular, the use of computer and telecommunications technology for transferring information gives rise to what we term the *electronic communication effect.* This means that information technology may (1) allow more information to be communicated in the same amount of time (or the same amount in less time) and (2) dramatically decrease the costs of this communication. These effects may benefit both markets and hierarchies.

In addition to these well-known general advantages of electronic communication, electronic coordination can be used to take advantage of two other effects: the *electronic brokerage effect* and the *electronic integration effect.* The electronic brokerage effect is of benefit primarily in the case of computer-based markets. A broker is an agent who is in contact with many potential buyers and suppliers and who, by filtering these possibilities, helps match buyers and suppliers to each other. The presence of the broker substantially reduces the need for buyers and suppliers to contact a large number of alternative partners individually (see Baligh & Richartz, 1967, and Malone, 1987, for detailed formal analyses of the benefits of brokering). The electronic brokerage effect simply means that electronic markets, by electronically connecting many different buyers and suppliers through a central data base, can fulfill this same function. The standards and protocols of the electronic market allow a buyer to screen out obviously inappropriate suppliers and to compare the offerings of many different potential suppliers quickly, conveniently, and inexpensively. Thus the electronic brokerage effect offered by an electronic market can (1) increase the number of alternatives that can be considered, (2) increase the quality of the alternative eventually selected, and (3) decrease the cost of the entire product selection process.

When a supplier and a procurer use information technology to create joint, interpenetrating processes at the interface between value-added stages, they are taking advantage of the electronic integration effect. This effect occurs when information technology is used not just to speed communication but also to change—and lead to tighter coupling between—the processes that create and use the information. One simple benefit of this effect is the time saved and the errors avoided by the fact that data need be entered only once. Much more important benefits of close integration of processes are possible in specific situations. CAD/CAM technology, for example, often allows both design engineers and manufacturing engineers to access and manipulate the design and manufacturing data to try out more designs and to create a product more acceptable to both sides. As another example, systems linking the supplier's and procurer's inventory management processes, so that the supplier can ship the products "just in time" for their use in the procurer's manufacturing process, enable the procurer to eliminate inventory holding costs and thus to reduce total inventory costs for the linked companies. The benefits of the electronic integration effect are usually captured most easily in electronic hierarchies, but they are sometimes apparent in electronic markets as well.

These advantages of electronic interconnections compared with existing nonelectronic coordination methods provide substantial benefits. The recipients of these benefits (either buyers or suppliers, or both) should be willing to pay for them (either directly or indirectly), and thus the providers of electronic markets and electronic hierarchies should, in many cases, be able to realize significant revenues from providing these services.

Shifting from hierarchies toward markets

Our prediction that information technology will be more widely used for coordinating economic activities is not a surprising one, even though our analysis of the three effects involved (electronic communication, brokerage, and integration effects) is new. In this section, we move to a more surprising and significant prediction: that the overall effect of this technology will be to increase the proportion of economic activity coordinated by markets.

Although the effects of information technology just discussed clearly make both markets and hierarchies more efficient, we see two arguments supporting an overall shift toward market coordination: The first is a general argument based on the analysis summarized in Table 3.1; the second is a more specific argument based on shifts in asset specifity and complexity of product descriptions.

General argument favoring shift towards markets

Our first argument for the overall shift from hierarchies to markets is a simple one, based primarily on two components. The first component is the assumption that the widespread use of information technology is likely to decrease the "unit costs" of coordination. As we noted, by coordination, we mean the information processing in tasks such as selecting suppliers, establishing contracts, scheduling activities, budgeting resources, and tracking financial flows. Because by definition, these coordination processes require communicating and processing information, it seems quite plausible to assume that information technology, when used appropriately, can reduce these costs. This is, of course, an empirically testable hypothesis, and there are already some suggestive data that support it (e.g., Crawford, 1982; Jonscher, 1983; Strassman, 1985).

The second component of our argument is based on the trade-offs summarized in Table 3.1. As we noted, and as Williamson (1981a) and numerous others have observed, markets have certain production cost advantages over hierarchies as a means of coordinating economic activity. The main disadvantage of markets is the cost of conducting the market transactions themselves. For a number of reasons (including the "opportunistic" ones emphasized by Williamson and the purely "informational" ones emphasized by Malone, 1987), these coordination costs are generally higher in markets than in hierarchies. An overall reduction in the "unit costs" of coordination would reduce the importance of the coordination cost dimension (on which markets are weak) and thus lead to markets becoming more desirable in some situations in which hierarchies were previously desirable. In other words, the result of lowering coordination costs, without changing anything else, should be to increase the proportion of economic activity coordinated by markets. This simple argument does not depend on the specific values of any of the costs involved, on the current relative importance of production and coordination costs, or on the current proportion of hierarchical and market coordination.

We find the simplicity of this argument quite compelling, but its obviousness appears not to have been widely recognized. There is also another, less obvious, argument that leads to the same conclusion. This second argument is based on shifts in our key factors for determining coordination structures: asset specificity and complexity of product description.

Changes in factors favoring electronic markets versus electronic hierarchies

As Figure 3.1 shows, some of the new, computer-based information technologies have affected both of our key dimensions in such a way as to create an overall shift from hierarchies to markets. Data bases and high-bandwidth electronic communication can handle and communicate complex, multidimensional product descriptions much more readily than traditional modes of communication can. Thus the line between high and low complexity has, in effect, shifted upward so that some product descriptions previously classified as highly complex, such as those of airline reservations, may now be considered low in complexity relative to the capabilities of the technology to communicate and manipulate them. The line should continue to shift upward for some time as the capabilities of information technology continue to evolve.

The dimension of asset specificity has also changed in such a way as to favor markets slightly over hierarchies. Flexible manufacturing technology allows a rapid changeover of production lines from one product to another. Thus some physical asset-specific components that are similar to other, nonspecific components may begin to be produced by more companies. Companies that in the past would not have tooled up for such a small market now may produce small numbers of these components without significant switch-over costs. Thus the vertical line in Figure 3.1 moves slightly right because some asset-specific components have become, in essence, less specific.

Both these changes enlarge the region of the figure in which market modes of coordination are favored, lending more support to our argument that there will be an overall shift in this direction.

Examples of shifts toward electronic markets

A dramatic example of this process has already occurred in the airline industry. When airline reservations are made by a customer calling the airline directly (with the "commission" received by the airline's own sales department), the selling process is coordinated by the hierarchical relationship between the sales department and the rest of the firm. When airline reservations are made through a travel agent, the sale is made (and the commission received) by the travel agent acting as an external selling agent for the airline. The selling process, in this case, is coordinated by the market relationship between the travel agent and the airline. Due, presumably in large part, to the greater range of choices conveniently available through the electronic market, the proportion of total bookings made by travel agents (rather than by customers dealing with airline sales departments) has doubled from 35 to 70 percent since the introduction of the American Airlines reservations system (Petre, 1985, pp. 43–44).

Similarly, there are many recent examples of companies such as IBM, Xerox, and General Electric substantially increasing the proportion of components from other vendors contained in their products (e.g., see *Business Week*, 1986; Prokesh, 1985). This kind of "vertical disintegration" of production activities into different firms has become more advantageous as computerized inventory control systems and other forms of electronic integration allow some of the advantages of the internal hierarchical relationship to be retained in market relationships with external suppliers.

EVOLUTION OF ELECTRONIC MARKETS AND ELECTRONIC HIERARCHIES

Motives for establishing an electronic market: Possible market makers

An electronic market may develop from a nonelectronic market or from an electronic hierarchy spanning firm boundaries. As Figure 3.2 indicates, any of several participants in an emerging electronic market may be its initiator or market maker, each with different motives. For a market to emerge at all there must be both producers and buyers of some good or service. (Depending on the nature of the good or service and on the coordination mechanism used, *producers* may also be called *manufacturers* or *suppliers*, and we use these three terms interchangeably. Similarly, we use the

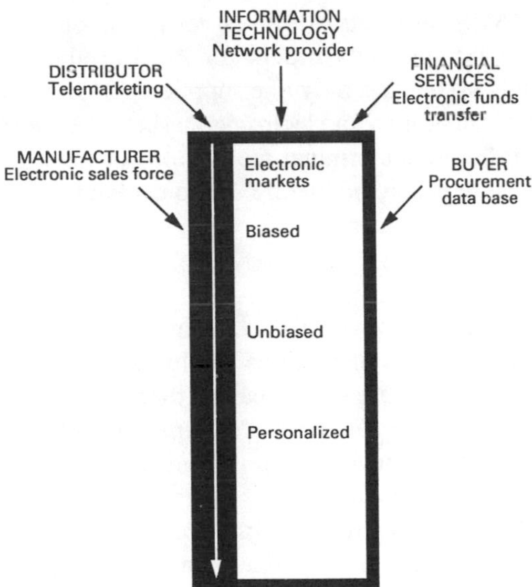

Figure 3.2. Evolution of electronic market makers. Multiple starting points lead to a common evolutionary path.

terms *buyers*, *procurers*, and *consumers* interchangeably.) In addition to these primary participants, an existing market may also include two other kinds of participants. First, there may be various levels of "middlemen" who act as distributors, brokers, or agents in the transfer of the goods being sold. We will usually use the term *distributors* to refer to all these levels. Second, there may also be various kinds of financial service firms such as banks and credit card issuers who store, transfer, and sometimes lend the funds needed in the transactions. Finally, we may regard as potential participants in any electronic marketplace the information technology vendors who can provide the networks, terminals, and other hardware and software necessary for a computer-based market. Each of these different kinds of market participants has different motivations and different possibilities for helping form electronic markets. Our framework suggests how these motivations and other forces such as the electronic brokering, electronic communication, and electronic integration effects may influence the evolution of electronic markets.

Producers

As the initial maker of a product, the producing firm is motivated to have buyers purchase its products rather than those of its competitors. This motivation has already led several producers to establish electronic interconnections with their buyers. In the airline industry, such electronic systems were originally established to encourage travelers to buy tickets from the airline providing the service; they were thus initially electronic hierarchies. Now, however, the systems provide access to tickets from all airlines, thus creating electronic markets with an electronic brokering effect (*Business Week*, 1985c; Cash & Konsynski, 1985; Petre, 1985). Another example of an electronic interconnection established by a producer is American Hospital Supply's ASAP system. Under this system, several thousand hospitals that buy American Hospital Supply's (AHS) products are given terminals on their own premises that allow them to enter automatically orders for AHS products (Jackson, 1985; Petre, 1985). Because this system has only one supplier (AHS), we would classify it as an electronic hierarchy rather than an electronic market. As we shall explain, our framework suggests that despite the original motivations of the producers, there are often strong forces that cause electronic hierarchies to evolve toward electronic markets that do not favor specific producers.

Buyers

In contrast with the producer, who would like to minimize the number of alternatives that the buyers consider, the buyers themselves would like to maximize the number of alternatives considered and the ease of comparing them. One way of doing this is for buyers to begin using computer data bases containing information about alternative products. In some cases, the buyers are powerful enough in a market that they can require suppliers to provide this information, thus creating an electronic market. For example, General Motors already requires its primary suppliers to conform to the computer hardware and communications standards established by the Automotive Industry Action Group (Cash & Konsynski, 1985). These systems can then be used to speed order processing and implement innovations such as "just-in-time" inventory management (*Business Week*, 1985a). Groups of buyers are currently developing similar electronic markets in the grocery, chemical, and aluminum industries as well (*Business Week*, 1985a). Unlike systems provided by producers, which are motivated by the desire to establish an attractive distribution channel for certain products, these systems are established by buyers to make supplier selection, order processing, and inventory management more efficient.

Distributors

In some cases, the initiative for a computer-based market may come from distributors rather than directly from buyers or suppliers. In the pharmaceuticals industry, for example, wholesale distributors such as McKesson have followed the lead of producers such as American Hospital Supply in setting up electronic connections with their customers (*Business Week*, 1985b). Like American Hospital, such distributors established the electronic links in order to try to monopolize the business of their customers, and at this stage, the systems are still electronic hierarchies rather than electronic markets. Just as with systems developed by producers, however, we expect that electronic links developed by distributors will often have an initial bias toward one or more producers but that these biases will usually disappear under pressure from competitive and legal forces. Although the benefits to the distributor may initially have had their source in the bias, the distributor may soon find that the greater efficiency offered by the electronic market over conventional markets allows adequate compensation to the distributor for running an unbiased market.

Financial services providers

By transferring the funds and/or extending the credit required for transactions, banks and other financial institutions are already participating in most markets. In some cases, this involvement can be the basis for providing a full-fledged electronic market. For example, some banks, such as Citicorp, provide to their credit card holders a telephone shopping service for a wide variety of consumer goods (Stevenson, 1985). The system keeps a log of the lowest retail prices available for all the products included. Cardholders can call for a price quotation, order the goods over the phone using their credit card, and have the goods delivered to their door. In a similar spirit, Citicorp and McGraw-Hill have formed a joint venture to disseminate information about alternative oil prices for crude oil and to match buyers and sellers (Bennett, 1985). Similarly, Louie (1985) described the evolution of the PRONTO home banking system at Chemical Bank, New York, from offering a single financial service (home banking) to becoming a full systems operator and providing home information services with stock prices and home-retailing information. The initial motivation of the financial institution in these cases is presumably not to favor the sale of any particular producer's products but to increase the volume of transaction processing and credit-based income for the financial institution.

Information technology vendors

In all of these examples, the hardware, networks, and often software necessary to create computer-based markets are provided by information technology vendors. Even though these examples demonstrate how the line between information technology vendors and other kinds of firms is beginning to blur, there are still some cases in which firms whose principal business is supplying information technology may be able to make computer-based markets themselves. For example, Western Union has a system for matching freight shippers with motor freight carriers and checking that the carriers have the necessary legal authorization and insurance coverage (Ives & Learmonth, 1984, p. 1199). It is easy to imagine other examples of information technology vendors' making markets. For example, a natural extension of the classified directory now provided by telephone companies would be an "electronic Yellow Pages," perhaps including capabilities for actually placing orders as well as locating suppliers. (A directory-only service of this type is already offered by Automated Directory Services; see Koenig, 1983.)

STAGES IN THE EVOLUTION OF ELECTRONIC MARKETS

We have seen that electronic markets may evolve from nonelectronic markets or from electronic or nonelectronic hierarchies. Frequently this evolution has an intermediate stage, a biased market, but eventually proceeds to an unbiased market. In the future, the evolution may continue to a personalized market.

From biased to unbiased markets

Some of the first providers of electronic markets attempted to exploit the benefits of the electronic communication effect in order to capture customers in a system biased toward a particular supplier. We believe that in the long run, the significant additional benefits to buyers possible from the electronic brokerage effect will drive almost all electronic markets toward being unbiased channels for products from many suppliers. For example, both American Airlines and United Airlines have introduced reservation systems that allow travel agents to find and book flights, print tickets, and so forth (*Business Week*, 1985c; Cash & Konsynski, 1985; Petre, 1985). The United system originally was established as an electronic hierarchy that allowed travel agents to book only flights on United. To compete with this system, American established a system that included flights from all airlines (thus making it a true market), but with American flights on a given route listed first. This shift to a biased market was possible both because airline reservations are not asset specific and because they can be described in standardized forms and manipulated in standardized processes that may be quickly and easily handled by the new technology. United soon adopted the same strategy, and by 1983 travel agencies that used automated reservation systems used one of these two systems in 65 percent of the reservations they made (Cash & Konsynski, 1985, p. 139). The significant bias in favor of their suppliers' flights that was introduced by these two systems eventually led other airlines to protest, and a ruling from the Federal Aviation Administration (FAA) eliminated much of the bias in the system. Now the systems continue to provide the same reservation service to other airlines, but for a significant fee.

A similar evolution may result in the case of American Hospital Supply's ASAP order entry system. American Hospital is apparently trying to prevent that outcome by making the shared processes themselves more asset specific. For instance, Jackson (1985, p. 137) listed many features built into the ASAP system to customize the system to a particular hospital's needs, in effect creating a procedural asset specificity in the relationship between buyer and seller. These features include purchase history files, computation of economic order quantities, and basic order file templates. In each case, powerful one-to-one hierarchical relationships are established between buyer and seller. However, most of the medical products sold through the system meet these criteria for electronic markets: They are not uniquely useful for specific customers, and their descriptions are relatively simple and standardized. Therefore, our model leads us to predict that this system (or its competitors) will move toward including products from many different suppliers. The same evolution is likely in the case of pharmaceutical distributors such as McKesson.

These examples show what we believe will be a common case: Producers who start out by providing an electronic hierarchy or a biased electronic market will eventually be driven by competitive or legal forces to remove or significantly reduce the bias.

From unbiased to personalized markets

A possible problem with unbiased electronic markets of the sort we have described is that they might overwhelm buyers with more alternatives than the buyers can possibly consider. This problem will be less important in commoditylike markets in which the product descriptions are well-known standards and in which the only dimension on which products are compared is price. But the problem will be particularly acute in markets for which the product descriptions have a number of related attributes that are compared in different ways by different buyers. Retail sales of many consumer products, for example, would fall into this category.

When electronic markets provide personalized decision aids to help individual buyers select from among the alternatives available, we will call them *personalized markets*. For example, at least one such system has been developed for airline reservations (Brown, 1986). Using this system, travel agencies and corporate travel departments can receive information about available flights, with each flight automatically ranked on a scale from 1 to 100. The rankings take into account "fares, departure times, and even the value of an executive's time."

It is easy to imagine even more sophisticated systems that use techniques from artificial intelligence to screen advertising messages and product descriptions according to the criteria that are important to a given buyer (e.g., see Malone et al., 1987, for a similar system that filters electronic messages of all kinds). Air travelers, for instance, might specify rules with which their own "automated buyers' agents" could compare a wide range of possible flights and select the ones that best match a particular traveler's preferences. A fairly simple set of such rules could, in many cases, do a better job of matching particular travelers' preferences than could all but the most conscientious and knowledgeable human travel agents.

In addition to techniques from artificial intelligence for specifying complex qualitative reasoning processes, there also are a number of normative mathematical models (e.g., Keeney & Raiffa, 1976), and descriptive behavioral models (Johnson & Payne, 1985; Payne, Braunstein, & Carroll, 1978; Russo & Dosher, 1983) that can help in designing such systems.

Clearly, these techniques will be more useful for certain products (e.g., those that are easily described and nonspecific) and certain buyers (e.g., industrial buyers doing routine purchasing rather than consumers buying on impulse). Ultimately, however, such personalized decision aids may be widely useful in both industrial and consumer purchasing for screening large amounts of electronically stored product information on behalf of particular buyers.

Another intriguing possibility is that some of the preference rules specified by buyers might be made available to suppliers. There clearly are cases in which protecting the privacy of buyers should preclude making this information available. In other cases, however, making the preferences of large numbers of buyers automatically available (perhaps anonymously) to suppliers, could dramatically improve the efficiency of certain kinds of market research and the responsiveness of suppliers. Instead of having to infer consumer decision rules from surveys or experiments, for example, suppliers might be able simply to observe the actual rules consumers had specified.

MOTIVES FOR ESTABLISHING ELECTRONIC HIERARCHIES

Although we have presented our reasons for expecting an overall shift toward electronic markets, there are still many cases in which asset specificity is high and product descriptions are complex and thus in which electronic hierarchies will be desirable. In particular, as Figure 3.3 suggests, electronic hierarchies will be established to improve product development or to improve product distribution. In this section, we discuss why and how companies may establish electronic hierarchies for each of these functions.

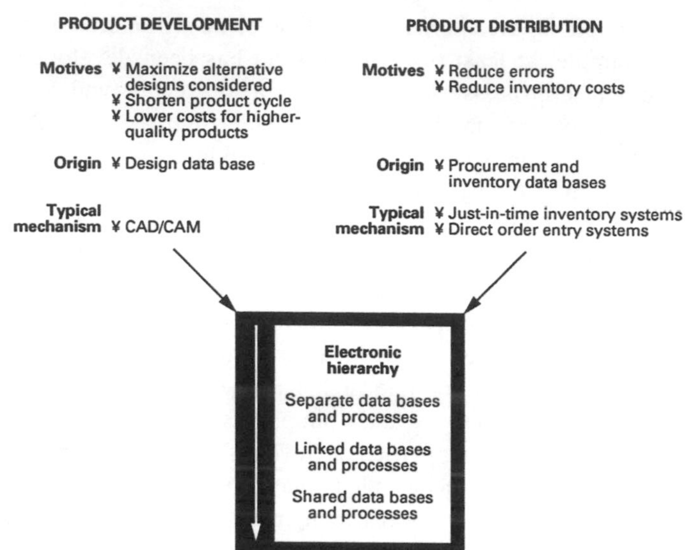

Figure 3.3. Evolution of electronic hierarchies: from separate to shared data bases.

Product development

In product development, CAD/CAM, electronic mail, and other information technologies can be used to enhance the hierarchical coordination between design and manufacturing groups. The electronic integration effect can be used, in this case, (1) to shorten the development cycle, (2) to increase the number of alternative designs considered, (3) to reduce development (i.e., coordination) costs, (4) to lower manufacturing costs (by involving manufacturing engineers in the design process), and (5) to produce a higher-quality product. The president of Xerox's newly integrated Engineering and Manufacturing Group, for example, says of such integration: "It is the key to faster and less costly development, to lower manufacturing costs, and to better products" (Hicks, 1984).

The key data that must be shared in the product development process are engineering drawings, parts descriptions, bills of materials, engineering change notices, machine tool configurations, and so forth. For example, in many companies the engineering change notice (ECN) process is considered a people-intensive, time-consuming, and error-prone administrative activity. Because the shared data base of an electronic hierarchy allows people directly involved in the change to work with the ECN process electronically, the large bureaucracy previously needed for administering this process coordination may be severely reduced (e.g., Miller & Vollmann, 1985).

Xerox's new electronic ECN process, for instance, has three parties: the design engineer, who is also responsible for the "manufacturability" of the change and the entering of the change in the spare parts ordering process; the manufacturing engineer, who designs the actual manufacturing process; and the manufacturing analyst, who updates the necessary manufacturing data bases to accommodate the change. In the previous process, a number of other people were also involved: the advanced manufacturing engineer, who worked with the design engineer to determine general manufacturability; the administrator of the record center where all data on the part were kept, who managed copying and distribution to necessary parties; the manufacturing configuration specialist, who provided information on the manufacturing bill of materials and maintained any changes required; and the spare parts planner, who entered and ordered spares for initializing the product in the distribution system. The electronic data base permits a significant reduction in administrative coordination costs and, more importantly, increases the quality and timeliness of the product development process as well.

Although this example is of electronic integration within one organization, there also are examples of linkages between design and manufacturing groups in different companies in both heavy manufacturing and the auto industry (Cash & Konsynski, 1985; Prokesh, 1985) In the design of semiconductor circuits, for instance, over 100 different processes and over 30 to 40 separate organizations have traditionally been involved (Feigenbaum & McCorduck, 1984; Strassmann, 1985). Use of the Mead Conway method for VLSI design and electronic integration between organizations has dramatically cut the number of processes and people necessary. Designers in remote organizations use standardized languages in functionally rich workstations and then send their standardized design data bases over a network to a supplier fabrication facility where they are linked to the supplier's manufacturing-process data bases. The end result is that the test circuits are delivered to the procurer at a much lower cost and in much less time.

Thus electronic integration of product design and development, whether within or between firms, uses linked or shared data bases to achieve more efficient and effective product development cycles. The electronic integration effect may also be realized in product distribution.

Product distribution

In product distribution systems, there are two main participants: the procurer and the supplier. The procurer's goal for establishing electronic hierarchies may be to have the inventory available to the factory production process "just in time," thus eliminating inventory carrying costs as well as all production control necessary to manage the staging of inventory (Nakane & Hall, 1983). That is, to lower inventory costs, procurers may raise the time specificity of the process. Firestone, for example, is part of the physical and electronic inventory system of two of the major car manufacturers, with the result that it, rather than the car manufacturer, carries the inventory of tires. Similarly, the large battery manufacturer that supplies the tire manufacturer's retail stores is tied into the store's physical and electronic inventory systems.

As we have seen, these electronic interconnections are allowing many manufacturers to rely more and more on external suppliers of components rather than on manufacturing the components themselves (e.g., Prokesh, 1985). One somewhat paradoxical aspect of this shift is that even though manufacturers are increasing the volume of components purchased externally, they are decreasing the number of suppliers from which these components are purchased (Prokesh, 1985, p. D5). This paradox can be resolved, however, by noting that the reasons given for minimizing the number of suppliers (e.g., to become preferred customers and thus increase leverage with the suppliers) amount to ways of intensifying the asset specificity of the products. In other words, these buyers are using information technology to "get the best of both worlds"—they are using electronic markets more often, but their relationships with each of the suppliers in these markets are becoming more like electronic hierarchies.

The supplier may be motivated to enter such a just-in-time arrangement for defensive reasons: Doing so may be a condition of doing business with the procurer. The supplier, however, may also perceive other advantages in an electronic arrangement. Jackson asserted that a buyer is unlikely to tamper with an established just-in-time relationship, "because changing would require another substantial investment in learning to work with the new vendor" (1985, p. 134). That is, the shared data bases and shared physical and electronic processes may become physically and humanly specific, as well as time specific, thereby making more likely a hierarchical rather than a market relationship. As we have seen, this is clearly a consideration in early systems such as that developed by American Hospital Supply. As we saw earlier, however, such electronic hierarchies frequently develop into biased and then unbiased electronic markets when the products themselves are not asset specific and are easy to describe in standardized terms.

In addition to these separate motives, both the procurer and the supplier may be motivated to reduce the time, cost, and errors produced by an extensive procurement system that requires repeated entries, transmissions, translations into different terms, and reentries of information between paper and computer systems of suppliers and procurers. For the automakers and component suppliers, for example, this costly process results in errors in approximately 5 percent of all procurer and supplier documents, according to an industry group (*Business Week*, 1985a). This group, the Automotive Industry Action Group, is establishing standard forms and processes for the three big auto companies and their many suppliers to use. Once these standards are established, the existing electronic hierarchies between buyers and sellers in this market are likely to evolve into electronic markets.

Relative power of participants

As these examples demonstrate, one of the critical factors in the establishment of electronic interconnections is the relative power of the participants. The interconnections that emerge are determined in part by the preexisting power relationships of the participants, and these power relationships may, in turn, be changed by the new electronic arrangements. For example, suppliers may enter into into a just-in-time inventory arrangement in order to continue doing business with a powerful buyer, and the knowledge that this arrangement gives the buyer about the inventory positions of all its suppliers may enhance the buyer's power even more.

Sometimes, merely agreeing on the standards for electronic systems can be the battleground on which many of the power issues are fought. For example, in the insurance industry, both the independent agents and the major commercial and property carriers are hotly contesting the control of standards (Benjamin, 1983). The large carriers would like to tie independent agents to their own systems and see their proprietary standards as a means to achieve this. However, the independent agents, through an industry association, are defining a set of standards for the principal insurance transactions that will give them the freedom to do business with multiple carriers. A number of large carriers have indicated that they will now live with the more general standards.

Stages in the evolution of electronic hierarchies

As we have seen, shared data bases, made possible by advances in information technology, are at the core of electronic hierarchies. They provide the mechanism for integrating processes across organizational boundaries by allowing the continuous sharing of information in easily accessible on-line form (Benjamin & Scott Morton, 1988).

Our basis for predicting the evolutionary path of these mechanisms is the observation that both the benefits and the costs of electronic integration become greater as the coupling between adjacent steps on the value-added chain becomes tighter. Thus we would expect organizations to obtain limited benefits at low cost before moving to greater benefits at a higher cost. Figure 3.3 indicates a plausible trajectory that this observation suggests: Stand-alone but mutually accessible data bases should appear first, then be replaced by electronically linked data bases, and, eventually, by fully shared data bases. We are not aware of good examples of all three stages of this trajectory occurring in a single system, but we can describe examples of systems at each of the three stages.

Stand-alone data bases

In this stage, stand-alone data bases, one or both parties make their data bases accessible to the other party in the electronic hierarchy. This often requires the other party to use a separate workstation. For example, the early versions of the American Hospital Supply order entry system required customers to use a separate workstation to access the AHS order entry programs and purchasing-history data bases (Harvard Business School, 1985). Even though the data base that is built up in this process is, in some sense, "shared" by the customers and AHS, it is not connected to the customers' accounting and other application systems, and so we classify it as a stand-alone data base.

Linked data bases

In this stage, linked data bases, the data bases are still separate, but a formal on-line mechanism passes information from one party's data base to the other. The most recent version of the AHS order entry system (see Harvard Business School, 1985) allows this kind of direct computer-to-computer communication. Orders are prepared by the customer's internal computer system and transmitted electronically to AHS, and then order confirmations are returned to the customer's computer and used to update the hospital's files. Another example of this level of linking is provided by the Mead-Conway VLSI design methodology. Here, electronic networks are used to transfer product design specifications from the CAD system on the designer's workstation to a manufacturing system that is located at a remote site and owned by another organization.

Shared data bases

In this final stage, shared data bases, one data base contains information of value to both parties in the electronic hierarchy. The engineering change notice process we described demonstrates a simple example of this situation, and great effort is currently being expended by CAD/CAM vendors and manufacturing companies to implement and use successfully this integrated engineering/manufacturing data base environment.

CONCLUSIONS AND STRATEGIC IMPLICATIONS

A casual reading of the business press makes clear that electronic connections within and between organizations are becoming increasingly important (e.g., *Business Week*, 1985c; Cash & Konsynski, 1985; Petre, 1985). The framework we have developed in this chapter helps explain many of these changes. We have shown how the greater use of electronic interconnections can be seen as the result of three forces: the electronic communication effect, the electronic brokerage effect, and the electronic integration effect. We have analyzed how factors such as the ease of product description and the degree to which products are specific to particular customers affect whether these interconnections will take the form of electronic hierarchies or electronic markets. Finally, and perhaps most importantly, we have argued that by reducing the costs of coordination, information technology will lead to an overall shift toward a proportionately greater use of markets rather than toward hierarchies to coordinate economic activity. By applying this framework, it is possible to see how many of the changes occuring today fit into a larger picture and to predict some of the specific evolutionary changes that are likely to occur as information technology becomes more widely used.

Our analysis has several implications for corporate strategy:

1. All market participants should consider whether it would be advantageous for them to try to provide an electronic market in their marketplace. For some participants, providing such a market may raise the sales of their current products or services. For all participants, it can offer a source of new revenues from the market-making activity itself.
2. All organizations should consider whether it would be advantageous for them to coordinate some of their own internal operations more closely or to establish tighter connections with their customers or suppliers by using electronic hierarchies.
3. Market forces make it very likely that biased electronic sales channels (whether electronic hierarchies or biased electronic markets) for nonspecific, easily described products will eventually be replaced by unbiased markets. Therefore, the early developers of biased electronic sales channels for these kinds of products should not expect that the competitive advantages that these systems provide will continue indefinitely. They should instead be planning how to manage the transition to unbiased markets in such a way that they can continue to derive revenues from the market-making activity itself.
4. All firms should consider whether more of the activities they currently perform in-

ternally could be performed less expensively or more flexibly by outside suppliers whose selection and work could be coordinated by computer-based systems.

5. Information systems groups in most firms should begin to plan the network infrastructure that will be necessary to support the kinds of internal and external interconnections that we have described.
6. Advanced developers of computer-based marketing technology should begin thinking about how to develop intelligent aids to help buyers select products from a large number of alternatives. Such intelligent aids may eventually be able to act, in part, as automated agents for the buyers. They may also, in some situations, be able to provide detailed information to suppliers about their customers' preferences.

In short, if our predictions are correct, we should not expect the electronically interconnected world of tomorrow to be simply a faster and more efficient version of the world we know today. Instead, we should expect fundamental changes in how firms and markets organize the flow of goods and services in our economy. Clearly, more systematic empirical study and more detailed formal analyses are needed to confirm these predictions, and we hope that the conceptual framework presented here will help guide this research.

ACKNOWLEDGMENT

This research was supported, in part, by the Management in the 1990s Research Program and the Center for Information Systems Research at the Sloan School of Management, Massachusetts Institute of Technology.

NOTE

1. In the terms used by Malone and Smith (1988; Malone, 1987), this table compares the performance that can be achieved with separate divisions in a product hierarchy with the performance that can be achieved with separate companies coordinated by a decentralized market (see Malone, 1987, Table 2). As Malone (1987, pp. 18–19) noted, this comparison is equivalent to a comparison of coordination by separate hierarchical firms and coordination by a market.

REFERENCES

Baligh, H. H., & L. Richartz (1967). *Vertical market structures.* Boston: Allyn & Bacon.

Barrett, S., & B. Konsynski (1982). Inter-organization information sharing systems. *MIS Quarterly* (special edition), December, p. 94.

Benjamin, R. (1983). What companies share is virtually a new game. *Information Systems News*, December 26, p. 11.

Benjamin, R., & M. S. Scott Morton (1988). Information technology, integration, and organizational change. *Interfaces.*

Bennett, R. A. (1985). Citibank, McGraw in a venture: Information service for oil. *New York Times*, September 10 (business section), p. 1.

Business Week (1985a). Detroit tries to level a mountain of paperwork. August 26, pp. 94–96.

——— (1985b). For drug distributors, information is the Rx for survival. October 14, p. 116.

——— (1985c). Information power: How companies are using new technologies to gain a competitive edge. October 14, pp. 108–116.

——— (1985d). Toyota's fast lane. November 5, pp. 42–44.

——— (1986). The hollow corporation (a special report), March 3, pp. 57–85.

Cash, J. (1985). Interorganizational systems: An information society opportunity or threat? *Information Society* 3:211.

Cash, J. I., & B. R. Konsynski (1985). IS redraws competitive boundaries. *Harvard Business Review*, March–April, pp. 134–42.

Chandler, A. D. (1962). *Strategy and structure.* New York: Doubleday.

Coase, R. H. (1937). The nature of the firm. *Economica N.S.* 4 (November).

Crawford, A. B. (1982). Corporate electronic mail: A communication-intensive application of information technology. *MIS Quarterly*, September, pp. 1–13.

Du Boff, R. B. (1983). The telegraph and the structure of markets in the United States, 1845–1890. *Research in economic history*, Vol. 8, pp. 253–77. Greenwich, CT: JAI Press.

Feigenbaum, E., & P. McCorduck (1984). *The fifth generation: Artificial intelligence and Japan's challenge to the world.* Reading, MA: Addison Wesley.

Harvard Business School (1985). American Hospital Supply Corp. (A) The ASAP system. HBS Case no. 0186–005.

Hicks, W. (1984). A new approach to product development. *High Technology*, October, p. 12.

Ives, B. I., & G. P. Learmonth (1984). The information system as a competitive weapon. *Communications of the ACM* 27 (December): 1193–1201.

Jackson, B. (1985). *Winning and keeping industrial customers.* Lexington, MA: Heath/Lexington Books.

Johnson, E., & J. Payne (1985). Effort, accuracy, and choice. *Management Science* 31 (April): 395–414.

Jonscher, C. J. (1983). Information resources and productivity. *Information Economics and Policy* 1:13–35.

Keeney, R. L., & H. Raiffa (1976). *Decision with multiple objectives: Preferences and value tradeoffs.* New York: Wiley.

Koenig, R. (1983). Call-in firms are taking on Yellow Pages. *Wall Street Journal.* March 1, p. 37.

Louie, B. (1985). Impact of information technology on the strategy-structure relationship. M.A. thesis, Sloan School of Management, Massachusetts Institute of Technology.

Malone, T. W. (1987). Modeling coordination in organizations and markets. *Management Science* 33:1317–32. (Reprinted in A. H. Bond & L. Grasser (Eds.), *Readings in Distributed Artificial Intelligence.* San Mateo, CA: Morgan Kaufman Publishers, 1988).

Malone, T. W., K. R. Grant, F. A. Turbak, S. A. Brobst & M. D. Cohen (1987). Intelligent information sharing systems. *Communications of the ACM*, 30:390–402.

Malone, T. W., & S. A. Smith (1988). Modeling the performance of organizational structures. *Operations Research* 36 (May–June): 421–36.

Miller, J. G., & T. E. Vollmann (1985). The hidden factory. *Harvard Business Review*, September–October, pp. 142–50.

Nakane, J., & R. Hall (1983). Management specifications for stockless production. *Harvard Business Review*, May–June, pp. 84–91.

Payne, J. W., M. L. Braunstein, & J. S. Carroll (1978). Exploring predecisional behavior: An alternative approach to decision research. *Organizational Behavior and Human Performance* 22:17–44.

Petre (1985). How to keep customers happy captives. *Fortune*, September 2, pp. 42–46.

Porter, M. E., & V. E. Millar (1985). How information gives you competitive advantage. *Harvard Business Review*, July–August, pp. 149–60.

Prokesh, S. E. (1985). U.S. companies weed out many operations. *New York Times*, September 22, pp. Al, D5.

Russo, J., & B. Dosher (1983). Strategies for multi-attribute binary choice. *Journal of Experimental Psychology: Learning, Memory, and Cognition* 9:676–96.

Stevenson, R. W. (1985). Credit card enhancements: Wider range of services. *New York Times*, April 30 (business section), p. 1.

Strassman, P. (1985). *Information payoff*. New York: Free Press.

Ware, M. (1982). A total integrated systems approach to CAD/CAM. *Computers*, January, pp. 105–16.

Williamson, O. E. (1975). *Markets and hierarchies*. New York: Free Press.

——— (1979). Transaction cost economics: The governance of contractual relations. *Journal of Law and Economics* 22:233–61.

——— (1980). The organization of work: A comparative institutional assessment. *Journal of Economic Behavior and Organization* 1:6–38.

——— (1981a). The economics of organization: The transaction cost approach. *American Journal of Sociology* 87:548–75.

——— (1981b). The modern corporation: Origins, evolution, attributes. *Journal of Economic Literature* 19:1537–68.

Yates, J. (1986). The telegraph's effect on nineteenth century markets and firms. Proceedings of the annual meetings of the Business History Conference, Columbus, OH, March 12–14.

CHAPTER 4

An Assessment of the Productivity Impact of Information Technologies

GARY W. LOVEMAN

The United States has recently suffered through a protracted period of low productivity growth and has experienced essentially no growth in real wages since 1973 (see Loveman & Tilly, 1988). Hope for a rebound in productivity growth is often linked to the continued improvement and diffusion of information technologies (IT),[1] which have recently undergone massive price declines and increased enormously as a proportion of capital spending.[2] Table 4.1 compares the evolution of computer prices with those for other components of producers' durable equipment: One dollar's worth of quality-adjusted computing power in 1970 cost $73.60 in 1950, and only 5 cents in 1984. Meanwhile, a 1970 dollar's worth of non-IT equipment cost only 59 cents in 1950 but rose to $2.54 in 1984. Changes in relative prices of this magnitude have straightforward implications from economic principles: Producers will substitute IT capital for other factors of production to the extent that is optimal given production technologies; output will rise as product prices fall; and total welfare will increase. The decline in the price of IT therefore has positive implications opposite to those precipitated for consumers by the earlier energy crisis, in which an important factor of production became radically more expensive.[3]

There is no doubt that firms have responded by investing heavily in IT. By the

Table 4.1. The declining relative price of computers (1982 = 100)

Year	Price deflator for computers	Price deflator for other producers' durable equipment
1950	93046	25
1955	32543	29
1960	11739	35
1965	3715	35
1970	1264	41
1975	637	58
1980	167	84
1984	63	105

Source: Gordon (1987), Tables 21 and 22.

mid-1980s, American firms were spending more than one-third of their total durable equipment budgets on IT. Indeed, the rise in investment was so substantial that despite much faster depreciation rates, IT's share of the total U.S. nonfarm business sector's stock of producer's durable equipment more than tripled from 1.8 percent in 1973 to 7.8 percent in 1985 (see Table 4.2). IT's share of equipment capital stocks varies enormously by industry (see Table 4.3) and tends to be highest in communications and services. The growth in IT's share from 1970 to 1985, however, has been fastest in industries such as durable manufacturing, construction, and trade, in which the initial shares were relatively low.

This story has all the ingredients for a happy ending, but unfortunately the ending, to date, is mixed at best. U.S. productivity growth remains sluggish, and in the absence of a presumption of a sudden deterioration in other factors, it is hard to document a large productivity boon from IT at the aggregate macroeconomic level.[4] At the disaggregated level of the firm, there has been little empirical research on the impact of IT on business performance. Although there are several interesting case studies of the experiences of individual firms, there has been scarcely any large sample econometric analysis of the relationship between IT and firm performance; that is, the productivity impact of IT capital has not been examined.[5]

The need for analysis at the firm level is clear, as that is where the relevant investment decisions are made. Thus, the return to IT at the firm level is a critical indicator of both IT's welfare effects and the efficiency with which IT is being utilized.[6] This chapter presents the results of an econometric analysis of IT capital productivity.[7] A unique data set is exploited that contains data from 1978 to 1984 at the business unit level for U.S. and Western European manufacturing companies.[8] The central finding is that for this sample, IT capital had little, if any, marginal impact on output or labor productivity, whereas all the other inputs into production—including non-IT capital—had significant positive impacts on output and labor productivity. Although different specifications and subsamples do yield somewhat different magnitudes, the nature of the result is surprisingly robust. In short, profit-maximizing firms in this sample would best have invested their marginal dollar in non-IT factors of production.

Table 4.2. IT's share of the equipment capital stock

Year	Share (%)
1978	1.8
1979	2.2
1980	2.6
1981	3.3
1982	3.8
1983	4.9
1984	6.3
1985	7.8

Constant dollar (1982) net stocks of fixed nonresidential private capital; shares are calculated as the stock of office, computing, and accounting machinery capital divided by total producers durable equipment. *Source:* U.S. Department of Commerce, Bureau of Economic Analysis, *Fixed Reproducible Tangible Wealth in the United States. 1982–1985.*

Table 4.3. High-tech capital as a share of total capital by industry (%)*

Industry	1950	1960	1970	1980	Change 1970–1985 %	Change 1970–1985 Ratio
Manufacturing	1.7	1.6	2.8	8.6	5.8	3.1
Durables	1.6	1.5	2.3	9.3	7.0	4.1
Nondurables	1.7	1.6	3.3	7.6	4.3	2.3
Mining	0.0	0.1	0.1	0.1	0.0	0.9
Construction	0.4	0.7	0.5	3.5	3.0	6.6
Transportation	0.4	0.5	0.6	1.1	0.5	1.9
Communications	20.0	30.6	40.8	53.4	12.6	1.3
Public utilities	0.5	0.6	1.1	3.1	2.1	2.9
Wholesale and retail trade	0.7	0.9	2.5	11.1	8.7	4.5
Finance, insurance, and real estate	6.1	5.7	6.0	14.4	8.5	2.4
Services	5.8	6.5	8.3	16.1	7.9	2.0

*High-tech capital consists of office, computing, and accounting machinery; communications equipment; instruments and photocopiers and related equipment. Capital stock data based on U.S. Department of Commerce, Bureau of Economic Analysis statistics for net stocks of nonresidential private capital, expressed in constant 1982 dollars.

Source: Roach (1987), Tables A–3 and A–4.

THE LITERATURE

Economists have long been interested in productivity growth, as it is what generates increased incomes and contributes to higher standards of living. The productivity growth slowdown affecting most industrialized Western economies since the early 1970s has sparked interest in identifying the sources of productivity growth. Perhaps the most extensive research in this field is on the relationship between research and development (R&D) spending—both private and public, and basic and applied—and productivity growth. The results of a number of studies at the firm level indicate that there is a large and significant positive relationship between various measures of firm productivity and investments in R&D. These studies also show that the effect did not decline significantly in the 1970s despite the overall productivity slowdown.[9] The methodology used in these studies is similar to that employed in this chapter, and the issues are also similar insofar as R&D produces intangible, information-intensive output. The most striking difference is that the implied average gross rate of return to R&D investment by U.S. manufacturers in the 1970s was at least 30 percent (see Griliches, 1986). As we shall show, this significant rate of return far exceeds any implied for IT in our sample.

Research on the relationship between IT and productivity is in its infancy. Roach (1987) disaggregated employment and output into two sectors each: information and production workers, and goods and information-intensive sectors. He then calculated labor productivity growth rates for each of the four categories and found that information worker productivity had fallen, or grown less, than production worker productivity had (see Table 4.4). Although the interpretation of these data is not straightforward, they do cast doubt on the notion that the growing share of information workers is the answer to the productivity problem.[10] Moreover, Roach compared industries with widely varying shares of high-tech capital and found no correlation with measured productivity growth.

Baily and Chakrabarti (1988) tackled white-collar productivity and IT as a part

Table 4.4. Information and production worker productivity (%)

	1986 versus average of 1970s		
	Output per worker	Output per production worker	Output per information worker
All industries	3.6	16.9	–6.6
Goods sector	10.8	20.0	–6.9
Manufacturing	30.1	45.9	4.2
Durables	31.1	49.5	2.0
Nondurables	28.4	40.3	7.5
Mining	–23.8	–7.1	–45.6
Construction	–26.0	–25.9	–26.6
Information sector	1.7	9.9	–2.6
Transportation, communications, and public utilities	–0.2	21.4	–20.6
Wholesale trade	11.6	74.2	6.4
Retail trade	6.7	9.6	4.6
Finance, insurance, and real estate	–7.9	9.8	–9.3
Services	4.3	7.4	2.6

Figures represent difference (in percent) between 1986 levels and average levels prevailing in the 1970s. All calculations are based on constant 1982 dollars. Information and production worker categories are defined in terms of occupational groupings consistent with those of "white-collar" and "blue-collar" employment, respectively. See Roach (1987), p. 24, for more definitional details.

Source: Roach (1987), Table 7.

of their broader inquiry into recent poor productivity growth. They argued that the current evidence does not show a significant productivity gain from IT and proposed three possible explanations:

1. Mismeasurement: IT is associated with changes in quality and customer service that are not captured by current price indices, thus leading to understated real output and productivity, and overstated inflation.
2. Distributional versus productive use of IT: IT is used as a marketing tool to redistribute among competitors a fixed level of output. In this case, private returns exceed social returns, as there is no social gain to the redistribution.
3. Organizational inefficiency: The intangible nature of IT makes it difficult for organizations to value information. This leads to a resource allocation problem, which is aggravated when bureaucratic behavior responds to an IT price decline by using more information technology capital and information workers rather than reducing the cost of a given output.

The central theme of the latter two explanations is that the failure of markets (internal and external) to value IT properly leads to misallocated resources and lower productivity growth. Baily and Chakrabarti examined these ideas further by simulating a simple model of firm behavior in which the firm produces marketing, customer service, and a final product via three different production functions. Marketing serves only to distribute a given demand among competitors, whereas customer service is of true value to consumers but is provided free of charge. The exercise is to simulate a 20 percent per-year decline in the price of IT and see how well the model predicts the "stylized facts" of rapid growth in IT use, customer services, and marketing and the declining relative productivity of information workers.

After trying various permutations of the model, Baily and Chakrabarti found that when information capital and information labor are poor substitutes in the production of services and marketing (i.e., the acquisition of IT requires more workers to use it), the model tracks the stylized facts rather well. They concluded that the main effect of the falling price of IT was on marketing and services, in which the former had no social gain, and output from the latter was not properly measured. IT is a poor substitute for labor, and so production becomes increasingly information worker intensive—and relative productivity drops—as the price of IT falls. Finally, Baily and Chakrabarti contended that it takes time for organizations to make transitions to new technologies and that productivity may begin to rise as the transition proceeds.

Osterman (1986) examined the substitutability between IT capital and two types of information workers—clerks and managers—between 1972 and 1978. He discovered that in the initial period following the introduction of computers, there is a large displacement effect for clerks and a smaller displacement effect for managers. However, two years later these displacement effects are partially offset by the greater employment of clerks and, especially, managers. Although the net employment effect is negative, the lower cost of information clearly leads to higher demand, which leads to an additional demand for information workers.[11] This result is consistent with the flavor, if not the magnitude, of Baily and Chakrabarti's claim about low substitutability between information workers and information capital.[12]

Finally, Bresnahan (1986) estimated the welfare gains from using mainframe computers in the financial services sector (FSS) between 1958 and 1972. His methodology was quite different from that used in this chapter. Bresnahan assumed that the nonregulated portions of the FSS are competitive, and so the firms act purely as agents for final consumers. Computer investments by firms are then effectively purchases by consumers. Price declines for computers lead to increased demand for them as inputs, cost reductions for FSS products, and, consequently, increased output in the final product market. However, service sectors lack good measures of real output (i.e., price indices), and so it is necessary to find alternative measures. Bresnahan showed that according to his assumptions, the area under the derived demand curve for an input—in this case mainframe computers by the FSS—is a welfare index.[13]

Bresnahan's results suggest that the gain to consumers from 1958 to 1972 was five or more times the expenditures by FSS firms on computer rentals. He concluded: "In current (1986) terms, the downstream benefits of technical progress in mainframe computers since 1958 are conservatively estimated at 1.5 to 2 orders of magnitude larger than expenditures, at least in this high-value use" (1986, p. 753). With this notable exception, there are no other large sample empirical studies of the productivity impact of IT at the firm level. The next section presents the data and methodology we used for this chapter.

DATA AND METHODOLOGY

The data

Analysis of the productivity impact of IT requires a framework that relates IT to output while adjusting for the influence of all relevant non-IT variables. Output may be measured in either physical or dollar terms. The latter choice is preferable in this case because it measures the firm's ultimate objective (e.g., sales or profits) toward which capital investments are made, and because it is insensitive to output that may have no value (e.g., CPU time, keystrokes, etc.). The construct appropriate for modeling the IT-productivity relationship is the production function. We will discuss several specifications of production functions, but they share the general form:

$$Q_{it} = Ae^{\lambda t}F(M_{it}, PS_{it}, L_{it}, K_{it}, C_{it}) \quad (1)$$

Q_{it} = real output by unit i in year t
M_{it} = real materials expenditure
PS_{it} = real non-IT purchased services expenditures
L_{it} = real total labor compensation
K_{it} = real non-IT capital
C_{it} = real IT capital
λ = rate of disembodied technological change
i = business unit index
t = year index
A = constant

The Management Productivity and Information Technology (MPIT) data base—a special adjunct to the larger and better-known Profit Impact of Market Strategy (PIMS) data base—contains most of the data necessary to estimate the production function. Data are available on roughly 60 manufacturing business units from the United States and Western Europe, observed annually for all or a portion of the period 1973 to 1984. Most business units are observed for five consecutive years—either 1978 to 1982 or 1979 to 1983—but the data for 1984 are rather thin. A business unit is defined as a unit of a firm "selling a distinct product(s) to an identifiable set of customers in competition with a well-defined set of competitors." Business units may be thought of as operating divisions or as product groups in a multidivisional organization. The 60 business units are drawn from roughly 20 firms, but the firms are by no means representative of the business community. Rather, they are predominantly Fortune 500 firms, and all are involved in manufacturing. The most important feature of the MPIT data base is the division of capital into IT capital and non-IT capital (machinery, land, structures, etc.). This, along with complete balance sheet and income statement data, provides the requisite input and output data to estimate a production function.

Despite the self-reported nature of the data, there is reason to believe that they are of fairly high quality. Business units do have latitude in defining some variables, but most of the variables used in this study are governed by common guidelines, such as accounting conventions. Moreover, the firms' self-interest in useful results from participation in the PIMS project, and careful review and consistency checks by the PIMS staff, suggest that the data are reasonably sound.

The data set does, however, suffer from several limitations, some of which constrain the options for econometrics. There are no input or output price indices, which eliminate the possibility of estimating cost functions, factor share equations, and factor demand equations.[14] This also affects production function estimation by requiring the use of aggregate price indices to derive real, or constant dollar, variables.

The specific variables are calculated as follows: Output is measured as sales less inventory changes, deflated by a price index unique to each of the six industry groups in the sample. The inventory adjustment results in a measure of production, and the output price indices are calculated from GNP industry-specific implicit price deflators to match the MPIT industry definitions with those used by the Commerce Department. Materials expenditures are deflated by the producer price index for intermediate materials and supplies. Real non-IT purchased services, such as travel and insurance, are a large input into production, but they do not aggregate well with either capital or materials. Therefore they are a separate input, deflated by the GNP implicit price deflator for business services. Data are available for total labor compensation and total employment. The former is used because it implicitly adjusts for labor quality and hours worked. This series is deflated by the U.S. Bureau of Labor Statistics hourly compensation index, disaggregated between durables and nondurables.

The capital stock numbers are, as always, less than ideal, but not uncharacteristically so. Each business unit reports the net book value and annual depreciation of its various categories of capital based on historical cost, all purchased or leased services, and its share of corporate (shared) assets. These measures capture the sum of capital resources as traditionally defined. Unfortunately, most firms treat in-house software development as an expense, and it thus is included in the labor input measure. The reported capital stock numbers were manipulated into more economically meaningful figures by adjusting the base figure for each unit and deriving subsequent years' figures by using deflated investment data and economic depreciation rates (see Appendix 1 for details).

The MPIT data base has several other useful features. First, a variety of organizational and strategic variables are included, such as the number of layers between different points in the organizational hierarchy, and industry concentration and market share. Second, all inputs are broken into two parts: those used in production and those used in management. The specifications exploit these unusual data. On the downside, we must emphasize that the final figures used for estimation are only as good as the price indices, which unfortunately are not business unit or firm specific. Furthermore, capital utilization figures are not available for the entire sample, which prevents adjusting for variations in utilization.

Table 4.5 offers a brief summary of the data used for estimation. The business units are large—1500 persons on average—and they tend to consider themselves as large players in their markets. Market share is defined as the percentage of sales in the "served market," in which the definition of the "served market" is left to the discretion of the business unit. The reported market shares are therefore likely to be larger than those that an economist would calculate, but the business units are nonetheless unlikely to face perfectly elastic demand.

The sample period was clearly one of low growth and much volatility for the business units, as mean sales growth was zero but the variance was quite large. Although all the businesses are manufacturers, they are engaged in many different subindustries, the largest being the poorly defined intermediate industrial and commercial goods sector. Finally, the businesses differ widely in their relative use of IT, but the average share of IT in total capital equipment or sales grew enormously from 1978 to 1982 as a result of rapid investment.

Table 4.5. The MPIT data, 1978–1984

Descriptive statistics					
Mean employment[a]					
Management					485
Production					1020
Median market share[b]					32%
Mean production growth[c]					0.0%
Standard deviation production growth[c]					25.9%
Industry composition					
Consumer products manufacture					
Durables					8.3%
Nondurables					23.3
Industrial/commercial manufacture					
Capital goods					1.7
Raw or semifinished materials					20.0
Components for incorporation into finished products					41.7
Supplies or other consumables					5.0
IT intensity[d]	1978	1979	1980	1981	1982
IT as a percentage of non-IT capital	5.4	5.5	6.8	8.5	10.4
IT as a Percentage of Sales	1.1	1.1	1.6	2.0	2.7

[a]Number of full time equivalents.

[b]Defined as percent of sales in served market. See text, "The Results," for a discussion of this series.

[c]Production is sales less inventory accumulation, adjusted for inflation.

[d]IT is defined in note 1, and all components are as defined in text and adjusted for inflation. The reported figures are averages of individual business unit values, and cover only 1978–82, because the sample is too small for 1983–84 to derive meaningful statistics.

The methodology

The productivity of IT capital is examined in the context of the general production function (Equation 1). Although productivity can be defined in various ways, all the definitions involve the ceteris paribus increase in output from an incremental increase in IT. Parameters from the estimated production functions measure the magnitude of this increase, or the size of the productivity effect, and the parameters differ depending on the specification of the production function. The investment decision follows from comparing the marginal cost with the marginal product, and the latter is fundamentally a function of these same parameters.

To make these ideas precise, consider the following simple example involving only labor and IT:

$$Q = L^{\alpha} C^{\beta} \tag{2}$$

The increase in output for a unit (or dollar) increase in IT, termed the *output elasticity* for IT, is given by β. If $\beta > \alpha$, IT is more productive on the margin. This does not, however, necessarily imply that more should be invested in C versus L, because it is also necessary to look at the marginal cost. In this example, the firm should invest if

$$\beta \times \frac{Q}{C} > \frac{Wc}{P} \quad \text{or} \quad \beta > \frac{Wc \times C}{P \times Q} \tag{3}$$

where Wc = the price of IT and P = the output price.

Clearly, to the extent that β is very low, further investment is indicated only if IT is very inexpensive relative to the final product and/or the share of existing IT in total output is small (i.e., Q/C is large).[15] Estimation of the parameters requires a specific functional form, and the one that imposes the least constraint is the "translog" production function. However, the generality of the translog function carries some costs and results from earlier work (Loveman, 1986) suggest that the more parsimonious Cobb–Douglas specification is preferable for this sample.[16] Therefore, the Cobb–Douglas formulation given in Equation 4 is used throughout the analysis:

$$Q = Ae^{\lambda t} M^{\beta_1} PS^{\beta_2} L^{\beta_3} K^{\beta_4} C^{\beta_5} \tag{4}$$

Here estimation of β_5, the output elasticity for IT capital and the parameter of primary interest, is straightforward. The Cobb–Douglas form does impose a constant unitary elasticity of substitution between inputs, but as Griliches noted (1986, p. 342), the use of Cobb–Douglas instead of a more complicated functional form should not make a critical difference in estimating the output elasticities.

The functional form models the behavioral relationship, but it is still necessary to consider the stochastic effects that generate the data and their econometric implications. In our case, stochastic elements enter the production model of the business unit from mainly three sources: (1) the technology, (2) production behavior, and (3) measurement of the variables. Because proper estimation hinges on the properties of the stochastic elements, we shall summarize these three sources of variation later.[17]

Production may deviate from the technological relationships specified in Equation 4 if there are characteristics specific to the business unit that are known to its management and exploited in the production process. These factors, such as particular management skills, access to unusually productive (or nonmarket) inputs, and the like, are included in the unit's optimization and are therefore embedded in the factor demands. This implies that observed input levels may be endogenous with respect to the production function; that is, the error term in the production function may be correlated with the input variable. Under these circumstances, ordinary least-squares estimates may be biased.

The business unit is also affected by various external forces not observed by the econometrician, most notably in input and output markets. Uncertain input quality, time delays between input purchases and output price determination, and imperfectly competitive markets all introduce stochastic terms that may or may not induce correlation between measured inputs and the stochastic term in the production function. Similarly, business unit production behavior such as bounded rationality or other failures in optimization may introduce stochastic effects common to both factor demands and the production function.

Errors in the measurement of the variables are a third important source of stochastic effects. Typically, errors in variables result from simple measurement error, failure to measure explicitly some important latent variable, or errors in aggregation. The crucial issue, of course, is not whether the variables are measured imperfectly but, rather, whether the measurement error is correlated with the disturbance term, resulting in least-squares estimates that are inconsistent.

Many of these stochastic effects, such as unobserved business unit characteristics, some external forces, and measurement errors, are time invariant. Therefore, transforming the data into growth rates eliminates the source of the bias, and this procedure is followed throughout this chapter. Important potential sources of biased estimates remain, and they are discussed in the context of the results.

The basic estimating equation is derived by rewriting Equation 4 in natural logarithms and differentiating with respect to time:

$$q = \lambda + \beta_1 m + \beta_2 ps + \beta_3 l + \beta_4 k + \beta_5 c + \epsilon_1 \quad (5)$$

where lowercase letters refer to growth rates of the respective Greek-letter variables, ε_1 is the error term, and β_5 is one measure of the productivity effect of IT. A simple alternative estimating equation is found by rewriting Equation 5 in terms of labor productivity (output per unit of labor input). Assuming that constant returns to scale $\sum_{i=1}^{5} \beta_i = 1$, Equation 5 can be rewritten as

$$q - 1 = \lambda + \beta_1(m-1) + \beta_2(ps-1) + \beta_3(k-1) + \beta_5(c-1) + \epsilon_1 \quad (5a)$$

where $q - 1$ = labor productivity, and β_5 measures IT's effect on labor productivity.

Another alternative would be to regress total factor productivity (TFP) on c to derive IT's effect on TFP. Unfortunately, the calculation of TFP requires a maintained assumption that business units are in equilibrium so that observed input shares equal the output elasticities. In our sample the production data are too volatile to make such an assumption plausible; hence we did not pursue the TFP approach.[18] A different approach is to argue that IT enhances coordination and results in a more effective utilization of labor. This broad concept is currently popular in the IT management literature (e.g., Zuboff, 1988), but the general idea of labor-augmenting technical progress has a much longer history. Following this tradition, the "true" labor input, L*, can be written as

$$L* = \theta L \quad (6)$$

where

$$\theta = \gamma(C) \quad (7)$$

and imposing a simple functional form:

$$\theta = \gamma C + \chi \quad (8)$$

Substituting Equation 7 into Equation 5 and rewriting in logarithms yields

$$q = \lambda + \beta_1 m + \beta_2 ps + \beta_3 l + \beta_4 k + \beta_6 c + \epsilon_2 \quad (9)$$

where

$\beta_6 = \beta_3 \times \gamma$
$\varepsilon_2 = \varepsilon_1 + \beta_3\, \varepsilon$
ε = i.i.d. error term

Estimating Equation 9 yields γ as β_6 / β_3, and γ measures the extent to which IT enhances the productivity of labor. These static specifications have an obvious shortcoming: Firms make IT investments that are quickly reflected on their books, but it takes time for software to be written or tailored, data bases to be accumulated, employees to be trained, and organizational changes to take place. Such considerations suggest a concave dynamic pattern of returns from IT, in which the payoff begins at some level, rises for a while, and then falls off.[19] Pakes and Griliches (1984) found support for this pattern of returns in a model in which firm profits were regressed on lagged investment. They discovered that the returns to capital investments rise over the first three years and then remain steady or fall slightly in the following years. It is possible to test for this pattern by making Equation 5 or 9 dynamic with respect to IT:

$$q = \lambda + \beta_1 m + \beta_2 ps + \beta_3 l + \beta_4 k + \sum_{i=1}^{n} \beta_{5i} c_{t-1} + \epsilon_3 \tag{10}$$

The β_{5is} estimates the impact on the output of current and previous years' investments in IT.

Finally, the existence of a distinction between production and management for all inputs in the data permits the testing of a different model. IT can be thought of as an input into the production of management, or coordination, with management itself being an input into final production. The production of management is thus nested within the overall production model:

$$Q = f(M, PS, L_p, K_p, C_p, I) \tag{11}$$

where

$$I = g(L_m, K_m, C_m) \tag{12}$$

and

I = management
p = production input
m = management input

Given one identifying restriction, it is possible to test for IT's contribution to the production of management and the final product, and for the productivity of management as an input into the production of the final product.

The next section discusses the results of estimating the models given by Equations 5, 5a, 9, 10, and 11.

THE RESULTS

Despite the broad range of models proposed in the preceding section, the data speak unequivocally: In this sample, there is no evidence of strong productivity gains from IT investments. The implied shadow value of IT does not favor further investment for the period covered by the data, and any implied rate of return is very low.

Static models

Table 4.6 presents the results of estimating the static model (Equation 5) and the labor-augmenting technological change model (Equation 9), using both the full sample and selected subsamples. Note first that the estimated output elasticities for *m*, *ps*, *l*, and *k* are of sensible magnitude and are statistically significant. Indeed, they

Table 4.6. Production function estimates: static model*

Variable	Full sample	IT intensity Low	IT intensity High	Industry Durables	Industry Nondurables	Market share Low	Market share High
	1	2	3	4	5	6	7
λ	.06	.04	.10	.01	.09	.13	−.05
	(.03)	(.04)	(.04)	(.04)	(.03)	(.04)	(.04)
m	.43	.34	.53	.39	.43	.55	.34
	(.03)	(.04)	(.05)	(.05)	(.05)	(.05)	(.04)
ps	.11	.16	.05	.06	.21	.12	.05
	(.02)	(.03)	(.03)	(.02)	(.03)	(.02)	(.04)
l	.57	.67	.41	.72	.45	.36	.77
	(.05)	(.06)	(.08)	(.10)	(.06)	(.06)	(.08)
k	.15	.10	.12	.08	.15	.18	.10
	(.05)	(.07)	(.08)	(.09)	(.07)	(.07)	(.08)
C	−.06	−.09	0.0	.04	−.11	−.12	.09
	(.03)	(.04)	(.06)	(.05)	(.05)	(.04)	(−.07)
y^a	−.11						
	(.06)						
n	231	113	118	114	117	112	119
R^2	.77	.84	.74	.78	.81	.80	.81

*Estimating equation is (5) in text. Estimates for y follow from (9). Variable definitions are given in text, The Data Standard errors are shown in parentheses.

[a]Standard error calculated using "delta method."

are consistent with both the observed factor shares and similar results from other studies.[20] The coefficients suggest mildly increasing returns to scale. There is evidence of disembodied technological change during this period, but the estimates are not precise and tend to vary considerably by subsample.

The estimated output elasticity for IT in the full sample, the parameter of central interest, is −.06, which, unsatisfyingly, suggests a reduction in output for a marginal increase in IT. Given the standard error of the estimate, with 95 percent certainty the true value lies between −.12 and 0. Within this interval it is impossible for the marginal product of IT or its rate of return to be positive.

Regressions on the full sample may mask important differences across firms such that the estimated parameters represent an average of the very good and the very bad. Two efforts were made to address this concern. First, dummy variables were introduced to control for industry effects, as were variables reflecting organizational structure.[21] The dummy variables allow the entire production function to shift according to given characteristics, but the output elasticity for IT is still constrained to be equal across all business units. The estimates, including dummy variables, were not significantly different from those for the full sample.

Heterogeneity among business units with respect to their use of IT is better captured by splitting the sample according to relevant identifiable criteria. Table 4.6 shows the results from three cuts: IT intensity, industry, and market share. IT intensity—IT as a percentage of non-IT capital—varies enormously across business units. In columns 2 and 3, the businesses were ranked by IT intensity and divided into two groups whose averages were 3 percent and 12 percent. There are many hypotheses that support making such a division, and one of the simpler ones is that businesses that use IT effectively tend to be the heaviest investors (i.e., investment flows to high returns). The results indicate that although high IT–intensity firms do apparently enjoy a higher productivity gain from IT, the estimated magnitude is still zero.

Businesses in different industries may also experience unequal returns from IT, owing to different technologies, management methods, or competitive circumstances. The simplest way to separate industries is by dividing between durable and nondurable manufacturers, and the results in columns 4 and 5 reveal a substantial differential. Durables producers have a positive, although insignificantly different from zero, productivity effect from IT, and nondurables producers have a significantly negative effect. Although the durables producers are clearly doing better with respect to IT, their performance still yields modest rates of return. In durables businesses in which the existing IT capital share in output is very small—less than 4 percent—additional investment may be indicated.

A final disaggregation was made on the basis of market share.[22] Businesses may enjoy high market shares if they have a unique technology or engage in anticompetitive activities, or high market share may follow from unusually effective management. Accordingly, the productivity of IT may vary across businesses of widely differing market shares. Columns 6 and 7 report estimates for subsamples divided by market share. The output elasticity for IT in the high market share group is the highest of any in this analysis, although its large standard error again makes it statistically insignificantly different from zero. The return to IT may be higher in this group, either because of better management of IT or because of restraints on competition. In any case, further investment may be optimal in these businesses, but it clearly is not in the low market share group.[23]

A simple alternative IT productivity measure is to estimate the effect of IT on labor productivity (Equation 5a in the text). This procedure requires the maintained assumption of constant returns to scale. The results of estimating Equation 5a, not reported in the tables, are twofold: Not surprisingly, the constant returns to scale assumption is rejected by an F-test, and the output elasticity on IT is negative and statistically insignificant.

Finally, the estimate for γ in the model given by Equation 9 is reported near the bottom of Table 4.6. As expected, IT does not enhance labor productivity.[24] In addition, γ was estimated for the various subsamples, but the results were not very interesting: Note that γ was higher (lower) when the output elasticity for IT was higher (lower).

Dynamic models

Estimates from the dynamic model (Equation 10) are shown in Table 4.7. It bears emphasizing that the introduction of dynamics reduces the sample size substantially: When two lags are used, $n = 111$, and with three lags, $n = 53$. The subsamples are, of course, even smaller. With this strong caveat in mind, the results generally support the notion of a pattern of returns to IT that is concave with respect to time.

Column 1 shows that when only two lags are used, the coefficient on non-IT capital is negative. The results from three lags—column 2—are more encouraging,

Table 4.7. Production function estimates: dynamic model*

			Industry			
	Full sample		Durable		Nondurables	
Variable	(1)	(2)	(3)	(4)	(5)	(6)
λ	−.12	−.25	−50	−2.16	.01	.41
	(.09)	(.22)	(.16)	(.07)	(.12)	(.25)
m	.44	.23	.44	.41	.34	.36
	(.04)	(.06)	(.05)	(.14)	(.09)	(.11)
ps	.07	.16	.04	.10	.14	.20
	(.02)	(.04)	(.03)	(.08)	(.06)	(.06)
l	.63	.54	.75	.53	.54	.50
	(.06)	(.08)	(.12)	(.30)	(.07)	(.08)
k	−.04	.24	−.10	.19	−.02	.41
	(.07)	(.12)	(.11)	(.17)	(.10)	(−16)
c	−.06	−.17	.05	−.09	−.06	−.27
	(.04)	(.06)	(.07)	(.15)	(.05)	(.06)
c_{-1}	−.04	−.11	.06	−.05	−.15	−.17
	(.05)	(.05)	(.08)	(.11)	(.06)	(.06)
c_{-2}	.09	.05	.25	.17	.05	−.16
	(.05)	(.08)	(.08)	(.20)	(.07)	(.10)
c_{-3}		−.09		−.02		−.10
		(.06)		(.15)		(07)
n	111	53	52	22	59	31
R^2	.84	.74	.90	.80	.77	.90

*Estimating equation is (10) in text. Variable definitions are given in text. The Data: subscripts refer to time (years). Standard errors are shown in parentheses.

as the non-IT coefficients are reasonable and the pattern of returns to IT rises and then falls as we hypothesized. Although this concave shape is appealing, its position is not, as the highest output elasticity is only .05, and the sum of the four elasticities is −.32. The estimated parameters again suffer from large standard errors, thus implying wide bounds for the true values, but the point estimates do not look good for the performance of IT.

The dynamic model was estimated for the various subsamples reported in Table 4.6, but the results were not very informative. In all cases, those subsamples that did better in the static model also had larger IT output elasticities in the dynamic model, but the problems found in the full sample also were present in the subsamples. The case of durables and nondurables illustrates the findings. The two-lag specification is again inappropriate, and durables do much better than do nondurables with three lags. However, the sum of the IT coefficients is essentially zero even for durables, and none of the coefficients is statistically significant at conventional levels.

Despite the negative overtone of these results, they are promising insofar as the concave patterns of returns is evident. Interview evidence suggests that, in many cases, IT projects require several years before they yield their highest returns. This suggests that if longer time series were available for the businesses in the sample, the estimated returns to IT might be much higher. The collection and analysis of such data are vitally needed for future research.[25]

Producing management models

The final estimates, presented in Table 4.8, suggest that the nested "production of management" model (Equation 11) is not consistent with the data. In order to identify β_6 and the αs separately, it is necessary to impose an identifying restriction. Two alternatives were used: constant returns in production (column 1) and constant returns in management (column 2). In both cases, the estimated parameters for the non-IT production inputs are sensible, but the output elasticities on both the management input and the inputs into the production of management, are not.[26] Although this more complicated specification is intuitively appealing, further research is needed to document its usefulness in characterizing actual production.

Table 4.8. Nested production function estimate

$$q = \lambda + \tau\,(\text{time}) + \beta_1 m + \beta_2 ps + \beta_3 1_p + \beta_4 k_p + \beta_5 c_p + \beta_6 (\alpha_1 1_m + \alpha_2 k_m + \alpha_3 c_m)$$

	Identifying restrictions[a]	
Coefficients	Constant returns in production[b]	Constant returns in management[c]
λ	.05	.05
	(.03)	(.03)
τ	–. 01	–.01
	(.01)	(.01)
β_1	.42	.42
	(.03)	(.03)
β_2	.10	.10
	(.02)	(.02)
β_3	.48	.48
	(.05)	(.05)
β_4	.19	.19
	(.07)	(.07)
β_5	.02	.02
	(.03)	(.03)
β_6	–.21	.03
	(.39)	(.05)
α_1	–.3	–2.0
	(.23)	(1.6)
α_2	.25	2.0
	(.32)	(2.2)
α_3	.14	1.0
	(.10)	(.07)
N	231	231
R^2	.78	.78

[a]Standard errors are shown in parentheses. The standard errors for β_6 and the as are calculated using the "delta method," and are conditional on the particular identifying restrictions.

[b] $\sum_{i=1}^{6} \beta_1 = 1$

[c] $\sum_{i=1}^{3} \alpha_1 = 1$

Evaluating possible biases

Now that the empirical findings have been presented, it is important to reconsider the possible sources of bias. If the estimates are biased, the true productivity effect from IT may be significantly higher than the results indicate. Because the equations were estimated in growth rates, time-invariant business unit effects—an important potential source of bias—are removed. This leaves time-varying simultaneity and measurement errors, and the lack of capital utilization measures, as remaining candidates.

In Appendix 2 we make some explicit calculations to estimate the likely sign and magnitude of the problem. The methodologies and results, which are rather technical, are also discussed at length in this appendix. The central finding is that under reasonable assumptions, the biases are likely to be small and of indeterminate sign. In the specific case of measurement error in the IT variable, the estimated output elasticity for IT is, if anything, biased upward. The main conclusions of the empirical analysis cannot, therefore, be attributed to biased estimation.

THE STORY

The empirical analysis in the preceding section has suggested that at least for this sample of manufacturing firms, it is very hard to demonstrate a significant positive relationship between accumulated IT expenditures and various productivity measures. Apparently, during the late 1970s and early 1980s, the marginal dollar would have been better spent on non-IT factors of production, including non-IT capital. Indeed, in many cases the results suggest substantial overspending on IT. The fact that firms were spending an ever-increasing share of their investment budgets on IT during this period, therefore, raises a substantial paradox that, we have argued, is replicated at the national level: Why, given the clear technological capabilities of IT and businesses' voracious appetite for IT, are the measured returns so low?

A solution to this paradox can be found among three lines of explanation:

1. The poor measured returns are an artifact of the period and sample under consideration, or the specific methodology applied in this study; the true long-term returns are substantial.
2. The true returns are large, but we lack the tools necessary to measure them.
3. A variety of identifiable organizational and strategic factors have reduced the payoff from IT.

Methodological concerns in this study

There is no doubt that the sample used in this study is not representative and is drawn from a difficult time period. The exclusion of nonmanufacturing firms ignores the majority of firms and employment and thus fails to consider this performance in industries such as financial services, for which the gains may have been substantial (see Bresnahan, 1986). Furthermore, Roach's (1987) data show that less than 20 percent of the U.S. IT capital stock resides in the manufacturing sector, that most is in the communications, finance, insurance and real estate, and service sectors.

Nonetheless, manufacturing is obviously a significant sector, and it happens to be the only one for which the necessary microdata are available. The problem here, however, is that the 1978–83 period was a historically bad time and displayed unusual turbulence for manufacturers throughout the industrialized world. The result may reflect in part the bad times being experienced by manufacturers and therefore be considered idiosyncratic to the time period. Although there is something to this point, the fundamental reasons are more elusive and will be discussed shortly.

A separate but perhaps more important problem is raised by the truncation of the data at typically five years per business unit. If the time lag between investment and payoff is longer than three years, then the dynamic model (Equation 10) will be too short temporally to capture the true relationship. Some other data set with longer time series evidence is necessary to evaluate this concern. However, anecdotal evidence suggests that three years is sufficient for many, but not all, projects.

Otherwise, the methodology used in this chapter is quite general, has been applied successfully in many related studies, and is not likely to be responsible for biasing the results downward significantly (see Appendix 2). What is most telling about our findings in this chapter is that they are remarkably robust for a wide variety of changes in specification, sample, and the like and that the non-IT parameter estimates are consistent with the findings of many other studies.

General methodological issues

IT raises a host of thorny methodological issues, as anyone knows who has tried to calculate explicitly the expected benefits of an IT system. When IT acts as a substitute for, say, labor, in an existing process, the cost–benefit methodology is straightforward. More generally, however, IT is used to enhance the quality of a product (operational quality, convenience, shorter development time, on-time delivery, easy service, etc.), or the quality of a decision (fewer errors, faster decisions, greater insight, etc.). In both cases, economic methods encounter significant problems. Perhaps the greatest problem is the lack of price indices that properly account for quality change. In many cases, changes in the competitive structure of the industry—often induced or abetted by IT—obscure the relationship between price and cost and further impede the construction of valid price indices. Because the relevant data are dollar denominated, the entire analysis is predicated on accurate price measurement. Failure to adjust properly for price and quality changes jeopardizes the whole undertaking. In Baily and Chakrabarti's (1988) model, inadequate measurement of improved customer service understates the true output from IT. Research on quality-adjusted price indices is clearly critical; yet the application of even existing research is still in its childhood.

IT's role in enhancing the information available to decision makers is also hard to evaluate, for here IT is one step removed from the final product. Subtle techniques may be needed to distinguish the contribution of IT from that of many other factors both before and after any given decision process. Regression techniques are, in principle, appropriate, but the model specifications are sufficiently imprecise and the data sufficiently noisy for the econometrics to be incapable of extracting the true relationships.

The obvious alternative to the general method used in this chapter is to estimate productivity relationships between direct physical measures of inputs and outputs, often at a finely disaggregated level (a department within a firm). This approach, however, suffers from several shortcomings. First and foremost, what ultimately matters is value—to the firm, individuals, or society. Physical output measures do not gauge the value that the market places on such output and are thus prone to finding large productivity gains for the enhanced output of low-value goods and services. This problem is acute in the case of IT, in which the output is typically an (intangible) intermediate good whose value may be very small (e.g., printed lines, data files, lines of code, instructions processed, etc.).

Second, the data for this sort of analysis necessary to control for exogenous factors are typically difficult to find. In fact, the scarcity of even the most basic data—output and IT input—often limits this method to very small sample or bivariate analysis.

Organizational factors

A third possible explanation for the paradox lies in the organizational factors, which are a real part of any enterprise. What makes IT unique is that instead of producing something tangible, it yields information (or data). Information (particularly idiosyncratic information), unlike tangible goods, may have no intrinsic value: It has value only when integrated with a structure that is capable of exploiting it effectively. The rapid drop in the price of computing power was coincident with a period of enormous institutional and organizational change in Western industrialized countries (see Piore, 1987; Piore & Sabel, 1984). Firms were making historically massive IT investments precisely at a time in which the organizational and strategic structures needed to utilize IT were undergoing their most profound changes. Many firms were in the midst of layoffs, leaving or entering markets, and so on and thus could not focus on using IT effectively from a business standpoint. The result was a growing IT capital stock and an associated group of managers, technologists, and the like immersed in volatile circumstances, without any coherent direction.

The absence of a significant productivity effect from IT therefore must be seen, at least in large measure, as a failure by managers to build organizations that effectively integrated IT with business strategy, human resource management, and efficient resource allocation. The claim for a lack of alignment between IT and business strategy and organization is heard so often today that it may already be a cliché. The challenge is to make this statement more precise in terms of specific factors that are either responsible for the misalignment or efficacious in correcting it. In an effort to identify such factors, a series of interviews was conducted with four of the Management in the 1990s sponsors, which include members of the manufacturing, services, and government sectors. Unlike the econometrics just discussed, no claims are made about the empirical validity of these interviews. They do, however, confirm the importance of several key issues, which can be grouped into two interrelated central problems that have limited the returns from IT: inadequate organizational structures and poor capital budgeting.

Organizational structures

There are no hard and fast rules for proper organizational structure, but it is possible to generate some basic principles. First, all firms operate along some continuum between centralization and decentralization, and many firms are frequently moving between various points. The trick is to recognize how the peculiarities of IT fit into a coherent overall picture. On the one hand, IT reduces the cost of communication and may, as Malone (1985) argued, favor market-mediated transactions over intrafirm transactions. This strengthens the case for decentralization, and indeed, for this and a variety of other perhaps more important reasons, the general thrust of organizational reforms in recent years has favored decentralization and increased autonomy for lower-level managers (see Piore, 1987; Piore & Sabel, 1984).

The costs of decentralization stem from the nature of IT. IT provides information, which offers gains of standardization, common access, common training, shared development, and so forth. There are thus clear benefits to some central control or direction for the use and development of IT: most notably, building an IT infrastructure (networking), educating, and pursuing a business strategy with IT. Not surprisingly, some firms first suffered the costs of decentralization when they discovered the growth in the number of marketing people visiting them from the same vendor, an increase in incompatible data bases, and systems that could not communicate directly.

Although the influence of IT on the degree of centralization varies by firm, the point here is that explicit consideration must be given to how the firm's IT activities fit with changes in its organizational structure. Decentralization, often motivated by other factors, may be best implemented with particular IT initiatives working in the opposite direction, for example, top-level IT policy review committees that oversee the internal consistency and efficiency of IT investments made by decentralized managers.

Second, the low productivity effect from IT suggests a failure by organizations to value properly the output from IT: In Baily and Chakrabarti's (1988) model this is evidence of a (internal) market failure. A key objective in organizational design must therefore be to put in place mechanisms that can better value IT. One part of this package is better measurement and more careful investment decisions. The other part is building organizations that facilitate the communication and transparency necessary to observe IT inputs and outputs and to channel the observations into the decision-making process. One simple example of a useful reform is integrating technologists with business people, who have heretofore been culturally and organizationally distant from each other.

Perhaps the most important insight to emerge from the interviews is that it is hard to incorporate IT into a changing organization until the organization itself is designed to accommodate change. In other words, the organization itself must be flexible and include human resource policies that provide coherent incentives for flexibility (see Osterman, 1988, chap. 4). In this context, IT systems must be built on elemental data that are basic to any particular organizational permutation, rather than being built on the basis of particular existing organizational structures.

A recent study of auto assembly plants by John Krafcik (1988) illustrates this argument. He examined the contribution of plant investments in robotics to productivity and product quality in a model that measures organizational structure and human resource policy. Krafcik's sample included assembly plants from North America, Japan, and Europe that featured different organizational schemes. His results showed no effect from robotics investments, after controlling for a measure of management policy.[27] This research underscores the need to nest IT effectively in organizational structure, human resource policies, and business strategy.

Capital budgeting

The achievement of significant returns from IT is predicated on effective capital budgeting. However, the evidence just shown indicates that investments in IT were not optimal and, indeed, that marginal dollars would have been better spent on other categories of capital, labor, or whatever. IT poses significant problems for calculating the expected gains and costs for a given investment, which makes the usual cost–benefit analysis quite difficult, and the need for better cost–benefit methods for IT is a plea heard often today. Complexity, however, is no excuse for failing to try to evaluate the expected returns and to use these calculations seriously in the investment decision. The main impediment to the better use of cost–benefit analysis is proper attribution of the gains from IT versus other factors; the ability to quantify noncontinuous benefits, such as using IT to stay competitive in a market that the firm would otherwise lose; proper accounting for secondary benefits, such as reduced floor space or shorter new product development time; proper measurement of the costs of not making the investment, such as loss of market share (i.e., proper baseline assumptions); and measuring expected gains when uncertainty allows several possible outcomes. Shortcomings in capital budgeting procedures, such as treating systems development costs as expense items, also contribute to nonoptimal investment analysis.[28]

Cost–benefit analysis must be applied not only to new projects but also to the maintenance of existing systems, which often account for an increasing share of total costs while contributing diminishing payoffs. In many firms there is no mechanism to trigger consideration of upgrade or replacement.

Even when cost–benefit analysis is adequate by traditional standards, it suffers from an additional problem. Most IT investments are made in the context of uncertainty over current and future product market conditions, organizational change, and improvements (or cost reductions) in the technology available for purchase in subsequent periods. In the case of irreversible investments—those that are sunk costs—there is value in waiting to make the investments until later periods when some of the uncertainty has been resolved.[29] This "option" value must be set against any costs, such as foregone revenue, but it is an important factor, tending to raise the required rate of return, that is seldom considered when weighing IT investment decisions. In fact, in some cases, senior managers, though not fully understanding the implications of IT, believed it to be of long-term strategic importance. For fear of being at a competitive disadvantage, firms often invested in IT more out of anxiety than clear thinking about its actual use. In many cases, firms bought into evolving technologies or systems too soon or too heavily, when waiting might have been better.

Finally, another possible cause of poor returns from IT stems from the IT budgetary process in many firms. A large portion of IT investments are responses to needs for particular services expressed by employees at various levels in the organization. A collection of these projects gradually becomes a budget as individual items percolate through the organization. They may be reviewed by an IT group for internal consistency, costs and benefits, and so on, but the budget goes to senior management having been formulated largely from below. Thus at least a significant portion of the budget is unlikely to reflect coordination with business strategy and organization. That is, because much of the IT budget originated relatively far below, it is difficult for it to be a product of executive business vision. The budgetary process has been complicated in recent years by the combination of organizational reforms favoring decentralization and the increased attractiveness of small systems and personal computers. The result has been a larger portion of the IT budget's falling under the authority of fewer senior managers, and an explosion of uncoordinated spending.

CONCLUSION: WHAT DOES THE FUTURE HOLD?

Managers' recognition of these problems reflects the fruits of several years' hard work, and progress has been made. Many firms have undergone substantive reorganization both to become more flexible generally and to use IT more efficiently. Today, information systems personnel and users are closer together organizationally and in terms of direction and motivation. Senior management is more familiar with IT and thinks much more about its role in overall business strategy. Budgetary control is often tighter, but more important, the IT budget is more carefully scrutinized, and projects are evaluated more thoroughly.

All of these factors suggest better times ahead for the use of IT, which would be a welcome boost to U.S. productivity. There are, however, several caveats. First, economics suggests that the highest-yielding reserves are mined first. This implies that today the marginal IT project may have a lower expected return than that of previous years. Opinions in the business community are mixed on this point. Some in the service industry agree, whereas others in manufacturing argue that there are several steps, or levels, in the use of IT. They contend that we are poised to jump up to a new level on which we go beyond the automation of known processes and the payoffs will be much higher. Improved standards and system integration will also help. Continued technological change, coupled with effective management, can override the diminishing returns problem.

Second, the software development (labor) share of total systems budgets has grown from much less than half to much more than half (due in part to the price decline of hardware). Productivity increases are thought to be much slower in software than in hardware, and this may constrain the future productivity impact of IT.[30]

These issues raise a question about the empirical results presented in this chapter. The data were generated from a period in which the state of the technology was dominated by large, mainframe computers and office automation. PCs came, to the greatest extent, later, as did robotics, expert systems, electronic integration, and so forth. There is no a priori reason to extrapolate the results from manufacturing in the late 1970s to early 1980s to current or future technologies. However, there simply is not any evidence to date that the returns from IT have increased.[31]

In sum, there is cause for no more than guarded optimism that the future productivity gains from IT will improve. Some firms (at least in the United States) have progressed toward better exploiting IT, but they have by no means solved all the problems. Indeed, there is as yet no compelling evidence that most firms have taken the measures necessary to improve significantly the returns from IT, irrespective of the particular state of the technology. History warns that we are prone to forgetting how radical things seemed when they first appeared; thus there is at least an element of hubris in attributing the low productivity gains of the earlier period to a "primitive" technology vis-à-vis today's standards.

APPENDIX 1

The net book value and depreciation data for each category of capital—land and buildings, non-IT equipment, and IT equipment—were used to derive annual "investment"[*] according to the identity:

$$NBV_t = (1 - \delta_a)NBV_{t-1} + I_t \qquad (1A)$$

where δ_a = reported depreciation rate and I_t = investment. This yields an investment figure for each year except the first for all firms in the sample. The net book value in the first year was deflated by the ratio of constant to historical cost, as defined by the Bureau of Economic Analysis (BEA)[†] for each category of capital, and this is the final value used in our analysis. For subsequent years, new capital stocks for each category were derived by first deflating the investment series by the implicit price deflator for each type of capital. Note that the new BEA quality-adjusted computer price index was used here[‡] and that the producers' durable equipment less office, computing, and accounting machinery price index was used for non-IT equipment. The new capital stock figures were then calculated using Equation 1A, but replacing δ_a with the economic depreciation rates (δ_e). Values of δ_e reported by Hulton and Wycoff (1981) were used for non-IT capital, and Oliner's (1986) estimate of δ_e for computers was used for IT capital. For IT equipment, δ_a differs substantially from δ_e : that is, δ_a is typically .12 in this sample and δ_e is .27. Given the importance of the assumed depreciation rate for this analysis, values of .20 and .37[§] were also used to test the sensitivity of the results to the choice of .27 for δ_e for IT equipment, and the parameter estimates were essentially unchanged. Note that δ_a and δ_e were similar for the other categories of capital.

Purchased IT services are a problematic and sizable component of the total IT input. This category includes telecommunications services, purchased data and software, time-sharing, and the like, and it is therefore not obvious what to do about capitalizing the total purchases number. Three alternatives were used to test the sensitivity of the results to different capitalization methods:

1. Total IT purchases were treated as investments and added to the IT capital stock, as we discussed.
2. Total IT purchases were doubled (assuming roughly a two-year average life) and added to the IT capital stock.

*Investment as calculated here includes write-offs and sales, thus allowing I_t to be negative. This, in fact, was often the case during the turbulent 1978–82 period when firms were restructuring. Because these are business unit data, internal transfer of assets within firms are reflected in the individual unit's balance sheets.

†I am grateful to John Musgrave at the Commerce Department's BEA for unpublished data. See also Musgrave, 1986.

‡For the 1978–84 period under consideration, the BEA price index does not differ markedly from that of Gordon, 1987.

§This is the δ_e for computers reported by Oliner, 1986.

3. Total IT purchases were tripled (assuming roughly a three-year average life) and added to the IT capital stock.

The results reported in the tables are from the first method, but the estimates were remarkably robust for changes in the capitalization procedure: That is, β_5 in Table 4.6 was –.055 for each of procedures 2 and 3.

Business units also use a portion of corporate capital, both IT and non-IT. The shares of corporate capital in total business unit capital are, however, small. Two methods were used to add the shares of corporate capital to the business unit stocks:

1. The corporate share was assumed to be rented at the user cost of capital,* and the flow was added to the relevant stock.
2. The corporate share was capitalized on the basis of δ_e for each type of capital.

The results presented in the tables are based on the first method, but the estimates were (not surprisingly) unchanged using the second method.

APPENDIX 2

The potential biases arise in all our specifications, but for simplicity, consider the static model given in Equation 5, in which k and c can be safely taken as predetermined, but simultaneity bias may follow from shocks to which the flexible inputs—m, ps, and l—respond contemporaneously. A positive correlation between ε_1 and m, ps, or l may be transmitted to β_5, and the sign of the bias is a function of the covariances among the inputs. The bias can be estimated as follows:

$$E(\beta - \mathbf{B}) = \text{bias} = E((X'X)^{-1}X'\epsilon_1) \tag{2A}$$

where β is the vector of parameters and $\mathbf{B}$ is the OLS estimates. Under the assumption of k, c predetermined, $\chi'\varepsilon_1$ is a column vector of dimension 5×1 in which the first three elements—ρ_1, ρ_2, ρ_3—measure the correlation between ε_1 and m, ps, and l, and the last two elements are zeros. Thus the bias can be rewritten as

$$\text{bias} = E(X'X)^{-1} \times \begin{pmatrix} \rho_1 \\ \rho_2 \\ \rho_3 \\ 0 \\ 0 \end{pmatrix} \tag{3A}$$

Note that ρ_1, ρ_2, and ρ_3 are presumably positive, but of unknown magnitude. It is, however, straightforward to calculate $(\chi'\chi)^{-1}$.

Given the small calculated covariances in the relevant rows of $(\chi'\chi)^{-1}$, even very large correlations between ρ's and ε_1 and c and ε_1 would not generate a significant negative bias to $\mathbf{B}_5$. For example, if ρ_1, ρ_2, and $\rho_3 = 1$, bias $(\mathbf{B}_5) = -.017$, which is clearly too small to influence the results.

The lack of a capital utilization measure can be analyzed in a similar fashion.

*I am grateful to Richard Kopcke, Federal Reserve Bank of Boston, for the user cost of capital data. See Kopcke, 1985, for details.

Let the "true" model be

$$q = \lambda + \beta_1 m + \beta_2 ps + \beta_3 l + \beta_4(\tau k) + \beta_5 c + \epsilon_2 \tag{4A}$$

where τ = capital utilization. Then $\varepsilon_2 = \beta_4 (1 - \tau) k + \varepsilon_1$. The size of the bias in $\mathbf{B}_5$ now hinges on the correlations between $\beta_4 (1 - \tau) k$ and the other inputs, and on the previously calculated row of $(\chi' \chi)^{-1}$. In this case, the ρ's need not all be positive, and given the alternating signs in the last row of $(\chi' \chi)^{-1}$, any bias in $\mathbf{B}_5$ is again likely to be small and of indeterminate sign.

The magnitude of any bias introduced by measurement error in the IT input variable can be estimated using the technique of Hausman and Griliches (1986). Consider the general model:

$$y_{it} = \beta \chi_{it} + \eta_{it} \tag{5A}$$

where χ^*_{it}, the true variable, is measured with error and the observed χ_{it} is defined by $\chi_{it} = \chi^*_{it} + \eta_{it}$; αi is a firm specific error; η_{it} is the usual error term; and v_{it} is a measurement error. Taking the kth difference yields

$$y_{it} - y_{it-k} = \beta(\chi_{it} - \chi_{it-k}) - \beta(v_{it} - v_{it-k}) = \eta_{it} - \eta_{it-k} \tag{6A}$$

If the measurement error is assumed to be i.i.d., then

$$\text{plim}\mathbf{B}_{ols,k} = \frac{\beta - \beta(v_{it} - v_{it-k})(v_{it} - v_{it-k})}{\sigma^2_{\chi,k}} \tag{7A}$$

$$= \beta - \left(\frac{2\beta\sigma^2 v}{\sigma^2_{\chi,k}}\right)$$

$$= \left(1 - \frac{2\sigma^2 v}{\sigma^2_{\chi,k}}\right) * \beta$$

where $\sigma^2_{x,k} = \text{var}(x_{it} - x_{it-k})$.

Equation 7A shows that **B** departs from the true β as the variance of the measurement error (σ^2_v) increases relative to $\sigma^2_{x,k}$. If v is not i.i.d. and, rather, is **AR**1, then the bias from the measurement error will be larger, and the formula given for the i.i.d. case will be a lower bound.

Calculating **B** for two different cases, such as first and second differences, yields an estimate of σ^2_v. In the case of the static model (Equation 5) on the full sample, $\sigma^2_v = 0.029$, which implies the usual result that $\mathbf{B}_5$ is biased toward zero. In other words, the true effect of IT is smaller (a negative number of higher magnitude) than the estimated effect. The central finding of no large positive productivity effect from IT is therefore not an artifact of bias from measurement error in the IT variable.

Calculation of any bias from mismeasurement of other variables, or the spillover from mismeasurement of the IT variable into the estimated coefficients for the other inputs, is much less tractable and will not be pursued here.

ACKNOWLEDGMENT

I am grateful to Chris Vellturo, Anil Kashyap, Brian Palmer, Michael Scott Morton, and seminar participants at the National Bureau of Economic Research, Cambridge,

Massachusetts, for their helpful comments and suggestions. Particular thanks are due to Ernst Berndt who has given me invaluable assistance throughout this project. Financial support from the Management in the 1990s Program is gratefully acknowledged. Thanks also to the many MIT90s Sponsors interviewees for their insights, some of which are reflected in this paper but are not explicitly attributed for reasons of confidentiality. I alone am responsible for any errors or omissions.

NOTES

1. For the purposes of the Management in the 1990s Program, IT is defined to include the following six broad categories: computers, software, telecommunications, professional work stations, robotics, and chips. With respect to the data used in this study, IT is defined to include computing machines, data bases, purchased software, telecommunications, telex and satellite equipment, and document generation equipment.

2. A recent headline story in *Business Week* (June 6, 1988) explored the "productivity paradox" surrounding the increased investment in IT and poor U.S. productivity performance.

3. See Bruno & Sachs, 1985. Furthermore, expectations are obviously important, as the price decline of IT was more easily anticipated than was the price rise of oil, and thus producers could modify technologies and input demand more smoothly in the former case.

4. Alternatively, the whole issue could be shrouded by mismeasurement. We shall return to this concern later.

5. One important exception is Bresnahan, 1986, discussed later.

6. IT could obviously have only normal returns in terms of firm profit but have large welfare gains if product prices fall as a result of cost reductions. The following analysis captures this effect via the estimation of production functions, which have dual representations as cost functions.

7. This terminology will be made more precise later.

8. The "business unit" is defined later.

9. See Griliches, 1986, for a brief review of this literature and new results for the 1970s.

10. For example, falling output per information worker could result from a transfer of tasks formerly done by production workers, thus raising the productivity of the latter. Alternatively, there could be problems in the information-handling activities per se. These considerations were raised by Baily and Chakrabarti (1988).

11. Osterman was referring to the offsetting increase in employment as an implication of the "bureaucratic reorganization hypothesis" in which the declines in information costs are associated with the reorganization of work.

12. Osterman's data do not distinguish among production, services, and marketing.

13. The derived demand curve for an input adjusts for equilibrium in the output market.

14. Furthermore, the firms in this sample cannot be characterized as facing perfectly competitive markets. Therefore, behavioral equations such as input demand functions risk misspecification from incorrect characterization of the profit maximization problem facing the firm.

15. In equilibrium, investment proceeds until $\beta = W_c{*}C / P{*}Q$. A low β leads to small C for given W_c.

16. The translog is a second-order approximation to an arbitrary function and, as such, places relatively little a priori structure on the data. In particular, the elasticities of substitution among the inputs are unconstrained. The costs associated with the translog include the need to estimate 21 parameters in our five input case, and the risk that if the data span a sufficiently large space, the approximation will be very crude. In addition, estimated translog

functions sometimes fail to obey fundamental economic principles, such as concavity-of-cost functions.

17. For more detail, see Loveman, 1986, and, more generally, Fuss & McFadden, 1978, pp. 249–72.

18. Berndt and Fuss (1986) develop a method for using TFP when firms are in temporary rather than long-run equilibrium. Unfortunately, their technique requires the constant returns assumption, which, as we shall show, is rejected in our data.

19. It is worth noting that accounting practices assume monotonic decline.

20. The mean factor shares in production (Q) for M, PS, L, K, and C are .4, .14, .32, .34, and .02, respectively.

21. Organizational structure is measured by the number of positions between various points in the hierarchy.

22. Although the self-reported market share numbers are unreliable, a ranking is less sensitive to consistent underestimates of the size of the market.

23. Strassman (1985) argued that firms that manage well overall also use IT effectively, and vice versa. Though similar in spirit to our result, his methods were quite different and were not based on a complete model of production or firm behavior.

24. Note that other than replacing the parameter on c with γ, the other coefficients in Equation 9 are as in Equation 5.

25. Some post-1984 MPIT data do exist, but they are largely new businesses in the sample rather than additional observations of existing businesses. Unfortunately, the proprietors of these data were not willing to make them available for academic research.

26. Reasonable perturbations in the returns-to-scale assumptions were not successful in yielding sensible parameter estimates.

27. Krafcik's "management index" is a composite measure that attempts to gauge production systems along a continuum between "fragile" (Japan) and "robust" (Western). The index is based on the percentage of assembly floor area used for postprocess repair; degree of emphasis on visual control of production; the degree to which the team concept is used; and the average level of unscheduled absenteeism.

28. See Kaplan, 1986, for a thorough discussion of the use of discounted cash flow in evaluating IT investments.

29. See McDonald & Siegel, 1986, for a detailed discussion of the option value of waiting to invest.

30. This claim is debatable, as new "case" tools may lead to significant productivity gains.

31. Recent evidence to the contrary includes Krafcik, 1988; Baily & Chakrabarti, 1988; and Roach, 1987.

REFERENCES

Baily, M. N., & A. Chakrabarti (1988). *Innovation and the productivity crisis.* Washington, DC: Brookings Institution.

Berndt, E., & M. Fuss (1986). Productivity measurement with adjustments for variations in capacity utilization and other forms of temporary equilibrium. *Journal of Econometrics* 33:7–29.

Bresnahan, T. F. (1986). Measuring the spillovers from technical advance: Mainframe computers in financial services. *American Economic Review* 76 (September): 742–55.

Bruno, M., & J. Sachs (1985). *The economics of worldwide stagflation.* Cambridge, MA: Harvard University Press.

Fuss, M., & D. McFadden (1978). *Production economics: A dual approach to theory and applications.* Amsterdam: North-Holland.

Gordon, R. J. (1987). The postwar evolution of computer prices. Cambridge, MA: National Bureau of Economic Research, working paper no. 2227.

Griliches, Z. (1986). Productivity, R&D, and basic research at the firm level in the 1970s. *American Economic Review* 76:141–54.

Hausman, J. H., & Z. Griliches (1986). Errors in variables in panel data. *Journal of Econometrics* 31:93–118.

Hulton, C. R., & F. C. Wykoff (1981). The measurement of economic depreciation. In C. R. Hulton (Ed.), *Depreciation, inflation and the taxation of capital*, pp. 81–125. Washington, DC: Urban Institute.

Kaplan, R. S. (1986). Must CIM be justified by faith alone? *Harvard Business Review*, March–April, pp. 87–95.

Kopcke, R. (1985). The determinants of investment spending. *New England Economic Review*, July–August, pp. 19–35.

Krafcik, J. F. (1988). Triumph of the lean production system. *Sloan Management Review*, Fall, pp. 41–52.

Loveman, G. (1986). The productivity of information technology capital: An econometric analysis. Mimeo, Department of Economics, Massachusetts Institute of Technology.

Loveman, G., & C. Tilly (1988). Good jobs or bad jobs: What does the evidence say? *New England Economic Review*, January–February, pp. 46–65.

Malone, T. (1985). Organizational structure and information technology: Elements of a formal theory. Management in the 1990s working paper no. 85–011, Sloan School of Management, Massachusetts Institute of Technology.

McDonald, R., & D. Siegel (1986). The value of waiting to invest. *Quarterly Journal of Economics* 101:707–27.

Musgrave, J. (1986). Fixed reproducible tangible wealth in the United States, 1982–85. *Survey of Current Business*, August, pp. 36–39. Washington, DC: Department of Commerce, Bureau of Economic Analysis.

Oliner, S. D. (1986). Depreciation and deflation of IBM mainframe computers: 1980–85. Federal Reserve Board working paper, Washington, DC.

Osterman, P. (1986). The impact of computers on the employment of clerks and managers. *Industrial and Labor Relations Review* 39 (January): 175–86.

——— (1988). *Employment futures: Reorganization, dislocation and public policy*. New York: Oxford University Press.

Pakes, A., & Z. Griliches (1984). Estimating distributed lags in short panels with an application to the specification of depreciation? Patterns and capital stock constructs. *Review of Economic Studies* 51 (April): 243–62.

Piore, M. J. (1987). Corporate reform in American manufacturing and the challenge to economic theory. Mimeo, Department of Economics, Massachusetts Institute of Technology.

Piore, M., & C. Sabel (1984). *The second industrial divide*. New York: Basic Books.

Roach, S. S. (1987). America's technology dilemma: A profile of the information economy. Special Economic Study, Morgan Stanley & Co., April.

Strassman, P. A. (1985). *Information payoff: The transformation of work in the electronic age*. New York: Free Press.

Zuboff, S. (1988). *In the age of the smart machine: The future of work and power*. New York: Basic Books.

CHAPTER 5

Determining User Needs for Novel Information-based Products and Services

ERIC VON HIPPEL

In the information age, needs for information-based products and services change and evolve more and more quickly. This represents a major problem for firms trying to serve those needs because, as I shall show, marketing research methods are not currently designed to function in environments marked by rapid change. I begin by reviewing the general problem facing marketing research in such environments. Then, I spell out a "lead user" marketing research methodology that can, I propose, help firms understand user needs for new products and services under the prevailing conditions in the field of information-based products and services. Finally, I review a successful case study using the method that I conducted with my colleague Glen Urban.

ROOT OF THE PROBLEM: MARKETING RESEARCH CONSTRAINED BY USER EXPERIENCE

Users selected to provide input data to consumer and industrial market analyses have an important limitation: Their insights into new product (and process and service) needs and potential solutions are constrained by their real-world experience. Users steeped in the present are thus unlikely to generate novel product concepts that conflict with the familiar.

The notion that familiarity with existing product attributes and uses interferes with an individual's ability to conceive of novel attributes and uses is strongly supported by research on problem solving (Table 5.1). We see that experimental subjects familiar with a complicated problem-solving strategy are unlikely to devise a simpler one when this is appropriate (see Luchins, 1942). Also, and germane to our discussion here, we see that subjects who use an object or see it used in a familiar way are strongly blocked from using that object in a novel way (see Adamson, 1952; Birch & Rabinowitz, 1951; Duncker, 1945). Furthermore, the more recently that objects or problem-solving strategies have been used in a familiar way, the more difficulty subjects will have employing them in a novel way (see Adamson & Taylor, 1954). Finally, we see that the same effect is displayed in the real world, in which

Table 5.1. The effect of prior experience on users' ability to generate or evaluate novel product possibilities

Study	Nature of research	Impact of prior experience on ability to solve problems
1. Luchins (1942)	Two groups of subjects (n =) were given a series of problems involving water jars (e.g., If you have jars of capacity A, B, and C, how can you pour water from one to the other so as to arrive at amount D?) Subject group 1 was given 5 problems solvable by formula B – A – 2C = D. Next, both groups were given problems solvable by that formula or by a simpler one (e.g., B – C = D).	81% of experimental subjects who had previously learned a complex solution to a problem type applied it to cases in which a simple solution would do. No control group subjects did so (p = NA)[a]
2. Duncker (1945)	The ability to use familiar objects in an unfamiliar way was tested by creating five problems which could be solved only by that means. For example, one problem could be solved only if subjects bent a paper clip provided them and used it as a hook. Subjects were divided into two groups. One group of problem solvers saw the crucial object being used in a familiar way (e.g., the paper clip holding papers), but the other did not (e.g., the paper clip was simply lying on a table unused).	The subjects were much more likely to solve problems requiring the use of familiar objects in unfamiliar ways if they had not been shown the familiar use just before their problem-solving attempt. Duncker called this effect *functional fixedness* (n = 14; p = NA)[a]
3. Birch & Rabinowitz (1951)	Replication of Duncker, 1945.	Duncker's findings confirmed (n = 25; p < .05).
4. Adamson (1952)	Replication of Duncker, 1945.	Duncker's findings confirmed (n = 57; p < .01).
5. Adamson & Taylor (1954)	The variation of "functional fixedness" with time was observed by the following procedure: First, subjects were allowed to use a familiar object in a familiar way. Next, varying amounts of time were allowed to elapse before the subjects were invited to solve a problem by using the object in an unfamiliar way.	If the subject uses an object in a familiar way, he is partially blocked from using it in a novel way (n = 32; p < .02). This blocking effect decreases over time.

Table 5.1. *continued.*

6. Allen &Marquis (1964)	Government agencies often buy R&D services via a "Request for Proposal" (RFP) that states the problem to be solved. Interested bidders respond with proposals outlining their planned solutions to the problem and its component tasks. In this research, the relative success of 8 bidders' approaches to the component tasks contained in two RFP's was judged by the agency buying the research (n = 26). Success was then compared with the previous research experience of the bidding laboratories.	Bidders were significantly more likely to propose a successful task approach if they had previous experience with that approach only, rather than previous experience with inappropriate approaches only.

[a]This relatively early study showed a strong effect but did not provide a significance calculation or present the data in a form that would allow one to be determined without ambiguity.

the success of a research group in solving a new problem is shown to depend on whether the solutions it has used in the past will fit that new problem (see Allen & Marquis, 1964). These studies thus suggest that typical users of existing products—the type of user-evaluators customarily chosen in market research—are poorly situated with regard to the difficult problem-solving tasks associated with assessing unfamiliar product and process needs.

As an illustration, consider the difficult problem-solving steps that potential users must follow when asked to evaluate their need for a proposed new product. Because individual industrial and consumer products are only components in larger usage patterns that may involve many products and because a change in one component can change perceptions of and needs for some or all other products in that pattern, users must first identify their existing multiproduct usage patterns in which the new product might play a role. Then they must evaluate the new product's possible contribution to these. For example, a change in a computer's operating characteristics may allow users to solve new types of problems if they also make changes in software and perhaps in other related products and practices. Next, users must invent or select the new (to them) usage patterns that the proposed new product makes possible for the first time and evaluate the utility of the product in these. Finally, because substitutes exist for many multiproduct usage patterns (e.g., many forms of problem analysis are available in addition to the novel ones made possible by a new computer), the user must estimate how the new possibilities presented by the proposed new product will compete (or fail to compete) with existing options. This problem-solving task is clearly a difficult one, particularly for typical users of existing products whose familiarity with existing products and uses interferes with their ability to conceive of novel products and uses when invited to do so.

The constraint of users to the familiar prevails even when sophisticated marketing research techniques are used, such as multiattribute mapping of product perceptions and preferences (see Shocker & Srinivasan, 1979; Silk & Urban, 1978).

"Multiattribute" (multidimensional) marketing research methods, for example, describe users' (buyers') perceptions of new and existing products in terms of several attributes (dimensions). If and as a complete list of attributes becomes available for a given product category, the users' perceptions of any particular product in the category can be expressed as the amount of each attribute that they perceive it to contain, and the difference between any two products in the category can be expressed as the difference in their attribute profiles. Similarly, users' preferences for existing and proposed products in a category can, in principle, be built up from their perceptions of the importance and desirability of each of the component products' attributes.

Although these methods frame users' perceptions and preferences in terms of attributes, they do not offer a means of going beyond the experience of those interviewed. First, for reasons just discussed, users are not well positioned to evaluate novel product attributes or "amounts" of familiar product attributes that lie outside the range of their real-world experience. Second, and more specific to these techniques, there is no mechanism to induce users to identify all product attributes that could be relevant to a product category, especially those attributes that are currently not present in any existing category member. To illustrate this point, consider two types of such methods, similarity–dissimilarity ranking and focus groups.

In similarity–dissimilarity ranking, data regarding the perceptual dimensions by which users characterize a product category are generated by asking a sample of users to compare products in that category and assess them in terms of their similarity and dissimilarity. In some variants of the method, the user interviewee specifies the ways in which the products are similar or different. In others, the user simply provides similarity and difference rankings, and the market researcher determines—via his or her personal knowledge of the product type in question, its function, the marketplace, and so on—the important perceptual dimensions that "must" be motivating the users' rankings.

The effectiveness of the similarity–dissimilarity method clearly depends on the analyst's qualitative ability to interpret the data and correctly identify all the critical dimensions. Moreover, by its nature, this method can explore only perceptions derived from attributes that exist in or are associated with the products being compared. Thus, if a group of evaluators is invited to compare a set of cameras and none has a particular feature—say, instant developing—then the possible utility of this feature would not be incorporated into the perceptual dimensions generated. That is, the method would have been blind to the possible value of instant developing before Edwin Land's invention of the Polaroid camera.

In focus group methods, market researchers assemble a group of users, familiar with a product category, for a qualitative discussion of perhaps two hours' duration. The topic for the focus group, which is set by the market researcher, may be relatively narrow (e.g., "35 mm amateur cameras") or somewhat broader (e.g., "the photographic experience as you see it"). The ensuing discussion is recorded, transcribed, and later reviewed by the researcher, whose task is to identify the important product attributes that have implicitly or explicitly surfaced during the conversation. Clearly, as with similarity–dissimilarity ranking, the utility of information derived from focus group methods depends on the analyst's ability to abstract, accurately and completely, from the interview data those attributes that the users felt were important to the products.

In principle, however, the focus group technique need not be limited to identifying only those attributes already present in existing products, even if the discussion is nominally focused on these. For example, a topic that extends the boundaries of discussion beyond a given product to a larger framework could identify attributes not present in any existing product in a category under study. If a discussion of the broad topic mentioned earlier, "the photographic experience as you see it," brought out user dissatisfaction with the time lag between picture taking and receipt of the finished photograph, the analyst would have information that would enable him or her to identify an attribute not present in any camera before Land's invention—that is, instant film development—as a novel and potentially important attribute.

But how likely is it that an analyst will take this creative step? And more generally, how likely is it that either method, similarity–dissimilarity ranking or focus groups, will be used to identify attributes not present in existing products of the type being studied, much less in a complete list of all relevant attributes? Neither method contains an effective mechanism to encourage this outcome, and discussions with practitioners indicate that in present-day practice, identification of any novel attribute is unlikely.

Finally, both of these methods conventionally focus on familiar product categories. This restriction, necessary to limit to a manageable number the number of attributes that "completely describe" a product type also tends to limit market research interviewees to attributes that fit products into the frame of existing product categories. Modes of transportation, for example, logically shade off into communication products as partial substitutes ("I can drive over to talk to him—or I can phone"), into housing and entertainment products ("We can buy a summer house—or go camping in my recreational vehicle"), and indeed, into many other of life's activities. But because a complete description of life cannot be compressed into 25 attribute scales, the analysis is constrained to a narrower—usually conventional and familiar—product category or topic. This has the effect of rendering any promising and novel cross category new product attributes less visible to the methods I have discussed.

In sum, then, we see that marketing researchers will face serious difficulties if they attempt to determine new product needs falling outside the real-world experience of the users they analyze.

LEAD USERS AS A SOLUTION

In many product categories, the constraint of users to the familiar does not lessen the ability of marketing research to evaluate needs for new products by analyzing typical users. In the relatively slow-moving world of steels and autos, for example, new models often do not differ radically from their immediate predecessors. Therefore, even the "new" is reasonably familiar, and the typical user can thus play a valuable role in developing of new products.

In contrast, in high-tech industries, the world moves so rapidly that the related real-world experience of ordinary users is often rendered obsolete by the time a product is developed or during the time of its projected commercial lifetime. For such industries I propose that "lead users" who do have real-life experience with novel product or process needs are essential to accurate marketing research. Although the insights of lead users are as constrained to the familiar as are those of other users, lead users are familiar with conditions that lie in the future for most—and so they are in a position to provide accurate data on needs related to such future conditions.

I define the *lead users* of a novel or enhanced product, process, or service as those who display two characteristics with respect to it:

1. Lead users face needs that will be general in a marketplace, but they face them months or years before the bulk of that marketplace will encounter them.
2. Lead users are positioned to benefit significantly if they can find a solution to those needs.

Thus, a manufacturing firm with a current strong need for a process innovation that many manufacturers will need in two years' time would fit the definition of a lead user with respect to that process.

Each of these two lead user characteristics contributes independently to the new type of product need and the solution data that such users are hypothesized to possess. The first is valuable because as we showed, users who have real-world experience with a need are in the best position to give market researchers accurate (need or solution) data regarding it. When new product and service needs are evolving rapidly, as is the case in many high-tech product and service categories, only those users "at the front of the trend" will have the current real-world experience that manufacturers must analyze if they are to understand accurately the needs that the bulk of the market will have tomorrow.

The utility of the second lead user characteristic is that users who expect to benefit from a solution to a need can provide the richest need and solution data to inquiring firms. The reason is that, as has been shown by studies of industrial product and process innovations (e.g., Mansfield, 1968), the greater the benefit a given user expects to obtain from a needed novel product or service, the greater will be that user's investment in precisely understanding the need and seeking a solution.

In sum, then, lead users are users whose current strong needs will become general in a marketplace months or years in the future. Because lead users are familiar with conditions that lie in the future for most others, I hypothesize that they can serve as a need-forecasting laboratory for marketing research. Moreover, because lead users often attempt to fill the need they experience, I hypothesize that they can provide, in addition to need data, valuable new product concept and design data to inquiring manufacturers.

TESTING THE METHOD

Glen Urban and I, with the able assistance of our student, David Israel-Rosen, conducted a prototype lead user market research study in the rapidly changing field of computer-aided design (CAD) products (Urban & von Hippel, 1988). (Over 40 firms compete in the $1 billion market for CAD hardware and software. This market grew at over 35 percent per year between 1982 and 1986, and the forecast is for continued growth at this rate for the next several years.) Within the CAD field, we decided to focus specifically on CAD systems used to design the printed circuit boards used in electronic products, or PC–CAD.

Printed circuit boards hold integrated circuit chips and other electronic components and interconnect these into functioning circuits. PC–CAD systems help engineers convert circuit specifications into detailed printed circuit board designs. The design steps that are or can be aided by PC–CAD include component placement, signal routing (interconnections), editing and checking, documentation, and interfacing to manufacturing. The software required to perform these tasks is very complex and includes placement and routing algorithms and sophisticated graphics. Some PC–CAD manufacturers sell only such software, while others sell systems that include both specialized computers and software. (Important suppliers of PC–CAD in 1985 included IBM, Computervision, Redac, Calma, Scicards, and Telesis.)

The method that Urban and I used to identify lead users and to test the value of the data they possess in the PC–CAD field had four major steps: (1) identifying an important market or technical trend, (2) identifying lead users with respect to that trend, (3) analyzing the lead users' data, and (4) testing the lead users' data on ordinary users.

IDENTIFYING AN IMPORTANT TREND

Lead users are defined as being in advance of the market with respect to a given important dimension that is changing over time. Therefore, before one can identify the lead users in a given product category of interest, one must specify the underlying trend on which these users have a leading position.

To identify an "important" trend in PC–CAD, we sought out a number of expert users. We found them by telephoning the managers of the PC–CAD groups in several firms in the Boston area and asking each: "Whom do you regard as the engineer most expert in PC–CAD in your firm? Whom in your company do group members turn to when they face difficult PC–CAD problems?"[1] After our discussions with expert users, it was clear to us that an increase in the "density" with which chips and circuits are placed on a board was and would continue to be an important trend in the PC–CAD field. Historical data showed that board density had in fact been steadily increasing over a number of years. And the value of continuing increases in density was apparent. An increase in density means that it is possible to mount more electronic components on a given-sized printed circuit board. This, in turn, translates directly into an ability to lower costs (less material is used), to decrease the product size, and to increase the speed of circuit operation (signals between components travel shorter distances when the board density is higher).

In addition, other equally important trends may exist in the field that would reward analysis, but we decided to focus on this single trend in our study.

IDENTIFYING LEAD USERS

In order to identify the lead users of PC–CAD systems capable of designing high-density printed circuit boards, we had to identify that subset of users who were

(1) designing very high density boards now and (2) were positioned to gain an especially great benefit from increasing the board density. We decided to use a formal telephone-screening questionnaire to accomplish this task and strove to design one that contained objective indicators of these two hypothesized lead user characteristics.

Printed circuit board density can be increased in a number of ways, each of which offers an objective means of determining a respondent's position on the trend toward higher density. First, more layers of printed wiring in a printed circuit board can be added. (The early boards contained only one or two layers, but now some manufacturers are designing boards with 20 or more layers.) Second, the size of electronic components can be reduced. (A recent important technique for achieving this is "surface-mounted devices" that are soldered directly to the surface of a printed circuit board.) Finally, the printed wires, "vias," that interconnect the electronic components on a board can be made narrower and packed more closely. Questions regarding each of these density-related attributes were included in our questionnaire.

Next, we assessed the level of benefit that a respondent might expect to gain by improvements in PC–CAD, by means of several questions. First, we asked about the users' level of satisfaction with existing PC–CAD equipment, assuming that great dissatisfaction would indicate an expect of much benefit from improvements. Second, we asked whether the respondents had developed and built their own PC–CAD systems, rather than buy the commercially available systems such as those offered by IBM or Computervision. (We assumed, as we noted previously, that users who make such innovation investments do so because they expect a high benefit from the resulting PC–CAD system improvements.) Finally, we asked the respondents whether they thought their firms were innovators in the field of PC–CAD.

The PC–CAD users we interviewed were restricted to U.S. firms and were selected from two sources: a list of the members of the relevant professional engineering association (IPC Association) and a list of current and potential customers provided by a cooperating supplier. The interviewees were selected from both lists at random. We contacted approximately 178 qualified respondents and had them answer the questions on the phone or by mail if they preferred. The cooperation rate was good, as 136 screening questionnaires were completed. One-third of these were completed by engineers or designers, one third by CAD or printed circuit board managers, 26 percent by general engineering managers, and 8 percent by corporate officers.

Simple inspection of the screening questionnaire responses showed that fully 23 percent of all responding user firms had developed their own in-house PC–CAD hardware and software systems. This high proportion of user-innovators that we found in our sample is probably characteristic of the general population of PC–CAD users. Our sample was well dispersed across the self-stated scale with respect to innovativeness, with 24 percent indicating that they were on the leading edge of technology, 38 percent up to date, 25 percent in the mainstream, and 13 percent adopting only after the technology was firmly established. This self-perception is supported by objective behavior with respect to the speed with which our respondents adopted PC–CAD: Half began using CAD between 1979 and 1985, 33 percent between 1974 and 1978, and 21 percent before 1969.

We next conducted a cluster analysis of screening questionnaire data relating to the hypothesized lead user characteristics, in an attempt to identify a lead user group. The two and three cluster solutions are shown in Table 5.2.

Note that these analyses do indeed indicate a group of respondents who combine the two hypothesized attributes of lead users and that effectively all of the PC–CAD product innovation is reported by the lead user group.

In the two-cluster solution, what we term the *lead user cluster* is, first, ahead of non–lead users in the trend toward higher density. That is, they reported more often using surface-mounted components, narrower lines, and more layers than did members of the non–lead cluster. Second, they appeared to expect a higher benefit from PC–CAD innovations that would allow them even more progress. That is, they report less satisfaction with their existing PC–CAD systems (4.1 versus 5.3, with higher values indicating satisfaction). Also, I believe that in order to increase satisfaction,[2] 87 percent of respondents in the lead user group reported building their own PC–CAD system (versus only 1 percent of non–lead users). Lead users also judged themselves to be more innovative (3.3 versus 2.4 on the four statement scale, with higher values more innovative) and were in fact earlier adopters of PC–CAD than were non–lead users. Twenty-eight percent of our respondents are classified in this lead user cluster. The two clusters explained 24 percent of the variation in the data.

In the three-cluster solution, the lead user group was nearly unchanged, but the non–lead group was separated into two subgroups. Non–lead group A (N-LA) had the lowest use of surface-mounted components, the widest line widths, the fewest layers, and the latest year of adoption and rated itself as lowest on adoption of innovations. Non–lead group B (N-LB) also differed from the lead user group in the expected ways except for one anomalous result: Group N-LB showed a higher usage of surface-mounted components than did the lead user group. In the three-cluster solution, 37 percent of the variation can be explained by cluster membership.

Table 5.2. Cluster analyses show user group with hypothesized lead user characteristics

	Two-cluster solution		Three-cluster solution		
	Lead user	Non–lead	Lead user	N-LA	N-LB
Indicators of user position on PC-CAD					
Density trend					
Use surface mount? (%)	87	56	85	7	100
Average line width (mils)	11	15	11	17	13
Average layers (number)	7.1	4.0	6.8	4.2	4.4
Indicators of user expected benefit from PC-CAD improvement					
Satisfaction*	4.1	5.3	4.1	5.2	5.2
Build own PC-CAD? (%)	87	1	100	0	0
Innovativeness**	3.3	2.4	3.2	2.1	2.8
First use CAD (year)	1973	1980	1973	1980	1979
Number in cluster	38	98	33	46	57

*7 point scale— high value more satisfied.
**4 point scale— high value more innovative.

A discriminant analysis indicated that "build own system" was the most important indicator of membership in the lead user cluster. (The discriminant analysis had 95.6 percent correct classification of cluster membership. The standardized discriminant function coefficients were build own .94, self-stated innovativeness .27, average layers .25, satisfaction –.23, year of adoption –.16, and surface mounting .152.)

ANALYZING LEAD USERS' INSIGHTS

The next step in our analysis was to select a small sample of the lead users identified in our cluster analysis to participate in a group discussion to develop one or more concepts for improved PC–CAD systems. Experts from five lead user firms that had facilities located near MIT were recruited for this group. The firms represented were Raytheon, DEC, Bell Labs, Honeywell, and Teradyne. Four of these five firms had built their own PC–CAD systems. All were working in high-density (many layers and narrow lines) applications, and all had adopted the CAD technology early.

The task set for this group was to specify the best PC–CAD system for laying out high-density digital boards that could be built with the current technology. (To guard against including "dream" features impossible to implement, we conservatively allowed the concept that the group developed to include only those features that one or more of them had already implemented in their own organizations. No one firm had implemented all aspects of the concept, however.)

The PC–CAD system concept developed by our lead user creative group integrated the output of PC–CAD with numerical control machines, had easy input interfaces (e.g., block diagrams, interactive graphics, icon menus), and stored data centrally with access by all systems. It also provided full functional and environmental simulation (e.g., electrical, mechanical, and thermal) of the board being designed, could design boards of up to 20 layers, could route thin lines, and could properly locate surface-mounted devices on the board.

TESTING PRODUCT CONCEPT PERCEPTIONS AND PREFERENCES

From the point of view of marketing research, new product need data and new product solutions from lead users are interesting only if they are desired by the general marketplace.

To test this matter, we decided to determine the PC–CAD users' preferences for four system concepts: the system concept developed by the lead user group, each user's own in-house PC–CAD system, the best commercial PC–CAD system available at the time of the study (as determined by a PC–CAD system manufacturer's competitive analysis), and a system for laying out curved printed circuit boards. (This last was a description of a special-purpose system that one lead user had designed in-house to lay out boards curved into three-dimensional shapes. This is a useful attribute if one is trying to fit oddly shaped spaces inside a compact product, but most users would have no practical use for it. In our analysis of preference, we think that the users' response to this concept can serve to flag any respondent's tendency to prefer systems based on system exotica rather than practical value in use.)

To obtain users' preference data regarding our four PC–CAD system concepts, we designed a new questionnaire that contained measures of both perception and preference. First, the respondents were asked to rate their current PC–CAD system on 17 attribute scales. (These were generated by a separate sample of users through triad comparisons of alternative systems, by open-ended interviews, and by technical analysis. Each scale was presented to the respondents in the form of a five-point agree–disagree judgment based on a statement such as "my system is easy to customize."[3] Next, each respondent was invited to read a one-page description of each of the three concepts we had generated (labeled simply J, K, and L) and to rate these on the same scales. All concepts were described as having an identical price of $150,000 for a complete hardware and software workstation system able to support four users. Next, rank-order preference and constant-sum paired comparison judgments were requested for the three concepts and the existing system. And finally, probability-of-purchase measures on an 11-point Juster scale were collected for each concept at the base price of $150,000 and alternative prices of $100,000 and $200,000.

Our second questionnaire was sent to 173 users (the 178 respondents who qualified in the screening survey less the five user firms in the creative group). Respondents were telephoned to inform them that a questionnaire had been sent. After a telephone follow-up and a second mailing of the questionnaire, 71 complete or near complete responses were obtained (41 percent), and the analyses that follow are based on these.[4]

LEAD USERS' CONCEPT PREFERRED

As can be seen from Table 5.3, our analysis of the concept questionnaire showed that the respondents strongly preferred the lead user group's PC–CAD system concept over the three others presented to them. Of the sample, 78.6 percent selected the concept created by the lead users' group as their first choice. The constant sum scaled preference value was 2.52 for the concept developed by the lead users' group. This was 35 percent greater than the users' preference for their own current system and more than twice as great as the preference for the most advanced existing commercially available product offering.

The concept created by the lead users' group was also generally preferred by users to their existing systems (significant at the 10 percent level based on the preference measures: $t = 12$ for proportion of first choice and $t = 2.1$ for constant sum).

Table 5.3. Test of all respondents' preferences among four alternative PC-CAD system concepts

PC-CAD concept	Percent first choice	Constant sum*	Average probability of purchase
Lead user group concept	78.6	2.60	51.7
Respondents' current PC-CAD	9.8	1.87	**
Best system commonly available	4.9	.95	20.0
User system for special application	6.5	.77	26.0

*Torgerson, 1958.
**Probability of purchase only collected across concepts.

And the lead users' group's concept was significantly preferred to the "special application" user system created to lay out curved boards. (The lead user concept was significantly better than the user-developed special application system on all measures at the 10 percent level (t = 12.3 for first choice, t = 7.9 for preference, and t = 8.5 for probability).[5]

Respondents maintained their preference for the lead users' concept even when it was priced higher than competing concepts. The effects of price were investigated through the probability-of-purchase measures collected at three prices for each concept. For the lead users' concept, probability of purchase rose from 52.3 percent to 63.0 percent when the price was reduced from $150,000 to $100,000 ($t$ = 2.3) and dropped to 37.7 percent when the price was increased to $200,000. Probability of purchase of the lead users' concept was significantly higher at all price levels (t greater than 4.4 in all paired comparisons), and it was preferred to the best available concept even when the specified price was twice as high as that of competing concepts. All three concepts displayed the same proportionate change in purchase probability as the price was changed from its base level of $150,000. The probability measures indicate substantial price sensitivity and provide a convergent measure of the attractiveness of the concept based on the lead users' solution content.

LEAD AND NON–LEAD USERS' PREFERENCES SIMILAR

The needs of today's lead users are typically not precisely the same as the needs of the users who will make up a major share of tomorrow's predicted market. Indeed, the literature on diffusion suggests that in general, the early adopters of a novel product or practice differ in significant ways from most of the users who will follow them (Rogers & Shoemaker, 1971). However, in this instance, as Table 5.4 shows, the product concept preferences of lead users and non–lead users were similar.

A comparison of the way in which lead and non–lead users evaluated PC–CAD systems showed that this similarity of preference was deep-seated. An examination of the PC–CAD attribute ratings and factor analyses derived from each group showed five factors in each, which explained the same amount of variation (67.8 for lead users and 67.7 for non–lead users). The factor loadings were also similar for the two groups, and their interpretation suggested the same dimension labels. Also, analysis showed that each group placed a similar degree of importance on each dimension (Urban & von Hippel, 1986).

Table 5.4. Concept preferences of lead versus non–lead users

PC-CAD concept	Percent first choice		Constant sum		Average probability of purchase	
	Lead	Non–lead	Lead	Non–lead	Lead	Non–lead
Lead user group concept	92.3	80.5	3.20	2.37	53.1	51.2
Respondent's current PC–CAD	7.7	11.1	2.64	1.56	—	—
Best system commonly available	0	2.8	.67	1.06	10.2	23.9
User system for special application	0	5.6	.52	.87	16.3	29.9

DISCUSSION

From the point of view of marketing research, I think that the results of this first test of a lead user method must be seen as encouraging. Lead users with the hypothesized characteristics were clearly identified; a novel product concept was created based on the lead users' insights and problem-solving activities; and the lead users' concept was judged to be superior to currently available alternatives, by a separate sample of lead and non–lead users. I should point out, however, that the high level of actual product innovation found among lead users of PC–CAD can be expected only in those product areas in which the benefit expected by such users is sufficient to induce the users' innovation. When the expected users' benefit is less, the need data available from lead users should still be more accurate and richer in "solution content" than the data from non–lead users, but they may not include prototype products such as those we observed in our study of PC–CAD.

According to our underlying hypothesis regarding the predictability of the sources of innovation on the basis of innovators' related expectations of benefit, I think that the lead user application has also shown encouraging results. Users who identified themselves as dissatisfied with existing products were shown as more likely to develop new ones responsive to their need.

ACKNOWLEDGMENT

The research reported on here has also been presented in Glen L. Urban and Eric von Hippel, "Lead User Analyses for the Development of New Industrial Products," *Management Science* 34 (May 1988): 569–82; and in Eric von Hippel, *The Sources of Innovation* (New York: Oxford University Press, 1988).

NOTES

1. PC–CAD system purchase decisions are made primarily by the final users in the engineering department responsible for the CAD design of boards. In this study we interviewed only these dominant influencers in order to find concepts and test them. If the purchase decision process had been more diffuse, it would have been appropriate to include other important decision participants in our data collection.

2. The innovating users reported that their goal was to achieve better performance than commercially available products could provide in several areas: high routing density, faster turnaround time to meet market demands, better compatibility with manufacturing, interfaces with other graphics and mechanical CAD systems, and improved ease of use for less experienced users.

3. The 17 attributes are ease of customization, integration with other CAD systems, completeness of features, integration with manufacturing, maintenance, upgrading, learning, ease of use, power, design time, enough layers, high-density boards, manufacturable designs, reliability, placing and routing capabilities, high value, and updating capability.

4. Ninety-four questionnaires (55 percent) were actually returned, but only 71 were judged complete enough to use. This subset consisted of 61 respondents who completed all items on both the screening and concept questionnaires, and an additional 10 who completed all items except the constant-sum paired comparison allocations.

5. As part of our analysis we tested for potential nonresponse bias by comparing early and later returns, but we found none. The returns from the first 41 percent of respondents showed the creative group concepts to be the first choice of 77 percent, and the returns from the last 59 percent showed the creative group concepts to be the first choice of 71 percent. The differences between the early and later returns were not significant at the 10 percent level ($t = .15$). Thus, there was no evidence of a nonresponse bias. A possible demand effect bias toward the lead user's group's concept could have been present, but the low preferences for the best available product and the curved board concepts argue against it. All concepts were presented in a similar format with labels of concept J, K, and L (the lead user group concept was labeled K). We did not expect any differential bias toward concept K.

REFERENCES

Adamson, R. E. (1952). Functional fixedness as related to problem solving: A repetition of three experiments. *Journal of Experimental Psychology* 44 (October): 288–91.

Adamson, R. E., & D. W. Taylor (1954). Functional fixedness as related to elapsed time and to set. *Journal of Experimental Psychology* 47 (February): 122–26.

Allen, T. G., & D. G. Marquis (1964). Positive and negative biasing sets: The effects of prior experience on research performance. *IEEE Transactions on Engineering Management* EM –11 (December): 158–61.

Birch, H. G., & H. J. Rabinowitz (1951). The negative effect of previous experience on productive thinking. *Journal of Experimental Psychology* 41 (February): 121–25.

Duncker, K. (1945). On problem-solving. Trans. L. S. Lees. *Psychological Monographs* 58 (Whole no. 270).

Luchins, A. S. (1942). Mechanization in problem solving: The effect of Einstellung. *Psychological Monographs* 54 (Whole no. 248).

Mansfield, E. (1968). *Industrial research and technological innovation: An econometric analysis.* New York: Norton.

Rogers, E. M., & F. F. Shoemaker (1971). *Communication of Innovations: A Cross-Cultural Approach.* New York: Free Press.

Shocker, A. D., & V. Srinivasan (1979). Multiattribute approaches for product concept evaluation and generation: A critical review. *Journal of Marketing Research* 16 (May): 159–80.

Silk, A. J., & G. L. Urban (1978). Pre-test-market evaluation of new packaged goods: A model and measurement methodology. *Journal of Marketing Research* 15 (May): 189.

Urban, G. L., & E. von Hippel (1988). Lead user analyses for the development of new industrial products. *Management Science* 34 (May): 569–82.

von Hippel, E. (1988). *The sources of innovation.* New York: Oxford University Press.

CHAPTER 6

Innovative Cultures and Organizations

EDGAR H. SCHEIN

Both students of organizations and managers are today increasingly concerned about the capacity of organizations to adapt to rapidly changing environmental conditions. The rate of change in the technological, economic, political, and sociocultural environments is picking up speed, and organizations are, therefore, finding it more and more important to figure out how to adapt.

Adaptation in turbulent environments requires more than minor adjustments to the present way of doing things. It often requires genuinely innovative ideas—new missions, new goals, new products and services, new ways of getting things done, and even new values and assumptions. Most important, adaptation means the developing of the capacity to manage "perpetual change." Organizations must "learn how to learn" (Argyris & Schon, 1978; Schein, 1980) and must become "self-designing" (Weick, 1977).

The difficulty is that organizations are by their nature and often by design oriented toward stabilizing and routinizing work. Organizations create cultures that are expressed in structures and processes that permit large numbers of people to coordinate their efforts and that allow new generations of members to continue to perform effectively without having to reinvent the organization each time (Schein, 1985). How then, can one conceptualize an organization that can function effectively and yet be capable of learning so that it can adapt and innovate in response to changing environmental circumstances? How can one conceive of an organization that can surmount its own central dynamic, that can manage the paradox of institutionalizing and stabilizing the process of change and innovation?

In this chapter I want to address some aspects of these questions and to present a point of view based on my research into the dynamics of organizational culture. In particular I want to focus on innovation as being itself a property of culture. In other words, what kind of organizational culture consistently favors innovation?

This question is of special interest at the present time because of the rapid advances being made in the field of information technology (IT). There is ample evidence to suggest that the introduction of IT into organizations not only forces cultural assumptions out into the open but that the potential of IT as a strategic aid to organizations will not be fulfilled unless, at the same time, those organizations develop (or already possess) what I define as *innovative cultures*.

The definition of *innovation* is itself a major problem. In this chapter I shall adopt a broad and imprecise definition—new ideas, behavior patterns, beliefs, values, and assumptions covering any aspect of the organization's functioning. In particular I want to ensure that we consider both (1) *content innovation*—new products, services, and ideas pertaining to the mission of the organization, and (2) *role innovation*—new ways of doing things, new definitions of roles, and new approaches to performing in roles (Schein, 1970; Van Maanen & Schein, 1979).

Defining what is "new" is, of course, also problematic. In analyzing a case of culture change in a large corporation, I found that some of the major changes that the organization felt it had made really reflected an affirmation of some of its most basic assumptions (Schein, 1985). What, then, had changed? Was there any innovation? My sense about this issue is that we must define innovation ultimately by the perceptions of both members of the organization and those outsiders who interact with the organization and, therefore, who are in a position to perceive changes. If both insiders and informed outsiders agree that something is really "new," then we are dealing with an innovation.

This definition will not satisfy the positivistic empiricist, however. Measuring consensus in perceptions is difficult and messy. But if we are to understand what really goes on in this organizational domain and if we are to arrive at better concepts and theoretical insights, at this stage we will be better off with the rich and messy insights of the ethnographer and the clinician (Schein, 1987).

In order to lay out these ideas efficiently, I have made minimal references to what is a vast literature on organization design and innovation. That is, my goal is not to summarize what we know but to be provocative and push into an area of cultural analysis that has not, to my knowledge, been much explored as yet.

A BASIC SOCIOTECHNICAL PARADIGM FOR ANALYZING ORGANIZATIONS

I shall start with some of my underlying assumptions about the nature of organizations. There are many models available for analyzing organizational systems. Many of them are flawed from the outset, however, because they conceptually separate the task and technical elements from the human and organizational elements. For example, most models of strategy and organization design advocate that one should start with a concept of mission or goal and then design the organization to fulfill that mission or goal. The human elements are typically thought of as something that follows and must be adapted to the mission and the technical/structural elements.

In contrast, a sociotechnical model would indicate that one must integrate the human considerations with the technical ones in the initial design process. The formulation of the organization's mission and goals is, after all, a product of human beings in entrepreneurial, technical, and managerial roles. The assumptions, beliefs, values, and biases of these human actors thus will limit and bias the technical and structural options considered, and they will certainly affect the organizational design.

Furthermore, if the people who will be using a given system (however it may have been invented) do not participate in its design, all kinds of unanticipated problems may arise that will make the system less effective than its technical designers had forecast. We see this especially in the realm of information technology in which the difficulties of implementation far outstrip the difficulties of invention.

For example, when an information system is designed, the human consequences are often either totally misunderstood or actively ignored. First a "small" example observed by Lotte Bailyn, in which the introduction of PCs to an executive group was slowed down by the frequently discovered fact that most executives cannot type and are not willing to learn to do so. The enthusiastic implementers had created a typing program to deal with this issue and, to provide effective feedback to the learners, arranged to have a bell ring every time a mistake was made (on the theory that an aural signal would get better attention than a visual signal would). But the signal was also public and no one wanted others to know when he or she was making errors, and so the system had to be redesigned with a less vivid but more private feedback signal.

A "larger" example occurred in one division of an aerospace company. The general manager needed detailed performance and schedule information for each project and program in the company and thus designed a system that would provide such detail. The system allowed him to identify schedule or performance problems as soon as they arose, so that he could check on what was going wrong. He felt he needed that information to deal with his outside stakeholders.

What this manager did not anticipate was that the project managers and engineers would feel threatened by the knowledge that their day-to-day behavior was being monitored. If the manager asked questions about problem areas, they found it difficult to respond because they had not had a chance to look at the reasons for the observed deviations from the established plan. The system designers should have expected this problem inasmuch as it is a well-known phenomenon in the psychology of control. What typically happens is that subordinates who feel threatened or embarrassed by revealed information attempt to subvert the system by refusing to enter data or by feeding in false information to protect themselves. Such behavior usually leads the system designers to invent more elaborate information devices that cannot be falsified, leading to an escalation of resentment and tension in the organization.

An even more dangerous outcome is that the subordinates become dependent on the boss to be the control system and cease to exercise whatever self-control they had once had (McGregor, 1960, 1967). They might feel that if the President has all the information, let's fix only those problems that he shows himself to be concerned about.

The sociotechnical solution is to involve all the people concerned with the system design. This was eventually done in the preceding case because the manager realized that creating resentment in his subordinates was counterproductive. The whole organization launched into a "redesign" of the system and invented a solution. It concluded that the manager had a valid need for the information but that he did not need it at the same time as all of the employees did. So the project members suggested a time delay; they would get the information as soon as it was available so that they could get to work on any problems that were identified. The manager would get the same information a couple of days later so that by the time he inquired about problems, or even before he inquired, the project teams could tell him what was wrong and how they were dealing with it. The time delay solved everyone's problems and led to a much more effective organization. The essential control stayed where the information was—in the project teams.

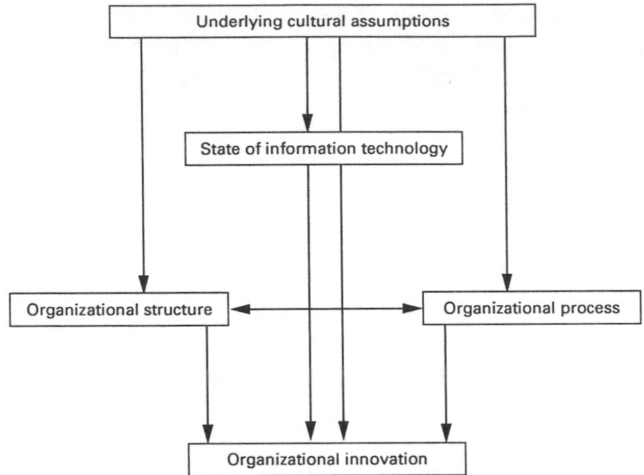

Figure 6.1. A sociotechnical model of organizational innovation.

Enough is known today about the human problems of information and control systems, about the design of equipment, and about the human problems of automation to make sociotechnical design entirely feasible. What usually stands in the way is cultural assumptions about the role of management and the role of technical designers in the initial creation of innovations. It is for these reasons that organizational culture must be analyzed first when defining the conditions for adaptation and innovation (see Figure 6.1).

This model emphasizes that one can study adaptation and innovation from the point of view of the organizational processes that must be included, from the point of view of the organizational structure that must be in place, and from the point of view of the information technology that must be available. However, inasmuch as the culture will determine how the technology is ultimately used and will influence both the structure and the processes that the organization uses, it is the cultural assumptions underlying innovation that will influence each of the other elements. Adopting a sociotechnical model reminds us that we cannot bypass the analysis of the cultural and human forces at work in organizations.

CULTURE

The overarching determinant of how organizations work is the culture that evolves in the organization as its members cope with the external problems of survival in the environment and their internal problems of integration (Schein, 1985). Culture can be defined as the pattern of learned basic assumptions that has worked well enough to be considered valid and, therefore, to be taught to new members as the correct way to perceive, think, and feel in relation to the problems of survival and integration.

Culture manifests itself in overt behaviors, norms, and espoused values, what can be thought of as the artifacts of the culture. Culture is also expressed in some of the less conscious and operational values that members share. But unless one deciphers the underlying, often implicit and unconscious, pattern of assumptions taken for granted, one has not really analyzed the culture.

A culture and its overt manifestations stabilizes the daily life of its members and provides meaning for what they do. Stability and hence predictability is essential to the members of an organization. Without predictability they cannot function and thus cannot avoid the anxiety that accompanies a loss of meaning. Culture, once in place, is therefore an inherently conservative force.

The "strength" of a culture is a function of several variables: (1) the strengths of the initial convictions of the organizational founders, (2) the stability of the group or organization, (3) the intensity of the learning experience in terms of the number of crises survived and the emotional intensity of those shared crises, and (4) the degree to which the learning process has been one of anxiety avoidance rather than positive reinforcement. The more the culture helps reduce anxiety, the more it will resist change.

Cultural assumptions tend toward a consistent paradigm to the extent that the culture's creators work from a consistent set of assumptions in the first place and to the extent that the organization's learning experiences provide consistence. If the members of an organization learn inconsistent things in order to survive and remain integrated, they will have inconsistent and possibly ambiguous assumptions with which they nevertheless feel comfortable (Martin, personal communication, 1987).

To the extent that culture is a learned product of group experience, there will be a culture wherever there is a group, in the sense of a set of people who share common experiences over a period of time. Inasmuch as most organizations are differentiated over time into many subgroups, there will be subgroup cultures in each of them, with their strengths varying as a function of the aforementioned factors. A total organization, then, can have a total culture as well as a set of subcultures, and any given member of the organization can simultaneously "possess" elements of all of the cultures of which he or she is a member (Van Maanen & Barley, 1984). Some of these will, of course, be family, community, occupational, and other groups that the person belongs to and identifies with outside the organization.

Given that members of organizations have multiple group memberships and that they will identify to different degrees with these various groups, it is not at all anomalous to have a strong overall culture that contains "deviant" elements, or to have entire subcultures that are deviant or countercultural because of their external connections, such as to a strong professional group or an international union (Martin & Siehl, 1983).

We know that cultures evolve and can be changed, but we have not analyzed carefully enough the characteristics of any given culture that would more or less facilitate change and innovation. Or, more directly, is it possible to conceive of a type of culture that would be innovative, that would have as its learning dynamic the invention of environmentally responsive new solutions rather than conservative self-preservation? And is it possible to conceive of a type of culture that would favor sociotechnical design innovations instead of those based on traditional technology?

INFORMATION TECHNOLOGY

Cultures are built around and respond to the core technologies that caused the organization to be created in the first place. One may expect organizational cultures to vary, therefore, according to the kind of core technology that is involved. Chemical, high-tech, heavy manufacturing, financial, and other service industries each will produce somewhat different "industry" cultures that will influence organizational cultures.

All organizations have in common the need to communicate, to get information to the right place at the right time in order to divide labor appropriately and coordinate the effort of the organization's members. The flow of information can be likened to the lifeblood of the system, and the information channels can be compared with the circulatory system. The state of IT in use at any given time is, therefore, likely to be an important determinant of the organization's capacity to learn. What, then, should be the characteristics of the information system to maximize the capacity of the organization to learn, adapt, and innovate?

Information technology is central to this analysis because its own evolution has enabled innovative leaps of extraordinary magnitude. Today some organizations are being designed on totally different premises by taking advantage of the IT's capabilities. We can conceptualize this best by distinguishing three kinds of utopian visions that have grown up around IT:

1. The vision to automate: Most of the critical functions in the organization are taken over by robots or computerized systems run by highly skilled and trained professional operators.
2. The vision to "informate": By building accurate models of critical processes in the organization, it is possible not only to automate such processes but also to make the processes themselves visible and understandable to everyone in the organization. This is what Zuboff (1988) calls "informating" the organization, and it obviously has tremendous implications for both workers and managers at all levels.

2a. Informating up: IT is used to aggregate and centralize as much information as possible about all the parts of the organization, in order to facilitate planning and control by top management. The organization becomes familiar to its top management.

2b. Informating down: The design of systems forces an analysis of the core production and other processes of the organization and makes them recognizable to the workers. Instead of understanding only a small piece of the total process, workers become familiar with the whole process and can thus make decisions that previously were made by various layers of management.

3. The vision to transform: A few organizations think of even more radical innovations by asking how one might organize the basic work, the communication patterns, and authority relations, to take advantage of the possibilities inherent in IT. Sociotechnical design considerations become primary in integrating the technical and human capabilities.

Such organizations may take a totally different form, being more like complex networks in which communication and authority chains shift around and change according to the requirements of the task and the motivation and skills of the people.

Adaptation and innovation are involved to varying degrees in each of these visions, but in the vision to automate and the vision to informate up, we are talking only of converting existing processes in order to be more efficient. Thus robots and various other kinds of machine-controlled work are important innovations in the production process, and sophisticated information systems that permit high levels of centralized control are innovations in the degree to which information can be rapidly collected and centralized, but it is only with informating down and transforming that we can get more radical innovation in the nature of the organization itself. In these instances, IT creates new concept of how work is to be done and how the management process itself is to be defined. What this means is that the cultural assumptions about the nature and use of IT will themselves be crucial determinants of how IT will be used to create further innovation.

ORGANIZATIONAL PROCESSES

Over time, every organization develops a set of processes, recurrent events that ensure that the principal task of the organization is fulfilled and that permit the members of the organization to coordinate effectively with one another. Such processes concern how members communicate with one another, how they solve problems and make decisions, how they implement decisions arrived at, and how they organize work, supervise, reward, punish, and, in general, deal with people (Schein, 1987, 1988).

Such processes reflect the culture as we defined it, but the basic cultural assumptions are largely implicit and invisible, whereas the processes that evolve over time are visible and can be analyzed. In order to understand any given organization, therefore, we need to specify both the underlying assumptions and the observable processes. In our analysis, then, the question is what kinds of cultural assumptions must be present to facilitate organizational processes that will increase the likelihood that the organization will be able to learn, adapt, and innovate?

ORGANIZATIONAL STRUCTURE

Some processes become stable and are articulated in rules, manuals, organization charts, and other more permanent documents reflecting how management feels that things should be done. The ultimate division of labor is embodied in job descriptions and organizational units and is the basic organization design in terms of who reports to whom and who is accountable for what, which is typically thought of as the "formal" structure. But as in the case of organizational processes, this structure really reflects the underlying cultural assumptions. One of the common misconceptions in this area is that structure can be analyzed as a factor separate from culture. If one starts with a sociotechnical model of organizations, one cannot separate structure from culture. One can, however, ask whether some formal structures are more likely to facilitate or encourage learning, adaptation, and innovation, and if so, what kinds of cultural assumptions will favor the evolution of such structures.

In most organizations one also finds an "informal" structure, those processes that are observed to be relatively stable but are supported only by implicit norms and are often regarded to be unsanctioned or even to contradict the formal structure. It is the existence of such counterstructures based on subcultures, or countercultures, that may determine what kind of innovation is possible.

The informal structure also includes "compensatory" or "parallel" structures that are designed to offset or supplement what may be weaknesses and dysfunctional elements in the formal structure (Schein, 1980, 1988). Such compensatory or parallel structures may be relatively permanent, such as standing committees, or they may be temporary processes, such as task forces and project teams formed to work only on specific and time-bound tasks.

Most organization theories acknowledge that without the informal organization, things simply would not be done effectively, and so the informal structure must be analyzed and understood if we are to comprehend the total system and how it works. In this chapter the question then becomes what kinds of cultural assumptions would favor the evolution of formal and informal structures that would be likely to lead to learning, adaptation, and innovation?

To sum up, I believe that in order to determine the necessary and sufficient conditions for an innovative organization, we must specify those cultural characteristics that favor the kinds of information technology, organizational processes, and formal and informal organizational structures that will increase the likelihood of such innovation.

CHARACTERISTICS OF AN INNOVATIVE CULTURE

Organizational cultures can be analyzed along many dimensions. I shall propose a few, as shown in Table 6.1, and hypothesize the assumptions necessary for innovative capacity. Table 6.1 can also be used as a diagnostic device for analyzing any given culture.

Organization–environment relationships

Hypothesis Cl: *The capacity of an organization to innovate increases to the extent that it assumes that its environments can be controlled, changed, and managed.*

Organizations can be distinguished by their shared assumptions regarding the degree to which they dominate or are dominated by their various environments. At one extreme we have organizations that seem completely dependent and assume that their existence and survival is out of their control. They act fatalistic and are passive in the face of environmental turbulence. They accept whatever niche the environment provides.

At the other extreme are organizations that share the assumption that their own behavior will influence the environment and that their survival and growth depend on the extent to which they can dominate some aspects of their environment. Also implied is the assumption that progress and improvement are possible, a basically optimistic orientation toward the environment.

Innovative capacity increases to the extent that members assume that innovation is possible and necessary, which derives from their optimistic assumption that the environment can be influenced. Organizations that pessimistically assume that they are dominated by others and/or that their environments are fixed find it difficult to conceive of new ideas and find it even more difficult to marshal the energy to try them out.

Table 6.1. Cultural dimensions that influence innovativeness*

1. Organization-environment relationship		
Environment dominant	Symbiotic	Organization dominant
		x
2. Nature of human activity		
Reactive, fatalistic	Harmonizing	Proactive
		x
3. Nature of reality and truth		
Moralistic authority		Pragmatism
		x
4. Nature of time		
Past oriented	Present oriented	Near future oriented
		x
Short time units	Medium time units	Long time units
	x	
5. Nature of human nature		
Humans are basically evil		Humans are basically good
		x
Human nature is fixed		Human nature is mutable
		x
6. Nature of human relationships		
Groupism		Individualism
		x
Authoritarian/paternalistic		Collegial/participative
		x
7. Subculture diversity/connectedness		
Low		High
		x

*The x on each dimension indicates the ideal condition for high innovativeness.

The nature of human activity

Hypothesis C2: *The capacity of an organization to innovate increases to the extent that it assumes that the appropriate human activity is to be proactive, to be oriented toward problem solving, and to improve things.*

All organizations make implicit assumptions about whether the appropriate behavior of their members is to be (1) reactive, fatalistic, and oriented to getting what pleasure one can out of one's lot in life (Dionysian); (2) to be proactive, optimistic, and oriented toward improving things (Promethean); or (3) to take the middle ground of trying to harmonize and compromise between one's own needs and whatever environmental constraints and possibilities exist (Apollonian). These assumptions are the individual-level counterpart to the assumptions relating the organization to its environment.

An innovator in the midst of reactive or harmonizing people will find it virtually impossible to get even an audience, much less a commitment to new ways of doing things. In Dionysian or Apollonian organizations, innovators are likely to be called whistle-blowers, boat rockers, or troublemakers and thus to be neutralized. And if the culture is too fatalistic, it will not, of course, attract or retain innovators in the first place.

One may wish to speculate whether there is an upper limit to activity orientation. If there are too many innovators and if the culture strongly encourages innovation, will that cause other problems that, in the end, will undermine innovation by making life too chaotic and unpredictable? I believe not, because if too much innovation becomes a problem, the organization will invent processes and structures that reduce innovation to a tolerable level. In other words, if the organization is going out of control, its own innovativeness will enable it to invent mechanisms to achieve greater discipline and control.

The reverse is not true, however. An organization that is too passive or fatalistic cannot invent "proactivity." It will stagnate until it fails or is taken over by others who will forcibly change the culture by replacing its employees with people oriented toward a different activity. I am hypothesizing, therefore, that one cannot have too much innovativeness but that one can have too much conservatism and passivity.

The nature of reality and truth

Hypothesis C3: *The capacity of an organization to innovate increases to the extent that it assumes that truth is to be arrived at by pragmatic (vs. moralistic) means.*

Organizations can be distinguished by the degree to which they share assumptions about how one determines whether or not something is true. When a complex decision has to be made regarding uncertain futures and information of uncertain validity, what criteria does the organization use to determine when it has enough and the right kind of information to make the decision?

At one extreme one finds a heavy reliance on tradition, dogma, the authority of moral principles, or the wisdom of elders. At the other extreme one finds pragmatism embodied in either a search for scientific verification or a trial- and error-attitude if formal verification is not possible or practical (England, 1975). If the decision is in a domain in which verification by physical means is not possible, pragmatism would imply that the decision makers debate the issues and subject each alternative to sufficient scrutiny that the one that survives can be accepted with some measure of confidence.

In organizations dominated by dogma or authorities of various sorts, it is not only difficult to articulate new ideas but even more difficult to obtain permission to try them out. An exception is, of course, the situation in which the innovator is the person in authority, a situation that arises from time to time in history but that is hard to specify as an organizational condition or to predict. To increase the innovative capacity generally, a positive value must be put on novelty, on breaking tradition, and on trying out new things even if they are risky, and such a value must be supported by an underlying assumption that "the truth" is not already known.

The pragmatic end of the continuum also implies a more positive attitude toward trial and error, risk taking, and the acceptance of unsuccessful efforts or failures. The more committed the organization is to dogmas, rules, systems, and procedures that become institutionalized, the harder it will be for its members to take the risks necessary for innovation to succeed. The message in such moralistic organizations is "try new things only if you are sure you will not break rules or fail," which is surely a prescription for conservatism and playing it safe.

The nature of time

Hypothesis C4A: *The capacity of an organization to innovate increases to the extent that it is oriented to the near future (vs. past, present, or far future).*

Hypothesis C4B: *The capacity of an organization to innovate increases to the extent that it uses medium-length time units (vs. short ones that do not allow innovation to develop or long ones that make innovation difficult to evaluate).*

All organizations hold implicit assumptions about the relative importance of the past, the present, and the future, and all organizations have implicit assumptions about the appropriate length of time units for different kinds of tasks. Some organizations measure themselves in short units such as weeks or months; others use intermediate units such as quarters and years; and still others use longer units such as five or 10 years. All organizations use all of these units for various different purposes, and as Lawrence and Lorsch (1967) pointed out years ago, the different functional units of an organization such as sales and research and development (R & D) have different assumptions about what it means to be "on time" and how long the units of work are.

It is likely that in each organization's culture, there are assumptions about the "really important" time units. The actual size of the relevant time units varies from company to company, so what is "past," "present," "near future," and "far future" must be determined for each organization, by getting the members' consensus on these units. The size of such time units is also influenced by the core technologies with which the organization is working. The development of new products, for example, takes much longer in the pharmaceutical industry than in the consumer goods industry.

Organizations that live in the past or present find it difficult to place a value on novelty, because they are focusing on what has worked or is working now. People with new ideas can be dismissed easily because their ideas do not "fit" what the organization likes to think about. On the other hand, if the organization is concentrating on the far future, it may not be able to launch any innovations because it assumes that there is always plenty of time to try things "in the future." A near-future orientation should, therefore, be most favorable to innovation.

It is also clear that too short a time orientation always makes innovation difficult because one can always show that short-run costs are too high to justify continuing the trial and error necessary for innovation. On the other hand, if the time units are too long, some innovations that fail will be allowed to continue too long; the organization will lose money; and the whole innovation process will be undermined because people will remember how they were hurt by past innovations. The organization's ability to decide on an optimal length of time for an innovation thus becomes an important determinant of its learning capacity.

This optimal length of time is subjectively defined in most organizations and must be measured within each organization. The precise length of the units is not as important as the members' ability to recognize that giving an innovation too little or too much time is equally destructive to the overall innovation process.

Optimal-length time units also play a role in selling an innovative vision, whether that comes from leaders or from other innovators in the organization. The vision of the future cannot exceed the ability of the organization's members to understand what is proposed, nor can it promise benefits that will be realized only by the next generation. To be motivated to implement something new, people have to be able to see the benefits that it will bring them within their own lifetime.

As Jaques argued (1976, 1982), the length of time over which organization members have "discretion" appears to vary with organizational rank. On the shop floor, supervisors check on employees by the hour or the day. At lower managerial levels, one has discretion over weeks, and so on up the ladder until the most senior management is supposed to define its tasks in terms of years. In communicating the future impact of proposed innovations, it becomes critical, then, to consider over what time units the audience is used to thinking. "Optimal" time units, in this context, are partly defined by the actual innovative task that is being proposed or undertaken.

The nature of human nature

Hypothesis C5: *The capacity of an organization to innovate increases to the extent that it assumes that people are ultimately neutral or good and, in any case, are capable of improvement.*

Organizations make implicit assumptions about human nature, both whether it is good, neutral, or evil and how malleable or fixed it is. If organizations are cynical about human nature (McGregor's Theory X), they will not encourage innovation or, worse, will suspect innovators of having ulterior motives. In such organizations, innovative capacity often is devoted to defeating organizational goals. Workers invent elaborate processes and devices to make life easier for themselves at the expense of organizational efficiency (Argyris, 1964; McGregor, 1960; Roethlisberger & Dickson, 1939).

On the other hand, if the organization holds optimistic assumptions about human nature (McGregor's Theory Y), it will expect people to be innovative, will encourage innovation, will listen to new ideas, and will be more likely to trust them. At the same time, for innovation to be encouraged, the organization's members must feel that they all are "perfectible" in the sense that their personality and contribution are not fixed. If one knows one can grow and improve, this knowledge (assumption) can act as a powerful stimulant to personal development and innovation.

The nature of human relationships

Hypothesis C6A: *The capacity of an organization to innovate increases to the extent that it assumes the ideal of individualism and the pursuit of individual diversity.*

Hypothesis C6B: *But if an organization has a few innovative individuals whose ideas are adopted, it can implement some types of innovation faster, to the extent that it assumes the ideal of groupism.*

Hypothesis C6C: *The capacity of an organization to innovate increases to the extent that it assumes that collegial or participative methods of decision making are the most appropriate.*

Hypothesis C6D: *But if an organization has innovative people in senior leadership roles, it can implement some innovations faster, to the extent that it assumes authoritarian or paternalistic methods of decision making.*

This dimension of culture pertains to prevailing assumptions about the ideal human relationship. Two dimensions are involved here:

1. The degree to which the organization assumes the ideal of "individualism" (that all good things come from individual effort) or "groupism" (that all good things come from the group, implying that all individuals must subordinate themselves to the group).
2. The degree to which ideal relationships are seen as collegial or participative (implying that power and influence in decision making depends on who has what expertise relevant to any given task to be accomplished) or as autocratic or paternalistic (implying that power and influence reside in positions, statuses, and roles or are a function of the individual's specific personality).

The hypotheses regarding these two dimensions are more complex and contingent because under certain conditions innovation can occur anywhere along them. Generally, a culture that values individuals and individual diversity has more ideas from which to draw and creates more incentives for ideas to be put forward. However, when it comes to accepting ideas and implementing them, the strongly individualistic organization may be at some disadvantage. In other words, in a groupist organization it is harder to get new ideas to be articulated, but if they are adopted, such an organization will be far more effective in implementing them because any individuals who may dissent will suppress their dissent for the sake of the group's welfare.

In such organizations the burden of innovation probably falls on the leaders, in that they are the most likely to be able to get an idea adopted in the first place. What the determinants are of innovativeness in the leaders of groupist organizations then becomes the secondary, but critical, question.

Collegial or participative decision making is more likely to identify the relevant areas in which innovation is needed, to advance good ideas, to stimulate creativity, and to produce a state of affairs in which everyone understands the idea so that it can be properly implemented. This assumption is central because collegial or participative decision making influences so many phases of the total innovation process, from invention to implementation, particularly if the new idea or process is complex and hard to understand.

If, on the other hand, an autocratic or paternalistic leader has innovative ideas that are sound, if the ideas are not too complex to communicate, and if the sociotechnical implications have been correctly thought through, it will be possible for the organization to implement such ideas more rapidly and more completely. The danger in this situation, however, is threefold: (1) that the leader will impose an idea that is wrong and the subordinates are neither motivated nor rewarded for pointing out the potential problems; (2) that the idea will not be successfully communicated, leading to paralysis and frustration; or (3) that the idea will be implemented incorrectly because the leader did not discover that the subordinates did not fully understand what he or she had in mind and/or did not accept the consequences of the innovation.

One additional point bearing on this assumption needs to be discussed: If predictions about the ultimate impact of IT are correct, then leaner, flatter, and more highly networked organizations are the likely consequence (Drucker, 1988; Malone, 1987). Such organizations cannot work effectively, however, if their managers are still operating from hierarchical models buttressed by autocratic or paternalistic assumptions (Schein, 1989). The basis of authority in such networks is more likely to be the degree of skill or expertise that any given member has at any given moment in time, relative to the task to be done. Positional authority will mean very little. Obviously such systems will function better if they hold collegial or participative assumptions in the first place.

Subcultural diversity

Hypothesis C7: *The capacity of an organization to innovate increases to the extent that it encourages diverse but connected subcultures.*

As organizations grow and mature, they develop subcultures as well as overarching cultures. The nature and diversity of such subcultures influence the organization's innovative capacity. For any given group, culture is a homogenizing force. However, if the organization contains in its total system enough diverse subsystems with their own diverse subcultures, it can innovate by empowering people and ideas from those subcultures that are most different from the "parent" yet are best adapted to a changing environment. Drawing on diverse subcultures is, in fact, the most common way that cultures evolve, and this process, if properly managed, is therefore one of the most important sources of innovation.

Such subcultures must be connected and part of a parent culture, or their elements will not be seen as relevant if introduced into the parent. For example, in a highly geographically decentralized organization, new ideas may well spring up in an overseas subsidiary, but these ideas can be imported by the parent organization only if the subsidiary is perceived to be part of the larger culture. If the ideas are brought in by transferring people from the subsidiary, those people will have credibility and influence only if they are perceived to be part of the larger culture and sympathetic to it.

It is this diversity-within-unity theme that accounts for so many current management statements that the effective organization is one that can both centralize and decentralize, that can be loose and tight at the same time. To restate the point, diversification and decentralization are effective as innovative forces only if the separate units are perceived to be, and feel themselves to be, connected to the whole. Conversely, if they do not feel connected, they will not be motivated to innovate on behalf of the whole. If they are not perceived to be connected, their ideas will not be perceived as relevant.

Summary

To summarize, in order to be innovative, an organizational culture must assume the following:

1. The world can change and change can be managed.
2. Humans are by nature proactive problem solvers.
3. Truth can be pragmatically discovered.
4. The most propitious time horizon is the near future.
5. Time units should be geared to the kind of innovation being considered.
6. Human nature is neutral or good and is, in either case, perfectible.
7. Human relationships are based on individualism and the valuing of diversity.
8. Decision making is collegial or participative.
9. Diverse subcultures are an asset to be encouraged, but subcultures must be connected to the parent culture.

Having stated these conditions for what must be true in the overall culture, what other conditions must be present in the state of information technology?

CHARACTERISTICS OF AN INFORMATION TECHNOLOGY FOR INNOVATION

I am assuming that any open system can function only if it can take in, move around, and appropriately process information. Information is the lifeblood, and information channels are the circulatory system, of the organization. If the organization is to be capable of innovation, what must be true of the information system?

Parenthetically, I am assuming that if these cultural conditions are not present, the organization is not likely to develop or implement an ideal information system, or if such a system should for some reason be present, it will misuse the system in ways that I shall describe shortly. So having an ideal system from a technological point of view will not by itself solve the problem of innovation. Technology alone will not cause things to happen. However, given the right conditions for innovation in the culture, it is possible to specify how an information system can enhance the chances for innovation.

Networking capacity

Hypothesis IT1: *The capacity of an organization to innovate increases to the extent that it has total networking capacity.*

My assumption here is that both the capacity to invent new ideas and the capacity to implement innovations may require at any given point in time connecting everyone to everyone else. I am not assuming that those connections have to be in operation at all times, only that it will favor innovation if the capacity is there. Especially important are channels between subcultures so that any new ideas that may arise in subcultures have a chance of being perceived by other subcultures and the parent culture.

The network does not have to be electronic. It can exist in the form of frequent meetings that include everybody, a heavy travel schedule that gets everyone to all parts of the organization, an efficient mail system, a good phone system, and the like. The more sophisticated technologies become more relevant as the constraints of time and space become more costly.

Routing and filtering capacity

Hypothesis IT2A: *The capacity of an organization to innovate increases to the extent that it can open and close channels as needed.*

Hypothesis IT2B: *The capacity of an organization to innovate increases to the extent that it can filter information into the channels as needed.*

My assumption here is that a fully connected network is not desirable at all times. For certain kinds of tasks and for certain stages of the innovation process, it may be more efficient to keep open only those channels that are necessary for efficient implementation. The organization must have the process capacity to diagnose its information needs, but it must also have the technical capacity to implement its diagnosis, in the sense of opening and closing channels as needed.

In arguing for this capacity I am not reverting to an authoritarian system, that is, some higher authority that opens or closes channels as needed. Rather, I am suggesting that such a capacity can be available in a collegial or participative system as well, in that members can choose to open and close channels themselves as they perceive this to be appropriate.

Just as the organization needs the technical capacity to open and close channels, so it needs the capacity to filter information flows into given channels (1) to avoid information overloads, (2) to prevent inappropriate information reaching some members, and (3) to ensure that appropriate information reaches those members who need it. Again, this implies diagnostic capacity along with the technical capacity of the system, and again, it implies that such filtering can be designed without reverting to an authoritarian hierarchical system. A good example of such a system is the Information Lens and Object Lens technology developed by Malone that allows the network's members to specify rules for routing and filtering that are then automatically implemented (Lai & Malone, 1988; Malone et al., 1989).

Connectivity to environment, "openness" of the system

Hypothesis IT3: *The capacity of an organization to innovate increases to the extent that it has several open channels to and from its environments.*

Organizations are open sociotechnical systems contained in several environments. If they cannot accurately track what is going on in those environments, they cannot identify those areas to which innovation is more or less important. Similarly, they cannot assess the effects of their own innovative and adaptive efforts if they cannot observe the effects of their innovative behavior on those parts of the environment that are intended to be affected.

Several channels to the environment are necessary, but they also must be connected to the appropriate decision points within the organization so that the incoming information can be processed correctly. Many organizations know a great deal, but this knowledge stays in departments that cannot effectively utilize, integrate, and act on it (Schein, 1980).

Capacity to evolve one's own IT system technologically

Hypothesis IT4: *The capacity of an organization to innovate increases to the extent that it can fully understand and implement innovations in information technology itself as these may apply to various aspects of the organization's tasks.*

What is implied here is the organization's ability to modify its own use of IT as new possibilities become available and as new ideas arise on how to use existing technology. This means that somewhere in the system there must be good information on current capacities and good information on future possibilities. Such information may come from internal or external sources, but it has to get to the right places to be acted on appropriately. Various aspects of IT such as office automation and CAD/CAM not only must be well understood but also must be flexibly adapted in order to support the organization's basic mission (Thomas, 1988).

INTERACTION OF CULTURE AND INFORMATION TECHNOLOGY

Implied in this analysis is that cultural assumptions can and will limit the degree to which IT can and will be used. The kind of information network just described is less likely to be installed in organizations that do not believe in proactivity, in mastering their environment, in participative decision making, and so on. But that is not the whole story. The technology itself can and will gradually affect organizational cultures by what it makes possible, and in some cultures the interaction between the culture and the technology can, in the long run, destroy adaptive capacity and innovation. In order to examine these interactions, we must first look at some of the properties of IT and show how they can become forces to unfreeze the present culture.

IT as a force unfreezing culture

If one thinks of the information technology community itself as being a subculture, one can identify some of its assumptions that, if implemented, lead to the unfreezing of other cultural assumptions. Specifically, the IT community assumes that it is intrinsically good for organizations to have more information, more widely distributed and more rapidly disseminated. The designers of IT are therefore likely to highlight the following properties of the technology:

1. Accessibility: More people can more easily access information that is electronically available in a network.
2. Rapidity: Information and feedback can be obtained much more rapidly by electronic means in computer-based networks.
3. Simultaneity: Information can be presented to large numbers of people simultaneously, even though they are geographically dispersed and are in different time zones.
4. Presentational flexibility: Information can simultaneously be presented in different ways to different people.
5. Complexity: Complex relationships and contextual factors in information can be more easily represented with computer aided systems (e.g., three-dimensional modeling).
6. System awareness: Creating information systems requires the accurate modeling of processes, and these models then become familiar to information users (the essence of what Zuboff meant by "informating").
7. System and network accountability: Networks enable all members to become aware of their mutual interdependence, that there is no necessary higher authority in the network, and hence that all members of the network are simultaneously accountable for the network's output.
8. Teamwork capacity: The combination of simultaneity and network accountability makes teamwork possible when every member realizes his or her part and when all contributions are clear, thus forcing mutual trust (i.e., any abuse by any member is immediately visible to all other members of the network).
9. Task-based authority: In a functioning network it is possible to designate decision-making power to whoever at any given moment in time has the most relevant information, and this authority can rotate among members of the network as the task changes.
10. Self-designing capacity: It is technologically and psychologically possible for the network to redesign itself continually and to adapt to changing circumstances if the necessary power and flexibility have been built in.

As we can see, these characteristics introduce a strong bias toward collaborative teamwork in that such work becomes not only much more feasible in an electronic environment but also more appropriate to the complex tasks that most organizations will face in the future.

What all of this means is that the introduction of IT is a force that may stimulate culture change by, first, forcing some cultural assumptions out into the open (i.e., assumptions about formal authority and managerial prerogatives) and, second, by clearly making alternative methods of coordination possible. Thus if either the leadership of an organization or some subculture within it introduces sophisticated IT networks, this will force cultural reexamination and reveal which cultural assumptions will aid or hinder further utilization of IT. The further implication of this argument is that the introduction of IT may be one of the most powerful ways of unfreezing a culture and starting a process of change toward more innovative capacity in general.

Presence of an IT subculture

Hypothesis I/C 1: *The capacity of an organization to innovate increases to the extent that it has somewhere inside itself a fully functioning, technologically sophisticated IT system that can be a demonstration of IT's capacity and a source of diffusion to other parts of the organization.*

In other words, there must be among the organization's subcultures at least one sub-subculture that is congruent with the assumptions of IT, or there will not be any place in the organization where IT can be appropriately utilized. However, such a subculture is only a necessary and not a sufficient condition for organizational innovation, because the larger culture may prevent diffusion of the innovation.

Destructive IT and culture interactions

Hypothesis I/C 2A: *Giving IT, for purposes of automation, to a management that operates under the assumptions of Theory X will in the short run improve productivity but in the long run will engender employee dependence and anxiety that will reduce the probability of innovation.*

Hypothesis I/C 2B: *Giving IT, for purposes of upward informating, to a management that operates under the assumptions of Theory X will allow such management a level of surveillance and control that will alienate employees, cause resistance, rebellion, refusal to use the system, falsification of data entry if possible, and, ultimately, total dependency and abdication of personal responsibility.*

Hypothesis I/C 2C: *Giving IT, for purposes of informating down, to a management that operates under the assumptions of Theory X will improve, in the short run, productivity and involvement but will, in the long run, be subverted by management's need to control and to assert what it regards as its prerogatives and rights.*

Hypothesis I/C 2D: *A Theory X management cannot transform an organization in terms of IT capabilities because the hierarchical control mentality will prevent the necessary employee involvement in system design and utilization.*

If one examines cases of IT implementation failure, there are some specific patterns that not only explain the failure but also point to certain interactions that, even if successful in the short run, can destroy the organization's longer-range capacity to innovate and adapt. These interactions are the cultural assumptions concerning participation and control and are shown in Table 6.2. The various IT visions are shown down the left side, and the two cultural extremes with respect to participation and control are shown along the top. These can most easily be characterized according to McGregor's Theory X and Theory Y, especially as they apply to the CEO or senior management as individuals.

The specific hypotheses in Table 6.2 have already been stated. The logic behind the first of these hypotheses derives from both earlier and current research on automation, especially the research by Hirschhorn (1987), which showed that workers in highly automated plants become anxious because of their high level of responsi-

Table 6.2. Positive and negative interactions between IT and culture

IT Vision	Theory X*	Theory Y*
Automate	Negative	Positive
Informate up	Very negative	Positive
Informate down	Very negative	Very positive
Transform	Not feasible	Very positive

*Theory X is used here as shorthand for hierarchical, authoritarian control orientation, based on cynicism about human nature. Theory Y is used here as shorthand for idealism about human nature and a belief in collegial or participative relationships that permit high degrees of self-control.

bility and the absence of supportive bosses. Because such workers often do not understand the complex technology, they become highly dependent on information that they do not understand. This combination of dependency and anxiety can lead to psychological denial and the inability to manage any crisis that may occur. That is, when the system sends alarm signals, the workers' anxiety level is so high that they assume that the information must be wrong and so ignore it.

The scenario underlying the second hypothesis has been played out in a number of organizations and may be the most dangerous because the subculture of IT plays directly into the assumptions of a control-oriented Theory X management. In the short run there is the illusion that the IT system has given management the perfect and ultimate control tool, especially if the system designers can also be categorized as Theory X. If one has control-oriented designers working with control-oriented managers, one is bound to get an organization that will look perfectly controlled but that will sooner or later fail for lack of employee commitment and involvement. And certainly there will be no motivation or capacity to innovate.

Evidence for the third hypothesis comes from Zuboff's study of the paper mill that dramatically increased its productivity as workers learned the logic behind the automated system they were using and discovered that they could run the plant perfectly well without lots of managerial control. But the managers were not willing to give up this control; they started to order the workers to do things that they already knew how to do, and to take credit for some of the improvements, leading workers to resent and consequently underutilize the system.

What is important to note is that the same system implemented with a Theory Y management would have entirely positive results, because the managers would be happy to have the workers exercise more control and take over the system. It is only the control need characteristic of the Theory X manager that produces the destructive negative results.

The fourth hypothesis is self-evident, in that the Theory X–dominated organization will not have transformational visions in the first place and so will not be able to elicit the innovative capacity to start a transformation process.

In summary, the capabilities of IT in combination with a hierarchically control-oriented management produce negative results in each of the IT visions, though those results may not show up initially. If the designers of the system are also operating from hierarchical control assumptions, they may do great harm to the organization in regard to its long-run ability to innovate and to adapt to changing environmental circumstances.

The implication is that the cultural assumptions concerning employee involvement, the importance of hierarchy as a principle of control, the prerogatives and rights of managers, and the nature of authority are the critical ones to examine in any IT project, because the potential of IT as a force for innovation will not be achieved if those assumptions are too close to Theory X.

SUMMARY AND CONCLUSIONS

We can summarize our hypotheses about IT by stating that an organization's capacity to innovate will increase to the extent that it has

1. The capacity to connect everyone.
2. The ability to open and close channels as needed.
3. The ability to filter information into the channels.
4. Several channels into and from the relevant environments and into the relevant decision centers.
5. The capacity to use the most advanced IT systems.
6. At least one fully functioning advanced IT system somewhere in the organization.
7. A Theory Y management that will use the IT applications appropriately and sensitively.

We noted that culture can constrain the ability to implement IT solutions, but at the same time, IT can be a powerful force to identify and unfreeze cultural assumptions if it can be introduced anywhere in the organization.

If the IT capacity is present and if the cultural assumptions favor innovation, the organization will develop processes and structures that will increase the likelihood of members' inventing and implementing those new ideas that will make the organization more adaptive in a rapidly changing environment.

The crucial point of this analysis is that if such technological and cultural conditions are not present, it is pointless to work on organizational processes and structures directly. People will simply resist the kinds of changes that may be necessary. Only if we can create the appropriate synergy between culture and IT capability can we achieve the long-range benefits that we are seeking.

The interweaving of cultural and technological factors is the essence of the sociotechnical model of organization design. I hope that these hypotheses will stimulate thinking about how to increase the probability of innovation and will serve as a kind of diagnostic grid to assess in any given group the degree of "innovativeness." Above all, I hope that by focusing on culture, I have made it clear why resistance to change and the desire of organizations not to innovate are entirely normal and understandable phenomena.

ACKNOWLEDGMENT

The ideas expressed in this chapter are the result of extended conversations with Tom Malone, Diane Wilson, and various other colleagues. Our goal was to identify the main characteristics of innovative, adaptive, and creative systems and cultures. Special thanks also to Lotte Bailyn, Marc Gerstein, Randy Davis, Bob McKersie,

Michael Scott Morton, and John Van Maanen for their insightful comments on an early draft of this chapter, and to the Management in the 1990s project for the financial support that made possible the research on which this chapter is based.

REFERENCES

Argyris, C. (1964). *Integrating the individual and the organization.* New York: Wiley.

Argyris, C., & D. A. Schon (1978). *Organizational learning.* Englewood Cliffs, NJ: Prentice-Hall.

Drucker, P. F. (1988). The coming of the new organization. *Harvard Business Review,* January-February, pp. 45–53.

England, G. (1975). *The manager and his values.* Cambridge, MA: Ballinger.

Hirschhorn, L. (1987). *The workplace within.* Cambridge, MA: MIT Press.

Jaques, E. (1976). *A general theory of bureaucracy.* London: Heinemann.

——— (1982). *The forms of time.* London: Heinemann.

Lai, K. Y., & T. W. Malone (1988). Object lens: A spreadsheet for cooperative work. Proceedings of the ACM Second Conference on Computer-supported Cooperative Work. Portland, OR, September.

Lawrence, P. R., & J. W. Lorsch (1967). *Organization and environment.* Boston: Harvard Graduate School of Business Administration.

Malone, T. W. (1987). Modeling coordination in organizations and markets. *Management Science* 33:1317–32.

Malone, T. W., K. R. Grant, K. Y. Lai, R. Rao, & D. A. Rosenblitt (1989). The information lens: An intelligent system for information sharing and coordination. In M. H. Olsen (Ed.), *Technological support for work group collaboration.*, pp. 65–88. Hillsdale, NJ: Erlebaum.

Malone, T. W., J. Yates, & R. I. Benjamin (1987). Electronic markets and electronic hierarchies. *Communications of ACM* 30:484–97.

Martin, J., & C. Siehl (1983). Organizational culture and counter-culture: An uneasy symbiosis. *Organizational Dynamics,* Autumn, pp. 52–64.

McGregor, D. (1960). *The human side of enterprise.* New York: McGraw-Hill.

——— (1967). *The professional manager.* New York: McGraw-Hill.

Roethlisberger, F. J., & W. J. Dickson (1939). *Management and the worker.* Cambridge, MA: Harvard University Press.

Schein, E. H. (1970). The role innovator and his education. *Technology Review* 72:33–37.

——— (1980). *Organizational psychology,* 3rd ed. Englewood Cliffs, NJ: Prentice-Hall.

——— (1985). *Organizational culture and leadership.* San Francisco: Jossey-Bass.

——— (1987). *Process consultation,* Vol. 2. Reading, MA: Addison-Wesley.

——— (1988). *Process consultation,* Vol. l, rev. ed. Reading, MA: Addison-Wesley.

——— (1989). An inquiry into the divine right of managers. *Sloan Management Review.*

Thomas, R. J. (1988). The politics of technological change: An empirical study. Sloan School of Management working paper no. 2035–88, July.

Van Maanen, J., & S. R. Barley (1984). Occupational communities: Culture and control in organizations. In B. M. Staw & L. L. Cummings (Eds.), *Research in organizational behavior,* vol. 6, pp. 287–365. Greenwich, CT: JAI Press.

Van Maanen, J., & E. H. Schein (1979). Toward a theory of organizational socialization. In B. M. Staw & L. L. Cummings (Eds.), *Research in organizational behavior,* vol. l, pp. 209–69. Greenwich, CT: JAI Press.

Weick, K. E. (1977). Organization design: Organizations as self-designing systems. *Organizational Dynamics,* Autumn, pp. 31–46.

Zuboff, S. (1988). *In the age of the smart machine.* New York: Basic Books.

PART II

STRATEGIC OPTIONS

A technology that affects organizations as deeply and profoundly as information technology does and that requires rethinking the nature of fundamental organizational processes, as well as establishing standards for an entire industry, necessarily also creates an opportunity to explore many strategic options.

Besen and Saloner begin Part II with a consideration of how the development and enforcement of standards affect, and in some instances can be used as a tool for, strategy. They show how standards can be used to advance or impede technological development and to enhance or constrain competition or to increase economic benefit from a technology. That standards can be used as a competitive weapon is certainly not news. But by looking at this concept systematically, as Besen and Saloner do, firms can understand better how to use standards developed outside the control of the affected firm.

The effect that technology has on strategy is communicated in the results reported by Venkatraman and Zaheer in Chapter 8. They found that the strategic use of information technology not only can lead to restructuring within the firm but also can allow shifts in interorganizational relationships that offer a strategic advantage. Using a quasi-experimental approach, Venkatraman and Zaheer show that the electronic integration of a supplier (in this case an insurance firm) with its sales agents has a selective effect on performance. They then measured the performance of the relationship between supplier and agent in different ways and discovered a statistically significant improvement in only one of the measures. This is not to say that the effect is not important. Rather, we should not always expect extensive, across-the-board effects from the introduction of technology. The effect may be greater in some ways than others, and so we should be careful to look at all possibilities. Measuring only a few possible outcomes can lead to false negative conclusions about impact (cf. Chapter 4). Venkatraman and Zaheer make an additional point: Those firms that expend more effort on training the users receive a greater benefit from the technology.

In regard to redesigning fundamental organizational processes, it is clear that to gain real benefits, a firm cannot simply superimpose the new technology on existing practices. Instead, it must examine what it is trying to accomplish and why it uses its established practices for this purpose. It must then decide where the organization wants to go and what the technology can create and enable in order to get there. In nearly all of the successful implementations reported in this volume, fundamental changes had to be made in the organization's operations in order to gain the full benefits of the technology.

The mutual interdependence of the organizational processes and the technology are the central issues in Chapter 9 by Henderson and Venkatraman. They emphasize four domains of strategic choice: business strategy, information technology strategy, organizational infrastructure and processes, and information technology infrastructure and processes. They then argue for the need for functional integration across the areas of business strategy and information technology strategy but connecting as well to what they call the "internal level" of infrastructure and processes, relating to both the organization and information technology.

Both Chapters 9 and 10 show how a strategy can be achieved by means of a creative relationship between the information systems designers and the managers, who will gain from effective implementation. In Chapter 10, Henderson and Cooprider examine the use of automated tools, in this case computer-aided software systems engineering (CASE), in information systems development. They develop a three-component (production, coordination, and organization) model of design aid technology that provides some badly needed structure for this little understood area.

Taking this to the level of structuring organizational relationships in Chapter 11, Crowston and Malone first offer an interesting review of the different approaches to considering the relations between organizational structure and information technology. Then they classify these into four different perspectives and use this analysis to point the way toward future research. In all of these cases, we are again seeing fundamental changes introduced in the nature of work, in order to benefit from the technology.

The required alignments often go beyond the bounds of a single firm. Thus Chapter 12, by Koh and Venkatraman, becomes important. The authors demonstrate the value of joint venture formation as reflected in stock market valuation. This is of particular interest to firms in the information technology sector, because of the proliferation there of joint ventures and other cooperative arrangements among firms. The data that Koh and Venkatraman use were taken from firms heavily involved in information technology.

Walker and Poppo return in Chapter 13 to the markets-versus-hierarchies discussion, initiated by Malone, Yates, and Benjamin in Part I, with an empirical study of transaction costs. They compare internal and external manufacturer–supplier relationships in a major manufacturing firm, which is an interesting way of partially testing the markets-versus-hierarchies hypothesis. The reader can assess where we stand after considering both sets of arguments.

CHAPTER 7

Compatibility Standards and the Market for Telecommunications Services

STANLEY M. BESEN AND GARTH SALONER

Not so long ago, technical standards in the United States telephone industry were determined primarily by the American Telephone and Telegraph Company. To be sure, AT&T had to coordinate with foreign telecommunications entities, independent telephone companies, and the United States Department of Defense, but the degree of coordination was relatively minor, and AT&T had substantial latitude in deciding on the standards that would be used. However, three forces have caused this situation to change dramatically.

First, because of the entry of large numbers of competing suppliers of equipment and services into the United States telecommunications industry, standard setting has moved from the technical concern of a single firm to a factor with important implications for competition. As a result, the processes by which standards are set are now subject to detailed scrutiny by both the regulatory authorities and the courts. In a sense, telecommunications standards have become too important to leave their determination solely to the telephone companies.

Second, the divestiture of the Bell Operating Companies from AT&T has, by fragmenting the telephone industry, reduced AT&T's ability to determine standards as it had in the past. Horwitt noted that "the market has changed [drastically] since predivestiture days, when Ma Bell set telecommunications standards and other carriers and equipment vendors had no choice but to follow. Now, AT&T is just one more vendor—albeit a formidable one—lobbying for industrywide adoption of the technologies and protocols it wants to use" (1986, p. 27). To an increasing degree, AT&T must accept the choices made by others rather than dictate the standards to which others must conform.

Third, the growing internationalization of telecommunications technology and services has resulted in a larger role for international standard-setting bodies. As a result, the autonomy that the United States previously possessed to set standards has been reduced, and the needed degree of coordination with suppliers in other countries has increased. According to Pool,

> Until now in the telecommunications field there have generally been two sets of standards, the CCITT standards of the International Telecommunica-

> tions Union followed in most of the world and the Bell System standards which prevailed in America (about half the world market). In the future CCITT standards will become more influential in this country, and AT&T will have an incentive to reduce its deviations from them. (1984, p. 119)

The major effort currently under way at the International Consultative Committee for Telephone and Telegraph (CCITT) to establish standards for Integrated Services Digital Networks (ISDN), in which the United States is only one of many players, is an important indication of this change.

THE DETERMINANTS OF THE STANDARD-SETTING PROCESS

There is no standard way in which standards are established. In some cases, standards are mandated by government agencies using administrative processes. In others, voluntary standards are decided on cooperatively, with information being exchanged, technologies being altered, and/or side payments being made to achieve a consensus. Finally, standard setting may be left to "the market," in which they emerge by dint of strength and influence.

Two factors that affect the nature and outcome of the standard setting process are especially important. The first concerns the private incentives that each of the interested parties—developers, manufacturers, buyers—have to promote the universal adoption of any standard. Such incentives may be weak because even when all parties may gain from the existence of a standard, the private costs of participating in its adoption may be higher than its benefits. This is likely to be the case for establishing systems of weights and measures and standards relating to the use of common terminologies.

The incentive to promote standards may also be weak when standardization eliminates a competitive advantage and thus devalues the benefits of having a standard. For example, Brock (1975) reported that IBM was unwilling to accept the COBOL-60 specifications for its business language because it wished to prevent the competition to which it would be exposed if there were a common business language. Horwitt (1987b) also found that American computer vendors such as IBM and telecommunications carriers such as Telenet were reluctant to adopt the CCITT X.400 electronic mail standard. Although adopting the standard would permit communication between subscribers to different electronic mail systems, it would also enable subscribers to move easily from one vendor to another.[1]

At the opposite extreme are cases in which the expected gains to all parties from promoting the universal adoption of a standard exceed the costs they incur from doing so. For example, Hemenway (1975, pp. 13 ff.) discussed how the early, highly fragmented automobile industry was plagued by incompatibility problems. All manufacturers stood to gain greatly if standards were established, but a high degree of participation was required if standardization was to be achieved. As a result, many paid the the costs of participation.[2] But with the later consolidation of the industry, the benefits of standardization have become less important.

The second factor affecting the way that standards are set is the extent to which the interested parties differ over which standard should be chosen. Varying preferences are especially unlikely when there are no significant differences among technologies, so that what is important is only that a standard be chosen, not what the standard is. Timekeeping and the use of calendars are examples in which no one cares which system is chosen so long as there is some generally accepted method.[3] Moreover, even when there are variations among technologies, so that the parties have different feelings about them, the same technology may still be everyone's preferred standard.

On the other hand, agents frequently prefer different standards. For example, manufacturers of VHS and Beta videocassette recorders would have different preferences as to which technology was adopted if standardization were attempted. Similarly, computer manufacturers who have designed their machines to work with specific operating systems would prefer different systems as the industry standard. Still another example is that some users of videotext prefer the North American Presentation Level Protocol Syntax (NAPLPS), with its sophisticated graphics capability, whereas others are content with the less expensive text-only ASCII standard (Besen & Johnson, 1986, pp. 80–84).[4]

When preferences differ, each party promotes as the standard the technology that maximizes its private benefits, not the one that maximizes the total social benefits.[5] In these cases, standard setting can no longer be viewed solely as a search for the technically best standard, or even as a process for establishing as the standard one of a number of "equivalent" technologies. Instead, standard setting is a form of competition in which firms seek to gain advantages over their rivals.

We can now identify four cases that differ in whether the interest in promoting any universal standard is large or small and in whether preferences are similar or diverse. The case in which there is a large interest in promoting a universal standard and the preferences are similar is what can be called the Pure Coordination Case. Here, either there are a number of possible standards to which everyone is indifferent, or the same technology is preferred by all, and the per-capita rewards to participation in standard setting are large enough to induce everyone to participate. The standardization process is simply a matter of agreeing on which alternative to use. Once it is reached, the agreement is self-enforcing, as no party has an incentive to deviate unilaterally. In the language of game theory, there are either multiple equilibria with identical payoffs or a unique equilibrium that is Pareto superior; that is, everyone prefers it to any other. The standardization process serves to select an, or the, equilibrium.

Much standardization is very close to the Pure Coordination Case. Although there may be some differences in preferences, these differences are small relative to the gains from achieving standardization. Here, standard setting is likely to be seen as an activity in which experts seek the best technical solution or, at least, choose a standard from a number that are equally good. In short, standard setting is a game in which everyone obtains a positive payoff, and moreover, it is one in which the choice that maximizes the payoff to any party maximizes the payoffs to all others. This view dominates descriptions of the standard-setting process that are produced by standard-setting organizations.

Even when preferences do not differ, standardization may not be achieved through private voluntary agreement. The reason is that the gains to any party may be so small relative to the cost of participating in the standard setting that "free rid-ing" by everyone results in no standard at all. In what might be called the Pure Public Goods Case, the per-capita gain from standardization is too small for anyone to find it worthwhile to participate in the process. Although everyone wants standardization, and the differences in preferences are small, no agent has a sufficiently large interest to establish a standard. This outcome is especially likely in industries that are highly fragmented or when the beneficiary of standardization is the public at large. Here, if standardization is achieved, it is likely to require government intervention, as in the establishment of standards for weights and measures, time, and language. Alternatively, several incompatible technologies may exist simultaneously.[6]

A third case involves large differences in preferences and little incentive to adopt a universal standard.[7] In the so-called Pure Private Goods Case, if there is no dominant firm, standardization cannot be expected to be achieved voluntarily. Here, private parties would not promote the creation of a formal standard-setting body, and if such a body were established, the objectives of participation would be to promote a favored candidate as the standard or to prevent the adoption of another. Unless side payments are possible, the most likely result is stalemate, with no party being willing to adopt the technology preferred by the others. Participants in standards meetings may attempt to stall the proceedings by, for example, continually introducing new proposals and not allowing the other participants enough time to examine them. The outcome will be the simultaneous use of incompatible technologies, the selection of a de facto standard through the market, or the failure of the technology to develop because of the absence of a standard.

Although in principle, government intervention can break a stalemate, such intervention may itself be the object of controversy, so that the government may be reluctant to intervene. The stalemate may also be broken if there is a dominant firm. However, if the dominant firm is opposed to universal standardization, it will be a Reluctant Leader and may attempt to prevent its rivals from producing compatible products.[8] For example, a firm with a large market share may be reluctant to promote its technology as an industry standard if it fears that the demand for the products of its rivals will increase at its expense if they can offer compatible products. For example, Ryan reported that Ashton-Tate attempted to prevent the adoption of its Dbase language as an industry standard. The firm's chairman was quoted as stating, "The Dbase standard belongs to Ashton-Tate and Ashton-Tate intends to vigorously protect it. It's proprietary technology" (Ryan, 1987, p. 133). The argument is that Ashton-Tate's large market share makes it less concerned than are its rivals about the benefits of compatibility.

Another possible example of reluctant leadership occurs when a firm is dominant because it controls access to an input that its rivals need to market either complete systems or individual components. Under certain circumstances, such a firm may prefer that its rivals be unable to offer components that are compatible with its "essential" input. The argument that IBM, for instance, attempted to make it difficult for competing manufacturers of peripheral equipment to offer products that were compatible with IBM's mainframes was an important element of the government's case in the 1969 Sherman Act antitrust suit against the company. A similar argument was made in the government's 1974 suit that led to the divestiture of the Bell Operating Companies from AT&T, when the essential input was access to the local distribution facilities of the operating companies.

In the fourth case, there are large differences in preferences, and each of the interested parties has a large interest in promoting the universal adoption of a standard. In this Conflict Case, a dominant firm may, if it desires, attempt to establish a de facto standard. Here, the dominant firm is a Cheerful Leader, and other firms may be forced to adopt the technology that it prefers. This is apparently what occurred in the emergence of the IBM personal computer as an industry standard.

In the absence of a dominant firm, the interested parties all participate eagerly in the standardization process. The process can be expected to involve side payments and coalition formation. For example, Horwitt found that a number of computer software and hardware vendors recently agreed

> to surrender market dominance based on proprietary products in favor of a standardized, public-domain Unix environment. One major thrust behind the standards is the vendors' realization that a fragmented Unix cannot effectively compete in the midrange system against emerging proprietary products from the likes of Digital Equipment Corp. and IBM. The vendors were reported as willing to cooperate with their competitors—or even to adopt a competing product—in order to hasten commercial availability of the multivendor programming and networking products that their customers demand. (1987a, p. 6)

Similarly, all major European equipment manufacturers, together with Digital Equipment and Sperry, have formed the X/Open Group to promote a standardized version of the Unix operating system. Their objective is to permit the portability of applications software among computers made by different manufacturers in order to "preempt any attempt by IBM to establish de facto minicomputer standards, as it has for mainframes and personal computers" (Gallagher, 1986, p. 121).

Firms can also be expected to promote their own products in the market during the standardization process in order to make more credible a threat to "go it alone." They may also ask the government to increase their leverage either in the market or in cooperative standard setting.[9] However, there will be considerable pressure for a standard to be adopted.

This four-way classification of the standards process is summarized in Figure 7.1.[10] As we have noted, when standard-setting bodies describe their activities, they typically characterize them as involving Pure Coordination. In these descriptions, the participants are willing to expend considerable resources to achieve compatibility, and any conflicts regarding what the standard should be reflect differences in technical judgments. Although standardization may not come easily in these cases, standard setting bodies will generally be able to achieve the needed degree of coordination. At the same time, the conventional description of standard setting fails to encompass a large and important number of cases in which differences about what the industry standard should be are not primarily technical—the Conflict Case—or when some of the parties actually prefer incompatibility—the Private Goods Case. Much of the remainder of this chapter examines situations in which the interests of the parties are not necessarily congruent because they raise the most interesting and difficult standardization issues from the point of view of public policy. However, we do not mean to suggest that the Pure Coordination Case is unimportant, and indeed, we offer a detailed analysis of the possible role for cooperative standard setting in this case.

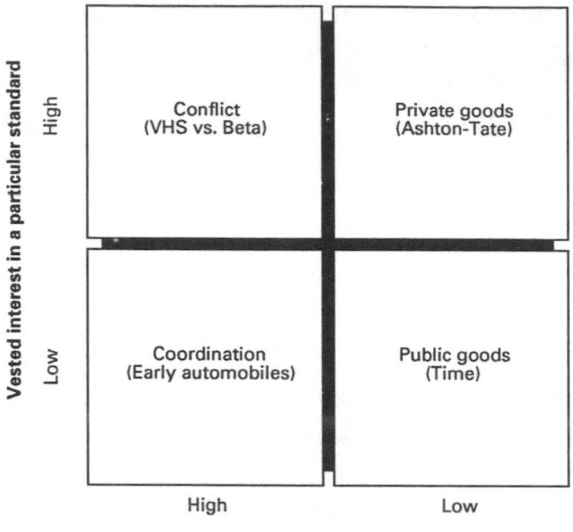

Figure 7.1. The determinants of the nature of the standards process (examples in parentheses).

Whether consensus will be achieved in private, cooperative standard setting depends on a number of factors, including (1) the importance of the benefits of standardization, (2) whether a small number of participants can prevent an effective standard from emerging,[11] (3) the extent to which the interests of the participants diverge, and (4) whether side payments are possible.

The prospect of achieving consensus becomes more likely as the benefits multiply from the network externalities that standardization produces. At one extreme, if consumers are reluctant to buy a good from a vendor because they fear that they may be "stranded" with the wrong technology, all vendors should be interested in agreeing on a standard. In such cases, firms may be willing to agree to conform to a standard that is not the one they prefer if the alternative is to have no sales at all. On the other hand, the more able a firm is to have sales even when there are no compatible products, the more reluctant it will be to conform to a standard other than the one it prefers.

If the success of a standard depends on obtaining agreement from all participants, standardization is less likely than when a smaller majority is required. When unanimity is required, any participant can hold out, refusing to support a standard unless he or she obtains a large share of the resulting benefits. This can be either an insistence that a preferred technology be chosen as the standard or a demand for payment in some other form. Because all participants can behave in this manner, consensus is unlikely. This may explain why standard-setting bodies typically require a less-than-unanimous consent for a standard to be adopted.[12]

Clearly, the more divergent the participants' interests are, the less likely it is that a consensus will emerge. When preferences are similar, the process of standardization is only learning that this is the case.[13] Once everyone knows that everyone else prefers the same technology, each can adopt the technology in complete confidence that his or her behavior will be emulated. Here, information sharing can promote the adoption of a standard that otherwise would not be used. By contrast, when preferences diverge, not only will such confidence be lacking, but each participant also will tend to exaggerate the differences in order to have his or her technology chosen. Thus, each participant may state that he or she will not follow the lead of another even if, in fact, he or she would. The result is to reduce the likelihood that anyone will attempt to start a "bandwagon."

Finally, the ability to make side payments may overcome what otherwise would be resistance to agreement on a standard. Especially when the difficulty in reaching agreement results from large divergences in preferences, if those who will gain most from the standard that is adopted share those gains with others, the reluctance to conform may be overcome. The sharing of gains need not involve cash transfers but can, for example, require that the "winners" license their technologies on favorable terms to the "losers."[14]

COOPERATIVE STANDARD SETTING IN PRACTICE

The analysis in the previous section suggests that there are a wide variety of circumstances in which cooperative standard setting is viable and productive. In fact, an important response to the need for coordinating product design is the evolution of a strikingly large and complex standard-setting community charged with the responsibility and authority to negotiate and adopt standards for their industries. In addition, liaisons and affiliations among standard-setting bodies have been formed across industries and national boundaries as the need has arisen. The result is a standards community comprising hundreds of committees and involving over a hundred thousand individuals. It is remarkable that for the most part, this community has formed at the initiative of industry participants and without governmental intervention or direction. Indeed, governmental agencies often take their guidance from the industry bodies and formally adopt as mandatory standards the voluntary standards that these bodies produce.

Voluntary standard setting

At some stage, usually fairly early in the development of a new product, manufacturers and purchasers often realize that they can achieve economies by adopting voluntary standards for some of the product's components or features. Using a subcommittee of an existing trade association or standard-setting organization, comments are obtained from all interested parties through a lengthy and formal procedure.[15]

Acceptable standards emerge under "the consensus principle," which generally refers to "the largest possible agreement . . . among all interests concerned with the use of standards" (Verman, 1973, p. 12).[16] A central clearinghouse is used to keep track of, and disseminate information about, standards. In the United States, this function is provided by the American National Standards Institute (ANSI), a private organization with more than 220 trade associations and professional and technical societies, and more than 1000 corporations as members (National Bureau of Standards, 1984).[17] ANSI approves a standard when it finds that its criteria for due process have been met and that there is a consensus among the interested parties. Some 8500 American National Standards have been approved in this manner (NBS, 1984, p. 71).

In the United States, the decisions of standard-setting bodies, and their operating procedures, have been subject to antitrust scrutiny. At least three organizations have been held to have violated the antitrust laws when they refused to certify that a new technology conformed to an industry standard.[18] As a result, the principle has been established that antitrust liability may be incurred by private voluntary standard-setting organizations if their actions are anticompetitive,[19] and these organizations must now expect their activities to be subject to challenge. Indeed, in one situation of which we are aware, a trade association actually refused to adopt an industry standard because it feared that it could avoid antitrust liability only by adopting costly procedures to ensure that its actions would be perceived as "fair."[20]

The need for standards transcends national boundaries. The same forces that formed national standards bodies also created organizations for international standardization. In 1946, delegates from 64 countries established the International Standards Organization (ISO).[21] In 1947, the International Electrotechnical Commission (IEC), formed some 43 years earlier, became affiliated with the ISO as its electrical division, thereby considerably expanding its scope. There are two striking features of the ISO: its extent and the rate of growth of its output. Of the roughly 7500 international standards that had been written by early 1985, some 5000 had been developed, promulgated, or coordinated by the ISO (Lohse, 1985). This contrasts with the mere 37 ISO recommendations that had been approved by the ISO's tenth anniversary in 1957 and the 2000 standards that had been written by 1972 (Sanders, 1972, p. 68).

As is the case with ANSI, the ISO is a nongovernmental, voluntary institution. It has 72 "full members" and 17 "correspondent members." The full members are national standards associations, such as ANSI, which have voting rights on the technical committees of the ISO as well as the Council and General Assembly.[22] The correspondent members are governmental institutions from countries that do not have national standards bodies. The standards are established by the 164 technical committees and their subcommittees and working groups, of which there are about 2000 (Lohse, 1985). It is estimated that the number of individual participants has grown from some 50,000 in 1972 (Sanders, 1972, p. 68) to over 100,000 today (Lohse, 1985, p. 20). Some 400 international organizations, including the CCITT, which we will discuss later, have a formal liaison with the ISO.

The same process for achieving consensus that characterizes national standard setting is present in the international arena.[23] Although the consensus principle is held as an ideal for the standards process at the international level as well (Sanders, 1972, p. 12), a draft international standard (DIS) must be formally approved by 75 percent of the full members who have elected to participate in the relevant technical committee. "Two or more negative votes receive special consideration" (Lohse, 1985, p. 22). Once a DIS has been approved by a technical committee, it must be adopted by the Council of the ISO as an international standard.

It is significant that the number of ANSI standards exceeds the number of international standards. Because international standardization is a fairly new phenomenon, it is often achieved at the national level before it is taken up internationally. Indeed, in its early years, the ISO was mainly concerned with coordinating existing national standards.

Standard setting in the telecommunications and computer industries

Telephone services have traditionally been provided by government-run (or in the United States, government-regulated) monopolies. In Europe these are the PTTs (Post, Telephone, and Telegraph Administrations), and in the United States, this position used to be held by AT&T. As long as these organizations had complete control over the design and use of the network, standardization within countries involved only a single firm. However, international standardization, requiring coordination among many firms, required consultation and agreement among national governments. It is not surprising, therefore, that there is a treaty-based organization to deal with standardization issues.

The International Telegraphic Union was formed by an agreement of 20 countries in 1865. In 1932, it merged with the organization created by the International Radiotelegraph Convention and was renamed the International Telecommunication Union (ITU).[24] The main goal of the ITU, which currently has 162 members, is to promote cooperation and development in telecommunications. The branches of the ITU most concerned with issues of standardization are the International Telegraph and Telephone Consultative Committee (CCITT) and the International Radio Consultative Committee (CCIR). The latter is concerned with matters specifically related to radio propagation and facilities, and the former deals with all other telecommunications issues.

The results of CCITT and CCIR deliberations are usually adopted as recommendations. Although these are not legally binding, countries find it in their interests to adhere to them in order to facilitate the interworking of national systems. Although rarely done, the ITU can adopt CCIR and CCITT recommendations as treaty agreements (known as regulations). Even though these have been restricted mainly to issues relating to radio, the 1988 World Administrative Telegraph and Telephone Conference considered regulations affecting "all existing and foreseen new telecommunications services."[25]

Because the CCITT is a part of a a treaty organization, the United States is represented there by a delegation from the Department of State. Two public advisory committees, the United States Organization for the International Telegraph and Telecommunications Consultative Committee (USCCITT) and the United States Organization for the International Radio Consultative Committee (USCCIR), advise the State Department on matters of policy and positions in preparation for meetings of the CCITT (Cerni, 1985).[26] The State Department is also able to offer accreditation to organizations and companies that allows them to participate directly in CCITT and CCIP activities. Historically, U.S. representation has been made in this way through companies providing telegraph and telecommunications services (Rutkowski, 1985, p. 25).

Several domestic voluntary standards organizations also take part in the telecommunications standardization process. One of the most important of these is Committee Tl, sponsored by the Exchange Carriers Standards Association (ECSA), which was organized after the divestiture of the Bell Operating Companies from AT&T to deal with standardization issues previously handled internally by AT&T.[27] This committee, whose members include exchange carriers, interexchange carriers, and manufacturers, develops interface standards for U.S. networks. Although the private sector plays a large role in the development of U.S. telecommunications standards, it does so subject to the substantial authority of the Federal Communications Commission (FCC) to regulate domestic and international communications under the Communications Act of 1934.[28]

Standardization decisions lie at the core of the establishment of telecommunications networks,[29] but the same is not true of computer hardware technology. Especially in the days when the mainframe reigned supreme, the major uses of computers were as stand-alone processors. Standardization issues revolved mainly around the ability of manufacturers of peripheral equipment to connect their products to the central processing units (CPUs) of other manufacturers. Because there were only a few mainframe manufacturers, and they provided integrated systems and thus were not dependent on the equipment of peripheral manufacturers, they had little incentive to ensure that the interfaces were standardized.[30]

Several factors have combined to increase the desirability of intercomputer communication. These include the desire to make corporate and external data available to a wide range of company employees, the need to share information generated in a decentralized way resulting from the emergence and rapid acceptance of the microcomputer, the increased use of computer technology in the service economy (e.g., banking, airline, and theater reservations), and the desire to access these and other potential services (e.g., education, library access, grocery ordering, and mail) from the home.

The first successes in standardizing data communications were not achieved until the mid-1970s. One of the most important early standards was CCITT Recommendation X. 25, which established interface specifications between data terminal equipment and public data networks.[31] These early standards were necessary for meeting immediate requirements—they were not components of a grand design that would ensure the compatibility of different protocols and system architectures (Folts, 1982).

The initiative for developing an overarching framework for information transfer between any two end systems was taken by the ISO. The ISO initiative is generally perceived as a bold and farsighted attempt to avoid the haphazard evolution of incompatible protocols. In contrast with many standards proceedings, this initiative anticipated future needs rather than merely reacting to them.

The result of this initiative was the Open Systems Interconnection (OSI) reference model, which provides a framework for structuring communication between separate end users. The term *open* conveys the ability of any end user to connect with any other. The forum in which such communication takes place is called the *OSI environment*. An *end user* is best thought of as a particular applications process (Folts, 1982). Thus, for example, an end user could be a person operating a manual keyboard terminal, or a production-line control program.

The communication between application processes requires that a number of functions be performed. The OSI Reference Model structures these functions into seven layers.[32] Broadly speaking, the upper three layers support the particular application being used. They provide the services that allow the application process to access the open system and to interpret the information being transferred to the application process. The lower three layers are concerned with transmitting the data from one applications process to another. The middle layer (the "transport" layer) links the application process support layers to the information transmission layers.

Contemporaneous with the blossoming of opportunities from intercomputer communication has been a major change in the technology of telecommunications networks. Voice communication requires both a transmission and a switching technology. The transmission technology carries the voice signal through the network, and the switching technology is responsible for its routing. The traditional analog technology amplifies the voice signal in such a way that it can be transmitted. Each time the signal is switched, the signal must be interpreted and then transformed again, and this process results in the accumulation of "noise."

The alternative digital technology immediately creates a digital representation of the voice signal. This digitized signal can then be switched repeatedly without decoding and redigitizing. Because the signals are in digital form, the switching is performed by computer. As the cost of computer technology has fallen, so has the cost of the digital technology. Accordingly, telecommunications networks are rapidly being transformed from analog to digital transmission and switching. Eventually, the entire telecommunications network will be digital, thereby forming an integrated digital network (IDN).

Once the telecommunications network transmits digital information, this network itself can be used for the kind of intercomputer communication just discussed. This vision of a single network that will be used for voice, data, facsimile, and video transmission is referred to as the integrated services digital network (ISDN). Because of the obvious connection between the work of the ISO on OSI and the interests of the CCITT in telecommunications, these two bodies are working together closely in developing standards for ISDN.[33]

NONCOOPERATIVE STANDARD SETTING

An alternative to setting voluntary standards through committees is for standards to evolve through the adoption decisions of market participants. In order to evaluate the utility of the committee system, or the desirability of imposing mandatory standards, it is necessary to understand how well "the market" would do in setting such de facto standards.

There are several dimensions along which the market's performance should be evaluated. These include whether the market selects the appropriate standard; whether inferior standards are abandoned when new, superior technologies become available; whether the appropriate trade-off between variety and standardization is made; and whether converter technologies are appropriately developed. These important economic issues were virtually ignored by economists until quite recently, but now a burgeoning theoretical literature is attempting to correct this failing.

The distinctive feature of the models discussed here is that the standardization create a demand-side economy of scale. In particular, when compatibility offers benefits, the users of a particular technology will obtain them when others adopt the same technology. Thus one individual's adoption decision confers a positive externality on other adopters. Because individual decision makers ignore these externalities in making their decisions, one cannot generally expect the outcomes to be efficient. Indeed, as we shall see, various kinds of inefficiencies can arise.[34]

Inertia and momentum in adopting a new standard

The benefits from standardization may make the users of a standardized technology reluctant to switch to a new, and perhaps better, technology, out of fear that others, bound together by the benefits of compatibility, will not abandon the old standard. If this is the case, it may be difficult for a new standard to be adopted. As a result, de facto standardization may retard innovation.

The first theoretical model of this phenomenon was created by Rohlfs (1974), who examined what would happen when a given number of agents simultaneously considered adopting a new technology.[35] Suppose that all potential adopters would adopt if each knew that the others would do so as well. However, no one would adopt if he thought that he would be alone. Rohlfs pointed out that there are generally multiple equilibria in this situation. One is for everyone to adopt the new technology, and another is for no one to adopt it. Similarly, if some subsets of users are in favor of adoption but others are not, still other equilibria are possible.

Consider four potential adopters. Suppose that 1 and 2 will adopt if the other does but that 3 and 4 will adopt only if the other does and 1 and 2 also adopt. Even if all four agents are better off adopting, it is conceivable that inertia will lead to an equilibrium in which only 1 and 2 adopt, if that outcome is somehow "focal."[36]

A second problem is that it may not be an equilibrium for all four to adopt, and yet that may be the most socially desirable outcome. This occurs, for example, when 3 and 4 are moderately reluctant to adopt the technology but their adoption would make 1 and 2 much better off. Because 3 and 4 ignore the benefits that they confer on 1 and 2 in making their adoption decision, there may be too little adoption.[37] Indeed, 1 and 2 may not adopt the new technology if they are unsure that 3 and 4 will do so.[38]

Farrell and Saloner (1985) demonstrated that some of these inertia problems could disappear if we allowed for sequential rather than simultaneous decision making and complete information. In that setting, they showed that when all agents prefer joint adoption of the new technology to the status quo, adoption is the unique equilibrium.[39] Moreover, if not all the agents prefer joint adoption of the new technology, the only equilibrium will be the largest set of possible adopters. Of those that do not adopt, there is no subset that desires to switch. This result suggests that the intuition about the possible innovation-retarding effects of standardization does not extend to a model in which the timing of the adoption decision is endogenous and the information is complete.

Although this model provides a useful benchmark, it suffers from a lack of realism along a number of dimensions. First, the assumption that all potential adopters are perfectly informed about one anothers' preferences is risky. Second, the model has a timeless quality. There are no transient costs of incompatibility, nor is adoption time-consuming. Finally, all potential adopters of the technology exist at the time the adoption is first contemplated. But in reality, some potential adopters will make their decision only sometime in the distant future.

More complete models have been developed to incorporate each of these features. The conclusion of all these studies is that the outcome of the adoption process may be inefficient. However, the inefficiency is not only that a socially efficient standard may not be adopted. It is also possible that a new standard may be adopted too readily; that is, it may be adopted when from a social point of view, it should not be.

For example, Farrell and Saloner (1985) studied what would happen when two potential adopters were imperfectly informed about each other's preferences. They discovered that the outcome resembled a "bandwagon": If one potential adopter were keen on adopting the new technology, it would do so early in the hope of inducing the other to follow. But if a potential adopter were only moderately keen, it would use a "wait-and-see" strategy, adopting only if the other were more eager and got the bandwagon rolling.

"Wait-and-see" behavior can have the effect of stalling the bandwagon even when both potential adopters hope for adoption. Thus, there may be too little standardization.[40] The converse is also possible. Suppose that two firms are currently using an existing technology when a new technology becomes available and that only one firm favors switching to the new technology. That firm may adopt the new technology, leaving the other with the choice of being the lone user of the old technology or switching as well. If the benefits of compatibility are large, the latter may find switching to be its best alternative. But the firm that opposes the switch may be hurt more than the firm that favors the switch benefits, so that firms in the aggregate would be worse off than if they had remained with the old technology.[41]

Not only has it been shown that incomplete information can lead to either "excess inertia" or "excess momentum" when adopting a new technology, but Farrell and Saloner (1986a) also provided two models in which this can occur even with complete information. The first model examines the case in which only new adopters consider a new technology but the installed base of users of an old technology does not find switching profitable. Excess inertia can arise here if the first potential adopters to consider the new technology are not prepared to give up the transient benefits from being compatible with the installed base of the old technology. They then adopt the old technology, swelling the ranks of the installed base and making the old technology even more attractive. In that case, the new technology cannot get off the ground. This can happen even if the new technology would be much preferred by most new users if it became established. The failure of the market in this case is that the first potential users to consider the new technology confer a benefit on later adopters that they do not take into account in making their adoption decisions. Cooperative standard setting will not be able to overcome this problem because, by assumption, early potential adopters highly value the benefits of compatibility with the installed base.

However, excess momentum can also be created when the new technology is adopted, but the harm imposed on users of the old technology, who are thereby stranded, exceeds the benefit to new adopters from the new technology. This result is important because it suggests that simple public policies aimed at encouraging the adoption of new technologies can exacerbate an existing bias in the market.[42]

The second model examines what happens when the adoption takes time. Here, all potential adopters of a new technology are users of an old one. The first adopter of the new technology will lose any compatibility benefits he currently enjoys until the others also adopt the new technology. At the same time, any user who does not switch to the new technology may find himself temporarily stranded with the old technology if other users switch before he does. If the first of these effects is strong, excess inertia may set in, with no potential adopter willing "to take the plunge," with the result that all remain with the old technology. If the latter effect is strong, excess momentum may be the response, with each potential adopter rushing to be the first to adopt out of fear of being temporarily stranded.

In these models, the potential adopters choose between the status quo and a single new technology. Arthur (1985) showed that the "wrong" technology may be chosen even when a sequence of first-time potential adopters are choosing between two new technologies.[43] As in thc Farrell and Saloner (1986a) model just discussed, the early adopters are pivotal. If most favor one of the technologies and adopt it, it will become relatively less expensive for the later adopters who, in turn, may find it uneconomical to adopt the other technology. However, if the majority of later adopters would have preferred the other technology society may have been better served by its adoption. In that case, the chance predisposition of early adopters to the socially inferior technology and the fact that they serve their own, rather than society's, interests, result in the the less preferred technology's being chosen as the standard.[44]

Communication, cooperation, and contracts

When an inefficient standard is established, for example, when a new standard is adopted despite the great harm inflicted on the installed base, the failure of the market to select the "right" standard can be avoided if all potential adopters can somehow coordinate their activity and make appropriate side payments. If such contracts and side payments can overcome any inefficiencies, it is important to know why they will not naturally arise within a market setting.

There are several possible reasons. The most important is that many of the agents whose adoption decisions are relevant are not active market participants at the time the new technology becomes available but arrive much later. In principle, one could imagine a scheme in which a fund is provided by current users to give subsidies to later adopters as they arrive. However, each current member of the installed base would have an incentive to ride free on the contributions of the others or, if a method of taxes and subsidies were used, to understate their true aversion to stranding.[45] Moreover, if as in Arthur's model, there is uncertainty about the preferences of future adopters, even a central authority may often err in its choice of a standard.[46]

An additional difficulty will arise if there is asymmetric information about the adopters' preferences. Farrell and Saloner (1985) explored the implications of communication in their asymmetric information bandwagon model and found that communication is a mixed blessing, in which potential adopters are unanimous in their desire to adopt the new technology and communication facilitates coordination and eliminates excess inertia. But if they have differing preferences, communication can actually make matters worse. A potential adopter who is only slightly averse to adopting the new technology will exaggerate his degree of aversion, making it even less likely that a bandwagon will get started. This suggests that there are circumstances in which inertia may actually be intensified if there is an attempt to set voluntary standards through industry committees.[47]

The development of translator devices or "gateway" technologies

In these analyses, the potential adopters faced the choice between two inherently and unalterably incompatible technologies. In practice, however, technical compatibility is not required in order for two components of a system to be able to communicate. When components have not been designed to be compatible, devices—variously known as translators, adapters, converters, or gateways—can often be used to permit them to interact.[48] Indeed, if translation were costless and technically perfect, standardization would be unnecessary.[49] However, translation is often costly, and something is often "lost" in translation. Nonetheless, there is a thriving business in the sale of devices that permit communication in the absence of compatibility.[50]

The existence of translators has a number of implications for standardization, most of which have not been addressed in the theoretical literature:

First, in some circumstances, the use of translators may be more efficient than the development of standards. Setting standards is costly, and if only a few users wish to combine incompatible components, it may be less costly for them to use translators than to try to achieve standardization. Moreover, if the principal uses of the incompatible components are to serve users with different needs, important benefits may be lost if standardization is required.

Second, translators are likely to be important during the period in which a number of incompatible technologies are vying to become the industry standard and consumers wish to have access to a larger "network" than any single technology can provide. The existence of translators permits the choice of a standard to be deferred until more information about the various technologies becomes available. This does not mean, of course, that either the market or standard-setting bodies will necessarily select the efficient standard after the period of experimentation, but better choices are possible if there are more data about the competing technologies.

Third, the existence of translators may promote the development of specialized uses for particular technologies and thus narrow the range of uses of each. David and Bunn (1987) argued, for example, that the development of the rotary converter for "translating" AC into DC electrical current delayed the development of high-voltage DC transmission.

Finally, the presence of translators may reduce the incentives to achieve standardization. As long as incompatible components can be combined into a system, consumers are likely to be less willing to demand that manufacturers standardize, and manufacturers are likely to be less willing to incur the costs of doing so.

Nonetheless, it is possible to overstate the extent to which translators can and will substitute for standards. There are likely to be cases in which translation is technically inefficient and/or in which the costs of achieving translation are high.[51] Several large communications users emphasized to us the value to them of having standardized communications networks and argued strongly that for them, translators are a poor substitute. They are thus likely to be an important force in promoting standardization.

STANDARDS AND COMPETITION

For the most part, none of the models discussed in the previous section take account of the prices for the different technologies that the potential adopters are considering. This is consistent with markets in which the various technologies are competitively supplied so that adopters face competitive prices. This feature of the models is important because if, instead, the technologies were offered by firms with some market power, the firms might have an incentive to behave strategically. In this section we examine three kinds of strategic actions: First, we analyze the effect of strategic pricing on the market's choice of technology. Second, we look at the effect of truthful advance announcements by firms that they propose to introduce a new product. Finally, we study the contention that leading or dominant firms, or firms with control over "bottleneck facilities," may use their positions to choose or change standards in order to disadvantage their rivals.[52]

Strategic pricing and product preannouncements

Katz and Shapiro (1986b) studied the implications of strategic pricing in a two-period model when there is competition between two technologies. The most interesting case they considered is one in which each technology was offered by a single firm and one technology had lower costs in the second period but higher costs in the first period.[53] They discovered that the sponsor of the technology that would be cheaper in the future had a strategic advantage. This is a somewhat surprising result, and its subtext is exactly the reverse of that in the models of the previous section, in which adopters tended to choose the technology that was more attractive at the time that they adopted it.

The reasoning behind Katz and Shapiro's result is the following: When each technology is provided by a single sponsor, that firm has an incentive to price very low early on, even below its cost, in order to achieve a large installed base and become the industry standard. However, potential adopters know that later on ("in the second period"), the firm will no longer have an incentive to use "promotional" pricing and so will charge a higher price. Potential adopters therefore expect the firm that will have the lower future costs also will have the lower future prices. If both firms charge the same first-period price, the potential adopters will therefore prefer the technology that will have lower future costs. Put differently, the firm that has higher first period costs can overcome that disadvantage by means of promotional pricing. However, the firm that has higher second-period costs cannot do the same, as consumers will rationally expect the firm to exploit its dominant position at that stage.

Strategic behavior results in lower prices for consumers. It does not, however, guarantee that the technology with the lower overall cost will be adopted. At the same time, however, a ban on promotional pricing may prevent the adoption of the technology with the lower cost.

Similar problems arose in the the model developed by Farrell and Saloner (1986a). Recall that in that model there was an installed base of users of an old technology when a new technology became available. As a polar case, they considered what would happen when the new technology is supplied by a competitive industry and the old technology is supplied by a monopolist. They showed that in some circumstances the monopolist is able to prevent the new technology from being adopted, by offering a discount to potential adopters.[54] This discount need not be offered to all adopters. Instead, there may be some critical installed base at which the old technology becomes invulnerable because the compatibility benefits from joining the installed base are so large. Once that point is reached, the monopolist need no longer offer a special inducement. There is thus a window of opportunity for the new technology that the monopolist may be able to close through strategic pricing. Moreover, this entry prevention tactic may be successful even when the new technology would have been superior from a social point of view.[55]

The Farrell and Saloner (1986a) model can also be used to demonstrate that a simple announcement that a product will be available in the future (a "product preannouncement") can determine whether or not a technology is adopted. To see this, suppose that the old technology is competitively supplied but that the new technology is supplied by a monopolist. By the time the monopolist is ready to introduce its product, the installed base on the old technology may make entry impossible. By preannouncing the introduction of a new product, the monopolist may thus be able to persuade some potential adopters to wait for its arrival. If that occurs, the new product will begin with an installed base of its own, making it the more attractive technology to later adopters. As in the case of strategic pricing, the preannouncement can result in the adoption of the socially less preferred technology, in this case because it leads to the stranding of the old technology's users.

Standards and "bottleneck" facilities

For the most part, the theory of noncooperative standard setting discussed thus far has focused on the market for a "primary" good, for example, computers, in which compatibility is sought or avoided because of its effect on demand in the primary market. In those analyses, the effect of compatibility, pricing, and preannouncement decisions in the primary market on the market for the secondary good was not analyzed in detail, because it is implicitly assumed that producers of the primary good do not participate in that market.

The situation in the telecommunications market is somewhat different. Here, one set of firms, the local telephone companies, is assumed to control the market for basic telephone transmission capacity, the primary market.[56] At the same time, these firms are, or would like to be, participants in the secondary markets for customer premises equipment (CPE) and enhanced telecommunications services. The questions that face regulators are (1) whether control of the primary market can be extended, through the use of standards or in other ways, to the secondary markets and (2) whether the local telephone companies will have the incentive to attempt to "leverage" their market power in this manner.[57]

The use of standards to increase profits in either the "system" market or in the market for a complementary good is analyzed in detail in Ordover and Willig (1981).[58] They considered a firm that is either the only supplier of one component of the system, the "primary" component, or that has a cost advantage in producing that component.[59] Other components of the system can be produced by rivals at the same cost.[60]

It is well known that if the firm has a monopoly over one component, it will often be able to obtain maximum profit without regard to the presence of rivals in the competitive market, as long as there are no constraints on the price, or prices, that it can charge. Consider the simplest case in which all consumers place the same value on a system and all firms have the same costs in producing all components but the "primary" one. Suppose that the cost of producing the primary component is 10; the cost of producing a secondary component by any firm is 5; and the value that each consumer places on a system, or its constituent components, is 25. If there are no constraints on the prices that the firm can charge, it can set the price of a system at 25, the price of the primary component at 20 = [25 – 5], and the price of the secondary component at 5. The firm obtains a profit of 10 = [25 – 10 – 5] on each system that it sells directly to consumers. Even when a consumer purchases only the primary component from the firm, it still obtains a profit of 10 = [20 – 10]. The firm is thus indifferent to whether consumers purchase the entire system or only the primary component from it, as its profits will be the same in either case. If rival firms can produce the secondary component more efficiently, say at a cost of 4, the profits of the firm will actually go up if it leaves the market for the secondary component to them. It can charge a price of 21 = [25 – 4] for the primary component and obtain a profit of 11 = [21 – 10], which is larger than the profit of 10 that it obtains from selling an entire system.

However, it may pay to eliminate a rival if there are limits on the prices that can be charged for the primary component. Thus in the previous example, if the firm can charge at most 12 for the primary component, say because of regulation, then as long as it can charge any price above its cost for the secondary component, it will wish to eliminate its rivals and dominate the secondary market as well. If it can, for example, charge 6 for the secondary component, its profits will be 3 = [12 + 6 – 10 – 5] if it can sell both components, or an entire system, whereas it can earn only 2 = [12 – 10] if it is limited to selling only the primary component. Indeed, if the firm can charge 13 or more for the secondary component, it can earn the entire monopoly profit even with the restriction on the price that it can charge for the primary component. If, however, there are rivals in the provision of the secondary component and if the firm must make the primary component available at a price of 12, its profits will be limited to 2 = [12 + 5 – 10 – 5]. This occurs because consumers will buy the secondary component from the firm's rivals if it attempts to charge a price in excess of 5. This is what gives the firm an incentive to eliminate its rivals. One way in which it can do so is to make its primary component incompatible with the secondary component manufactured by its rivals.

The firm may also wish to eliminate its rivals if different consumers place different values on systems and these differences are proportional to their use of the secondary component. Suppose, for example, that there are two consumers, one that places a value of 25 on a system consisting of one of each component and the other that places a value of 40 on a system consisting of one primary component and two secondary components. The firm's costs are the same as in the previous example.

If there is no competition in the secondary market, the firm can offer the primary component at a price of 10 and each of the secondary components at a price of 15, and capture the consumers' entire surplus. Its profits in this case are 45 = [40 + 25 – 10 – 10]. But if there are rival suppliers of the secondary component who can produce at a cost of 5, so that the firm must obtain its profits entirely from the primary component, it will sell the primary components for 20 and earn profits of only 20 = [20 + 20 – 10 – 10].[61] Eliminating a rival is desirable because it permits price discrimination that would not otherwise be possible.[62] Once again, a possible strategy for eliminating rivals is to design the primary component so that it is incompatible with the components produced by rivals.

The two elements necessary in order to use the types of strategies that Ordover and Willig analyzed are present in the telephone industry. First are the regulatory constraints on the prices that can be charged for the primary product, that is, access to the transmission network. These constraints take the form of limits on both the overall rate of return that the firm can earn and the prices of individual services. Second, the primary product may be a "bottleneck" or "essential facility" that will be needed if the suppliers of enhanced services or CPE are to be able to sell their wares.[63]

At the same time, one of the assumptions in the examples that Ordover and Willig presented must be questioned. In their examples, the firm that controls the primary market does not, as a result, have a cost advantage in producing the secondary goods. In such cases, no loss in efficiency results from banning the participation of suppliers of the primary good in the secondary markets. Similarly, there is no loss from requiring them to participate in these markets through separate subsidiaries, so that instances of anticompetitive behavior can be more easily detected.

In addressing the effects of the limitations placed on AT&T by its Computer II decision, however, the FCC noted that

> the inability to realize . . . scope economies was one cost of structural separation for AT&T's provision of CPE; and we believe the elimination of such costs could well result in efficiencies for AT&T's provision of enhanced services, to the extent that such services could be integrated into or colocated with AT&T's basic network facilities.[64]

And when examining the effects of similar restraints on the BOCs, the commission observed "that structural separation imposes direct costs on the BOCs from the duplication of facilities and personnel, the limitations on joint marketing, and the inability to take advantage of scope economies similar to those we noted for AT&T."[65] If the economies of scope noted by the FCC are important, a blanket ban on BOC participation in the CPE and enhanced services markets, although it might prevent anticompetitive behavior, might also prevent efficient supply.[66]

We conclude that the conditions are present under which standards might be used to disadvantage the competitors of those who control access to the telecommunications transmission system. To prevent these and other forms of anticompetitive behavior, the FCC and the courts have either prohibited the telephone companies from providing certain services or have required that these services be provided through fully separated subsidiaries. If telephone companies have lower costs than these competitors, however, either a blanket prohibition or a separate subsidiary requirement may be economically inefficient. As a result, the FCC has begun to pursue an alternative approach under which the restrictions on the telephone companies are eliminated and, at the same time, a regulatory framework to make more difficult the anticompetitive use of standards is established.

TELECOMMUNICATIONS STANDARDS, TELEPHONE REGULATION, AND THE FCC

Until the 1960s, standardization was not a major telecommunications policy issue, as there were no competing providers of equipment, or of communications services, who might be adversely affected by the standards that were chosen by AT&T.[67] But beginning with the FCC decision in the Carterfone case,[68] which introduced competition into the supply of equipment to telephone customers, standards have become an increasingly important policy concern. In adopting its equipment registration program, in which it sought to eliminate technical barriers to the entry of independent equipment suppliers, the commission required, with one minor exception, that "all terminal equipment be connected to the telephone network through standard plugs and jacks."[69] And in its Computer II decision, [70] in which it sought to promote competition in the market for equipment and enhanced services, the FCC required that technical information that independent suppliers might need to compete had to be provided to them on the same terms as to the subsidiaries of the telephone companies. In this regard, the commission singled out "information relating to network design and technical standards, including interface specifications [and] information affecting changes which are being contemplated to the telecommunications network that would affect either intercarrier connection or the manner in which CPE is connected to the interstate network" (paragraph 246).[71]

The decisions by the FCC to require standardized interconnection for terminal equipment and to provide technical information to independent suppliers were part of an effort designed to enable independent equipment vendors to compete effectively in the supply of this equipment. Although the commission did not itself participate in the process of establishing interconnection standards, leaving their determination to the industry, its policy has been enormously successful, at least as judged by the wide variety of equipment that is now available and by the sharp declines in the market shares of the telephone companies.[72]

Under the modified final judgment (MFJ) that settled the government's antitrust suit against AT&T,[73] the Bell Operating Companies are "prohibited from discriminating between AT&T and other companies in their procurement activities, the establishment of technical standards, the dissemination of technical information . . . and their network planning."[74] Moreover, the MFJ "requires AT&T to provide [the] Operating Companies with, inter alia, sufficient technical information to permit them to perform their exchange telecommunications and exchange access functions. . . . The Operating Companies, in turn, are prohibited from discriminating in the establishment and dissemination of technical information and procurement and interconnection standards."[75]

Finally, in its Computer III decision,[76] the FCC indicated that it would waive its requirement that the operating companies provide enhanced services only through separate subsidiaries if competitors were given a comparably efficient interconnection (CEI) and an open network architecture (ONA) plan acceptable to the commission had been offered. The requirement of CEI is intended to give competing suppliers access to the telephone transmission system on the same basis as the subsidiaries of the telephone company that are providing the same services. ONA means that the components of the telephone system are to be made available to competing suppliers on an unbundled basis so that they can be combined with the services of these suppliers in any manner desired. The nature and identities of these components—the basic service elements—in ONA are likely to be contentious issues, as they will affect the potential for competition. Competing suppliers will undoubtedly wish to have highly disaggregated components with which they can interconnect easily. The telephone companies are likely to argue for a higher level of aggregation.

Both the interfaces with the basic service elements and the number and nature of these elements are standards issues. The first involves an obvious standards concern, as the design of these interfaces will determine whether a competing supplier can employ a particular element in offering its services. Less obvious is why the second is a standards issue. If components can be obtained only on a bundled basis, the interface between them will be completely inaccessible to the competing supplier. But the economic effect of an inaccessible interface will be exactly the same as if it were accessible but incompatible with the supplier's equipment. Providing components only on a bundled basis is the limiting case of incompatibility.

Two broad lessons can be drawn from this history. First, the range of services that independent suppliers can offer to telecommunications customers has increased markedly over the last three decades as the restrictions previously imposed by AT&T have been eliminated by regulation. Indeed, the initial effect of many regulatory interventions was either to deny AT&T, and later the BOCs, the ability to provide certain services or to restrict the way in which the services could be offered.

Second, eliminating the restrictions placed on the provision of services by the telephone companies is conditioned on imposing behavioral constraints designed to facilitate competition from independent suppliers. These constraints include requirements that information about network design changes be promptly given to competing vendors; that these vendors be offered a "comparable" interconnection to the telephone system, provided that the telephone company itself offers such a service; and that the components of the network be available on an "unbundled" basis so that customers can acquire from the telephone companies only those portions of network services that they desire.

THE DETERMINATION OF TELECOMMUNICATIONS STANDARDS

Next we shall discuss how standards can be used as a competitive weapon. This section examines two cases of standard setting in telecommunications, ISDN and open network architecture, to illustrate both phenomena.

ISDN standardization

A worldwide effort, involving literally thousands of individuals, is currently under way to develop standards for ISDN.[77] This effort is intended to define the architecture of ISDN and to promote common ISDN standards in different countries. Those countries attempting to set ISDN standards through the CCITT are interested in creating compatibility among their various national telecommunications networks in order to achieve the demand-side economies of scale discussed earlier. As we have already seen, however, even when compatibility is highly valued, it may not be easily achieved. The principal reasons are that even if all countries value compatibility, they may not agree on what the single standard should be and that some countries may prefer a degree of incompatibility to shelter their domestic telecommunications suppliers from foreign competition. As a result, achieving agreement on common standards is likely to be a slow process, and differences among national systems may persist. Indeed, there is some danger that the slowness of the process may encourage the development of incompatible systems by those unwilling to wait for international consensus.

In attempting to achieve standardization among national ISDNs, the CCITT has not confined its activities to specifying a single dimension of each interface through which information can move. Instead, it has pursued a strategy of attempting to achieve compatibility at a variety of "layers," ranging from the physical interconnections that will be permitted to the forms in which data will be recognized.[78] Because communication must be effected at all layers at each interface, the specification of standards is quite complex.

Moreover, not only are the various interface specifications being specified, but so is the architecture of the ISDN. This means that the standards will encompass where the interfaces will be and whether they will be accessible by users or independent suppliers. Clearly, the more alike the various national systems are, the simpler and less costly the required interfaces between them will be. But the fact that the architecture of ISDN will be specified by CCITT may create problems in those countries, such as the United States, where there are a large number of competing suppliers of telecommunications services.[79]

The concern is that the design of ISDN, in particular restrictions on user access, can be used to limit the competition faced by the operators of the transmission network. As a result, there may be significant conflicts between users and suppliers. Rutkowski put the point succinctly: "Users generally have an interest in maximizing their service options, while providers (particularly telephone network providers) have an interest in limiting those options to maximize their operating efficiencies and minimize losses to competitive providers" (1985, p. 46).

From the perspective of establishing standards, the most significant aspect of the development of ISDN is the increased number of interfaces at which the telecommunication network can be accessed and the ways in which such access can take place.[80] Whereas before the Carterfone decision "access" was available only at an AT&T-supplied terminal, subscribers—or providers of enhanced services—can now obtain access to the system at a number of points using several different types of equipment. ISDN is likely to increase this number further, but there must be a significant degree of standardization of interfaces and terminals in order for this to occur.

Consider a message that must "access," that is, pass through, a particular node in the telecommunications network if it is to reach its intended destination. To obtain access, a number of components are required to establish a "path." The first such component is the subscriber's terminal equipment. This can be either a device with a standard ISDN interface, for example, a digital telephone, or one that requires an adapter to access a digital network. Second, network equipment is required to perform switching and concentration functions. An example of such a device is a digital exchange. The third component is the network termination equipment that lies between the transmission system and the subscriber's premises. This is the connection between the subscriber's premises and the local telephone loop. Certain types of equipment permit the second and third components to be combined. Finally, there is the link between the local loop and the network itself.

The subscriber can use these components in various ways and, depending on the regulatory regime, may choose to obtain many or few of them from the telephone company. In the United States, for example, a subscriber may employ a terminal requiring an adapter, as well as the adapter and both types of termination equipment from the telephone company.[81] Alternatively, she may obtain the adapter from an independent vendor and the termination equipment from the telephone company. Or she may also purchase the "switch" from an independent vendor and only the last link from the telephone company. Or she may acquire all of the components from independent vendors. Similarly, a subscriber may use a terminal that does not require an adapter but may purchase any or all of the remaining components from independent vendors.[82]

The ISDN model currently under consideration does not contemplate an interface at which a subscriber, or an independent service provider, can obtain access to the system without going through the telephone company's local loop.[83] This is consistent with the views of most Post, Telephone, and Telegraph Administrations and probably with those of the BOCs, which would like to require use of this loop. It is not, however, consistent with the views of independent suppliers, who wish to maximize the number of points at which they can obtain access so that they can use as much or as little of telephone company–supplied services as they desire. Thus, even if there were no controversy regarding the designs of the interfaces that were actually offered, there might still be a dispute over how many were offered and where they were located.[84]

United States policy is likely to vary from international ISDN standards if the latter do not permit access to the network without using the local loop. For example, U.S. vendors can expect to obtain access through the telephone company network, and indeed, there have even been discussions of whether a comparably efficient interconnection requires that the equipment of these vendors be located at telephone company central offices.[85] One continuing policy concern is thus likely to be which interfaces will be available to independent suppliers and on what terms.

One way to assuage this concern is for the telephone companies to provide, as they are currently required to do, unbundled private line service, that is, pure transmission capacity, along with ISDN.[86] Thus, ISDN would not completely replace the existing telecommunications system, but some elements of the old system would remain. As a result, independent suppliers would have substantial freedom to construct their own networks using telephone company–provided private lines and other components of their own choosing. These systems would employ none of the "intelligence" in the telephone company's ISDN but would be able to offer many, or all, of the same services. As a result, even if all of the elements of an ISDN were not available on an unbundled basis, enough other resources would be available to make feasible the provision of competitive offerings. This would also protect competing vendors against the possible manipulation of the design of interfaces for strategic purposes. Thus, although a requirement that private line service continue to be provided does not appear to be a standards issue, it may be a partial substitute for a complete agreement on standards.[87]

Still another way to prevent carriers from using standards in an anticompetitive manner is to limit their ability to offer certain types of services, or to limit the way in which they may do so.[88] As we have already noted, however, drawing the line between the provision of basic (transmission) and other services is becoming increasingly difficult. It will become even more difficult with the introduction of ISDN, in which the network itself will contain a substantial amount of intelligence. Moreover, economies may be lost if such restrictions are imposed. In any event, existing restrictions are being relaxed, so that competition between exchange carriers and independent service suppliers is likely to increase. The result is that these suppliers will remain concerned about where they can obtain access and what the nature and terms of that access will be. Regardless of how ISDN standardization issues are resolved by the CCITT, these issues are unlikely to go away any time soon.

Open network architectures

The Bell Operating Companies are currently involved in developing open network architecture (ONA) plans which, if accepted by the FCC, will relieve the companies of some of the restrictions they face in offering enhanced telecommunications services. The FCC will require that ONA plans offer users the opportunity to purchase unbundled basic service elements (BSEs) so that users can configure their own telecommunications networks using as much or as little of the BOC networks as they desire. Two standards issues are raised by these developments. First, what will the basic service elements be? Second, will the BOCs offer standardized ONA plans?

The choice of BSEs is a standards issue, because offering them to parts of the network only on a bundled basis is economically equivalent to making it impossible for users to connect to the interface between them. As in the case of ISDN, network users want the elements of the network to be offered in small "bundles" so that they can purchase from the BOCs only those portions that they want. Other elements will be purchased from other vendors or provided directly by the user, which may itself be an independent service provider. On the other hand, the BOCs will presumably want to offer more aggregated bundles so as to limit the choices of users. Alternatively, the BOCs can make available many small elements but, by failing to standardize their interfaces, may force users to buy more elements from the BOCs than they may want. For these reasons, considerable controversy is likely to meet the announcement of the ONA plans.

Whatever the ONA plans contain, there will also be the issue of whether they will be the same for all BOCs. Although some large telecommunications users have expressed concern that the lack of uniformity will increase their costs,[89] there is currently no formal mechanism to coordinate the standards that will be used in the various regions of the United States.[90]

The economic theory of standards suggests three possible reasons that standardized ONA plans may not emerge: (l) large differences in preferences among the BOCs, (2) difficulties in coordinating the BOCs even if preferences are similar, and (3) the desire of some or all BOCs to achieve a competitive advantage by adopting different ONA plans.[91] If the BOCs do not adopt uniform plans, the outcome may be (1) the absence of a national standard, with the resulting slow development of new technologies because users who operate in different regions will find the costs of employing incompatible technologies to be too high; (2) the simultaneous use of incompatible technologies in different regions despite the higher costs and lower benefits for users; or (3) the emergence of one technology as the standard through a "bandwagon" in which those BOCs using other technologies are forced to switch to the standard.

A uniform national standard may fail to develop rapidly if users, uncertain about whether a national standard will emerge and what that standard will be, adopt a "wait-and-see" posture. If the fear of being stranded with the wrong technology results in such behavior by a large number of users, "excess inertia" may result.[92] Excess inertia is especially likely if the BOCs have different preferences, but it can also occur if such differences do not exist. A coordinated standard-setting process might overcome this inertia.

A second possibility is the rapid adoption of incompatible technologies in different regions. This is likely if there are many customers whose communications are confined to a single region, so that incompatibility is not important to them and/or if the benefits of using the new technologies exceed translator costs for users who communicate between regions. Note that although the new technologies develop rapidly in this case, the cost of incompatibility to users—in terms of translator costs or services not used because their benefits are less than the cost of translation—may still be substantial, and the outcome may be less efficient than if there were a common standard.

Third, one technology may emerge as the national standard. This can occur if a bandwagon that is started by early adopters changes the offerings of those BOCs using other technologies. Once again, however, it is important to observe that the winning technology is not necessarily the one that is most economically efficient.

Finally, of course, the BOCs may adopt standardized ONA plans. As we noted earlier, three conditions seem especially important for this to occur. First, there are no great differences in the preferences of the various BOCs, which may exist here as long as none of the companies has made significant investments in a particular technology. Second, the growth of the market is highly dependent on the existence of a common standard, because users place a great value on compatibility. Finally, the competitive advantages from incompatibility are small. If these conditions are met, standards may result through agreements among the BOCs. Recently, the Exchange Carriers Standards Association announced formation of the Information Industry Liaison Committee to "act as an ongoing national forum for the discussion and voluntary resolution of ONA issues."[93] Although the committee is not a formal standard-setting body, its presence may still promote agreement on common standards.

We do not mean to suggest that the absence of a formal mechanism to achieve national uniformity will necessarily produce inefficient outcomes or that the existence of such a mechanism will always overcome these inefficiencies. Rather, the main lesson of the theory just discussed is that there is no guarantee that uncoordinated standard setting by the BOCs will achieve the efficient outcome and that there are many instances in which it will not. Moreover, it may be difficult to tell even after the fact whether the outcome is an efficient one. The emergence of a common standard and rapid diffusion are still consistent with the choice of the "wrong" technology.

CONCLUSION

Two lessons can be drawn from the economic theory of standard setting. The first is that even when everyone benefits from standardization, there is no guarantee that standardization will be achieved or, if it is, that the "right" standard will be chosen. The second is that standards may be used as tools of competitive strategy, with firms either seeking incompatibility or promoting their preferred technology as the standard in order to gain an advantage over their rivals. Moreover, both problems are present whether de facto standardization occurs through the market or voluntary standards are chosen cooperatively.

Not surprisingly, both lessons can be applied to telecommunications. The fragmentation of the industry, among regions in the United States, internationally, or among user groups, may create coordination problems. The central role played by telecommunications carriers may create competitive ones. The examples of ISDN and ONA are only two instances of the growing importance of standards issues in this industry.

Much may be learned about the best way to set standards, by observing the performances of the differing approaches to telecommunications standardization being pursued in the United States and Western Europe. In the United States, standardization dictated by AT&T has been replaced by a system in which individual participants have substantial autonomy and voluntary standard setting has become more important. In Europe, by contrast, a system in which individual countries have had substantial freedom to establish their own standards appears to be evolving into one in which countries forgo some independence to obtain the benefits of more rapid technical change.

ACKNOWLEDGMENT

This chapter will appear also in R. W. Crandall and K. Flamm, eds., *Changing the Rules: Technological Change, International Competition, and Regulation in Communications* (Washington, DC: Brookings Institution, forthcoming). The authors wish to acknowledge helpful comments by John Arcate, Stephanie Boyles, Donald Dunn, Joseph Farrell, Hendrik Goosen, Charles Jackson, Leland Johnson, Ian Lifschus, Walter Richter, Leonard Strickland, and Clifford Winston on earlier drafts of this chapter.

NOTES

1. By contrast, in Europe the strong demand for X.400 products has apparently forced U.S. vendors to support the standard in order to participate in the electronic mail market.

2. If everyone benefits from having a standard, but the benefits are unequally distributed, those who obtain the largest benefits may be willing to incur the costs of setting standards, and those who receive smaller benefits take a "free ride." This outcome, in which a public good is provided by those users who receive the largest benefits, has been referred to as "the exploitation of the great by the small." See Olson (1965) for a discussion of this issue. Olson offers,

among other examples, the case of international alliances in which large countries often pay a disproportionate share of the costs.

3. The hour has not always had a fixed length. At one time, day and night were each defined to have 12 hours. As a result, the length of an hour fluctuated over the year; see Hemenway (1975, p. 5). Similarly, many types of calendars have been used throughout history; see *Collier's Encyclopedia* (1979, vol. 5, pp. 136–45).

4. In many cases, even if agents have no preferences when a technology is first introduced, they may develop them once they have adopted a particular technology. Thus, although it makes little difference in principle whether cars drive on the left- or right-hand side of the road, once a convention has been adopted, the owners of automobiles and the operators of trams or buses will usually favor the status quo. For example, when Sweden decided to switch from the left- to the right-hand side of the road in the late 1960s, a national referendum voted overwhelmingly against the change (Kindleberger, 1983, p. 389). Similarly, owners of railroads with incompatible gauges will each prefer the gauge used by their rolling stock. In the case of railroads, another interested group is the workers who are employed to change the settings of the wheels of the rolling stock as it passes from one gauge to another. Their interests are therefore in opposing any standardization, as their jobs are at stake (Nesmith, 1985). This suggests that instances in which agents are indifferent may be rare once there is a substantial installed base of equipment.

5. This assumes that side payments are not possible.

6. Paradoxically, when standardization cannot create a competitive advantage, so that achieving a consensus should be easy, the incentive to free ride is greatest.

7. This does not mean that there are no benefits from standardization, but only that the distribution of benefits is very sensitive to the standard that is chosen.

8. See Braunstein and White, 1985, for a discussion of allegedly anticompetitive standards practices in the computer, photography, and telecommunications industries.

9. The case of AM stereo may be apposite. After the FCC decided not to adopt a standard but to leave standard setting to "the market," some of the contenders succeeded in having the FCC revoke Harris's type acceptance. This forced both Harris to withdraw temporarily from competition and stations using its system to cease operating in stereo, an example of using governmental processes to gain a competitive advantage. Later, Harris dropped out of the competition, and stations using its technology switched to using Motorola's, an example of coalition formation. See Besen and Johnson, 1986, for a fuller account.

10. Note that all firms in an industry may not be in the same cell. The examples of dBase and Unix are apparently cases in which the dominant firm prefers that no standard be adopted, because it thereby retains a competitive advantage, and smaller firms prefer that a standard be chosen, because that enhances their ability to compete.

11. This can arise either when all participants want a standard but differ strongly as to what that standard should be, or when some participants do not want any standard at all. In the latter case, those firms that do not want a standard will not participate in the process, as apparently occurred in the case of the COBOL and dBase standards.

12. When less than unanimity is required, a small number of firms may agree to support a standard, leaving to others the decision as to whether to conform. A number of computer and hardware manufacturers, not including IBM, discussed the creating a standard for extending the bus for the IBM PC AT from 16 to 32 bits; see Editorial, "Inside the IBM PCs," *Byte*, 1986 extra ed., pp. 6, 8. The third section considers the rules relating to the adoption of voluntary standards by committees.

13. See Farrell and Saloner, 1985, for an analysis of the role of information in standard setting.

14. An alternative is the adoption of "compromise standards" that borrow aspects of the technologies that the different participants prefer in a way that leaves none with an advantage. One reason that this approach may be used is that arranging for side payments is often difficult.

15. See Sullivan, 1983, for more details about this process.

16. The consensus principle is explicitly not taken to imply unanimity (Sanders, 1972). Certainly it does not imply a simple unweighted majority of industry participants. Hemenway noted, for example, that "a number of negative votes of groups that are only distantly concerned with the subject matter may be discounted in the face of the affirmative votes of parties that are vitally affected by the standard" (1975, p. 89).

17. Originally organized in 1918 as the American Engineering Standards Committee, comprising four engineering societies—mining, civil, chemical, and mechanical—its name was changed to the American Standards Association in 1928. At that time, its membership was opened to trade associations and government bureaus. Finally, from 1966 to 1969 it was reorganized under the name of ANSI, and its role shifted from creating standards to coordinating them; see Sullivan, 1983, p. 33, and Hemenway, 1975, p. 88, for additional details.

18. See *American Society of Mechanical Engineers, Inc., v. Hydrolevel Corporation*, 456 U.S. 556 (1982); *Radiant Burners, Inc. v. People's Gas Light & Coke Co.*, 364 U.S. 656 (1961); and *Indian Head, Inc. v. Allied Tube & Conduit Corporation*, United States Court of Appeals for the Second Circuit, 1987, slip opinion. See also Federal Trade Commission, 1983, for an extended analysis of the potential for anticompetitive behavior in the development of standards.

19. However, collective activity to influence government standard setting is generally immune from liability under the antitrust laws. The Noerr–Pennington Doctrine adopted by the courts offers substantial antitrust immunity to firms acting collectively to influence legislative or regulatory behavior; see Fischel, 1977, and Hurwitz, 1985, for useful discussions of the doctrine.

20. See the discussion in Besen and Johnson, 1986, of the behavior of the National Association of Broadcasters in deciding whether to adopt an AM stereo standard.

21. The ISO was preceded by the International Federation of the National Standards Association (ISA), formed in 1926 by about 20 of the world's leading national standards associations. The ISA disbanded in 1942 because of the war (Sanders, 1972, p. 64). In 1981 the ISO changed its name to International Organization for Standardization but retained the abbreviation ISO (Rutkowski, 1985, p. 20).

22. The ISO accepts as a member the national body that is "most representative of standardization in its country." Most of these (more than 70 percent) are governmental institutions or organizations incorporated by public law (Rutkowski, 1985, p. 21).

23. See Lohse, 1985, and Sanders, 1972, for more details on the functioning of the ISO.

24. See Bellchambers, Hummel, and Nickelson, 1984, for details of the history of the ITU.

25. Resolution no. 10 of the Plenipotentiary Conference of the ITU (in 1982 in Nairobi) (cited in Rutkowski, 1985, p. 261).

26. "Membership [in the USCCITT] is extended to all parties interested in telecommunications standards, including users, providers, manufacturers, national standards organizations, and Government Agencies" (Cerni, 1985, p. 38).

27. See Rutkowski, 1985, for details of ESCA and other voluntary standards organizations; and Lifschus, 1985, for a description of the activities of Committee Tl.

28. Title I gives the FCC general jurisdiction over communications services; Title II, specific jurisdiction over common carrier telecommunications services; and Title III, jurisdiction over the use of radio stations.

29. This is not to say that they are essential, because translators often can substitute for interface standards. But whether standards or translators are used, the issue of whether or how to standardize naturally arises.

30. Users of computer languages, on the other hand, had obvious incentives to achieve standardization and used the typical voluntary committee structure.

31. These protocols are essential to packet-switched networks. In such a network, data to

be transmitted from one user to another are arranged in "packets." In addition to the data, each packet includes such information as the users' addresses. Protocols establish, among other things, call origination and acceptance formats, error checking, speed and flow parameters; see Rybczynski, 1980, for the details of X.25.

32. See Folts, 1982, or Tannenbaum, 1981, for a more detailed description of OSI.

33. Technical Committee 97, headquartered at ANSI in New York, is the ISO subcommittee responsible for ISDN standards (Rutkowski, 1985, p. 17).

34. Two other issues concerning the effect of standardization on market structure and firm behavior are also important. The first is whether in the presence of benefits from compatibility, firms can take strategic actions to disadvantage their rivals. When an individual firm has the ownership rights to a given technology (such a firm is often called a *sponsor* of the technology in this literature), the adoption of the technology as a standard confers some monopoly power. Thus each firm may be expected to take measures to encourage the adoption of its technology as the standard, and to protect and extend its monopoly power once it has been achieved.

The second issue is of particular importance in such markets as telecommunications, in which customers use a primary product (e.g., the telephone network) in conjunction with secondary services (e.g., customer premises equipment and enhanced telecommunications services). In such markets the question arises as to whether firms with a dominant position in the primary market can use their control of interface standards to extend their dominance to the secondary market. These two issues are discussed in the fifth section of this chapter.

35. The model is actually cast in terms of agents' choosing whether or not to join a telecommunications network, but the analogy to the choice of a standard is complete.

36. How 1 and 2 manage to coordinate their behavior is, of course, important. The point of the example, however, is that 3 and 4 may not be successful in achieving coordination even if 1 and 2 can do so. Note that this is an example of Pure Coordination if all four agents are better off adopting. If this is the case, a standard-setting body will succeed in promoting adoption of the new technology.

37. Dybvig and Spatt (1983) demonstrated that in some cases, simple subsidy schemes may alleviate both problems.

38. Note that this is an example of Conflict and cannot be resolved by replacing noncooperative standard setting with a standard-setting body. Agents 3 and 4 will not switch even if 1 and 2 agree to do so.

39. The proof uses the following backward-induction argument. Suppose that there are n potential adopters and that n-1 has already adopted the technology. In that case, the nth adopter will as well. Therefore, consider the n-1th adopter when n-2 has already adopted. That potential adopter knows that if he adopts, the final adopter will also, and so he, too, adopts. The same logic can be applied all the way back to the first adopter. This explains why a standard setting body can succeed in achieving universal adoption only in the first of the two examples we discussed.

40. Postrel (n.d.) extended Farrell and Saloner's (1985) results to the n-agent case.

41. Thus, although "bandwagons" may overcome the need to employ cooperative standard setting to achieve efficient adoptions, they may also promote inefficient ones. Moreover, in the latter case, cooperative standard setting may not only fail to overcome this tendency, but it may actually promote it.

42. Rosenberg (1976) and Ireland and Stoneman (1984) also showed that such policies can have the unexpected effect of slowing the adoption of a new technology. That is, an adopter of a new technology knows that these policies offer an incentive to new innovation, increasing the chance that the new technology will itself soon be obsolete. See David, 1986c, and David and Stoneman, 1985, for a discussion of these and other implications of public policy aimed at hastening the adoption of a technology.

43. In the simplest version of Arthur's model, the demand-side externalities arise from "learning by using," in which each time a potential adopter selects one of the technologies, the costs to later users of the same technology are reduced. However, the model can easily be extended to the case of compatibility; see David, 1986b, for a discussion of this point.

44. Cowan, 1986, analyzed the same phenomenon from a different perspective. As in Arthur's model there is learning by using. In addition, however, potential adopters are unsure which technology is better. Each trial of a technology elicits some information about its desirability. Thus, as in the other models, there is a connection between the welfare of late adopters and the decisions of early ones. Because early adopters ignore the value of the information they give to late ones, from a social point of view there may be too little exploration of the value of alternative technologies.

45. This free rider problem would arise, of course, even if the model were "timeless."

46. David, 1986b, calls such a central authority a "blind giant."

47. Another portion of the literature addresses the trade-off between standardization and variety. Farrell and Saloner (1986b) showed that when the degree of standardization is left to market forces, too little variety may be provided if the existence of a historically favored technology prevents an otherwise viable alternative from getting off the ground. Matutes and Regibeau (1986) addressed the case in which products are combined in "systems," and they demonstrated that standardizing the product interface can increase the variety of systems by facilitating "mix-and-match" purchases. But it can also lead to higher prices. The compatibility of components may also have implications for technology adoption. Berg (1985) compared a regime in which there are two competing technologies with one in which there is only one technology. In the former, one of the technologies may eventually become the de facto standard. In that case, the adopters of the abandoned technology may find that compatible components are no longer provided. The realization of this possibility tends to dampen the demand for both technologies, leading to slower technology adoption. Farrell and Gallini (1986) showed that a monopolistic supplier of the primary good may encourage competition in the component market in order to mitigate this problem.

48. See Braunstein and White, 1985, for a brief discussion of translators as a substitute for standards.

49. By "technically perfect," we mean that messages sent in either direction and then returned are identical to those that were originally transmitted.

50. Some examples of translation devices are: (l) Word For Word, which is a "software document converter that converts files and documents from one PC-compatible word processing system to another" (advertisement in *Byte*, 1986 extra ed., p. 229); (2) a series of products offered by Flagstaff Engineering that "can connect your incompatible computer systems using diskette, tape, communications, or printed media" (advertisement in *Byte*, September 1986, p. 320); and (3) PC<>488 which "allows your IBM PC/XT/AT or compatible to control IEEE-488 instruments" (advertisement in *Byte*, November 1986, p. 155).

51. Also, Katz and Shapiro (1985) discovered that firms providing incompatible technologies will generally not have the correct incentives to provide converters.

52. See Adams and Brock, 1982, for an example of this view.

53. They also studied the case in which both technologies are competitively supplied. Their results in that case are similar to those of Farrell and Saloner (1986a), discussed in the previous section.

54. The same advantage exists when a monopolist is the supplier of a new technology that is incompatible with one offered by a competitive industry.

55. Katz and Shapiro (1986a) found the same results for their two-period model.

56. Whether this presumption is true is not addressed in this chapter, although the conclusions would be affected if there were effective competition in the transmission market. Similar issues arise in countries where a single entity controls the entire telecommunications

system and competes with outside suppliers. This explains the large role given to the achievement of common standards by the Commission of the European Communities. The commission is concerned with "the promotion of Europe-wide open standards, in order to give equal opportunity to all market participants" (1987, p. 5).

57. This is akin to the issues raised in the various antitrust cases involving IBM, in which it was alleged, among other things, that IBM manipulated its interconnection standards to extend its putative monopoly in the market for mainframe computers to the market for peripheral equipment. This chapter is not the occasion to revisit the issues raised in these cases. We raise the examples of the IBM case only because they present analogies to policy questions in the telephone industry. For a vigorous defense of IBM's actions, see Fisher, McGowan, and Greenwood, 1983.

58. See also Ordover, Sykes, and Willig, 1985. Ordover and Willig actually described several ways in which firms might attempt to exercise such leverage. These include refusing to sell the primary good to a rival, selling only complete systems and not their components, selling both systems and components but setting high prices for components if purchased separately, "underpricing" components that compete with those sold by rivals, and "overpricing" components that are needed by rivals to provide complete systems. Thus, standards are only one of many tools that a firm can use strategically to disadvantage its rivals and to increase its profits. It should also be observed that these all are variants of the "raising rivals' costs" strategies analyzed in detail in Krattenmaker and Salop, 1986.

59. It should be clear that the component is called primary not because it is any more necessary than any other component but because of the advantage that the firm has in producing it.

60. The ability to use standards in such an anticompetitive manner will be severely limited if efficient, low-cost translators are available. For example, a firm that seeks a competitive advantage by designing interfaces that cannot directly accommodate the products of its rivals will find the strategy unsuccessful if users can easily connect incompatible devices by using translators.

61. The firm's profits will be the same if it sells only one primary component at 30. The analysis assumes that the firm cannot offer only complete systems at discriminatory prices.

62. This is analogous to the argument that firms vertically integrate forward in order to permit them to practice price discrimination; see Gould, 1977.

63. To the extent that suppliers of enhanced services or CPE can "bypass" the local transmission facilities of a telephone company, the ability of the telephone company to use standards anticompetitively is reduced.

64. Federal Communications Commission, Report and Order in the Matter of Amendment of Sections 64.702 of the Commission's Rules and Regulations (Third Computer Inquiry); and Policy and Rules Concerning Rates for Competitive Common Carrier Services and Facilities Authorizations Thereof; and Communications Protocols under Section 64.702 of the Commission's Rules and Regulations, CC Docket no. 85–229, Adopted May 15, 1986, released June 16, 1986, paragraph 80.

65. Communications Protocols, paragraph 90.

66. See Phillips, 1986, for a forceful statement of the proposition that substantial efficiency losses will result if the BOCs are confined to offering basic service.

67. Of course, consumer welfare could depend on the choices that were made.

68. Use of the Carterfone Device, 13 FCC 2d 420, reconsideration denied, 14 FCC 2d 571 (1968).

69. 56 FCC 2d 593 (1975), p. 611.

70. Second Computer Inquiry, 77 FCC 2d 384 (1980).

71. Although the requirement that competitors be given information limited the ability of AT&T to use standards to disadvantage its rivals, AT&T might still prefer standards different from those desired by its rivals.

72. In the early 1980s, AT&T's share of the customer premises equipment market had declined to somewhat over 60 percent (U.S. House of Representatives, 1981), and by 1986 its share of total lines shipped had fallen further to about 36 percent for handsets, 25 percent for key systems, and 20 percent for PBXs (Huber, 1987). In the United Kingdom where the entry of independent suppliers of terminal equipment did not begin until much later than in the United States and where a somewhat different equipment registration program exists, non–British Telecom suppliers have captured half of the addition of the installed base of telephones since 1980 and about 10 percent of the key system market (Solomon, 1986).

73. *United States v. Western Elec. Co.* (American Tel. and Tel. Co.), 552 F. Supp 131 (D.D.C. 1982).

74. Ibid., p. 142.

75. Ibid., p. 177.

76. 60 RR 2d 603 (1986).

77. Rutkowski, 1985, contains an extensive description of this process.

78. These layers are patterned to a substantial degree on those in the Open Systems Interconnection (OSI) reference model.

79. Although not as far along as in the United States, this development is also occurring in the United Kingdom and Japan.

80. The introduction of open network architecture in the United States will have a similar effect. One article argued that the effect of ONA is likely to be an increase in the number of interfaces by "an order of magnitude." See Editorial, "Part 68 Is Not Compatible with ONA," *Telecommunications* 21 (North American ed.), January 1987, p. 8.

81. Conceivably he might purchase the various components from different parts of the company.

82. Of course, this wide range of options is available only where competitive suppliers exist. In many countries, all components must be acquired from the telephone company.

83. In the language of CCITT, this is not a "reference point"; see Rutkowski, 1985, pp. 145–46.

84. Note that denying access is equivalent to providing an interface that is totally incompatible with the equipment of one's rivals.

85. Note that denying access to independent vendors at the central office may be equivalent to the strategy, discussed by Ordover and Willig (1981), of not making certain components of a system available to rivals, depending on the costs of the alternatives.

86. This is apparently contemplated by the CCITT, but in any event, it is likely to be an element of United States telecommunications policy.

87. Alternatively, it can be thought of as providing an alternative interface. Also note that the pricing of private lines as well as of competing telephone company offerings affects the nature of competition. As Ordover and Willig (1981) observed, "underpricing" components that compete with those sold by rivals and "overpricing" components that are needed by rivals may be part of a competitive strategy. Thus, even if private lines are available, they will not be an attractive alternative to ISDN if they are very costly.

88. This is, of course, the approach taken in Computer II and in the modified final judgment.

89. Betts (1986) described a large user who "is worried that the lack of standard protocols will increase cost for equipment, staff expertise and software and complicate operating procedures as well as hamper the diagnosis and resolution of network problems" (p. 1) and quoted the counsel for the International Communications Association, a group of large users, that "we have an overall concern that we may end up with seven separate, incompatible, ONA plans" (p. 15).

90. But see the following discussion of the Information Industry Liaison Committee.

91. A particular technology may be favored because it reduces the competition that a BOC faces from suppliers of equipment that compete with equipment offered by the BOC or be-

cause it reduces the ability of other suppliers to offer equipment that provides services that could otherwise be offered through the network. The stated goal of the proposed European policy to achieve common telecommunications standards among countries (Commission of the European Communities, 1987) is to promote competition.

92. Besen and Johnson (1986) conjectured that the absence of an AM stereo standard may be responsible for the slow rate of diffusion of that technology by radio stations and listeners. Inertia can also result if the benefits to users are reduced because incompatibility raises their costs.

93. "ECSA Sponsoring Information Industry Liaison Committee on 'Open Network Architectures'," *Telecommunications Reports*, October 19, 1987, p. 15.

REFERENCES

Adams, W., & J. W. Brock (1982). Integrated monopoly and market power: System selling, compatibility standards, and market control. *Quarterly Review of Economics and Business* 22:29–42.

Arthur, W. B. (1985). Competing technologies and lock-in by historical small events: The dynamics of allocation under increasing returns. Center for Economic Policy Research Discussion Paper no. 43, Stanford University, January.

Bellchambers, W. H., J. Francis, E. Hummel, & R. L. Nickelson (1984). The International Telecommunication Union and development of worldwide telecommunications. *IEEE Communications Magazine* 22 (May): 72–83.

Berg, S. V. (1985). Technological externalities and a theory of technical compatibility standards. Mimeo, University of Florida.

Besen, S. M., & L. L. Johnson (1986). Compatibility standards, competition, and innovation in the broadcasting industry. Rand Corporation, R-3453–NSF, November.

Betts, M. (1986). Open nets trigger fears. *Computerworld*, November 3, pp. 1, 15.

Braunstein, Y. M., & L. J. White (1985). Setting technical compatibility standards: An economic analysis. *Antitrust Bulletin* 30:337–55.

Brock, G. (1975). Competition, standards and self-regulation in the computer industry. In R. E. Caves & M. J. Roberts (Eds.), *Regulating the product*. Cambridge, MA: Ballinger.

Cerni, D. M. (1985). The United States organization for the CCITT. *IEEE Communications Magazine* 23 (January): 38–42.

Collier's Encyclopedia (1979). New York: Macmillan.

Commission of the European Communities (1987). Towards a dynamic European Community. Green paper on the Development of the Common Market for Telecommunications Services and Equipment, June.

Cowan, R. (1986). Backing the wrong horse: Sequential technology choice under increasing returns. Mimeo, Stanford University, December.

David, P. A. (1986a). Narrow windows, blind giants, and angry orphans: The dynamics of system rivalries and dilemmas of technology policy. TIP working paper no. 10, Stanford University, March.

——— (1986b). Some new standards for the economics of standardization in the information age. TIP working paper no. 11, Stanford University, August.

——— (1986c). Technology diffusion, public policy, and industrial competitiveness. In R. Landau & N. Rosenberg (Eds.), *The positive sum strategy: Harnessing technology for economic growth*. Washington, DC: National Academy of Sciences.

David, P. A., with J. A. Bunn (1987). "The battle of the systems" and the evolutionary dynamics of network technology rivalries. TIP working paper no. 12, Stanford University, January.

David, P. A., & P. L. Stoneman (1985). Adoption subsidies vs. information provision as instruments of technology policy. TIP working paper no. 6, Stanford University, April.

Dybvig, P. H., & C. S. Spatt (1983). Adoption externalities as public goods. *Journal of Public Economics* 20:231–47.

Farrell, J., & N. Gallini (1986). Second-sourcing as a commitment: Monopoly incentives to attract competition. Working paper no. 8618, Department of Economics, University of California at Berkeley, December.

Farrell, J., & G. Saloner (1985). Standardization, compatibility, and innovation. *Rand Journal of Economics* 16:70–83.

——— (1986a). Installed base and compatibility: Innovation, product preannouncements, and predation. *American Economic Review* 76:940–55.

——— (1986b). Standardization and variety. *Economics Letters* 20:71–74.

Federal Trade Commission, Standards and Certification, Bureau of Consumer Protection, (1983). *Final staff report*, April.

Fischel, D. R. (1977). Antitrust liability for attempts to influence government action: The basis and limits of the Noerr–Pennington Doctrine. *University of Chicago Law Review* 45:80–122.

Fisher, F. M., J. J. McGowan, & J. E. Greenwood (1983). *Folded, spindled, and mutilated: Economic analysis and U.S. v. IBM.* Cambridge, MA: MIT Press.

Folts, H. C. (1985). A tutorial on the interconnection reference model. *Open Systems Data Transfer* 1 (June):2–21. Reprinted in W. Stallings (Ed.), *Computer communications: Architecture, protocols, and standards.* Silver Spring, MD: IEEE Computer Society Press.

Gallagher, R. T. (1986). Europeans are counting on Unix to fight IBM. *Electronics*, July 10, pp. 121– 22.

Gould, J. R. (1977). Price discrimination and vertical integration: A note. *Journal of Political Economy* 85:1063–71.

Hemenway, D. (1975). *Industrywide voluntary product standards.* Cambridge, MA: Ballinger.

Horwitt, E. (1986). Protocols don't stand alone. *Computerworld*, October 20, pp. 27, 29.

——— (1987a). Vendors pull together to boost Unix standards. *Computerworld*, January 26, p. 6.

——— (1987b). X.400 flies in Europe, lags in U.S. *Computerworld*, November 2, pp. 49, 53.

Huber, P. W. (1987). The geodesic network. 1987 report on competition in the telephone industry. U.S. Department of Justice, Antitrust Division, January.

Hurwitz, J. D. (1985). Abuse of governmental process, the First Amendment, and the boundaries of Noerr. *Georgetown Law Review* 74:601–62.

Ireland, N., & P. L. Stoneman (1984). Technological diffusion, expectations, and welfare. Paper presented to the TIP workshop at Stanford University, February.

Katz, M. L., & C. Shapiro (1985). Network externalities, competition, and compatibility. *American Economic Review* 75:424–40.

——— (1986a). Product compatibility choice in a market with technological progress. *Oxford Economic Papers* 38:146–65.

——— (1986b). Technology adoption in the presence of network externalities. *Journal of Political Economy* 94:822–41.

Kindleberger, C. P. (1983). Standards as public, collective and private goods. *Kyklos* 36:377–96.

Krattenmaker, T. G., & S. Salop (1986). Anticompetitive exclusion: Raising rivals' costs to achieve power over price. *Yale Law Journal* 96:209–93.

Lifschus, I. M. (1985). Standard committee Tl-telecommunications. *IEEE Communications Magazine* 23 (January):34–37.

Lohse, E. (1985). The role of the ISO in telecommunications and information systems standardization. *IEEE Communications Magazine* 23 (January):18–24.

Matutes, C., & P. Regibeau (1986). Compatibility and multiproduct firms: The symmetric case. Mimeo.

National Bureau of Standards (1984). *Standards activities of organizations in the U.S.* Prepared for the Office of Product Standards Policy, R. Toth, (Ed.). Washington, DC: U.S. Government Printing Office.

Nesmith, A. (1985). A long, arduous march toward standardization. *Smithsonian*, March, pp. 176–94 .

Olson, M. (1965). *The logic of collective action*. Cambridge, MA: Harvard University Press.

Ordover, J. A., A. O. Sykes, & R. D. Willig (1985). Nonprice anticompetitive behavior by dominant firms toward the producers of complementary products. In F. M. Fisher (Ed.), *Antitrust and regulation: Essays in memory of John J. McGowan*, pp. 115–30. Cambridge, MA: MIT Press.

Ordover, J. A., & R. D. Willig (1981). An economic definition of predation: Pricing and product innovation. *Yale Law Journal* 91:8–53.

Phillips, A. (1986). Humpty Dumpty had a great fall. *Public Utilities Fortnightly*, October 2, pp. 19–24.

Pool, I. de S. (1984). Competition and universal service. In H. M. Shooshan (Ed.), *Disconnecting Bell: The impact of the AT&T divestiture*. New York: Pergamon.

Postrel, S. (n.d.). Bandwagons and the coordination of standardized behavior. Mimeo.

Rohlfs, J. (1974). A theory of interdependent demand for a communications service. *Bell Journal of Economics* 5:16–37.

Rosenberg, N. (1976). On technological expectations. *Economic Journal* 86:523–35.

Rutkowski, A. M. (1985). *Integrated services digital networks*. Dedham, MA: Artech House.

Ryan, A. J. (1987). Esber: Dbase language not for public domain. *Computerworld*, October 19, p. 133.

Rybczynski, A. (1980). X.25 interface and end-to-end virtual circuit service characteristics. *IEEE Transactions in Communications* COM-28 (April):500–10. Reprinted in W. Stallings (Ed.), *Computer communications: Architecture, protocols, and standards*. Silver Spring, MD: IEEE Computer Society Press.

Sanders, T. R. B. (1972). *The aims and principles of standardization*. Geneva, Switzerland. International Organization for Standardization.

Solomon, J. H. (1986). Telecommunications evolution in the UK. *Telecommunications Policy* 10:186–92.

Sullivan, C. D. (1983). *Standards and standardization: Basic principles and applications*. New York: Marcel Dekker.

Tannenbaum, A. S. (1981). Network protocols. *Computing Surveys* 13 (December): 453–89. Reprinted in W. Stallings (Ed.), *Computer communications: Architecture, protocols, and standards*. Silver Spring, MD: IEEE Computer Society Press.

U.S. House of Representatives (1981). Telecommunications in transition: The status of competition in the telecommunications industry. A report by the majority staff of the Subcommittee on Telecommunications, Consumer Protection and Finance, of the Committee on Energy and Commerce, November 3.

Verman, L. C. (1973). *Standardization, a new discipline*. Hamden, CT: Ardon Books.

CHAPTER 8

Electronic Integration and Strategic Advantage: A Quasi-Experimental Study in the Insurance Industry

N. VENKATRAMAN AND AKBAR ZAHEER

The subject of information technology (IT) and its potential for strategic advantage has gained currency in recent years. The evolving literature is largely dominated by conceptual frameworks (e.g., McFarlan, 1984; Porter & Millar, 1985; Wiseman, 1985) and detailed case studies of popular examples and applications such as McKesson's Economost system (Clemons & Row, 1988), American Airlines' SABRE reservation system (Copeland & McKenney, 1988), and American Hospital Supply's ASAP system (Harvard Business School, 1985, 1988; Venkatraman & Short, 1990). It can be reasonably argued that a major reason for considering IT-based applications as potential sources of strategic advantage lies in the capability for electronic integration among firms that can change the basis of competition in a marketplace (Barrett & Konsynski, 1982; Cash & Konsynski, 1985; Johnston & Vitale, 1988). *Electronic integration* is defined as the integration of two or more independent organizations' business processes by exploiting the capabilities of computers and communication technologies.[1] We shall elaborate on this issue later.

Although the role and benefits of interorganizational systems (IOS) in particular and electronic integration in general have achieved the status of conventional wisdom, the extent of research support for arguing their importance is rather limited. The current literature is restricted to discussing the nature and levels of IOS (Barrett & Konsynski, 1982), descriptive and normative frameworks in which managers can assess the role of IOS in their organizational contexts (Cash & Konsynski, 1985; Johnston & Vitale, 1988), and theories concerning the role of IOS in changing market characteristics (Bakos, 1987; Malone, Yates, & Benjamin, 1987). There is a marked lack of empirical research studies that focus on the specific effects—if any—of such systems on business performance. Indeed, much of the support is based on anecdotes, personal opinions, and experiences rather than on systematic research studies. Thus, a formal, empirical assessment of the role and benefits of electronic integration appears necessary and timely.

Toward this end, this chapter discusses the results of a quasi-experimental study on the effects of electronic integration in the insurance industry, with particular attention to the commercial lines of the property and casualty (P&C) business. The uniqueness of this study lies in

1. Its quasi-experimental design, with an experimental sample of independent insurance agents who are electronically interfaced (with a dedicated system) and a matched control sample (based on size, state, and location category) of agents who are not electronically interfaced with this particular insurance carrier.
2. The use of objective, longitudinal performance data on these agents from the carrier's records to identify the specific performance effects of electronic integration.

This study offers an opportunity to test systematically an implicitly accepted, but largely untested, proposition regarding the benefits of electronic integration.

BACKGROUND: THEORETICAL CONCEPTS AND EARLIER RESEARCH

Strategic advantage through electronic integration

The emerging stream of electronic integration and strategic advantage is characterized by limited theorizing, mostly inductive attributions. In this chapter, we shall set the stage for a deductive approach to assessing the effects of electronic integration by developing theoretical arguments from multiple perspectives: institutional economics, especially the transaction-cost theory (see Williamson, 1975, for disciplinary arguments, and Malone, Yates, & Benjamin, 1987, for a specific discussion of multiorganizational coordination mechanisms enabled by information technologies), the industrial organization economics and applied game-theory perspective (see, e.g., Bakos, 1987; Rotemberg & Saloner, 1989), and macroorganizational theories of organization–environment adaptation (see, e.g., Thompson, 1967).

According to Malone, Yates, and Benjamin (1987), developments in information technologies are expected to give rise to three effects: (1) the electronic communication effect, reducing costs of communication while expanding its reach (time and distance); (2) the electronic brokerage effect, increasing the number and quality of alternatives and decreasing the cost of transactions; and (3) the electronic integration effect, increasing the degree of interdependence among the participants in the business processes. Thus, electronic integration is expected to alter the nature of interrelationships in a given market with the potential to become both efficient (as in reduced costs) and effective (as in increased capabilities for assessing available options leading to better decisions) for the firms involved in electronic integration.

This issue needs to be further clarified by discussing the form of IOS deployed, which can be either a common infrastructure through a third-party system (i.e., ANSI .X12 standards) or a unique, proprietary system installed to develop and implement a firm-level electronic integration strategy (e.g., Baxter's ASAP network or American Airlines SABRE network). In the former case, the benefits of electronic integration cannot be differentially appropriated, as other competitors have access to the same technological capabilities, whereas in the latter the firm chooses to commit its strategic investments with the expectation of deriving firm-level advantages.

Following Rotemberg and Saloner (1989), we distinguish between cooperative advantage (i.e., the advantage accruing to a set of firms joining in the creation of a common network) versus competitive advantage (i.e., the advantage to the firms differentiating at the level of the network used to develop business relationships) in our discussion of benefits of electronic integration. Our basic thesis is that if a firm can successfully differentiate its IOS network, then the competitive advantage gained from such a network may be greater than the cooperative advantage of standardization. The reasons for selecting one form over the other are based on complex factors, including market structure and the firm's specific strategic choices to compete in a given market (Porter, 1980; Rotemberg & Saloner, 1989). In addition, there is a strong possibility of dynamic movement across the forms of competitive and cooperative advantage as the structural and competitive conditions change, as in the case of the automatic teller machine networks. Thus, the overall argument is that these systems create or enhance entry barriers, thus providing the incumbents with greater opportunities for exploiting efficiency and effectiveness.

A complementary strand in understanding the role and effects of electronic integration is provided by the macroorganization theories of organization–environment interaction. Thompson (1967) drew up propositions that outline specific actions for competitive versus cooperative postures in a given market. These are rooted in the belief that firms seek to minimize uncertainty in their task environments. Electronic integration can be argued to be an efficient mechanism for organizations to use to increase their ability to process information (Galbraith, 1973), thus coping with environmental uncertainty. Consequently, electronic integration is expected to enhance organizational effectiveness.

Conceptualizing electronic integration

We distinguish electronic integration from the common platforms of electronic data interchange (EDI), and we also differentiate among interorganizational systems (IOS). Specifically, EDI provides the technical platform rooted in a set of standards for informational exchange among participants in a marketplace; IOS builds on these common EDI standards (when necessary) to design and deploy different ways of interconnecting multiple organizations (for a good classification of IOS, see Konsynski & Warbelow, 1989). Even within a single category of IOS (say upstream or downstream linkages), there can be differences in the functions of several organizations. As an example, not all airline reservation systems offer the same functions for travel agencies. In addition, even within a specific IOS, a firm may choose to exercise different business options for its interconnected partners. Consequently, we need to distinguish system features, as do Konsynski and Warbelow (1989), from the strategic choices to exploit the ways of developing interorganizational relationships for specific business purposes; this is termed *electronic integration*. In other words, the applications within an IOS (say, a reservation system) can be the same for several organizations, but the strategic effects may be different. Although there are obvious interrelationships among EDI, IOS, and electronic integration, we argue that it is useful to distinguish among them when delineating the theoretical linkages underlying the role and impact of information-based advantages in the marketplace.

Earlier assessments of evidence

In addition to the limited theorizing, the extent of empirical support for the benefits of electronic integration is also sparse. The American Hospital Supply Corporation's (AHSC, now Baxter International) ASAP system is a classic, overworked illustration in this area. Although no systematic assessment of its effects is available, by 1984 over 4500 customers were linked through this system, which carried over 100,000 products. Further, AHSC increased its sales by an average of 13 percent per year between 1978 and 1983, and a typical hospital order through this system averaged 5.8 items, as compared with an industry average of 1.7 items.[2] Baxter executives and industry observers credit the system for the company's success in the competitive hospital supplies marketplace.

In contrast, Clemons and Row (1988) made a more thorough analysis of McKesson's Economost system. According to them, since the system was first introduced nationally in 1975, McKesson's drug sales grew from $922 million to $4.8 billion, an increase of 422 percent, whereas its operating expenses rose by only 86 percent; McKesson also greatly reduced the number of personnel in order entry and sales. Similarly, airlines reservation systems have been studied in detail (e.g., Copeland & McKenney, 1988). Although the exact data are not available, it is widely acknowledged that the proportion of tickets booked through the SABRE system was much higher for American Airlines' flights than for any other airline whose schedules were also displayed on the system.

Need for systematic assessments

Although there appears to be strong face validity in the results reported in these case studies, from a research point of view they need to be supplemented using more formal criteria of social science research. For this purpose, we use the following six criteria provided by Terpstra (1981) in his assessment of research studies on organization development effects: the presence of a probability sample, an adequate sample size for analysis, the use of a control group, random selection for treatment, pre- and posttests, and the use of significance levels for assessing the effects of treatment. For a systematic evaluation of electronic integration effects, all or most of these criteria need to be satisfied.

THE PROPERTY AND CASUALTY INSURANCE MARKET

The U.S. insurance industry can be divided broadly into the life and health and the property and casualty (P&C) markets, each with its distinctive products and channels of distribution. P&C insurance offers protection against such risks as fire, theft, accident, and general liability. The P&C market can be further broken down into personal and commercial lines, the former covering individuals (e.g., automobile and homeowner insurance) and the latter indemnifying commercial policyholders against general liability and workers' compensation. The industry generated about $200 billion in premiums in 1988.[3]

The P&C insurance market relies, particularly for its commercial lines, on direct writers and independent agents for distribution of its products to the customer. The former has no ownership rights of renewals and is exclusive to one carrier, whereas independent agents—by definition—represent multiple carriers. They are compensated by commissions and retain the rights to their policies and accounts, even if their relationship with the insurance carrier issuing the policy is terminated (Stern & El-Ansary, 1977). The P&C market is composed of over 3600 insurance carriers, as there are few barriers to entry. This level of fragmentation and low market power makes for intense price-based competition. Approximately 300 carriers have multiple offices (Frost & Sullivan, 1984), and 20 to 30 are major carriers, accounting for about 50 percent of revenues.

Further, the industry is on the threshold of a major industry transformation along several dimensions. First, there has been a reduction in the number of independent agents by as much as 25 percent during 1980–86[4] to around 42,000, because of the consolidation of agency operations. Second, there is a growing trend in forward integration by carriers through mechanisms such as direct writing, commissioned-employee arrangements, and exclusive agencies. Third, more and more agency automation systems ("back-office" automation) are being installed, which, in order to be efficient, require larger business volumes with the resulting scale economies. Finally, electronic integration between insurance carriers and independent agents is another force that appears to be changing the competitive characteristics of the marketplace; a recent survey estimated that 28 percent of all independent agents were integrated with at least one insurance carrier.[5]

Within the P&C market, personal lines—because of their relatively standardized and regulated nature—have been prime targets of automation by large insurance carriers. In contrast, commercial lines are less regulated and considerably more complex and thus have only recently been subjected to computerized policy processing. It is not coincidental that expert systems—which have lately seen a surge of development—have had a significant role in the computerized processing of commercial lines. But we shall limit this chapter to the commercial lines, for two reasons: (1) Because of the significance of resources committed to computerized policy processing of complex commercial lines, it is an attractive setting for testing theoretical propositions; and (2) the recent deployment of electronic interfacing allows a more systematic design for the collection of pre- and postdata, to be described later.

The nature of electronic integration

Industry standards for electronic policy information transfer between the carrier and the insurance agents were set by the industry organization, ACORD, and in 1983, the Insurance Value Added Networks (IVANS) were established. According to Malone and his colleagues (1987), Rotemberg and Saloner (1989), and Thompson (1967), the installation of a common network will favor the independent agents, as it will enable them to interface with multiple carriers in providing efficient service in the market. Specifically, the agents reduce their dependencies on a few carriers while exploiting the full benefits of electronic integration and brokerage effects. Indeed, in Malone and his colleagues' (1987) terminology, such a move would have propelled the industry from a decentralized marketplace toward an electronic market, owing to significant reductions in the "unit costs of coordination" of the delivery of the insurance.

Hence, it is not surprising that the agents seem favorably disposed to using a common network and that some carriers are obviously less enthusiastic, as they believe that a "true interface" between the agent and all the relevant carriers would force them to compete more on price alone. The reason is that the cost of accessing and evaluating alternative quotes is dramatically reduced, thereby improving the bargaining power of the agents relative to that of the carriers. The existence of common rating systems for standard policy modules accelerates the movement toward predominantly price-based competition. Consequently, some leading insurance carriers (like Aetna, CIGNA, Travelers, St. Paul) decided to pursue the route of competitive advantage rather than cooperative advantage (Rotemberg & Saloner, 1989), by developing and installing systems with proprietary interface standards operated through private networks. This initiative could give the carriers means of competing other than that based predominantly on price. It appears, however, that the medium-sized carriers have stronger incentives to pursue cooperative strategies, given the high costs of private systems and networks that give scale benefits to the larger players.

Electronic integration and the focal carrier's business strategy

The focal carrier considers electronic integration with its agents to be central to its business strategy. The carrier's business strategy in the P&C market can be broadly described as (1) reducing the number of agents in order to concentrate on a limited number of high-potential agents (with a significant share of business with this carrier), (2) controlling loss ratios (which are closely related to the agent's share of business; i.e., the largest share carrier has the best loss ratios), and (3) creating product differentiation (through higher service levels).

This business strategy is supported by electronic integration, by installing a commercial policy-processing system at selected independent agents. The focal carrier has committed a significant level of strategic investments by developing and installing the system and the network at no cost to the agents and by bearing the entire expense of hardware, software, communications, and the associated training. The characteristics of the system are (1) on-line policy quotation, which enables the agent to obtain more quickly the relevant information on a potential quote (i.e., within a day or two) than with the traditional communication with the carrier with a typical time lag of one to three weeks, and more important, the ease of information exchange enabled through dedicated linkages implies that the focal carrier can at least be considered for obtaining a quote; (2) multiple-option flexibility, which enables the agent to explore on-line alternative scenarios of policy specifications at remote locations and thereby to offer better service; (3) risk evaluation, which provides an efficient basis for evaluating the risk propensity of a prospective policy with the capability offered by the back-end expert systems, with the potential of reducing loss ratios; (4) policy issuance, which allows agents to initiate more quickly the issuing of a policy at remote carrier locations (two weeks instead of six weeks) and which reduces paper handling; (5) endorsements, which allow the agents to provide postissuance support (including minor modifications), with the opportunity to offer greater service to the customers; and (6) claims handling, which automates the steps in settling claims, resulting in more efficient and a higher level of service.

Delineating levels of analysis

When dedicated electronic integration has two roles, that of the focal carrier (i.e., the deployer of the system) and that of the agent (i.e.,where the system is deployed), it is important to differentiate the effects of the two roles. At the level of the agent—who has not shared in the costs of development of the system—the net benefit is the result of the following components: (1) greater efficiency through electronic integration after recognizing some displacement of administrative data entry costs, (2) more business because of the agent's ability to use the system features as a means of differentiating in the marketplace, and (3) the costs associated with greater dependence on the focal carrier with a possible shift in relative bargaining power.

For the carrier—who has invested in the proprietary network—benefits are likely to arise from increased revenues and higher-quality insurance business. Specifically, we contend that the six characteristics of the system have different impacts on the efficiency dimension (i.e., increased number of policies and new policies) and the effectiveness dimension (i.e., increased revenues) of the focal carrier, as shown in Table 8.1. The rationale is as follows: Given the greater "ease of doing business" created by system characteristics such as on-line policy quotation, computerized policy issuance, endorsements, and claims handling, the expectation is that the agents will be motivated to bring relatively more business to this carrier than before (rollover effects) and that the interfaced agents will be able to compete more efficiently and effectively in their markets, resulting in greater growth in businesses relative to their counterparts, who may not have this source of differentiation. The efficiencies in information processing enabled by these system characteristics will ensure that these agencies can service a larger account base than before. The assumption here is that the different information-processing capabilities (such as timeliness, accuracy, efficiency, and expert-system support) are critical to differentiating the commercial insurance product because of its inherent complexity. Thus, the agent's capability—to quote, issue, and underwrite policies tailored to the customer's requirements and differentially from those competitors who are not electronically interfaced—is considerably enhanced. In this chapter, therefore, we examine the effects of electronic integration at the level of the focal carrier, by aggregating his or her performance across a set of interfaced agents.

There are interesting parallels with other settings of electronic integration. For example, the ASAP system reportedly brought more business to American Hospital Supply owing to the easy use of its system and its capability to assist in a variety of business transactions such as order status and tracking. Similarly, because American Airlines received a greater proportion of business based on the "display bias" on the

Table 8.1. Impact of system characteristics on efficiency and effectiveness

System characteristics	Impact on efficiency	Impact on effectiveness
On-line policy quotation	Primary	Secondary
Multiple option flexibility	Secondary	Primary
Risk evaluation	Secondary	Primary
Policy issuance	Primary	—
Endorsements	Primary	Secondary
Claims handling	Primary	Secondary

screen, the expectation is that the focal, interfaced carrier would always be considered as a potential underwriter of a particular business (as long as it offers the product line). Given these similarities, this chapter provides a formal empirical basis for assessing the effects of dedicated electronic integration as a source of competitive advantage.

Assessing the effects of electronic integration

Assessing organizational effectiveness is a thorny issue in organizational sciences (Cameron & Whetten, 1983), including information systems (IS) research, which uses several different constructs. There are two dominant approaches to assessing the expected benefits for the focal carrier, namely:

1. Cost-versus-benefit approach, requiring a direct economic assessment of all costs associated with this initiative compared with the actual realized benefits according to specific performance criteria.
2. Benchmarking approach, requiring an assessment of performance improvements for the interfaced agents against a matched sample of agents who are not interfaced.

The cost–benefit approach is complex for the following reasons: (1) The costs were incurred over a period of several years over successive iterations of the system, thereby making a direct cost-versus-benefit comparison somewhat difficult; (2) given the carrier's strategy of adopting a proprietary system to create sources of firm-specific competitive advantage, some of the benefits cannot be directly measured in terms of short-term improvements in performance; (3) the system is conceived by the firm as a strategy involving several business lines over many years, thus making any precise cost allocation for a given business nearly impossible; and finally, (4) a direct cost-versus-benefit assessment does not discount the possibility that the agents without the technology could have modified their product offering along other dimensions over which they have control, such as better service and lower prices, to compensate for the lack of system functions.

In contrast, the benchmarking approach has the following benefits: (1) It can control the temporal context of industry cycles if both sets of agents face the same external conditions; (2) it isolates the specific IT-based gains by using a matched sample; and (3) it avoids arbitrariness in cost allocation and focuses on effects relative to a benchmarked sample.

Using strategic advantage

The conceptualization and use of strategic advantage in general, and IT-based strategic advantage in particular, are a major challenge. In this chapter we view IT-based strategic advantage along two complementary dimensions: efficiency (in terms of the number of new business policies and the number of policies in force) and effectiveness (in terms of the total number of written premiums and the total number of commissions).[6] The indicators in parentheses for the two dimensions were decided on in discussions with the company executives, and they are consistent with the general literature on insurance operations and reflect a goal-centered view (Cameron & Whetten, 1983). With a benchmarking approach, the efficiency view cannot be based on the conventional cost-versus-benefit logic. Hence, we view efficiency gains as the ability of the interfaced agents to exploit the information-processing capabilities of the system (as shown in Table 8.1) to realize additional slack in order to pursue more business opportunities in the marketplace than otherwise possible. This is distinct from exploiting those system capabilities that have a more pronounced impact on raising the level of revenues or increases in market share for the carrier.[7]

Hypothesis

The general hypothesis for the study is stated in a null form as follows:

H0: *Electronic integration will not increase the performance of the interfaced agents as compared with that of the noninterfaced agents.*

There are two alternative hypotheses, termed here as the *strong-form* and the *weak-form* alternatives. The strong-form hypothesis, that both dimensions of strategic advantage would emerge as significant, is stated as follows:

$Halt_{strong}$: *Electronic integration will increase the performance (both efficiency and effectiveness) of the interfaced agents as compared with that of the noninterfaced agents.*

The rationale for expecting the strong-form hypothesis to hold is as follows: For the efficiency dimension, consistent with the theory developed in the previous section and elaborated in Table 8.1, we expect the system to lower the costs of coordination between the focal carrier and the agent and to enhance the information-processing capability (e.g., faster turnaround of policy quotes, policy issuance, and claims processing) of the dyad. Similarly, for the effectiveness dimension, we expect the agent to use these capabilities, such as seeking more comprehensive "what-if" insurance options, customizing the insurance products in order to differentiate the insurance services (Etgar, 1976), and obtaining a higher share of the market, higher revenues, and shifts in the carriers' market share (rollover effects).

The weak-form alternative hypothesis states that only the efficiency dimension would be significant in the two groups and is stated as follows:

$Halt_{weak}$: *Electronic integration will increase the efficiency of the interfaced agents' performance, as compared with that of the noninterfaced agents.*

This hypothesis takes a restrictive view of the effects of electronic integration and expects mainly efficiency effects; there are not likely to be effectiveness gains, for the following reasons: First, the policy is a substantial business expense for the insured, which will be decided according to various factors, including price. Thus, the agent may not be able to direct the business to the interfaced carrier because of electronic integration alone, without competitive prices. In a highly competitive market, therefore, improved service levels through faster quotes and customization may not outweigh higher prices. Second, because insurance products are bought annually and regularly, the speed of response by itself may not be a good reason for an insurance customer to switch to another company. Third, even if the agent has been able to use his or her information-processing capabilities to obtain more business, this effect may not be observable within a relatively short period of six months after the introduction of the system.

RESEARCH DESIGN

Designing the quasi experiment

As we mentioned, our research design contained a quasi-experimental study of the performance effects of electronic integration in the commercial lines of the P&C market, with a particular focus on the electronic integration by one major carrier. The essential characteristics of the design required the following five steps:

1. Identifying a random sample of agents that are electronically interfaced with the carrier (termed here the experimental group).
2. Identifying a "benchmarking set" of noninterfaced agents who are matched using three criteria—size (in terms of premium volume), location category (metro, small city, suburban versus rural), and geographic category (state or region). In other words, a corresponding agent in the same-sized category, in the same state, and in the same location category was selected (termed here the control group).[8]
3. Identifying the date of electronic integration. This was the later of the two dates on which the two most significant commercial lines of business were electronically interfaced, as identified by the carrier for each agent.
4. Selecting a "performance effects window" six months[9] before interfacing and six months after interfacing.
5. Analyzing the performance effects of integration.

This quasi-experimental design needs some explanation. As shown in Figure 8.1, the design we adopted is the untreated control group design with pretest and posttest (Cook & Campbell, 1979). This is different from the pure experimental design version in which the experimental subjects are assigned randomly from a com-

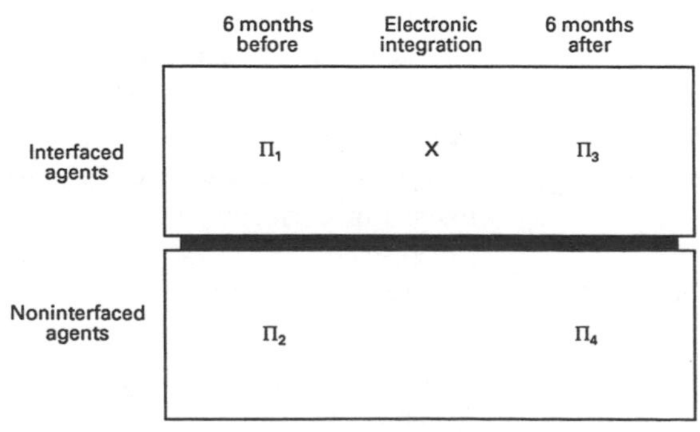

Figure 8.1. The design of the quasi-experimental study.

mon population. We could not influence the selection of agents to be interfaced; however, we were fortunate to obtain a reasonable, matched control group. This design controls for the major threats to validity and satisfies five of Terpstra's six criteria (1981).

The integration with the agents began in 1985 and is still continuing. The sample was restricted to those integrated in one calendar year in which a significant number of interfacings occurred, which was 1987. The sample size for the two groups are approximately 70 for each.[10]

Data

Data on the four performance indicators were obtained from the internal records of the insurance carrier. For each agent, the performance levels were obtained for six months before the integration and for six months after the integration (excluding the month of interfacing). Given that all the data were obtained from the internal records, there are no compelling reasons to expect different measurement systems for the two groups (one of the common threats to validity in this type of design). The measurement error—if any—is the same for the two groups of agents.

Table 8.2 presents the correlations among the four indicators of performance. To summarize, there is a significant correlation between the two indicators of effectiveness, namely, total written premium and commissions ($r = 0.92$, $p < .001$), implying a high level of convergence across indicators. However, the correlation coefficient between the two indicators of efficiency, namely, number of policies and number of new business policies, is low ($r = 0.18$, $p < .10$), implying poor convergence across them. Hence, it is inappropriate to treat these two indicators as reflecting the same construct of efficiency. Accordingly, we separated the two, with the number of policies reflecting the construct of operating efficiency and the number of new policies reflecting a new construct of performance, termed *new business*.

Performance attributable to integration was assessed as the slope (in terms of differences) rather than as absolute levels. The reason is that the inherent differences in the performance levels before integration was corrected by focusing on the changes in performance. Discussions with the managers of the carrier indicated that there were no other major confounding factors across the two groups. Thus, if the performance differences were found for the electronically interfaced group in comparison with the control group, they could be attributed with confidence to electronic integration, subject to assessing the equivalence of the groups at the time of selection.

The performance differences across the two groups were assessed using t-tests.[11] Because the data on percentage changes in performance appeared not to conform to

Table 8.2. A matrix of zero-order correlations among the indicators

Indicator	Total premium	Commissions	Number of policies	New business policies
Total premium	1.00			
Commissions	0.92	1.00		
Number of policies	0.06	0.11	1.00	
New business policies	0.42	0.45	0.18	1.00

Correlations greater than 0.19 are statistically significant at p-levels better than 0.05 ($n = 124$).

standard normal distributions, we rescaled the data on percentage changes in performance using a natural log transformation. The values for skewness and kurtosis—which far exceeded the normal range in the original scale—now exhibited values within acceptable range for normal distribution.[12] Our interpretations and conclusions, therefore, are based on the transformed data.

RESULTS AND DISCUSSIONS

Table 8.3 summarizes the results of the analysis, with three important patterns emerging: First, the interfaced group had consistently better performance levels before integration (along all the four criteria) than did the noninterfaced group (all the t-values are significant at $p < .05$). This was largely attributed to the fact that the carrier obviously selected its better-performing agents for electronic integration, and thus a true experimental design could not have been possible. This further rein-

Table 8.3. Performance effects of electronic integration

Performance indicator	Interfaced Mean	Interfaced SD	Noninterfaced Mean	Noninterfaced SD	t-test difference
Effectiveness	(n = 72)		(n = 72)		
1. Total written premium (before)[a]	171.5	271.1	97.6	131.7	2.08**
Total written premium (after)	215.6	459.1	103.0	125.6	2.01**
Change (%) in total premium[b]	30.7	74.8	47.7	199.5	–0.68
Change (%) in total premium (log transformed)[c]	4.70	0.63	4.57	0.85	1.02
	(n = 72)		(n = 72)		
2. Commissions (before)[d]	26.7	52.5	13.1	13 7	2.13**
Commissions (after)	32.4	83.6	13.7	14.1	1.87*
Change (%) in commissions	26.5	73.6	30.4	132.1	–0.22
Change (%) in commissions (log transformed)	4.70	0.61	4.55	0.75	1.03
Operating efficiency	(n = 78)		(n = 78)		
3. Number of policies in force (before)	326.4	625.9	139.4	103.8	2.60***
Number of policies in force (after)	358.0	744.1	140.9	96.1	2.56***
Change (%) in number of policies in force	11.7	32.6	8.0	34.2	0.69
Change (%) in number of policies in force (log transformed)	4.69	0.22	4.64	0.27	1.13
New business	(n = 68)		(n = 68)		
4. New business policies (before)	8.3	9.9	4 3	3.2	3.16***
New business policies (after)	9.6	15.8	3.3	2.3	3.25***
Change (%) in new business policies	19.1	80.2	7.6	155.6	0.54
Change (%) in new business policies (log transformed)	4.63	0.53	4.34	0.72	2.65***

*** $p \leq .01$ ** $p \leq .05$ * $p \leq .1$

[a]Figures in thousands of dollars per month, averaged over a six-month period.

[b]Change is calculated as (after-before) *100/before for each agent and mean values reported for entire sample.

[c]Due to high skewness in the distributions, log transformations provide more appropriate comparisons of percentage changes.

[d]Figures in thousands of dollars per month, averaged over a six-month period.

forces the need to assess percentage changes in the two groups rather than absolute differences.

Second, the interfaced group continued to report consistently better performance levels after integration (along all four criteria) than did the noninterfaced group (three t-values are statistically significant at $p < .05$ and one at $p < .10$). Thus, a posttest-only design would not have provided the required results to assess the impacts of electronic integration.

The third pattern, pertaining to the differences in performance, addresses the hypothesis. For operating efficiency, the differences in performance levels for the total number of policies in force was not statistically different from those of the noninterfaced (control) group ($t = 1.13$; ns).[13] For effectiveness, neither difference in performance levels for the two indicators was significant. For the total written premium, the difference was not statistically different from that of the noninterfaced (control) group ($t = 1.02$; ns), and for the total number of commissions, the difference was again not significant ($t = 1.03$; ns). However, for the construct of new business, the difference was statistically significant ($t = 2.65$; $p < .01$).[14] Thus, we found minimal support for the weak-form alternative, but we could not reject the null hypothesis in favor of the strong-form alternative hypothesis.

SYNTHESIS

This chapter tried to assess the collective performance of a group of agents who were electronically interfaced against a corresponding group who were not interfaced electronically with the focal carrier. The results support the performance increase for the new business dimension of strategic advantage, but overall performance differences for the effectiveness and operating efficiency dimensions are absent. Thus, according to the underlying hypothesis we were testing, the weak-form alternative was minimally supported, and the strong-form alternative did not receive empirical support. Indeed, it is interesting that the system capabilities seem to have had a pronounced impact on new business policies, further reinforcing the expectation that the technology plays an important part in enhancing the efficiency of processing new business leads. Collectively, our results raise interesting questions pertaining to the strategic benefits of electronic integration.

The strategic benefits of electronic integration seems to have reached the status of an implicitly accepted truism in the professional circles, albeit with scant theorizing and little empirical demonstration. The results of this chapter thus call for more systematic theorizing (i.e., reasons for expecting strategic benefits under different contingencies) as well as an empirical demonstration of those effects. Specifically, such theorizing should be based on the specific information attributes modified through electronic integration and the consequent impacts. Thus, we caution against overly optimistic and indiscriminate prescriptions on the role and benefits of electronic integration.

In reference to this research setting, although increases in new policies are an important criterion in the insurance business, it is equally important to focus on the quality of the insurance sold by these agents. If the agents merely use the available information-processing capabilities for enlarging their policy base, but not for attracting and selecting the business with the better risk profile, then electronic integration will serve only a short-term objective (increase in policies) with potentially dysfunctional longer-term consequences (poor risk policies). Thus, it is critical to assess effectiveness also, using criteria such as loss ratios, especially in those cases in which electronic integration also involved the decentralization of underwriting authority to the agents.

RESEARCH IMPLICATIONS

Two categories of research implications emerged from this study.

Theoretical models

It is clear that electronic integration activities across segments of the business processes of interdependent firms are increasing. But there is a glaring lack of theoretical models that explain the role and benefits of electronic integration, although there has been some preliminary theorizing using disciplinary perspectives such as transaction cost analysis (Malone et al., 1987), industrial organization economics (Rotemberg & Saloner, 1989), and game-theoretic models (Bakos, 1987). We believe that theoretical models should focus on the structure of electronic integration (including the conditions and characteristics of business relationships enabled by the specific functions of the interorganizational systems as well as their consequent benefits for the different participants) and also on the process of electronic integration (including the roles, responsibilities, and control of business activities even within the same interorganizational system of a single organization).

The structure of electronic integration could be rooted in disciplinary perspectives such as industrial organization economics, game theory, agency theory, and transaction costs, and it could deal with choices pertaining to firm boundaries, the shifts in business activities affected by integration, the selection of partners, risk sharing, and the different benefits for the participants. In contrast, the process of electronic integration could be grounded in perspectives such as organization theory, political science, and social networks, and it could deal with the changes in relative roles and responsibilities, the transformation of business processes, and shifts in the control of activities. Recognizing the interdependencies among these issues, a comprehensive research perspective on electronic integration should devote equal attention to both types of models.

Empirical demonstrations

The theoretical models should be accompanied by systematic empirical examinations using multiple research designs. This chapter adopted a quasi-experimental design to examine empirically a basic proposition derived from the current theoretical perspectives and provided minimal support for efficiency benefits from electronic integration. Future research should consider (1) approaches similar to that used in this chapter (such as experiments and quasi experiments) that allow for rigorous examination of the effects, (2) firm-level characteristics of partners interfaced with the focal carrier to delineate differential performance based on variations in the business practices that use electronic integration, and (3) possible longitudinal assessments to identify the sustainability of effects as well as the robustness of the results across business cycles.

The empirical studies should be sensitive to another temporal dimension in assessing the impacts, namely, the time lag for ascertaining the steady-state effects. This study adopted a six-month window (after integration) to assess the effects. Because electronic interfacing is not a case of implementing a marginal administrative technology, could there be a lag due to learning? In other words, is it possible that the performance improvements were not observed within a six-month window owing to a slow internal process transformation that may not have yet fully exploited the capabilities offered by integration? There is some earlier support for arguing that the effects of technology are not instantaneous and that organizations need to transform in order for maximal gains from IT (Rockart & Short, 1989). Although we did not explore the question of learning effects, it also is something to be considered in future designs. Ideally, it should reflect an assessment of not only the time lag but also the specific process actions taken by the implementing organization to use fully the potential offered by electronic integration. We now are in the process of designing a longitudinal extension with complementary primary data from the agents on their process changes to capture the potential learning effects.

CONCLUSION

This chapter focused on the effects of electronic integration (through a dedicated, proprietary system) of one major carrier with independent agents. We assessed the effects of electronic integration from the perspective of the focal carrier and in terms of the increases in performance reported by a sample of interfaced agents, as compared with those of a matched set of noninterfaced agents. The results provide minimal support for the weak-form hypothesis of efficiency effects, owing to electronic integration, but no support for the effectiveness hypotheses.

ACKNOWLEDGMENT

This is an expanded version of a paper presented at the Tenth Annual International Conference on Information Systems, Boston, December 4–6, 1989, and published in the *Proceedings*. We gratefully acknowledge the support provided by the Management in the 1990s Research Program, MIT, and thank the executives of the insurance company that wishes to remain anonymous. The associate editor, Benn R. Konsynski, and the five reviewers of Information Systems Research provided constructive suggestions for improving the manuscript.

NOTES

1. For an overview of the technical connectivity issues, see Wang and Madnick, 1988.
2. *Business Week*, 1980.

3. Standard & Poor's industry surveys.

4. d'Adolf, 1987, p. 27.

5. Ibid., p. 28.

6. It is important to recognize that the commission structure remained unchanged during the period of our study, thereby discounting the possibility that the agents could have bargained a higher commission structure for incurring the efforts associated with this interfacing operation.

7. We would liked to have considered the impact on two other effectiveness measures, namely, market share changes and loss ratios, but unfortunately data were not available.

8. According to Cook and Campbell (1979), there is a possibility of bias due to the non-equivalence in the control group because the experimental group could be chosen for their meritorious earlier performance. Suitable corrections may have to be made to mitigate the confounding effects if the expected results are observed in this quasi-experimental study.

9. Discussions with the managers and agents indicates that this is an appropriate window. There is an obvious trade-off: If the "window" is too small, the effects may not be observed, but if the window is too large, the impact of other confounding effects (e.g., internal changes such as process redesign and differential learning as well as external changes such as consolidation and mergers) cannot be ruled out in this design.

10. The sample sizes for the two groups are exactly the same given the design of quasi experiments, but because of missing data on some of the performance measures, the numbers vary across the four performance indicators, from 68 to 78.

11. One of the reviewers pointed out that in this quasi-experimental design, there is a strong possibility of a negative correlation between the interfaced and the noninterfaced groups, resulting in the standard t-test's being biased. In order to address this concern, we tested the hypotheses using a variant of the t-test, which is discussed separately.

12. For instance, the values of skewness before the transformation and after the transformation are as follows: premium, 5.51 (0.22); commissions, 2.62 (0.22); number of policies, 3.11 (0.88); and new business policies, 6.41 (0.55). This supports the use of the transformed values.

13. The variant of t-test that corrects for the bias in the correlated samples is Sandler's A-test (Bruning & Kintz, 1987, p. 16). The A-values support the results of the t-test. For instance, they were not significant in the three cases in which the t-tests were not significant. In the case in which the t-test was significant, the Sandler's A test had a value of 0.099 ($p < .001$).

14. As noted in note 8, we tested for the equivalence of the two groups in terms of the growth rates of new business policies before integration. The t-statistic was 0.80 (not significant), providing confidence in the results.

REFERENCES

Bagozzi, R. P. (1980). *Causal models in marketing*. New York: Wiley.

Bakos, Y. J. (1987). Interorganizational information systems: Strategic implications for competition and coordination. Ph.D. diss., Massachusetts Institute of Technology.

Barrett, S., & B. Konsynski (1982). Interorganization information-sharing systems. *MIS Quarterly* (Special Issue) 6:93–105.

Blois, K. J. (1972). Vertical quasi-integration. *Journal of Industrial Economics* 20:253–72.

Bruning, J. L., & B. L. Kintz (1987). *Computational handbook of statistics*. Glenview, IL: Scott-Foresman.

Business Week (1980). Information Processing. September 8.

——— (1985). Information power. October 14.

——— (1986). Information business. August 25, pp. 82–90.

Cameron, K., & D. Whetten (1983). Organizational effectiveness: One model or several? In K. S. Cameron & D. A. Whetten (Eds.), *Organizational effectiveness: A Comparison of multiple perspectives*, pp. 1–24. New York: Academic Press.

Cash, J. I., & B. Konsynski (1985). IS redraws competitive boundaries. *Harvard Business Review* 63:134–142.

Clemons, E. K., & M. Row (1988). McKesson Drug Company: A case study of Economost—A strategic information system. *Journal of Management Information Systems* 5 (Summer):37–50.

Cook, T. D., & D. T. Campbell (1979). *Quasi-experimentation: Design and analysis issues for field settings*. Boston: Houghton Mifflin.

Copeland, D. G., & J. L. McKenney (1988). Airline reservation systems: Lessons from history. *MIS Quarterly*, September, pp. 353–70.

d'Adolf, S. V. (1987). It's a smaller agency world. *Independent Agent*, August.

Etgar, M. (1976). Channel domination and countervailing power in distributive channels. *Journal of Marketing Research* 13:254–62.

Frost & Sullivan (1984). The market for insurance company automation. Report, New York, April.

Galbraith, J. R. (1973). *Organization design*. Reading, MA: Addison-Wesley.

Harvard Business School (1985). Case no. 9–186–005. American Hospital Supply Corporation (A) The ASAP system. Cambridge, MA: Harvard Business School.

——— (1988). Case no. 9–188–080. Baxter Healthcare Corporation: ASAP Express. Cambridge, MA: Harvard Business School.

Johnston, H. R., & M. R. Vitale (1988). Creating competitive advantage with interorganizational information systems. *MIS Quarterly*, June, pp. 153–65.

Keen, P. G.W. (1986). *Competing in time: Using telecommunications for competitive advantage*. Cambridge, MA: Ballinger.

Konsynski, B. R., & A. Warbelow (1989). Cooperating to compete: Modeling interorganizational interchange. Mimeo, Harvard Business School.

Malone, T. W., J. Yates, & R. I. Benjamin (1987). Electronic markets and electronic hierarchies. *Communications of the ACM*, June, pp. 484–97.

McFarlan, F. W. (1984). Information technology changes the way you compete. *Harvard Business Review* 62:98–103.

Porter, M. E. (1980). *Competitive strategy*. New York: Free Press.

Porter, M. E., & V. E. Millar (1985). How information gives you competitive advantage. *Harvard Business Review* 63:149–60.

Rockart, J. F., & J. Short (1989). IT in the 1990s: Management of interdependence. *Sloan Management Review*, Spring, pp. 1–12.

Rotemberg, J., & G. Saloner (1989). Information technology and strategic advantage. Unpublished manuscript, Management in the 1990s Research Program, Sloan School of Management, Massachusetts Institute of Technology.

Standard and Poor's Industry Surveys (1990). *Insurance and Investment*, July 12. New York: Standard and Poor's Corporation.

Stern, L., & R. El-Ansary (1977). *Marketing channels*. Englewood Cliffs, NJ: Prentice-Hall.

Terpstra, D. (1981). Relationship between methodological rigor and reported outcomes in organization development evaluation research. *Journal of Applied Psychology* 66:541–43.

Thompson, J. D. (1967). *Organizations in action*. New York: McGraw-Hill.

Venkatraman, N., & J. E. Short (1990). Strategies for electronic integration: From order-entry to value-added partnerships at Baxter. Center for Information Systems Research, Massachusetts Institute of Technology, working paper no. 210.

Wang, Y. R., & S. E. Madnick (1988). Connectivity among information systems. Center for

Information Systems Research, Massachusetts Institute of Technology, working paper no. 176.

Williamson, O. E. (1975). *Markets and hierarchies*. New York: Free Press.

Wiseman, C. (1985). *Strategy and computers: Information systems as competitive weapons*. Homewood, IL: Dow Jones-Irwin.

CHAPTER 9

Strategic Alignment: A Model for Organizational Transformation via Information Technology

JOHN C. HENDERSON AND N. VENKATRAMAN

As organizational transformation emerges as an important theme among both management scholars and practitioners, it is perhaps a truism that the organizations of the 1990s will be significantly different from those of the last few decades. Although several factors are thought to influence and propel the organizational transformation process, as the chapters in this volume demonstrate, a major force lies in the recent developments and capabilities offered by information technologies (IT) namely, computers and communication technologies. This is mainly due to the acceleration in recent years of the power and capabilities of these technologies, with a corresponding improvement in the cost–performance ratio (Scott Morton, 1991). Over the last few years, several different arguments have been offered to highlight the potential of IT to influence competitive characteristics (see, e.g., Keen, 1986; McFarlan, 1984; Parsons, 1983; Porter & Millar, 1985; Rockart & Scott Morton, 1984; Wiseman, 1985) as well as to enable and shape business transformations, but there is a glaring lack of systematic frameworks to conceptualize the logic, scope, and patterns of organizational transformation enabled by information technology (IT). To help address this deficiency, this chapter develops and presents a conceptual model with a set of propositions and management implications.

Our chapter is based on a pivotal premise, that the role of information technology in organizations has shifted beyond its traditional, "back-office support" role toward that as an integral part of organizations' strategy. Following King (1978), Rockart and Scott Morton (1984), and others, we differentiate among three major roles for IT: administration, operations, and competition. The administration role signifies the scope of IT as the automation of accounting and control functions, which is reasonably well understood in the traditional literature on management information systems (see, e.g., Ein-dor & Segev, 1978; Ives, Hamilton, & Davis, 1980). Indeed, the importance of technology for streamlining the activities of payroll, accounts payable, and accounts receivable is taken for granted and so will not be elaborated here. We state only that this role requires the deployment of an efficient IT platform (including hardware, software, and communication systems) for administration and control and is independent of the organization's strategic management. The operations role is an extension of the first role and is distinguished by the creation and deployment of a technology platform that creates the capability of automating the entire set of business processes, as opposed to only the administrative activities. This role requires the deployment of an IT infrastructure that responds to and supports the chosen business strategy (King, 1978).

According to Grant and King (1982), Hax and Majluf (1984), and Hofer and Schendel (1978), strategic management can be viewed as a hierarchy of three levels of strategies: corporate strategy (concerned with the portfolio of and interrelationships among businesses), business strategy (focusing on a strategy that maximizes the best firm-specific advantages to compete in the marketplace), and functional strategy (reflecting the efficient allocation of resources allocated to a particular function). In this hierarchy, IT strategy is at the functional level, to allocate efficiently its resources to support the chosen business strategy. Thus, in these two roles, IT strategy reflects a functional efficiency orientation (King, 1978).

In contrast, the competitive role represents a significant point of departure. Extending beyond an internal, efficiency focus, organizations can now deploy new IT applications that use the information and technological attributes to obtain different competitive advantages in the marketplace (Cash & Konsynski, 1985; Copeland & McKenney, 1988; McFarlan, 1984; Venkatraman & Kambil, 1991). Increased attention is now being paid to the potential role of IT to influence structural characteristics of markets (e.g., Clemons & Row, 1988) as well as to shape the basis of competition (see, e.g., Malone, Yates, & Benjamin, 1987; Rotemberg & Saloner, 1991). But it is becoming clear that a limited consideration of the first two roles for IT in modern corporation is not adequate, as it can have dysfunctional consequences.

More important, the role of IT has significant implications for organizational transformation. The reason is that the mere superimposition of powerful IT capabilities on the existing organizational structure and processes is unlikely to yield superior competitive benefits, a conclusion supported by one of the central messages from the MIT research project, Management in the 1990s (Scott Morton, 1991), that the successful organizations can be distinguished by their ability to use IT capabilities to transform their businesses (structures, processes, and roles) to obtain new and powerful sources of competitive advantages in the marketplace.

While we are on the threshold of the competitive role, we also note that the existing frameworks are limited in their ability to provide insights and guidance. The administrative role is supported by frameworks such as critical success factors (Davis, 1979; Rockart, 1979), and the second operational role is supported by frameworks like business system planning (IBM, 1981) or value chain analysis (Porter & Millar, 1985). However, we cannot obtain insights into using a competitive role, as it is sufficiently different from the other two, from these frameworks.

Nevertheless, several frameworks have been proposed to address the challenge of recognizing the competitive role of IT. These include Parsons's (1983) articulation of the different impacts of IT on the marketplace; McFarlan's (1984) adaptation of Porter's competitive strategy framework to a context characterized by the deployment of IT applications; Rockart and Scott Morton's (1984) adaptation of Leavitt's (1965) organization theory model; and other frameworks rooted in a set of convenient dimensions (e.g., Hammer & Mangurian, 1987; Wiseman, 1985). Based on a general assessment of these frameworks (for a systematic approach to organizing these frameworks, see Earl, 1988), we argue that they are useful for describing and highlighting the emerging interconnection between IT capabilities and organizational actions but that they fail in not articulating the logic and rationale for exploiting IT capabilities and the complexities of the organizational transformation required to use technological capabilities. More specifically, they fail to address simultaneously the business (external) and organizational (internal) requirements of transformation enabled and shaped by new and powerful IT capabilities. This chapter addresses this need by offering a model to link organizational transformation and the exploitation of IT capabilities in its competitive role.

PROPOSED STRATEGIC ALIGNMENT MODEL

Our proposed model is depicted in Figure 9.1. It is based on four domains of strategic choice: business strategy, organizational infrastructure and processes, IT strategy, and IT infrastructure and processes.

Business strategy

If we view organizational transformation from a "voluntaristic," as opposed to a "deterministic," perspective (Astley & Van de Ven, 1983; Miles & Snow, 1978), then business strategy is a central concept. The concept of strategy is overarching, however (Andrews, 1980; Hax & Majluf, 1984), and covers a broad terrain with

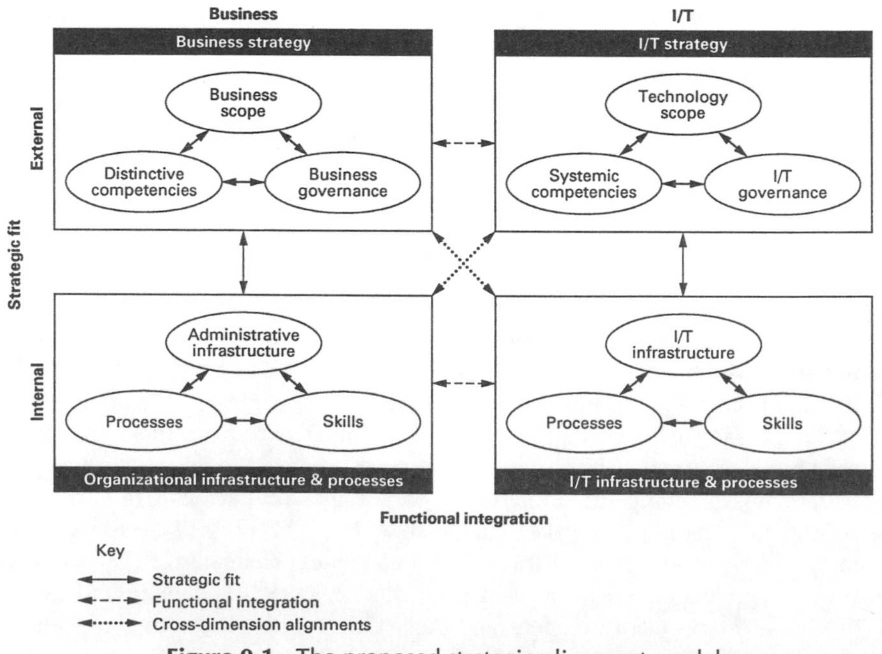

Figure 9.1. The proposed strategic alignment model.

multiple meanings, definitions, and conceptualizations (Venkatraman, 1989b; Venkatraman & Grant, 1986). Nevertheless, most discussions deal with three central questions: (1) business scope—choices pertaining to product–market offerings (Hofer & Schendel, 1978); (2) distinctive competencies—those attributes of strategy (e.g., pricing, quality, value-added service, superior distribution channels) that contribute to a distinctive, comparative advantage over other competitors (Porter, 1980; Snow & Hrebiniak, 1980); and (3) business governance—choices of structural mechanisms to organize the business operations (e.g., strategic alliances, joint ventures, licensing) that recognize the continuum between markets and hierarchy (Jarillo, 1988; Williamson, 1985).

Organizational infrastructure and processes

The relevance of including organizational infrastructure and processes need not be extensively justified in the context of organizational transformation. But given the challenge to specify a parsimonious set of dimensions, we consider the following: (1) administrative infrastructure, including organizational structure, roles, and reporting relationships (Galbraith, 1974); (2) processes, the articulation of work flows and the associated information flows for carrying out key activities (Thompson, 1967; Zuboff, 1988); and (3) skills, the capabilities of the individuals and the organization to execute those tasks that support a business strategy (Fombrun, Tichy, & Devanna, 1984; Scott Morton, 1991).

Information technology strategy

The concept of IT strategy is relatively new and hence open to differing definitions and assumptions. As we did with business strategy, we conceptualize IT strategy as having three dimensions: (1) an information technology scope, referring to the types and range of IT systems and capabilities (e.g., electronic imaging systems, local- and wide-area networks, expert systems, robotics) potentially available to the organization; (2) systemic competencies, focusing on those distinctive attributes of IT competencies (e.g., higher system reliability, interconnectivity, flexibility) that help create new business strategies or better support existing business strategies; and (3) IT governance, choosing structural mechanisms (e.g., joint ventures, long-term contracts, equity partnerships, joint R&D) to obtain the required IT capabilities, such as the deployment of proprietary versus common networks (Barrett & Konsynski, 1982; Rotemberg & Saloner, 1991; Venkatraman, 1991) as well as strategic choices pertaining to the development of partnerships to exploit IT capabilities and services (Henderson, 1990; Johnston & Lawrence, 1988; Johnston & Vitale, 1988; Koh & Venkatraman, 1989).

Information technology infrastructure and processes

Like an organization's infrastructure and processes, the IT infrastructure and processes have three characteristics: architecture, or those choices pertaining to applications, data, and technology configurations (see, e.g., Parker, Benson, & Trainor,

1988; Zachman, 1986); processes, which are concerned with the work processes central to the IT infrastructure's operations, including processes for systems development, maintenance, and monitoring and control systems (Bostom & Heines, 1977; Henderson, Rockart, & Sifonis, 1987; Janson & Smith, 1985; Markus & Robey, 1988; Martin, 1982a, 1982b; Raghunathan & King, 1988; Rockart & Short, 1989); and finally, skills, those choices pertaining to the knowledge and capabilities required to manage effectively the IT infrastructure within the organization (Martin, 1982a, 1982b; Mumford, 1981; Strassman, 1985).

DISTINCTIVE FEATURES OF THE MODEL

Before proceeding further, we shall describe the distinctive features of our proposed strategic alignment model.

Distinguishing IT strategy from IT infrastructure and processes

The first feature of our model is the distinction between IT strategy and IT infrastructure and processes, and it is critical, given the general lack of consensus on what constitutes IT strategy. So, we build from the literature on business strategy, which clearly separates the external alignment (positioning the business in the external product–market space) from the internal arrangement (designing the organizational structure, processes, and systems) (see, e.g., Snow & Miles, 1983). In the IT arena, given the historical predisposition to view it as a functional strategy, such a distinction had neither been made nor believed necessary. But as we consider the capability of using the emerging IT capabilities to redefine market structure characteristics as well as to reorient the attributes of competitive success, the limitation of a functional view becomes readily apparent.

Indeed, the hierarchical view of the interrelationship between business and functional strategies is increasingly being questioned, given the prevalent feeling that the subordination of functional strategies to business strategy may be too restrictive to exploit the potential sources of competitive advantage that lie at the functional level. Accordingly, functions are being considered as sources of competitive, firm-specific advantage. The principal emerging themes include "strategic marketing management," recognizing the exploitation of sources of marketing advantages at the business strategy level (e.g., Wind & Robertson, 1983); "strategic human resource management," highlighting the consideration of human resource profiles and capabilities in the formulation and implementation of strategies (e.g., Fombrun, Tichy, & Devanna, 1984); notions of "manufacturing as a competitive weapon," illustrating the potential sources of advantages in production and manufacturing and exploring the linkage between finance and corporate strategy (Myers, 1984). A common theme is the recognition of an external marketplace, in which these function-specific advantages can be used, and an internal organizational function, in which the functions should be managed efficiently.

In the strategic alignment model, we distinguish IT strategy from IT infrastructure and processes, using four different business examples to illustrate this difference. First, the decision by American Express to commit much of its resources to its electronic imaging technology platform in order to provide value-added services (by providing copies of receipts with its monthly statements) as a means of differentiating its travel-related services is related to its IT scope and systemic capabilities, which are conceptually different from its internal management of its data centers or its global telecommunications network. Both are necessary for an efficient use of IT capabilities, but one falls within the purview of external domain, and the other is concerned with internal operations. Second, Eastman Kodak's decision to outsource its data center operations to IBM is related to critical "make-versus-buy" choices (IT governance) in the IT marketplace and is logically distinguished from its decision of centralizing and decentralizing systems development activities across its different business units.

The third example is McGraw-Hill's custom-publishing strategy in its textbook business. It devised a strategy of offering custom textbooks as an alternative to standard textbooks, using its sophisticated electronic imaging technology infrastructure in a three-way joint venture with Eastman Kodak and R. R. Donnelley & Sons. This IT-based business capability reflects McGraw-Hill's IT strategy, which shapes and supports its business strategy, and is conceptually different from its internal IT infrastructure and operational systems. Finally, Baxter Healthcare—known for its analytical systems automated purchasing (ASAP)—announced the formation of a joint venture with IBM for providing software, hardware, and information-based services to the hospitals, thus reflecting its IT governance posture of collaboration, which is separate from its internal management of the information systems function. Together these four business examples show the importance of the three dimensions of IT strategy portrayed in Figure 9.1 and they argue for separating IT strategy from the internal management of information systems (IS).

Differentiating strategic alignment from bivariate fit and cross-domain alignment

Our proposed strategic alignment model is more than the articulation of the underlying axes, the four domains, and their constituent dimensions. It derives its value from the different relationships among the four domains. There are three dominant types of relationships in the model depicted in Figure 9.1, termed *bivariate fit*, *cross-domain alignment*, and *strategic alignment*.

Bivariate fit

The simplest relationship is a bivariate one linking two domains, either horizontally or vertically. The bivariate relationship between the organization's business strategy and its infrastructure and processes refers to the classic strategy-structure fit that has been a dominant theme in organizational strategy research (Chandler, 1962; Rumelt, 1974; for an overview, see Venkatraman & Camillus, 1984). Correspondingly, we specify a bivariate relationship between the IT strategy and IT infrastructure and processes in this model, highlighting the need to connect an organization's external positioning in the IT marketplace with its approach to managing IS in its organizational context. These two relationships represent the classic strategy formulation–

implementation perspectives for the two strategies considered here: business strategy and IT strategy.

In contrast, the other two bivariate relationships link the domains horizontally. The links between business strategy and IT strategy (i.e., articulating the required IT scope and developing systemic competencies and IT governance mechanisms) reflect the ability to use IT strategy to shape and support business strategy. This is relevant to the competitive role of the IT function discussed earlier. In addition, the link between organizational infrastructure and processes and IT infrastructure and processes points up the need to ensure internal coherence between the organization's requirements and expectations, on the one hand, and the delivery capability within the IS function, on the other hand, which is consistent with the notion of viewing IS as a "business within a business" (Cash et al., 1988).

Benefits and limitations of bivariate fit

A major benefit of the bivariate fit perspective is its simplification of the relevant domain, invoking ceteris paribus conditions. If, for instance, the organizational and IS infrastructures can be reconfigured easily, then a bivariate interconnection between business and IT strategies will suffice. However, most instances of organizational transformation require adaptation across multiple domains, thus limiting the value of bivariate perspectives. An obvious approach is to consider multiple bivariate relationships, which can lead to an error of "logical typing" or "reductionism" (Bateson, 1979; Venkatraman, 1989a).

Indeed, a major controversy in the literature on organizations is distinguishing between bivariate relationships according to a few variables and multivariate, holistic relationships among those variables representing an organizational system (McKelvey, 1975; Miller & Friesen, 1984; see also Alexander, 1968). The main dispute is that if one were to decompose the system into a set of bivariate relationships, there might be internal logical inconsistencies (or mutually conflicting directions) among multiple pairwise contingencies. As Child remarked, "What happens when a configuration of different contingencies are found, each having distinctive implications for organizational design?" (1975, p. 175). Extending this argument to our context of strategic IT management, the limitation is considering external perspectives only (through business and IT strategies without any regard for the internal considerations) or internal perspectives only (by integrating the IS functions and activities into the overall organizational infrastructure). Alternatively, the bivariate fit can separate business and IT perspectives, which have been contended to be dysfunctional (see, e.g., King, 1978; McLean & Soden, 1977; Pyburn, 1983). This calls for recognizing mutivariate relationships or, more precisely, cross-domain relationships.

Cross-domain alignment

The first type of multidomain relationship has three domains, linked sequentially. This can be conceptualized as a triangle overlaid on the model shown in Figure 9.1. Although eight combinations of cross-domain alignments are possible, we argue that four are important and managerially relevant to our discussion here. These are summarized in Figure 9.2 and are labeled strategy implementation, technology exploitation, technology leverage, and technology implementation.

	Label	Cross-domain perspective	Common domain anchor	IT planning method example
1	Technology exploitation		Technology strategy	Opportunity identification (Sharpe, 1989) Value chain analysis (Cash, 1985)
2	Technology leverage		Business strategy	G/CUE (Gartner Group, 1989)
3	Strategy implementation		Business strategy	CSF (Rockart, 1979) Enterprise modeling (Martin, 1982 a, b)
4	Technology implementation		Technology strategy	Service-level contracting (Leitheiser & Wetherbe, 1986)

* Domain anchor

Figure 9.2. Four dominant perspectives of IT planning.

As it is depicted in Figure 9.2, strategy implementation is a cross-domain perspective that assesses the implications of implementing the chosen business strategy through an appropriate organizational infrastructure and management processes as well as the design and development of the required IT infrastructure and processes. This is perhaps the most common and widely understood cross-domain perspective, as it corresponds to the classic hierarchical view of strategic management (see, e.g., the three-level hierarchy in Hax & Majluf, 1984). Given its widespread acceptance, it is not surprising that several different analytical methodologies are available to carry out this perspective, in which the more popular approaches include critical success factors (Rockart, 1979), business systems planning (IBM, 1981), and enterprise modeling (Martin, 1982b).

As shown in Figure 9.2, technology exploitation reflects the ability of IT strategy to influence business strategy. Within the "competitive role" for IT, this perspective is concerned with exploiting emerging IT capabilities to influence new products and services (i.e., business scope), influence the key attributes of strategy (distinctive competencies) and to develop new forms of relationships (i.e., business governance). Unlike the previous perspective, which considers business strategy as given (or a constraint for organizational transformation), this perspective allows the modification of business strategy by means of emerging IT capabilities. Beginning with the three dimensions of IT strategy, this perspective seeks to identify the best strategic options for business strategy and the corresponding decisions pertaining to organizational infrastructure and processes.

Examples of the technology exploitation perspective include the exploitation by Baxter Healthcare (previously, American Hospital Supply Corporation) through its proprietary ASAP electronic order-entry system to deliver superior, value-added service to its hospital customers and the consequent implications for redesigning the internal organizational processes (see, e.g., Venkatraman & Short, 1990); the attempt by Federal Express to create a new standard for overnight delivery though its COSMOS/PULSAR system and the corresponding implications for redesigning its internal processes; and the ability of American Express, IDS division, to use its IT infrastructure to develop capabilities for electronically filing income tax returns and to use this information to tailor its financial products to individual needs (Venkatraman & Kambil, 1991).

Although much of the current excitement about IT in its competitive role is in the technology exploitation perspective, the discussion has been at the level of the bivariate fit between IT strategy and business strategy (see, e.g., McFarlan, 1984; Wiseman, 1985). We believe that any consideration of the attractiveness of the emerging IT capabilities without corresponding attention to the redesign of internal operations would be seriously limited, with negative consequences for organizational transformation. The reason is that performance is clearly a function of both the formulation and the implementation of strategies, and too little attention to any one at the expense of the other can obscure the best possible mode for organizational transformation.

As seen in Figure 9.2, technology leverage is a cross-domain perspective that assesses the implications of implementing the chosen business strategy through the appropriate IT strategy and the articulation of the required IS functional infrastructure and systemic processes. The underlying rationale is that business strategy is best executed by using the emerging technological capabilities rather than by the designing an efficient internal organization. For example, USAA, a leading American insurance company, decided that the best strategic option was to institute a superior document-handling system based on state-of-the-art electronic imaging technology. This was accomplished through a joint development venture with a key vendor, necessitating fundamental changes to the internal IT infrastructure, its data, applications, and configurations.

Another example is American Express Travel Related Services, whose business strategy was anchored on two technology-based competencies: the quick approval of purchases and the provision of copies of receipts to the cardholders. American Express's approval of a charge card (i.e., without any preset spending limit) typically has a longer lead time than does a corresponding transaction for its competitors' credit cards (with a preset spending limit). It was imperative that American Express at least match the response time of its leading competitors, for if it failed, the cardholder might switch to an alternative, faster-transacting card. This business strategy required a systemic competence involving expert systems (authorizer's assistant) and corresponding changes in the internal IS organization for developing, maintaining, and controlling the systems. The second component, termed *ECCB* (enhanced country club billing) refers to American Express's provision of copies of all charge slips with the customer's monthly statement. Although cardholders expressed satisfaction with this service, the cost of traditionally maintaining and distributing the slips was becoming prohibitive. However, an optical scanning, storage, and laser-printing system allowed a more efficient delivery of the same level of service.

According to the proposed strategic alignment model, these examples highlight the impact of business strategy (distinctive competence) on IT strategy (IT governance and systemic competencies, respectively) and the corresponding implications for IT infrastructure and processes (e.g., IS architectures). Again, the limitations of a bivariate fit perspective are apparent. Either a formulation view (e.g., the impact of business scope on IT scope or systemic competencies) or an implementation view (i.e., the implications of systemic competencies or new IT governance for internal IS operations). Some new analytical perspectives are beginning to reflect technology leverage. For example, Gartner's G/CUE (Gartner Group, 1989) examined an organization's business strategy and identified implications for IT strategy, with respect to key trends in the IT markets via technology scanning, and also the implications for moving from the current IT infrastructure to the desired state.

In Figure 9.1, technology implementation is concerned with the strategic fit between the external articulation of IT strategy and the internal implementation of the IT infrastructure and processes with their corresponding impact on the overall organizational infrastructure and processes. In this perspective, the role of business strategy is minimal and indirect and is best viewed as providing the necessary administrative support for the internal organization. This perspective is often viewed as a necessary (but not sufficient) to ensure the effective use of IT resources and to be responsive to the growing and fast-changing demands of the end user population. Analytical methodologies even partially reflecting this perspective requires a systematic analysis of the IT markets as well as possible service-contracting approaches. Examples of analytical methods include end user need surveying (Alloway & Quillard, 1983), service-level contracting (Leitheiser & Wetherbe, 1986), and architectural planning (Zachman, 1986).

To summarize our discussion of four cross-domain perspectives, we drew up the following propositions:

P1: *The effectiveness of strategic IT management will be significantly greater for any cross-domain perspective than for any bivariate fit relationships.*

P2: *On average, the four cross-domain perspectives for strategic IT management will be equally effective.*

The rationale for the first proposition is derived from the preceding discussion of the limitations of bivariate relationships in a complex organizational system and the need to integrate across external and internal domains as well as across business and technology domains. The rationale for the second proposition is based on the principle of equifinality, that is, several equally effective approaches to exploiting technology for organizational transformation, in which the universal superiority of one approach over another cannot be proved ahead of time.

Further, according to Figures 9.1 and 9.2, it is clear that these four perspectives reflect a top-down orientation, in which either a business strategy or an IT strategy direct the subsequent internal (organizational) considerations. As recognized earlier, it is entirely conceivable to consider corresponding bottom-up orientations. For example, the organization infrastructure could serve as a domain anchor for a process that considers the impact of organizational capabilities on business strategy and the subsequent implications for IT strategy. Such perspectives would signal recognition of the current organizational infrastructure or IT infrastructure as the relevant starting points for deriving implications for the external, strategic choices. Thus, although the top-down orientations reflect both the preference of strategic managers and the rational, analytic approach adopted here, it is important to recognize that the proposed strategic alignment model does accommodate the possible existence of internally consistent, bottom-up analysis of cross-domain relationships. In the interest of space and given the relatively limited attention so far to these perspectives, however, we shall not discuss them here.

Strategic alignment

The final relationship in our proposed model is strategic alignment. This means simultaneous or concurrent attention to all four domains, and it can be conceptualized in its weak and strong forms. In its weak form, it can be thought of as a single-loop transformation process across the four domains, and in its strong form, it can be viewed as a double-loop transformation process. The notion of a loop requires specifying a starting point and a particular direction of transformation; hence the distinction between a single-loop and a double-loop process (see Argyris, 1977, 1982). The former accommodates only one single direction of transformation, whereas the latter recognizes the centrality of both possible directions. We shall elaborate the logic underlying strategic alignment by invoking two theoretical concepts: completeness and validity.

Completeness is a central concept of strategic alignment because it is clear that not considering any one of the four domains will leave unrecognized one domain and its consequent relationships. As we stated, each of the four dominant cross-domain perspectives fails to recognize (i.e., take as given and fixed) one of the four domains. For instance, technology exploitation (Figure 9.2) does not recognize critical issues pertaining to IT infrastructure, and so it is incomplete. Given the critical interplay among the four domains, we argue for the importance of completeness or, more formally, a single-loop transformational process.

Validity refers to the degree of attention to overcoming the possibility of bias by means of unrecognized or hidden frames of reference. A major concern, raised by Churchman (1971), Mason and Mitroff (1981), and Weick (1979) in the context of a decision-making process, refers to the possible threat to the validity of decisions introduced by the existence of a domain anchor or a fixed reference frame that remains unchallenged (for a discussion in the IS context, see Henderson & Sifonis, 1988). Following Mason and Mitroff (1981) and Argyris (1977, 1982), we call for an analytical method that challenges the assumption of a given domain anchor. More formally, the analytical method should incorporate a double-loop transformational process.

Figure 9.3 schematically represents the different types of relationships just discussed, excluding bivariate fit—which was argued to be myopic and dysfunctional. Specifically, there are two types of cross-domain perspectives: unidirectional and focused. The distinction is that the latter recognizes the potential sources of invalidity (or biases) and corrects the pairing of the cross-domain perspectives. Extending beyond cross-domain perspectives, there are two forms of strategic alignment, the weak form, represented as a single loop, and the strong form, specified as a double-loop process. Thus, we developed the following proposition:

P3: *The effectiveness of strategic IT management, under ceteris paribus conditions, is significantly greater for a complete process than for any type of cross-domain alignments.*

We believe that much of the failure to translate the available opportunities into using IT for superior organizational performance lies in the incompleteness of the process just described. In other words, though adequate attention may be given to the four domains, it may not still represent a complete process, as depicted in Figure 9.3. To illustrate: In our field research, we encountered a strategic IT management process that paid attention to all the four domains represented in our strategic align-

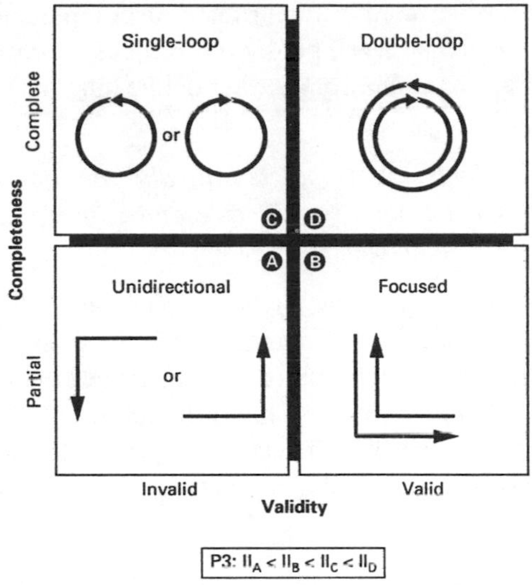

Figure 9.3. Strategic IT management effectiveness.

ment model (Figure 9.1) but still was considered ineffective by the managers. Detailed interviews and further analysis of their process indicated that the first step reflected technology exploitation, and the second, strategy implementation. Both analytical steps were supported by well-known analytical methodologies. However, as shown in Figure 9.2, such a process does not address the relationship between IT strategy and IT infrastructure and processes. That is, although we twice assessed the relationship between business strategy and organizational infrastructure and processes, we did not evaluate the feasibility of translating IT strategy into appropriate systems and processes in the IS function. Indeed, migration problems across different generations of systems emerged as a major contributor to the project's failure. More formally, we termed this as an incomplete process, and hence it is weaker than a process that considers consistent, cross-domain perspectives.

Other propositions derived from Figure 9.3 are as follows:

P4: *On average, the unidirectional perspective is the least effective process for strategic IT management.*

The rationale for this proposition is that this perspective reflects neither completeness nor validity. In other words, it carries the risks associated with incompleteness as well as the failure to challenge the domain anchor. In the absence of both critical requirements of strategic IT management, it is straightforward to argue that this proposition is the least effective one.

P5: *On average, single-loop (i.e., complete but invalid) and focused (incomplete but valid) processes will be equally effective and superior to a unidirectional process for strategic IT management.*

Our rationale for this proposition rests on the importance of completeness and validity in addressing strategic IT issues. Although both forms of strategic IT processes are currently used (Boynton & Zmud, 1987; Rockart, 1979), there is no earlier theory regarding the relative importance of completeness versus validity. Thus, although we contend that the single-loop and focused processes are superior to a unidirectional process, we refrain from further delineating the relative effectiveness of these two approaches.

P6: *On average, double-loop (i.e., complete but valid) and focused (incomplete but valid) processes will be equally effective and superior to a unidirectional process for strategic IT management.*

Essentially, this proposition means that a complete and valid process will be the most effective approach to strategic IT management. Such an approach not only addresses all the four relevant domains, but it also challenges the assumptions inherent in the domain anchors. However, it has a major limitation in terms of high levels of resources, in both time and costs, which need to be recognized and managed depending on the specific contingencies that the organization faces.

STRATEGIC ALIGNMENT AS AN ELEMENT OF ORGANIZATIONAL TRANSFORMATION

This chapter created a model of organizational transformation that addresses the requirements of using the emerging developments in information technologies. This model is based on the need to achieve alignment across internal and external domains as well as functional integration across business and IT areas. We argued for the value of the model with propositions for research and practice. Although the chapter provided some support for the conceptual validity of the model, the empirical validity leading to the confirmation or falsification of the propositions requires systematic field research. We are in the midst of establishing the key constructs and collecting multiperiod data to test the propositions offered here.

Over two decades ago, Thompson noted, "Survival rests on the co-alignment of technology and task environment with a viable domain, and of organizational design and structure appropriate to that domain" (1967; p. 147). These observations are equally valid today and apply well to the present context of exploiting IT capabilities for organization design. Our position is that strategic alignment—especially between business and IT strategies across external and internal domains—is an important element of the larger organizational transformation process. Specifically, we described the usefulness of the model as a descriptive model, a prescriptive model, and a dynamic model.

Strategic alignment as a descriptive model

On the first level, the proposed strategic alignment model can be viewed as a descriptive model of organizational transformation. Specifically, it can be used to identify the key factors to be considered (i.e., the four domains and the 12 constituent dimensions shown in Figure 9.1) as well as an alternative direction of transformation (i.e., the different cross-domain perspectives shown in Figure 9.2). The power of the model lies in the parsimonious delineation of the dimensions and the conceptual separation of IT strategy from its infrastructure and processes. From a research point of view, this model can be used to describe and categorize examples of exploiting IT as a lever for business transformation. From a management decision-making point of view, this model identifies the different alternatives to using IT for business transformations. We are aware of several organizations adopting this as the central model in their strategic management process, in which IT plays a critical role in business transformation.

Strategic alignment as a prescriptive model

At a second level, the proposed model can be viewed as prescribing certain alternatives and approaches. Prescriptive frameworks derive their logic and rationale from underlying theoretical arguments and/or empirical results. Although there is preliminary theoretical support for some of the cross-domain perspectives, we will not yet see it as a prescriptive model until we test these propositions with empirical data. The reason is that we agree with Mintzberg, who observed, "There has been a tendency to prescribe prematurely in management policy—to tell how it should be done without studying how it is done and why. . . . Prescriptions become useful only when it is grounded in sophisticated description" (1977, pp 91–92). We believe that the strategic management of IT is in a similar position—with excessive prescription based on isolated cases, which is counterproductive to both theory and practice. We are now in the midst of accumulating empirical observations using this conceptual model to understand the patterns of realizing value from IT investments, with the ultimate aim of transforming this into a prescriptive model.

Strategic alignment as a dynamic model

Implicit in our discussion is that strategic alignment is a dynamic concept, best viewed as "shooting at a moving target." One of the managers we interviewed in connection with this research project stated that this model is best viewed as a "journey and not as an event." This is analogous to Miles and Snow's argument that the organizational adaptive cycle—which provides a means of conceptualizing the major elements of adaptation and of visualizing the relationships among them—is a central concept of strategic management (1978, p.27). It is also consistent with Thompson, who pointed out that alignment is

> not a simple combination of static components. Each of the elements involved in the [co-] *alignment has its own dynamics* [and] *behaves at its own rate,* governed by the forces external to the organization.
>
> . . . If the elements necessary to the co-alignment are in part influenced by powerful forces in the organization's environment, then organization survival requires adaptive as well as directive action in those areas where the organization maintains discretion. . . . As environments change, the administrative process must deal not just with which domain, but how and how fast to change the design, structure, or technology of the organization. (emphasis in original; 1967, pp. 147–48)

Accordingly, we view the strategic alignment model as a dynamic model of strategic IT management requiring the organization to identify the areas in which it should maintain discretion (in both the business and IT domains) and the approaches to transforming the internal organization structures and processes. We recognize, however, that a dynamic perspective does not imply the need to manipulate and adapt all dimensions at all times, nor is it predictable at specific trigger points (Child, 1975; Miles & Snow, 1978; Thompson, 1967). Indeed, the key strategic IT management challenge lies in identifying those strategic dimensions that must be modified under different contingencies for enhancing organizational performance. It is our hope that our detailed research project will offer some normative guidelines for recognizing and responding to critical contingencies.

Thus, in closing: Our view of business transformation recognizes the organization as the nexus of key streams of actions with complex variables. These streams are dynamic in scope, moving in different directions and pace. We believe that the challenge of organizational transformation is best conceptualized as a dynamic strategic alignment process with particular considerations of those strategic components that matter at that point in time, and our argument is that IT occupies that role at present and will in the foreseeable future. We hope that this chapter has provided a parsimonious model to conceptualize and manage one area of complexity inherent in managing today's organizations.

ACKNOWLEDGMENT

The authors would like to acknowledge the contributions to this research made by Christine Bullen, Gary Getson, Charles Gold, Jim Sharpe, Cesar Toscano, and other persons who served on our academic and industry advisory panels. This research was funded by the IBM Corporation.

A version of this chapter was prepared for inclusion in Thomas Kochan and Michael Useem, eds., *Transforming Organizations* (New York: Oxford University Press, 1991). Our thanks to Tom Kochan and Michael Useem for their constructive comments on our previous drafts.

REFERENCES

Alexander, C. (1968). *Notes on the synthesis of form*. Cambridge, MA: Harvard University Press.

Alloway, R. M., & J. A. Quillard (1983). User managers' systems needs. *MIS Quarterly* 7:27–41.

Andrews, K. R. (1980). *The concept of corporate strategy*, rev. ed., Homewood, IL: Irwin.

Argyris, C. (1977). Double loop learning in organizations. *Harvard Business Review* 55:115–125.

——— (1982). Organizational learning and management information systems. *Data Base* 13 (Winter-Spring):3–11.

Astley, W. G., & A. Van de Ven (1983). Central perspectives in organization theory. *Administrative Science Quarterly* 28:245–73.

Barrett, S., & B. Konsynski (1982). Inter-organization information sharing systems. *MIS Quarterly* (Special Issue), December, pp. 93–105.

Bateson, G. (1979). *Mind and nature*. New York: Dutton.

Benjamin, R. I., J. F. Rockart, M. S. Scott Morton, & J. Wyman (1984). Information technology: A strategic opportunity. *Sloan Management Review* 25:3–10.

Bostom, R. P., & J. S. Heines (1977). MIS problems and failures: A socio-technical perspective, Parts I and II. *MIS Quarterly* 1:17–32; and 1:11–28.

Boynton, A. C., & R. W. Zmud (1987). Information technology planning in the 1990s: Directions for research and practice. *MIS Quarterly* 11:61.

Cash, J. I., & B. Konsynski (1985). IS redraws competitive boundaries. *Harvard Business Review* 63:134–142.

Cash, J. I., H. W. McFarlan, J. I. Mckenney, & M. R. Vitale (1988). *Corporate information systems management: Text and cases.* Homewood, IL: Irwin.

Chandler, A. D. (1962). *Strategy and structure: Chapters in the history of American enterprise.* Cambridge, MA: MIT Press.

Child, J. (1975). Managerial and organization factors associated with company performance—Part II, a contingency analysis. *Journal of Management Studies* 12:12–27.

Churchman, C. W. (1971). *The design of inquiring systems: Basic concepts of systems and organization.* New York: Basic Books.

Clemons, E. K., & M. Row (1988). McKesson Drug Company: A case study of Economost—A strategic information system. *Journal of Management Information Systems* 5:37–50.

Copeland, D. G., & J. L. McKenney (1988). Airline reservations systems: Lessons from history. *MIS Quarterly* 12:353–70.

Daft, R. L., & K. E. Weick (1984). Toward model organizations as interpretive systems. *Academy of Management Review* 9:284–95.

Davis, G. B. (1979). Comments on the critical success factors method for obtaining management information requirements. *MIS Quarterly* 3:57–58.

——— (1982). Strategies for information requirements determination. *IBM Systems Journal* 21:4–30.

Dickson, G. W., R. L. Leitheiser, J. C. Wetherbe, & M. Niechis (1984). Key information systems issues for the 1980's. *MIS Quarterly* 8:135–59.

Earl, M. (Ed.) (1988). *Information management: The strategic dimension.* Oxford: Clarendon Press.

Ein-dor, P., & E. Segev(1978). Strategic planning for management information systems. *Management Science* 24:1631–1641.

Fombrun, C. J., N. M. Tichy, & M. A. DeVanna (1984). *Strategic human resource management.* New York: Wiley.

Galbraith, J. R. (1974). Organization design: An information processing perspective. *Interfaces* 4:28–36.

——— (1977). *Organization design.* Reading, MA: Addison-Wesley

Gartner Group (1989). *G/customer user evaluation.* Stamford, CT: Gartner Group.

Grant, J. H., & W. R. King (1982). *The logic of strategic planning.* Boston: Little, Brown.

Hammer, M., & G. E. Mangurian (1987). The changing value of communications technology. *Sloan Management Review* 28:65–71.

Hax, A. C., & N. S. Majluf (1984). *Strategic management: An integrative perspective.* Englewood Cliffs, NJ: Prentice-Hall.

Henderson, J. C. (1990). Plugging into strategic partnerships: The critical IS connection. *Sloan Management Review* 31:7–18.

Henderson, J. C., J. F. Rockart, & J. G. Sifonis (1987). Integrating management support systems into strategic information systems planning. *Journal of Management Information Systems* 4:5–23.

Henderson, J. C., & J. G. Sifonis (1988). The value of strategic IS planning: Understanding consistency, validity, and IS markets. *MIS Quarterly* 12:187–200.

Hofer, C. W., & D. E. Schendel (1978). *Strategy formulation: Analytical concepts*. St. Paul, MN: West Publishing.

IBM (1981). Information systems planning guide. Business systems planning report no. GE20–0527–2, 3rd ed., July.

Ives, B., S. Hamilton, & G. B. Davis (1980). A framework for research in computer Based management information systems. *Management Science* 26:910–34.

Ives, B., & G. P. Learmonth (1984). The information system as a competitive weapon. *Communications of the ACM* 27:1193–1201.

Janson, M. A., & L. D. Smith (1985). Prototyping for systems development: A critical appraisal. *MIS Quarterly* 9:305–16.

Jarillo, J. C. (1988). On strategic networks. *Strategic Management Journal* 9:31–42.

Johnston, H. R., & P. Lawrence (1988). Beyond vertical integration—The rise of value-adding partnerships. *Harvard Business Review* 66 (July-August):94–101.

Johnston, H. R., & M. R. Vitale (1988). Creating competitive advantage with interorganizational information systems. *MIS Quarterly* 12:153–65.

Keen, P. G. W. (1986). *Competing in time: Using telecommunications for competitive advantage*. Cambridge, MA: Ballinger.

King, W. R. (1978). Strategic planning for management informations systems. *MIS Quarterly* 2:27–37.

Kling, R. (1980). Social analyses of computing: Theoretical perspectives in recent empirical research. *Computing Surveys* 12:61–110.

Koh, J., & N. Venkatraman (1989). Joint ventures in the information technology sector: An assessment of strategies and effectiveness. Sloan School of Management working paper no. 1908–89, December.

Leavitt, H. J. (1965). Applied organizational change in industry. In *Handbook of organizations*, chap. 27. Chicago: Rand McNally.

Leitheiser, R. L., & J. C. Wetherbe (1986). Service support levels: An organized approach to end-user computing. *MIS Quarterly* 10:337–49.

Malone, T. W., J. Yates, & R. I. Benjamin (1987). Electronic markets and electronic hierarchies. *Communications of the ACM* June, pp. 484–97.

Markus, M. L., & D. Robey (1988). Information technology and organization change: Causal structure in theory and research. *Management Science* 34:583–98.

Martin, J. (1982a). *Application development without programmers*. Englewood Cliffs, NJ: Prentice-Hall.

——— (1982b). *Strategic data planning methodologies*. Englewood Cliffs, NJ: Prentice-Hall.

Mason, R. O., & I. I. Mitroff (1973). A program for research on management information systems. *Management Science* 19:475–87.

——— (1981). *Challenging strategic planning assumptions: Theory, cases, and techniques*. New York: Wiley.

McFarlan, F. W. (1984). Information technology changes the way you compete. *Harvard Business Review* 62:98–103.

McFarlan, F. W., & J. L. McKenney (1983). *Corporate information systems management: The issues facing senior executives*. Homewood, IL: Irwin.

McKelvey, B. (1975). Guidelines for the empirical classification of organizations. *Administrative Science Quarterly* 21:571–97.

McKinsey & Company, Inc. (1968). Unlocking the computer's profit potential. *McKinsey Quarterly* Fall, pp. 17–31.

McLean, E. R., & J. V. Soden (1977). *Strategic planning for MIS*. New York: Wiley.

Miles, R. E., & C. C. Snow (1978). *Organizational strategy, structure and process.* New York: McGraw Hill.

Miller, D. (1981). Toward a new contingency approach: The search for organizational gestalts. *Journal of Management Studies* 18:1–26.

Miller, D., & P. H. Friesen (1984). *Organizations: A quantum view.* Englewood Cliffs, NJ: Prentice-Hall.

Mintzberg, H. (1977). Policy as a field of management theory. *Academy of Management Review* 2:88–103.

Mumford, E. (1981). Participative systems design: Structure and method. *Systems, Objectives, Solutions* 1:5–19.

Myers, S. C. (1984). Finance theory and financial strategy. *Interfaces* 14:126–37.

Myers, W. (1985). MCC: Planning the revolution in software. *IEEE Software* 2:68–73.

Parker, M. M., & R. J. Benson, with H. E. Trainor (1988). *Information economics: Linking business performance to information technology.* Englewood Cliffs, NJ: Prentice-Hall.

Parsons, G. L. (1983). Information technology: A new competitive weapon. *Sloan Management Review* 24:3–14.

Porter, M. E. (1980). *Competitive strategy: Techniques for analyzing industries and competitors.* New York: Free Press.

Porter, M. E., & Millar, V. E. (1985). How information technology gives you competitive advantage. *Harvard Business Review* July-August, pp. 149–60.

Pyburn, P. J. (1983). Linking the MIS plan with corporate strategy: An exploratory study. *MIS Quarterly* 7:1–14.

Raghunathan, T. S., & W. R. King (1988). The impact of information systems planning on the organization. *Omega* 16:85–93.

Rockart, J. F. (1979). Chief executives define their own data needs. *Harvard Business Review* 57:81–93.

Rockart, J. F., & M. S. Scott Morton (1984). Implications of changes in information technology for corporate strategy. *Interfaces* 14:84–95.

Rockart, J. F., & J. E. Short (1989). IT in the 1990s: Managing organizational interdependence. *Sloan Management Review* 30:7–17.

Rotemberg, J., & G. Saloner (1991). Information technology and strategic advantage. In M. S. Scott Morton (Ed.), *The corporation of the 1990s.* New York: Oxford University Press.

Rumelt, R. P. (1974). *Strategy, structure and economic performance.* Cambridge, MA: Harvard University Press.

Scott Morton, M. S. (1991). *The corporation of the 1990s.* New York: Oxford University Press.

Sharpe, J. H. (1989). Building and communicating the executive vision. IBM Australia, Ltd., working paper no. 89–001, February.

Snow, C. C., & L. Hrebiniak (1980). Strategy distinctive competence and organizational performance. *Administrative Science Quarterly* 25:317–336.

Snow, C. C., & R. E. Miles (1983). The role of strategy in the development of a general theory of organizations. In R. Lamb (Ed.), *Advances in Strategic Management*, Vol. 2, pp. 231–59. Greenwich, CT: JAI Press.

Strassman, P. (1985). *The information payoff.* New York: Free Press.

Thompson, J. D. (1967). *Organizations in action: Social sciences bases of administrative theory.* New York: McGraw-Hill.

Venkatraman, N. (1989a). The concept of fit in strategy research: Toward verbal and statistical correspondence. *Academy of Management Review* July.

——— (1989b). Strategic orientation of business enterprises: The construct, dimensionality and measurement. *Management Science* 35:942–62.

——— (1991). Information technology-induced business reconfiguration: The new strategic management challenge. In M. S. Scott Morton (Ed.), *The corporation of the 1990s*, pp. 122–58. New York: Oxford University Press.

Venkatraman, N., & J. C. Camillus (1984). Exploring the concept of "fit" in strategic management. *Academy of Management Review* 9:513–25.

Venkatraman, N., & J. H. Grant (1986). Construct measurement in organizational strategy research: A critique and proposal. *Academy of Management Review* 11:71–87.

Venkatraman, N., & A. Kambil (1991). Strategies for electronic integration: Lessons from electronic filing of tax returns. *Sloan Management Review* (Winter):33–43.

Venkatraman, N., & J. E. Short (1990). Strategies for electronic integration: From order-entry systems to value-added services at Baxter. MIT Center for Information Systems Research working paper no. 210.

Weick, K. E. (1979). *The social psychology of organizing,* 2nd ed. Reading, MA: Addison-Wesley.

Williamson, O. E. (1985). *The economic institutions of capitalism: Firms, markets and relational contracting*. New York: Free Press.

Wind, Y., & T. S. Robertson (1983). Marketing strategy: New directions for theory and research. *Journal of Marketing* 47:1–17.

Wiseman, C. (1985). *Strategy and computers: Information systems as competitive weapons*. Homewood, IL: Dow Jones–Irwin.

Zachman, J. A. (1986). A framework for information systems architecture. IBM Los Angeles Scientific Center Report no. G320–2785, March.

Zani, W. M. (1970). Blueprint for MIS. *Harvard Business Review* 48:95–100.

Zmud, R. W., A. C. Boynton, & G. C. Jacobs (1986). The information economy: A new perspective for effective information systems management. *Data Base* 16:17–23.

Zuboff, S. (1988). *In the age of the smart machine*. New York: Basic Books.

CHAPTER 10

Dimensions of IS Planning and Design Aids: A Functional Model of CASE Technology

JOHN C. HENDERSON AND JAY G. COOPRIDER

In today's business environment, a critical management issue is "time-to-market": the length of time it takes an organization to convert a product concept into a viable product that is available in a specific market. The Xerox Corporation, for example, believes that its improved ability to manage time-to-market while retaining or improving quality has been a major factor in its efforts to rebuild its competitiveness (Harvard Business School, 1989). Extending this notion, Hewlett-Packard focused on the "time-to-break-even" as a measure of success for product development (personal communication, 1988). This perspective directly incorporates aspects of quality and maintainability while highlighting the importance of rapid response.

It is not surprising that the information systems (IS) function in a business faces this same challenge. As information technology becomes an integral part of an organization's competitive strategy, IS faces increased demands to improve the "time-to-market" for IS products and services. In fact, researchers and practitioners such as Hackathorn and Karimi (1988), Kull (1984), Brooks (1987), and others suggested that IS's inability to reduce the backlog of demand for systems products and meet the growing demand for new IS products represents a significant management challenge.

Although many factors affect an organization's ability to deliver high-quality products in a short time (Ancona & Caldwell, 1987), one way to address this issue is to use computer-aided planning and design (CAD–CAM) tools. We see, for example, Xerox, Ford and many other organizations using CAD–CAM technologies to enhance their capacity to develop quickly and deliver products to specific markets. Similarly, we have seen the growth of a major industry that seeks to deliver comparable design aid technology to the IS function. Sometimes referred to as CASE (computer-assisted software engineering), this technology is targeted at those who wish to use automation to affect the timing, cost, and quality of products and services delivered by IS. Beck and Perkins (1983), for example, found that 56 out of the 97 organizations they surveyed used automated tools as a means of improving their IS planning and design processes.

The impact of these tools on the productivity of software developers and, ultimately, on time-to-market is unclear. Semprevivo (1980) and Necco, Gordon, and Tsai (1987), for example, reported that design aid technology improves designers' productivity. In contrast, Card, McGarry, and Page (1987) and Lempp and Lauber (1988) found that after controlling for factors such as experience and task complexity, the use of software development aids did not have a significant effect on productivity and only a relatively weak effect on quality.

Such conflicting results can be attributed to many factors. For example, some of the studies addressed the impacts of productivity on narrowly defined tasks such as encoding specifications or developing flow representations (Case, 1985). In contrast, other studies examined the entire system design life cycle (Card et al., 1987). Perhaps more fundamental is the lack of a precise definition of design aid usage. It is often unclear whether usage refers to access (e.g., whether such technology was available to the team) or measures actual usage behavior. Furthermore, it is not clear that the level of aggregation defined by the usage variables in most studies is sufficiently precise to predict the impact of performance. For example, if a macrousage variable is employed (e.g., "did I use this package?"), teams may indicate similar design aid usage levels but actually utilized different subsets of functions. As a result, the impact of the technology can easily be mixed, leading to an overall assessment across design teams that indicates little or no impact.

The need to define and measure technology usage behavior more precisely suggests a need to develop a model of design aid technology that corresponds more closely to key designer behaviors. That is, rather than define this technology in economic terms (e.g., costs), technology terms (e.g., PC based or networked), or other more general terms (e.g., having an embedded design language or structured code compiler), we must create a model of design aid technology that is function oriented. Such a model would then directly relate the usage of a tool to the design team's performance.

The existing literature on IS planning and design offers a starting point. Hackathorn and Karimi (1988) and Welke and Konsynski (1980), for example, differentiated between design methodologies and design tools. Methodologies define the logical disciplines underlying IS planning and design activities, and tools represent these principles in a software application. Hackathorn and Karimi (1988), Beck and Perkins (1983), and others supported the notion that software engineering and information engineering require the application of sound engineering principles to the task of IS planning and design. Understanding these principles offers one means of mapping the functions of design aid technology onto key usage behaviors.

The difficulty lies in the diverse set of concepts, principles, and subsequent methodologies that can be used to create a design aid environment. Chikofsky and Rubenstein (1988), for example, claimed that there is as yet no accepted definition of CASE technology that satisfies this range of design concepts and methodologies. In a similar vein, Osterweil recognized this inherent diversity and argued that a research program in software engineering must address all design-related activities:

> The task of creating effective environments is so difficult because it is tantamount to understanding the fundamental nature of the software processes. A specific environment does not merit the name unless it provides strong, uniform support for the entire process it is intended to facilitate; that is not possible unless the process is fully appreciated and understood. (Osterweil, 1981, p. 36)

In the following sections, we describe the development of a functional model of design aid technology. We refer to this as a functional CASE technology model (FCTM). However, we use the term *CASE* in a broad sense, encompassing a wide range of planning and design activities. This interpretation is consistent with an emerging view of CASE that emphasizes the focus of design on the entire programming environment (Acly, 1988; Holt, Ramsey, & Grimes, 1983).

A FUNCTIONAL CASE TECHNOLOGY MODEL (FCTM)

There are several reviews of functions found in various CASE environments. Hackathorn and Karimi (1988), for example, categorized CASE technology in terms of the design life cycle addressed and the extent to which the environment provides for a range of support, from conceptual to explicit design techniques. The function of the CASE technology is then implied by the method(s) incorporated in the environment and the aspect of planning and development for which the support environment is intended. Thus, a tool that embraces the Gane–Sarson (Gane & Sarson, 1979) method can be expected to provide features such as functional decomposition or data flow diagrams. Of course, the tool may offer much more in the context of communications or analysis. Such distinctions, however, are not clear.

Reifer and Montgomery (1980) provided a more general schema, beginning with a general model of design having three components: input, process, and output. Each component was decomposed until 52 functions were distinguished. They believe that this taxonomy permits the classification of all current software development tools (at the time of their study) and allows an easy comparison and evaluation of tools. Although one could argue the validity of such an ambitious claim, their taxonomy does provide a direct linkage to design behavior. For example, Reifer and Montgomery identified features such as tuning, structure checking, scheduling, auditing, and editing. Clearly, such a model can be linked to the actual behaviors of designers. Similar approaches were discussed by Rajaraman (1982) and Houghton and Wallace (1987).

These models, however, appear limited. For example, the function associated with teams is not clearly identified. Features such as those found in COLAB (Stefik et al., 1987) or PLEXSYS (Konsynski et al., 1984–85) that support groups through structured processes for brainstorming, communication, voting, negotiation, or other team behaviors appear to be lacking. To the extent that improving the "time-to-break-even" will involve the use of teams (as suggested by Ancona & Caldwell, 1987; Cooprider & Henderson, 1990, and others), we need to incorporate these functions into CASE and, indeed, into any functional model of planning and design technology.

In this research, we pursue an objective consistent with the earlier research that attempts to characterize the key dimensions of design support technology. That is, we want to develop a functional model of design support (CASE) technology. To achieve this objective we used a four-step process. First, we interviewed leading designers of CASE-related technology in order to generate those functions that could be of value to an IS planner or designer. The specific functional definitions we discussed in the interviews were required to correspond to observable design behaviors.

Second, the complete set of generated functions was reviewed by 25 practicing designers familiar with CASE technology, to refine ambiguous items and eliminate any obvious redundancies. Third, based on a review of the design literature, we drew up a classification scheme as a basis for sorting each function generated during the interviews. This Q-sort was carried out by an independent group of 34 IS designers experienced in CASE technology. The intent of this step was to evaluate the model's robustness. Finally, we used the model to evaluate currently available CASE products. This step represents one test of the model's ability to represent adequately and discriminate among actual CASE environments.

In the first step, we used open-ended interviews with leading CASE designers (both academics and practitioners) in order to draw up a list of possible CASE functionalities. We conducted total of 11 interviews, each lasting from two to three hours. Each interview subject had had extensive personal involvement in CASE technology research or had had actual development experience with several commercial CASE products. Our subjects included three academics and eight practitioners.

The interviews consisted of giving the subject a list of functions extracted from the literature. To ensure adequate discussion, we divided the lists into five sections. The subjects reviewed each functional description, noting any ambiguity or bias in its definition. At the end of each section, we discussed any problems with definitions and added new functions. The order of presentation of each section was randomized across subjects.

A total of 124 distinct functionalities were generated through the interviews. The second step was a clarification procedure to combine or eliminate vague or redundant functional definitions. To do this, we asked three to five expert users for each of eight existing CASE products to evaluate their product using the 124 functions. Each subject indicated the ease of use of a given function on a one-to-five scale, with one being "very difficult to use or nonexistent" and five being "very easy to use or essentially automatic." The reliability of each functional definition of a given product can be assessed by analyzing the variance (or correlation) across subjects. If the definition was clear, the subject experts were to assign the same ease-of-use rating to a given function. We reviewed and eliminated or refined functional definitions with high variance or low interrater reliability (below .8). As a result of this process, we defined 98 different functions.

The third step in the process was developing a model that reflected the scope of these 98 functions. This model, called the Functional CASE Technology Model (FCTM), was created in two stages. First, we reviewed the relevant design literature in order to define a general model. Then, 34 expert CASE users sorted each of the 98 functionalities into one of the dimensions defined by this model. The extent to which this Q-sort process resulted in a consistent sorting pattern across subjects was seen as evidence that the earlier model was a meaningful abstraction and could be used to represent a wide range of CASE functionality. That is, the model represents more than a unique artifact of the researchers' interpretation of the existing literature.

An alternative approach for developing such a model was discussed by Sherif and Sherif (1967). In their approach, they asked the subjects to cluster similar attributes, thereby creating a subject-specific model. The models generated by the subjects could then be analyzed for underlying similarities and, hence, formed the basis for generating an overall model. The strength of this approach lies in its ability to eliminate the bias created by an earlier model. Such an approach requires extensive time, however, and may result in dimensions that have little theoretical grounding. In this case, the time needed to cluster 98 items far exceeded the time that the subjects were willing to spend. Further, years of both theoretical and empirical research on IS planning and design provided a basis for developing a tentative model. Given these two factors, the Q-sort testing strategy was used.

Two dimensions of CASE technology

Reviews of the organizational literature on technology (Fry, 1982; Fry & Slocum, 1984; Slocum & Sims, 1980; Withey, Daft, & Cooper, 1983) reveal a diversity of approaches to measuring technology. Perrow (1967) defined technology as the actions used to transform inputs into outputs. In that context, technology is a production variable, affecting the way that inputs are converted to desired outputs. Economists have long characterized technology as production technology concerned with creating, processing, and handling physical goods. Thus, as illustrated in Figure 10.1, one perspective of CASE technology is to view it as an underlying production technology.

This perspective on planning and design technology focuses on transforming inputs into outputs (Kottemann & Konsynski, 1984). At an individual level, Simon (1976, 1981) contended that bounded rationality ultimately limits the capacity of human information processing and, hence, the transformation process. This information-processing perspective is often used to characterize the planning and design task (Thomas & Carroll, 1979) and provides a basis of describing the production of design aid technology. We define production technology as a function that directly affects the capacity of persons to generate planning or design decisions and their subsequent artifacts or products.

A second perspective that has been used to evaluate technology is coordination. Williamson (1975) noted that constraints on human information processing can arise from the bounded rationality of a particular agent and from the communication requirements stemming from the interaction between agents. Bakos and Treacy (1986) also identified the need to reflect both the bounded rationality of individuals and the communication costs in a general model of information technology. Thompson (1967) argued that coordination is necessary for interdependence among

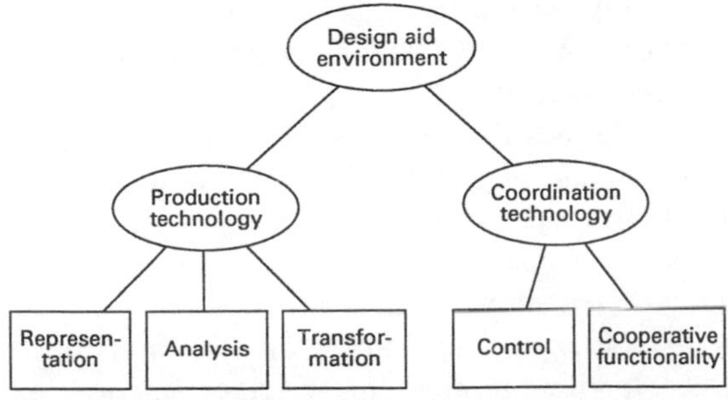

Figure 10.1. Two functional dimensions of IS planning and design technology.

business processes. Interdependence implies that the performance of one or more discrete operations has consequences for the completion of others. The concept of interdependence is a fundamental principle in designing organizations (Galbraith, 1977; McCann & Galbraith, 1981; Thompson, 1967). Different types of interdependence create different coordination structures among the participants.

Winograd and Flores (1986) claimed that in all but the most routine jobs, workers request and initiate actions that affect the economic, political, or physical conditions of those around them. They also described organizations as "networks of directives and commissions" and stated that the coordination of action is central to this work environment. Given this characterization of organizations, they suggested that a major benefit can be gained from the technology used in organizations to request, create, and monitor their commitments.

Malone defined coordination as "the additional information processing performed when multiple, connected actors pursue goals that a single actor pursuing the same goals would not perform" (1988). Applying these ideas about coordination to programming environments, Holt, Ramsey, and Grimes (1983) suggested that a coordination system can serve as an appropriate foundation stone of CASE technology. Malone; Winograd and Flores; Holt, Ramsey, and Grimes; and other researchers discovered a major role of computer technology: better enabling or supporting coordination activities. Consistent with this perspective, we define coordination technology as a function that enables or supports the interactions of multiple agents in executing a planning or design task. Because a design team consists of multiple agents with a variety of goals and skills, coordination technology may emerge as an important dimension of CASE technology.

Taken together, we conceptualize design aid technology as a combination of production and coordination technology. Next, we shall build from these two perspectives of technology the components of CASE technology. In each section we shall examine the relevant research on IS planning and design aids and define these two dimensions as distinct subdimensions or components (see Figure 10.1).

Production technology: Representation

The first component of production technology is labeled *representation* to emphasize the notion of abstracting or conceptualizing a phenomenon. Schon (1984), Zachman (1986), and others identified the process of evolving abstractions and presenting them in a communicable form as an activity essential to planning and design. Zachman (1986), for example, listed categories of functions such as process flow diagrams, functional charting, or entity modeling that reflect alternative means to represent concepts or phenomena. Kottemann and Konsynski (1984) created a hierarchy of knowledge representation that includes names or labels, domain set specifications, association or relations mapping, and complete meaning that suggests the need for several representation functions. From our perspective, each of these categories indicates a need for a specific function to support the process of generating an external representation of a planning or design concept.

Specifically, the representation component is defined as a function enabling the user to define, describe, or change a definition or description of an object, relationship, or process. Our interviews resulted in a range of functions that appear to carry out this conceptual component. We shall describe these functions later but make some general observations now. The generated representation functions reflect a general notion of knowledge representation and acquisition. For example, functions such as the ability to describe a process as an information flow or the ability to represent an organization's authority relationships indicate basic requirements to represent knowledge.

A second aspect of the representation dimension shows the requirements for adapting or changing representations and for storing or retrieving representations. For example, the ability to combine many entity or process representations into a single complex object supports the user in an adaptation or change task.

Finally, the ability to use alternative modes of representation (e.g., text versus visual representation) is demonstrated. In fact, as suggested by Konsynski and associates (1984–85), our subjects viewed the ability to shift among alternative representations as an important function.

Production technology: Analysis

The dimension of analysis reflects the problem-solving and decision-making aspects of planning and design. Simon (1981), for example, portrayed design as a problem-solving process and emphasizes the importance of tasks evaluating multiple alternatives and choices made by the designer. In a similar vein, we defined the analysis component to be a function that enables the user to explore, simulate, or evaluate alternative representations or models of objects, relationships, or processes.

Similar to the functional building blocks of a decision support system (Keen & Scott Morton, 1978; Sprague & Carlson, 1982; Treacy, 1981), the analysis functions show the need to compare, simulate, evaluate, ask "what if" with respect to a criterion, and choose or optimize. It is interesting to note that some functional definitions imply an embedded intelligence in the design aid. For example, the ability to suggest problem resolutions based on previously used solutions indicates the use of expert system and artificial intelligence (AI) concepts in the development of design aids.

In each case, the function in this (analysis) dimension assumes the existence of a knowledge base (often a model) and seeks to manipulate this knowledge in order to investigate alternatives, resolve conflicts, or support a choice. It is a proactive analysis process that builds on or adds to knowledge. Thus, we would expect the result of using analysis to be the enhancement or adjustment of a given representation (i.e., the use of modeling). The significant interaction between these two dimensions suggests that they constitute components of the more general dimension of production technology.

Production technology: Transformation

The nature of planning and design has been conceptualized as a process or series of transformations (Kottemann & Konsynski, 1984; Zachman, 1986). A transformation is an internally complete and consistent change in a design concept or artifact. The need for completeness and consistency reflects the attribute that a transformation is a nonrandom purposeful activity and hence can be repeated. For example, converting a logical data model into a set of definitions represented in the language of a given data base system is a transformation.

In general, the notion of transformation has been the mechanism to represent important aggregates or chunks of design activity. At a macrolevel, the system design life cycle describes a series of design transformations. Researchers such as Zachman (1986) and Hackathorn and Karimi (1988) demonstrated a range of transformations that are central to IS planning and design processes. We defined the component of transformation to be a function that executes a significant planning or design task, thereby replacing or substituting for a human designer or planner.

This dimension of CASE technology shows a straightforward capital–labor substitution. It differs from analysis in that it replaces human activity rather than only providing support. In this sense, it is analogous to the distinction between decision support systems and process automation. Of course, transformation technology can enhance the overall performance of humans by allowing the redistribution of human resources. Still, at a task level, the intent of the transformation function is direct substitution for the human resource.

As might be expected, the bulk of the generated transformation functions address activities late in the design cycle (e.g., code generation). As such, they often depend on a few functions' being available in the representation component. However, as we shall explain, current technology often does not effectively link these two functional components.

A second observation is that the ability to deliver the transformation function often implies embedding intelligence into the CASE technology. For example, the ability to normalize automatically a data model is an emerging type of transformation function that extensively uses expert systems and AI technology. As we see more use of intelligent CASE technology, we may expect to see new functions for this dimension.

Coordination technology: Control

The focus of the components of technology discussed thus far has been production oriented. That is, the technology has directly influenced a person's ability to produce aspects of the design. In this capacity, the technology represents a classic productivity-enhancing investment, that is, a trade-off between capital and labor. Through the investments in technology, the task of a designer is accomplished with fewer resources.

The use of technology to reduce the cost of coordination can, however, enable a design team to achieve new levels of efficiency and effectiveness. For example, Applegate, Konsynski, and Nunamaker (1986) and Stefik and associates (1987) described technology that is intended to improve the productivity of meetings, in part through enhanced communication. Such technology not only can affect the efficiency or effectiveness of a given meeting but also improve the team's decision making or problem solving throughout the design life cycle.

Our interviewees identified those technologies that focus on the need to coordinate individuals. It was interesting that during the interviews the subjects seemed to shift from conceptualizing the planning or design process as an individual activity to one involving a group or team. When this shift occurred, the design aid function pointed to issues such as the need to exchange information, enforce policies or security measures, or understand or resolve conflicts.

It is not surprising that one aspect of design aid technology that emerges from the design literature contains a component of coordination: control, or a notion of a manager–employee or principal–agent relationship in a planning or design process. That is, design activities have an explicit or implicit contract to deliver a product or service to a customer for a given price. In order to ensure that the contract is fulfilled, a control system or monitoring system is required. Similarly, among the activities of a design team, a project leader may contract with an individual. Again, the project leader requires some information to ensure that this person does, in fact, carry out the contract in the intended way.

In addition to the need to monitor, the principal or manager may want to restrict the activities of a given agent or employee. For example, he or she may want to restrict the agent's access to particular data or prevent his or her changing some aspect of an existing or proposed system. At a more abstract level, the project leader must be able to communicate project goals (even the means to achieve these goals) and to ensure that the resources of the team are allocated in the best way to achieve the goals.

Of course, requirements to control the activities of a group have long been recognized by the developers of computer-aided design technology. Houghton and Wallace (1987), Reifer and Montgomery (1980), and others found several functions spanning notions of project management, configuration control, and access control. We defined control as a function that enables the user to draw up and enforce rules, policies, or priorities that will govern or restrict the activities of team members during the planning or design process.

Two general types of relations appear in this component: resource management and access control. Resource management enables a manager to ensure that the behavior of individuals, and therefore the utilization of resources by the design team, is consistent with the organization's goals. The capability to budget, to identify a critical path or set of activities, to monitor progress or service levels, and to communicate or enforce appropriate goals are examples of this function. In essence, this function supports several traditional control activities. As we shall explain later, CASE technology's ability to achieve effective internal control (i.e., substitute individual control for managerial control) has major implications for performance.

A second function is access or change control, which implies that issues of security and access must be carefully managed. Access control includes configuration control, authorization management, and the ability to identify and audit the activity of designers, particularly when these activities change existing work or directly pertain to a team policy. In essence, these functions assume that the design team will use and produce a valuable asset. Hence, access to those assets must be monitored and controlled.

Coordination technology: Cooperation

The control dimension addresses the need to establish and enforce goals, policy, procedures, standards, and priorities during a design process. It is the traditional concept of manager and employee that assumes the need to enforce a work contract. Information is required both to ensure the effective execution of a task and to monitor the contract.

An alternative mode of coordination assumes that the participants operate on a peer-to-peer level. In this mode, the interaction among individuals is based on shared goals and a perception of mutual gain from a given interaction. Thus, cooperative behavior is not enforced by a set of rules. Rather, such interaction reflects a sense of peer involvement in which exchange is often voluntary.

Davis and Smith (1983), Henderson (1988), and Malone (1988) described the concept of cooperative behavior in this manner. For example, Davis and Smith argued that the need for cooperation among experts arises from shared goals and a knowledge interdependence among the experts with respect to these goals. In this research we defined the cooperative function as enabling the user to exchange information with another individual(s) for the purpose of influencing (affecting) the concept, process, or product of the planning/design team.

Our interviews generated several functions that we modeled as cooperative functions that show the role of CASE technology as both a communication channel and a facilitation aid. Reifer and Montgomery (1980) saw communication as an important aspect of computer-aided design technology. Certainly in a group context, communication is a key issue. The basic cooperative functions address the need for several communication functions, from basic messages to enhancements such as the ability to attach a note to a diagram. In essence, these functions provide a platform for electronic interaction among members of a team.

The second class of cooperative functions uses technology to help facilitate group interaction, such as providing for electronic brainstorming or managing the degree of anonymity of input (i.e., votes). Applegate, Konsynski, and Nunamaker (1986) described technology that offers this function. For example, the user of PLEXSYS technology can choose among several structured group processes and adapt the technology to facilitate the execution of the particular approach chosen. The technology affects the process through efficiency (e.g., the ability to capture the output of a brainstorming session) and by changing parameters of the group process within an efficiency level. For example, the technology can permit a significantly larger group size than is often associated with a brainstorming session. To the extent that participation and involvement affect the success of a project, this increased capacity can have significant benefits. These functions, particularly those that implement structured group processes, contain aspects of control. For example, electronic brainstorming imposes an interaction protocol on the members of the team. This association between control and cooperation is to be expected, as they both are components of the same dimension of coordination. The key distinction is that cooperation assumes a peer relationship among participants and is based on a concept of sharing. It functions primarily as a conduit or enabler of information exchange. Control, in contrast, assumes a hierarchical relationship and provides a way of exchanging the information necessary to establish, monitor, and enforce this hierarchy. Each relates to coordination but does so from a different perspective.

A third dimension of CASE technology: Organizational technology

Simon (1976) found that the bounds of rationality can be extended not only by increasing individual computational power but also by institutionalizing organization-wide standards or procedures to help individual performance. This capability, which we refer to as *organizational technology*, can be described as organizationwide mechanisms through which an organization provides "institutionalized help" to individuals and groups in order to overcome the cognitive burdens of information processing. March and Simon (1958) argued that by establishing organization infrastructures, which they call *standard operating procedures*, the organization can reduce the burdens of information processing because search procedures are somewhat automated in the standard operating procedures. Similarly, Galbraith (1977) contended that implementing a vertical information system and the implied standards of data and language associated with such a system is one strategy to enhance a firm's information-processing capacity.

Organizational technology is viewed in this context as an institutionalized support technology. Recent research in areas such as organizational decision support systems (King & Star, 1990) and the use of IS for creating an "information economy" (Zmud, Boynton, & Jacobs, 1986) has highlighted the need to differentiate the characteristics of information technology support for organizational processes (e.g., organizational decision making) from group and individual processes. The feedback that we received from our interviews underscored the need to distinguish organizational technology from the other dimensions of technology. A design team performs its work in a larger organizational context as it interacts with other teams or stakeholders in order to obtain resources, make decisions, and exchange inputs and outputs. In this regard, organizational technology is concerned with the environment in which these interactions occur. In this light, we define organizational technology as a function and as an associated policy or procedure that determines the environment in which production and coordination technology will be applied to the planning and design process. Representing any production or coordination technology requires deciding either to conform to or deviate from standards of technology and procedures. These decisions affect the ability of organizations to support the design process. Decisions to deviate from standards, for example, reduce organizations' ability to use specific production or coordination technologies as well as teams' ability to use these functions for several design teams or processes.

As we shall discuss later, our interviews and our empirical analysis revealed some confusion about the definitions of functions in organizational technology. One explanation for this confusion is that organizational technology is not completely independent of production and coordination. Rather, organizational technology enables the use of production and coordination technology. For example, the organizational technology of standardizing a particular design methodology affects production (e.g., which diagrams or models are used) and coordination (e.g., providing a common language for teams to communicate results). For this reason, Figure 10.2 shows organizational technology as affecting production and coordination rather than as being separate and independent.

Organizational technology: Support

One component of organizational technology addresses the skills required to use the technology rather than directly focusing on specific planning and design tasks. At issue is the range of support required to help the design aid user learn about and use the design aid in the most effective way possible. We refer to this component as *support technology* and defined it as a function to help an individual user understand and use a planning and design aid effectively.

Our interviewees considered support functionality to be essential to gaining an impact from using CASE. They identified functions ranging from passive (e.g., an on-line help function) to proactive, which uses domain knowledge or past user be-

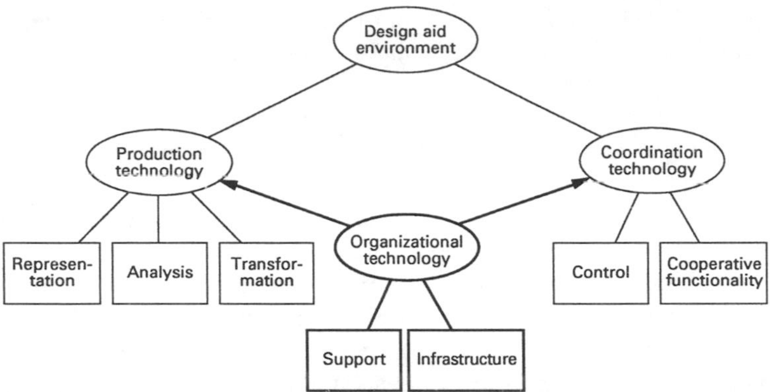

Figure 10.2. Organizational technology: three dimensions of IS planning and design technology.

havior patterns to diagnose or recommend appropriate action (e.g., explaining why a particular function should be used in a particular situation).

Many characteristics of "user-friendly" systems incorporate such support functions. For example, Houghton and Wallace (1987) described support functions that reflect the skills (expert to novice) of a typical user population. Note that general interface technology is not incorporated as a support function. For example, the use of a mouse or point-and-click is a feature that affects the (physical or mental) effort necessary to exercise a function. As such, this aspect of the design environment should be incorporated into the ease-of-use measure of a set of functions.

Organizational technology: Infrastructure

Computer-based design tools can provide organizationwide infrastructures for developing complex software. Often, complex software is built module by module by several design teams. If the teams do not proceed carefully, the idiosyncrasies of an undisciplined team can lead to an expensive failure. Design aid tools can help the design team manage the complexities of development by providing a common foundation for the development of IS. As a result, the organization can introduce parallelism and share scarce talent among teams. The infrastructure enforces the use of consistent techniques throughout the organization.

Because the enforcement of organization wide infrastructure comes primarily by limiting what design teams can do with the tools, there is the possibility that an inflexible infrastructure can stand in the way of designing effective systems. Therefore, although the ultimate power of infrastructure technology is its ability to extend the range of solutions and approaches that can be handled by the design team, its actual impact on the development process is unclear.

Ultimately, the ability to develop and sustain an organizational infrastructure requires the use of standards. As we suggested, standards can increase organizational flexibility and limit the creative process of planning and design. For example, Lempp and Lauber (1988) argued that the emerging standards for computer-aided design technology and practice are a strategic concern to organizations that depend on information technology.

A major purpose of the infrastructure is to make skills and data portable. Portable skills and data are promoted through standardized relationships among various activities of the design life cycle. The ability to introduce design processes simultaneously is enhanced. For example, adopting a standard structure for representing the knowledge generated in a design process enables sharing this knowledge with other teams. Similarly, it provides a basis for teaching designers about the knowledge that is available and how other teams function. As a result, organizational performance can be improved by a team's ability to anticipate when coordination is required.

Our interviewees came up with few examples of functions that could be thought of as standards, and so they were not included in our subsequent analyses. However, the debriefings with members of organizations frequently emphasized the importance of a technology infrastructure, and the discussion of infrastructure often included system utilities and architectures. For example, one function focused on the ability to port between technology platforms, and another highlighted the ability to function in a highly distributed environment. The need for consistency in the data definition storage structure with emerging standards for a central repository was also often mentioned.

In essence, these discussions brought out the need to incorporate a dimension of design aid technology that can support organization change and flexibility. As such, we defined the infrastructure of organizational technology as standards that enable portability of skills, knowledge, procedures, or methods across planning or design processes.

Summary

We introduced three general dimensions and seven components of planning and design technology: production, coordination, and organizational technologies as the relevant dimensions, with production as being composed of three components (representation, analysis, and transformation), coordination as two components (control and cooperation) and organizational technology as two components (support and infrastructure). In addition, we described organizational technology as enabling production and coordination technology rather than as being an independent dimension.

Several observations seem appropriate. A distinction often made between design support environments is the ease of a function's use. For example, two design aid environments may support data flow diagramming, but they may differ in their ease of use. Ease of use can be viewed as a measure of the effort required to exercise the function and, thus, as a relative measure of cost. Combining a functional model with the notion of ease of use permits the researcher to explore the usability of CASE technology.

Second, the level of functional specificity reflects the goal of creating a correspondence between the functional model and usage behavior. For example, interviewees rejected as too general the use of "documentation" as a function. Rather, documentation is a (passive) form of representation that requires a particular function. The need to develop a parsimonious model in a research setting (particularly one that requires the users of a system to describe their usage behaviors) argues against a micromodel. The function described in this chapter thus reflects the subjects' judgment of an appropriate level of aggregation.

Finally, we do not claim that the list of 98 functions that we described and will detail shortly is all the functions needed for planning and design technology. Rather, the functions specified for each component we view as spanning the scope of the component. The convergence found in the Q-sort process and the ability to discriminate among actual products support our conclusion that these functions can be grouped under the proposed definitions of the components.

Evaluating the FCTM

A final concern in the development of functions is the ability to associate reliably a particular function with actual CASE products. As we noted in our discussion of a functional CASE technology model, a reliability check resulted in a total of 98 functions forming the pool with which to define the functions' dimensions just described. In the following sections, we first used a Q-sort test to examine the robustness of the proposed model. The test consisted of giving independent experts in CASE technology the definitions of each component[1] and asking them to sort the 98 functions into these categories. The extent to which the subjects sorted the functions in the same way we saw as evidence that the proposed model was a good characterization of CASE technology. A second test then examined the extent to which the model discriminated between CASE products in an interesting and useful way. Next, we shall present the results of this Q-sort and the application of the model to evaluate eight commercially available CASE products.

Empirically analyzing the FCTM

A summary of the results of the Q-sort test is shown in Table 10.1. A total of 34 subjects (not involved in the previous development of this model) sorted the functions according to the definitions described earlier. We tabulated the results according to the category receiving the most assignments. As Table 10.1 shows, we assigned 50 functions to production technology, 26 to coordination technology, and 22 to organizational technology.

The detailed results of the Q-sort test are shown in the right-hand columns of Table 10.2. The functions are listed in the order of declining frequency of mention by the 34 subjects. Following the description of each function is the percentage of respondents who placed it into the relevant component. For example, for item 1 in Table 10.2, 88 percent of the respondents placed "Represent a design in terms of process or flow models" into representation.

Even if these assignments do not indicate agreement on a primary component, there may still be agreement on the more general dimensions of production, coordination, or organizational technology. If this is true, there is support for the premise that these general dimensions adequately reflect CASE technology. The last three columns of Table 10.2 show the percentage of respondents sorting the specific functionality into the production dimension (representation, analysis, or transformation), the coordination dimension (control or cooperative functionality), and the organiza-

Table 10.1. Summary profile of components of design aid technology

Component	A Number of functionalities associated by a majority of respondents	B Number of additional functionalities associated by a plurality of respondents	C Total number of functionalities
Representation	9	9	18
Analysis	17	2	19
Transformation	11	2	13
Production technology	37	13	50
Control	12	4	16
Cooperative functionality	9	1	10
Coordination technology	21	5	26
Support	13	9	22
Organizational technology	13	9	22

tional dimension (support). For example, function 15 in Table 10.2 ("Map the existing systems onto a functional description of the organization") was placed by only 42 percent of the respondents into the representation component, but fully 94 percent of the respondents placed it into the general production technology dimension (i.e., sorted it into representation, analysis, or transformation).

A simple chi-square goodness-of-fit test (with a .05 level of significance) is used to test the hypothesis that assignments are random. The results of this simple test is shown in Table 10.2 at both the component level (i.e., the six components that were used in the sort) and at the dimension level (i.e., production, coordination, and organization). At the component level, there are only two functions for which the chi-square test of uniform distribution is not rejected (transformation 13 and support 22). Although this is a weak test, it does support the conclusion that the six components do differ significantly. At the dimension level, only 12 functions failed to reject the test of a random assignment. Again, this supports the conclusion that these dimensions differ.

A more specific review of the assignment patterns is even more revealing. For representation, only nine of the 18 items received more than 50 percent as a primary selection, but all nine of the functions below 50 percent appear to be regarded as general production functions.

The sorting results for analysis appear more consistent, with 17 of 19 functions receiving more than 50 percent primary assignments. Again, the two items below 50 percent appear to be general production functions with fairly uniform distributions across representation, analysis, and transformation.

The transformation component has 11 of 13 functions exceeding 50 percent. In general, the functions appear to be within the production dimension. The two functions that fall below 50 percent are ambiguous. Both functions 12 and 13 fail to reject the chi-square test at the dimension level, suggesting that there is a significant overlap between the production and control aspects of these functions.

In the control component, 12 of 16 functions received more than 50 percent of the primary assignments. This distribution of assignments suggests support of this

Table 10.2. Detailed profile of components of design aid technology

	Component selected	Dimension selected (%)		
		Production	Coordination	Organization
A. Functionalities of representation (production technology)				
1. Represent a design in terms of process or flow models	88	94	3	3
2. Represent a design in terms of data models	82	94	3	3
3. Construct several types of models (data, process, functional)	77	91	0	9
4. Customize the language or conventions used for representation	70	76	15	9
5. Represent relationships between information requirements and goals	68	91	9	0
6. Represent authority relationships of target systems organization	65	82	9	9
7. Provide the option of drawing diagram lines exactly where wanted	65	73	9	18
8. Combine many entities or processes into a single complex object	59	85	3	12
9. Show an object's attributes by selecting it in a diagram	52	82	0	18
10. Maintain descriptions of existing systems to interact with target	47	76	18	6
11. Provide flexible naming conventions	47	56	18	26*
12. Maintain a single master definition of each process, object, etc.	44	62	26	12*
13. Move between different types of models	44	70	9	21
14. Redraw a diagram so that it is uncluttered and easy to read	42	79	3	18
15. Map the existing systems onto a functional organizational description	42	94	6	0
16. Combine structurally equivalent processes or objects	35	91	0	9
17. Simultaneously display several screens showing different versions	34	59	16	25*
18. Choose a first-cut model from among stored generic models	30	70	6	24
B. Functionalities of analysis (production technology)				
1. Test for consistency between a process model and a data model	85	91	9	0
2. Check for the structural equivalence of objects or processes	82	91	0	9
3. Check for unnecessary or redundant model connections	79	88	9	3
4. Detect inconsistencies in models, definitions, etc.	79	88	9	3
5. Identify the design impact of proposed changes in a design	79	88	6	6
6. Search the design for similar objects	74	88	0	12

Table 10.2. *(continued)*

	Component selected	Dimension selected (%)		
		Production	Coordination	Organization
7. Use analytical decision aids to measure performance	73	88	6	6
8. Detect and analyze system errors from execution of target system	73	88	6	6
9. Identify schedule impacts of a proposed design change	70	82	18	0
10. Search design for complex relationships	68	70	12	18
11. Suggest problem resolution based on previously used solutions	65	76	3	21
12. Estimate the process performance characteristics of a design	64	76	15	9
13. Search design for objects with specified characteristics	59	70	6	24
14. Simulate the production environment of the target system	58	88	3	9
15. Identify where predefined criteria or rules have been violated	56	65	35	0
16. Trace relationships between detailed specifications and planning efforts	50	76	18	6
17. Identify the differences between separate versions of an object	50	65	20	15
18. Recommend a general model incorporating many limited perspectives	41	88	3	9
19. Perform an operation on only a portion of a design	35	82	9	9
C. Functionalities of transformation (production technology)				
1. Generate executable code from a screen mockup	91	94	3	3
2. Generate executable code in several procedural languages	91	94	3	3
3. Generate code compatible with a variety of physical environments	79	85	12	3
4. Generate standard code for generic programs	79	82	9	9
5. Generate executable versions of a design for testing/evaluation	79	94	3	3
6. Generate a logical specification into a physical one	74	97	0	3
7. Transform a high-level representation into a more detailed one	68	97	0	3
8. Provide documentation as a by-product of design	59	74	0	26
9. Perform reverse engineering	59	91	0	9
10. Generate screen mockups	53	94	6	0
11. Import data from and export data to external files/packages	50	56	31	13
12. Create templates for tasks and deliverables	38	50	38	12

Table 10.2. *(continued)*

	Component selected	Dimension selected (%)		
		Production	Coordination	Organization
13. Propagate a change in an object to all places the object appears	32	70	21	9
D. Functionalities of control (coordination technology)				
1. Specify who can review various parts of the design work	79	6	94	0
2. Provide product management information	79	15	82	3
3. Maintain a record of who is responsible for each part of product	71	6	82	12
4. Maintain a record of changes made in the design	65	9	82	9
5. Provide management information for more than one product	64	15	82	3
6. Specify who can modify various parts of the design work	64	12	85	3
7. "Freeze" a portion of a design to protect it from changes	62	15	79	6
8. Manage the quality assurance path for a project	55	9	85	6
9. Alter rules that control the way certain functions are performed	55	24	67	9
10. Provide assistance in analyzing project management priorities	52	33	55	12
11. Estimate how long a specific task or project will take	52	36	52	12
12. Remind members of team about approaching deadlines	52	6	85	9
13. Follow rules in merging separate versions of models, diagrams, etc.	49	27	70	3
14. Produce metrics for comparing projects complexity, quality, etc.	49	30	52	18*
15. Maintain list of requirements for design and how satisfied	46	49	45	6*
16. Temporarily ignore a problem/ inconsistency so work can continue	29	41	32	27*
E. Functionalities of cooperative functionality (coordination technology)				
1. Maintain a dialogue with other users of the tools	91	3	91	6
2. Allow a group of users to work simultaneously on a single task	91	6	91	3
3. Send messages to others who use the tools	88	3	91	6
4. Allow concurrent use by several users of dictionary/diagram/etc.	85	6	91	3
5. Provide group interaction support (brainstorming, NCT, etc.)	85	9	88	3
6. Attach electronic notes to objects for other to read	62	20	65	15
7. Allow giving of anonymous feedback or input	53	6	88	6

Table 10.2. *(continued)*

	Component selected	Dimension selected (%)		
		Production	Coordination	Organization
8. Notify designer if a change is made in design that affects his work	53	9	88	3
9. Build a catalog of macros that other users can access	50	24	50	26
10. Help the designer and end user evaluate design alternatives	41	47	44	9*
F. Functionalities of support (organizational technology)				
1. Provide aids for quick references to basic command/functions	97	3	0	97
2. Provide on-line help for a specified command/feature	94	3	3	94
3. Provide instructional materials for learning the tools	91	3	6	91
4. Provide context-specific on-line help	88	6	6	88
5. Identify external sources of information on specific topics	84	16	0	84
6. Provide options about how to interact with the tools	76	21	3	76
7. Build templates or examples of work for use in tutorials/demonstrations	59	18	23	59
8. Explain why an action or alternative has been recommended	55	42	3	55
9. "Browse" in other segments of the tool while using graphics mode	50	47	3	50
10. Explain why part of a design has been identified as inconsistent	50	47	3	50
11. Anticipate user's mistakes from his pattern of previous errors	50	32	18	50
12. Allow the undoing of a series of commands	50	41	9	50
13. Generate outputs in a variety of media	50	26	24	50
14. Incorporate new command "macros" into command structure	49	39	12	49
15. Generate presentation-quality printed reports and documents	47	38	15	47
16. Provide individual change pages of documents	43	24	33	43
17. Graphically magnify a model to see greater levels of detail	38	59	3	38
18. Build a general access library of customized models	35	35	30	35
19. Prepare, edit, store, send, and retrieve documents	32	53	15	32
20. Store versions of a design for later "roll-back"	32	38	30	32
21. Link a design to a library of models/systems for testing	30	49	21	30*
22. Develop, run, and store completely customized reports	29	59	12	29**

*failed χ^2 test for 3 dimensions. **failed χ^2 test for 6 components.

component and a consensus with respect to the coordination dimension. For the four functions not receiving more than 50 percent primary assignments, function 13 appears to reflect a general coordination perspective, and functions 14, 15, and 16 failed to reject the chi-square test for differences at the dimension level. These functions appear to overlap with support and analysis, suggesting a significant level of ambiguity in their functional descriptions.

The cooperation component received only 10 assignments, but nine of those received more than 50 percent as a primary assignment. In general, these functions appear to reflect a coordination perspective, but the subjects distinguished them from the control component. Function 10 did not receive more than 50 percent primary assignments and also failed to reject the chi-square test at the dimension level. This function shows significant overlap with both analysis and support.

Finally, the support component had 22 functionalities, with only 13 of the 22 receiving primary assignments. This component appears to be difficult for subjects to differentiate clearly. Although six functions have strong agreement as support, the remaining functions reflect aspects of both production and coordination. Two of the nine functions receiving fewer than 50 percent primary assignments failed the chi-square test. Function 21 failed to reject the test at the dimension level, and function 22 failed to reject the weaker component-level test. The sort pattern across those assignments with less than a 50 percent primary sort appears to overlap significantly with at least one other dimension. These results may mean a need to redefine the support component. An alternative explanation is given in Figure 10.2. The organizational dimension of technology affects the support environment mainly through its impact on the production and coordination dimensions. Because of this, it is often difficult to isolate the functions of organizational (and hence support) technology from those of production and coordination.

In sum, the sorting results supported each of the component concepts. Only 13 of the 98 functions failed to reject the chi-square test at the dimension or component level. Twenty-seven functions received less than 50 percent as a primary sort, although 13 of these 27 had support as their first or second choice, indicating the difficulty of separating this component. Of the remaining 14 functions, eight showed a general production perspective and one a general coordination perspective, thereby providing additional support for the dimension-level concepts.

As the next step in the analysis, we used the technology components to compare eight commercially available CASE products. The comparison will be used to determine whether the FCTM is a useful tool for evaluating possible CASE environments.

Comparing CASE products

In this section, the FCTM is used to characterize eight commercially available CASE products. The products were selected in order to cover the full system development life cycle. The life cycle was divided into three general categories: planning, design, and construction. For comparison, we selected two products that appear to target each of these. We also chose to evaluate two products that purported to integrate all three components. To ensure that the products did in fact reflect these components, 25 expert users were asked to indicate the level of support that the product provided for the seven tasks shown in Table 10.3. These perceptions supported the conclusion that both the tools selected for evaluation span the life cycle and have distinctive product features.

A summary of the product evaluations appears in Table 10.4. In each case, three to five expert users of a product were asked to evaluate its ease of use with respect to the 98 functions. A five-point scale (Table 10.4) was used for evaluation. A function was considered to exist if the average response of the subjects was greater than 3.0.

Several conclusions can be drawn from Table 10.4. First, the model differentiates products in an expected way. For example, the products that target planning and conceptual design focus on representation, although they are relatively weak on transformation. Similarly, those products targeting construction provide higher levels of transformation and are weaker on representation.

Second, only one product significantly covers the control function. Furthermore, all products are weak on cooperation. This result suggests that current products may have a limited impact on team performance.

Third, the products do provide support, but there is significant variation among them. A more detailed analysis shows that there is general support in the form of basic help commands, but the availability of advanced, intelligent support is quite limited.

A final observation is reflected in the summary "Total used" row in Table 10.4, which indicates the number and percentage of all possible functions that appear in at least one product. The results suggest that claims for integration and coverage by CASE products are at best limited to notions of production technology. There is a significant gap between possible and available functions in coordination, analysis, and intelligent forms of support. Even within the production dimension, the degree of support can vary significantly.

A detailed listing of the available functions of the eight CASE tools is shown in Table 10.5. As with Table 10.4, a particular function was considered to exist for a specific product if the expert users of that product rated the ease of using that function as being greater than 3.0. We can use Table 10.5 to compare specific functions across products. For example, the support functions of "provide on-line help" and "quick reference to basic commands" (1 and 2) are generally available across the life cycle. But more sophisticated or intelligent support such as "the ability to anticipate user mistakes based on past errors" (11) is absent.

These results suggest that the FCTM is a useful way to characterize design aid technology. Though clearly not the only possible perspective, this model does ap-

Table 10.3. Life cycle coverage by product

	Product							
Design activity	A	B	C	D	E	F	G	H
IS planning	4.5	3.71	1.88	2.8	2.0	1.1	3.5	2.4
Requirement definition	3.25	3.86	4.0	3.3	2.8	1.8	4.5	3.2
Conceptual design	3.0	3.57	4.50	3.67	2.8	2.3	4.8	4.0
Detailed design	2.0	2.29	3.63	3.0	4.0	3.4	4.6	4.6
Implementation	1.33	1.86	2.1	1.6	4.6	4.7	3.1	3.1
Testing	1.0	1.43	1.6	1.0	3.2	4 3	2.2	1.7
Maintenance	2.0	1.43	2.5	1.8	4.2	4.8	3.9	2.5

Scale: 1.0 very little support, 2.0 some support, 3.0 adequate support, 4.0 good support, 5.0 extensive support.

Table 10.4. Summary of product evaluations

Case	I Representation		II Analysis		III Transformation		IV Control		V Cooperative functionality		VI Support	
Tool	No.	%	No.	%	No.	%	No.	%	No.	%	No.	%
Possible	18	100	19	100	13	100	16	100	10	100	22	100
A	7	39	5	26	2	15	0	0	1	10	4	18
B	5	28	2	11	1	8	0	0	1	10	3	14
C	11	61	3	16	2	15	3	19	2	20	8	36
D	9	50	5	26	2	15	0	0	0	0	8	36
E	2	11	0	0	5	38	0	0	3	30	1	5
F	3	17	4	21	7	54	1	6	2	20	5	23
G	13	72	5	26	4	31	9	56	4	40	14	64
H	10	56	3	16	4	31	0	0	3	30	8	36
Total Used	17	94	9	47	11	85	9	56	4	40	17	77

Example: the user can instruct the tools to redraw a diagram on the screen so that it is uncluttered and easy to read. Scale: 1 = does not exist or is very difficult to use; 2 = difficult to use; 3 = adequate ease of use; 4 = easy to use; 5 = very easy to use, essentially automatic.

pear to be reliable and valid for several functions and it does differentiate among products. Next, we shall consider the implications of the FCTM and possible items for future research.

IMPLICATIONS AND FUTURE RESEARCH

Our research led to the development of a model of design aid technology with three general dimensions: production, coordination, and organization. Each of these general dimensions has a number of subdimensions. Production technology consists of representation, analysis, and transformation; coordination technology, of control and cooperation, and organizational technology, of support and infrastructure. A Q-sort technique was used to map specific functions onto these components and their related dimensions. The results of this analysis point to a reasonably strong consensus among those involved in the sorting process, implying that these dimensions provide a useful way of categorizing major functions. Further, when this model is applied to existing products, important differences are revealed.

The results of applying the FCTM to current products highlighted two significant limitations (at least for the products included in this study). First, the products supported a relatively weak level of analysis. Because the ability to support the critical thinking process of design is crucial, these results suggest that increasing the level of analysis technology is promising. Second, the products offered a limited amount of support for cooperative activities in the design process. The ability of these tools to assist in coordinating the activities of several designers within and across teams is a major area for enhancing the functions of these tools.

Our debriefings emphasized the importance of the organizational dimension of technology. This emphasis means that the users of design aids must pay careful attention to the availability of support and the building of technology infrastructures through the use of standards and relevant support.

Table 10.5. Detailed listing of CASE tool functionality

CASE tool	1	2	3	4	5	6	7	8	9	10	11	12	13	14	15	16	17	18	19	20	21	22
A. Representation																						
A			x			x		x	x	x		x			x							
B			x					x		x		x	x									
C	x	x	x	x		x	x	x	x		x	x	x									
D	x	x	x			x		x	x			x	x				x					
E								x			x											
F								x			x	x										
G	x	x	x		x	x	x		x	x	x	x	x				x	x				
H	x	x	x			x	x		x			x	x			x		x				
B. Analysis																						
A	x									x			x		x	x						
B													x						x			
C										x			x		x							
D	x									x			x		x			x				
E																						
F				x						x			x	x								
G										x			x		x	x			x			
H													x					x	x			
C. Transformation																						
A								x					x									
B													x									
C										x	x											
D							x						x									
E	x		x	x				x		x												
F	x			x	x	x		x		x			x									
G								x		x	x	x										
H					x			x		x	x											

The selection of a design aid tool requires fitting the function to the characteristics of the user's design task. In this sense, one cannot conclude that coverage across all functions is inherently valuable. Rather, one must recognize how specific functions address the behavior of a designer or design team. One interpretation of this is that the relative value of the identified dimensions and even the specific functions within a dimension may not be equal across all task environments. Therefore, one important line of future research would be to establish empirically the organizational and specific design activities that increase the importance of specific functions or dimensions.

This research represents an initial attempt at examining systematically the underlying dimensions of design aid technology. Although the results of the work are encouraging, we note some concerns. The methodology we used was a limited test of the construct validity of the dimensions and their components. Future research should include a more formal testing of the underlying validity of these dimensions of technology. The model presented in this research offers the representation interpreted by several expert designers and users. Clearly, one has to be concerned that their consensus might reflect a bias of the design community that would omit or understate innovative or emerging functions. Nevertheless, the degree of convergence shown by the data and their usefulness for classifying current products indicates that it is a meaningful starting point.

Table 10.5. *(continued)*

CASE tool	1	2	3	4	5	6	7	8	9	10	11	12	13	14	15	16	17	18	19	20	21	22
D. Control																						
A																						
B																						
C				x		x	x															
D																						
E																						
F				x																		
G	x		x	x		x	x	x			x	x			x							
H																						
E. Cooperation																						
A						x																
B				x																		
C						x				x												
D																						
E				x		x				x												
F.				x						x												
G				x		x			x	x												
H				x		x				x												
F. Support																						
A	x	x	x	x																		
B	x	x				x																
C	x		x						x				x				x	x	x			x
D	x	x	x	x			x		x								x					
E															x							
F	x					x									x	x						x
G	x	x	x			x	x		x	x		x	x	x	x		x	x	x			
H	x	x	x						x				x		x			x	x			

A primary focus for future research will be measuring the usage behavior of actual design teams with respect to the dimensions of technology described in the FCTM. By using the FCTM as a basis for conceptualizing usage behavior, the relationship between the usage behavior of design teams and their actual performance can be empirically demonstrated. In this way, the FCTM will be able to characterize the performance impact of IS planning and design aids.

ACKNOWLEDGMENT

This research was funded by the Management in the 1990s project. The authors wish to thank the reviewers for their comments and suggestions.

NOTE

1. As discussed in the section on organizational technology, the infrastructure component resulted from feedback during debriefing, and thus it is not included in the Q-sort test.

REFERENCES

Abdel-Hamid, T.K., & S. E. Madnick (1985). Impact of schedule estimation on software project behavior. Working paper no. 127, Center for Information Systems Research, Massachusetts Institute of Technology.

Acly, E. (1988). Looking beyond CASE. *IEEE Software*, March, pp. 39–43.

Adelson, B., & E. Soloway (1985). The role of domain experience in software design. *IEEE Transactions on Software Engineering* SE-11 (November): 1351–60.

Ancona, D. G., & D. F. Caldwell (1987). Management issues facing new-product teams in high-technology companies. In D. Lewin, D.B. Lipsky, & D. Sockell (Eds.), *Advances in industrial and labor relations*, Vol. 4, pp. 199–221. Greenwich, CT: JAI Press.

Andriole, S. J. (1986). *Software development tools: A source book*. Princeton, NJ: Petrocelli Books.

Applegate, L. M., B. R. Konsynski, & J. F. Nunamaker (1986). A group decision support system for idea generation and issue analysis in organizational planning. In *Proceedings* of the Conference on Computer-supported Cooperative Work, Austin, TX, December 3–5, pp. 16–34.

Bakos, J. Y., & M. E. Treacy (1986). Information technology and corporate strategy: A research perspective. *MIS Quarterly* 10:107–119.

Banker, R. D., S. M. Datar, & C. F. Kemerer (1987). Factors affecting software maintenance productivity: An exploratory study. In *Proceedings* of the Eighth International Conference on Information Systems, Pittsburgh, December 6–9, pp. 160–75.

Beck, L. L., & T. E. Perkins (1983). A survey of software engineering practice: Tools, methods, and results. *IEEE Transactions on Software Engineering* SE-9:5 (September): 541–61.

Brooks, F. P., Jr. (1987). No silver bullet: Essence and accidents of software engineering. *IEEE Computer*, 20 (April): 10–19.

Bruns, G., & S. L. Gerhart (1986). Theories of design: An introduction to the literature. MCC Technical Report no. STP-068–86, Microelectronics and Computer Technology Corporation, Austin, TX.

Card, D. N., F. E. McGarry, & G. T. Page (1987). Evaluating software engineering technologies. *IEEE Transactions of Software Engineering* SE-13 (July): 845–851.

Case, A. F., Jr. (1985). Computer-aided software engineering (CASE): Technology for improving software development productivity. *Data Base* 17 (Fall): 35–43.

Chikofsky, E. J., & B. L. Rubenstein (1988). CASE: Reliability engineering for information systems. *IEEE Software*, March, pp. 11–16.

Connor, A. J., & A. F. Case, Jr. (1986). Making a case for CASE. *Computerworld*, July 9, pp. 45–46.

Cooprider, J. G., & J. C. Henderson (1990). Technology-process fit: Perspectives on achieving prototyping effectiveness. In *Proceedings* of the Twenty-third Hawaii International Conference on System Sciences, January, pp. 623–30.

Dart, S. A., R. J. Ellison, P. H. Feiler, & A. N. Habermann (1987). Software development environments. *IEEE Computer* 20 (November): 18–28.

Davis, R., & R. G Smith (1983). Negotiation as a metaphor for distributed problem solving. *Artificial Intelligence* 20 (January): 63–109.

Durfee, E. H., & V. R. Lesser (1987). Using partial global plans to coordinate distributed problem solvers. In *Proceedings* of the Tenth International Joint Conference on Artificial Intelligence, Milan, Italy, August 23–28, pp. 875–83.

Durfee, E. H., V. R. Lesser, & D. D. Corkill (1987). Coherent cooperation among communicating problem solvers. *IEEE Transactions on Computers* C-36 (November): 1275–91.

Frenkel, K. A. (1985). Toward automating the software-development cycle. *Communications of the ACM* 28 (June): 578–89.

Fry, L. (1982). Technology-structure research: Three critical issues. *Academy of Management Journal* 25:532–52.

Fry, L. W., & J. W. Slocum, Jr. (1984). Technology, structure, and workgroup effectiveness: A test of a contingency model. *Academy of Management Journal* 27 (June): 221–46.

Galbraith, J. R. (1977). *Organization design*. Reading, MA: Addison-Wesley.

Gane, C., & T. Sarson (1979). *Structured systems analysis: Tools and techniques*. Englewood Cliffs, NJ: Prentice-Hall.

Glass, R. L. (1982). Recommended: A minimum standard software toolset. *ACM SIGSOFT Software Engineering Notes* 7 (October): 3–13.

Hackathorn, R. D., & J. Karimi (1988). A framework for comparing information engineering methods. *MIS Quarterly* 12 (June): 203–20.

Hanson, S. J., & R. R. Rosinski (1985). Programmer perceptions of productivity and programming tools. *Communications of the ACM* 28 (February): 180–89.

Harvard Business School (1989). Xerox Corporation: Executive support systems. Harvard Business School case no. N9–189–134, Harvard University, April.

Henderson, J. C. (1988). Involvement as a predictor of performance in IS planning and design. Working paper no. 175, Center for Information Systems Research, Massachusetts Institute of Technology, August.

Holt, A., H. Ramsey, & J. Grimes (1983). Coordination system technology as the basis for a programming environment. *Electrical Communication* 57:307–14.

Honda, K., M. Azuma, A. Komatubara, & Y. Yokomizo (1985). Research on work environment for software productivity improvement. In *IEEE Proceeding* of 9th COMPSAC Computer Software & Applications Conference, Chicago, October 9–11, pp. 241–48.

Houghton, R. C., Jr., & D. R. Wallace (1987). Characteristics and functions of software engineering environments: An overview. *ACM SIGSOFT Software Engineering Notes* 12 (January): 64–84.

Keen, P. G. W., & M. S. Scott Morton (1987). *Decision support systems: An organizational perspective*. Reading, MA:Addison-Wesley.

Kemerer, C. F. (1988). Software production economics: Theoretical models and practical tools. Working paper no. 168, Center for Information Systems Research, Massachusetts Institute of Technology.

King, J. L., & S. L. Star (1990). Conceptual foundations for the development of organizational decision support systems. In *Proceedings* of the Twenty-third Annual Hawaii International Conference on System Sciences, January, pp. 143–51.

King, W. R. (1984). Evaluating an information systems planning process. Working paper, Graduate School of Business, University of Pittsburgh.

Konsynski, B. R., J. E. Kottemann, J. F. Nunamaker, Jr., & J. W. Stott (1984–85). PLEXSYS-84: An integrated development environment for information systems. *Journal of Management Information Systems* 1 (Winter): 64–104.

Kottemann, J. E., & B. R. Konsynski (1984). Dynamic metasystems for information systems development. In *Proceedings* of the Fifth International Conference on Information Systems, Tucson, AZ, November 28–30, pp. 187–204.

Kull, D. (1984). To raise productivity work smarter, not harder. *Computer Decisions* 16 (March): 164–89.

Lempp, P., & R. Lauber (1988). What productivity increases to expect from a CASE environment: Results of a user survey. In *Productivity: Progress, Prospects, and Payoff*, Proceedings of 27th Annual Technical Symposium, Gaithersburg, MD, June 9, pp. 13–19.

Malone, T. W. (1988). What is coordination theory? Working paper no. 2051–88, Sloan School of Management, Massachusetts Institute of Technology.

March, J. G.,& H. A. Simon (1958). *Organizations*. New York: Wiley.

Martin, C. F. (1988). Second-generation CASE tools: A challenge to vendors. *IEEE Software,* March, pp. 46–49.

McCann, J., & J. R. Galbraith (1981). Interdepartmental relations. In P. C. Nystrom, & W. H. Starbuck (Eds.), *Handbook of Organizational Design*, Vol. 2, pp. 60–84. New York: Oxford University Press.

McIntyre, S. C.,B. R. Konsynski, & J. F. Nunamaker, Jr. (1986). Automating planning environments: Knowledge integration and model scripting. *Journal of Management Information Systems* 2 (Spring): 49–69.

Necco, C. R., C. L. Gordon, & N. W. Tsai (1987). Systems analysis and design: Current practices. *MIS Quarterly* 11 (December): 461–76.

Osterweil, L. (1981). Software environment research: Directions for the next five years. *IEEE Computer* 14 (April): 35–43.

Perrow, C. (1967). A framework for the comparative analysis of organizations. *American Sociological Review* 32 (April): 194–208.

Rajaraman, M. K. (1982). A characterization of software design tools. *ACM SIGSOFT Software Engineering Notes* 7 (October): 14–17.

Reifer, D. J., & H. A. Montgomery (1980). Final report, software tool taxonomy. Management Consultants report no. SMC-TR-004, National Bureau of Standards, no. NB795BCA0273, June.

Schon, D. A. (1984). Problems, frames and perspectives on designing. *Design Studies* 5 (July): 132–36.

Semprevivo, P. (1980). Incorporating data dictionary/directory and team approaches into the systems development process. *MIS Quarterly* 4 (September): 1–15.

Sherif, M., & C. W. Sherif (1967). The own categories procedure in attitude research. In M. Fishbein (Ed.), *Readings in attitude theory and measurement*, pp. 190–98. New York: Wiley.

Simon, H. A. (1976). *Administrative behavior: A study of decision-making processes in administrative organization*, 3rd ed. New York: Free Press.

Simon, H. A. (1981). *The sciences of the artificial,* 2nd ed. Cambridge, MA: MIT Press.

Slocum, J. W., Jr., & H. P. Sims, Jr. (1980). A typology for integrating technology, organization, and job design. *Human Relations* 33 (March): 193–212.

Sprague, R. H., Jr., & E.D. Carlson (1982). *Building effective decision support systems*. Englewood Cliffs, NJ: Prentice-Hall.

Stefik, M., G. Foster, D. G. Bobrow, K. Kahn, S. Lanning, & L. Suchman (1987). Beyond the chalkboard: Computer support for collaboration and problem solving in meetings. *Communications of the ACM* 30 (January): 32–47.

Thomas, J. C., & J. M. Carroll (1979). Psychological study of design. *Design Studies* 1 (July): 5–11.

Thompson, J. D. (1967). *Organizations in action*. New York: McGraw-Hill.

Treacy, M. E. (1981). Toward a behaviorally grounded theory of information value. In *Proceedings* of the Second International Conference on Information Systems, Cambridge, MA, December 7–9, pp. 247–57.

Wasserman, A. I. (1982). Automated tools in the information system development environment. In H. J. Schneider, & A. I. Wasserman (Eds.), *Automated tools for information systems design*, pp. 1–9. New York: North-Holland.

Weiderman, N. H., A. N. Habermann, M. W. Borger, & M. H. Klein (1986). A methodology for evaluating environments. In *Proceedings* of the ACM SIGSOFT/SIGPLAN Software Engineering Symposium on Practical Software Development Environments, Palo Alto, CA, December 9–11, pp. 199–207.

Welke, R. J., & B. R. Konsynski (1980). An examination of the interaction between technology, methodology and information systems: A tripartite view. In *Proceedings* of the First

International Conference on Information Systems, Philadelphia, PA, December 8–10, pp. 32–48.

Williamson, O. E. (1975). *Markets and hierarchies*. New York: Free Press.

Winograd, T., & F. Flores (1986). *Understanding computers and cognition*. Norwood, NJ: Ablex.

Withey, M., R. L. Daft, & W. H. Cooper (1983). Measures of Perrow's work unit technology: An empirical assessment and a new scale. *Academy of Management Journal* 26 (March): 45–63.

Zachman, J. A. (1986). A framework for information systems architecture. Report no. G320–2785, IBM Los Angeles Scientific Center, Los Angeles.

Zmud, R. W., A. C. Boynton, & G. C. Jacobs (1986). The information economy: A new perspective for effective information systems management. *Data Base,* Fall, pp. 5–16.

CHAPTER 11

Information Technology and Work Organization

KEVIN CROWSTON AND THOMAS W. MALONE

Ever since at least 1958, when Leavitt and Whisler (1958) predicted that the use of information technology (IT) would lead to the demise of middle management, researchers have speculated about the effects of IT on organizations. Even though many of the early predictions have not come true, new kinds of information technology are now increasingly affecting how people work, often in ways that we are just beginning to understand. As the cost of the underlying technology continues to drop, IT is almost certain to become more and more pervasive and may even make possible new kinds of work organization that we can as yet only barely imagine.

In this chapter, we discuss the relationship between the use of IT and work organizations. We first review theories that can help analyze organizations, technology, and the link between the two. We suggest four perspectives on organizations—rationalist, information processing, motivational, and political—that can be used to interpret organizational structure. Using these four perspectives, we review the results of empirical studies of the use of IT to determine what changes have been made in the past and can be expected in the future. Our goal here is not to predict inevitable impacts but, rather, to discover possible outcomes, both good and bad, and to illuminate the factors that may lead to them. In many cases we believe that the results of using IT are not fixed but can instead be greatly influenced by conscious choice. We conclude with some ideas about the kinds of future research that will be useful and some implications for the design of systems, work, and organizations.

THEORETICAL BASES

We begin our investigations by presenting three components of a theoretical basis for studying the effects of IT on organizations. First, we need a theory about organizations that describes their important features and shows which features will reflect the use of IT. Second, we need a body of theory about technology, again to identify the features of IT that are essential to its use in organizations. Finally, and perhaps most important, we need somehow to link some parts of these two bodies of theory. These theories are necessary for both research and practice. For research, a strong theoretical basis is needed to demonstrate the important attributes of the items of interest and to identify linkages that need to be investigated. For practice, a good theory summarizes a body of research and provides implications to guide the design of new systems.

The theories in these three areas, however, are social theories, which differ from theories in sciences such as physics. The reason for this is partly the relative youth of the social sciences, but largely the differences in the objects of study. With social phenomena more than with many physical phenomena, there are often many factors, any of which may be important. Although many theories do make specific predictions about outcomes, a perhaps more important function is to suggest which of the many possible factors are the relevant ones. In this latter sense, consistent sets of these theories can be grouped together into perspectives. Different perspectives point to different key issues; that is, they complement rather than contradict one another. Before examining the results of past studies, then, we will briefly discuss various perspectives on organizations, technology, and the link between the two.

Perspectives on organizational structure

Obviously, there are many kinds of organizations, and different kinds of organizations will be differently affected by the use of IT. To reduce the scope of this chapter somewhat, we have focused on formal work organizations, especially corporations. Even so, there is tremendous diversity, and unfortunately, we do not know which differences matter most. At some level, we do not really know what organizations are, and our intuitive notions are difficult to make precise. For example, task (what the organization does) is clearly important. Organizations in information-intensive industries such as insurance or banking should be quicker to show the effects of the use of IT, as computers are particularly useful for processing large quantities of information. Identifying task as a dimension, however, only partially addresses the problem, unless we can next identify the important dimensions of tasks.

The body of theory in this area, which should describe the principal dimensions of organizations, is not very well developed or coherent. There are many incomplete theories of organizations that may be part of a more comprehensive theory, but these components are not yet well integrated or well supported empirically. Different studies have often used incompatible definitions of the same key variables, making their results difficult to compare. These differences are due partly to the exploratory nature of many of these studies and partly to the different perspectives that researchers have of organizations, reflecting the interdisciplinary nature of the field (Pfeffer, 1982) and the prior theoretical commitments of the researchers (Hirschheim, 1986). For example, Hirschheim claimed that researchers who are optimistic about the effects of using IT are more likely to consider IT as a tool and to adopt what he calls a *functionalist paradigm*. These researchers view the world as composed of immutable objects and so concentrate on developing causal explanations of observed phenomena. Pessimists, by contrast, are more likely to view IT in its social setting and thereby adopt an *interpretivist paradigm*. These researchers see the world as a social construct and attempt to understand their findings in the framework of their subjects, rather than building causal models. Each perspective leads researchers to examine different phenomena and variables. Studies based on different assumptions about organizations have often talked past one another and focused on different features of the organizations studied. In particular, interpretivists often choose to perform detailed case studies to find out how users come to understand the technology they use and how it fulfills their social needs.

A number of authors have proposed ways of classifying the perspectives. Pfeffer (1982) suggested two dimensions: perspective on action and level of analysis. Pfeffer first observed that an organization's actions can be viewed in three ways; as purposeful (i.e., intendedly rational), externally constrained (e.g., by a lack of some resource), or emergent (e.g., random but retrospectively rationalized).

Pfeffer then distinguished between theories that treat organizations as the units of analysis (e.g., market economics) and those that examine the subunits that comprise organizations. Given our interest in the effects of IT on organizational structure, we shall focus mainly on the latter set of perspectives. Here we can differentiate between perspectives that examine characteristics of the subunits, such as the level of skill required for a particular job or how much autonomy a worker has in performing a task, and those that treat features of the organization as a whole, such as the arrangement of the divisions or the patterns of communication within the firm.

Kling (1980) offered six perspectives, divided into two groups that he named *systems rationalist* and *segmented institutionalist*. Research based on the systems rationalist perspective sees organizations as directed toward some common goal, such as increased efficiency or profit, and views as legitimate the authority of managers in higher levels of the firm to decide how to achieve these goals. In this perspective, IT is simply a tool that can be used to advance some organizational goals. The segmented institutionalist perspective, by contrast, examines the use of computing more broadly. It acknowledges the effects of the technology on individuals and groups other than the actual users of the technology, and it recognizes their possibly conflicting interests.

In this chapter we shall discuss the effects of IT on organizations, drawing on theories from four complementary perspectives proposed by Malone (1985): rationalist, information processing, motivational, and political (see Table 11.1). The first three of these perspectives correspond roughly to the three that Kling (1980) calls *systems rationalist*. The rationalist perspective assumes that organizations are composed of purposely rational agents, operating toward some defined goal, typically profit maximization. It concentrates on economic efficiency and rationally structuring the firm. The information-processing approach shares many of these characteristics but looks instead at the organizational processes and communications patterns of the firm. The motivational perspective recognizes that workers may have interests different from those of the management of an organization, but it typically assumes that these goals can be matched by properly designing the jobs of individual workers. That is, if a job is sufficiently motivating, the workers will presumably be more satisfied and will want to perform well. The political view is one example of Kling's *segmented institutionalist* perspectives. It assumes that different groups in the organization may have conflicting goals that cannot be reconciled. Power determines which group achieves its goals, and IT may be used as a means to increase power.

Each perspective suggests a different approach to the study of IT and organizations, and each makes different predictions about the effects likely to be encountered. For example, Robey (1981) noted that a rationalist view of organizations expects the

Table 11.1. Central issues of four organizational perspectives

Perspective	Central issues
Rationalist	Employment
	Job loss
	Administrative intensity
	Levels of hierarchy
	Centralization / Decentralization
	Differentiation
	Formalization
Information processing	Patterns of communication
	Weak links
	Social context cues
Motivational	Individual motivations
	Skill variety
	Task meaningfulness
	Autonomy
	Interpersonal motivations
Political	Power
	Vertical distribution
	Horizontal distribution

use of IT to be associated with changes in the organization, as IT allows work to be done in new and different ways. A political view expects that IT will be used by those with power in the organization to support their position, reinforcing rather than changing the organization's structure.

Some perspectives may be more useful than others for analyzing the effects of the use of IT. For example, it is unclear how the use of an electronic mail system will affect the distribution of power in a firm: It may either concentrate or disperse it. It is clear, however, that the use of electronic mail will facilitate and reduce the cost of some types of communications, pointing to an information-processing-based analysis.

Perspectives on technology

The second necessary basis for studying the impacts of IT on organizations is one theory of technology. Our ability to develop technology itself is probably more advanced than our theories of organizations, but our understanding of the uses of technology is probably behind our understanding of organizations. It is still difficult to identify the relevant dimensions of technology or to measure it, although it is clear that there are large differences between, for example, personal computers and mainframes. The task to which the IT is applied also makes a difference. For example, a payroll system has greatly different functions and is likely to have different effects than an electronic mail system does. Few researchers, however, have attempted to characterize IT precisely or even to define it. Many studies have used very crude measures of IT (such as total dollar investment in IT), and as yet there are no good typologies of the various kinds of systems. Several have been proposed, but they are either too rough to distinguish usefully the different uses of technology (e.g., Bakos,

1985) or to focus exclusively on technical details, omitting use altogether (e.g., Barrett & Konsynski, 1982). Similar problems have been noted for studies of technology in general (e.g., Fry, 1982).

Some preliminary characterizations of technology have been made, however. Markus and Robey (1990) noted that past researchers identified such dimensions as batch processing versus interactive systems, decision support versus decision-making systems, and administrative versus technical systems. Robey (1983) differentiated among administrative systems, production-scheduling systems, and central coordination systems and found that each system had a different effect. For example, he observed that systems designed simply to automate existing procedures tended not to lead to any organizational changes.

Past studies of IT have viewed it in different ways. Markus and Robey (in press) identified three different conceptions of IT. First, a researcher can simply measure IT as an independent variable and attempt to correlate its use (and perhaps other factors) with organizational changes. Alternatively, IT can be analyzed as a special kind of production technology. For example, some researchers (e.g., Perrow, 1979; Woodward, 1980) listed ways in which an organization's structure depends on the nature of the technology it uses. Finally, the use of IT may be an alternative organizational design strategy. For example, Galbraith (1974, 1977) proposed ways in which an organization can increase its information-processing capacity, including through the use of IT.

One distinction that we will make is between the use of IT as a production technology and as a coordination technology. IT can be used as a production technology, to produce directly some output—for example, by producing account statements in a bank, by keeping track of policyholders in an insurance company, or by controlling a machine tool in a factory. These uses should be distinguished from employing IT as a coordination technology—for example, by providing the data necessary to integrate more closely two stages in a production line or to make some decision more easily.

The link between structure and technology

The final necessary component of a theoretical basis for research in this area is a link between some aspects of the two bodies of theory just outlined. Unfortunately, few past studies have explicitly described the nature of the link they were drawing. Markus and Robey (1990) discussed three different kinds of links that have been used in past research: the technological imperative, the organizational imperative, and the interactionist perspective.

Technological imperative

The *technological imperative* assumes that the technology will have some determined effects on the structure of the firm (see Figure 11.1). For example, Woodward (1980) found that the formality of a company's structure seemed to depend on the type of production technology it used: Job shops using unit production were relatively informal; mass production companies were much more formal; and continuous flow production companies were again informal. The focus of such research is predictive in that it attempts to forecast what changes will occur in response to using IT. This view

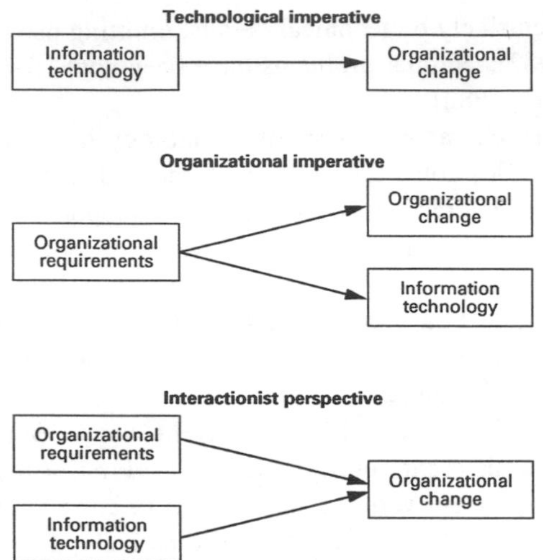

Figure 11.1. Links between organizational structure and technology.

can be adapted somewhat by assuming that the effects of IT are contingent on other factors, such as the firm's environment. There may be many other factors that need to be examined, however. For example, Leavitt and Whisler (1958) hypothesized that different groups would be variously affected because they differ in ease of measuring outcomes, economic pressures, and acceptance of job programming.

Organizational imperative

Markus and Robey (in press) called their second view the *organizational imperative*. This view reverses the direction of causality by assuming that managers make organizational changes (including adopting certain kinds of IT) in response to certain organizational needs (see Figure 11.1). Markus and Robey described this view as prescriptive, as most authors have attempted to propose what IT a manager should use under different conditions. For example, Galbraith (1974, 1977) offered four methods to increase an organization's information-processing capacity. This view concentrates on the managers' intentions, however, ignoring possible unintended side effects of using IT. It also discounts possible nonrational goals for using IT, such as increasing political power. Furthermore, such studies have only mixed empirical support. For example, Child (1972) found no conclusive evidence that organizations with different forms performed differently under the same conditions.

Interactionist perspective

A final view suggested by Markus and Robey (in press) is an *interactionist perspective*, which holds that the result of using IT is a complex interaction between what the technology allows and what the organization and the managers want (see Figure 11.1). They pointed out that unlike the other perspectives, this view does not allow predictions about the effect of IT. In fact, they claimed that this view shuns prediction for understanding the underlying reasons for a change, leading to a focus on *post hoc* analyses. Such an approach may, however, be most appropriate to studies of complex organizations, which are affected in many ways besides by technology.

We take a modified interactionist point of view. We believe that in many cases IT acts as an enabling factor that makes possible certain kinds of organizational change. If those changes are desirable, they may then occur. Certain kinds of change may be especially desirable and thus especially common, but different effects are still possible. Kling (1980) expressed a similar view, noting that IT does not have deterministic impacts but, rather, common impacts that may vary under different conditions, depending on the particulars of the organization being studied, the way the technology is used, and, perhaps most important, the goals of those using it. Rather than attempting to predict changes due to particular systems, then, we hope to suggest conditions under which different uses of technology are likely to be desirable.

SURVEY OF EMPIRICAL RESEARCH

Our aim in studying past research is not to predict what must happen but to illuminate possible outcomes, including some that may not usually be considered, and to suggest the factors that lead to these outcomes. To do this we will present a variety of scenarios as examples of possible changes. In each case we will try to tell a plausible story about how the IT had the effect that was observed.

As a basis for this presentation we will draw on a number of different kinds of evidence. First, this subject has been a source of much interest and coverage in the popular business press. These articles describe the experiences of specific firms and provide interesting examples of the effects that IT could have. On a more rigorous theoretical level is a long tradition of studies of the links between different kinds of production technology and aspects of organizational structure. A number of writers have summarized this body of literature (Fry, 1982), and we will attempt to determine where these findings are applicable. Finally, there are many studies of the impact of IT in particular and some summaries of this body of research in general (Attewell & Rule, 1984; Rice, 1980; Robey, 1981).

Unfortunately, this body of literature has several limitations that make it difficult to draw general conclusions. First, the findings are mostly out of date: Many of the studies are more than five years old, and the data they draw on are older still. These studies examine traditional applications such as payroll systems, even though the technology has rapidly advanced. There are few studies that investigate the use of technologies such as personal computers or electronic mail, even though these kinds of applications are likely to have enormous and quite different impacts. Second, it is difficult to generalize from these earlier studies because they were often quite vague about how the technology was actually being used. This makes it difficult to trace the mechanism through which some application affected the firm. Finally, the methodologies employed were sometimes weak, making the strength of the conclusions questionable.

Studies of the organizational effects of IT have viewed IT and organizations in different ways, and many effects have been noted. Each organizational perspective suggests different kinds of effects that should be studied. To organize our survey, therefore, we have grouped the effects based on the four perspectives just discussed (see Table 11.1). Some effects (such as centralization) have been widely studied, however, and so we will survey these issues from several perspectives.

Rationalist perspective

In this section we will draw mainly from classical organization theory, with its focus on rationality and efficiency, and we will consider several features of organizations suggested by this perspective.

Employment

Organizations differ in size, and intuitively we would expect different-sized organizations to behave differently. Variations in size are reflected in several interrelated measures, including the number of employees, the number of levels of management in a hierarchical organization, the number of employees reporting to a specific manager (the manager's span of control), and the ratio of production workers to administrative workers in a firm (the firm's administrative intensity). Obviously, these features are interrelated, and a change in the structure of an organization may affect a combination of them. For example, a firm may reduce its head count either by eliminating some employees from all parts of the organization, thereby reducing the number of employees reporting to a single manager, or even by eliminating an entire level of management.

Studies of these aspects of size have not found consistent results, partly because there may be no general effects. In addition, however, past studies have often treated these various factors independently, making it difficult to see any more general patterns. In addition, different uses of IT have not been separated, further clouding the issue, as the actual effect seems to depend heavily on how the technology is used. In this section, we will differentiate between the use of IT for production and for coordination functions.

Job loss

An early common prediction was that the widespread use of IT would replace most routine workers, thus causing massive unemployment (e.g, Mumford & Banks, 1967; Myers, 1967), and in fact, systems have often been cost justified on the basis of reducing the number of employees (e.g., Matteis, 1979). For instance, Rice (1980) cited a study of 33 companies (Sanders, 1977) in which 90 percent cut the number of employees (one company laying off thousands of workers) or increased their output with the same number of staff. The prediction of an overall reduction in employment due to the use of IT is difficult to support empirically, however, as most studies have, examined only a few firms or a few industries, and more comprehensive census data are difficult to interpret unequivocally (Attewell & Rule, 1984). Furthermore, other factors may more strongly affect employment, thereby masking the effect of using IT.

In fact, it is interesting to note that IT may, in some cases, increase rather than decrease employment. For instance, Osterman (1986) listed several means by which the use of IT may affect clerical employment. First, computers might be used simply to replace clerks. Second, the use of IT may itself create some new jobs, such as that of data entry clerks or positions in the data-processing department. Third, the use of computers may make the firm more efficient, increasing the demand for its products and thus indirectly its total level of employment. Finally, coordination may be viewed as a complementary input in the production process. For instance, if IT makes coordination more effective and less expensive, the demand for coordination and therefore for both IT and the clerks who provide it may increase. This analysis holds only for coordination functions, however, suggesting that clerks employed in production functions are more likely to be displaced by the use of IT. The total effect of using IT on the employment of managers may be less, as fewer managers are involved in production than in coordination. Osterman combined these effects in a microeconomic production function and calculated the rate of substitution between clerks and computers. Using census data from 1970 through 1978, he found that the use of computers initially led to decreased employment but that this effect was partially offset by a subsequent increase in employment due to greater coordination. As he pointed out, however, this later increase may involve a different set of workers than were initially displaced.

Administrative intensity

The jobs of most managers are so far less affected by the automation of production functions than are those of clerks. In this case, the smaller number of production workers and the unchanged number of managers and other coordination workers indicate that the administrative intensity (the ratio of administrative to production workers) may actually rise if IT is used to automate production functions. Osterman (1986) also predicted that the use of IT would affect the jobs of workers in production more than those in coordination, again increasing administrative intensity. A number of studies agree with this general prediction. For instance, Stabell and Forsund (1983) found that an increased use of computers is associated with higher levels of administrative intensity. Scharek and Barton (1975) noted a reduction of low-level personnel. Whisler (1970a) found that the companies he studied cut the number of clerical employees they employed but that the supervisory and managerial levels stayed about the same. Blau, Falbe, McKinley, and Tracy (1976) and Rice (1980) also observed a higher proportion of professionals, and *Business Week* (Office Automation, 1984) described a firm that changed from 70 percent clerical to 60 percent professional, with an overall reduction of 20 percent. Zuboff (1983a) and Nolan and Pollock (1986) explained this change graphically as a shift from a triangular hierarchy to a diamond-shaped firm, thicker in the middle than at the bottom or top.

Levels of hierarchy

One of Leavitt and Whisler's (1958) original predictions is that the number of levels of hierarchy in organizations will decrease as computers are used to perform the functions of those middle managers. So far, however, there is no conclusive evidence that this prediction has been realized. Changes in levels of hierarchy seem to depend on the way the IT is used, and different studies have reported opposite findings. *Business Week* (Office Automation, 1984), for example, discussed firms that are reducing bureaucratic functions with computers and thus trimming the number of levels of hierarchy. Also, Crowston, Malone, and Lin (1987) studied the use of a computer conferencing system used to help eliminate a level of hierarchy. They found, however, that new central staff specialist positions were created at the same grade level as those eliminated, leaving the total employment approximately unchanged. Whisler (1970a) found little evidence of changes in hierarchical levels in his studies but noted one case in which the number of levels rose at the upper level and fell at the lower level, keeping the total the same. Blau and colleagues (1976) hypothesized that IT could actually increase the levels of hierarchy, as it could be used as an impersonal means of control and could shorten the feedback loop even if the number of levels were raised. Similarly, Pfeffer and Leblebici (1977) found that the use of IT as a means of control led to more levels of hierarchy and more departments when controlling for the size of the firm.

Centralization and decentralization

Centralization is perhaps the most commonly investigated organizational effect of using IT. When examining this literature, however, it becomes apparent that the concept of centralization has been variously defined and that the effect of IT differs depending on which construct is considered. We will look mainly at the centralization or decentralization of decision making. Even so, IT may affect decisions differently, simultaneously causing both centralization and decentralization.

We can think of the use of IT as a means of lowering the cost of coordination. This often seems to lead to increased centralization, but this effect is not inevitable. We will study two kinds of reasons—economic and motivational—that an organization might choose either to centralize or decentralize, and we will suggest how cheaper coordination can aid either process.

Economic reasons

Reduction of buffer inventories. One motive for centralizing is to reduce buffer inventories between groups by more tightly coordinating their interaction (e.g., "just-in-time" inventories). This closer integration often requires some decisions to be made at a higher level and to be implemented by each group. In some cases, IT is used explicitly for coordination. For example, production-scheduling systems attempt to coordinate more closely deliveries of raw materials with their use, thus requiring closer cooperation between the purchasing and the production departments. Argyris (1970) hypothesized that IT might be used to strengthen the integration between departments and thus lower the level of interdepartmental competition. Mann and Williams (1960) and Whisler (1970a) found a related effect. In some cases, low-level workers in different departments cannot simply work out a solution to some shared problem, as they might have in the past, because their results must fit an often inflexible information system. Instead, intervention by higher levels of management and by the data-processing staff is necessary, thereby increasing centralization.

Economies of scale. Another reason to centralize is to take advantage of economies of scale. In general, as a functional group grows, it becomes more efficient in production, as it can take advantage of economies of scale and share capacity among the different parts of the firm that require its services. For example, a centralized copying center can realize several advantages. First, because it does more copying, a central service can purchase paper and other raw materials in bulk and buy larger and more efficient copiers. Because the service is shared among many users, there is less variation in the load, and so each machine can be used more efficiently. Furthermore, the service can afford to buy more specialized but less frequently used equipment and to train people in its use. These greater efficiencies are offset, however, by the higher cost of coordination, both within and among groups. For example, to get service from such a centralized copying plant might require filling out a requisition, arranging for billing, delivery, and so forth, thereby lengthening the service time. Rush service might be difficult or expensive to negotiate. Furthermore, the central service will need a manager and perhaps other administrative personnel to ensure its smooth operation. If each department had its own private copier, many of these costs would disappear. A greater use of IT may lower the cost of the necessary coordination, thus favoring greater centralization. Scharek and Barton (1975) observed a shift to functional hierarchies, that is, hierarchies in which the subunits are organized around a single function rather than including a number of functions. Whisler (1970a) reported the replacement of departments selling different types of insurance, with various departments performing specific tasks for all policies. Both Osterman (1986) and Rice (1980) discussed using task pools for word processing or routine clerical operations, another form of functional specialization. Malone and Smith (1988) and Malone (1987b) presented a simplified model of an organization based on the information processing necessary to coordinate the assignment of tasks to different agents within the organization. Using this model, they identified trade-offs among different organizational structures based on their production and communication costs and the robustness of the organization in face of the agents' failure. Malone and Smith (1988) showed how this model was consistent with the historical development of American firms (e.g., as discussed by Chandler, 1962) and argued that as the use of IT lowers coordination costs, the trade-off shifts in favor of functional hierarchies.

As the cost of coordinating falls further, however, more decentralized organizational forms such as markets may become desirable (Malone & Smith, 1988). Markets are assumed to have lower production costs, as they can further exploit economies of scale and average uncorrelated demand across many firms, but higher coordination costs, as more communication is necessary to find a supplier and contracting with an outside party means higher levels of risk and uncertainty. As the cost of coordination drops, however, these factors become less important. Malone, Yates, and Benjamin (1987b) contended similarly that using IT may lead to a greater use of markets and especially of computer-mediated markets, which may offer more efficient coordination.

The use of IT may also allow a physical decentralization of work. Many organizations are already geographically dispersed and coordinated using telecommunications. Olson (1982) stated that "telecommuting" may allow individuals to work at home instead of at a central office. Becker (1986) presented a number of arguments against home work and suggested satellite work centers instead.

Motivational and political reasons

Another commonly discussed possibility is that centralizing decision making is inherently desirable to managers and that decentralization takes place only because no single person can control the necessary resources (e.g., information, employees) because of limitations in humans' information-processing capacity (Simon, 1957). These constraints force managers to delegate control over some decisions in order to focus on more important issues (Schultz & Whisler, 1964). The use of IT may lessen these constraints in two ways: first, by providing easier access to and facilitating more complete analyses of data regarding the firm's operations and, second, by providing a mechanism to program jobs and to control workers. The use of IT may thus permit decisions to be made at a higher level and ensure their implementation by subordinates. Leavitt and Whisler (1958) and Pfeffer (1978) found that IT enables centralization and that firms will therefore recentralize. As Zuboff (1983b) pointed out, it may often be difficult for a manager to have information about a problem and refrain from acting on it.

Alternatively, a manager may want to encourage the decentralization of decisions in order to increase workers' autonomy (which may be desirable for reasons discussed later). Some authors have predicted that IT will encourage greater participation in decisions by lower-level workers. IT provides ways to control the premise of the decision, by allowing more equal access to data or by controlling the way in which a decision is made, and to monitor the results, by providing quicker feedback. Given the ability to ensure that decisions are made consistent with their wishes, managers may be willing to delegate the actual decision. Systems used to provide individual support may also encourage decentralization, as they enlarge an individual's capacity to analyze data or enforce the use of common decision analysis tools. IT can also support lateral ties between low-level workers, allowing them more easily to exchange information and thus coordinate their own activities, as suggested by Galbraith (1974, 1977) and found by Robey (1981).

Other structural features

Differentiation. Another possible impact of using IT is the development of more differentiated or segmented jobs. Differentiation is difficult to define or measure precisely. Researchers in this area have measured, for example, the number of job titles used in a given organization or the number of different departments. It seems certain that using IT will require some new jobs and departments, such as a data-processing or telecommunications group, if only to manage the complex technology. Carter (1984), for example, found that using IT in newspapers did lead to the creation of new specialties, such as data-processing manager. It is less clear how using IT will affect other functions in an organization. Earlier, we argued that IT could lead to a reintegration of some tasks (e.g., handling all aspects of issuing a letter of credit, instead of a single step in a multistep process (Matteis, 1979). Such a reintegration would minimize the differentiation between jobs or departments. Or a higher level of functional specialization could raise the degree of differentiation. The empirical evidence is mixed: Mohrman (1982) cited some evidence that technology reduces the differences among roles, whereas other researchers (e.g., Carter, 1984) reported an increase.

Formalization. IT is often hypothesized to affect the degree of an organization's formalization. Here formalization refers to the degree to which the organization depends on the formal rules and regulations in operation. An informal organization, sometimes called an organic organization, is one in which few rules and formal procedures are used. For example, companies with production lines often have rigid work rules, whereas most research laboratories are administered according to individuals' interactions and not formal rules.

The use of IT can affect the level of formality in an organization in many ways. Most older centralized transaction-processing systems are inflexible. Because such systems can do things in only one way, rules are needed to limit actions to this process. The system itself embodies many rules about how the job should be done, again substituting the use of rules and regulations for individual decision making. A system may also make it easier to spot errors and identify their sources, thus further controlling work (Mann & Williams, 1960). On the other hand, Pfeffer (1978) pointed out that using IT may encourage the evaluation of outcomes instead of process and make the enforcement of rules both easier and less necessary by more quickly providing feedback about the outcomes of actions, thus decreasing formality. Finally, because smaller organizations are typically less formal, IT may lessen formality by reducing organizational size. For example, Woodward (1980) found that heavily automated manufacturers, such as oil refineries, had few actual production workers, thus lowering the level of formality among the remaining, mostly managerial or professional, workers.

The use of IT for individual support or for communications may well have different effects. On the one hand, Olson (1982) noted that using telecommunications to allow workers to work at home resulted in less personal interaction and therefore more formal evaluations. On the other hand, both Foster and Flynn (1984) and Pfeffer and Leblebici (1977) found that using IT could lead to less formalized interactions. Culnan and Markus (1987) cited research that showed how the use of electronic mail could undermine the formal hierarchy, again pointing to less formality. Huber (1984) suggested that as informal processes or "soft" data become more important to organizations, these organizations may become more formal about ensuring their existence.

Information-processing perspective

One problem with classic organization theory is that because it focuses on organizational structure, it does not address what IT is particularly useful for—processing information. A potentially useful way to examine the impacts of IT on organizations is to examine the kinds of information that the organization uses and the ways that it processes this information (Galbraith, 1974, 1977; Tushman & Nadler, 1978). Tushman and Nadler (1978, p. 292) outlined three basic assumptions of such an information-processing perspective: Organizations must deal with work-related uncertainty; organizations may be viewed as information-processing systems; and organizations may be regarded as composed of sets of groups or departments. In this view, organizational structure is the pattern and content of the information flowing between the subunits and the way they process this information.

Patterns of communication

IT can affect the pattern and content of organizational communications in many ways. First, the use of IT may lead to changes in the structure of an organization, leading to new patterns of communication or changes in the content or quantity of existing kinds of communication. Integrating jobs, a possible outcome of using IT, can lead to fewer needs for communication, as a single person can do the job with no need to communicate with coworkers, an effect noted by Whisler (1970b). For example, storing transaction data in a commonly accessible data base may make requests for information unnecessary. Such changes may also affect the level of social interactions. Some researchers claim that by integrating tasks, the use of IT eliminates the need and opportunity for workers to interact. For example, Crawford (1982), in a study of using electronic mail, discovered a decrease in the amount of face-to-face communication. Zuboff (1983a) hypothesized that social isolation will be further increased if workers can work at home instead of in an office. On the other hand, Foster and Flynn (1984) found that the use of IT can lead to more frequent personal contacts, suggesting that different uses of IT will have very different effects.

Second, IT may be used to provide new media for communication, such as electronic mail or computer conferencing, again leading to new patterns of communication. These kinds of systems have been somewhat more heavily studied, and some important characteristics of these systems have been identified. For example, computerized media may be preferable to other kinds of communication because they can be faster and cheaper (Crawford, 1982). Furthermore, computerized communication has a low incremental cost per message; that is, it costs the sender about the same to send a message to one person as it does to two; if the system supports mailing lists, it may be as easy to send mail to hundreds of people, specifying only the name of the list. Crawford noted that this form of bulk mailing eliminates the need for secretaries to duplicate and mail multiple copies of memos. Finally, electronic mail or conferencing are asynchronous: Only one of the recipients needs to be present at a time, making communications easier to arrange (e.g., across time zones). By thus reducing the cost of communications, IT may make coordination less expensive, with the possible results just enumerated. Huber (1984) observed that such uses of IT will be necessary to allow organizations to deal with the more complex and more turbulent postindustrial environment, with more available information.

The ability to address communications by other than the name of the recipient (e.g., to a mailing list for electronic mail or to a specific conference for computer conferencing) means that a sender may not know the person with whom he or she is communicating, but only the area of interest. Computers can be used to support this sort of communication. For example, the Information Lens system (Malone et al., 1987a) is designed to help users of an electronic mail system obtain more of the information in which they are interested and fewer irrelevant messages.

Weak links

By providing new communications channels, computerized media may facilitate the formation of "weak" (acquaintance) ties. For example, Freeman (1984) studied the use of computer conferencing by scientists and found that people became aware of one another and one another's work, even though they had not met in person, thereby suggesting that the computer system allowed these contacts to develop more easily. Easier formation of weak ties may also lead to a shift from hierarchical to "all-channel" communications in companies. Some studies have shown an initial increase in vertical communication, followed by a shift to more evenly distributed communications as new horizontal links are formed and the formal reporting system begins to decline in (relative) importance (Culnan & Markus, 1987). (Interestingly, similar results were noted for the introduction of the telephone, which provided comparable improvements over earlier communications media.) Weak links can be valuable new sources of information (Feldman, 1986). Users of electronic mail in two studies reported that as many as 60 percent (Culnan & Markus, 1987) or 70 percent (Sproull & Kiesler, 1986) of the messages they received were messages that they felt they would not have received from another source, and 50 percent of the messages they sent to people with whom they would otherwise not have communicated. Some of this new information may be unnecessary, however, contributing only to computerized junk mail. In the two studies, much of the new information was not work-related. Some of it, however, included valuable data that were difficult or time-consuming to collect in any other way, such as users' opinions of proposed changes in system features.

Social context cues

Computerized media currently provide fewer social context cues than do many other kinds of communication media. These cues regulate many kinds of interaction, and their absence may change the nature of computerized communications. Because the recipient may know only the sender's name, and the sender may know nothing at all about the recipient, cues such as age, sex, race, appearance, or status may be eliminated. Computerized media, in their current text-only format, provide only a limited bandwidth channel. This limitation eliminates subtler kinds of communications such as body language and tone of voice. Finally, because many kinds of computerized communications are asynchronous, users are deprived of any feedback as they communicate. (Note that none of these limitations is unique to computerized communications: Written memos also are asynchronous and text only, and they may be written without knowledge of all the possible recipients.) Sproull and Kiesler (1986) claimed that this lack of social context cues leads to less inhibited communications, which may have either positive or negative effects. For example, people may be more willing to speak out over an electronic system that preserves some anonymity than in a public meeting, and what they say may be considered more seriously. On the other hand, they may also be more willing to express extreme opinions ("flaming") (Kiesler, Siegel, & McGuire, 1984).

Motivational perspective

The perspectives discussed in preceding sections capture many important aspects of coordinating the activities of people in organizations, but they may not have included some of the most significant factors about why people are there in the first place.

Some factors that affect motivation and satisfaction at work, such as pay, benefits, or working conditions, are primarily extrinsic to the tasks being performed. Hertzberg (1968) hypothesized that these "hygiene" factors may lead to dissatisfaction if they are below some acceptable level but that they are not positive "motivators" for greater effort. In other words, these extrinsic factors may affect which goals people choose and whether they choose to participate in the organization at all (e.g., see March & Simon, 1958, chap. 4), but these factors alone do not usually lead to highly involving and satisfying jobs.

Another set of factors, however, are intrinsic to the tasks being performed, and they seem to be particularly important to determining the degree of involvement and satisfaction in an activity (e.g., see Hertzberg, 1968). We divide these factors into two groups: (1) individual motivations that may be present in any activity and

(2) interpersonal motivations that depend for their appeal on interactions among people. Even though there are no firm conclusions about the overall consequences of IT for these motivations, Attewell and Rule (1984) discovered that a number of previous surveys show more cases of increased rather than decreased job satisfaction after the introduction of IT.

Individual motivations

Malone (1982) discussed several recommendations for how individual motivational factors such as challenge, fantasy, and curiosity can be used to make user interfaces more interesting and enjoyable. For example, for some users, challenge can be enhanced by incorporating successive layers of complexity in an interface, with each layer being mastered in turn as users become more skilled. When we expanded our focus to include designing systems to be used by groups of people, it became clear that computers make it possible and sometimes desirable to redesign whole jobs and organizations as well as individual programs. Hackman and Oldham (1980) pointed to five factors that contribute to highly motivating work. Skill variety, task variety (i.e., doing a whole job rather than a piece of one), and task significance were thought to contribute to experienced meaningfulness, autonomy to experienced responsibility, and feedback to knowledge of actual results. Workers who feel they are responsible for an important job and who can tell how well they are doing it are believed to be more motivated to do well. These factors are related to the four suggested by Malone (1982); for example, the concept of "skill variety" in well-designed jobs can be seen as another way of increasing the challenge of a job. Next, we shall discuss the possible effects of IT on skill variety, task identity, and significance and autonomy.

Skill variety

Deskilling. One particularly common prediction of the effect of IT is *deskilling*; that is, IT can be used to strip a job of its content, leaving only a dull routine. For example, instead of directly solving some problem, a worker might instead feed the relevant data to a computer and have it solve the problem. This approach may have some advantages for the organization, as it ensures a more consistent solution to the problem, but the resulting job may be less desirable for the worker.

Schultz and Whisler (1964) believe that computers can replace the lowest-level clerical and analytic functions, thus displacing an employee if that was all the person did. Clerks would still be needed to prepare data for the computer, but these new jobs may have lower skill requirements than the jobs they replace. Glenn and Feldberg (1977) described this process as the "proletarianization of clerical work." They noted that clerical jobs are becoming more like factory jobs, with more subdivisions of work and specialization of workers due to automation and the use of scientific management principles from classic organization theory as management tries to control workers and to minimize the variability of their output. Similar deskilling was discovered by Mann and Williams (1960), Whisler (1970b), and Scharek and Barton (1975). As the flow of work becomes more like an assembly line, an individual clerk's pace becomes regulated by the needs of processes on either side, and the need for interaction and the resulting opportunities for social ties to form are thereby reduced.

Zuboff (1983b) pointed out that a system embodies assumptions about how the work should be done, resulting in a loss of flexibility for the worker. The system may also clarify the ambiguity of work, diminishing workers' opportunities to display mastery of their jobs. Formal rules replace discretion or specific knowledge, thus reducing the inner motivation to work. Many of these effects may also apply to jobs of middle managers. As computers are used to handle more and more analyses, middle managers may be reduced to messengers or eliminated altogether.

Upgrading. The opposite prediction is *upgrading*. Instead of doing the job that the worker did, computers can be used to automate the repetitive parts, leaving the more interesting components for the humans and producing a more desirable job requiring a higher level of skills or having more responsibilities. For example, Zuboff (1983b) presented a case in which the automation of a paper mill increased the role of the first-line production workers, as they could control more than the single functions they used to. The jobs therefore required more skill, and the operators began to perform some of the functions of the managers. Mann and Williams (1960) also found some cases of job enlargement and the system's elimination of many routine jobs.

The use of IT may also upgrade the jobs of middle managers. Instead of simply collecting and presenting data, managers may be able to analyze and interpret them. That is, their role may change from giving orders to convincing others of their interpretations. Argyris (1970) reasoned that managers would have to be better educated in order to deal with the greater flow of data.

Deskilling and upgrading. In practice, both deskilling and upgrading seem likely to occur simultaneously. Attewell and Rule (1984) reported both effects and noted that it is difficult to determine which predominates. They presented some evidence that there are now more skilled jobs and fewer unskilled ones but pointed out that it is hard to determine the cause for this shift. They concluded that past studies have not been well designed, again making firm conclusions difficult.

Task meaningfulness

The category of task meaningfulness refers to Hackman and Oldham's (1980) notion that jobs are more satisfying when they involve the completion of a "whole" and identifiable piece of work ("task identity") that has a substantial impact on the lives of other people ("task significance"). In computer games and in some unavoidably dull jobs, it is possible to use fantasy to make an activity more meaningful (e.g., the task of controlling a factory process can be mapped into a fantasy display of piloting a spaceship (Carroll & Thomas, 1980). However, the implication of this category name is that the organizational use of computers should be designed to make the tasks themselves as meaningful as possible. For example, one of the reported benefits of an early office automation project was that bank clerks had their jobs restructured so that they no longer performed isolated clerical steps in a process they did not understand but instead handled all the steps in dealing with their assigned customers (Lorsch, Gibson, & Seeger, 1975; Matteis, 1979).

Autonomy

The use of IT can change an individual worker's degree of autonomy in doing his or her job. Many researchers believe that computer systems offer new possibilities for supervising and controlling workers (e.g., "A New Era for Management," 1983;

Briefs, 1981; Zuboff, 1983b). Using a computer system may make it easier for a worker's superiors to control his or her work (e.g., by providing quicker feedback on a worker's performance) and make it clear who is not performing. Blau and colleagues (1976), however, found increased control only in routine jobs.

Increased control by supervisors. Argyris (1970) suggested that a centralized information system may reveal previously hidden information, thereby limiting an employee's perceived freedom to act and making the system seem threatening. Zuboff (1983b) argued similarly that because the system makes information more widely available, a subordinate may become less willing to act independently on data that his or her superior will also see.

Increased control by system. A system may also become itself an impersonal source of authority (Zuboff, 1983b). One form of such a loss of autonomy is the computer system's taking control of the pace of work and determining how quickly the work must be done. Zuboff (1983b) believes that computers give quicker feedback, thus increasing the pace of work indirectly, even if it is not set explicitly. Attewell and Rule (1984) reported mixed findings on this topic: Of the studies they surveyed, 25 percent reported an increase in time pressure; 50 percent, no change; and 25 percent, a reduction in time pressure.

Increased autonomy for workers. A system can also have the opposite effect. As we noted, for example, automating the routine parts of tasks can allow the reintegration of several previously separate jobs, resulting in a job that can be done independently and without direct supervision. Managers may also be more willing to delegate responsibility, as their subordinates' results can be tracked by the system.

Walton (1982) provided examples of both increased control and increased autonomy and pointed out that the designers of systems can choose the technology is used. Attewell and Rule (1981) summarized a number of studies by noting that most workers do not report an increase in perceived control or in their control over their subordinates but that their feelings of control and being controlled increase at higher levels of the hierarchy. Kling (1980) also reported that using IT seemed not to change radically the nature of work for the workers he studied.

Interpersonal motivations

When we are concerned with group interactions, three kinds of interpersonal motivations (cooperation, competition, and recognition) can be as important as individual motivations are (see Malone & Lepper, 1987). Systems can be designed to engage these interpersonal motivations. For example, one of the problems that may arise in a text-sharing system is how to motivate people to contribute information. In addition to economic pricing schemes, intrinsic motivations may be used for this purpose. For example, people's motivation for recognition may be engaged by a system in which rankings of the most widely read messages in different categories can be displayed along with their authors' names. This approach should be even more effective if messages that are rated by some readers as being valuable are then automatically redistributed to a wider audience.

Political perspective

A central construct for political analyses of organizations is power. A political view sees the organization as composed of shifting coalitions that compete for resources. Power can be loosely defined as the ability of one person or group to influence the actions of another (Bariff & Galbraith, 1978). Power has many sources, such as the "legitimate" authority of a superior in a hierarchical organization, the promise of rewards, the control of access to necessary resources (perhaps including information), or expertise. Other measures of a group's power include work flow pervasiveness (the number of other groups that depend on this group), immediacy (how quickly the loss of a group's services is felt), and substitutability (the extent to which some other group can substitute for this one).

The use of IT affects the distribution of power in many ways. First, IT affects access to information, a potentially valuable resource. In some settings, it is possible that IT will be used primarily for its symbolic value rather than for any particular function, making the IT itself a potential resource (Feldman & March, 1981). Second, IT affects how people do their job, again changing the nature of the relationship among groups. One (likely) possibility is that IT will be used largely to reinforce the firm's existing power structure, for if it did not, power holders in the organization would be unlikely to encourage its use (Kling, 1980; Pfeffer, 1978). It also seems clear that using IT can greatly increase the power of those who control it (Pfeffer, 1978). We will examine two different distributions of power: vertical (i.e., between levels in the firm), and horizontal (i.e., between groups at the same level).

Vertical distribution of power

One way that IT can affect the vertical distribution of power in a firm is by changing who has access to information. For example, a computer system may provide an easier way to monitor the results of subordinates' actions and to speed the flow of information upward in the company, thus centralizing power. For example, Leavitt and Whisler (1958) discovered that in companies with computer systems, the junior managers no longer controlled which information was summarized and reported. Similarly, Zuboff (1983b) found that managers of automated plants felt that they no longer controlled information about production and so lost power. Before the introduction of a computer system, for example, the plant managers chose when and how to report problems that the plant experienced; with the system, they found out about them at the same time as everyone else did. Many systems may encourage this process, as they are often designed primarily to meet the needs of managers. For example, Grudin (1987) observed that multiuser systems may require many people to work with them, though benefiting only the manager.

IT can also be used to decentralize, thus moving power down in the organization. For example, a universally accessible data base can reduce top management's monopoly on companywide information. The use of IT may thus change the basis of power by making information a less scarce resource. To the extent that vertical power is thereby equalized, other sources of power will become more important. One common prediction is that power will be based on competence and knowledge rather than on hierarchical position (Argyris, 1970; Foster & Flynn, 1984). Zuboff (1983b) found that when the system made more information equally available, power was not telling someone what to do (i.e., based on hierarchical position) but, rather, convincing them to accept one's interpretation of the data. Attewell and Rule (1984) reported that most studies found either no change or a reinforcement of the existing power structure, although they noted that the use of IT seems to be "compatible with a wide variety of lateral and vertical power relationships in organizations" (Attewell & Rule, 1984, p. 1189).

Horizontal distribution of power

The use of IT can also change the balance of power between groups at the same organizational level of a firm. For example, a common computer system may lead to greater data sharing and thus power equalization between groups at the same level. This cooperation may then lead to greater coordination, allowing better performance, as the two groups can jointly optimize, rather than each trying to do the best it can alone.

As we mentioned, using IT can greatly increase the power of the group that controls the technology. IT may become critical to the firm's operation: most banks, for example, would be completely unable to function if their computer systems failed. The group controlling the computer systems may also control access to data, a potentially scarce resource. The IT group thus may be in a position to mediate between other groups, for example, by setting corporate standards for computer equipment or software, thus defining the functions available even to users of personal computers. Schultz and Whisler (1964) suggested that these staff members assume some of the functions of the line managers and that they therefore should be tied to top management and to the firm's strategic goals.

IMPLICATIONS FOR FURTHER RESEARCH

Our review of the literature has revealed several shortcomings that should be addressed by further research. First, it is clear that the field needs better conceptualizations and uses of the two major dimensions: technology and organization. Until there is wider agreement on the meanings of these central terms, it will be difficult to compare and integrate different pieces of research. Typologies of technology and organization may also serve other functions, for example, by detecting relationships that have not been adequately studied.

The perspectives we have discussed reveal appropriate variables to investigate and provide theories of likely kinds of interactions as well as methodologies to investigate them. For example, we believe that one of the most important characteristics of IT is that it processes information and that analyzing the kinds of information that an organization uses and the ways that this information is processed provides considerable insight into organizational functions, as well as a basis for the design of systems.

Second, the field needs a better research design. As in any social science, cause and effect are complex. There are many possible variables, and it is difficult to identify which are most important and to control the rest. Simple correlational studies are inadequate because they omit too many possibly significant variables and relationships, and so research designers should be cautious about making generalizations from such studies. In general, it seems premature to concentrate on only a few variables. In the short run, this may mean a greater use of methodologies such as case studies that emphasize understanding at the expense of generalizability. Most important, we need to be able to identify the implications of using IT and to provide guidance for the designers of systems. Malone (1985) proposed changing the focus from explanatory or predictive theories (i.e., if X, then Y) to theories of design (i.e., in order to achieve Y, do Z).

IMPLICATIONS FOR THE DESIGN OF SYSTEMS AND WORK

As we have seen, there appear to be few inevitable results of the use of IT and many possible outcomes, depending on factors such as the organizational context, the type of IT used, and management's motivations. Because there are no general theories for predicting the outcomes of particular situations, our advice to designers is simply to use the frameworks and examples we presented to consider in advance the possible outcomes of using IT.

Walton (1982) pointed out that past studies of implementing computer systems often concentrated on ways to overcome resistance to a new system. He argued that these efforts should be extended to the design phase as well, to avoid, rather than merely to overcome, problems. He noted (Walton & Vittori, 1983) that even though managers seem to realize that using IT can have organizational side effects, there has been little effort to predict or reduce them. Walton suggested that organizations need explicit normative models, stating what kind of effects are desirable. New systems should be explicitly assessed for their organizational impacts, and the design process should allow the systems to evolve as their effects change or become clearer. Each individual or group within an organization may judge systems differently, however. One issue for a designer, then, is to determine the clients of his or her design, that is, whose value systems will be used to guide the design.

In the remainder of this section, we will briefly propose how the four perspectives we discussed suggest principles for designing systems, work, and organizations.

Rationalist perspective

The rationalist perspective assumes that the organization has an identifiable goal, such as profit maximization, and that IT should be used to achieve that goal more efficiently, for example, by reducing costs or increasing the quality of the output. This can be done by analyzing the functions of different parts of the organization and automating where it is cost-justified to do so. Because much current systems design attempts to follow this perspective, we will not discuss it further, except to note that for systems used for coordination it may be difficult to identify inputs and outputs or to place a value on them, thus making cost justification problematic (Crowston & Treacy, 1986).

Information-processing perspective

In the information-processing view, IT has a major effect, by providing cheaper coordination and thus making coordination-intensive forms more practical. A company might take advantage of economies of scale by creating larger functional departments, using IT to provide the necessary coordination among different groups. For example, different divisions of a company could all use data stored in one centralized data base, rather than each having partial information or passing information among themselves. Alternatively, a company could use marketlike structures, again coordinated by using IT. Airlines, for example, now provide an electronic marketplace for selling tickets.

Systems like electronic mail or computer conferencing may have several advantages. First, they may be more efficient media for existing communication: faster, asynchronous, and possibly less expensive. Second, electronic media may lead to new patterns of communication, either encouraging people to participate more actively or helping form weak links, which can provide new data. Systems like the Information Lens (Malone et al., 1987a) may be used to help process quantities of semistructured data.

Work redesign can be based on the "object-oriented" modeling technique discussed by Crowston and colleagues (1989). The resulting model of the organization may reveal places where the information flow can be streamlined or where IT can be better used to support the necessary processing. Possible organizational structures for a given task can be compared by estimating the costs of different kinds of communications links, to determine which will be the most effective.

Motivational perspective

In the motivational perspective, the client of a new information system is the workers and only indirectly the organization. A successful design is one that increases the workers' satisfaction and improves their attitudes toward work.

A motivational design may start by analyzing the costs and rewards of a job for the person holding it. Hackman and Oldham (1980), for example, provided an instrument that attempts to measure the motivating aspects of a job. They also listed those characteristics of an organization that should be checked to assess its readiness for changes. If the conditions are such that a work redesign is likely to fail or to have little effect, they suggested that it not be attempted.

Sirbu (1980) offered several ideas for software design that enhance the motivating aspects of the users' jobs. He found that rather than enforcing restrictions on users' actions, designers provide ways of holding them accountable for what they do, thus increasing their autonomy. To increase feedback, Sirbu feels that any monitoring reports generated be shared with the users, not restricted to their managers. Finally, he believes that systems offer opportunities to master new skills and perform new tasks, thus widening the users' repertoire of skills.

A design methodology for creating motivating work is sociotechnical design. Sociotechnical design attempts to improve simultaneously the social and the technical subsystems of a job in order to achieve the most effective job design. Pava (1983) provided a good introduction to this technique and discussed its applications to the design of information systems.

Political perspective

The political perspective suggests that it is important to determine the client of a design, as different groups may have conflicting goals and value systems. It may be useful, therefore, to secure support from an existing power holder, such as top management. A designer should also analyze the firm's existing power structure in order to identify vested interests both for and against the system, which may be at the root of resistance to change. Zuboff (1983b), for example, suggested examining carefully any sources of resistance to a new system. She noted that although the immediate complaints may disappear, the underlying problems may continue indefinitely to damage the work setting. Involving users in designing the system may improve it by revealing the designers' implicit assumptions about the nature of the problem, as well as improving the eventual users' feelings of ownership of the system.

CONCLUSION

One theme of this chapter is that a system designer is an organizational change agent, whether intentionally or not. Designers must be aware that their systems are not neutral objects but instead reflect a theory of how the surrounding organization does or should work. Furthermore, the effects of information technology (IT) are not deterministic: Similar systems can and do have widely different effects, depending on the particulars of the organization and the intentions of the managers who deploy them. Designers should therefore be explicit about which effects are desirable and attempt to predict and control the effects that the system does have.

To understand these potential impacts we need to understand organizations, technology, and the link between the two. Unfortunately, the body of theory in these areas is neither well developed nor integrated. Indeed, different researchers approach these topics from different perspectives, often arriving at contradictory findings or simply talking past one another.

Each of these perspectives provides only a partial view of the relationship between organizational structure and IT, however, and designers should be cautious about predictions that acknowledge only one view. Only when a system is viewed from all these perspectives can designers begin to predict and to design the effects of their systems on work organization.

REFERENCES

Argyris, C. (1970). Resistance to rational management systems. *Innovation* 11:28–35.

Attewell, P., & J. Rule (1984). Computing and organizations: What we know and what we don't know. *Communications of the ACM* 27:1184–92.

Bakos, Y. (1985). Toward a more precise concept of information technology. In *Proceedings of the Sixth International Conference on Information Systems*, pp. 17–24. Indianapolis: Society for Information Management and the Institute of Management Sciences.

Barrett, S., & B. Konsynski (1982). Inter-organization information sharing systems. *MIS Quarterly* 6:93–104.

Bariff, M. L., & J. R. Galbraith (1978). Intraorganizational power considerations for designing information systems. *Accounting, Organizations and Society* 3:15–27.

Becker, F. D. (1986). Loosely-coupled settings: A strategy for computer-aided work decentralization. *Research in Organizational Behavior* 8:199–231.

Blau, P. M., C. M. Falbe, W. McKinley, & P.K. Tracy (1976). Technology and organization in manufacturing. *Administrative Science Quarterly* 21:20–81.

Briefs, U. (1981). Re-thinking industrial work: Computer effects on technical white-collar workers. *Computers in Industry* 2:76–81.

Carroll, J. M., & J. C. Thomas (1980). Metaphor and the cognitive representation of computer systems. Technical report no. RC8302. Yorktown Heights, NY: IBM Watson Research Center.

Carter, N. M. (1984). Computerization as a predominate technology: Its influence on the structure of newspaper organizations. *Academy of Management Journal* 27:247–70.

Chandler, A. D., Jr. (1962). *Strategy and structure: Chapters in the history of the American industrial enterprise*. Cambridge, MA: MIT Press.

Child, J. (1972). Organizational structures, environment and performance: The role of strategic choice. *Sociology* 6:2–22.

Crawford, A. B., Jr. (1982). Corporate electronic mail—A communication-intensive application of information technology. *MIS Quarterly*, 6 (September): 1–13.

Crowston, K., T. W. Malone, & F. Lin (1987). Cognitive science and organizational design: A case study of computer conferencing. *Human Computer Interaction* 3:59–85.

Crowston, K., & M. E. Treacy (1986). Assessing the impact of information technology on enterprise level performance. In *Proceedings of the Seventh Annual Informational Conference on Information Systems*, pp. 299–310. San Diego, CA: Society for Information Management and the Institute of Management Sciences.

Culnan, M. J., & M. L. Markus (1987). Information technologies. In F. M. Jablin, K. H. Roberts, L. L. Putnam, & L. W. Porter, (Eds.), *The Handbook of Organizational Communication: An Interdisciplinary Perspective,* pp. 420–43. Newbury Park, CA: Sage Publications.

Feldman, M. S. (1986). Constraints on communication and electronic messaging. In *Proceedings of the CSCW '86 Conference on Computer-supported Cooperative Work,* pp. 73–90. Austin, TX: Microelectronics and Computer Technology Corporation.

Feldman, M. S., & J. G. March (1981). Information in organizations as signal and symbol. *Administrative Science Quarterly* 26:171–86.

Foster, L. W., & D. M. Flynn (1984). Management information technology: Its effects on organizational form and function. *MIS Quarterly* 8 (December): 229–35.

Freeman, L. C. (1984). The impact of computer-based communication on the social structure of an emerging scientific specialty. *Social Networks* 6:201–21.

Fry, L. W. (1982). Technology-structure research: Three critical issues. *Academy of Management Journal* 25:532–52.

Galbraith, J. R. (1974). Organization design: An information processing view. *Interfaces* 4:28–36.

——— (1977). *Organization design*. Reading, MA: Addison-Wesley.

Glenn, E. N., & R. L. Feldberg (1977). Degraded and deskilled: The proletarianization of clerical work. *Social Problems* 25:52–64.

Grudin, J. (1987). Social evaluation of the user interface: Who does the work and who gets the benefit? In *Proceedings of Human-Computer Interaction—INTERACT '87*, pp. 805–11. Amsterdam: Elsevier Science Publishers B.V. (North-Holland).

Hackman, J. R., & G. R. Oldham (1980). *Work Redesign*. Reading, MA: Addison-Wesley.

Hertzberg. (1968). One more time: How do you motivate employees. *Harvard Business Review* 46 (January–February): 53–62.

Hirschheim, R. A. (1986). The effect of a priori views on the social implications of computing: The case of office automation. *ACM Computing Surveys* 18:165 96.

Huber, G. P. (1984). The design of post-industrial organizations. *Management Science* 30:928–51.

Kiesler, S., J. Siegel, & T. W. McGuire (1984). Social psychological aspects of computer-mediated communication. *American Psychologist* 39:1123–34.

Kling, R. (1980). Social analyses of computing theoretical perspectives in recent empirical research. *ACM Computing Surveys* 12:61–110.

Leavitt, H. J., & T. L. Whisler (1958). Management in the 1980's. *Harvard Business Review* 36 (November–December): 41–48.

Lorsch, J. W., C. F. Gibson, & J. A. Seeger (1975). First National City Bank Operating Group (A, A1, B, B1). Case nos. 9–474–165, 9–475–061, 9–474–166, & 9–475–062. Boston: Harvard Business School Case Program.

Malone, T. W. (1985). Designing organizational interfaces. In *Proceedings of the CHI '85 Conference on Human Factors in Computing Systems,* pp. 66–71. San Francisco: Association for Computing Machinery.

——— (1987a). Computer support for organizations: Towards an organizational science. In J. Carroll (Ed.), *Interfacing thought: Cognitive aspects of human computer interactions*. Cambridge, MA: MIT Press.

——— (1987b). Modeling coordination in organizations and markets. *Management Science* 33:1317–32.

——— (1990). Organizing information processing systems: Parallels between human organizations and computer systems. In W. Zachary, S. Robertson, & J. Black (Eds.), *Cognition, computation, and cooperation.* Norwood, NJ: Ablex (Reprinted from *Organizational Computing*).

Malone, T. W., K. R. Grant, F. A. Turbak, S. A. Brobst, & M. D. Cohen (1987a). Intelligent information-sharing systems. *Communications of the ACM*, 30:390–402.

Malone, T. W., & M. R. Lepper (1987). Making learning fun: A taxonomy of intrinsic motivations for learning. In R. E. Snow and M. J. Farr (Eds.), *Aptitude, learning, and instruction: III Conative and effective process analysis*. Hillsdale, NJ: Erlbaum.

Malone, T. W., & S. A. Smith (1988). Modeling the performance of organizational structures. *Operations Research* May-June, pp. 421–36.

Malone, T. W., J. Yates, & R. I. Benjamin (1987b). Electronic markets and electronic hierarchies. *Communications of the ACM* 30:484–97.

Mann, F. C., & L. K. Williams (1960). Observations on the dynamics of a change to electronic data-processing equipment. *Administrative Science Quarterly* 5:217–56.

March, J. G., & H. A. Simon (1958). *Organizations*. New York: Wiley.

Markus, M. L., & D. Robey (1990). Information technology and organizational change: Causal structure in theory and research. *Management Science*.

Matteis, R. J. (1979). The new back office focuses on customer service. *Harvard Business Review* 57:146–59.

Mohr, L. B. (1971). Organizational technology and organizational structure. *Administrative Science Quarterly* 16:444–59.

Mohrman, A. M., Jr. (1982). The impact of information-processing technology on office roles. Paper presented at the annual meeting of the World Futures Society, Washington, DC.

Mumford, E., & O. Banks (1967). *The computer and the clerk*. London: Routledge & Kegan Paul.

Myers, C. A. (Ed.) (1967). *The impact of computers on management*. Cambridge, MA: MIT Press.

Newell, A., & H. A. Simon (1976). Computer science as empirical inquiry: Symbols and search. *Communications of the ACM* 19:113–26.

A new era for management (1983). *Business Week*, April 25, pp. 50–86.

Nolan, R. L., & A. J. Pollock (1986). Organization and architecture, or architecture and organization. *Stage by Stage* 6:1–10 (available from Nolan, Norton and Co., Lexington, MA).

Office automation (1984). *Business Week*, October 8, pp. 118–42.

Olson, M. H. (1982). New information technology and organizational culture. *MIS Quarterly* 6 (special issue): 71–92.

Osterman, P. (1986). The impact of computers on the employment of clerks and managers. *Industrial and Labor Relations Review* 39:175–86.

Pava, C. (1983). *Managing new office technology*. New York: Free Press.

Perrow, C. (1967). A framework for the comparative analysis of organizations. *American Sociological Review* 32:194–208.

——— (1979). *Complex organizations: A critical essay*, 2nd ed. New York: Random House.

Pfeffer, J. (1978). *Organizational design*. Arlington Heights, IL: Harlan Davidson.

——— (1982). *Organizations and organization theory*. Boston: Pitman.

Pfeffer, J., & H. Leblebici (1977). Information technology and organizational structure. *Pacific Sociological Review* 20:241–61.

Reif, W. E. (1968). *Computer technology and management organization*. Iowa City: Bureau of Business and Economic Research, University of Iowa.

Rice, R. E. (1980). Impacts of computer-mediated organizational and interpersonal communication. In M. Williams (Ed.), *Annual review of information science and technology*, Vol. 15. New York: Knowledge Industry Publications.

Robey, D. (1976). Information technology and organization design. *University of Michigan Business Review* 18:17–22.

——— (1981). Computer information systems and organization structure. *Communications of the ACM* 24:679–87.

——— (1983). Information systems and organizational change: A comparative case study. *Systems, objectives, solutions* 3:143–54.

Sanders, D. H. (1977). *Computers in society: An introduction in information processing*, 2nd ed. New York: McGraw-Hill.

Scharek, P., & L. Barton (1975). Comments on the influence of information technology on organizational structure in the insurance industry. In E. Grochla & N. Szyperski (Eds.), *Information systems and organizational structure*. New York: Walter de Gruyter.

Schultz, G. P., & T. L. Whisler (Eds.) (1964). *Management organization and the computer*. Glencoe, IL: Free Press of Glencoe.

Simon, H. A. (1957). *Administrative behavior*, 2nd ed. New York: Free Press.

Sirbu, M. (1980). Programming organizational design. In *Proceedings of the Fifth International Computer Communications Conference*, pp. 349–54. Atlanta: International Council for Computer Communications.

Sproull, L., & S. Kiesler (1986). Reducing social context cues: Electronic mail in organizational communication. *Management Science* 32:1492–512.

Stabell, B. B., & F. Forsund (1983). Productivity effects of computers in administration. An exploratory empirical investigation. Paper presented at the Seminar on the Assessment of the Impact of Science and Technology on Long-term Economic Prospects, United Nations Economic Commission for Europe, Rome.

Tausky, C. (1970). *Work organizations: Major theoretical perspectives*. Itasca, IL: Peacock.

Tushman, M., & D. Nadler (1978). Information processing as an integrating concept in organization design. *Academy of Management Review* 3:613–24.

Walton, R. E. (1982). Social choice in the development of advanced information technology. *Technology in Society* 4:41–49.

Walton, R. E., & W. Vittori (1983). New information technology: Organizational problem or opportunity? *Office: Technology and People* 1:249–73.

Whisler,T. L. (1970a). *The impact of computers on organizations*. New York: Praeger.

——— (1970b). *Information technology and organizational change*. Belmont, CA: Wadsworth.

Wilson, D. (1985). The reinvention of microcomputers: Toward an analytical framework. Ph.D. diss., Harvard University.

Woodward, J. (1980). *Industrial organization: Theory and practice*, 2nd ed. Oxford: Oxford University Press.

Zuboff, S. (1983a). New worlds of computer-mediated work. *Harvard Business Review* 61 (September-October): 142–52.

——— (1983b). Some implications of information systems power for the role of the middle manager. Working paper no. 84–29. Boston: Harvard Business School.

CHAPTER 12

Joint Venture Formations and Stock Market Reactions: An Assessment in the Information Technology Sector

JEONGSUK KOH AND N. VENKATRAMAN

A central area of research in contemporary strategic management research is concerned with "hybrid organizational arrangements" (Borys & Jemison, 1989) at the "interorganizational" or the "network" level (Powell, 1990) involving mechanisms such as joint ventures, technology licensing, cooperative research and development (R&D), and marketing arrangements (Contractor & Lorange, 1988; Harrigan, 1985; Kogut, 1988a; Mariti & Smiley, 1983). Within this general stream, joint venture is an important mechanism that can give a firm new and powerful sources of competitive advantage (Harrigan, 1988) and distinctive competencies (Kanter, 1989; Powell, 1990).

Research on joint ventures spans disciplinary boundaries. As represented in Figure 12.1, we categorize the existing research into four types using two dimensions: (1) the dominant theoretical perspective, classified as either the strategic behavior or the transaction cost perspective, and (2) the research focus, namely, whether the focus is on the motives for the formation of joint ventures or on their impacts.

The first type of studies—termed *strategic motives* of parents—seeks to explain the motives for joint venture formations based on a firm's capability to offer distinct products and/or services. These motives primarily relate to enhancement of both market power (Boyle, 1968; Fusfeld, 1958; Mead, 1967; Pate, 1969; Pfeffer & Nowak, 1976a, b) and operating efficiency (Backman, 1965; Berg & Friedman, 1977, 1978; Rockwood, 1983; Stuckey, 1983). The second type—termed *impacts of joint ventures*—is concerned with two questions: What is the impact of joint venture formations? and What are the conditions under which joint ventures have greater impact? For this type, there have been few empirical examinations of such questions (notable exceptions are: Harrigan, 1988; McConnell & Nantell, 1985).

In contrast, the third type—termed *efficient governance mechanisms*—is grounded in the transaction cost perspective (Williamson, 1975) and seeks to explain the motives for forming joint ventures, by invoking a logic that this mechanism best minimizes the sum of production and coordination (transaction) costs as compared with other kinds of governance mechanisms (see, especially, Balakrishnan & Koza,

Theoretical perspective	Focus	Motives for JV formation	Impacts of JV
	Strategic behavior	**Type (A)** Explanation of JV formation based on a firm's ability to offer products or services to compete effectively	**Type (B)** Expectation of higher performance when firms form JVs to maximize their ability to offer products or services to compete effectively
		Empirical studies: Berg & Friedman, 1977; Duncan, 1982	Empirical studies: Harrigan, 1988; McConnell & Nantell, 1985
	Transaction cost perspective	**Type (C)** Explanation of JV formation based on minimization of production and coordination costs of governance	**Type (D)** Expectation of higher performance when firms choose the modes that best minimize production and coordination costs
		Empirical studies: Shan, 1986; Teece, Pisano, & Russo, 1987	No empirical study

Type A: Strategic motives of parents
Type B: Effectiveness of JV strategies
Type C: Efficient governance mechanisms
Type D: Effectiveness of governance mechanisms

Figure 12.1. Joint ventures: theoretical perspectives and research focus.

1989; Hennart, 1988; Kogut, 1988a). In other words, these studies explore the rationale and the contexts for the superiority of joint ventures over other mechanisms like vertical integration or long-term contracts. (Examples of studies in this type include Shan, 1986; and Teece, Pisano, & Russo, 1987.)

Extending this theoretical perspective into a normative realm, the fourth type—termed *effectiveness of governance mechanisms*—argues that if firms indeed choose the modes that best minimize production and coordination costs, they are likely to perform better than do those that do not adopt the prescribed modes. However, there are no reported empirical studies belonging to this type.

Let us consider the two prominent studies belonging to the second type. McConnell and Nantell examined 136 joint ventures (JV) from a cross section of industries using an event-study methodology and concluded that joint ventures are, on average, value-creating activities for the parent firms. Although they noted that their results are "supportive of the 'synergy' hypothesis" (1985, p. 519), they did not further examine the relationship of differential characteristics (strategies) of JV formations and their impacts. We argue that such an extension would help explain the factors affecting the variations in the value-creating ability of joint ventures from a strategic management research perspective.

Harrigan's (1988) study, in contrast, focused on the JV as the unit of analysis and attempted to isolate the differential effects of joint venture characteristics. Specifically, she found, using cross-sectional data, that characteristics or strategies—such as partners' and parent venture relationship traits—had little impact on joint venture effectiveness, and she concluded that industry-level traits are more important determinants of JV success. Given that several authors have contended that the value from JV formations depends on their characteristics (see, e.g., Berg, Duncan, & Friedman, 1982, on the technological, knowledge-acquisition characteristic), the differential role of joint venture characteristics is an important area of research in strategic management.

Taking these two studies as the point of departure, this chapter examines the impact of JV formations on the market value of the parents. Two objectives are the goal of this study:

1. An assessment of the impact of JV formations (within one sector of the economy, the information technology sector) on the stock market valuations for the parents using an "event-study" methodology.
2. A further identification of the differential role, if any, of four strategic factors—pertaining both to the degree of relatedness between the product-market segments of the parents and the joint ventures and to areas of partner asymmetry such as the degree of relatedness and relative size—on the stock market valuations.

A related methodological objective is to explore the nature of the relationship between stock market reactions to the announcement of joint venture formation (intended JV strategies) and managerial assessments of the role and effects of JV (realized strategies) of providing preliminary support for using stock market returns as one referent in evaluating the role of JV.

THEORETICAL PERSPECTIVES

The joint venture as a value-creating mechanism

Potential benefits. The range of benefits accruing via joint ventures is extensive but can be organized into four categories: (1) economies of scale—by placing the parents' distinct activities under one entity (e.g., in 1986 GTE Corporation and United Telecommunications, Inc., formed US Sprint, which combined the GTE–Sprint long-distance telephone company and GTE Telenet, a data transmission network, with United Telecommunications' US Telecom, a long-distance telephone company, and Data Communications Corporation (Uninet), a United Telecommunications public data transmission network); (2) access to complementary assets—by pooling the partners' complementary assets such as production, marketing, design, and manufacturing (e.g., in 1983 AT&T and Philips formed AT&T/Philips Telecommunications Systems to manufacture and market AT&T's network switching equipment, through which AT&T's technology was linked to Philips' marketing skills); (3) cost or risk sharing—through joint projects in areas characterized by extremely high development costs coupled with uncertain demand and/or a short product life cycle or technology life cycle (e.g., in 1982 Knight-Ridder and Tele-Communication, Inc., formed TKR Cable Company to acquire, develop, and operate CATV systems); and (4) shaping the scope and basis of competition—by co-opting existing or potential competitors within regulatory constraints (e.g., in 1984 IBM formed Trintex, a videotex-service venture, with CBS and Sears, Roebuck, which pitted IBM against its chief rival AT&T, which had a two-year head start in the two-way electronic service field).

Potential costs. Following Porter and Fuller (1986) we recognize three categories: (1) coordination costs—which are incurred when ongoing coordination is needed between the partners that may be difficult when they have divergent interests (e.g.,

Moxon & Geringer, 1985); (2) erosion of competitive position—which occurs when an existing competitor is made more formidable by transferring proprietary expertise and market access as well as lowering entry barriers (e.g., Bresser, 1988); and (3) creation of an adverse bargaining position—which may occur if one partner is able to capture a disproportionate share of the value created by the joint venture because of the other partner's adverse bargaining position resulting from specialized and irreversible investments (Balakrishnan & Koza, 1988).

Rationale for JV formation. Powell noted:

> Firms pursue cooperative agreements in order to gain fast access to new technologies or new markets, to benefit from economies of scale in joint research and/or production, to tap into sources of know-how located outside the boundaries of the firm, and to share the risks for activities that are beyond the scope of the capabilities of a single organization. (1990, p. 315)

Such an argument, also consistent with the transaction costs literature, recognizes that a parent will consider forming a joint venture if the possible benefits exceed the corresponding costs associated with forming and operating this interorganizational arrangement. Although each parent considers a specific set of benefits and costs to arrive at its decision, we are concerned with the aggregate assessment by the stock market of intended JV formation strategies. Thus, our approach to assessing the intended JV strategies is rooted in the "event study" model that determines the impact of an event on a firm's stock prices by estimating the normal (or expected) return to its stock in the absence of the event (Fama et al., 1969).

Thus, following Harrigan (1985), Contractor & Lorange (1988), Porter & Fuller (1986) and earlier empirical findings presented in McConnell and Nantell (1985), our first hypothesis is as follows:

H1: *The abnormal returns associated with the event of joint venture formations are expected to be positive for the participating parents.*

We propose and test H1 in the spirit of an empirical replication of McConnell and Nantell's (1985) findings, but with a different time frame and minimum overlap in the JV sample frame, given that most "lawlike findings" in social science research require constructive replication and triangulation across settings.

Stock market reactions to different JV strategies

A general observation that the formation of JVs has a positive value by itself is of limited use for both theory and practice; hence, an important extension is to identify whether differential strategies lead to differential values. For this purpose, we begin from the accumulated evidence in the research stream on diversification and mergers that combining related resources creates more value than does combining unrelated resources, a conclusion that is popularly termed the *relatedness hypothesis* (e.g., Bettis & Hall, 1982; Rumelt, 1982; Singh & Montgomery, 1987). The theoretical underpinning is that when a company operates related businesses, it is possible for the firm to exploit its "core factor," leading to economies of scale and scope, efficiency in resource allocation, and an opportunity to use particular technical and managerial skills (Rumelt, 1982; Chandler, 1990). We extend this set of theoretical arguments to the realm of JV formations (see also McConnell & Nantell, 1985), to hypothesize that related joint ventures are expected to outperform unrelated ones. Thus, we consider the role of JVs in influencing product-market segments and also the degree of the JV's relatedness to the focal parent's portfolio.

Role of joint ventures in influencing product-market segments. Joint ventures are formed for different reasons and expectations. In conceptualizing the role of JV in influencing the product-market activity of the parents, we adopt the framework of Salter and Weinhold's (1979) adaptation of Ansoff's (1965) classical framework of corporate strategy. Thus, as shown in Figure 12.2, the role of JV can be viewed along two dimensions: product expansion, or adding new products, and market expansion, or serving new customers. In the identical category, parents and joint ventures are in the same product-market segments; in the related-supplementary (RS) category, the proposed joint ventures give the parents access to new customers and markets rather than new products; in the related-complementary (RC) category, they give the parents new products rather than access to new markets; and in the unrelated category, the parents and joint ventures are in different product-market segments. Figure 12.2(b) illustrates this role classification using this framework.

Each role represents different resource combinations and, therefore, different opportunities for creating market value (Shelton, 1988). Opportunities for value creation are maximized when the JVs are closely related to their parents in terms of product and/or market scope. Duncan (1982) argued that monopoly gains are most likely when there is overlap in the product-market segments of the parents and joint ventures, and Fusfeld (1958) discussed the case of iron and steel firms' using JVs to enhance their market power through complex channel linkages. In a similar vein, Borys and Jemison (1989) proposed that "hybrid" arrangements that involved pooled interdependence (i.e., a common pool of resources on which each partner can draw,

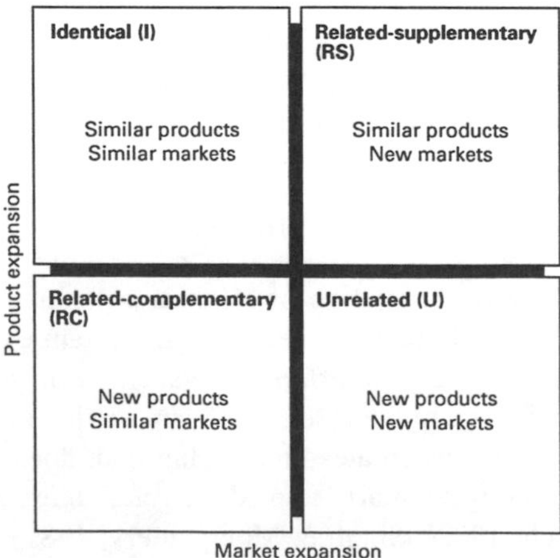

Figure 12.2. Role of joint ventures in influencing product–market scope. **(a)** Role clarification.

as reflected in similar business scopes) are more likely to be successful than are those involving sequential interdependence (e.g., supplier or marketing arrangements). Thus, we expect that joint ventures in the identical category (similar products and markets) will create a higher value than will those JVs belonging to the RS, RC, and unrelated categories.

In contrast, when JVs play no significant role in expanding either products or markets, they are expected to contribute minimally to the market value of the parents. These reflect minimal opportunities of interdependence and sharing of intercorporate resources, except financial resources. So, we believe that the identical type has the best opportunities and the unrelated type has the worst opportunities. However, the existing theory is weak in distinguishing between the roles of RS and RC categories. Thus, the hypothesis for differential value based on the patterns of relatedness outlined in Figure 12.2a is stated as follows:

H2: *Parents forming joint ventures in the identical category will, on average, report the highest abnormal returns, and parents forming joint ventures in the unrelated category will, on average, report the lowest abnormal returns.*

Degree of relatedness with the focal parent's portfolio. An extension of the considerations of relatedness allows us to examine the division of benefits from the joint venture formation between parents for the same joint venture. Suppose that parent 1 and parent 2 equally own a joint venture and that although all of parent 1's product-market segments are related to the specific area of the JV operation, only a small fraction of parent 2's business operation is related to the JV's business. Then, it can be argued that the particular JV gives parent 1 more opportunities than it gives parent 2. Specifically, by taking support from the market power (Pfeffer & Nowak, 1976a, b) and operating-efficiency arguments (Contractor & Lorange, 1988; Porter & Fuller, 1986), the formation of JV provides parent 1 with a greater opportunity to exploit economies of scale and scope in operations than that offered to the other parent. Lewis (1990) cited several instances in which joint ventures and other collaborative mechanisms were used successfully to increase bargaining power, inhibit opponents' moves, and raise entry barriers. Consequently, we expect that the same JV will influence the market value of parent 1 more than it will parent 2. This hypothesis formally recognizes the asymmetry in the value derived by the partners based on the differential contributions to the product-market scope of operations.

Parent 1	Parent 2	Joint venture	Role for parent 1	Role for parent 2
Control Data	NCR	CPI[a]	I	I
AT&T	Ricoh	AT&T Ricoh[b]	RS	I
IBM	MCA	DiscoVision[c]	RC	I
Warner Commun.	Amex	Warner-Amex[d]	I	U
S. NE Telephones	CSX	LightNet[e]	I	U

[a] To develop and make computer peripherals
[b] To make and market AT&T's small telephone systems in Japan
[c] To develop, manufacture, and market videodisc players and their discs
[d] To construct and operate cable systems
[e] To launch railroad communication services

(b) Market expansion.

The formal hypothesis is as follows:

H3: *The parent with the higher sales portion of businesses related to the joint venture's business in an equally owned joint venture will, on average, report a higher abnormal return than will the parent with a lower sales portion.*

Related versus unrelated partner. The third characteristic is concerned with the degree to which the partners are operating in related businesses. As argued by Borys and Jemison (1989) and Harrigan (1988), significant asymmetries between the partners are harmful to venturing performance, as their heterogeneity exacerbates differences in how the partners value their joint venture's activities. Further, there is minimal "common ground" on which to develop the process of intercorporate sharing of skills and capabilities. Although we are not saying that such ventures should not be attempted, we are arguing that they are likely to be assessed less favorably by the stock market than will those joint ventures with a greater overlap of activities and processes. Thus, our premise is that the more "distant" the partners are in relation to each other, the fewer opportunities they will have for strategic and organizational compatibility.[1] Pfeffer and Nowak (1976a) concluded that horizontal JVs increased their market power, and Duncan (1982) reported a positive, significant impact of related JVs on average rates of returns. Thus

H4: *Firms with related joint venture partners will, on average, report higher abnormal returns than will those with unrelated partners.*

The empirical results for the relatedness hypothesis have been mixed, however, and Barney (1988) described specific conditions that enhance the probability of deriving greater value for mergers between strategically related firms. Within the context of joint ventures, Balakrishnan and Koza (1988) employed a transaction cost framework to show that joint ventures are superior to markets and hierarchies when the costs of valuing complementary assets are not trivial. They hypothesized that investors will respond less favorably to joint ventures between related partners that are well informed about each other's business, as a joint venture may not be a value-maximizing mechanism when the costs of valuing and acquiring complementary assets are trivial. The parents' management should have chosen acquisition, and the failure to do so is a signal to the market about either the inefficiency of the management or the managerial motives behind the decision. Thus, it is important to test this hypothesis empirically.

Large versus small partner. An important variable in the choice of joint venture formation pertains to the relative size of the partner. In recent years, the incidence of joint ventures in which large and small firms join to create a new entry into the marketplace has been increasing (Hlavacek, Dovey, & Biondo, 1977; Roberts, 1980), with the smaller partner providing technological resources and the larger partner supplying the financial resources. The question is whether the smaller or the larger partner derives more value in these ventures, ceteris paribus. In the mergers and acquisitions literature, there is a growing body of research on the "relative size hypothesis." This provides some evidence that the abnormal return of the acquired firm (small firm) in a merger is larger than that of the acquiring firm (large firm) but that the gains in dollar value are approximately equal (Asquith, Bruner, & Mullins,

1983; Bradley, Desai, & Kim, 1983). Indeed, Asquith, Bruner, and Mullins (1983) contended that the failure of most studies of mergers to detect any effect of the merger on the acquiring firms is due to the fact that in most cases, the acquiring firms are significantly larger than the acquired firms. Thus, if the dollar value of gain in a merger is divided evenly between the acquiring and the acquired firms and if the acquiring firm's market value is 10 times that of the acquired firm, then a 10 percent abnormal return to the shareholders of the acquired firm will translate into an 1 percent abnormal return to those of the acquiring firm (McConnell & Nantell, 1985).

We believe that it may not be straightforward to apply this argument from the mergers and acquisitions research stream to joint ventures, because in order to derive equal benefits, the small partners may offer resources and capabilities that are proportionately similar to those of the larger partner. So, it is unclear whether there will be any greater gain for the smaller partner compared with that for the larger partner. Obviously, the way in which benefits from the formation of a joint venture are divided between the smaller and larger partners is an important issue in understanding the relevance of the relative size in the selection of partner(s). Without a strong theory already in place, we frame our hypothesis in a null form:

H5: *The abnormal return of the smaller partner in an equally owned joint venture will be, on average, no different from that of the larger partner, and the dollar value of their gains will be approximately equal.*

METHODS

Sample frame

This study is designed with a focused sample. The specific sector we are considering is labeled the *information technology (IT) sector*, which has been growing in importance over the last decade. We broadly defined the IT sector to include the areas of the economy that directly and/or indirectly deal with products and components, such as electrical and electronics machinery, equipment, and supplies, measuring instruments and optical goods, communication, computer and data processing, and electronic imaging and video. The sample includes joint ventures reported in the *Wall Street Journal* and referenced in the *Wall Street Journal Index* between 1972 and 1986. In order to be included in the final sample, the common stock returns for at least one of the parents had to be available on the daily returns file of the Center for Research in Security Prices (CRSP) over a period beginning 270 days before the announcement of the joint venture. The sample was screened to eliminate parents that made announcements regarding earnings, dividends, mergers, or other important firm-specific information during the arrangement announcement period.

This search and screening procedure yielded a sample of 239 firms in 175 joint ventures. Table 12.1 summarizes the number of joint ventures and the participating parents in the joint venture industry.

Table 12.1. Number of joint ventures and parents by joint venture industry

Joint venture industry	Joint ventures	Parents
Manufacturing sector		
Electronic components	19	20
Electronic equipment	8	8
Precision controls	11	11
Computer and peripherals	31	42
Tape and disc	6	8
Photo and office equipment	7	10
Communications equipment	20	23
Subtotal	102	122
Nonmanufacturing sector		
Motion pictures	15	23
Cable services	21	38
Communications services	26	41
Software and data processing	11	15
Subtotal	73	117
Total	175	239

Analytical methodology

Model. The principal analytical methodology we used to test these hypotheses is the standard residual analysis technique based on the market model. The procedure described here follows the methods used by Dodd, Dopuch, and Hollhausen (1984) and Brown and Warner (1985). The day on which the initial article describing a joint venture appeared in the *Wall Street Journal* was numbered event day $t = 0$. The trading days before that day were numbered event days $t = -1$, $t = -2$, and subsequent trading days were numbered event days $t = +1$, $t = +2$, and so on.

Daily market model parameters were estimated for each firm using 200–day returns beginning with event day $t = -270$ and ending with event day $t = -71$.

$$R_{it} = a_i + b_i R_{mt} + u_{it} \qquad t = -270 \text{ to } t = -71$$

where

R_{it} = common stock return of firm i on day t

R_{mt} = rate of return on the CRSP value-weighted index on day t

a_i and b_i = ordinary least-squares estimates of market model parameters

u_{it} = market model errors

A firm was included only if it had a minimum of 100 days of returns. The impact of the announcement of the security's price was measured over the two-day trading period consisting of $t = -1$ and $t = 0$. Henceforth, this two-day trading interval will be referred to as the *announcement period.* The analytical methodology we followed is the same as the conventional approach used in previous studies adopting the event-study model. In the interest of space, we have not provided details that are already available in sources such as Brown and Warner (1985), Lubatkin et al. (1989), McConnell and Nantell (1985), and Friedman and Singh (1989).

Selecting a relevant time frame. One of the most important issues in using an event study is to select the relevant time frame—daily or monthly returns data with important trade-offs between the two (see Lubatkin & Shrieves, 1986, for a discussion relevant to strategic management research). We justify the use of daily returns data in this research for the following reasons: First, McConnell and Nantell (1985) reported two-day average abnormal returns of 0.73 percent; thus, it seemed that the magnitude of abnormal returns associated with joint ventures would be significantly small compared with that of abnormal returns associated with events such as mergers. Using monthly data may cause the effect of extraneous events to outweigh that of joint ventures. Although the use of daily data may understate abnormal returns associated with joint venture formation, it, however, makes it possible to capture at least a lower-bound estimate that can be attributed directly to joint venture formation. Second, because the major firms in the information technology sector tend to form multiple joint ventures, many firms may have to be excluded from the sample, thus reducing sample size and introducing a bias. Third, it is also important to note that this daily time frame has been adopted by studies of some areas in strategic management in which a corporate action is the outcome of a series of related events or tactics, each of which increases or decreases the probability of the final outcome. Key themes include mergers and acquisitions (e.g., Chatterjee, 1986; Shelton, 1988; Singh & Montgomery, 1987) and CEO succession (e.g., Beatty & Zajac, 1987; Friedman & Singh, 1989; Lubatkin et al., 1989).

Statistical tests. We employed two tests in addition to the conventional t-test to assess the possible impact of outliers. The first is the binomial z-statistic constructed based on the efficient-market assumption that the sign of the parent's abnormal return will follow a binomial distribution, with the probability of its taking a positive sign being 0.5 (Brown & Warner, 1985). So, if the announcements of joint ventures have no significant effect on the returns to the shareholders of the parents, then the abnormal returns of the parents during the announcement period will be normally distributed. That is, one-half of the parents will have positive abnormal returns, and the other half, negative abnormal returns. The other test we used was the median signed rank (Wilcoxon) test, which takes into account the magnitude as well as the sign of each parent's abnormal return (Hollander & Wolfe, 1973).

The construct validity of the dependent variable measure

There is some concern that the stock market reaction around the date of announcement of an event like the acquisition (or joint ventures) may not reflect the success of implementing the strategy (see, e.g., Porter, 1987; Ravenscraft & Scherer, 1987). Regarding the link between expected performance (initial stock market reaction) and the long-term actual performance of acquisitions (realized strategies), some preliminary support has been found in the mergers and acquisitions stream (e.g., Healy, Palepu, & Ruback, 1990), in which it is relatively easy to adopt accounting data to make meaningful comparisons. In contrast, in the case of joint ventures, it is difficult to use publicly available aggregate data to delineate the portion attributable to a particular joint venture sources, thus requiring us to resort to primary data collection.

We tested for the convergent validity between the measures of stock market reaction and managerial assessments. For managerial assessments, we attempted to obtain the name and address of the CEO for every firm in our sample (parents). We sent letters to the CEOs with a two-page questionnaire describing the purpose of our study and a request to forward it to the manager most knowledgeable about the status and benefits of each of the joint ventures. Several companies (especially those who entered into the joint venture in the 1970s) had terminated their JV operations and could not identify knowledgeable informants to give the required data. We received usable data on managerial assessments of the JV performance from 56 parents (representing nearly 25 percent of the study sample). It is important to recognize that the sample is biased in favor of those joint ventures formed in the 1980s.[2] Each manager was asked to judge the JV in relation to five objectives using a scale on which 5 indicated much better than expectations, down to 1, much worse than expectations. The five indicators were (1) contributions to sales, (2) profitability, (3) technological expertise, (4) marketing capabilities, and (5) the sharing of financial risks. These indicators are consistent with those of Mariti and Smiley (1983) Harrigan (1985), and Contractor and Lorange (1988). A summated index was calculated, as these indicators covary consistently, as indicated by Cronbach $\alpha = 0.71$.

We estimated the association between abnormal returns (market) and management assessment using two different statistics: a parametric Pearson correlation coefficient and a nonparametric Mann–Whitney test to ensure robustness of results under differing distributional assumptions. The correlation coefficient was $r = 0.389$ ($p < 0.01$), and the Mann–Whitney coefficient was $W = 286$ ($p < 0.01$).[3] These statistics support the construct validity (especially the convergent validity of the measures) of the market-based measurement scheme. A very high coefficient of association should not be expected, because this approach does not formally recognize the process underlying the realization of benefits from this form of intercorporate arrangement (see, e.g., Jemison & Sitkin, 1986). The upper bound for such a correlation coefficient is much less than one (although we cannot theoretically specify it), and we believe that these results provide preliminary but consistent support for the validity of stock market reaction as a valid referent for assessing significant strategic events.

RESULTS

H1: Stock market reaction to JV formations

Table 12.2 presents the estimated abnormal returns associated with joint ventures and the test statistics. The two-day announcement-period average abnormal return is 0.87 percent, and all three tests indicate that the null hypothesis can be rejected at the 0.01 level of significance. In addition, we divided the sample into manufacturing and nonmanufacturing sectors (see Table 12.1) to test the stability of the results and found that the results were not statistically different between the two subsamples.

Next, we multiplied the two-day announcement-period abnormal return for each firm by the security's total market value as of event day $t = -3$. The cross-sectional average of the dollar values is $12.6 million. It is useful to note that the unexpected

Table 12.2. Stock market reaction to the formations of joint ventures and other cooperative arrangements

Type (Number of firms)	Mean AR (t-stat.)[a]	Positive ARs (B-stat.)[b]	Wilcoxon (z-stat.)[c]
Joint ventures	0.87%	58%	(3.30)**
(*n* = 239)	(5.28)**	(2.52)**	
Technology exchange	0.80	57	(1.67)
(*n* = 102)	(2.66)**	(1.39)	
Licensing agreements	0.40	48	(–0.33)
(*n* = 60)	(0.95)	(–0.26)	
Marketing agreements	0.01	37	(–3.21)**
(*n* = 91)	(0.04)	(–2.41)**	
Supply agreements	–0.13	46	(–0.18)
(*n* = 50)	(–0.27)	(–0.57)	

**$p < 0.01$
[a]Student t statistic with 99 degrees of freedom.
[b]Binomial sign test statistic with normal approximation.
[c]Wilcoxon test statistic with normal approximation.

average change in wealth from joint ventures is greater than the total market value of the equity of a significant fraction of all companies listed on the New York and American stock exchanges. Although this does not reflect the total value created by joint venture formation, it is a lower-bound estimate of the value of joint venture formation. Further, the average value of managerial assessment for the subsample available to test this hypothesis is 3.99 (standard deviation: 0.22), which is statistically different ($p < 0.01$) from the midpoint of the 5-point Likert scale, lending further support to this hypothesis.

Exploratory comparison of stock market reactions to alternative cooperative mechanisms

An important premise underlying this study is that the stock market reactions to JV formations, on average, will be significantly different from zero. A rival hypothesis is whether other cooperative arrangements would also be perceived significantly by the stock market. To test this rival hypothesis, we looked at whether other cooperative mechanisms were differentially perceived by the stock market. Specifically, we considered mechanisms, such as technology exchange, licensing, marketing, and supply agreements. This analysis is exploratory, given the infancy of theoretical and empirical work in this stream, in which their relative attractiveness cannot be theoretically distinguished. Indeed, Powell observed that "there is no clear cut relationship between the legal form of cooperative relationships and the purposes they are intended to achieve. The form of the agreement appears to be individually tailored to the needs of the respective parties, and to tax and regulatory considerations" (1990, p. 313). Hence, our interest is in determining whether there is any discernable pattern in the degree of market reactions to the different mechanisms.

For this analysis, we adopted the same search-and-screening procedure as in the case of joint ventures. This process yielded a sample of 102 firms in 76 technology exchange agreements, 60 firms in 45 licensing arrangements, 91 firms in 77 marketing agreements, and 50 firms in 38 supply agreements. The estimated average abnormal returns associated with these four types of cooperative arrangements are also presented in Table 12.2. The average abnormal return during the announcement period for technology exchange agreements is 0.8 percent, ($p < 0.01$), which confirms the importance of technology access as a motive for cooperation in this sector. Because the binomial z-statistic and the Wilcoxon test do not reject the null hypothesis, even this result could be due to a few outlier observations. Further, all three tests indicated that the other three mechanisms were not perceived significantly by the stock market.

We could not, however, normalize the values for these mechanisms using any common basis, as technology exchange agreements might involve complex barter or technology access; marketing agreements might involve complex nonlinear, graded percentage-of-sale fee structures; licensing and royalties might involve future options; and so forth. Hence, our observations are that JVs and technology license arrangements are viewed significantly positively (i.e., different from zero) and that the other three arrangements are not viewed significantly by the market.

H2: Roles of joint ventures

We used two dimensions—"adding new products" and "serving new customers"—to create a classificatory scheme for the roles of joint ventures shown in Figure 12.2. The product dimension is used to distinguish between truly new products and those similar to existing products of the parent(s), based on whether parents or divisions involved in joint venture formation already had operations in the businesses with the same SIC codes at the four-digit level as the businesses of their newly created joint ventures. The market dimension is used to distinguish between market expansion and new market operations and according to whether joint ventures allowed their parent firms to expand into new geographic markets of the parents' existing businesses or to serve customers in new industries (businesses). Thus, based on data obtained from published announcements of the joint venture activities, we divided the full sample into four groupings, as shown in Table 12.3: Identical (91 parents), Related-Supplementary (54 parents), Related-Complementary (73 parents), and Unrelated (17 parents). Four parents were removed owing to the lack of adequate data.

Table 12.3. Pattern of abnormal returns: results of testing the differential roles of joint ventures for hypothesis 2

	Categories			
Test statistics	Identical ($n = 91$)	Related supplement ($n = 54$)	Related complement ($n = 73$)	Unrelated ($n = 17$)
Average abnormal return	1.32%	0.60%	0.68%	0.37%
(t-stat.)	(5.20)**	(1.50)	(2.21)*	(0.80)
Firms with positive abnormal returns	62.6%	53.7%	57.5%	52.9%
(Binomial z-stat)	(2.41)**	(0.54)	(1.29)	(0.24)
Wilcoxon Test (z-stat)	3.15**	0.71	1.68†	0.29

†$p < 0.10$ *$p < 0.05$ **$p < 0.01$

All three tests allowed us to reject the null hypothesis of no synergistic effect at the .01 level of significance for the Identical sample. For the Related-Complementary sample, the t-test and the Wilcoxon test permitted the rejection of the null hypothesis at the .05 and .10 levels of significance, respectively. However, the null hypothesis cannot be rejected for the Related-Supplementary and Unrelated samples according to any of the three tests. Thus, the results indicate the following: (1) The formation of joint ventures, on average, will have significant positive effects on the market values for the parent firms if the joint ventures strengthen some existing product–market segments or market new products in the existing markets; whereas (2) the formation of joint ventures, on average, will create no appreciable increase in the market value for the parents if the joint ventures either develop new customers or enter into new, unrelated product–market segments.

These findings basically support H2. Inconsistent with the underlying theoretical argument is, however, the finding that the Related-Supplementary joint ventures, on average, create no appreciable increase in market values. This is clearly contradictory to Shelton's (1988) finding in the area of acquisitions that combining assets in a related-supplementary fashion creates the greatest values with the least variance. A possible explanation is that in the information technology sector (especially in the telecommunications equipment and computer industries), tailoring products to the needs of customers in new geographic markets is often necessary and expensive, so that such costs may outweigh benefits such as economies of scale.[4]

H3: Degree of relatedness with the focal parent's portfolio

Next, we identified a subsample in which both or all parents were included in the full sample (n = 119). We had to exclude those parents not listed in the CRSP data base that were either foreign-owned or smaller, privately held corporations, as the required data were not available for all the relevant parents. For each JV included in the subsample, based on data from COMPUSTAT segment tapes as well as 10-K reports, the parent with the higher sales portion of businesses related to the JV business was put into the "parent-with-opportunity" sample, and the other parent with the lower sales proportion was put into the "parent-without-opportunity" sample. In the case of a joint venture involving more than two parents, those parents that were more or less similar in the sales portion of related businesses were placed into the same sample. Any two businesses were classified as related if they shared at least one of the following characteristics: (1) similar products and/or markets, (2) similar production technologies, and (3) similar science-based research. The "parent-with-opportunity" sample contained 58 parents, and the "parent-without-opportunity" sample consisted of 61 parents.[5]

Table 12.4 shows that the tests did not reject the null hypothesis of no synergistic effect for the "parent-without-opportunity" sample, whereas the t-test and the Wilcoxon test did reject the null hypothesis at the .01 and .1 levels of significance for the "parent-with-opportunity" sample. Note that the relatively weak support provided by the Wilcoxon test and the lack of support from the binomial z-test stems from the peculiar distribution of the data, as shown by the corresponding significance levels associated with the binomial z-statistic and the Wilcoxon test for the full

Table 12.4. Pattern of abnormal returns: results of testing the differential effects of relatedness with the focal parent's portfolio for hypothesis 3

Test statistics	Full paired ($n = 119$)	Parent with opportunity ($n = 58$)	Parent without opportunity ($n = 61$)
Two-day announcement period average	0.75%	1.40%	0.14%
Abnormal return (t-stat.)	(3.01)**	(3.79)**	(0.44)
Firms with positive abnormal returns	51.3%	58.6%	44.3%
Binomial z-stat.	(0.28)	(1.31)	(−0.90)
Wilcoxon test (z-stat.)	0.36	1.71†	−1.17

†$p < 0.10$ **$p < 0.01$

paired sample. Nevertheless, the results support the hypothesis that the parent with more businesses related to the joint venture's business derives more benefits from the joint venture than does the other parent(s).

H4: Related versus unrelated partner

We placed parents into the "related-partner" sample if they had partners with operations in related businesses. Thus, the "unrelated-partner" sample consisted of parents with partners that had operations in unrelated businesses. Relatedness was used as in the test of H3. In the case of joint ventures involving multiple partners, parents with at least one related partner were put into the "related-partner" sample. Again, owing to inadequate information, three parents were excluded. The "related-partner" sample consisted of 183 parents, and the "unrelated-partner" sample had 53 parents.

As shown in Table 12.5, all three tests rejected the null hypothesis of no significant impact at the .01 level of significance for the "related-partner" sample, whereas no test rejected the null hypothesis for the "unrelated-partner" sample. This finding provides strong support for H4, as it appears that joint ventures involving related partners are more effective for the parents than otherwise. This finding is at odds with Balakrishnan and Koza's (1988) competing hypothesis and thus is an important area for further inquiry.

Table 12.5. Pattern of abnormal returns: differential effects of related versus unrelated partner for testing hypothesis 4

Test statistics	Related partner ($n = 183$)	Unrelated partner ($n = 53$)
Two-day announcement period	1.05%	0.12%
Abnormal return average (t-stat.)	(5.27)**	(0.36)
Firms with positive abnormal returns	61.7%	45.3%
Binomial z-stat	(3.18)**	(−0.69)
Wilcoxon test (z-stat.)	4.16 **	−0.89

**$p < 0.01$

H5: Large versus small partner

We formed a subsample of joint ventures in which both or all parent firms were included in the full sample. For each joint venture included in the subsample, the parent with the larger market value of its common stock three trading days before the announcement of the JV formation was placed into the "large-partner" sample, and the other parent with the smaller market value was placed into the "smaller-partner" sample. In the case of a joint venture involving more than two parents, those parents that were more or less similar in size were put into the same sample. The "large-partner" sample contained 59 parents, and the "small-partner" sample contained 60 parents. The remaining 120 parents in the full sample were placed into the "all-other" sample. This third sample contained parents for which the partner's common stock was not listed on either the New York or the American Stock Exchange during the period of this study.

Table 12.6 shows that the shareholders of the smaller partner earned a significantly positive abnormal return, whereas those of the larger partner earned an insignificant abnormal return. This result is not consistent with McConnell and Nantell's (1985) finding that shareholders appear to gain when firms enter into joint ventures, regardless of the relative size of their partner. Moreover, the result that smaller partners, on average, earn higher gains in dollar value ($19.2 million) than do larger partners ($2.3 million) is not consistent with the "relative size hypothesis" of the merger studies. It may be argued that having a larger firm as a joint venture partner will be more beneficial.

The stock market perceives that a small firm with a large firm as the joint venture partner can derive significant benefits such as the spillover of the large partner's reputation to the small firm. For example, the large firm's endorsement of the small firm as a partner may be a valuable asset. On the other hand, the asymmetry in size is likely to lead the smaller partner into an adverse bargaining position. Indeed, the overall control over major decisions in the joint venture may be in the large partner's hands.

Table 12.6. Pattern of abnormal returns: differential effects of the results across large versus small partner for hypothesis 5

	Categories			
Test statistics	Full ($n = 239$)	Large partner ($n = 59$)	Small partner ($n = 60$)	All other ($n = 120$)
Two-day announcement period average abnormal return (t-stat.)	0.876 (5.28)**	0.44% (1.38)	1.13% (3.18)**	0.94% (3.97)**
Firms with positive abnormal returns (binomial z-stat.)	58.2% (2.52)**	39.7% (–1.58)	62.7% (1.96)*	64.8% (3.26)**
Wilcoxon test (z-stat.)	3.30 **	–1.95	2.45 **	4.26**
Gains in dollar ($ mil.)	$12.6	2.3	19.2	14.3
Average market value ($ mil.)	$6,073	10,010	1,429	6,489
Average sales ($ mil.)	$8,227	12,387	2,367	9,150

*$p < 0.05$ **$p < 0.01$

DISCUSSION

Impact of joint venture formations on the market value

"Does the stock market react positively to joint venture formations?"—We set out to address this question under ceteris paribus conditions based on earlier research that the formation of joint ventures (McConnell & Nantell, 1985; see also Woolridge & Snow, 1990) does have a positive and significant impact on the market value of the participating firms. Our results were consistent with our expectations, thus providing an independent empirical corroboration of an important theoretical axiom using a focused sample frame and a more recent time period. Further, our exploratory calibration of the relative valuations of different intercorporate cooperative mechanisms revealed that joint ventures and technology exchange were viewed positively relative to other mechanisms. This is consistent with the general expectation that within the IT sector, a significant area of business competence is technology. This exploratory result pertaining to different cooperative mechanisms, however, begs for a more systematic theorizing so as to distinguish among the differential avenues for creating value along a contingency framework.

Differential values of joint venture strategies

"Does the stock market differentially value the different joint venture strategies?"—We next examined a set of strategies that could lead to differential valuation and demonstrated that the magnitude and significance of value creation from joint ventures varied across different types of joint ventures and different types of partners (H2 through H5). Harrigan's (1985, 1988) findings were derived from multiple sectors, but we focused on one sector, thereby mitigating industry effects in isolating the differential effects of joint venture strategies. We showed that stock market reacts differently to the strategies adopted to form joint ventures under differing conditions.

Specifically, we found that the parents forming JVs in the Identical and Related-Complementary categories reported higher gains in abnormal returns than did those parents forming other types of JVs; the parents with a higher proportion of business operations with the JV operations earned higher abnormal returns than did other parents; the parents with related partners received a greater increase in the value than did those with unrelated partners; and finally, the smaller partner benefited more from JV formation than did the larger partner.

If we juxtapose the results relating to joint ventures with those of technology exchange and marketing agreements, we can highlight the importance of technology-based competence in this sector. Because of rapid technological changes and consequent competitive pressure, firms form the Identical-type joint ventures to acquire complementary technologies and to strengthen their product-market scope (as described for the CDC–NCR venture). We developed a sector-specific conjecture that access to complementary technologies contributes greatly to value creation as shown by the significantly positive abnormal returns for the Identical-type joint ventures and technology agreements. Further, our results were consistent with those of Mariti and Smiley (1983) involving 70 cooperative agreements in Europe and is in general agreement with the knowledge-acquisition aspect of joint ventures (Berg & Friedman, 1980; Powell, 1990).

In contrast, market access, another important motive for forming cooperative arrangements, did not appear to be viewed significantly by the stock market, as indicated by the lack of expected findings associated with the Related-Supplementary joint ventures and marketing agreements. These findings are at odds with their strategic significance and popularity, especially with the conventional wisdom that new marketing and distribution channels are essential to supporting the creation of new products and intensifying globalization. Although a partial explanation can be found in the specifics of the sample studies, a useful line of inquiry would be to develop a more careful analysis of various cooperative arrangements in order to understand the factors in the different sectors that lead to an increased valuation of JV formations by the market.

Extensions

Need for a contingent research framework

A useful line of inquiry would be to develop a framework that recognizes, at minimum, the following four issues: (1) the industry and market structure factors that delineate the key characteristics for forming joint ventures and other cooperative arrangements; (2) the strategic (i.e., firm-level) factors that capture the specific goals and capabilities that could indicate the appropriateness of the different arrangements; (3) the level of analysis (i.e., parent or the JV) corresponding to the different theoretical and methodological requirements; and (4) the timing of assessing the impact of JV (*ex-ante* versus *ex-post*). Such a framework could both organize the research questions and synthesize the results.

Delineating the process of deriving value from joint ventures

There is considerable value in focusing on the process of creating value by means of cooperative arrangements. For example, our research relied on the collective ability of the stock market to process the required information to judge the impact of JV (intended) strategies. This should be complemented by a process theory that reconciles the important differences between intended and realized JV strategies. Such an attempt could build from Jemison and Sitkin's (1986) discussions of the process of deriving value from acquisitions and could adopt a goal-centered approach to organizational effectiveness (Cameron & Whetten, 1983). Such an extension would go a long way in developing a much-needed integration between market-based assessments (relying on financial theory) and a larger conceptualization of organizational effectiveness.

ACKNOWLEDGMENT

This research was supported by the Management in the 1990s Research Program and the research consortium on Managing Information Technology in the Next Era (MITNE), at MIT. This is a significantly revised version of the paper presented at the Academy of Management Meetings at Washington, DC, in August 1989. Harbir

Singh's comments and suggestions during this study are acknowledged, but without implicating him in any way. We thank the two reviewers for their constructive comments and suggestions on the previous drafts.

NOTES

1. Lewis (1990) provides an interesting set of case illustrations of the possible costs and difficulties of persuading unrelated partners to work together effectively.
2. No other distinguishing differences could be observed, thus supporting the representativeness of this subsample in relation to the overall study sample.
3. We tested the robustness of this result by dividing the sample into large and small subsamples, but the coefficient was not statistically different across the subsamples.
4. For instance, a *Financial Times* article (June 10, 1986) reported that Ericsson invested $100 million to modify one of its switching systems for the U.S. market; ITT invested $200 million (20 percent of its worldwide R & D) to adapt a central office switch to the LATA Switching Generic Requirements of the U.S. market.
5. One of the reviewers pointed out that the relative share of the two parents in the JV is an important issue in understanding the differential opportunities. We agree with this observation entirely, and indeed in the 80 percent of the cases for which the data were available, the split was 50–50, lending confidence to the assumption regarding equal share between the two parents. Further corroboration is provided by Berg and Friedman (1980) and Harrigan (1985), who noted that the majority of joint ventures are equally owned, although their control structure may vary. In addition, in our questionnaire to obtain managerial assessments of JV performance, we asked them to indicate the ownership structure, and 52 out of 56 indicated that the JV was equally owned.

REFERENCES

Ansoff, H. I. (1965). *Corporate strategy: An analytical approach to business policy for growth and expansion.* New York: McGraw-Hill.

Asquith, P., R. F. Bruner, & D. W. Mullins (1983). The gain to bidding firms from merger. *Journal of Financial Economics* 11:121–40.

Backman, J. (1965). Joint ventures in the light of recent antitrust developments: Joint ventures in the chemical industry. *Antitrust Bulletin* 10:7–24.

Balakrishnan, S., & M. Koza (1988). Information asymmetry, market failure and joint-ventures: Theory and evidence. Unpublished manuscript, University of California at Los Angeles.

Barney, J. B. (1988). Returns to bidding firms in mergers and acquisitions: Reconsidering the relatedness hypothesis. *Strategic Management Journal* 9 (special issue on strategy content): 71–78.

Beamish, P. (1984). Joint venture performance in developing countries. Ph.D. diss., University of Western Ontario.

Beatty, R., & E. Zajac (1987). CEO change and firm performance in large corporations: Succession effects and manager effects. *Strategic Management Journal* 8:305–17.

Beaver, W., P. Kettler, & M. Scholes (1970). The association between market determined and accounting determined risk measures. *Accounting Review* 45:645–82.

Berg, S., J. Duncan, & P. Friedman (1982). Joint venture strategies and corporate innovation. Cambridge, MA: Olegeschlager, Gunn and Hain.

Berg, S., & P. Friedman (1977). Joint ventures, competition, and technological complementarities. *Southern Economic Journal* 43:1330–37.

——— (1978). Technological complementarities and industrial patterns of JV activity, 1964–1965. *Industrial Organization Review* 6:110–16.

——— (1980). Causes and effects of joint venture activity: Knowledge acquisition vs. parent horizontality. *Antitrust Bulletin* 25:143–68.

Bettis, R. A., & W. K. Hall (1982). Diversification strategy, accounting determined risk, and accounting determined return. *Academy of Management Journal* 25:254–65.

Boyle, S. E. (1968). An estimate of the number and size distribution of domestic joint subsidiaries. *Antitrust Law and Economics Review* 1:81–92.

Borys, B., & D. B. Jemison (1989). Hybrid arrangements as strategic alliances: Theoretical issues and organizational combinations. *Academy of Management Review* 14:234–49.

Bradley, M., A. Desai, & E. H. Kim (1983). Specialized resources and competition in the market for corporate control. Working paper, University of Michigan.

Bresser, R. (1988). Matching collective and competitive strategies. *Strategic Management Journal* 9:375–85.

Brown, S. J., & J. B. Warner (1985). Using daily returns: The case of event studies. *Journal of Financial Economics*, 14:3–31.

Cameron, K. S., & D. A. Whetten (1983). Some conclusions about organizational effectiveness. In K.S. Cameron & D.A. Whetten (Eds.), *Organizational effectiveness: A comparison of multiple methods*, pp. 261–77. New York: Academic Press.

Chatterjee, S. (1986). Types of synergies and economic value: The impact of acquisitions on merging and rival firms. *Strategic Management Journal* 7:119–39.

Contractor, F. J., & P. Lorange (1988). Cooperative strategies in international business. In F. J. Contractor & P. Lorange (Eds.), *Cooperative strategies in international business*, Lexington, MA: Lexington Books.

Dodd, P., P. Dopuch, & R. Hollhausen (1984). Qualified audit opinions and stock prices. *Journal of Accounting and Economics* 6:3–38.

Duncan, J. L. (1982). Impacts of new entry and horizontal joint ventures on industrial rates of return. *Review of Economics and Statistics* 64:339–42.

Fama, E. F., L. Fisher, M. C. Jensen, & R. Roll (1969). The adjustment of stock prices to new information. *International Economic Review* 1:1–21.

Friedman, S., & H. Singh (1989). CEO succession and stockholder reaction: The influence of organizational context and event context. *Academy of Management Journal* 32:718–44.

Fusfeld, D. (1958). Joint subsidiaries in the iron and steel industry. *American Economic Review* 48:578–87.

Harrigan, K. R. (1985). *Strategies for joint ventures*. Lexington, MA: Lexington Books.

——— (1988). Strategic alliances and partner asymmetries.in international business. In F. J. Contractor & P. Lorange (Eds.), *Cooperative strategies in international business*, pp. 205–26. Lexington, MA: Lexington Books.

Healy, P., K. Palepu, & R. Ruback (1990). Does corporate performance improve after mergers? Working paper no. 3149–90, Sloan School of Management, Massachusetts Institute of Technology.

Hennart, J. F. (1988). A transaction cost theory of equity joint ventures. *Strategic Management Journal* 9:361–74.

Hlavacek, J. D., B. H. Dovey, & J. J. Biondo (1977). Tie small business technology to marketing power. *Harvard Business Review* 55:106–16.

Hollander, M., & D. A. Wolfe (1973). *Nonparametric statistical methods*. New York: Wiley.

Jemison, D., & S. Sitkin (1986). Corporate acquisitions: A process perspective. *Academy of Management Review* 11:145–63.

Jensen, M. J., & R. Ruback (1983). The market for corporate control: The scientific evidence. *Journal of Financial Economics* 11:5–50.

Kanter, R. M. (1989). *When giants learn to dance*. New York: Simon & Schuster.

Kogut, B., (1988a). Joint ventures: Theoretical and empirical perspectives. *Strategic Management Journal* 9:319–32.

——— (1988b). A study of the life cycle of joint ventures. In F. J. Contractor & P. Lorange (Eds.), *Cooperative strategies in international business*. Lexington, MA: Lexington Books.

Lewis, J. (1990). *Partnerships for profit*. New York: Free Press.

Lubatkin, M., K. Chung, R. Rogers, & J. Owers (1989). Stockholder reactions to CEO changes in large corporations. *Academy of Management Journal* 32:47–68.

Lubatkin, M., & R. Shrieves (1986). Towards reconciliation of market performance measures to strategic management research. *Academy of Management Review* 11:497–512.

Mariti, P., & R. H. Smiley (1983). Co-operative agreements and the organization of industry. *Journal of Industrial Economics* 31:437–51.

McConnell, J., & J. Nantell (1985). Common stock returns and corporate combinations: The case of joint ventures. *Journal of Finance* 40:519–36.

Mead, W. J. (1967). Competitive significance of joint ventures. *Antitrust Bulletin* 12:819–51.

Moxon, R. W., & J. M. Geringer (1985). Multinational ventures in the commercial aircraft industry. *Columbia Journal of World Business* 20:55–62.

Pate, J. L. (1969). Joint venture activity, 1960–1968. *Economic Review*, Federal Reserve Bank of Cleveland, pp. 16–23.

Pfeffer J., & P. Nowak (1976a). Joint ventures and interorganizational interdependence. *Administrative Science Quarterly* 21:398–418.

——— (1976b). Pattern of joint venture activity: Implications for antitrust research. *Antitrust Bulletin* 21:315–39.

Porter, M. (1980). *Competitive strategy*. New York: Free Press.

——— (1987). From competitive strategy to competitive advantage. *Harvard Business Review* May-June, pp. 43–59.

Porter, M., & M. Fuller (1986). Coalitions and global strategy. In M. Porter (Ed.), *Competition in global industries*, pp. 315–43. Boston: Harvard Business School Press.

Powell, W. (1990). Neither market nor hierarchy: Network forms of organization. In B. Staw & L. L. Cummings (Eds.), *Research in organizational behavior*, Vol. 12, pp. 295–336. Greenwich, CT: JAI Press.

Ravenscraft, D. J., & F. M. Scherer (1987). *Mergers, sell-offs and economic efficiency*. Washington, DC: Brookings Institution.

Roberts, E. B. (1980). New ventures for corporate growth. *Harvard Business Review*, July-August, pp. 134–42.

Rockwood, A. (1983). The impact of joint ventures on the market for OCS oil and gas leases. *Journal of Industrial Economics* 31:452–68.

Rumelt, R. P. (1982). Diversification strategy and profitability. *Strategic Management Journal* 3:359–69.

Salter, M. S., & W. A. Weinhold (1979). *Diversification through acquisition: Strategies for creating economic value*. New York: Free Press.

Shan, W. (1986). Technological change and strategic cooperation: Evidence from commercialization of biotechnology. Ph.D. diss., University of California at Berkeley.

Shelton, L. M. (1988). Strategic business fits and corporate acquisition: Empirical evidence. *Strategic Management Journal* 9:279–87.

Singh H., & C. A. Montgomery (1987). Corporate acquisition strategies and economic performance. *Strategic Management Journal* 8:377–386.

Stuckey, A. (1983). *Vertical integration and joint ventures in aluminum industry.* Cambridge, MA: Harvard University Press.

Teece, D., G. Pisano, & M. Russo (1987). Joint ventures and collaborative arrangements in the telecommunications equipment industry. International Business working paper no. IB-9, University of California at Berkeley.

Williamson, O. E. (1975). *Markets and hierarchies: Analysis and antitrust implications.* New York: Free Press.

Woolridge, J. R., & C. C. Snow (1990). Stock market reaction to strategic investment decisions. *Strategic Management Journal* 11:353–64.

CHAPTER 13

Profit Centers, Single-Source Suppliers, and Transaction Costs

GORDON WALKER AND LAURA POPPO

Do organizations and markets govern transactions differently? This question has motivated a large body of research that has reached divergent conclusions. Proponents of transaction cost theory (Williamson, 1985) have found that organizations and markets differ in their governance capabilities. Other authors (Eccles & White, 1988; Granovetter, 1985; Stinchcombe, 1983), however, believe that the transaction cost argument is stated too strongly, and they argue that organizations and markets are not discrete institutions to which the theory can be straightforwardly applied.

A central hypothesis of transaction cost theory is that interunit relationships in which supplier assets are specialized have lower transaction costs inside an organization than when the relationship is between organizations (Demsetz, 1988; Klein, Crawford, & Alchian, 1978; Riordan & Williamson, 1986). Asset specialization will increase the buyer's loss if the supply relationship is terminated. The potential for a higher loss gives the supplier an opportunity to bargain for a greater share of the value of the relationship. Thus, as the supplier's assets become specialized, it should be more reluctant to bear the costs of adapting to changes in the buyer's needs. Such a difficulty in bargaining between units is managed more effectively, according to transaction cost theory, by organizational authority than by contracting in the market. Organizational authority is more effective because it controls resource allocation to the units and has better information about their costs (Williamson, 1975, p. 154).

A substantial amount of research (Anderson & Schmittlein, 1984; Masten, 1984; Monteverde & Teece, 1982; Walker & Weber, 1984) has produced results that are consistent with this logic. The standard test of the theory, when examining how transactions are governed, is to predict whether an activity is performed inside or outside an organization by the extent to which the activities' assets are specialized. These tests have shown for several types of functions (e.g., sales force, manufacturing component fabrication, research and development) that assets in the firm tend to be more specialized than are the assets of independent suppliers.

There are two potentially troubling characteristics of these studies. First, they have not compared transaction costs inside the organization with transaction costs between the organization and its outside suppliers under comparable degrees of asset specialization. This comparison was required to demonstrate that an organization has superior governance capabilities relative to the market. Second, the causes of asset specificity in interunit relationships have not been spelled out. This omission is significant, as assets inside an organization may become specialized after they are vertically integrated. The inference that an organization lowers transaction costs by vertically integrating operations with high asset specificity may therefore be incorrect. These omissions make it difficult to respond to critics who contend that the theory overstates the effect of supplier asset specificity on vertical integration (Coase, 1988; Demsetz, 1988; Dore, 1983) and understates the bureaucratic and interunit bargaining costs that vertical integration entails (Eccles & White, 1988; Perrow, 1986).

These criticisms are particularly relevant to research on organizations and markets that do not conform to ideal types. In many organizations, in-house units may be governed in the same way that market suppliers are. Multidivisional corporations decentralize control over interdivisional supply relationships. Decentralization induces a marketlike incentive system favoring coordination within the divisions, organized as profit centers, at the expense of coordination among them (Chandler, 1962; Galbraith, 1973; Williamson, 1975). Evans and Grossman (1983) argued that such a marketlike incentive system is both more costly and less effective than the market itself. Williamson (1985, p. 140) also expressed reservations about the effectiveness of "high-powered incentives" within a corporation. Finally, Eccles and White (1988) described cases in which profit centers in multidivisional corporations prefer relationships with independent suppliers to in-house relationships because the latter are more difficult to manage.

Conversely, market suppliers may be governed in the same way that organizational units are (Bradach & Eccles, 1989; Stinchcombe, 1983). The existence of "quasi firms" (Eccles, 1981) and long-term contracts (Joskow, 1985) as substitutes for vertical integration (Kleindorfer & Knieps, 1982) has long been observed. MacNeil (1978), furthermore, described markets in which the supplier's expectation of an enduring business generates effective norms of conflict resolution. MacNeil called this type of supply relationship *relational contracting*. A critical test of the theory would compare the effect of asset specialization on transaction costs within decentralized corporations with its effect in hybrid market supply relationships, like relational contracting. This is precisely our purpose in this chapter.

HYPOTHESES

Asset specificity

Decentralized multidivisional firms are composed of profit centers that may supply one another with goods and services. Corporate management must weigh the effect on corporate performance of poor interdivisional adaptation to ongoing changes in a supply relationship against the effect of higher profitability in the supplying division. Increasing asset specificity in the supplying profit center may raise the costs of poor interdivisional adaptation beyond divisional gains. Therefore, when divisions with specialized assets do not facilitate adaptation with their internal customers, corporate management may intervene to reduce the potential loss or signal that intervention will occur if coordination does not improve (Eccles & White, 1988). This threat of intervention reinforces the effectiveness of other coordination mechanisms developed to resolve interunit conflict over specialized assets (Thompson, 1967, chap. 5; Galbraith, 1973).

For relational contracting with outside suppliers, we argue the reverse: As asset specificity increases, governance becomes weaker rather than stronger. Although relational contracting lowers conflict resulting from asset specialization (Williamson, 1979), its effectiveness is based on supplier expectations rather than on the force of organizational authority. In transaction cost theory, because expectations do not bind as strongly as authority does (Dow, 1987), increasing asset specificity exposes the latent incompatibility between the corporation's interests and those of outside suppliers. Relational contracting practices are therefore strained. Therefore our hypothesis is as follows:

Hypothesis 1 (H1): *The effect of supplier asset specificity on transaction costs should be lower in a multidivisional corporation than in relational contracting with market suppliers.*

Preselection investment in technology

Potential suppliers may invest in new technology to increase the probability that they will be selected to supply the input. However, once the supplier is chosen, this investment may influence subsequent conflict with the buyer. To signal commitment to the buyer and influence the selection decision, part of the supplier's investment should not be redeployable (Klein & Leffler, 1981; Williamson, 1983).[1] According to H1, because the adaptation costs associated with these specific assets (Williamson, 1985, p. 179) should be better managed within the organization than in the market, we hypothesize

Hypothesis 2 (H2): *The effect of supplier preselection investment in technology on transaction costs should be lower for relationships between profit centers than for relational contracting with outside suppliers.*

Supplier market competition

Supplier asset specificity and supplier market competition have often been confounded (Walker & Weber, 1984). In fact, almost by definition, as supplier assets become more specialized, the competitiveness of the supplier market should decrease. However, the argument for the effect of market competition on transaction costs is somewhat different from that of asset specificity. Because the availability of competitors makes it easier for the buyer to switch suppliers, it raises the credibility of a buyer's threats to terminate the relationship. The more credible the threat of termination is, the less the supplier should haggle with the buyer over adaptation costs. But this proposition should not be equally true for relationships between profit centers and for relational contracting with outside suppliers.

Williamson (1985, p. 151) argued that organizations have a bias toward maintaining authority over internal transactions, whatever the level of asset specialization. Corporate encouragement to buy inside may also reflect the need to maintain volume in some inputs, for example, labor and capital, or functions, for example, advertising and basic research, that have large economies of scale. Thus, an internal procurement bias would lower the threat of termination for profit centers. Conversely, in market supply, both the authority relation and the economies of scale in inputs and functions are absent. The ancillary costs of termination are thus reduced, and the credibility of termination threats is raised. We thus hypothesize

Hypothesis 3 (H3): *The influence of supplier market competition on transaction costs should be lower for relationships between profit centers than for relational contracting with outside suppliers.*

The comparability of inter profit center relationships and relational contracting

Our hypotheses assume that differences between internal and external suppliers are not due to variation in the technology of the inputs supplied. Rather, technological differences may be related to the product's life cycle (Harrigan, 1983) or to management's choice of technology to increase demand for the end product (Riordan & Williamson, 1986). Such differences are important, as they may influence the supplier's value to the corporation.

In markets in which new technology determines product success, performance is higher the earlier in a technology's life cycle the effective interunit adaptation occurs. The corporation is therefore likely to coordinate relationships with specialized suppliers more extensively when their technologies are new. If asset specialization for inside and outside suppliers occurs at different stages in the technology's life cycle, the corporation will value the relationships with these suppliers differently. The results for H1 will therefore be biased.

The dynamics of supplier market competition are also likely to differ across the stages of the technology's life cycle (Harrigan, 1983; Stigler, 1951). Technology diffusion and the entry of new firms into the market are important to competition in the early stage of an industry; but in the mature stage, competition is shaped by increasing consolidation. If the dynamics of competition differ between profit centers and outside suppliers, the results for H3 may be biased.

Furthermore, managers may choose among different technologies to enhance demand for the end product (Riordan & Williamson, 1986). If the choice of a technology determines the degree of asset specificity and is made simultaneously with the decision whether to make or buy (Williamson, 1985, p. 89), then the inputs supplied inside the corporation may differ technologically from those produced by outside suppliers. Because economic losses due to interunit conflict are higher for technologies that enhance demand, technological differences between inside and outside suppliers may confound H1 and H3. To control for the effect of technology, we predicted both asset specificity and market competition according to an input's technological age. Age of technology refers to both the product's life cycle and the input's demand-enhancing features. We compared these predictions across profit centers and market suppliers to identify the technological differences between them.

METHOD

Research setting

The assembly division. We studied the supply relationships of one large assembly division (over $2 billion in revenues) in a very large U.S. manufacturing corporation. The division produces a number of consumer products for sale to the corporation's customers. The consumer products vary in design but are sufficiently similar to be built from a generic set of about 250 inputs. In addition to having design differences, inputs may be manufactured with varying grades of material that affect the quality of the consumer product.

The design, production, and marketing of consumer products are organized through product programs in the assembly division. These programs form an important subdimension of the division's structure, which is organized first around functions, for example, engineering, marketing, and operations. Purchasing personnel within the operations department establish and manage relationships with suppliers, both inside and outside the corporation. The purchasing function is organized first by product program and then by type of input, for example, electronics and plastic moldings.

Supply relationships with component manufacturing divisions. Over 50 percent of the inputs to the assembly division come from component-manufacturing divisions, operated as profit centers, in the corporation. The component divisions sell their output to the assembly division, to other corporate units, and to customers in the market outside the corporation. Supply relationships between the assembly division and the component divisions were virtually mandated until several years before we began our study (see Eccles, 1985, for a description of inter profit center contracting modes). At that time, corporate management perceived that the production costs of the assembly division's product–market competitors were lower than were the assembly division's costs for products of equal quality. Lower costs meant that these competitors were earning a greater financial return than was the assembly division. They were also a threat to the assembly division's market share. Market share in turn was a critical determinant of the division's costs because of the large economies of scale required for efficient operations. Furthermore, it was apparent that competitors were less vertically integrated than in the corporation investigated here. Because a major source of the assembly division's costs were inputs from the component divisions, it was necessary to assess the production-cost competitiveness of these divisions. The corporation therefore released the assembly division from its mandated relationships with the component divisions and allowed it to force them to compete with potential outside suppliers. This new policy of exchange autonomy (Eccles, 1985) created a more adversarial atmosphere between the assembly division and the component divisions than had existed under the policy of mandated relationships.

Relationships with outside suppliers. At the time of our study the assembly division's relationships with its outside suppliers strongly resembled MacNeil's (1978) concept of relational contracting. This resemblance was due to a policy that the assembly division had implemented, three years before our data were collected, to reduce its supplier base and change its practices for managing suppliers. Under the new policy, the assembly division moved from competitive bidding to a system based on the assembly division's target price for the input. In addition, before the new policies were implemented, suppliers were contractually obligated to absorb changes in material costs. The new policies replaced this obligation with negotiated adjustments based on an evaluation of supplier costs. Suppliers, moreover, were expected to improve continuously their productivity and quality. These changes raised the level of information exchanged with suppliers, especially regarding costs. The relationship with the supplier, under these terms, was expected to last for the duration of the consumer product program, which could exceed five years. Because the supplier was likely to be the only source of the input to the program, the supplier expected to form a lasting, exclusive relationship. This expectation was likely to lead the suppliers to mollify any minor conflicts over cost allocation, consistent with relational contracting behavior.

The new policy was not risk free. Because an outside supplier was likely to be the single source of an input, it was highly likely that the supplier's assets would become at least partly specialized over time in accordance with the assembly division's operating practices. More specialized assets would raise the division's cost of switching to a new supplier if the current supplier performed poorly. This potential attenuation of the supplier's markets for the division's inputs may also have made it more difficult to assess the competitiveness of outside suppliers' performance.

To reduce the potential supplier–management problems associated with high switching costs and low supplier–market competition, the division chose suppliers that consistently performed better than their competitors did. The likelihood that future assembly division requirements would be met effectively was thereby increased, for two reasons: (1) The capabilities of the suppliers were higher, and (2) the consistently high performance of the suppliers represented an investment in reputation that would be damaged if they began to take advantage of their new close relationship with the assembly division. Finally, because an outside supplier chosen in the supplier-reduction program was likely to deliver more than one input to the division and was expected to meet all of the division's demand for each input, the division constituted a larger percentage of the supplier's total volume. The division's bargaining position in conflicts with the supplier was thereby strengthened.

Background field research

To ground our theory in the experience of assembly division managers, we interviewed personnel in purchasing, engineering, and logistics over a period of three years. The supplier-reduction program and the exchange-autonomy policy with component divisions were implemented during this period. Five group meetings were held with the purchasing and engineering managers. In these meetings the managers presented cases illustrating the determinants of both in-house and outside supplier performance. These cases provided important data on the type of information that purchasing managers had about suppliers and on their perceptions of successful supplier relationships. During the last two years of this field research we visited a component division to investigate the differences between selling inside and outside the corporation. We also observed the extent to which the component division made its investment decisions in response to assembly division requirements. Finally, over an eight-month period during the third year, we observed weekly meetings between assembly division personnel and market suppliers that were part of the assembly division's cost-reduction program. The interview, case, and observation data gathered during this phase of the study suggested that the theory we proposed could be closely applied to the supplier–management problems of the assembly division. These data also suggested how we should use our variables.

Variables

Transaction costs

We defined transaction costs as the difficulty experienced by the assembly division in reaching agreement with its suppliers on the allocation of adjustment costs. Difficulty in reaching interunit agreement on cost allocation specifically measures the intensity of bargaining over adjustment costs. Although the structure and intensity of the bargaining situation may be affected by institutional factors, as we hypothesized, they do not determine its definition or measurement. Thus we believe that our narrow use of transaction costs excludes any obvious confounding by institutional factors and thus addresses the critiques of both Demsetz (1988) and Dow (1987) regarding transaction cost measurement. Demsetz (1988) asserted that the costs an organization incurs in managing its resources are not comparable to transaction costs. He defined management costs quite broadly, more as general administrative costs than as expenses related to coordinating specific activities. Transaction costs, however, are defined narrowly as the "costs of negotiating" in relationships with suppliers (Demsetz, 1988, p. 151, n. 5). Similarly, Dow (1987) argued that in both organizations and markets, the assessment of interunit agreement must be separated from the institutional resources required to achieve it. This implies that the efficiency of transactions should be compared across institutions, independent of the institutional factors that shape transaction characteristics (Dow, 1987, p. 19). If this criterion is not met, Demsetz's critique of transaction cost theory in terms of the incomparability of management and transaction costs must be considered.

Dow also contended that interunit adaptation and agreement on how it should be achieved are important to evaluating the efficiency of interunit relationships. Our definition of transaction costs combines these elements. Adjustment costs in supply relationships represent the costs of adaptation directly and are a focal point of supplier–management practice because of price competition in the assembly division's product market. Agreement on cost allocation is an important goal of negotiations with suppliers, as it is a condition for effective adaptation.

We measured allocation difficulties for two causes of adjustment cost: engineering changes and changes in the costs of raw material inputs to component fabrication. Engineering changes and changes in material costs have different origins, but both may lead to higher transaction costs. Engineering changes originate in the assembly division but are not under the control of division purchasing. Purchasing does experience, however, the ensuing conflict with the supplier over the adjustment costs associated with the changes. In contrast, material cost changes originate in the markets supplying the division's suppliers. A division supplier must decide whether to absorb the costs and lower its profits or to attempt to pass them on to the assembly division by requesting a price increase. Our measures of transaction costs are (1) the difficulty of agreeing with the supplier on the allocation of costs due to engineering changes for the part (measured on a seven-point Likert-type scale) and (2) the difficulty of agreeing with the supplier on the allocation of costs due to changes in material costs for the part (measured on a seven-point Likert-type scale).

Asset specificity

Asset specificity has been used in many ways (Williamson, 1985; chap. 4). We measured the construct in terms of the uniqueness of the supplier's technical labor skills and manufacturing equipment for producing the product delivered to the assembly division. This use is consistent with Klein, Crawford, and Alchian (1978, p. 300), who argued that unique assets enable suppliers to appropriate quasi rents in the contracting process, and with Walker and Weber (1984), who used supplier proprietary technology as an (inverse) measure of supplier–market competition. We measured asset specificity as (1) the extent to which the production of the part requires technical labor skills that are relatively unusual for the supplier (measured on a seven-point Likert-type scale) and (2) the extent to which the production of the part requires manufacturing equipment that is relatively unusual for the supplier (measured on a seven-point Likert-type scale).

Preselection investment in technology

We used the supplier preselection investment in new technology with one measure. Our hypothesis for the supplier technology investment required that the investment be made in order to increase the supplier's chances of selection. If the investment was made for other reasons, the proportion of nonredeployable assets was likely to be small. We measured whether the supplier invested in new technology to enhance the likelihood of being selected as a supplier for this category of part (measured as yes or no).

Supplier market competition

Walker and Weber's (1984) supplier market competition construct was measured in part by variables that denoted the degree of competition directly. These variables were highly correlated (coefficient alpha = .7 for three variables) and had strong predictive validity. We chose to measure the variable that was most correlated with the construct ($r = .975$) as the indicator of supplier market competition in our study: the extent to which there are enough potential suppliers to ensure adequate competition at the commodity level for providing the input (on a seven-point Likert-type scale).

Age of input technology

We used the age of the input technology with two variables that pertain to input's design and manufacturing process: (1) the newness of the input's design technology (measured on a seven-point Likert-type scale) and (2) the newness of the manufacturing process used to produce the input (measured on a seven-point Likert-type scale).

Data Collection

Sample selection

We chose our sample of supplier relationships by drawing a random subset of 100 from the assembly division's 250 generic inputs. To collect data on the supplier relationships for this sample, we focused on supplier relationships for two consumer product programs in the assembly division. Both of these programs were affected by the assembly division's new policies regarding the selection and management of suppliers both inside and outside the corporation.

Questionnaire data

We constructed a questionnaire to distribute to the purchasing managers of the assembly division who were responsible for selecting and managing suppliers for the two programs. During the background fieldwork for the study, purchasing managers had demonstrated substantial knowledge about the division's internal suppliers and its external supplier markets. A subset of these managers reviewed the questionnaire to evaluate the accuracy and relevance of its concepts and language. The uses of the variables just listed reflect the judgments of these managers. After it was reviewed, the questionnaire was sent to purchasing managers who were asked to provide information on their relationships with suppliers for each input in the sample. We received usable questionnaires on 99 inputs. Forty-four inputs were secured from internal profit centers and 55 from outside suppliers. Thirty-two of these inputs were repeated for both consumer product programs. Consequently, we received information on 67 of the 100 inputs in our random sample.[2] Eighty-nine percent of the market suppliers in our sample were single-source suppliers, and all but one of the remaining 11 percent had contracts that guaranteed a fixed percentage of the division's volume.

Key-informant bias

We measured the variables by using the managers' responses to the questionnaire items. The use of this kind of subjective data has been common in research on transaction costs (Anderson & Schmittlein, 1984; Masten, 1984; Monteverde & Teece, 1982; Walker and Weber, 1984); and although none of these studies has measured transaction costs directly, their results have shown strong construct and predictive validity for transaction cost determinants. There are several causes for concern about using subjective data, however.

Results of our analyses of variables measured using subjective responses may have limited external validity because they may be confounded by perceptual bias. Our use of purchasing managers as key informants may have biased our results toward the perspective of this function in the assembly division. However, Heide and John (1990) found in industrial components industries that buyers' and suppliers' perceptions of the degree to which the suppliers' assets were specialized were strongly and significantly correlated. Their results indicated that the buyers had extensive and reliable knowledge of the supplier market, the kind of knowledge that the assembly division's purchasing personnel displayed in our conversations with them. Heide and John's findings also suggest that the emphasis that transaction cost studies placed on the judgment of the buying unit was not misplaced. Transaction cost research on vertical integration typically focuses on the buyer, as the buyer's experiences and interpretations of the supplier's behavior determine subsequent integration or deintegration decisions. The significant correlation of the buyer's and supplier's judgments of supplier asset specialization is evidence that the buyer can accurately perceive the causes of potential supplier opportunism.

Key-informant bias may also be present due to differences in the supplier selection and management practices of the two consumer product programs to which our respondents belong. We tested for these differences, as we shall describe later. Finally, each manager may have had his or her own bias when responding to our instrument. Unfortunately, because information on each product in our sample was provided by a single manager, we were unable to separate true information about the product from systematic respondent bias due to individual differences. Because our questions referred to objective phenomena in the managers' experiences with suppliers and were clearly understood by our respondents, we feel confident that the subjective bias in our data is low. Nonetheless, we addressed this problem in a variety of ways.

ANALYSIS

Hypothesis testing

We represented the hypotheses as a multiple-indicator structural equation model (Bagozzi & Phillips, 1982) estimated using the maximum-likelihood method of LISREL VI (Joreskog & Sorbom, 1984). The model for the hypotheses, using our measures, is shown in Figure 13.1. In Figure 13.2 we present the model using Greek letters, by convention, to represent the parameters we estimated.

We tested the hypotheses by constraining the parameter representing a hypothesized relationship to be equal for both groups of suppliers and then by allowing the parameter to be different between the groups. The difference in chi-square between

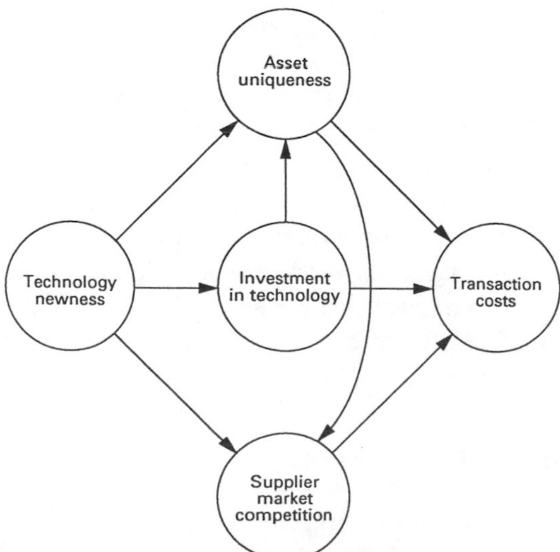

Figure 13.1. Predictors of transaction costs.

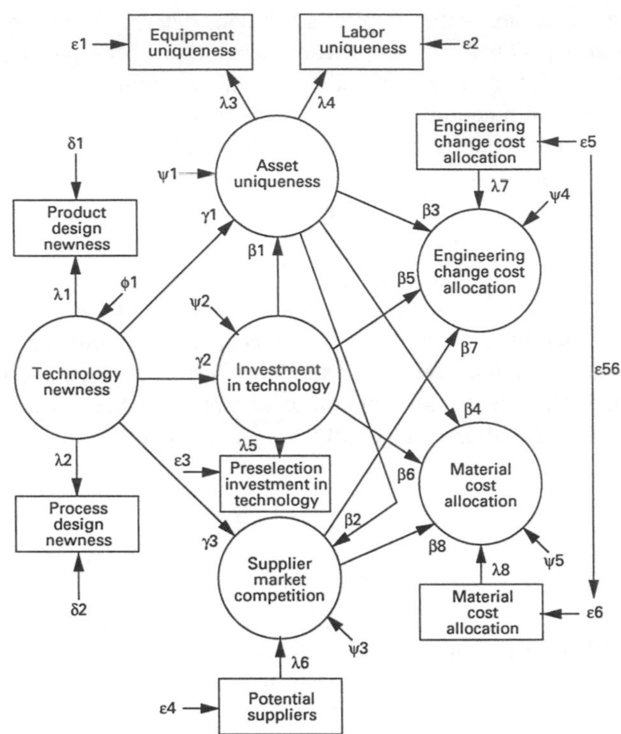

Figure 13.2. Model predicting transaction costs, including both measurement and causal paths.

these two estimates of a parameter indicates whether there is a difference between profit centers and market suppliers.

Comparison of means for types of supplier

By analyzing the moments matrices of profit centers and market suppliers, we tested our hypotheses and compared the means of the two types of suppliers at the same time (see Byrne, Shavelson, & Muthen, 1989; Joreskog & Sorbom, 1984, chapter 5). We compared the means on the five constructs in our model: difficulty in allocating adjustment costs, asset specificity, preselection investment in technology, supplier market competition, and age of input technology. This test replicates the conventional transaction cost assessment of the organization–market dichotomy. To the extent that the means of the two types of supplier do not differ on these constructs, the market–organization dichotomy is blurred.

Jackknife estimates of the parameters

Maximum-likelihood estimation of structural equation models assumes that each variable has a normal distribution. However, Monte Carlo tests have shown that although the estimates are robust for strong violations of this assumption (Sharma, Durvasula,

& Dillon, 1989), the standard errors of these estimates are not robust. Because our variables clearly violate the assumption of multivariate normality, we jackknifed (Mosteller & Tukey, 1977, chapter 7) the maximum-likelihood results to obtain new estimates and standard errors that are not based on distributional assumptions.

Model specification

To eliminate a Heywood case (an estimate of a negative variance) that appeared in our initial run (for δ_2 in Figure 13.2), we estimated the parameters in the model following Rindskopf's (1984) method. As Rindskopf did, we reconstructed the model so that error terms were estimated as exogenous variables; we then squared the parameters estimating the error terms to calculate the error variances, which could not be negative. However, for simplicity, the results are reported using the notation in the model shown in Figure 13.2.

Assessment of key informant bias

We assessed potential key-informant bias in our results in three ways. First, it is possible that bias was introduced because respondents belonged to the two product programs that may have differed on unobservable characteristics. We assessed this potential confounding of our results by regressing the two programs on all the variables in a logistic regression. If these variables predict the programs, thereby indicating significant differences between them, the programs may confound the structural equation model results. Second, key-informant bias might be present in the effect of outliers on the maximum-likelihood estimates. The jackknife procedure assesses this effect. The closer the jackknife estimates are to the maximum-likelihood values, the less likely it is that problem outliers exist in the data. Finally, key-informant bias might be manifested through correlated measurement error (Phillips, 1981). If the fit of our model to the data is good without specifying correlated measurement error, whatever bias might exist will add little to the explanatory power of the model. To assess the goodness of fit of the model to the data, we report the χ^2 goodness-of-fit test using the maximum-likelihood estimates. This test is a rough approximation of fit, as it is sensitive to sample size and assumes that the data are multivariate normal. Consequently, we also used the Type 2 parsimonious normed-fit index (Mulaik et al., 1989), which takes into account both sample size and the parsimony of the model.

RESULTS

The correlation matrices, means, and standard deviations of the variables are shown in Table 13.1. The correlation matrices for profit centers and outside suppliers indicate that the two types of transaction costs, although significantly correlated, are not adequate indicators of a single construct. The correlations between the two variables are not high enough to suggest a strong coefficient of reliability. Furthermore, the correlations between the two indicators and the other variables are clearly different

Table 13.1. Means, standard deviations, and correlations

Variable	Mean	S.D.	1	2	3	4	5	6	7
Profit centers									
1. Product design newness	3.33	1.38	—						
2. Process design newness	3.20	1.69	.79	—					
3. Labor uniqueness	3.81	1.71	.43	.50	—				
4. Equipment uniqueness	4.64	2.09	.46	.50	.84	—			
5. Investment in technology	1.61	.50	–.45	–.71	–.42	–.41	—		
6. Supplier market competition	3.93	1.60	–.08	–.02	–.52	–.62	.08	—	
7. Engineering cost allocation	3.34	1.77	–.15	–.10	.11	.23	–.04	–.55	—
8. Material cost allocation	2.89	1.56	–.29	–.26	–.36	–.42	.03	.01	.30
Outside suppliers									
1. Product design newness	2.80	1.78	—						
2. Process design newness	2.46	1.59	.73	—					
3. Labor uniqueness	3.19	1.91	.33	.46	—				
4. Equipment uniqueness	3.61	2.00	.53	.64	.60	—			
5. Investment technology	1.71	.46	–.16	–.40	–.31	–.32	—		
6. Supplier market competition	5.10	1.56	–.36	–.19	–.08	–.45	.17	—	
7. Engineering cost allocation	2.80	1.69	.02	.23	.31	.19	–.29	–.00	—
8. Material cost allocation	2.76	1.60	.06	.20	.28	.25	–.39	–.10	.58

in magnitude, suggesting low concurrent validity and strong potential for interpretational confounding (Burt, 1976). Consequently, we predicted each indicator separately. To control for potential bias due to common measurement properties of the two transaction cost indicators, we estimated the covariance between their measurement errors (ε_{56}).

Table 13.2 presents the results for construct validation. The covariance between the indicators of transaction costs (ε_{56}) is statistically significant and does not differ across the two types of supplier ($\chi^2 \text{dif}_1 = .78$, $p = .62$). This result suggests that both measures are related to an unobserved construct, but not so strongly that it constitutes a latent variable in the model. We shall elaborate later on the implications of this finding for the measurement of transaction costs.

The results also show that our measures of asset uniqueness have significantly less error in profit centers than in outside suppliers ($\chi^2 \text{dif}_3 = 11.3$, $p = .01$). However, the reliability of the construct (Bagozzi, 1980, p. 181) in each group is acceptable (.89 for the profit centers; .78 for the outside suppliers). The two types of suppliers do not differ in the measurement of technology newness ($\chi^2 \text{dif}_3 = 7.09$, $p = .07$; reliability = .87).

Table 13.3 shows that the two types of suppliers differ in their mean values only for the construct of market competition. Profit centers have less competition than market suppliers do, consistent with Walker and Weber's (1984) results. These findings support our assertion that the two types of supply relationships are embedded in hybrid institutions.

Table 13.4 shows the findings for the three hypotheses and other causal paths. H1 is supported: Asset uniqueness leads to lower interunit conflict for profit centers than for outside suppliers (for engineering cost allocation, $\chi^2 \text{dif}_1 = 3.95$, $p = .047$; for material cost allocation, $\chi^2 \text{dif}_1 = 8.51$, $p = .004$). Interestingly, higher levels of asset uniqueness lead to lower levels of conflict for profit centers but have no effect

Table 13.2. Maximum-likelihood estimates for construct validation of technology newness, asset uniqueness, and transaction costs

Parameter	Unstandardized M.L.E.	Standardized M.L.E.	Jackknife estimate of M.L.E.	χ^2 difference profit centers to outside suppliers
Technology newness				7 09
λ1	1.00	.76	—	
λ2	1.36	1.00	1.78 + (.14)	
δ1	1.07	.65	—	
δ2	0.00	0.00	—	
Asset uniqueness				11.3*
Profit centers				
λ3	1.00	.75	—	
λ4	1.45	.96	1.44 + (.12)	
ε1	.87	.21		
ε2	.46	04	—	
Outside suppliers				
λ3	1.00	.75	—	
λ4	1.49	.99	1.56 + (.12)	
ε1	1.49	.62	—	
ε2	.45	.04	—	
Transaction costs				
ε_{56} ·	.44	.44	.42 + (.06)	.78

*p < .05 *Standard errors are in parentheses

on conflict for outside suppliers (compare estimates of β_3 and β_4 between the two types of suppliers).

In contrast, both H2 and H3 are disconfirmed. Preselection investment in technology leads to greater difficulty in reaching interunit agreement regarding cost allocation (β_5 and β_6) for both profit centers and outside suppliers. The coefficients are not significantly different between the two types of suppliers (engineering cost allocation, $\chi^2 dif_1 = .60$, p = .44; material cost allocation, $\chi^2 dif_1 = .00$, p = 1.0). Furthermore, contrary to expectations, supplier market competition predicts lower interunit conflict for profit centers than for outside suppliers (engineering cost allocation, $\chi^2 dif_1 = 13.9$, p = .001; material cost allocation, $\chi^2 dif_1 = 5.78$, p = .017). Like asset specificity, higher market competition leads to less conflict (β_7 and β_8) for the component divisions but has no effect on outside suppliers.

Table 13.3. Differences in construct means between profit centers and outside suppliers

Variable	Unstandardized M.L.E.	Standardized M.L.E.	Jackknife of M.L.E.	Jackknife of S.E.
Technology newness	.55	.44	.36	.27
Asset uniqueness	.34	.24	.39	.26
Investment in technology	.02	.04	.03	.06
Supplier–market competition	–.81	–.47	–.82$^+$	.26
Engineering cost allocation	–.16	–.09	–.16	.60
Material cost allocation	.12	.07	.07	.33

$^+|T| > 2$

Table 13.4. Results for hypotheses

Parameter	Unstand-ardized M.L.E.	Stand-ardized M.L.E.	Jackknife estimate of M.L.E.	χ2 difference profit centers to outside suppliers
Hypothesis 1				
Profit centers				
β3	–.40	–.32	–.45 + (.17)*	3.9*
β4	–.99	–.88	–1.03 + (.23)	8.5*
Outside suppliers				
β3	.27	.21	.23 + (.28)	
β4	.22	.19	.19 + (.22)	
Hypothesis 2				
β5	–.67	–.18	–.76 + (.20)	.60
β6	–1.09	–.32	–1.07 + (.31)	.00
Hypothesis 3				
Profit centers				
β7	–.82	–.80	–.85 + (.18)	13.9*
β8	–.51	–.55	–.55 + (.21)	5.8*
Outside suppliers				
β7	.13	.13	.11 + (.22)	
β8	.03	.04	–.02 + (.12)	
Estimates for other causal paths				
γ1	.62	.54	.77 + (.11)	.74
γ2	–.22	–.57	–.29 + (.03)	3.75
γ3	.42	.30	.52 + (21)	.31
β1	–.23	.08	–.26 + (.39)	1.07
β2	–.85	.69	–.83 + (.15)	.27
Estimates for error terms				
φ3	1.19	.96	.83 + (.09)	
ψ11	1.07	.76	1.12 + (.08)	
ψ22	.39	.83	.39 + (.02)	
ψ33	1.25	.72	1.56 + (.24)	
ψ44	1.51	.86	1.57 + (.17)	
ψ55	1.35	.85	1.33 + (.15)	

*p < .05 *Standard errors are in parentheses + |T| > 2

The effects of technological age on asset specialization and supplier market competition do not vary between profit centers and outside suppliers (χ^2dif$_1$ = .74, p = .39; and χ^2dif$_1$ = .31, p = .58, respectively). Thus, we can be reasonably certain that technology differences between the two types of suppliers do not bias our results. Interestingly, for both types of suppliers, newer technology relates to both greater asset uniqueness and greater supplier market competition (γ_1 and γ_3, respectively).

Asset uniqueness and supplier market competition are negatively related (β2), as expected. But contrary to expectation, preselection investment in technology does not affect asset uniqueness (β1). These results are the same for both profit centers and outside suppliers (χ^2dif$_1$ = .27, p = .61; and χ^2dif$_1$ = 1.07, p = .31, respectively).

Table 13.5. Logistic regression of product program on product technology and predictors of transaction costs

Variable	Parameter	S. E.	χ^2	p
Intercept	2.15	2.17	.97	.33
Supplier–market competition	–.18	.20	.78	.38
Labor uniqueness	.17	.19	.86	.36
Equipment uniqueness	–.25	.21	1.54	.22
Investment in technology	–.04	.62	.00	.94
Engineering cost allocation	–.02	.16	.02	.89
Material cost allocation	–.04	.17	.04	.83
Product design newness	–.12	.23	.30	.58
Process design newness	–.19	.27	.54	.46

Likelihood ratio: χ^2 (59 df) = 91.03; p = .005.

Finally, key-informant bias does not appear to confound our findings. The logistic regression results presented in Table 13.5 show that none of the variables we studied is related to the two product programs. Thus the programs are not an important omitted variable in the model. Also, in general, the jackknife values are reasonably close to the maximum-likelihood estimates, suggesting that outliers are not a major contributor to the results.

The chi-square goodness of fit for the model shows that we cannot reject it ($\chi^2 dif_{44} = 52.99$, p = .17). This statistic suggests that there is no unspecified systematic structure of the error terms that might represent key-informant bias. Also, the Type II parsimonious-normed goodness-of-fit index is .96. The model is thus a good fit to the data, controlling for the number of parameters estimated and our small sample size.

DISCUSSION AND CONCLUSIONS

Do organizations and markets govern transactions differently? Our answer is a highly qualified yes. The basic proposition of transaction cost economics is sound: Supplier asset specificity within the corporation is associated with lower transaction costs than is asset specificity in the market. Our results, however, stretch and reshape the theory in ways that partially support its critics. These changes are related to the hybrid characteristics of the organization and markets we studied.

Decentralization in the corporation and relational contracting with market suppliers affect supplier relations in ways that strike at traditional research on transaction costs. The means of the profit centers and outside suppliers differ only in their degree of market competition. Thus a conventional test of transaction cost theory, which compares the level of asset specificity inside and outside an organization, would fail. This failure supports arguments (Eccles & White, 1988; Stinchcombe, 1983) that hybrid organizations and markets are more similar than transaction cost theory proposes. Moreover, because in-house and market supply have the same level of interunit conflict, a process of institutional selection based on transaction costs would not favor one type of supplier over the other.

Although in-house and market supply relationships appear to be hybrid or non-standard, H1 is supported. This result is confounded by neither age of technology nor extent of competition. We infer that the coordination mechanisms the division uses to manage specialized inputs in-house are simply more effective than are the mechanisms available in the market. This is the essence of the transaction cost theory of vertical integration. But because the support of H1 may be related to better in-house management of new technologies rather than to specialized assets, we estimated the direct relationship between the age of the technology and both types of cost allocation. The estimates were not significant ($\chi^2 dif_1 = .53$, for engineering change cost allocation difficulties; $\chi^2 dif_1 = .52$, for material cost allocation difficulties).

How much in-house coordination mechanisms represent the old centralized control of profit center relationships, as opposed to new practices, has important implications for interpreting the results for H1. Two examples, both focused on the relationship between new technology and asset specialization, highlight the difference between old and new mechanisms. One important and enduring practice is that a large, relatively powerful centralized engineering staff coordinates the development of new technologies in the component divisions. Technologies that create unique assets are especially salient, as they can give the corporation an edge over its competitors. The corporation will gain, however, only if a component division successfully adapts a technology to an assembly division's needs. For this reason and because successful adaptation of the technology leads to learning about its generalizability, staff engineers have an incentive to help resolve problems between the profit centers and the assembly division. We frequently observed staff engineers in consultative roles, in both the assembly division and the component divisions, but we observed no such role for these engineers in relationships with outside suppliers.

An example of a new coordination mechanism developed to improve the effectiveness of supplier operations, both inside and outside the corporation, is "early sourcing," which has long been a practice in Japanese manufacturing firms (see Rubinger, 1985) and is becoming widely adopted by U.S. manufacturing organizations (*Purchasing*, 1984). The major goals of early sourcing are to use the supplier's technological expertise and to create a product design compatible with the supplier's manufacturing facilities, thereby leading to lower costs and higher quality. Suppliers participating in early sourcing are brought into the process of developing a product either as it is being designed by the buyer's engineers or as the technology itself is being developed. This practice contrasts with traditional supplier involvement, which typically occurs after the first product prototype is made, long after the technology development and the product design have been completed. Early sourcing gives the buyer more information about the supplier's capabilities and its cost structure. Furthermore, inputs that are early sourced from component divisions tend to be produced with more unusual assets than are early-sourced inputs from outside suppliers.[3] Therefore, because of better information, negotiations over cost allocation for unique assets in the profit centers may be less difficult than negotiations for comparable assets in outside suppliers.

We cannot say whether H1 is supported because of the vestiges of centralization or the successful management of decentralization, or both. If only old centralized practices are effective and they decline as decentralization takes hold, we should expect to see transaction costs rise in the corporation. If effective new practices can replace the old, then transaction costs will remain lower for unique assets in the corporation.

These alternative scenarios for interunit coordination show that our results for H1 support the transaction cost framework more as a theory of organization design than as a theory predicting changes in the boundary of the firm. The important difference between transaction cost theory and other theories of organization design is that it compares relationships inside an organization with market contracting. The theory is silent, however, on how to compare coordination mechanisms between organizations or within the same organization over time.[4] Such a comparison would be a necessary part of analyzing a single organization's move from central to decentralized control over supplier relations. Further development of the theory is therefore required to address the issues that our supportive findings raise.

It seems clear, moreover, that although H1 is supported, the corporation is unlikely to integrate vertically any specialized outside suppliers. By lowering the potential for opportunistic behavior, relational contracting reduces the transaction costs associated with specialized market suppliers, even though they have new technology and low competition. Because specialized outside suppliers do not cause the corporation to incur high transaction costs, they are unlikely to be candidates for integration. This finding supports Coase (1988) in his assertion that asset specificity is not a sufficient condition for vertical integration (cf. Klein, 1988; Williamson, 1988).

Relational contracting not only decreases the threat of vertical integration, but it also reduces the threat that outside suppliers will be terminated. Decentralization has the opposite effect on in-house units: It increases the threat of termination. The net outcome is that market competition leads to greater cooperation in-house, contrary to H3. Thus in-house suppliers are apparently not protected by an internal procurement bias. Because market incentives are viable within the corporation for standard inputs, the costs of managing them are likely to be low and may approach the costs of managing standard inputs with new technology in the market under relational contracting. This result challenges the assumption in transaction cost theory that the market manages all standard assets more efficiently (e.g., Masten, 1984; Riordan & Williamson, 1986; Williamson, 1981).

Neither decentralization nor relational contracting has a salubrious effect on the behavior of suppliers that have made preselection investments in new technology. Unexpectedly, these investments do not involve specialized assets, suggesting that these suppliers are unlikely to participate in buyer programs such as early sourcing. Nor are the markets for these products highly competitive. Therefore, within the corporation, profit centers with new technology investments are influenced by neither the coordination mechanisms to manage specialized suppliers nor the discipline of market competition. Outside the corporation, relational contracting may break down because of the need to cover the high fixed costs of new investment in an emerging market.

External validity

Our variables may have limited external validity because they do not measure dollar prices or costs. This limitation is characteristic of research on transaction cost theory. The "microanalytic" focus that Williamson (1985, p. 403) advocated has led researchers to measure managerial experience in a number of institutional contexts.

Generalizing the constructs underlying these measures and the logic connecting the constructs is a primary research task to which our study contributes.

Our measurement of transaction costs illuminates some problems in developing a single, generalizable construct. The covariation of measurement error between the transaction cost indicators (ε_{56}) may represent their shared content: the difficulty of agreeing on adjustment cost allocation. In turn, the poor convergent validity of the measures may be due to unshared content: the different causes of adjustment costs—engineering changes and material cost changes—that they capture. This result indicates that estimating the process of achieving agreement with a supplier may be separated from the substantive issues about which the agreement is reached.

Measuring more broadly defined transaction costs is therefore likely to be at least as complex as our problem here, as they include both interunit conflict and governance costs. To minimize this complexity, future researchers may choose to decompose broad concepts into their unique contents, for example, product design changes, and to predict each content with a separate theory. This theory should be tailored to the practices and policies that can be tied to the specific content predicted. Because our predictions for engineering and material cost changes were similar, we believe that their institutional contexts were comparable.

Several distinguishing characteristics of our sample and method should be discussed. First, in contrast with previous transaction cost studies, which typically analyze convenience samples, we analyzed a random sample from the complete product list of the division. Thus we can be reasonably confident that our results generalize to the population of assembly division inputs. Second, like Walker and Weber (1984), but unlike the authors of other previous studies, we simultaneously tested our hypotheses and estimated a measurement model. We thereby identified the part of the covariance among the variables that is due to measurement alone. Third, our knowledge of how our theory applies to the institutional context in which it was tested not only increased the study's internal validity but also indicates the type of organization and supplier relationships to which our model and results apply. Because supplier reduction and "outsourcing" programs have been adopted by many U.S. manufacturing firms, we believe that our model may have reasonably wide applicability.

Conclusion

Although our findings defend the core of transaction cost theory, they raise questions concerning how the theory should be applied to complex economic institutions facing strong competition in their product markets. Corporate decentralization and relational contracting diminish the role of asset specialization as a necessary condition for low transaction costs in-house and as a sufficient condition for high transaction costs in the market. Therefore, how the theory should be used to predict shifts in the current boundaries of the corporation is unclear.

We suspect that the effect of in-house asset specialization on transaction costs reflects both enduring supplier governance practices and new policies designed to improve supplier performance. How and when, in the history of an organization, supplier asset specialization determines the organization's boundaries thus becomes a critical question. Careful research on the separate origins and consequences of in-house and market governance is therefore a necessary and central research agenda for transaction cost theory.

ACKNOWLEDGMENT

This research was supported by the Reginald Jones Center, Wharton School, the Management in the 1990s Program at MIT and by a grant from the National Science Foundation, no. SES-8800310. We appreciate the comments of Bruce Kogut, Dan Levinthal, Marshall Meyer, Oliver Williamson, and two anonymous reviewers.

NOTES

1. The theory here concerns the contracting problems faced by the buyer after the supplier has invested in new technology to obtain the buyer's business. We did not examine the motivations that led the supplier to make the investment. Presumably, one of these would be the large size of the order that the supplier received from the buyer.
2. To see whether the subsample of 67 was representative, we compared the proportions of in-house and market suppliers in this sample with their proportions in the sample of 100. The proportions were not statistically different between the two samples.
3. Regressions show a significant relationship between early sourcing and asset uniqueness ($p < .10$) for profit centers, controlling for technology newness, but no relationship for outside suppliers. Like technology newness, early sourcing has no direct effect on transaction costs.
4. Williamson's theory (1975, chap. 8; 1985, chap. 11) regarding the efficiency of the multidivisional form addresses the problem of reducing unnecessary coordination between divisions rather than improving necessary coordination.

REFERENCES

Anderson, E., & D. Schmittlein (1984). Integration of the sales force: An empirical examination. *Rand Journal of Economics* 13:206–13.

Bagozzi, R. P. (1980). *Causal models in marketing*. New York: Wiley.

Bagozzi, R. P., & L. W. Phillips (1982). Representing and testing organizational theories: A holistic construal. *Administrative Science Quarterly* 27:459–89.

Bradach, J., & R. H. Eccles (1989). Price, authority and trust: From ideal types to plural forms. *Annual Review of Sociology* 15:97–118.

Burt, R. S. (1976). Interpretation of confounding and unobserved variables in structural equation models. *Sociological Methods and Research* 5:3–52.

Byrne, B. M., R. J. Shavelson, & B. Muthen (1989). Testing for the equivalence of factor covariance and mean structures: The issue of partial measurement invariance. *Psychological Bulletin* 105:456–66.

Chandler, A. D. (1962). *Strategy and structure*. Cambridge, MA: MIT Press.

Coase, R. H. (1988). The nature of the firm: Influence. *Journal of Law, Economics and Organization* 4:33–48.

Demsetz, H. (1988). Theory of the firm revisited. *Journal of Law, Economics and Organization* 4:141–62.

Dore, R. (1983). Goodwill and the spirit of market capitalism. *British Journal of Sociology* 34:459–82.

Dow, G. (1987). The function of authority in transaction cost economics. *Journal of Economic Behavior and Organization* 8:13–38.

Eccles, R. H. (1981). The quasi-firm in the construction industry. *Journal of Economic Behavior and Organization* 2:335–58.

——— (1985). *The transfer pricing problem.* Lexington, MA: Lexington Books.

Eccles, R. H., & H. White (1988). Price and authority in inter profit center transactions. *American Journal of Sociology* (supplement) 94:S17–S51.

Evans, D. S., & S. J. Grossman (1983). Integration. In D. S. Evans (Ed.), *Breaking up Bell*, pp. 95–126, New York: Macmillan.

Galbraith, J. (1973). *Designing complex organizations.* Reading, MA: Addison Wesley.

Granovetter, M. (1985). Economic action and social structure: The problem of embeddedness. *American Journal of Sociology* 91:481–510.

Harrigan, K. R. (1983). *Strategies for vertical integration.* Lexington, MA: Heath.

Heide, J. B., & G. John (1990). Alliances in industrial purchasing: The determinants of joint action in buyer–supplier relationships. *Journal of Marketing Research* 27:24–36.

Joreskog, K. G., & D. Sorbom (1984). *Lisrel VI: Users guide.* Mooresville, IN: Scientific Software.

Joskow, P. L. (1985). Vertical integration and long-term contracts. *Journal of Law, Economics and Organization* 1:33.

Klein, B. (1988). Vertical integration as organizational ownership: The Fisher Body-General Motors relationship revisited. *Journal of Law, Economics and Organization* 4:199–213.

Klein, B., R. Crawford, R., & A. Alchian (1978). Vertical integration, appropriable rents, and the competitive contracting process. *Journal of Law and Economics* 21:297–326.

Klein, B., & K. B. Leffler (1981). The role of market forces in assuring contractual performance. *Journal of Political Economy* 89:615–41.

Kleindorfer, P., & G. Knieps (1982). Vertical integration and transaction-specific sunk costs. *European Economic Review* 19:71–87.

MacNeil, I. R. (1978). Contracts: Adjustments of long-term economic relations under classical, neoclassical and relational contract law. *Northwestern University Law Review* 72:854–906.

Masten, S. (1984). The organization of production: Evidence from the aerospace industry. *Journal of Law and Economics* 27:403–18.

Monteverde, K., & D. J. Teece (1982). Supplier switching costs and vertical integration in the automobile industry. *Bell Journal of Economics* 13:206–13.

Mosteller, F., & J. Tukey (1977). *Data analysis and regression.* Reading, MA: Addison-Wesley.

Mulaik, S. A., L. R. James, J. Van Alstine, N. Bennett, S. Lind, & C. D. Stilwell (1989). Evaluation of goodness-of-fit indices for structural equation models. *Psychological Bulletin* 105:430–45.

Perrow, C. (1986). *Complex organizations: A critical essay.* New York: Random House.

Phillips, L. W. (1981). Assessing measurement error in key-informant reports: A methodological note on organizational analyses, *Journal of Marketing Research* 18:395–415.

Purchasing Magazine (1984). Medal of excellence. June 6.

Rindskopf, D. (1984). Using phantom and imaginary latent variables to parameterize constraints in linear structural models. *Psychometrika* 49:37–47.

Riordan, M., & O. E. Williamson (1986). Asset specificity and economic organization. *International Journal of Industrial Organization* 3:365–78.

Rubinger, B. (1985). Technology policy in Japanese firms. *Technology in Society* 7:281–96.

Sharma, S., S. Durvasula, & W. R. Dillon (1989). Some results on the behavior of alternate covariance structure estimation procedures in the presence of non-normal data. *Journal of Marketing Research* 26:214–21.

Stigler, G. J. (1951). The division of labor is limited by the extent of the market. *Journal of Political Economy* 59:185–93.

Stinchombe, A. (1983). Contracts as hierarchial documents. Unpublished manuscript, Stanford Graduate School of Business, Stanford University.

Thompson, J. D. (1967). *Organizations in action.* New York: McGraw-Hill.

Walker, G., & D. Weber (1984). A transaction cost approach to make-or-buy decisions. *Administrative Science Quarterly* 29:373–91.

Williamson, O. E. (1975). *Markets and hierarchies.* New York: Free Press.

——— (1979). Transaction cost economics: The governance of contractual relations. *Journal of Law and Economics* 22:3–61.

——— (1981). The economics of organization: The transaction cost approach. *American Journal of Sociology* 87:548–77.

——— (1983). Credible commitment: Using hostages to support exchange. *American Economic Review* 73:519–40.

——— (1985). *The economic institutions of capitalism.* New York: Free Press.

——— (1988). The logic of economic organization. *The Journal of Law, Economics and Organization* 4:65–94.

PART III

THE ORGANIZATION AND MANAGEMENT RESPONSE

In Part III, we will examine the impact of information technology at the interface between the individual and the organization, and we will see the effect of leadership on organizational attitudes toward the technology. We also will see how a major telecommunications firm managed the problems associated with job displacement, how workers react to computer-based monitoring of their performance, and the effectiveness of "telecommuting."

As the chapters in this volume have shown repeatedly, organizations must almost always undergo some change in existing practices or structure in order to derive full benefit from information technology. Understanding the ways in which information technology can affect organizational structure and the ways in which organizations can adapt to and accomplish the needed changes, often involving worker displacement, is the subject addressed in Part III.

In Chapter 14, Schein first takes us to the executive level and explains how CEOs, too, can encourage or impede the diffusion of information technology through an organization. He then takes us back to the old saw that "actions speak louder than words" and shows the chief executive's behavior to be critical to determining the adoption of technology. The impact of information technology is mediated by what people choose to do or not to do and can have an organizationwide effect.

Carroll and Perin then explain to us in Chapter 15 that there are a variety of levels at which an organization can use information technology. They contrast three firms' approaches to introducing microcomputers. Without telling their story for them, we shall say only that it is clear that how seriously an organization views the technology makes a difference in the way in which it approaches implementation and in the benefits it derives from the technology. Carroll and Perin bring us back again to the basic lesson: Until we reexamine the nature of the business and consider how information technology can be used (or when it cannot be used) to accomplish the organization's tasks,we will not gain full benefit. We are reminded of a thesis completed at MIT as part of the Management in the 1990s Program but too late to be included in this volume. In this thesis (Robertson, 1990) the author argued that there are three levels at which an organization implementing a computer-aided design (CAD) system can view its investment. At one level, it can be seen as an investment in "physical capital." In other words, it is simply a device for improving an existing process, that is, an automated or electronically augmented drafting board. At a deeper level, CAD can be viewed as an investment in "human capital." From this perspective it extends existing human capabilities and introduces new processes. The designer can now work more effectively in three dimensions and make design tradeoffs that were much more difficult or impossible with traditional approaches. Finally, the organization can view CAD as an investment in "social capital." In this sense, CAD becomes a catalyst for more effectively managing relationships among the organizational units involved in the design. One of the more contentious interunit relationships is between product design and manufacturing engineering. CAD can improve this relationship by allowing these two units to share design information and thereby to influence each other's problem-solving approaches.

Using the presence or absence of design changes to enable a product to be manufactured, Robertson analyzed the effect of users implementing CAD at these three levels. Those groups that saw CAD only at the first level, as an improved drafting instrument, drew no benefit. Those who went to the second level and saw CAD as a way to extend the designer's capabilities drew some benefit, in needing fewer redesigns for manufacturing compatibility. But those who used the system to improve communication and relationships between product design and manufacturing engineering groups needed the fewest redesigns. It was at this third level of implementation that organizations drew the greatest benefit.

In Chapter 16, Pentland uses three criteria to assess the introduction of laptop computers to U.S. Internal Revenue Service agents. He looked first to see whether they used the technology, and then, he inquired about their satisfaction with it. Finally, he asked agents whether the laptop computer enabled them to do more work in a given time. Use, he found, is related to satisfaction. Heavier users were more satisfied. Satisfaction, in turn, is related to performance. But the direct link between use and performance was, at best, very weak and short of statistical significance. In fact, if one controls for satisfaction, it will turn slightly (although again not significantly) negative. Once again, we have the problem of improper fit between the technology and the nature of the work. Pentland reports that many agents felt compelled (although this was never explicitly communicated, nor was it IRS policy) to use the laptops. Some agents therefore used them even when a calculator and columnar pad would have been quicker. This use, even when the agent realized that the technology did not fit the task well, naturally led to a perception of poorer performance. So, for those cases for which the technology was suitable, processing time was shorter; when it was inappropriate, processing was prolonged. The net result is a nonsignificant relation between use and performance.

Chalykoff and Kochan focus on a different type of job and a different application of information technology. In Chapter 17, they show that the incorporation of information technology for monitoring employee performance and providing feedback produces surprising results. The monitoring of employees as they use computers, telecommunication systems, or similar applications of information technology is a practice that has produced considerable dispute but that is becoming more widespread. Chalykoff and Kochan's results will surely be cited in these arguments for a long time to come. They found that an unexpectedly high proportion of employees, for example, preferred computer-aided monitoring, of which they were unaware, over direct monitoring with the supervisor present. Evidently, they felt they could be more relaxed and perform better if they did not know when they were being monitored.

At another extreme, in Chapter 18 Bailyn demonstrates that when employees are completely out of sight of their supervisor, for example, when working at home and "telecommuting," the employees become concerned lest management forget them. She goes on to show that the popular press's reports of large numbers of workers staying at home and connected to the organization by computer are somewhat exaggerated. The home-based operation does not always provide as much freedom as might be imagined, and it can lead to a fear of second-class status compared with that of peers who are in full-time direct contact with management. Westney and Ghoshal, in their examination in Chapter 19 of one of the possible sources of stimulants for organizational change, return us to a strategic level in the organization. They examine the intelligence function, how organizations collect and process information on competitors and markets on a worldwide basis. In this instance, this does not mean changes necessitated by information technology but, rather, the ways in which information processing can provide a basis for organizational adaptation and change. This is an obvious application for information technology that has been largely neglected. An enormous body of information on markets and competitors is processed by large companies. But their use of technology, according to Westney and Ghoshal, has been far from systematic and not very effective. It thus appears to be a great opportunity for innovation, and the globalization of industry makes this an imperative, as traditional methods for collecting and processing information of this sort are not effective given the geographic dispersion of sources.

Little, in contrast, goes to the other extreme, and in Chapter 20 he discusses applications that have been highly developed and utilized. In the consumer goods area, information technology provides marketers with information in a way that Little says represents a discontinuity in their capabilities. Consumer preferences can be monitored, and this information can rapidly be made available to decision makers in marketing, R&D, and production organizations. All of this results from the collection and quick processing of information at the retail level, coupled with the timing of marketing strategies and advertising. This is an area that is now highly developed and in which organizations have created a structure that enables them to use this technology effectively.

Allen and Hauptman show in Chapter 21 how research, development, and engineering organizations, which process abstract and complex forms of information, can use information technology to substitute for traditional organizational forms. The two organizational structures used in this activity, project teams and functional departments, each specialize in making possible a particular form of communication. The project team coordinates work efforts, and the functional department transfers specialized knowledge among its members. Some interesting innovations, based on information technology, can be used for these same purposes. These allow the organizational designer to choose an organizational structure that promotes one of these two forms of communication and to augment it by using information technology to achieve the other type of communication.

No matter what the tone, set by the CEO or others, and no matter whether the outcome is widespread adoption or "wait and see," the economic effect on the organization can be widespread. In Chapter 22, Lynch and Osterman explain why this is true in the case of a major telecommunication provider. As the nature of work changes, so do the requirements for those who perform the work. How do organizations adapt to this? What strategies can they use? How are choices made among retraining programs, transfers, quits, layoffs, retirements, early retirements, and so on? Lynch and Osterman describe the answers to these questions for several occupational types and connect their results to a strong theoretical base. Then by means of this theoretical structure, they demonstrate how to apply what they have learned to other situations.

Kochan, MacDuffie, and Osterman take us through another case, in Chapter 23, explaining how as a consequence of a shift in the work being performed, a major corporation reallocated talent in the organization. This is a problem that companies will face more and more often in the next several years. Learning about the experience of this company, which managed the process humanely and effectively is a valuable lesson. The process, which was expensive in the short run, had the long-term payoff of maintaining the employees' loyalty and commitment to the company. This is clearly an example that runs counter to the currently popular belief about American firms' favoring the short term over the long term.

REFERENCE

Robertson, D. C. (1990). CAD systems and communication in design engineering: A test of the information process model. Ph.D. diss., Sloan School of Management, Massachusetts Institute of Technology.

14

The Role of the CEO in the Management of Change: The Case of Information Technology

EDGAR H. SCHEIN

Few people would question the assumption that CEOs have a major impact on changes in their organizations. Yet there is surprisingly little analysis of just what this impact is likely to be; whether it will vary by industry, company, or the CEOs' attitude and style; and what empirical data can be gathered to begin to shed some light on these issues.

We decided in 1987 to interview CEOs in a variety of companies and, with the assistance of a number of our Sloan Fellows and other graduate students, were able to interview 94 executives, all of whom were current or past CEOs, and, in a few cases, COOs or presidents of divisions in conglomerates or multidivisional companies. What is distinctive about this research is that it draws exclusively on the responses of the chief executives, a point of some importance inasmuch as most of them felt that becoming a CEO changed their role and attitudes.

Our interviews focused on the CEOs' personal attitudes toward and use of information technology (IT), and they tried to elicit some of the underlying assumptions behind these behaviors and attitudes. Common dimensions and variables were chosen for the interview protocol and subsequent analysis, but because we felt it essential to get the CEOs' spontaneous views, we asked our interviewers to allow the CEOs to tell their story in their own way. We then combined the protocols according to theme and found that the coding reliability was sufficient to pursue our analysis and to develop constructs, but not high enough to allow us to generalize from this sample to the population of CEOs.

This chapter fits the CEOs' responses into a framework that allows us to analyze how they affected their organizations' changes.

GENERIC CEO ROLES IN THE CHANGE PROCESS

Table 14.1 shows a model of the change process that Kurt Lewin originally proposed and I elaborated in order to explain changes that contained planned, nonvoluntary,

Table 14.1. A stage model of planned change

Unfreezing: Creating motivation to change
Disconfirmation
Induction of anxiety / guilt
Creation of psychological safety
Creating change throuqh cognitive redefinition
Stimulating imitation or identification
Stimulating scanning
Refreezing: Stabilizing the change
Integration into personality
Integration into key relationships and social system

sometimes coercive elements (Lewin, 1952; Schein, 1961, 1972, 1987). Lewin correctly foresaw that in living systems any given stable state was a "quasi-stationary" equilibrium that could be unfrozen, moved, and refrozen, but he did not detail how one actually unfreezes a system, moves it, and then refreezes it. Because organizations usually develop stable routines and cultures, any organizational change tends to occur according to the stages identified in this model.

As Table 14.1 shows, one can logically analyze and order the steps necessary in each stage of the change process, though these steps often occur either out of sequence or simultaneously. Most of these steps take place through the intervention of a person labeled for this purpose a *change agent*, and it is these interventions on which I wish to focus. The question we shall consider is whether and how CEOs act as change agents and during which of these steps.

Disconfirmation: The CEO as a disconfirmer

CEOs are uniquely suited to be disconfirmers because of their power position in the organization, the information to which they have access, and the responsibilities they have for maintaining the organization's health. If things are not going right in their view, they are obligated to change the organization by disconfirming the present state. Normal routines that have become habits in an organization will not change unless someone ceases to respond in the expected manner. Such disconfirming responses will obviously have more weight if they come from the CEO than from someone lower in the hierarchy.

For example, one of our respondents decided to start the change toward a greater use of IT by announcing that he was personally going to start using a desktop terminal and would henceforth send all important communications to his subordinates by means of electronic mail. In other words, if they sent something by the old system, he would simply not answer, and if they did not get a terminal of their own, they would miss important messages from him.

Disconfirmation in its simplest form means that things that used to work no longer work. External circumstances can disconfirm, as when sales fall off or the price of the company's stock falls, but more typically in organizational change, it is a human change agent who starts the process by sending different signals, such as when a CEO announces that a major downturn in business will require downsizing, that a change in technology will require reorganization, that a merger will require a realignment of people, or, as in the preceding example, that he will change his own behavior in such a way as to force others to change theirs. In each case, the initial impact of the message can be described as a disconfirmation of the present behavior, values, and assumptions.

If there is no disconfirmation from any source, there will be no motivation to change. In a complacent organization, therefore, one of the CEO's first functions is to generate information or announce decisions that will have a disconfirming effect. But that is not enough, as many CEOs find.

Inducing anxiety and/or guilt: The CEO as the "bad parent"

Disconfirming messages will have an impact only if they pertain to something important to us. For example, if the CEO ceases to respond to subordinates' behavior in an area not relevant to their concern, they may simply not pay attention. However, if the CEO's continuing to behave in the old way makes the subordinates feel anxious because some important goals may not be met or makes them feel guilty because some valued ideals will not be met unless a change occurs, then the message will be heeded and discomfort will motivate some activity. It is this step that leads to quips like "no pain, no gain" or the common assertion among change agents that unless the system is "hurting somehow," there will be no change.

CEOs are in a good position to cause anxiety or guilt because they are symbolically and psychologically in a parent role. Even if they do not try to be parental, many subordinates will, for their own psychological reasons, attribute parental power to them and react strongly to any signals that the CEO is pleased or displeased with them.

Probably the best example is the CEO who states outright or subtly implies to his subordinates that their failure to learn to use IT means either that they will fail in their work (anxiety induction) or that they are technologically "backward" (guilt induction). Whether or not it is intended, change is forced when the subordinates feel obsolete, out of touch, or in some other way uncomfortable about maintaining their old behavior.

Creating psychological safety: The CEO as the "good parent"

If too much anxiety or guilt is created, however, there is the danger that the targets of the change will react defensively. One of the most likely defenses in this situation is denial, which in this case means that the subordinates cease to "hear" the disconfirming signals or rationalize them away. Subordinates say to themselves: "The boss doesn't really mean it; he is just showing off his own new toy; he won't persist if I don't go along," and so on.

Given this state of affairs, there will be no motivation and readiness for change unless the target also feels psychologically safe. In other words, giving up the old behavior, value, or assumption creates anxiety, and people will not tolerate that kind of anxiety unless they feel some support during the transition period (Schein, 1985).

In the case of the introduction of IT, people may feel embarrassed by the slowness of their learning or their inability to type, or their poor grammar or spelling, all of which they hid before by dealing directly with a secretary. A common error here is to assume that such resistance to change is only a lack of motivation or an unwillingness to make an effort to learn something new. Much more likely is the defensive avoidance that results from an inability to face one's own presumed inadequacies if one does not feel psychologically safe.

CEOs should and do attend to this problem in a variety of ways. One of the most common we found was to be totally inflexible on the ultimate goals to be achieved (i.e., that desktop workstations would eventually be used by all senior management) but to be highly flexible and supportive on (1) the pace of their introduction, (2) the degree to which some subordinates could continue to use their secretaries to enter data or memos, and, most important, (3) the amount and type of training help the CEOs would provide, no matter what the cost. Subordinates could use individual coaches if "going to class" caused tension, and in some cases, this meant individual coaching for long periods of time. Some CEOs felt that sending their subordinates to formal classes would threaten them further, and they arranged for an instructor who would provide the psychological safety necessary to learn something new.

We cannot count how many CEOs played each of these three unfreezing roles, because local circumstances varied or we did not have the data. However, we heard many stories about the disconfirming and anxiety/guilt-inducing roles. It was less common to hear stories from CEOs about the necessity of providing psychological safety, even though they were often in the best position to offer it. We thus have to assume that they either were less sensitive to the need for this step or were less willing to talk about it because it appears to be more "soft."

Creating change through cognitive redefinition: Stimulating imitation or identification, with the CEO as a role model

Ultimately, unfreezing creates a motivation and a readiness to change. The change target recognizes the need to learn something new and starts to look around for relevant information. For the change to last, the target not only must learn new behaviors but also must cognitively redefine the issue so that new perceptions, attitudes, and feelings are created as well. Sometimes such cognitive redefinition occurs before the change in behavior, sometimes afterward in an effort to reduce dissonance (Festinger, 1957). But if it does not occur at all, we are dealing only with temporary change of the sort that one sees when people are coerced but not convinced.

The most common source of new information is someone else in the organization who seems to be "doing it right," in the sense that his or her behavior is being positively confirmed. Such role models not only offer behavioral cues regarding what to do, but more important, they permit the target to identify psychologically with the model and thereby absorb some of the new cognitive point of view.

Many of the CEOs we interviewed explained how using IT enabled them to think in a fundamentally different way about "managing the business" and that part of their problem was to explain these new concepts. For some of their subordinates, this meant new assumptions about what a manager does and how a business can and should be managed. If the CEOs felt comfortable with their own vision and level of understanding, they would become willing role models, teachers, and objects of psychological identification. If they did not, they could deliberately stay away from the situation, conceal their own behavior to a greater degree, and disconfirm efforts by their subordinates to imitate or identify with them.

Some CEOs were outspoken about not wanting to be role models. They sent the message "Do what I say, not what I do," a situation that arose frequently with entrepreneurs who often recognized that their own personal style was unusual and not necessarily the correct model for others. Another reason that some CEOs intentionally tried not to be role models was that they wanted to avoid cloning themselves. That is, they believed that an effective organization needs innovative behavior, and so they stimulated as much as possible people's efforts to learn in their own way and from their own sources.

If the CEOs felt that they personally were the wrong role model but that a correct model existed and that learning from a role model was the best way to learn, they could, of course, manage the change by bringing into the organization consultants, trainers, or other executives who represented what they wanted to teach.

Stimulating cognitive redefinition through scanning: The CEO as a process consultant

Imitation and identification enable rapid learning, with the result that behavior can be standardized fairly quickly. However, if the goal is for the new behavior to be innovative, then this change mechanism is a disadvantage because it prematurely funnels all changes into the same channels. If CEOs wish to avoid such premature channeling, they must create circumstances that will "help the subordinate to learn" by becoming more of a process consultant and/or by sending subordinates "out into the world" to find out what is out there and to learn from it (Schein, 1969, 1987, 1988).

The essence of process consultation in this context is for the CEO to become interested in the subordinate as a learner and to provide whatever help the subordinate appears to need in order to learn the new behavior, much as a coach elicits from an athlete what he or she can do best. The CEO as process consultant does not advise, teach, or tell. Instead he or she listens, helps the subordinate identify what the problem is, and helps him or her figure out what he or she will do about the problem. The CEO may offer options and alternatives but never recommends any particular course of action as the correct one.

The best example of this kind of behavior is that described by McGregor in regard to the CEO who wanted his company to have a better management development program. McGregor advised him not to design and impose such a program, but simply to say to his key subordinates that starting now he was expecting them to develop better management development processes (disconfirming and inducing anxiety), that he did not know how to do this (refusing to be a role model), but that he would begin to measure their performance and determine part of their annual bonus according to how well they were doing (inducing anxiety), and that he would supply resources and help if anyone needed it. This CEO provided psychological safety through his tone and demeanor and by offering his subordinates whatever resources they needed to enact the program. He also requested quarterly reviews to discuss what they had done (disconfirming and inducing anxiety), but during those reviews he functioned as a process consultant rather than as a teacher or boss (stimulating scanning).

This combination of circumstances forced the subordinates to scan their environment, to seek help from consultants, to read, to consult other companies, to create task forces, and in other ways to obtain information on what to do and how to do it. They were not under orders to come up with a common program (another way of creating psychological safety), and so each could create his or her own solutions. The quarterly reports served as a good vehicle for the CEO to approve the innovative efforts and to provide help. By the end of the year the company had an active and effective management development program.

In our interviews we saw many examples of this kind of forced scanning. The CEO would announce that the company had to learn to use IT better, would disclaim any special visions or skills in this area, but would expect reports on progress. Often with the help of the IT department, key subordinates would create committees or task forces to scan the environment, learn about IT, and begin to redefine in their own heads what tools and processes they needed. They would then be in a position to educate the CEO.

If this scanning process was to work, however, the steps required for unfreezing had to have taken place. We found good examples of CEOs who had earlier disconfirmed the present practice by asserting that "something" was not right, without, however, offering a vision or a solution themselves.

Refreezing: Consolidating and stabilizing the change in the change target and the surrounding social system: The CEO as a reinforcer

One of the most frustrating aspects of organizational change is that new behaviors and attitudes do not stick once the initial "Hawthorne effect" is gone. If the new behavior or attitudes are not "refrozen," the system will either revert to its original state or move in some undesirable new direction. This means that the new response must fit into both the personality of the change target and his or her relevant relationships. Otherwise a new unfreezing process will begin because of personal discomfort or disconfirmation by others in the system.

In order to avoid either of these unwanted outcomes, change agents generally favor projects that involve as much of the total system as possible, and they encourage change mechanisms that draw more on scanning than on identification or imitation. If a person learns through scanning, he or she will automatically incorporate only those things that fit into his or her personality, whereas with imitation and identification he or she often adopts a behavior to please the role model, only to drop it when the role model is no longer an audience.

The implications for the CEO's behavior are obvious. If the CEO is the original change agent, he or she must view as his or her change target entire groups or subsystems, not isolated individuals, and he or she must avoid becoming the object of imitation. Finally, because he or she is the principal audience for and the reinforcer of change, when the change goes in the right direction, he or she should strongly confirm the new behavior and attitudes.

We discovered in our interviews that many CEOs were sensitive to these kinds of issues, but only at an intuitive level. They did not talk as articulately about group norms and the subtleties of change as they did about unfreezing and setting a direction for change. And how they chose to reinforce the change had much to do with their vision of IT and the longer-range goals they saw for it.

Summary

I have tried to show that one can classify CEO change agent behavior according to a model of the change process. By identifying the separate components of the change process, one can analyze what may be missing and on what behavior, therefore, the CEO should concentrate.

In ongoing change programs one sees many of these roles being played simultaneously and repeatedly as the change works its way through the system. Each time a new subsystem is encountered, a new unfreezing, changing, and refreezing cycle must begin. The CEOs who are effective change agents constantly monitor what is needed and supply the missing functions rather than trying to play all of the roles themselves. And their consistency over long periods of time with respect to what they confirm and disconfirm is critical to the ultimate success of the total change effort.

FACTORS INFLUENCING CEO CHANGE AGENT BEHAVIOR

Having identified the generic change agent roles, we now need to know what, if anything, will determine how a given CEO will actually behave whether initiating and managing change. All of the following factors can be thought of as "partially causal" or influential, and they probably act in complex combinations rather than as single forces (see Figure 14.1). In terms of change theory, each factor can be thought of as either a "driving" force leading to increased pressure for the system to move in a certain direction or as a "restraining" force leading to resistance (Schein, 1985, 1987).

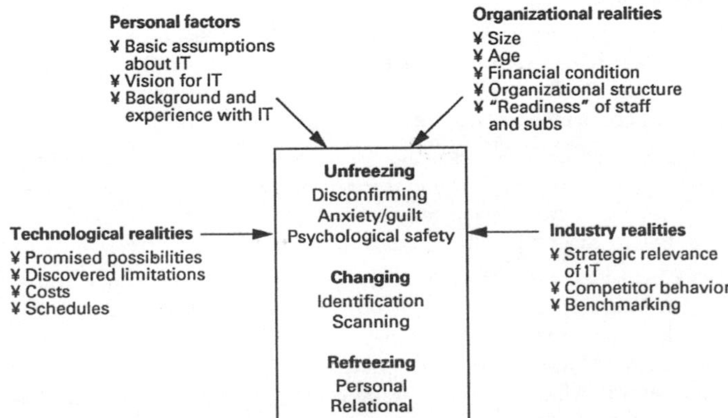

Figure 14.1. CEO change roles and their determinants.

The CEO's basic assumptions about information technology

It was our own assumption that whether or not they were explicitly aware of it, all CEOs had certain assumptions about IT and a vision of what it could or could not do for them. A typology of such assumptions based on the faith that IT is a good thing for organizations and a conviction that those things will or will not come about, is shown in Table 14.2 and Figure 14.2.

Though the coding was not always totally reliable, we were able to agree enough on the basic types to give a rough approximation of how many of our CEOs fell into each category, as shown in Table 14.3 (based on the 84 cases analyzed later).

In regard to the assumptions, one can see a degree of realism. A few CEOs were optimistic about the potential of IT, but most of them were realistic about the difficulties of changing their organizations. Both of these groups would be expected to exert driving forces, in that they would try to unfreeze and change their organizations. Those who were ambivalent and those who saw IT as "merely a tool," were more cautious in their approach to implementation and would thus be expected to be equally on the restraining force side as on the driving force side. There were few real skeptics, and so one would not expect strong restraining forces from CEOs except in the form of caution about the potential costs of IT.

Specific visions of IT

For those CEOs who had a positive vision of IT, we wanted to distinguish the nature

Table 14.2. A typology of CEO assumptions about IT

IT Utopian idealist	This CEO sees nothing but benefits deriving from the increased use of IT in all areas of his business and personal life. He may not see all these benefits in actual use, but he believes firmly that in time all the benefits will be realized.
IT Realistic utopian	This CEO sees great potential benefits in IT, but is not sure that they will all be realized because of hidden costs, resistances in others, and various other sources of difficulty that are not inherent in IT, but in its implementation.
IT Ambivalent	This CEO sees some benefits in some areas but sees potential harm in other areas and/or perceives that the costs may in the end outweigh the benefits; therefore, he is ambivalent in the sense of wanting to push ahead, but being cautious and doubtful at the same time.
IT Realistic skeptic	This CEO is basically doubtful about the benefits of IT, short-run or long-run, but realizes that the appeal of the technology will bring much of it into organizations anyway; given this reality the CEO must control carefully what is introduced so as to minimize potential harm or excessive costs.
IT Utopian skeptic	This CEO believes that IT is primarily harmful in that it undermines other effective managerial processes. It is not merely excessively costly, but actually harms organizational effectiveness by encouraging the use of tools, categories of information, and processes of doing work that are less effective than what is presently or potentially possible in terms of other managerial models; he therefore sees his role to be to minimize the harm that IT can do, to undermine its implementation in any way possible, and to control its costs to the utmost degree.

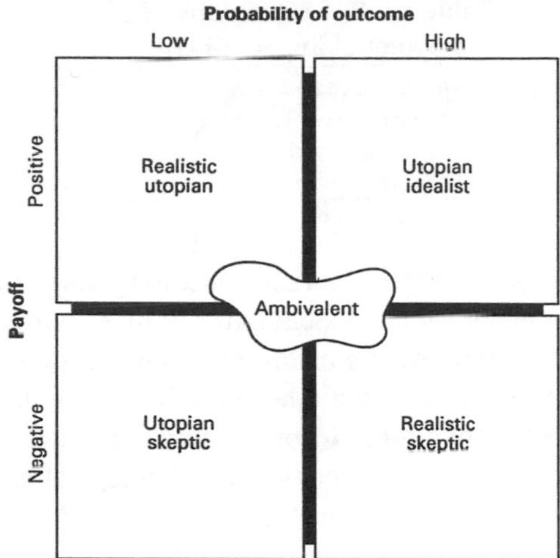

Figure 14.2. CEOs' assumptions about IT.

and strength of that vision in order to determine further how they would behave in the change agent role. Because we were limited to our interview data, we do not have detailed information about this aspect of CEOs' attitudes and behavior, but it is nevertheless important to outline the possibilities. For this purpose, we differentiated several levels of the "impact" of IT on organizations, as shown in Table 14.4.

The vision to automate

Some CEOs in our sample saw the ultimate role of IT to be a way of replacing expensive, unreliable human labor with sophisticated robots, systems, and other IT devices. The promise of IT for them was that it would ultimately save money, improve quality, and thereby make the organization more effective. They tended to look at their organizations from a manufacturing point of view and were preoccupied with cost and/or technological issues.

Such CEOs tend to be less utopian and more ambivalent or skeptical. The change agent role that they would be most likely to play is either to disconfirm the current cost structure by insisting on automation or by disconfirming the current use of technology by insisting on technological upgrading. In both cases they would focus more on the primary role of IT in the manufacturing process and would be relatively less sensitive to the possible role of IT in the management system or its impact on the management system of the automation they were advocating.

Table 14.3. Number of CEOs holding different assumptions.

	Payoff	Probability of occurrence	Number	%
Utopian idealist	+	+	17	20
Realistic utopian	+	–	46	55
Ambivalent	+	+	19	23
Realistic skeptic	–	+	2	2
Utopian skeptic	–	–	0	0
Total			84	100

Table 14.4. CEO visions of the potential impact of IT

The vision to *automate*
The vision to *informate up*
The vision to *informate down*
The vision to *transform*

As we also pointed out, though this vision has long-range implications technologically and may entail major capital expenditures, it often proves to be shortsighted because the human implications are not carefully thought through and the systems in the end do not work as well as they should because they do not take advantage of the operators' creativity and innovation. In other words, the deeper assumption that human behavior can be automated in a complex technological environment may not be valid in some cases.

The vision to "informate up": Control utopia

The term *informate* is taken from Zuboff (1988) and refers to the impact of IT on making previously concealed parts of a system's processes more visible to people both higher up and lower down in the organization. Some CEOs saw IT to be the "ultimate management control tool." They assumed that by installing the right kind of information system, they would be completely informed about every aspect of every operation in their organization. Such information would enable them to pinpoint problems rapidly and to set into motion remedial measures.

Needless to say, such a vision appeals to the control-oriented executive and probably is functionally similar to the automation solution, except that what is being automated here is not the production process but the control process. The human organization is being replaced with an information system. Toward this ultimate goal a number of CEOs insisted on installing terminals on their own and their subordinates' desks in order to facilitate the introduction of a complete communication network and a common information and control system.

Some of the resistance that CEOs encountered from their subordinates was probably motivated by the subordinates' recognition that once such a system was installed, it could easily be abused by a control-oriented CEO. Abuse here would be micromanagement by the CEO, thereby undermining the rest of the organization and possibly even the validity of the information fed into the system because of the employees' tendency to falsify input data in reaction to the discomfort and anxiety that the system created. Unfortunately, the system designers often collude with this type of CEO by reassuring him or her that they can make the system invulnerable to any kind of falsification.

According to our model of change, the CEO who is oriented toward control via an upward-informating system will be an effective disconfirmer but will have trouble unfreezing the system because he will not be sensitive to the need to provide psychological safety. He may successfully coerce change, but the change will be only superficial and will be unstable because it will not require any cognitive redefinition by the subordinates, who are the change targets.

Such CEOs may be utopian regarding the potential of IT, but they are expressing an extreme degree of skepticism about human behavior, what McGregor would have labeled "Theory X." The very existence of the complete information and control system signals to the rest of the organization that top management does not trust the human organization to inform and control itself adequately (McGregor, 1960).

The vision to informate down

"Informating down" is what Zuboff observed to be the consequences of computerizing production processes and creating automated factories. If the production process was to be automated, it first had to be viewed as a complete system. In order for the operators to manage the new processes, they thus had to understand this complete system. Zuboff observed that not everyone could make the transition from manual work, but for those who could, the production process would be clear. One consequence was that supervisors no longer would have the power that special knowledge or understanding had previously given them, as this "knowledge power" would now be distributed throughout the work force. For many middle managers, this loss of power was a direct threat, but for CEOs looking to create the "factory of the future," this could be a positive vision if they also had a Theory Y set of assumptions about human nature (McGregor, 1960) and were willing to push operational control down in the organization.

In our interviews we could not always tell whether or not the executives advocating this kind of IT solution were genuinely interested in "informating" their organizations, or whether they were secretly hoping for lower costs and more centralized control. But at least in their words, these CEOs were advocating a much more radical IT usage than what was proposed in either of the preceding visions.

In any case, such CEOs would be much more sensitive to the issues of creating psychological safety, both for operators who had to change their concept of what their work would be in the future and for middle managers whose role might disappear altogether. They would also realize that changes of this magnitude would not occur without strong external and internal disconfirmation and the induction of guilt/anxiety, and thus they were forced to consider all of the stages of getting a change process started.

The vision to transform

A few CEOs saw IT as the basis for completely transforming their organization and industry. They could see how IT would change the organization's relationship to its suppliers and customers; how the introduction of networking, executive support systems, teleconferencing, and other IT innovations would alter the company's products, markets, and organizational structure; and how these in combination would alter organizational boundaries, interorganizational relationships, and even the management process itself.

The role of hierarchy would change, in that distributed information would make local problem solving and lateral information sharing much more feasible, and the role of the executive team in the strategy process would change if modeling and various kinds of decision support tools would make it possible to develop alternatives more rapidly. In a sense, IT would make it possible to be simultaneously more centralized in regard to basic strategy and goals and more decentralized in regard to implementation and control.

Power and authority would shift away from position and status toward knowledge and information, and leadership would become more widely distributed as one of the requirements of the task to be accomplished. More emphasis would fall on groups and teamwork, and boundaries between jobs and roles would become more fluid. That, in turn, would require a higher level of professionalization in the work force in order to deal with higher anxiety levels resulting from role ambiguity (Hirschhorn, 1988).

We encountered a few executives who seemed to be pushing toward this kind of vision, but most of them acknowledged that it would take some time before IT itself would be good enough and cheap enough to make this possible. They correctly foresaw that such transformations would require major cultural change that would take some time and effort to accomplish. Perhaps most troubling to them was the implication that the current work force might not be well enough educated or trained to fulfill the necessary roles in the transformed organization, an issue that is also present in the informated organization.

Such CEOs clearly fell into our utopian idealist category, and their behavior in terms of the change model seemed to be oriented toward consistent but careful unfreezing, because of their concern that their organizations might not be ready to handle the level of change required. They were, in this sense, another group sensitive to psychological safety as an issue in the change process.

In summary, the assumptions held by the CEOs were obviously critical to both how they viewed the potential of IT and how optimistic they felt about implementing various IT projects in their organizations. But clearly, their own assumptions were not a sufficient explanation of their behavior. We found in the interview data that other factors operated as well, as powerful driving and restraining forces.

Technological realities and limits

For many CEOs, a major restraining force limiting their vision of IT was their perception that the technology was not yet good enough or cheap enough to deliver on its potential. Their change agent behavior would then be to press harder on the IT community to improve the technology itself while at the same time restraining their organization in order not to "waste money" on solutions that might not work well anyway.

Such perceptions might arise either from a lack of experience with computers or, paradoxically, from great experience with computers, in that the CEOs could see through some of the promises that their own IT people were making. And we found a surprising number of CEOs who argued that desktop workstations were not an appropriate tool for them in their role as CEO, even though they had used them extensively and happily in all of their previous jobs. They felt that IT did not have the capacity to deal with the soft, probabilistic, rapidly changing kind of information that they had to deal with in their role as CEO. As a consequence, such CEOs might strongly resist using IT in the executive suite but encourage its use at lower levels.

Industrial realities

One of the most powerful forces determining CEOs' attitudes and behavior was the behavior of their competitors in their industry. CEOs often seemed unsure how to use IT, how much to invest in it, how to assess its potential benefits, and whether or not there were operational or strategic benefits to be derived, and so they scanned their competitors and at least tried to stay even. What other companies were doing thus became a kind of benchmark for some CEOs, especially those who had less personal experience with IT. They would override their own convictions about IT if they found it necessary to do or not to do certain things simply because their competitors were or were not doing them.

In those companies in which the CEO was using this kind of benchmarking, IT managers could use information about what other companies were doing, as a change lever of their own to disconfirm the CEOs present behavior and get him started on a change process of his own. In such situations the IT manager acquired unusual power unless the CEO had his own network of peer contacts to check out what other companies were doing.

A second powerful industry reality was the degree to which the industry was involved with information products and therefore had already learned a great deal about IT. Particularly in the financial services, transportation (airlines), and telecommunications industries, CEOs appeared to have generally more insight into the realities of IT, and because of this benchmarking, we found the same kind of IT usage in all of these companies. Some of the more aggressive CEOs who initiated total IT change programs were found in companies that were already familiar at the product level with the necessity for sophisticated IT solutions.

In contrast, the manufacturing industry seemed to be heterogeneous, with some companies trying very hard to introduce IT at all levels and others viewing it with skepticism. Those CEOs who had been most "burned" by past IT projects that had failed or had proved to be overly expensive, came mainly from manufacturing companies.

Organizational realities

Organizational size and age appeared to make a difference. Larger, older, multidivisional companies tended to have CEOs who delegated the major IT decisions and implementation programs to special task forces and to divisional management. In contrast, in young and/or small companies' CEOs said they had to be directly involved with IT matters at all times. They could not afford to delegate such decisions or to hire IT staffs.

The more structurally decentralized the company was, in regard to having multiple divisions and geographic units, the more the CEO felt constrained by the presence of multiple subcultures that would be hard to tie together. Not only was the initiative for IT innovations more likely to be in the units, but the innovations themselves also were more likely to be operational ones that were motivated and managed at the unit level. Companywide integration efforts such as electronic mail and common information and control systems were much more difficult to implement in multi-unit structures. In such organizations CEOs often became the monitor and controller of IT, regardless of their own feelings about it.

The company's financial condition was cited as a factor restraining IT experimentation if money was in short supply and the company was trying to become more profitable. Even if the CEO was utopian in his personal vision, he often had to put IT projects lower on the priority list. On the other hand, if money was plentiful, we found energetic utopian CEOs willing and able to push through entire IT systems single-handedly, even though no one could prove that the innovations were cost effective or strategically critical.

Finally, the state of the senior management's and employees' training was cited by some CEOs as a constraining force. Sometimes these were experienced, knowledgeable CEOs with a thorough background in IT who recognized that they had to move slowly because their people were not ready for some of the more sophisticated IT applications.

Personal experience with computers and IT

Many of the CEOs were knowledgeable about and experienced in the use of computers and IT. Such knowledge could work as either a driving or a restraining force, however, because it also meant greater insight into the problems of IT, its probable costs, its technological limitations, and its tendency to promise more than it could deliver.

Summary

The six sets of factors identified by our CEOs as major influences on their decisions with regard to IT are, of course, interrelated and interactive. The most striking result, therefore, is the diversity of situations we encountered at the CEO level. We were seeking the common elements in how CEOs would structure their own behavior as change agents and found, instead, that the multiplicity of technological, industry, organizational, and personal forces operating made such generalizations very tenuous.

At the same time, we could see that not every CEO's situation was unique. But there were common patterns, and so we set out to cluster the common factors in a set of "implementation scenarios" (Sutherland, 1988).

CEOS' IMPLEMENTATION SCENARIOS

The scenarios we identified were based on coding all 94 interviews and looking for patterns and clusters in the data (see Table 14.5). The coding was not precise or reliable enough to warrant actual correlations and factor analysis, and so these clusters were determined more on inspection, as will be seen. The clusters accounted for 84 of the cases, as will be shown in Table 14.6. The 10 cases that did not fit any cluster were omitted from this analysis. The results should be seen as a basis for further hy-

Table 14.5. CEO implementation scenarios

The delegating skeptic
The information-dependent service manager
The hands-on adopter
The positively focused

potheses rather than generalizable findings, though we found in follow-up interviews in selected companies clear examples of each scenario.

"Delegating skeptics"

The "delegating skeptics," comprising 20 percent of the population we interviewed, were characterized by a pattern of attitudes and self-described behaviors that reflected their basic doubts about IT. They were older than the other groups, were found mostly in manufacturing companies, and played an essentially passive cost containment role vis-à-vis IT.

They did not believe that CEOs should be involved in IT decisions; they tended to respond to rather than initiate IT issues; they made IT implementation decisions primarily in terms of their cost; they did not see any reason for the personal use of terminals (only 12 percent used terminals); they saw the negative consequences of IT as being equal to its positive consequences in terms of the overall human impact of IT; and they were the highest group in the number of negative effects of IT they cited, with "waste time and resources" at the top of this list.

In our change model, these CEOs would be a restraining force on IT implementation. They would not unfreeze the system or be any kind of role model, though they would encourage refreezing if they saw benefits. One can presume that their IT vision was limited to automation and perhaps informating up. In terms of their assumptions, 65 percent were rated as "ambivalent" and only 35 percent were rated as "realistic utopians."

"Information-dependent service managers"

Most of the "information-dependent service managers," comprising roughly 14 percent of the group, were in charge of medium-sized financial service organizations such as banks and insurance companies that had had to develop their IT systems in order to remain competitive. They tended to be the youngest group, and they seemed to take IT for granted.

In terms of IT-related decisions, they were predominantly in the "routine review" category. They, like the skeptics, tended to respond rather than initiate; they saw little need to get involved with implementation issues (partly because their organizations had mature, competent IT departments); and they saw themselves as supporting IT implementation in their companies.

On personal use, the group was divided, with 69 percent reporting no use. In regard to the positive and negative aspects of IT, this group was the most positive in terms of human impacts and saw the fewest number of negatives overall. They were highest in seeing IT as something that "helps people think," "improves service and company performance," "cuts personnel," "makes more information available," "saves costs and time," and "provides major strategic or competitive benefits."

I would guess that this group is the most committed to IT, with 31 percent utopian idealists and 62 percent realistic utopians. Interestingly, one of these CEOs was a realistic skeptic, but he clearly did not interfere with his company's program. One would also hypothesize that this group would be high in seeing the transformation

Table 14.6. Characteristics of CEOs in different implementation scenarios (%)

	DS*	ID*	HOA*	PF*
Age				
Over 60	35	8	29	24
Under 50	12	31	22	29
Industry				
Manufacturing	71	0	57	29
Financial services	6	100	19	6
Other services and miscellaneous	24	0	24	65
Company size				
Under 3000 employees	41	15	32	18
3000 to 50,000 employees	35	85	46	35
Over 50,000 employees	24	0	22	47
What role is appropriate for CEO in making decision?				
Little or no role	59	23	3	29
Review by exception only	29	8	16	29
Routine review	12	69	35	29
Hands on active in all decisions	0	0	46	12
What was your most recent role?				
None or review by exception	94	46	27	41
Routine or active	6	54	73	59
What role is appropriate for CEO in adopting and implementing IT?				
Little or no role	82	92	5	35
Support/set example	12	8	43	41
Be routinely personally involved	6	0	51	24
What was your own most recent involvement?				
None	100	88	14	41
Created supportive environment	0	12	32	24
Personally involved	0	0	54	35
How appropriate is it for CEO to personally use IT?				
Critical	6	23	27	47
Depends/matter of style	41	54	57	29
Not helpful/inappropriate	53	23	16	24
Do you personally use a terminal?				
Some or extensive use	12	31	49	41
None	88	69	51	59
Perceived level of IT implementation in company?				
Aggressive implementation	0	38	73	64
Supportive to implementation effort	53	54	27	30
Passive/support based on cost	47	8	0	6

potential of IT, partly because it is already happening in their businesses and partly because they see the strategic potential of IT.

As change agents they presented a mixed picture of being positive and supportive but not likely to initiate or be strong role models. The unfreezing forces in their companies had probably begun to operate years ago owing to economic and competitive pressures, and further active change projects have tended to be delegated more to the IT group.

Table 14.6. *(continued)*

	DS*	ID*	HOA*	PF*
What are the main barriers to implementation?				
Human interface/user problems	24	85	46	65
Lack of management involvement or control	24	54	30	29
Systems integration/networking	41	77	32	24
Cost	47	69	54	41
Low output/waste of capacity	41	15	41	18
Attitude toward overall human impacts of IT				
Mostly positive	0	92	16	77
More positive than negative	24	8	60	18
Negatives equal positives	77	0	24	6
Positive aspects of IT				
Helps people think	47	92	49	41
Makes people more efficient	47	62	59	65
Makes more information available	18	54	35	12
Improves company performance	29	62	54	53
Cuts personnel cost	0	62	24	41
Areas of positive impact on IT				
Production/operations/manufacturing	71	77	81	82
Managerial decision support	77	31	87	59
Strategic/competitive advantage	35	77	59	47
Cost savings	23	85	46	23
Time savings	6	85	38	18
Negative aspects of IT				
Impedes thinking	24	0	30	0
Impedes communication	24	0	16	6
Causes skills to deteriorate	24	8	11	0
Wastes time and resources	59	8	41	12
People resist learning it	24	15	38	24
Number of negatives cited				
None	12	61	13	59
One	29	39	35	41
Two or more	59	0	52	0
Basic assumptions about IT				
Utopian idealists	0	31	16	41
Realistic utopians	35	62	70	35
Ambivalent	65	0	11	24
Realistic skeptic	0	8	3	0
Utopian skeptic	0	0	0	0

*DS = Delegating skeptic; ID = Information dependent; HOA = Hands-on adopter; PF = Positively focused.

"Hands-on adopters"

The "hands-on adopters," comprising 40 percent of the total, were distinguished mainly by their belief that CEOs should actively participate in IT decisions (only 19 percent favored review by exception or no involvement) and in IT implementation (only 5 percent favored little or no CEO role). Almost half stated that CEOs should initiate IT projects (compared with 0 and 15 percent in the preceding two groups), and their companies were the highest in the percentage of full-scale, aggressive implementation of IT. This group was spread over small, medium, and large companies but was predominantly in the manufacturing sector. In age they were average.

This group was the highest in favoring personal use by CEOs and highest in actual reported use (49 percent reported some or extensive use). Their attitude toward positive and negative aspects of IT was balanced in that they saw more positives than negatives, but only 16 percent said that the effect of IT was "mostly positive," and 24 percent said that the positives and negatives were about equal. They cited most of the positives that the information dependents saw, but they found many more negatives, almost as many as the skeptics did (41 percent saw IT as wasting time and resources; 38 percent said that people resist learning it; and 30 percent said that it impedes thinking).

What we have in the hands-on adopters is predominantly realistic utopians (70 percent), with the remainder scattered among the other categories. By virtue of their close involvement with IT decisions and implementation projects, they had acquired a more balanced and realistic point of view of IT, suggesting that their IT visions probably varied all the way from automation to transformation, depending on other factors.

It is in this group that one would find the most active change agents among the CEOs, probably playing the whole gamut of change roles. Being the most active users, they were also the most likely to be role models, but being realistic they would see the value of encouraging scanning. It is in this group that one would expect to see the most effective creation of psychological safety.

"The positively focused"

The "positively focused" CEOs, comprising another 20 percent of the total, were distinguished by their positive, idealistic stance on IT, combined with a rather hands-off approach and some evidence of Pollyannaish thinking about IT. The hands-on adopters felt positive, but they also saw all the problems because they were close to them. The positively focused, in contrast, were often in very large companies (47 percent were in companies of over 50,000 employees), in which their own involvement in IT was minimal because the real action was down in the divisions. Only a few of them felt that they had to impose common systems at the corporate level if divisional opposition were strong, but they felt that they had to get their money's worth out of IT anyway because of its utilization at lower levels.

A number of them were in service-oriented industries like telecommunications and airlines, in which the use of IT is so central to their business that there is little problem getting money for implementing IT. One hypothesis that Sutherland suggested is that these companies can afford to be idealistic because they have not faced the cost issues that plague manufacturers. Their attitudes are derived more from their background in the utilities industries in which direct competition and hence cost control were not central issues.

The positively focused tended to have little or no involvement in IT decisions because they had excellent technical staffs to whom they delegate, but they were more likely to initiate and be supportive of implementation efforts than were the information-dependent or skeptical groups. Their companies, along with those of the hands-on adopters, were the most aggressive implementers. They were the highest group in terms of their belief that using IT was critical to the CEO, but only 41 percent of them were personal users.

Like the information dependent, the positively focused were very positive about the human impacts of IT and saw virtually no negatives (hence the Pollyanna label) when compared with the hands-on adopters. As might be expected, they were predominantly utopian idealists (41 percent) and realistic utopians (35 percent). The remainder were ambivalent.

I expected to find many CEOs in this group with strong visions of organizational transformation. In a number of cases that we analyzed, we found CEOs not only encouraging implementation throughout but also strongly unfreezing their immediate executive team by strongly disconfirming the old ways and providing psychological safety in order to make the transition feasible. Some of our best examples in the early section of this chapter on executive change agent roles came from this and the hands-on adopter groups.

SUMMARY AND CONCLUSIONS

What we have, then, in the implementation scenarios is two groups that are relatively uninvolved, but for opposite reasons. The information-dependent CEOs are knowledgeable, take IT for granted, and comfortably delegate IT issues. The delegating skeptics are cynical, aloof, and controlling, seeing IT as just another expensive tool to be watched carefully.

Then we have two groups that are involved, but in very different ways. The hands-on adopters personally push through IT projects and thereby become familiar with all the problems and prospects that this technology will bring to organizations. On the other hand, we have the positively focused who are in organizations that can afford to implement IT, who need IT in terms of their core business, but who do not need to be personally and directly involved in projects and therefore are less familiar with IT's problems and prospects.

The change agent roles of these different executives, of course, differ with their basic orientation and the situation of their organizations. As we noted, all of the CEOs were driven by the state of affairs in their industry. Only a few had utopian transformation visions that went substantially beyond what other companies in their industry were doing. Those few are singled out as heroic change agents by academics and the media, but the reminder from our data is that they are a distinct minority.

We concluded that CEOs find themselves in complex force fields and, accordingly, vary their behavior as change agents. They feel that the realities of their particular situation in terms of the size, age, structure, and financial condition of their companies, the technological possibilities and limitations, industry benchmarks, employee readiness, and the credibility and skill of their IT management all must be taken into account when deciding how far and how fast they should push the adoption of new IT tools. Many of them believe, therefore, that this calls for CEOs to be an integrative force instead of IT zealots, though they acknowledge that future generations of CEOs will have been educated much more thoroughly in the possibilities of the computer and IT, thus enabling them to take more of a hands-on adopter stance.

For the IT skeptic it is reassuring to realize that there are a good many CEOs out there who are cautious, who have been burned, and who therefore are quite realistic about the limitations of today's IT solutions. On the other hand, for the IT utopian it is reassuring to find that 40 percent of our CEOs do involve themselves actively in IT projects, even if they personally do not use desktop workstations, and many more take IT for granted as a technology and a set of tools that will help their companies in many ways.

REFERENCES

Buzzard, S. H. (1988). An analysis of factors that influence management of information technology in multidivisional companies. M.A. thesis, Sloan School of Management, Massachusetts Institute of Technology.

Carey, D. R. (1988). Information technology: Attitudes and implementation. M.A. thesis, Sloan School of Management, Massachusetts Institute of Technology.

Donaldson, H. M. (1987). Executive assumptions about information technology in the service industries. M.A. thesis, Sloan School of Management, Massachusetts Institute of Technology.

Festinger, L. (1957). *A theory of cognitive dissonance*. New York: Harper & Row.

Glassburn, A. R. (1987). A study of chief executive officer attitudes toward the use of information technology in executive offices. M.A. thesis, Sloan School of Management, Massachusetts Institute of Technology.

Harman, P. E. (1987). Executive assumptions about information technology in the banking industry. M.A. Thesis, Sloan School of Management, Massachusetts Institute of Technology.

Hirschhorn, L. (1988). *The workplace within*. Cambridge, MA: MIT Press.

Homer, P. B. (1988). A study of information technology innovation in high technology firms. M.A. thesis, Sloan School of Management, Massachusetts Institute of Technology.

Kelly, M. L. (1987). Attitudes and expectations of senior executives about information technology within the consumer electronics industry with emphasis on Japan. M.A. thesis, Sloan School of Management, Massachusetts Institute of Technology.

Kennedy, H. E. (1987). CEO assumptions concerning information technology in high technology firms. M.A. thesis, Sloan School of Management, Massachusetts Institute of Technology.

Lasswell, S. W. (1987). Chief executive officer attitudes concerning information technology: A study of high technology and aerospace companies. M.A. thesis, Sloan School of Management, Massachusetts Institute of Technology.

Lewin, K. (1952). Group decision and social change. In G. E. Swanson, T. N. Newcomb, & E. L. Hartley (Eds.), *Readings in Social Psychology*, rev. ed. New York: Holt.

McGregor, D. M. (1960). *The human side of enterprise*. New York: McGraw-Hill.

North, J. B. (1987). Attitudes of telecommunications executives about information technology. M.A. thesis, Sloan School of Management, Massachusetts Institute of Technology.

Pilger, D. R. (1987). Chief executive officer attitudes toward information technology in the automotive and manufacturing industries. M.A. thesis, Sloan School of Management, Massachusetts Institute of Technology.

Schein, E. H. (1961). *Coercive persuasion*. New York: Norton.

——— (1969). *Process consultation*. Reading, MA: Addison-Wesley.

——— (1972). *Professional education: Some new directions*. New York: McGraw-Hill.

——— (1985). *Organizational culture and leadership*. San Francisco: Jossey-Bass.

——— (1987). *Process consultation*, Vol. 2. Reading, MA: Addison-Wesley.

——— (1988). *Process consultation*, Vol. 1, rev. ed. Reading, MA: Addison-Wesley.

Shuff, R. F. (1988). A model of the innovation process in information technology. M.A. thesis, Sloan School of Management, Massachusetts Institute of Technology.

Stewart, N. S. (1987). Chief executive officers: Assumptions about information technology in the insurance industry. M.A. thesis, Sloan School of Management, Massachusetts Institute of Technology.

Sutherland, D. J. (1988). The attitudes and management behaviors of senior managers with respect to information technology. M.A. thesis, Sloan School of Management, Massachusetts Institute of Technology.

Zuboff, S. (1988). *In the age of the smart machine*. New York: Basic Books.

CHAPTER 15

How Expectations About Microcomputers Influence Their Organizational Consequences

JOHN S. CARROLL AND CONSTANCE PERIN

In the six years since the introduction of the IBM personal computer (PC), the ways that many people work have changed rapidly. By current estimates, there is one computer workstation for every 20 workers in the United States, and by 1990 some predicted that there would be one for every two or three in most industries (Keen, 1985). As their price has come down, managers find it easy to purchase PCs as discretionary office equipment or furniture. That simple transaction can put on an employee's desk a stand-alone workstation of power comparable to that of the typical large mainframe computer of the 1960s.

Although we might view this technological change as representing progress, anyone familiar with the uses of microcomputers in organizations readily encounters some paradoxes. In 1987, during a presentation to 50 graduates of the Senior Executive Program of the Sloan School on this subject, one person raised his hand and interjected, "We know that microcomputers are increasing in numbers, but how do we stop them?" About one-half of this group thought that although the investment in small systems was getting to be enormous, companies had little to show for it.

After initial enthusiasm, organizations may find few genuinely effective uses for microcomputers beyond routine tasks. One estimate suggests that 25 percent of microcomputers are "orphans" that end up unused (Young, 1984) or, as we have heard, "30–pound paperweights." *Fortune* reports that "U.S. business has spent hundreds of billions [on IT] . . . but white-collar productivity is no higher. . . . Getting results usually entails changing the way work is done, and that takes time" (1986, p. 20). On the other hand, anecdotes abound about the ways that efficiency has improved and how new services and reorganizations have become possible (e.g., Harris, 1987).

The aim of this chapter is to suggest how both managers and employees might think about what to expect from microcomputers, because those expectations, we believe, are an important source of the consequences observed. We base our discussion on three case studies of computer implementation in three large organizations, on numerous discussions with other companies, consultants, and experts, and on our reading of an expanding literature.

EXPECTATIONS AND CONSEQUENCES

Two broad categories of beliefs, assumptions, and scenarios have dominated expectations of information technologies and their organizational integration. One frame of reference is that of "technology push," which has also provided the basis for much of the research on the impact of microcomputers (and the impact of information technology more generally). This "technological imperative" (Markus & Robey, 1988) assumes that the impact of technology is inherent in the technology itself—that is, its speed, efficiency in information handling, and independence from centralized data-processing units. For example, microcomputers by themselves have been predicted to lead to reductions in the work force, dramatic decreases in middle management, and greater centralization of decision making and control (Leavitt & Whisler, 1958).

Yet several reviews of research documenting the impact of microcomputers suggest fewer direct relationships and more ambiguity. Inconsistent, mixed, and null results have been found on issues of centralization and decentralization, quality of work life, work force reductions, deskilling, and other variables (Attewell & Rule, 1984; Kling, 1980; Robey, 1977). To some extent, these inconsistencies are due to a lack of differentiation between those studies that looked at mainframe end user computing, and those that investigated microcomputers, differences in work processes, and clerical versus professional workers (Invernizzi, 1988; Kling & Iacono, 1988a). More complex theories addressing a wider set of contingencies have not yet been developed.

One controlling assumption that underlies the technological imperative as a frame of reference is that a PC is a tool whose known attributes will yield predictable results. For example, at one of our case sites, the manager responsible for introducing PCs saw them as being "fancy adding machines." From such a perspective, management "implements" and "diffuses" technology as if it were a tangible tool—the language itself reinforces the assumption of finite utility and suggests that the implementation of PCs is viewed as being little different from the replacement of inkwells and gas lamps by ballpoint pens and electric lights.

The second conventional frame of reference views PCs and information technologies as offering capabilities whose realization depends on the ingenuity of the vendors, software developers, users, consultants, and other experts. This process is called *reinvention*, by which the technology is changed as it is introduced (Wilson 1985; cf. "reengineering," Rice & Rogers, 1980). In contrast with the "technology push" perspective of hardware whose functions are already known, PCs are assumed to offer a bundle of possibilities and options: Their add-on boards, telecommunications, and software together suggest functions that could develop as a result of use.

In this view, PCs are not considered to be fully preprogrammed or bounded. Their impact is emergent (Markus & Robey, 1988); that is, it is dependent on complex interrelationships among the work itself, the nature of the technology and the organization, and the implementation strategy (Invernizzi, 1988; Kling & Iacono, 1988a). This broad-gauged expectation is analogous to the difficulties of specifying the impacts of investments in employee education, given the variable impacts on different people in different situations. A better educated work force might be more productive, more creative, be capable of greater decentralization and better communication, require less management, and so on. Or the better-educated work force, faced with a stodgy organization, may become dissatisfied and less productive. From the reinvention perspective, many factors may mediate technological changes, and many consequences are possible.

A set of case studies was designed, therefore, on the premise that the kinds of expectations with which an organization approaches new information technology do much to define the consequences that will be observed. Aside from these frames of reference, we had no prefigured definitions of the other kinds of expectations; the purpose of the case studies was to find out how expectations and their organizational consequences might best be characterized. We anticipated only that in managing the implementation of microcomputers, senior management and staff would typically make strategic and political choices about hardware, software, training, support, and personnel based on assumptions about and expectations of microcomputer use.

From the literature, we knew that managers are more likely than not to make these choices with only the vaguest notions of how microcomputers will influence the larger organization as they change work processes, communication patterns, and the distribution of authority (Walton & Vittori, 1983). We also knew that although the major responsibility for creating innovative applications is placed on end users, management may have overly high expectations about the "friendliness" of the machines, and employees may have fears about their abilities and changes in their jobs (Zuboff, 1982).

Nor is "end user computing" often based on strategic planning (Rockart & Flannery, 1983), as illustrated in a paradoxical story told to us by a group of management consultants who specialize in designing and implementing management information systems. Their services are often sought by large organizations because the brand assortment of personally owned PCs has so proliferated that maintenance and purchasing need to be systematized and standardized. Employees have brought in their own PCs, they say, because "that's the only way I can get my work done." "End user computing isn't a management brainwave—it's more a grass-roots process," these consultants observe. Yet in their own branch of a national consulting firm, there is no networked system, either local or national, even though these consultants can think of many business uses it could serve—writing joint proposals, coordinating marketing efforts, and sharing the results of their engagements. Senior partners seldom use PCs: "It's out of character to have a PC on your desk if you're an upper-level manager here."

A recent survey of CEOs' attitudes toward PCs (Schein & Wilson, 1987) reinforces the previous observation: "Personal interaction with a terminal or a PC is not part of the CEO's job," and "It isn't worth my trouble to master the mechanics." As data-processing and management information system departments integrate their functions with business units, an important question is whether and how those patterns of nonuse may change.

CASES IN MICROCOMPUTER INTRODUCTION

Our case studies examined organizations in three companies that are in the process of introducing new technologies. In two of these cases, the sites are the companies' accounting functions, experienced in mainframe applications but newly introduced to

PC-based technology. The third site is a high-tech firm in which an advanced development group is testing a networked workstation having multitasking and windowing capabilities, which the group itself developed.

Site 1: RESOURCE

We conducted two sets of interviews about 16 months apart in a production accounting group (numbering about 200 at the time of our first visit) and with other employees in supportive roles, in a very large corporation exploring and selling natural resources. This group keeps track of the revenues and taxes associated with thousands of leases. The work entails repetitive, high-volume calculations, and the accountants' career ladders consist mainly of moving from shorter- to longer-term projects.

Until the introduction of PCs, shorter-term projects had to be done by hand because they were too small and changeable to be programmed by central data processing. Monthly and quarterly closings typically created machine overloads, and accountants took to their sleeping bags in the office while waiting for turnaround results. At the time of our first interviews, four PCs had been introduced within the past year, each equipped with dual floppies and a hard-wired connection to the mainframe system. By the second interviews, the size of the group had doubled to 400, as a consequence of a corporate acquisition, which brought new employees from another state and about eight additional microcomputers (with hard disks).

Expectations

The manager of the group had originally been motivated to try out the PCs after seeing that an industry competitor had introduced them. With four machines for 200 employees, his vision of their use was obviously limited. He saw them as being "fancy adding machines" in a well-defined niche; he expected Lotus 1–2–3 packages to automate manual spreadsheets and 10-key calculators. The PCs were expected to be used only for the short-term reports previously prepared manually. The company was still oriented to using a mainframe and accustomed to a slow turnaround. Its expectations were thus somewhat increased efficiency, reduced drudgery, and a more professional appearance to reports.

With these limited objectives, the rules for PC use were seemingly loose: Any employee could take training, but mostly on their own time, and anyone could suggest or develop 1–2–3 applications. Nevertheless, the manager forbade the accountants to use PCs for writing their analyses and memos; he regarded writing as "typing," and he insisted that they continue to send handwritten memos to the word-processing pool.

This group manager did not use a microcomputer at the office, but his family used one at home. Nor did supervisors habitually use computers; in general, management saw PCs as being tools for soldiers, not for generals.

Implementation

Consistent with this low-key approach, employees were little prepared for the appearance of the first PCs. Most accountants found out about them from coworkers or their supervisor, or just by seeing them around. Few knew or cared about the manager's decision to bring in the machines.

An organizationwide center provided training on a voluntary basis. After an introductory session and one hour of training time per week on company time, employees were expected to take any further training on their own time, at lunch or after work. Besides "learning by doing," coworker tutoring was common: Twenty-three names came up as local "experts" familiar with more sophisticated techniques, but they were widely distributed among work groups on the floor. Average use was about 10 percent of work time, with the heaviest users spending one-third of their time using PCs. Except for peak use periods, there was little difficulty getting on the machines.

By the second visit, there was some evidence that PC use had reached a steady state and might be decreasing. Users reported having spent more time during the learning phase than now. When they were developing larger applications, initiated by senior managers, the use was also heaviest. Most of the obvious ways of automating spreadsheets had been thought of, although some people felt they still had some new ideas to work out. The accounting group's user logs bear out these observations: During the nine months before our first interviews, total reported PC use had increased by about 20 percent, largely due to the continuous addition of new users. The predominant trend for individual users was downward, for on average, each user reported spending only half the time that he or she had spent in their first month or two of use.

Consequences

For the most part, microcomputers found a useful niche in the accountants' work. Even workers who had never used the mainframe were using PCs, and longer-term employees were "less inclined" to use PCs than were newer and younger accountants. Most users reported saving time as they did their old tasks in new ways: The clerical aspects of accountants' work had amounted to about 25 percent of total work time, and so there was general agreement that the microcomputers were a "good thing." Although most reported that their work processes were essentially the same as they had been before PCs, about 20 percent said that they had time now to "find problems" and do more "in-depth verification" of trends and fluctuations. They reported that the machine capabilities stimulated their creativity and allowed them to consider the meanings of the numbers in new ways. About 25 percent had new responsibilities for application development and training brought about by the microcomputers themselves.

About 20 percent of the users voiced concerns that the PCs might be overused. Some spreadsheets, they said, might better have been left as manual operations or not drawn down from other computer systems. Management instituted an approval system for new PC applications, one clear expression of its view of their limited utility. The restrictions placed on word processing were another such expression, yet accountants themselves had different opinions about the value of PCs for their word processing. Some argued that a fast turnaround was important for certain documents, and others argued that the results on draft printers took longer and looked worse. One group found the word-processing restriction both ridiculous and onerous, and, at some risk, bootlegged a draft printer into its area for short documents requiring immediate delivery or for internal consumption.

During the second round of interviews, we observed a second wave of consequences, triggered by new employees who were more experienced with and enthusiastic about PCs. These relocated employees also were accustomed to an organization that was less hierarchical and centralized. By this time, moreover, one of these employees was assigned the job of "systems administrator" to provide PC information, evaluation, and planning to the 400 accountants. Yet microcomputers remained a minor factor in their work processes; they were generally seen as being more a convenience than a necessity. Lotus 1–2–3 remained the principal application software.

Overall, although microcomputer competence was felt to be somewhat important, it was not a substitute for getting one's work done. Yet, it might open up better work assignments or a new job, even though it was not considered to be an element of the formal review of older and "established" employees. One senior supervisor viewed computer training as being relevant to employees' "personal" development, not their "professional" development. This supervisor would rather have the accountant at his desk getting out a report than having him taking training on company time. At the same time, among new hires, Lotus 1–2–3 training had been built into their accounting education, and computer competence was beginning to play more of a role in career considerations.

Site 2: COMMCO

COMMCO is the largest company of a multistate, multicompany telecommunications corporation. In COMMCO's Comptroller's Department, which has approximately 1000 employees, we studied the use of microcomputers in two groups: the Revenue District, with 160 mostly clerical employees; and the Chief Accountant's Division, with 47 employees who are mostly managerial-professional. We conducted individual and group interviews with employees from the two groups, upper management, and personnel from related organizations such as Information Systems and Training. There were, again, two rounds of interviews about eight months apart.

End user computing had been slowly emerging throughout the companies and within the parent corporation. Several years before our first visit, COMMCO's Comptroller's Department had purchased dozens of Victor PCs, only to scrap them in favor of the IBM PCs and minicomputers currently in use. However, those at the corporate level in Information Systems had largely ignored end user computing, realizing only much later that they had "missed the boat," as they put it. By then, the Comptroller's Department had taken charge of small-systems computerization throughout COMMCO and has continued to maintain this policy initiative. Technical support by Information Systems is now separate from the Comptroller's control over policy and authorization, but the relationship is cooperative.

Expectations

Management's view of end user computing is ambitious. The impetus and vision come from the executive level. Management foresees a microcomputer on nearly every manager's desk and perhaps one for every two other employees on average, based largely on an image of a leaner company whose future and productivity are to be enabled by new technology.

Microcomputers are used primarily for spreadsheet and data base work and also for word processing and decision support. A range of future uses is envisioned as part of an integrated process tying together the corporate mainframe, departmental minisystems, and widely distributed micros. The multiple computer systems are expected to serve tasks of different magnitudes and to provide communication linkages among the systems. Tasks in the Chief Accountant's Division center on storage and retrieval of information about taxes, rates, depreciation, regulatory rules, and preparation of various reports; in the Revenue Department, employees are billing customers and receiving payments, checking for accuracy, and writing reports.

Implementation

We came onto this site about one year after the first orders for the IBM PCs. In the Chief Accountant's Division, 47 people were using 32 micros as well as 22 minicomputer terminals. In the Revenue Division, 161 people had 15 micros and 11 terminals. The small-systems initiative was based on several policy elements:

1. a simple ordering procedure and a rule-of-thumb justification of a one-year payback.
2. Encouragement and support for a standard family of hardware and software, and the possibility of ordering anything that was justifiable.
3. Wholesale in-house computer education from top to bottom. Starting in March 1985, 500 to 600 employees per month were taking courses in Intro PC, Lotus 1–2–3, Crosstalk, and dBase; advanced courses were gradually being introduced.
4. Encouragement to anyone in COMMCO to learn about microcomputers and to develop applications.
5. Some skilled PC users deliberately placed around the organization and given the responsibility of writing applications and helping users.

By the time of our second interviews, an experimental program was in place at an Information Resource Center, which combined the educational classroom facilities with technical support personnel who reported to corporate Information Systems, and policy/administrative personnel who reported to the Comptroller's group.

Consequences

It is uniformly believed that microcomputers have saved large chunks of time and reduced drudgery. The time savings are used both to reduce time pressure and to redirect effort. There is less overtime and work backlog, with people being able to get to their normal work and perform it under less time pressure and with monthly and quarterly closing times being less hectic. Fewer tasks are done by hand. The reduction in repetitive tasks has permitted some jobs to be reconfigured in ways that make them more meaningful to workers—instead of having three people adding up numbers on the same job, each of whom sees only a dismembered portion of it, workers now are getting more meaningful chunks of work from start to finish because labor-intensive input crunching is reduced. Most employees report that their work has more variety because of PCs.

With some extra time for exploration, employees are doing more analysis of output, more "as if" simulations, and coming to understand better the meanings of the numbers. In addition, new analytic functions and new reports have appeared that were impractical in the past. Management can rely on a much wider range of accessible information. The microcomputer system can be viewed as a jointly accessible resource: a distributed data base that allows each person or person–program unit to make independent inquiries. Of course, some of the dollars reflected in time savings are used up by new jobs that have been created to serve both computers and users.

These new tools have captivated some employees. We encountered one "local hero," a clerk who had previously spent most of his time pushing numbers around pieces of paper (adding, adding, adding)—until he won a computer as a door prize at a retail store. In the office, he had previously been obliged to wait his turn to use a PC, but because he now had his own at home, he soon became a lead user, reduced 30 hours of his weekly paperwork into three automated hours, and became an area computer consultant. Later, he moved into the Information Resource Center in the official role of general consultant to microcomputer users. Another records clerk, previously untrained, created 42 applications immediately upon being trained "just to get rid of the mounds of paper" on his desk. Having discovered this new competence, he was considering going back to school and making a major career change.

The patterns of microcomputer use were very different in the Chief Accountant's group and the Revenue operating group. Most of the managerial level accountants in the Chief Accountant's group had PCs on their desks for making sophisticated analyses, such as data base development for court cases on rate change requests. The few clerks were having difficulty finding an available machine but did not feel free to use the PC sitting on a manager's desk, although managers would occasionally use the clerks' machines. When asked what would happen if the group were given another microcomputer, one clerk said, "They'd hire another manager." By the time of our second visit, microcomputers had become as much a part of the workplace as desks were, and just about everyone had taken a basic introduction to micros and had some task to do on them. The few who remained untrained felt completely left out. Microcomputer literacy thus had moved from being a technical specialty to being a basic job requirement.

In the Revenue group, there are few managers and many workers who make phone calls, pull up records on the mainframe computer, chase down bad bills, and so forth. The second- and third-level managers were busy with human resource management, which left them little to do personally on a micro. Their secretaries and clerks were becoming the lead users (cf. von Hippel, 1986), but their use was less widespread and less sophisticated than in the Chief Accountant's group. Although secretaries were using minicomputer terminals for word processing, as yet the general usefulness of these tools remained undemonstrated. Schedule routines went unused by managers; electronic mail and other functions were not yet available. The general sense was that there were many applications to be written, but little time and few resources for proceeding more quickly.

It is difficult to know whether these differences arose from the match between tasks and computer resources, the relative availability of computer resources, or the relative skill levels of the managers. It was our impression that the Chief Accountant's group had more success because they had the power to request resources and successfully cultivated the belief that their work required them. The operating group seemed to align its tasks with the minicomputers that were not well supported and not yet very effective.

We came away with the impression of an established company shaking itself up, trimming down, and educating for the future through the medium of computerization. Microcomputers have become an integral part of many work processes. Generally, the PCs are considered to have proven their worth. When asked what they would do if their micros were taken away, the employees' responses ranged from "I would die" to "I would kill you." Changes in jobs and organizational structure are encouraged, and a spirit of experimentation pervades the company. The vision of top management and the sense in the ranks are of change and progress—and in the ranks, some anxiety about job security. Some employees expressed concern for the less well-educated population of this region whose future jobs were rapidly disappearing.

The most troublesome technical problems involved computer systems integration. There was not yet an easy way to communicate across machines, either from PC to mainframe or from PC to PC. Many people downloaded information from mainframe to minis or micros, but the procedures were slow and not well known. Examples abounded of rekeying data to replace these linkages. The first application in Revenue was to audit random bills from each of 30 types of customers. Being able to check twice as many bills as they could manually, employees caught a $4 million error that they credit to the PCs. On the other hand, pulling these bills daily from the mainframe and rekeying these data into a PC exemplifies the lack of system integration. One clerk in Revenue spent about 200 hours taking information from a 3000–page report residing on the mainframe and rekeying it into his PC for an annual report analysis. Local area networks were on order to help solve this intermachine communication bottleneck.

Generally, it was agreed that the minicomputers were not yet cost effective and that the next two years of the lease were definitely an experiment. Managers and technical employees recognized that new technologies could vastly increase their functions or completely outmode them. Our impression was that the minis were undersupported. They require technical expertise; yet the departments were choosing moderately trained people for the job. In some cases, those assigned to manage the minis did not think very highly of them.

Finally, there were some hints that the scope of microcomputer applications might be changing. For the most part, small-scale projects were the first to be automated. Concern was expressed that the exhaustion of simple automation applications would mean fewer opportunities for creative computer use by those at lower skill levels. In addition, as the frontier of use shifted to advanced projects, it was unclear whether there was sufficient time and skilled staff to move into a mode involving new tasks that spanned the organization.

Site 3: HITECH

HITECH is a large engineering and manufacturing company in the computer industry. The organization markets and itself uses a continuously growing bundle of information technology tools and products. This site consists of a 45-person advanced engineering group providing internal assistance in designing, planning, and implementing companywide end user computing. Its customers are, in the short run at least, the rest of HITECH.

Our observations centered on a new workstation, developed in this group, which included sophisticated functions and enhancements, such as multitasking with multiple windows, at high speed, on large high-resolution screens, and with a user-friendly front end including mouse and icons. The standard software included a multitasking, multiuser operating system, mail, word processing, office productivity tools, spreadsheet, videotext, and worldwide electronic conferencing. Recently developed window management software was available to only some of the users. The multitasking in separate windows provided Macintosh-like capabilities in a powerful networked workstation. Depending on their specific jobs, employees could assemble other software for project management or software development, for example. Through the interface to larger computers, they shared common resources such as data bases and printers.

This technology is itself state-of-the-art, beyond what is now commercially available. As both developers and users, these skilled computer professionals have invested highly in it and in creating the future "bells and whistles" that will enhance profits and their careers.

Everyone in this organization was accustomed to using a PC or terminal connected into the corporate worldwide network—thousands of terminals worldwide, and growing 100 percent annually. All of the members of the advanced engineering group that we studied had networked terminals, and some had more than one on their office desk and another at home. Hundreds of technical topics are available on the conferencing system, and there are recreational conferences as well (e.g., hobbies and games). Some employees who never contribute to the technical conferences do, however, read them as a means of self-training and preparation for requesting new assignments.

Most people spend over 50 percent of their time on the computer, and most prefer electronic mail and computer conferencing to the telephone. When the main computer system goes down and it is no longer possible to use individual systems, just about all work comes to a standstill; employees report that they stand around chatting until the system gets fixed or it is time to go home.

Expectations

The company's strategic vision evokes the "technology imperative," which they define this way: Because organizations are changing in unforeseen ways, the most effective strategy for claiming the "technological high ground" is to engineer a new technology and get it into the hands of people who will find ways of making it work for themselves. They believe, in fact, that the results of new technologies cannot be predicted without actually trying them. The manager's strategy (he is an engineer) is to "intrusively dump this new workstation onto the group." These lead users were expected to take on the simultaneous role of innovators (cf. von Hippel, 1986). If users find a technology useful or make it more usable, then the development process will continue on the basis of that experience. The group manager expressed his belief that "if something is useful, the human will adapt and make use of it," and if the technology is not adopted, it is the "failure of technology, not the human." If people do not find it useful, then we move on; he also said that he had "some scars" from failed projects, but those were par for the course and to be expected in his position.

Accompanying this engineer's technological strategic vision is a mistrust of centralized planning and management. The belief is that those at the top should set a direction and offer "energy" to company efforts, but the design process should be—is necessarily—decentralized, unpredictable, and self-managing. These employees, mostly engineers and computer scientists, want the organizational system to support taking initiative, scrounging for resources, and using marketlike mechanisms rather than standard routines. Organizationally, there is an aggressive emphasis on innovation through decentralization. The "plan" for technology use consists of "driving a stake up the hill," providing a new technology that people will use to pull themselves up toward an unfolding future.

As a group serving all internal computing functions worldwide, its products are expected to find a useful niche within other research and development (R&D) organizations and, as well, within administrative functions—marketing, financial analysis, orders, and manufacturing. Yet the group manager observed while demonstrating the workstation to us, "I don't know why, but administrative employees seem to use these capabilities less than we do in engineering."

Implementation

Because part of their work is to explore and to push the new equipment to its limits—to make it work, however possible—the "implementation" phase at this site is uniquely based on a "reinvention" framework. Although all group members had the new machine at their work space by the time of our interviews, their critical responses were colored by their anticipation of still another, currently secret, new development that will make even this new system wholly obsolete "in about 18 months."

No workstations were then available within the company outside this R&D environment, and so we were unable to make comparative observations of actual use. The expectation is, however, that the experiences of this group itself will be on the basis first of revisions and then of the company's internal marketing and distribution strategy.

Consequences

Given these specialists' ability to imagine the ideal workstation, this version received mixed reviews. The multiwindowing capability was seen as being a great improvement: "Like working with different pieces of paper on my desk, I can follow multiple streams of consciousness"; "I can work on one thing while another is processing." The large screens and icon menus made the new workstations easier to use, they said. On the other hand, they expected a transparent interface operating at the speed of thought: A computer should respond instantaneously to their cognitive processing and have no awkward translations of their requirements. Most people felt the system was faster than the one that preceded it, but several wanted it to be faster still. What some called "minutes" of waiting time for responses seemed to us like a few seconds.

"There are more tools available now than I have time to learn how to use," said one computer scientist. Documentation is scanty, and learning occurs by doing or by consulting peers. As welcome as its new features are, this workstation represents, to this group, an incremental, evolutionary process, not a discontinuity with previous ways of working.

EXPECTATIONS OF AUTOMATING, INFORMATING, AND NETWORKING

Viewing these three cases as representing a continuum characterized by organizational expectations helps make sense out of the variations among them. At one end of this continuum is the expectation that microcomputers will speed up well-understood tasks such as word processing and spreadsheet entry and analysis, directed toward enhancing efficiency and reducing head count. That is, microcomputers are expected only to "automate" specific processes, a view closely related to the traditional view of technology as substituting capital investment for labor costs.

Beyond this scenario of automating specific tasks is a second cluster of expectations that Zuboff (1985) labeled *informating*. In this process, organizations expect information technology to enhance the information-handling capabilities of computer users, who are, in turn, expected to use these data to gain a deeper understanding of the organization's workings.

The automate–informate continuum extends further to include a third "networking" point (Perin, 1988), what Rockart and Short (1989) call a "wired society." When the information technology systems are interconnected, the expectation is that employees will be able to transcend their own organization's limitations of resources, information, and experience by calling on those elsewhere in the company and across company boundaries. In contrast with automating and informating, in which the focus is largely internal to each unit and to the organization as a whole, networking for messaging and conferencing can reveal and transcend boundaries around functions and problems and focus attention on external interdependencies.

This continuum of expectations of microcomputer use helps explain, first, why the scope and scale of organizational consequences differ and, second, why conventional understandings of centralized and decentralized management and cost control have different consequences, depending on whether the organization or any of its units is automating, informating, or networking.

Scope and Scale of Organizational Consequences

The automating scenario has the narrowest goals and expected consequences, affecting mostly task efficiency. For example, at RESOURCE, PCs are used for specific tasks, replacing some of the manual work with computer calculations, encapsulated from any broader organizational or social contexts. The investment in information technology is made in a risk-averse way: A few microcomputers are introduced with bounded uses, and priority is given to the purity of mainframe data bases. The larger organization experiences few reverberations and is deliberately protected from unplanned change. Management policies offer just enough education to automate current tasks, but they do allow each worker or work group to define its requirements and evolve its own new skills and routines.

Thus, in a context in which management expects small efficiency gains, provides equipment and support in a narrowly defined area, and constrains the range of workers' discretion, the results rest most heavily on the function of the technology (Danziger & Kraemer, 1986). At best, the desired efficiencies are obtained, as at RESOURCE.

Informating defines a wider spectrum of expected consequences, in which information technology is regarded as being capable of enhancing strategic uses of data, analysis, and communication. It makes greater demands on organizational adaptability, as work, roles, and relationships may become transformed and reinvented, as is beginning to happen at COMMCO. COMMCO combines automating and informating. End user computing is not entirely encapsulated but is seen instead as being essential to a wider organizational strategy of productivity improvement. Rather than computerizing tasks, as RESOURCE does, COMMCO is "computerizing" people by investing in their training and supporting their tools, and depending on attrition to reduce their costs. By providing more discretion and more resources, COMMCO increases the range of possible consequences and also the range of organizational and personal variables that can affect the way that information technology is used (Danziger & Kraemer, 1986; Kling & Iacono, 1988). COMMCO is also hoping to computerize the organization as a whole through its first-level attempts at systems integration; its vision extending to the networking, transcending end of the continuum.

Networking has the widest consequences, internally and externally, when networks of data warehouses, electronic mail, and computer conferencing become the resources on which team and project work depends. As organizations rely on networks for distant resources of data and analysis, for worldwide discussions unconstrained by location or time zones, and for access to an international community of interests, networking can make the greatest demands of all on organizational adaptability as it incorporates external contexts over which it has least direct control. HITECH faces all of those possibilities, given its commitment to local and wider area networks and the technology to support and extend them.

HITECH is a clear example of a company already passing the informating point along the continuum and at the networking pole, such that the entire organization is expected to participate in the consequences of its technology strategy. Even so, not all company functions participate at the same rate or intensity: R&D employees find electronic mail and conferencing essential to their work, but administrators and managers make little use of this companywide resource. Within any one company, then, each organizational unit may take its own position along the continuum.

Centralized–decentralized management and cost control

Underlying its automating strategy, RESOURCE exhibits some of the Theory X (McGregor, 1960) mistrust of workers, that is, management specifies what people should and should not do with computers. Efficiency is one concern of centralized control: Will employees waste their time or produce inferior work that others could do better and more cheaply? Controlling the social structure is another: Accountants are ordered to send handwritten copy to the typing pool because doing their own reports and memos on the computer is "typing," considered to be work inappropriate to their role.

At RESOURCE, the user logs serve the dual purpose of rationing access to a scarce resource and recording the number of users and hours of use. It is not surprising that an accounting organization would want to justify the cost of microcomputers by means of monitoring and control systems. The stated assumption was that the number of PCs to be provided depended on utilization, and near-constant use was the primary justification for getting more PCs. A payback analysis was required along with each purchase order, in which managers had to show that the computer would pay for itself in about a year. Considering how these figures may have been "cooked," management did not really know whether usage could be evaluated seriously on cost-justification grounds alone. As Schein (this volume) points out, one form of the "vision to informate" is to informate the control process by keeping closer track of workers and attempting to micromanage the company, which is "similar to the automation solution."

At the other extreme is HITECH, at which informating and networking are the norm, and engineers are in the driver's seat and they mistrust management. Centralized controls at HITECH accept the need for each organization to accumulate resources and negotiate with others in pursuit of its vision or interests. The inefficiencies of continual negotiation between centralization and decentralization are perceived as being part of the cost of maintaining initiative and creativity. It is evident that the marketlike organizational structure and processes of HITECH is compatible with easy networking. It is not clear whether the increased costs of this high volume of communication are justified by the enhanced flexibility it permits (cf. Malone, this volume).

COMMCO is committed to informating and sees networking only indistinctly on its horizon. These expectations lead it to take a middle ground in controlling computer proliferation. By providing opportunities and support, it channels computer growth in a managed direction yet does not forbid other initiatives. At the same time, only the "approved list" of hardware and software is supported; only certain courses are taught internally, making it much easier and safer for employees to go in the approved direction. However, they could experiment if they were willing to bear the risk individually.

The automating organization will inevitably rely on cost justification alone, a tactic necessary to any short-term view of costs and profits. Unless informating and networking strategies are expected to materialize over time, it may be adequate. But given the users' creativity and the various unforeseen contexts that can lead to applications developments, it may be a nearsighted way of thinking about new technologies. For at any point along the automate–informate network continuum, the organization itself may be transformed in ways that may enhance its ability to incorporate new technologies or to resist them.

SCRIPTING THE AFFINITIES BETWEEN TOOLS AND WORK

If management is to manage expectations, that is, to develop and communicate appropriate expectations, then it needs to understand their sources and nature and to have a method for structuring and discussing them. We believe that management should consider the relationships among work processes, work groups, organizational structures and processes, and business strategy in terms not only of goals or end states but also of ways to get from the current situation to the desired one. Most important, these relationships should be thought out in reasonable detail, with what one might call a "process theory" (Markus & Robey, 1988) of the introduction of microcomputers to replace the uncritical acceptance of the "technological imperative" scenario in which technology is believed to have inherent characteristics that have inevitable impacts on work.

Sources of expectations

If expectations are important contributing causes of the impact of new information technology, as we have argued, then what are the sources of these expectations? Expectations arise from a variety of sources inside and outside the organization.

General expectations about the relation of technology to work, authority, prestige, and efficiency arise from a person's location in a bureaucratic hierarchy and the nature of accountabilities and types of production processes in which he or she participates. In conditioning the impact of a new technology, the same technology can have different effects in different organizations (Barley, 1988). Further, individuals or groups within the organization may be especially influential in shaping expectations. Consider, for example, the difference in the vision of microcomputers by the manager at RESOURCE and the executive at COMMCO, or the information systems (IS) group at COMMCO who saw that they had "missed the boat" because they had inappropriate expectations about microcomputers. Lead users with previous computer experience and an affinity for the technology may turn out to be somewhat unusual, however, as illustrated by the engineers at HITECH who have difficulty understanding why the administrative side of the company is not using the new technology, which it, in turn, perceives to be "for the engineers."

A major source of expectations comes from outside the organization. For example,

> Vendors and the mass media have convinced many naive computer users that computer use is as simple as pushing a button. This image of "easy to use" systems has led many managers to have unrealistic expectations about what their workers can do in a specific time period with little or no training. (Kling & Iacono, 1988a, p. 19)

The failure of its vendor to deliver on its promises upset several of our interviewees at COMMCO. Consultants provide key information that shapes expectations about IT, as do the writing of popular academics and consultants such as Tom Peters, Peter Drucker, Shoshanna Zuboff, and Paul Strassman. Expectations also arise from other organizations whose experiences with technology become known. To wit, the manager who introduced PCs to the accounting group at RESOURCE had first seen them in operation at a competitor.

Finally, vague expectations may crystallize or change while planning and implementing the technology. New information about computers, their users, and uses may establish a range of possible outcomes. Pilot projects or feedback from early users may clarify the likely benefits and problems of new technologies. HITECH uses its development group to evaluate the potential of new technology and to decide how to alter it to achieve or raise that potential. Given the array of sources of expectations and their mutual relationship with outcomes, any causal relation between expectations and impacts must be modified in two ways: First, expectations join forces with a web of influences, and second, expectations can be altered as the implementation proceeds.

Scripts

To support the management of expectations, we propose the metaphor of a "script" (Schank & Abelson, 1977) as a way of making more concrete the notion of tracing the expected relationship between new technology and its consequences. A script is a series of events or episodes, similar to a "scenario" but at a concrete level of actions and work processes. Just as it does in a play, the script outlines the actors, their roles, the objects and setting, and the expected sequences of actions and consequences. Uncertain consequences can be represented by alternative scenarios, a method common in strategic planning exercises (e.g., Wack, 1985). Uncertain processes (getting from scene A to scene B) can be improvised by the actors or can be represented as cycles of action and feedback until effective strategies are found.

On the one hand, scripts can be written in detail that controls people in an authoritarian, "top-down" implementation of microcomputers, or in vague images and goals, which often accompany "grass-roots" development or technology that is "parachuted" onto desks. Striking a balance between tighter and looser scripts is critical. Workers and supervisors should feel free to improvise and develop their own ideas (to some extent), but management should have a script outlining how the goals will be accomplished.

Writing microcomputer introduction scripts requires some rethinking of the policy and structural linkages among the significant events in which all the actors participate, and then asking what difference the PCs will make to them. For example, time savings remain a prominent goal in the introduction of microcomputers. But scripts are incomplete; for example, we see little curiosity about the ways that the possible time "savings" will be "reinvested" in revised work processes and activities that are intended to affect the firm's competitive position and the value-added chain. We will return to this issue of the broader strategic implications of the details of microcomputer implementation at the end of this chapter.

Research on technology implementation often documents trends and relationships at levels of abstraction removed from managers' everyday concerns with computers, workers, and organizational policies and structures. Thinking in terms of scripts suggests that managers might instead "walk through" the steps by drawing on live situations or reports of others' experiences as a way of foreseeing what might happen. Our three cases demonstrate several important dimensions of such scripts: (1) affinities between technology and work, representing the kinds of end states that could be achieved, and how (2) support for microcomputers and (3) the management of conflict are central to scripting the implementation process.

Affinities

The primary disappointments with information technology stem from tools that are inadequate to work processes. By writing scripts, the natural affinities among tools, work processes, employees' requirements, and the organizational structure would be identified. The more familiar notions of "fit" and "functionality" only partially capture the image that we want to convey: Fit and function both imply that the criteria for effectiveness are embodied in the person or the process or the tool, any one of which independently controls the outcomes. Affinity, by contrast, suggests an active mutuality in which person, process, tool, and organizational structure all work together so well and so interdependently that they cannot be conceived or evaluated apart from one another.

The automation of a single work process by a particular piece of software represents an easily envisioned affinity, such as the use of Lotus 1–2–3 at RESOURCE to replace handwritten spreadsheets and the spread of minicomputer-based word processing among the secretaries at COMMCO. The "bootlegged" printer at COMMCO shows how one group of accountants refused to disavow the affinity between its work processes and localized word processing. When machine-user interfaces are "unfriendly" or when software developers write applications without having involved users in their design, affinities often remain unsurfaced and unacknowledged.

The success of automation in replacing hand calculations by spreadsheet programs for accounting, or in automating back rooms of paper and paper pushers in the banking industry, demonstrates a ready affinity between tool and work process. Yet even such obvious affinities may have complex organizational consequences, such as changing career paths and reorganizing jobs, or strategic consequences, such as the consolidation in the banking industry necessitated by the high fixed costs of huge computer systems (Steiner & Teixera, 1988).

Informating requires a wider scope of planning and design work to achieve that mutuality because multiple tasks and less structured tasks are affected. It requires a functional yet flexible technology alongside user trials and feedback. Creativity is more central, because end users (and others) are creating or reinventing the technology and their organizational relationships as they work with it or use its outputs.

Networking requires even wider organizational design efforts, especially in foreseeing the new kinds of social relationships that can develop through conferencing and electronic mail. Criteria for allowing employees data access, for example, may reinvent organizational policies. Software applications for networked project teams may transcend conventional boundaries. Malone (1987) suggested that the lower costs of communicating with new information technologies will enable more use of communication-intensive mechanisms such as decentralized buying and selling within companies and less hierarchical forms of coordination that do not rely on authority and rules. These enabled structural consequences are most likely to occur when organizational leadership, creativity, and strategy are aligned.

The significance of affinities can be seen on a broader scale in the divergent ways that automobile plants have incorporated new production technologies. Investments in hundreds of millions of dollars in new robotics, flexible manufacturing systems, and other hardware are found to have had virtually no impact on efficiency and quality in plants that have not simultaneously reconsidered old-style human resource policies and associated social structures, including rigid job classifications and adversarial labor-management relations. Only those organizations adopting human resource policies of employee consultation and feedback seem to be able to demonstrate that they benefit from moderate or high levels of new technology (Kochan, 1988)—evidence for the prerequisite affinity among tools, policies, work processes, employee requirements, and organizational policies.

Although HITECH's overall vision is to move the entire organization toward "enterprise computing," in which the new workstation is a linchpin, management lacks a clear understanding of its affinities to work processes other than those in R&D functions. The product is assumed to speak for itself; yet one manager of an information analysis group has an image of its being "more engineering oriented, self-contained, and multitasking. I think of it as being very elaborate and more than my group will need." Despite being aware that "the administrative side of the house hardly uses the existing computers and their communication functions," the company has no research under way to discover what low-frequency users are doing instead or what kinds of hardware and applications might make more strategic sense for them. Nonetheless, upper management continues to be concerned about efficient "asset utilization," unaware of this gap in basic "consumer" or marketing information. Moreover, organizational policies contradict this "enterprise" strategy, which declares that upper management will use these workstations but the organizational structure delegates such tasks to staff and specialists. Scripting would surface such gaps and paradoxes.

The more that is known about the affinities between specific jobs and new technologies, the more likely that organizations will experience positive changes in levels of computer use, user satisfaction, and performance. Bikson's research showed that the key variables to account for positive changes were "job design characteristics . . . [s]pecifically, variety and challenge in work along with adequacy of resources for task performance" (1987, p. 165), including exclusive workstation use and the functions of the tools. Function outweighed user friendliness, but effective use "requires better learning support for employees than many organizations are prepared to provide" (p. 174). In short, identifying affinities between technology and work processes needs to be the paramount scripting concern, but scripts that ignore the implementation process, for example, by leaving training to personal time with weak organizational incentives, are likely to be self-defeating.

Because we know more about the uses of specific functions such as word processing and spreadsheets than we do about generic computer functions such as communication and file management, and because such single functions can be automated apart from broader work and organizational arrangements, it has been easier to automate specific functions than to informate or network to support generic functions (Bikson, 1987). It is a substantial challenge to develop scripts that contain more technological and organizational elements, each of which is as yet only partially understood.

Scripting support for microcomputer use

In regard to support and training, there seems to be little recognition that computer use requires skills that must be taught and retaught if not used regularly (some say about three hours daily). This early investment in the education process represents, of course, a loss of some immediate productivity. Further, those without a technical background or who use computers infrequently may spend still more time to relearn commands at almost every use. Although this process is inevitable when microcomputers are available, we see little evidence of scripts that take account of these everyday complexities.

In our case studies, management seems to expect too much for too little. RESOURCE put only a few PCs in place for hundreds of people and expected users to keep learning on their own time. Little support was made available for decentralized application development. At COMMCO, high expectations helped employees get going and work through some initial problems, so that by the time more problems emerged, the PC user base was broad enough and the pool of resources adequate for solving them. It is not clear, however, that COMMCO's problems with minicomputers will so readily be resolved, given the inadequacy of the resources supporting them. Many organizations are likely to follow a limited script in which they parachute PCs into work groups and hope for productivity gains with minimal support. Although some companies set up extensive training programs, information centers, and devices such as computer-assisted learning packages, our impression is that these mechanisms are used because they have good reputations, not because they have been carefully worked into an organizational script.

Conflict

The scripting metaphor should help managers foresee organizational conflicts over implementation. The classic script, one now thought to be outdated, included conflicts over access and control between data processing and information systems, on the one hand, and organizational end users on the other. At COMMCO, there is a conflict between corporate worry over microcomputer proliferation and a local logic that encourages it. At RESOURCE, there is a conflict over the permitted uses of microcomputers. At HITECH, where decentralization is an overarching script, local scripts require the continuous management of conflicts and negotiations among many semiautonomous units. Management should be in the position to answer questions about the consequences of such conflicts and to offer ways of dealing constructively with them.

Another type of conflict arises over enactment. Scripts may be unrealistic in matching the actors to their roles or foreseeing contingencies in different situations. Without having identified the "ecology of interests" (Kling, 1980), most scripts leave people to improvise, therefore, and they muddle through as best they can. HITECH seems almost premised on improvisation, whereas to the RESOURCE managers improvisation is undesirable.

LINKING STRATEGIES AND TACTICS FOR MICROCOMPUTER IMPLEMENTATION

How organizations position the decision to invest in microcomputers influences their expectations and implementation consequences. Do they see the decision as being only local and tactical or as integrated into a broader strategic vision, or both? Models dealing with these relationships are just beginning to appear, such as Henderson and Venkatraman's (this volume) strategic alignment model that links (1) business strategy, (2) the technology platform, (3) IT strategy, and (4) organization and management. Scripts that build out from expectations to work processes and then to strategy can help implement these models.

The predominance of limited scripts for introducing microcomputers suggests either widespread strategic ambivalence or simple ignorance of the consequences of the tactical issues, or both. The ambivalence and resistance of middle managers to information technology that may threaten their jobs is commonly observed, yet those at the top are also unlikely to integrate the relationship between the technology and productive processes into their strategic visions. Interviews with CEOs of high-tech firms reveal that by and large they "do not see IT as a CEO-level issue," and they generally categorize its functions as being tactical or "just a tool" (Kennedy, 1987, pp. 97–98).

Schein (this volume) finds that CEOs vary greatly in their assumptions about and visions of the likely impacts of IT, and the manner in which they implement (or delegate, or reject) IT. Although CEOs may be the most visible and influential individuals in their organizations, our cases suggest that a similar analysis of variations can be made for line managers, staff, and workers. Such beliefs are important to the way that IT enters and affects the company.

It is true, of course, that the competitive advantage that some organizations attain by investing in microcomputers and other information technologies cannot be easily transferred. Because models of strategies have not been readily available, many companies leap into new technologies in order to be in the vanguard in a "social movement" (Kling & Iaconno, 1988b) or to keep abreast of their competition. The social pressures can outweigh any cost–benefit analyses; for example, organizational expectations may be based on beliefs that computers

- Symbolize an orientation toward the future and toward adaptation.
- Increase worker satisfaction and interest.
- Attract different kinds of people to the company.
- Educate workers for newer technologies yet to come.
- Quicken the pace of information flow and adaptation.

Recent research suggests that one consequence of microcomputer implementation is that line managers have, or ought to have, more control over the allocation of resources (Danziger & Kraemer, 1986, p. 211). Line managers are left to figure out a workable script incorporating conflicting demands for cost cutting versus resources for computer support, standardization versus creativity, centralized control versus decentralized flexibility, and formal role relationships versus new centers of competence and mutual interest that microcomputers can foster. Although meeting these demands may appropriately give greater control to line managers, it is likely that such negotiations cumulatively become organizationally and strategically critical. They need to be placed higher—and earlier—on the list of strategic concerns. As Rockart and Short (1989) pointed out, "The economic, behavioral, and political consequences of today's striking new uses of information technology should be well thought out and the requisite change processes effectively managed by those responsible for the management of the business itself."

What consequences does such line activity have for strategic planning and control, given "only" tactical changes in work design, training efforts, or organizational policies? How are line and staff managers communicating about the implementation consequences? In writing and rewriting implementation scripts, these actors are also defining activities important to the value-added chain. These can provide significant information in the search for new forms of electronic and organizational integration (Benjamin & Scott Morton, 1986). In their daily work, employees may be reinventing both the machines and the organization itself. In the 1990s, management needs to script the conceptual and practical linkages between such tactical and strategic consequences of microcomputers.

ACKNOWLEDGMENT

We appreciate the assistance of John Roberts, Elaine Yakura, Roger McPeek, and George Roth in collecting the data, and Frank Basa, Walton Yuen, and Sarbani Thakur who assisted in other aspects of this project.

REFERENCES

Attewell, P., & J. Rule (1984) Computing and organizations: What we know and what we don't know. *Communications of the ACM* 27:1184–92.

Barley, S. R. (1987). Technology, power, and the social organization of work: Towards a pragmatic theory of skilling and deskilling. In S. Bacharach & N. DiTomaso (Eds.), *Research in the sociology of organizations*, Vol. 6, pp. 33–80. Greenwich, CT: JAI Press.

Benjamin, R. I., & M. S. Scott Morton (1986). Information technology, integration, and organizational change. Management in the 1990s working paper no. 86–017. Sloan School of Management, Massachusetts Institute of Technology, April.

Bikson, T. (1987). Understanding the implementation of office technology. In R. E. Kraut (Ed.), *Technology and the transformation of white-collar work*, pp. 155–76. Hillsdale, NJ: Erlbaum.

Bowen, W. (1986). The Puny Payoff from Office Computers. *Fortune* May 26, pp. 20–24.

Danziger, J. N., & K. L. Kraemer (1986). *People and computers: The impact of computing on end users in organizations*. New York: Columbia University Press.

Foster, L., & D. Flynn (1984). Management information technology: Its effects on organizational form and function. *MIS Quarterly* December, pp. 229–36.

Harris, C. L. (1987). Office automation: Making it pay off. *Business Week* October 12, pp. 134–46.

Invernizzi, E. (1988). Information technology, flexibility, and organizational design equifinality: Is any prediction possible? Unpublished manuscript, Management in the 1990s, Sloan School of Management, Massachusetts Institute of Technology.

Keen, P. (1985). Computers and managerial choice. *Organizational Dynamics* Autumn, pp. 35–49.

Kennedy, H. E. (1987). CEO assumptions concerning information technology in high technology firms. M.A. thesis, Sloan School of Management, Massachusetts Institute of Technology.

Kling, R. (1980). Social analyses of computing: Theoretical perspectives in recent empirical research. *Computing Surveys* 12:61–110.

Kling, R., & S. Iacono (1988a). Desktop computerization and the organization of work. Unpublished manuscript, Department of Information and Computer Science, University of California at Irvine.

——— (1988b). The mobilization of support for computers. *Social Problems* 35:226–43.

Kochan, T. A. (1988). Human resources and technology in the auto industry. Paper presented at the Management in the 1990s Seminar Series, Sloan School of Management, Massachusetts Institute of Technology, February 11.

Leavitt, H. J., & T. L. Whisler (1958). Management in the 1980s. *Harvard Business Review* 36:41–48.

Malone, T. W. (1987). Modeling coordination in organizations and markets. *Management Science* 33:1317–32.

Markus, M. L., & D. Robey (1988). Information technology and organizational change: Causal structure in theory and research. *Management Science* 34:583–98.

McGregor, D. (1960). *The human side of enterprise*. New York: McGraw-Hill.

Perin, C. (1988). Place-time habits vs. high-tech options: Professional level work in the 1990s. Sloan School of Management working paper, Massachusetts Institute of Technology.

Rice, R., & E. Rogers (1980). Reinvention in the innovation process. *Knowledge* 1:499–514.

Robey, D. F. (1977). Computers and management structure: Some empirical findings re-examined. *Human Relations* 30:963–76.

——— (1983). Information systems and organizational change: A comparative case study. *Systems, Objectives, Solutions* 3:143–54.

Rockart, J., & L. Flannery (1983). The management of end user computing. *Communications of the ACM* 26:776–84.

Rockart, J., & J. E. Short (1989). IT in the 1990s: Managing organizational interdependence. *Sloan Management Review* 30:7–17.

Schank, R. C., & R. P. Abelson (1977). *Scripts, plans, goals, and understanding*. Hillsdale, NJ: Erlbaum.

Schein, E. H., & D. D. Wilson (1987). CEOs look at information technology: What do they see? Paper presented at the annual meeting of Management in the 1990s, Sloan School of Management, Massachusetts Institute of Technology.

Steiner, T. D., & D. Teixera (1988). Technology is more than just a strategy. *McKinsey Quarterly*, Winter, pp. 39–51.

von Hippel, E. (1986). Lead users: A source of novel product concepts. *Management Science* 32: 791–805.

Wack, P. (1985). Scenarios: Uncharted waters ahead. *Harvard Business Review,* September-October, pp. 73–89.

Walton, R., & W. Vittori (1983). New information technology: Organizational problem or opportunity? *Office: Technology and People* 1:249–73.

Wilson, D. D. (1985). The reinvention of microcomputers: Toward an analytical framework. Ph.D. diss., Harvard University.

Young, T. (1984). The lonely micro. *Datamation,* April 1, pp. 100–18.

Zuboff, S. (1982). New worlds of computer-mediated work. *Harvard Business Review*, September-October, pp. 142–152.

——— (1985). Automate/informate: The two faces of intelligent technology. *Organizational Dynamics*, Autumn, pp. 4–18.

——— (1988). *In the age of the smart machine: The future of work and power*. New York: Basic Books.

CHAPTER 16

End User Computing in the Internal Revenue Service

BRIAN T. PENTLAND

Phase 1 of the automated examination system (AES) constituted a major shift in the technology of field audits in the Internal Revenue Service (IRS). Until 1986, all field audits had been conducted essentially by hand on 14-column ledger pads and hand calculators. Reports were handwritten, as clerical help for typing was a scarce resource reserved for other uses. In 1986, the IRS began issuing laptop personal computers to revenue agents, the accounting professionals who conduct field audits of corporate and individual tax returns. With more than 14,000 revenue agents participating in the process, AES is certainly among the largest end user computing implementations in history and provides a unique opportunity to study how variations in management policy and training can influence the ability of employees to integrate new technology into their work.

In this chapter, I have chosen to view implementation primarily as a learning process. As a learning process, implementation starts when the equipment or training is first given to users and ends when the technology is fully integrated into the flow of work.[1] This choice stems partly from the unique character of the organizational setting and technology, which I shall describe later in some detail. But it also stems from the fact that every investment in innovative technical capital requires the creation of new skills among potential users (Tomer, 1988). Without adequately trained users, even the best-designed equipment will sit idle or be used at less than full potential.

In the case of AES, those planning and managing the implementation were aware of the need for users to be given training and skills development. Although users in all locations were issued identical hardware and software, they were not supplied with identical training, support, incentives, and learning time needed to master the new tools. The result was systematic variations in the success of the implementation, as measured by levels of use, user satisfaction, and performance. Because of the uniformity of tasks, technology, and organizational context, this research provides a good opportunity to isolate the effects of training and management policy on implementation success.

Sources of data

The data reported in this chapter were drawn from two sources. First, I conducted open-ended interviews during a series of field visits between February and July 1987. I interviewed more than 80 persons, either individually or in groups. They represented two regions, four districts, and 11 revenue agent groups, as well as the national AES Project Office and Examination Division management.[2] Within each district, I talked to agents from at least two (sometimes three) field audit groups. These groups and individuals were chosen on an ad hoc basis, with availability, convenience, and individual consent being the main concerns. Those interviewed had been issued computers three to nine months earlier. The interviews were unstructured, lasting between one and two hours each. Taping was generally not allowed, so the raw data consists of expanded interview notes. Quotations are taken directly from these notes, with names, places, and other identifying references omitted to protect confidentiality.

Second, I conducted a sample survey (n = 1110) of revenue agents.[3] In order to capture possible group effects, this sample was clustered by field audit group (the first level administrative unit of the Examination Division, consisting of 12 to 14 revenue agents and their group manager). A total of 138 groups were included in the sample, 128 of which had more than three respondents per group. The overall response rate (at the individual level) was estimated to be 85 percent. The survey includes respondents from all seven IRS regions and 48 out of 64 district offices. This sample is completely independent of the sites selected for interviews.

PART 1: THE AUTOMATED EXAMINATION SYSTEM

The idea of an automated examination system (AES) started in 1979 as part of a productivity initiative in a district in the Western region. AES has the goal of making an examination, as nearly as possible, a paperless process. The concept is to have electronic "work centers" for each occupation. When the entire system is in place, the paper flow between steps in the audit process can be reduced to an electronic flow.

The laptop portables are only the first of several phases. The complete system is planned to include networks of minicomputers and mainframes on a national basis, on-line access to taxpayer records, on-line legal research, and artificial intelligence for classification and selection of returns. The expected benefits, beyond simply eliminating paper, include faster information access, improved management control, higher examination quality, and about 20 percent more productivity overall.

It is important to note that the "automation" in AES pertains most directly to the support functions, examination support and processing (ESP), and planning and special programs (PSP). A paperless process would result in significant staff reductions in these areas. Likewise, it should be clear that auditing requires that a person of considerable skill and knowledge be present to handle the interaction, look at and consider the evidence, make decisions, and so on. Only certain limited aspects of a revenue agent's work can be done or even affected by computer.

Phase 1 of AES: Hardware and software

Phase 1 was limited to a laptop portable computer and software for use in field audits.[4] Although the computers had internal modems and software for telecommunications, agents generally had nothing to dial into. The first phase of AES was completely "stand-alone": one agent, one computer. In this initial phase, productivity was expected to rise only 2 to 3 percent at most.

Two main software programs were provided with the PC. The first, called the 1040 Workcenter, was designed as a comprehensive tool for auditing 1040 returns and all the associated schedules. This program was originally issued on 18 floppy disks (later reduced to 12 and then nine). The Workcenter is a menu-driven program that guides one through the audit and produces standardized work papers. This program was written by the national AES project office in conjunction with consultants from Arthur Andersen, with the input of literally hundreds of revenue agents from the field in all stages of design and testing. As noted, the 1040 Workcenter was intended as one piece of a vast hierarchical network of computing power. Consequently, the main menu on the Workcenter included nonworking selections for "legal research" and other functions intended for later phases of implementation.

The other main piece of software was a commercial package called Enable, which is a general word-processing, spreadsheet, database, and communications package. As shipped, Enable contains no tax-related applications, but it is possible to write programs and templates in Enable that can be used for auditing. This program was delivered off the shelf to AES users and also required several diskettes to run. It is interesting that the 1040 Workcenter can integrate spreadsheet computations calculated using Enable. That is, one can use the Workcenter and Enable together in the same audit.

As might be expected, the number of diskettes needed in the software was discouraging for the revenue agents, and almost everyone complained about the inconvenience of disk swapping:

> Trouble is, you have to keep switching disks, and it's very time-consuming. It's a beautiful machine and I even like the software, but the disk switching is horrible.
>
> I would never take that thing into the field and embarrass myself in front of some attorney by playing floppy-swappy. No way. I don't see how anyone can use it the way it is now.

When we consider the success of the AES implementation in terms of productivity improvements, problems like those described here will play an important role in analyzing the findings.

How the laptop affects work

Only some parts of the revenue agent's work are directly affected by the computer. Out of all the tasks an agent must do to complete an audit, only the preparation of certain materials for the case file—work papers, revenue agent report (RAR), and tax computations—can be done by computer. The PC is not applicable to activities such as reviewing books and records, doing legal research, interviewing taxpayers, making appointments, and doing paperwork. When asked if he felt that the laptop had changed his job, one manager explained as follows:

> The computer may change the job somewhere down the road, when it's more than just a fancy calculator or typewriter. Things like direct access to the service center and legal research, those will be important. But for the time being, it does not really change the job.
>
> The computer will never do an audit. You still have to look at the books and records, and you still have to deal with taxpayers. The computer may save time on some computations, which is a big help, but it won't do the job for you. The basic job is still done with the little green shield and the white sleeves rolled up. You just can't get away from that.

This basic impression was confirmed by agents and managers in all districts. The much-studied "impacts on the organization" are not very important in this case as of yet, because the organization and the work remain essentially unchanged. It could hardly be otherwise, because the scope of Phase 1 was constrained by legal and organizational requirements for examinations and by conditions negotiated with the National Treasury Employees Union (NTEU), which represents the revenue agents.

For legal reasons, uniform procedures must be followed. The steps of conducting an audit are formalized in the *Internal Revenue Manual* (and in the voluminous history of litigation surrounding the IRS) and cannot be changed easily. Organizationally, the inputs and outputs of the examination process flow to and from many other IRS functions (e.g., appeals, collection), which were not as yet being automated. As a result, the ways that case files are assembled and audits move through the system did not change:

> Once we get the final tax computation and the RAR, there's no difference between pre-and post-AES, as far as the agent goes. The paper trail stays the same from there on out. The case folders are assembled the same way, the folder is ready to go from the manager's desk to review and ESP for final processing.

The NTEU was generally cooperative about planning for AES, but it also restricted the implementation process. In addition to helping shape policy on issues of equipment security, liability for loss or damage, and home use, the union had a major impact on the evaluation of revenue agents. As part of the introduction process, NTEU negotiated for a learning period during which agents could not be evaluated—positively or negatively—on their use of the computer. That is, managers could require the use of the PC or threaten an agent with a poor evaluation for not using it. Likewise, they could give credit to those who excelled at it. As a result, use of the computer was officially discretionary.

Auditing on the laptop

Where the laptop does change things, of course, is where the pencil meets the paper. The most apparent change is that RARs and work papers are now typed instead of handwritten. Some agents say their work papers are more terse, others that they are more verbose; the difference seems to correlate to typing speed. But there was virtually unanimous agreement that typewritten work looks "more professional" than does handwritten work. In fact, better-looking work papers seemed to be the biggest, most widely recognized benefit of the new technology, as the following quotations suggest:

> All the reports were handwritten and they looked like hell. Now the reports look more professional. We can edit them on the screen, review them, and then print them. It gets rid of scribbles on paper, piles of notes, which are hard to follow. The PC doesn't really save time, but it forces me to be more logical in my approach. It's the greatest tool they ever gave me.
>
> A 30–to-50 page handwritten pencil report to collect $50,000 or send someone to jail? That's silly! So a computer output looks more professional, for sure. But on a personal level, it enhances people's self-image, too.

The effect of the laptop on the details of how an agent organizes and conducts an audit is a more elusive issue. In part, it hinges on the way in which the different media—software versus pencil and paper—support the auditor's thought process. Many agents felt that the computer was somewhat of a mixed blessing, good for some specific tasks but not very helpful overall. This finding was strongly confirmed by the survey, in which almost 75 percent of the respondents agreed that "the laptop allows me to do some things faster" and only 15 percent agreed that "on the whole, the laptop reduces time on case." (This finding is discussed in more detail later.) One senior agent, AES instructor, and self-proclaimed "PC evangelist" summarized the general problem of auditing on the computer in this way:

> Examination is an art, not a science. You're getting multiple kinds of information from multiple sources. It's much easier to assimilate this with paper and pencil, so you can just flip between the pages and put new things down as they come up.

Apparently, the problems of keeping the audit straight are increased by the computer. This was described vividly by a senior agent who had taught several classes as an AES instructor and had used a PC for auditing since the earliest pilot programs in 1985.

> You know I'm still figuring out how to deal with the PC. It's like an obstacle course in my mind. Paper is much easier mentally to deal with. It's difficult to adjust to keeping things on diskette, remembering what you have and where it is—especially with a spreadsheet. It's so hard to see a spreadsheet on that small screen.

Agents using the Workcenter had similar complaints:

> It's so clumsy when you try to do a bank deposit analysis. You'd like to have a sheet of paper for each account and have them all in front of you at once so that you can enter transfers easily. But with the PC, there's a screen for each account and month. It's so confusing to remember which screen is for which account.

> It's not transparent. You are constantly aware of the fact that you are using a program, rather than the fact that you are doing an examination. It's hard to tell what the program is doing with all of the numbers you put in.

These comments point to problems in the design of the system and perhaps to the unsuitability of a task such as auditing to automation of any kind. The data available here do not provide much insight into these questions, because the underlying task and technology variables are controlled for. And there is no basis for comparison among different tasks or technologies within this study, so we can only wonder whether people using different technologies for the same tasks would have the same difficulties.[5]

Distinctive features of AES as end user computing

It is worthwhile summarizing and emphasizing some of the points from the preceding discussion that make AES distinctive as an end user computing application. These contextual variables are keys to understanding the implementation process at the IRS, and they also limit how much we can generalize from the findings of this research, as other situations will differ.

1. Use is discretionary. By agreement with the National Treasury Employees Union (NTEU), revenue agents cannot be evaluated positively or negatively for their use or nonuse of the laptop computer. The only official incentives for use are indirect; if agents feel that the computer will help them do their job better (and thus get a better evaluation), they can choose to use it. As a result, revenue agents had the opportunity to vote on AES with their keyboards or their pencils.
2. Phase 1 used strictly stand-alone systems. The rule with AES is "one agent, one case, one computer." Agents work independently on their cases, and their computer systems operate independently. Data are entered and retrieved only by the individual user, and there is no reason for sharing data. With no pressure or benefit to interact with other users, the decision to use the computer is purely personal.
3. Users are not managers. Unlike users of decision-support systems and other end user applications that frequently appear in the MIS literature, revenue agents are not managerial employees. Rather they are "street-level" personnel (Danzinger & Kramer, 1986), the technical specialists who actually conduct audits, the product of the Examination Division. Thus the computer and software are production tools.
4. Users are professionals.[6] Although revenue agents are not managers, they also are not clerks or secretaries. All revenue agents are accountants, and many are CPAs. Their duties require extensive knowledge of tax law and considerable skills in auditing and accounting. And unlike most federal employees, revenue agents must charge their time on an hourly basis to specific audits in their inventory.
5. All users are doing approximately the same kinds of tasks. Although there is some specialization within the Examination Division, by far the largest contingent of revenue agents work "general program" cases. These are small to moderate corporations, as well as complex individual returns. All the data reported here are from general program agents and their managers.

6. All users received the same technology. This study, therefore, controls for technology, because every agent received an identical laptop portable computer with identical software and similar teaching materials, all of which were developed (or purchased) and distributed by the national office.

PART 2: THE IMPLEMENTATION PROCESS

This part of the chapter uses the interview data to describe the implementation process and form some hypotheses about how certain variables influence the success of implementation. Treating implementation as a learning process focuses on whether a particular variable promotes or hinders the learning process. Conceptually, every hypothesis asks the same questions: Does this variable (e.g., on-the-job training) contribute to learning and thereby to the success of the implementation?

Training

Training marks the first step of the implementation process as I define it here. The entire group of revenue agents (12 to 14) received Phase 1 training together with their manager. The collective training process built shared knowledge as they helped one another with problems, cursed about the printer paper, laughed at one another's "beeps," and traded little war stories (a favorite pastime among IRS agents). Van Maanen (1978) observed that collective processes encourage new initiates to share notes and help one another with problems. This can give rise to shared meanings that divert from and even subvert the "official" view.

The general outline of the AES training cycle was as follows: Laptops were issued on the first day, and agents could take them home that night. The training schedule for AES varied somewhat because the districts had some latitude in customizing and administering the training to meet the needs of their agents. The format for training was as follows:

1. Classroom: four days, covering hardware, disk handling, DOS familiarization, and the 1040 Workcenter.
2. "OJT" period: three weeks, for on-the-job training in the use of the Workcenter in the field doing training audits.
3. Classroom: three days, exercise in Enable word-processing and spreadsheets.
4. "OJT" period: two weeks, for on-the-job training in the use of Enable and the Workcenter in the field.

Classroom training

AES training begins in the classroom, which is the classic formal socialization setting. Training is conducted in special rooms with desk space and outlets for all of the laptops set aside specifically for this purpose. The agents participating are clearly "in training" and insulated from their regular duties. Lectures and exercises were alternated so that agents got immediate practice on each topic covered. The content of the classroom training was provided by standard texts written in the national office. Each class had two or three instructors, so that there was always at least one "rover" to give people individual help during the exercises. In each of the four districts where I conducted interviews, agents reported that it was among the best IRS training sessions they had ever attended.[7]

Nonetheless, there is a gap between what is taught in the classroom and what is needed to apply the tools to real cases. As part of the fieldwork required in studying this implementation, I attended classroom training sessions for Workcenter and Enable. According to the instructors and the opinions of many students in the classes, the material covered was necessary but not sufficient for using the computer in the field. One manager explained it this way:

> You see the training familiarizes them with the PC and the software, but not really with the use of the system in the field. There's another level of competence that they need to be able to really use it. There's a big difference between the skills you get in class and what you need in the field.

On-the-job training

The purpose of on-the-job training (OJT) is to help bridge the gap between classroom skills and real-world skills. OJT is intended to give informal, personalized attention to agents doing their regular work with the laptop. OJT thus forms a sharp contrast with the formal classroom setting, although formal group workshops are a common part of OJT. At least one on-the-job instructor (OJI) is assigned to each group during OJT.

Although the general format for OJT was determined by the national office, the quality actually delivered varied quite markedly between districts. In two of the districts I visited, the on-the-job instructors were not really available for helping the trainees. This seemed to stem from a heavy overall workload, which meant that the instructors had to work on their own cases during the training period. As a result, they could not give trainees their undivided attention, as explained by this trainee:

> The OJI was not very good. They scheduled three Mondays for OJT, but then the person who was the OJI just went over to his desk and started working on something else. So when you had a question, it was like "What are you bothering me for?"
>
> Another thing was the training audits. We got these training audits, but we didn't get them far enough in advance so that we could schedule a meeting with the taxpayer during the OJT period and start the audit. By the time people had started their training audits, a lot of them had forgotten how to use the software.

By contrast, the OJT in the other two districts was outstanding. This agent was initially very negative about AES, but OJT turned her around:

> I had an attitude problem: Training messed up my schedule, and I resented it. . . . I did not want to start using the PC. The first case I took it on, I didn't plan to. Most everyone had someone go with them on early PC visits. My group manager came on an individual return, and the OJI came with

> me to do a partnership. These visits worked out very well. These visits were vital in getting me to use the PC and feel comfortable.
>
> The instructors have been incredible. I don't think they've been given the credit they deserve in bringing us on-line. They did a lot of things above and beyond the call of duty, but totally necessary.

Clearly, the formal training process, classroom and OJT, is important to the success of the implementation. The hypotheses arising from these observations are simply that good classroom training and good on-the-job training will promote the success of the implementation.

Taking time to learn

In order to incorporate the PC into their daily work, revenue agents needed to take additional time on the job to learn. Each district officially had only one full-time support person assigned, and that person was responsible for coordinating hardware maintenance. In some districts, AES trainers would often provide unofficial, ongoing support. But ultimately, most users were on their own after the training period. They had to invest a considerable amount of time figuring out how to address new situations with the available tools so that they could work more quickly next time. The interviews suggested that this was true of all users, even those with significant previous computer experience and good training. In effect, agents and their managers were being asked to take time now in order to save time later. But taking that time conflicted with important organizational values regarding time and performance, which created a dilemma for the revenue agents.

"Time on case" is an important measure of performance at the IRS, and along with various other measures, it is used to allocate resources and establish program priorities. Time is tracked by case; agents bill their time to the case in their inventory using a form called the 4502. This form is not only the revenue agent time sheet; it also provides data about the status of audits in process. Although time is tracked and reported back to management at the district branch and group levels, along with other statistics, it is not used to review managers or agents or to establish quotas.

Nonetheless, the emphasis on time is woven deeply into the fabric of the organizational culture. Part of the felt pressure on time stems from the way that newcomers are informally socialized by their peers. According to a branch manager with 24 years at IRS,

> From my first day in the service, the people all around me said, "Keep time on case low, or they'll get you for it. And stay away from fraud cases, because the time on case is way too high, and they'll get you for it for sure." But the managers *never* say that to the agents; I don't, my boss never did, and nobody else does. But I'd bet you anything that if you go down to the first floor and ask them, they'll probably tell you, "Keep time on case low and stay away from fraud cases."

Time becomes critical to revenue agents in other ways as well. For example, cases must be opened within the statute of limitations for taxation. Once opened, there is pressure from the taxpayer and from management to complete them quickly. There are priority cases (e.g., from the Tax Compliance Measurement Program,

TCMP) that have stringent deadlines for completion. So elapsed time is also important in addition to the cumulative time spent working on the case. Although there has been an effort in recent years to deemphasize time on case as a performance statistic (in favor of quality), keeping time on case low is still an important cultural norm for the revenue agent in the field.

An AES instructor (a GS-12) pointed out the problem that this norm presents to agents learning to use the laptop:

> It's pounded into their heads from the very beginning—time on case, time on case, keep it low, keep it low. So it's really hard for the agent to accept that it's OK for them to take time to learn.

The problem is simply that learning to use the computer takes a considerable amount of time that agents generally feel they cannot afford to take. In all of the sites visited, management espoused the official policy of allowing agents to take extra time if needed. But an agent in one district expressed some skepticism about how the policy worked out in practice:

> You have to force yourself to use the computer right now. It really doesn't save any time at first. They tell you that you have all the time in the world to do these exams with the PC, but in practice it doesn't work out that way. After the exam, they'll ask, "Why all the hours on the exam?" and it really doesn't help to say, "Because I used the PC." The pressure is always on to keep the hours down and the yield up.

Similarly, agents in another district needed approval from their group manager to put extra hours on a case. But in the two other districts, management seems to have gotten the message across, so that agents felt more free to learn.

> The management has said that time is not a problem, as long as you're working and learning. Time on case is on the back burner. There is historically a strong emphasis on time, so this is unusual. We don't feel any pressure at all to meet time-on-case criteria for stuff we do with the PC. They really don't seem to care, for the time being, anyway. They expect time to go up.

Thus, a crucial feature in this implementation process was the extent to which management could free agents from the usual norms of keeping time low and allow them the time they needed to learn. The hypothesis here is that those sites at which a lenient policy regarding time on case was effectively communicated and enforced, the implementation should be more successful.

Discretionary use?

Although using a computer was officially optional, this policy apparently received rather different interpretations in various districts. According to a manager in one site, "Official word has been that in 18 months, the PC will be a critical element. In the meantime, we'll get you help." "A critical element" is part of the revenue agent's job description.[8] As mentioned earlier, the NTEU had explicitly excluded computer use from the revenue agent's review criteria. The group manager grades agents on the basis of standards set for the critical elements, which include accuracy of work, timeliness, and the like. Promotions and awards are contingent on performance on critical elements, as is continued employment. An agent who fails a critical element should start looking for another job.

In two of the districts where I conducted interviews, it seemed to be common knowledge that PC use would definitely be required in the near future (although group managers did not yet use it for employee reviews). But in the other two districts, agents and managers had a much more circumspect attitude: "Maybe, somewhere down the line, it might be required." In general, there was very little urgency to learn the technology. The significance of this belief can be seen by comparing the following two remarks, the first from an agent who does not believe the PC will be mandatory, and the second from one who does.

> The main thing is, it's not mandated. If we don't have to do it and we have a choice of using pencil and paper, which is faster, most people are going to use pencil and paper. It should be mandatory, the time to work on the PC, otherwise people will put it off and never get around to it.
>
> The computer becoming a critical element is a big item, a real big item. It doesn't matter if you like it or not, you'll have to use it. What are you gonna do about it? It's become a real topic of conversation in the last six months, lots of templates, lots of interest.

Because agents are under pressure to complete examinations "in a timely manner" (i.e., as quickly as possible), they are reluctant to do anything they do not have to do, especially if it takes extra time. Learning to use the laptop certainly takes extra time up front, and it may not save much time later. Working from this premise and the norms on time, optional use may lead to no use. On the other hand, the belief that computer use will soon be required is a powerful incentive for learning.

The learning curve and the forgetting curve

If implementation is a learning process, and learning leads to use, then there should be an improvement in reported levels of use over time. In other words, there should be a learning curve of some kind. Almost everyone interviewed believed strongly that "once they got up to speed, they'd use the computer a lot more." Of course, a new user cannot just wait until he or she gets up to speed. As suggested in the quotation, users need to "force themselves" to use the computer until they get better through practice.

Some users, however, were forced to wait before putting their training into use, because of a job assignment mechanism used in IRS called a *detail*. One interviewee completed his training in January and then was detailed at the Taxpayer Service Division to answer questions until April 15. He had forgotten nearly everything he learned in his training by the time he was in a position to put his knowledge to use. And although the learning curve may be rather gradual, the forgetting curve (as experienced by this agent) seems to be quite precipitous. Until new skills have had a chance to be reinforced through experience on the job, they appear to be quite volatile and slip away quickly.

PART 3: ANALYSIS AND RESULTS OF SURVEY DATA

This part of the chapter uses results from a survey of revenue agents to test the hypotheses generated from the interview data.

Implementation success: Use, performance, and satisfaction

A central problem for any implementation research is developing measures of success. Frequently, user satisfaction is taken as a proxy for success on the assumption that users are well motivated and knowledgeable about whether their needs are being met (Doll & Torkzadeh, 1988). Use is another important measure of success, as use is a prerequisite for benefits (Trice & Treacy, 1988). When clear performance measures exist, they are probably the most desirable, as they relate most closely to the underlying cost-benefit aspects of the project.

In this survey we had indicators of all three kinds of implementation success: use, performance, and satisfaction. Measured in terms of use or satisfaction, the implementation of AES was fairly successful. Two-thirds of the revenue agents used the computer for at least 10 hours per week, and more than 78 percent believe that it is an appropriate and helpful tool (Table 16.1). However, only 15 percent believe that the computer saves overall time on case. This is true even though almost 75 percent believe that it is faster for some tasks, as shown in Table 16.1.

The discrepancy between the efficiency of the laptop for some tasks and its overall impact is accounted for by more than 60 percent of the respondents using the laptop for tasks that would be faster to do by hand. Unfortunately, there are no data in the survey regarding the relative frequency or importance of tasks that were sped up or slowed down by the laptop. But it seems that for the mix of tasks to which agents apply it, the laptop is a mixed blessing. It is faster for some, slower for others, and, according to more than 60 percent of them, slower overall on balance. The impact of AES on the overall productivity of users is ambiguous at best and quite possibly negative.

Relationships among use, performance, and satisfaction

The results shown in Table 16.1 are supported by the correlation matrix shown in Table 16.2. Although use correlates with satisfaction ($r = 0.46$) and satisfaction correlates with performance ($r = 0.54$), use and performance correlate rather weakly ($r = 0.14$). The first two relationships make sense, given the norms in the IRS for working quickly and saving time: Satisfied agents use the PC more, and they believe that it helps them save time. But the weak relationship between use and performance tends to confirm that revenue agents are using the PC whether or not they believe it reduces overall time on case. This interpretation is strengthened by the correlations among use, performance, and the tendency to use the laptop even when it is slower. Agents who used it even when it was slower used it more ($r = 0.31$), and as a result, they reported a somewhat lower overall performance ($r = -0.17$).

There are several possible explanations of these results. First, the respondents (with between three and 24 months of experience at the time of the survey) may not yet be fully up to speed. They are investing time now in learning, hoping to save

Table 16.1. Raw indicators of implementation success

	Percent	*n*
Use: "How many hours per week do you currently use the laptop?"		
Zero (Do not use)	4.7	51
Less than 1 hour per week	3.6	40
1 to 5 hours per week	13.9	152
5 to 9 hours per week	12.7	138
10 to 14 hours per week	16.0	174
15 to 19 hours per week	14.6	159
20 hours or more per week	34.5	376
Total	100.0	1090
Satisfaction: "The laptop is an appropriate tool for Revenue Agents."		
Strongly agree	32.2	355
Agree	45 9	305
Not sure	12.4	137
Disagree	6.4	71
Strongly disagree	3.1	33
Total	100.0	1101
Performance: "On the whole, the laptop reduces time on case."		
Strongly agree	4.3	47
Agree	10.7	118
Not sure	23.8	264
Disagree	32.5	356
Strongly disagree	28.7	315
Total	100.0	1100
"The laptop allows me to do things faster."		
Strongly agree	26.8	296
Agree	47.6	525
Not sure	11.0	121
Disagree	8.8	97
Strongly disagree	5.8	64
Total	100.0	1103
Do you ever use the laptop on something that you know would be faster by hand"		
Frequently	18.1	198
Sometimes	52.6	577
Rarely	16.8	184
Never	12.5	137
Total	100.0	1096

time later. If this is true, then there should be a positive relationship between the time since training and performance. Another possibility is that the fit between the technology and the task is such that it simply does not save time to use the computer, regardless of how much or how well one uses it. This possibility has already been discussed and is beyond the scope of the data available here to answer. A third possibility is that some other factor (e.g., management policy) is causing agents to use the laptop whether or not they normally would; that is, whether or not it saves time.

Regardless of how one interprets these data, there is an important message for research on MIS implementation: Not all measures of success are equal. In particular, a project that looks like a success in terms of use can still be a failure in terms of

Table 16.2. Correlations among use, performance, and satisfaction[a]

	Use	Performance	Satisfaction	Some things faster
Use				
Performance	0.14*			
Satisfaction	0.46*	0.54*		
Some things faster	0.44*	0.50*	0.74*	
Use even if slower	0.31*	–0.17*	0.01	0.01

*$p \leq 0.0001$ $n = 945$

[a]The correlation is shown in this table are computed using scales for use, performance and satisfaction as described in the text. These scales estimate the underlying constructs more reliably than the single indicators used in Table 16.1.

actual productivity improvements. Although measures of productivity are notoriously difficult to find, one should not assume that use can serve as a proxy. In order to insulate the results here from this pitfall, I used each of the three measures to analyze the effects of training, management, and other variables on implementation success.

Variables that influence implementation success

In my analysis, I measured each aspect of implementation success using a scale that combines multiple items from the survey, including those presented in Table 16.1. The indicators were combined to create more reliable estimates of the underlying constructs, with three indicators of use combined to create a scale.[9] I measured satisfaction by four items regarding the appropriateness and helpfulness of the computer in the work,[10] and I gauged performance by means of two items that ask whether overall time on case is higher or lower with the laptop.[11] These variables and the reliability of the resulting scales are summarized in Table 16.3.

Table 16.3 also describes the variables used for the constructs identified in the qualitative discussion, as well as some additional variables that were included as controls. Two variables measured specific aspects of training. The first (INSTRUCT) is perceived experience and training ability. The second (OJT) counts the number of distinct activities included in on-the-job training (e.g., full-time instructor, instructor came to field, had training cases, had workshops).

The perception that management policy on time on case was helpful was measured by TOC POLICY. The perception that use would soon be required was measured by HAVETO. Because not all respondents were trained simultaneously, it was useful to have a measure of time since training. This variable (TIME) was measured on a seven-point interval scale (with three-month intervals) and can be used to look for learning curve effects. Likewise, the gap between training and actual use (GAP) was measured by a four-point interval scale (with one-week intervals). This variable can be used to estimate the "forgetting" effects described earlier.

Finally, a set of control variables was included. The prior experience of the agent with computers was measured by PRIOR. The grade level of the agent (GRADE) was an important proxy for a variety of different effects. Most revenue agents start at GS-7 or GS-9 and progress automatically to GS-11 in their first two years. Promotions to GS-12 and GS-13 are competitive but generally reflect more seniority. Thus, grade level captures job tenure, but more important, it captures dif-

Table 16.3. Independent and dependent variables

Variable	Number of items	Alpha	Description
Use	3	0.78	Combines number of tasks automated, number of system features used and hours of use.
Satisfaction	4	0.86	Items on appropriateness, effectiveness and helpfulness.
Performance	2	0.72	Does it take more or less time to complete your work with the PC?
INSTRUCT	2	0.82	Instructor ability and experience
OJT	4	0.74	Quality of on-the-job training
TOC POLICY	1		How helpful was management policy regarding time on case?
HAVETO	4	0.70	I use the computer because I feel I have to, I will be evaluated on it, etc.
TIME	1		Time between training and date of survey (February 1988).
GAP	I		Gap between training and first use of computer on the job.
PRIOR	1		Prior experience with computers (before AES training).
GRADE	1		Grade level of respondent.
Gender	1		Gender (1 = male; 2 = female)
Age	1		Age of respondent (seven-point scale)

ferences in the kinds of work that agents do as they become more skilled. Junior agents do large numbers of simple audits, mostly 1040s, and senior agents do fewer but more complex cases. Finally, gender and age are included as generic controls, with age measured on a nine-point scale with five-year increments (1 = 25 or under, 9 = more than 60).

Predicting implementation success

Table 16.4 presents a set of three regressions (one for each outcome measure), with all of the management, training, and control variables included as predictors. These regressions can be used to test the hypotheses stated earlier. The entries in Table 16.4 are standardized regression coefficients, and a significant, positive coefficient indicates a positive influence on the outcome measure.

In addition to the variables discussed so far, the regressions in Table 16.4 include seven dummy variables that represent the influence of the seven IRS regions. The regions are included to test and to control for regional differences. Although it is beyond the scope of this analysis to explain why the outcomes varied by region, it is clear from the results in Table 16.4 that they did. Controlling for these regional differences helped give a clearer picture of the variables in which we are interested. Note that regional differences were among the strongest effects shown in Table 16.4.

Table 16.4. Use, performance, and satisfaction

Independent variable	Dependent variable		
	Use	Performance	Satisfaction
INSTRUCT	0.06	0.09*	0.16**
OJT	0.08*	0.09	0.03
TOC POLICY	0.17**	0.11**	0.19**
HAVETO	0.14**	–0.17**	–0.07
TIME	0.19**	0.0L	0.04
GAP	–0.20**	–0.04	–0.09*
PRIOR	0.21**	0.05	0.17**
GRADE	–0.12**	–0.01	–0.06
Gender	0.03	–0.03	–0.02
Age	–0.04	–0.03	–0.02
Regions			
North Atlantic	–0.26**	–0.05	–0.16**
Mid-Atlantic	–0.13**	–0.08	–0.12**
Southeast	–0.09	–0.15**	–0.09
Southwest	0	0	0
Central	0.01	–0.07	–0.08
Western	–0.10*	0.09	–0.01
Midwest	–0.02	–0.02	–0.09*
Adjusted R^2	0.31	0.12	0.20
Df Regression	16	16	16
Df Residual	1008	965	1014
F value	30.02	9.19	16.97

*P < 0.01 **p < 0.001

Effects of training

The ability and experience of training instructors had a small, positive influence on all three measures of success, with the strongest influence on satisfaction. On-the-job training also had a small, positive influence on use, but a small negative influence on perceived time savings and no significant influence on satisfaction. These findings seem to contradict the importance placed by some interviewees on on-the-job training. If performance or satisfaction were the only outcome measures, we would have to reject the hypothesis that on-the-job training contributes to implementation success.[12] The relatively minor effect of on-the-job training may have been due to the relatively low variation in the indicator used in the survey. A better measure of the quality of OJT might produce different results.

Effects of management policy

The results regarding time-on-case policy and discretionary use are quite interesting. As expected, the policy that allowed agents to take the time they needed to learn (TOC POLICY) had a positive influence on use, performance, and satisfaction. This suggests the wisdom of encouraging users to continue learning on the job and establishing policies that allow them to do so. The outcome with respect to performance tends to contradict the possibility that the self-reported performance measure is based solely on expectations. The positive coefficient on TOC POLICY indicated that telling users that time on case was expected to increase (and that this was all right) actually reduced time on case. The management policy regarding the discretionary use (HAVETO) told quite a different story. Table 16.4 shows that this policy (or its absence) has an opposite effect on use and performance. Discretionary use seemed to lead to lower levels of use but to higher levels of performance and satisfaction, whereas mandatory use had the opposite effects. Generally, agents used the computer more if they felt they had to, but they reported that it took them longer to do their work. This pattern is consistent with the results in Tables 16.1 and 16.2. It appears that the tendency of management in some locations to require use caused some agents to use the computer for tasks that they could have done faster by hand, thus lowering their overall productivity.

It may be that those agents who felt obligated to use the computer were investing more time in learning, regardless of the immediate efficacy of doing so. Some care should be taken in interpreting this finding, however, because the self-reported performance data reflect the subjective impression that having to use the PC takes longer, rather than its actually taking longer. But with this caveat in mind, this is an important finding for the debate concerning control-oriented implementation strategies, because it suggests that although a policy of mandatory use can promote use, it can also reduce productivity.

Learning and forgetting

As expected, the time since training (TIME) had a fairly strong positive influence on use: The longer an agent had had the PC, the more he or she used it. But it had little or no effect on perceived performance and satisfaction. This was a rather surprising outcome, because it suggests that performance does not improve with experience, that there is no learning curve for the laptop. This finding also tends to rule out inexperience as an explanation of the low productivity results shown in Table 16.1, because productivity apparently does not vary with experience.

Another interpretation for this result is that people probably do improve over time but that they are weakly influenced by changes in their own performance (i.e., they are poor judges of time, biased by prior expectations, and so on). Perceived performance would be relatively insensitive to actual performance if that were the case. Depending on whether success is measured by use or by performance and satisfaction, one would either accept or reject the idea that implementation success improves over time.

The results regarding the gap after training (GAP) were also somewhat ambiguous. Agents who were unable to start using the computer immediately after training used it significantly less. But like the learning curve, the forgetting curve did not seem to apply very strongly to perceived performance or satisfaction.

Prior experience, grade level, gender, and age

Prior experience with computers (PRIOR) had a significant positive influence on use and satisfaction but not on performance. This finding contradicted the expectation that persons with prior skills should be able to use a tool more effectively. Either the skills are irrelevant, or the tool is not particularly helpful. The weight of the evidence here is accumulating for the latter interpretation. Notwithstanding this ambiguity in the performance outcome, the message in this finding is familiar and clear: Implementation success can be enhanced by selecting employees with appropriate prior training or experience.

Grade level affects use, with higher-grade agents using the computer less often than lower-grade agents do. This difference is probably more a function of the complex nature of the audits done by higher-grade agents. Gender and age apparently had no effect at all on use, performance, or satisfaction. After controlling for differences in grade level, the old timers appeared to be just as successful at using the new tools as the younger agents were.

PART 4: CONCLUSION

As we mentioned at the end of Part 1, the nature of the task and the technology in the Examination Division set some limits on how much we can generalize from these results. Revenue agents work alone and so do their computer systems. The fact that using the computer was basically discretionary and that the choice was purely personal are critical features of this situation. Nonetheless, there are some important lessons to learn from this case.

The first lesson is what it means to have a successful implementation. According to the data presented here, high levels of use are not necessarily associated with large increases in productivity, which is an important objective of the computerization effort.

Whether this shortfall reflects the need for more training, a poorly designed system, or both, is a question that lies beyond the scope of this analysis. But if productivity failed to improve over time, would the implementation be a failure? As mentioned in Part 1, revenue agents greatly value the improved work they are able to produce with the computer.

The value-added from the computer might lie in better-looking, more readable work products rather than improved productivity per se. The laptop may provide other symbolic benefits to revenue agents, by adding to their professional "front" and by allowing them to keep up with their counterparts in the private sector.[13] Ultimately, the best justification for AES may not be economic after all.

But if economic justification is important, then productivity needs to be measured. The findings here make it clear that use is not a good proxy for productivity. Rather, user satisfaction is a much better indicator of productivity improvements, although it would presumably capture the more intangible symbolic benefits as well.

The next lesson concerns the importance of training. Although the survey data are somewhat ambiguous with respect to performance improvements, it is clear that good instructors and on-the-job training are necessary ingredients for successful implementation. It is also clear that training should be immediately put into use, for the gap between training and actual use experienced by some agents was among the strongest negative influences on use. The fact that a gap could be so devastating points to the value of what was lost and to its extreme volatility.

Of course, the learning process does not stop after training. The data here suggest that management has an important role in creating an atmosphere in which learning can continue on the job. In the context of AES, that meant giving agents some breathing room from the usual time pressures, to experiment with the computer without being penalized. This single management policy was the strongest, least ambiguous predictor of success in the implementation effort.

One of the great mysteries of this research was the substantial differences between regions. For example, the North Atlantic and Mid-Atlantic regions had significantly lower levels of use and satisfaction than did the rest of the country. I have no explanation for these differences, but the IRS personnel offered a variety of folk theories on the subject during follow-up interviews. All of these theories were somewhat plausible; none could be tested (with the available data); and they usually involved a broad generalization of "People are different there."[14]

Whether or not the people are different there, something certainly was, because the outcomes were different. The lesson here is that implementation success may depend on a broader set of contextual factors as well as on more identifiable factors, such as training and management support. If these differences do arise from contextual factors, such as regional culture or labor markets, then they are likely to fall outside the organization's control. If the findings here are any indication, they are just as important as anything else management does.

NOTES

1. This view leaves out some important earlier steps, such as design. A more complete picture of the implementation process (cf. Kwon & Zmud, 1987) would include earlier steps, which are equally vital to the overall success of the technology.
2. The Examination Division is the part of the IRS that conducts audits; there are separate divisions for Collection, Taxpayer Services, and so on. In this paper, I use *IRS* for brevity, but I refer only to the Examination Division. Note also that although the term *division* is used in district field offices, the term *function* would be better for the Examination Division at the national level.
3. This survey was designed and administered by Price Waterhouse under contract to the IRS. The sample also included an additional 500 group managers whose responses are not analyzed in this paper.
4. Each agent and group manager received a portable MS-DOS computer with two 5–1/4 inch floppy disk drives, a gray LCD screen, and an external power supply. The unit folds like a small, rather thick briefcase and weighs about 12 pounds.
5. Another interpretation for these comments is that these users were still learning to use the system. Although this is certainly a consideration for the population of revenue agents as a whole, these particular comments came from two of the most experienced AES users that I interviewed, one of whom had been an avid home user for years. If these individuals still are not "up to speed," then the possibility of an average user's becoming fluent in a reasonable time must be questioned.
6. The term *professional* has a technical sociological definition (cf. Etzioni, 1969) that is not fully met by IRS revenue agents. For example, it is not evident that their loyalty is primarily to their profession. Rather, their loyalty is to their employer, the IRS, because other members of the accounting profession at large are their adversaries. There is also an ongoing debate in the IRS on the status of the revenue agents, with some older agents claiming that they are now merely "tax technicians," not "real professionals."
7. The basic model of classroom training followed by OJT is used in all IRS training; Revenue agents learn tax law, auditing, and IRS procedures in the same general format.
8. "Critical elements" are part of the contract negotiated with the IRS by the NTEU.
9. The three items are (1) number of tasks automated (e.g., computations, work papers, document requests, etc.); (2) number of features used (e.g., world processing, spreadsheet, workcenter, etc.); and (3) hours of use per week.

10. The four items, measured on a five-point scale, are (1) The laptop enhances my ability to contribute to my job; (2) the laptop is appropriate equipment for revenue agents; (3) the laptop enhances my pride in my work; and (4) the laptop allows me to do more.

11. One of the items refers to the particular respondent ("Do you spend more or less time on cases?"), and the other item is ambiguous as to its reference ("Overall, the laptop reduces time on case."). Because the items correlate strongly (0.56, $n = 1000$), they combine to make a reasonable scale ($r = 0.72$).

12. Technically speaking, we would fail to reject the null hypothesis that OJT does *not* contribute to implementation success.

13. Pentland (1988) described in some detail the symbolic and presentational value of the computer.

14. According to one such folk theory, easterners do not like to be told what to do, whereas people in other parts of the country are more likely to go with the flow. In short, easterners have an "attitude problem." Although I do not subscribe to this particular theory, it does indicate the kinds of regional differences that might in fact be operating.

REFERENCES

Benson, D. H. (1983). A field study of end user computing: Findings and issues. *MIS Quarterly* 7:35–46.

Danzinger, J. N., & K. L. Kraemer (1986). *People and computers: The impacts of computing on end users in organizations*. New York: Columbia University Press.

Doll, W. J., & G. Torkzadeh (1988). The measurement of end-user computing satisfaction. *MIS Quarterly,* June, pp. 259–74.

Etzioni, A. (Ed.) (1969). *The semi-professions and their organizations.* New York: Free Press.

Kwon, T. H., & R. W. Zmud (1987). Unifying the fragmented models of information systems implementation. In R. J. Boland & R. A. Hirschheim (Eds.), *Critical issues in information systems research.* Chichester: Wiley.

Pentland, B. T. (1988). AES in the IRS: An interactionist view of enduser computing in the Internal Revenue Service. Paper presented at the Academy of Management, Division of Technology and Innovation Management, Anaheim, CA, August.

Rivard, S. (1987). Successful implementation of end-user computing. *Interfaces* 17 (May-June): 25–33.

Rockart, J. F., & L. S. Flannery (1983). The management of end user computing. *Communications of the ACM* 26:776–84.

Tomer, J. F. (1988). *Organizational capital: The path to higher productivity and well-being*. New York: Praeger.

Trice, A., & M. Treacy (1988). Utilization as a dependent variable in MIS research. *Database*, Fall-Winter, pp. 33–41.

Van Maanen, J. (1978). People processing: Strategies of organizational socialization. *Organizational Dynamics*, Summer, pp. 18–36.

CHAPTER 17

Computer-aided Monitoring: Its Influence on Employee Job Satisfaction and Turnover

JOHN CHALYKOFF AND THOMAS A. KOCHAN

In the last few years, few human resource issues have spawned as intense a public debate as computer-aided monitoring has. To the critics, monitoring conjures up images of repressive managerial control practices associated with an earlier period of American industrialization, namely "19th century garment industry sweatshops" (9 to 5, 1986). Moreover, the capability of information technology to electronically monitor employees' interactions with clients is viewed as an invasion of privacy and ultimately denigrating to employees (Nussbaum & duRivage, 1986; Shaiken, 1987).

On the other hand, proponents view monitoring as essential to conducting business and largely beneficial to employees for their training ("Telephone Monitoring," 1987). Monitoring employees' interactions with the organization's clients, it is argued, both provides feedback to employees and helps ensure the satisfaction of customers in their dealings with the organization.

Although negative consequences of the technology—high stress, low levels of job satisfaction, absenteeism, and high turnover (Jacobson, 1984; Nussbaum & duRivage, 1986; Shaiken, 1987)—have been reported, the limited anecdotal evidence and a handful of case studies available to date provide little in the way of testable hypotheses for determining the validity of these claims. But there are a few studies that do help establish a testable framework for sorting out these competing claims. For example, in a careful case study of an insurance office, Attewell (1987) examined managers' views of the role of monitoring in the workplace, and its actual use. His findings suggest that managerial orientations toward monitoring and managers' use of monitoring are much more benign than the critics claim. The U.S. Congress Office of Technology Assessment stressed the importance of performance feedback in work settings where computer-aided monitoring takes place. The report argues that because performance is monitored continually in these settings and "employees perceive that rewards or punishments could ensue from an evaluation of their performance, they are especially interested in feedback" (1987, p. 56).

Although these studies provide a useful empirical and theoretical starting point for assessing the impact of information technology, none has linked characteristics of the monitoring process to standard employee-level job outcomes such as job satisfaction and turnover intention. Yet this focus is needed to uncover the actual role that monitoring plays in the employment relationship and the extent to which its potentially negative effects are inherent or can be mitigated by attention to feedback processes.

This chapter addresses these issues by testing the extent to which satisfaction with computer-aided monitoring plays a central role in mediating the relationships between its antecedents and employee job satisfaction and turnover propensity. We then compare the explanatory power of this mediating role with the effects of monitoring on job satisfaction and turnover propensity that occur because of employees' opposition to monitoring.

Because no previous study has developed and tested a theoretical model related to employees' attitudinal responses to computer-aided monitoring, we conducted 91 primary interviews with employees, supervisors, and managers in five offices of the Automated Collection System (ACS), which is part of the Tax Collection Division of the United States Internal Revenue Service (IRS). The interviews were essential to drawing up theoretical propositions unique to computerized work settings. The offices at which the interviews were conducted used computer-aided monitoring of employee performance. Computer-aided monitoring in these offices is referred to as *telephone monitoring* and consists of objective and subjective components. The subjective component requires supervisors to listen in on employees' work-related calls, usually without the employee's knowledge of the monitoring, while they simultaneously view on a video display terminal the case that the employee is working on. The objective component is continuous computer tracking of performance indicators such as the employee's average talk time, number of calls completed, and number of calls attempted. We next present the results of our interviews with managers supervisors and employees.

RESULTS OF THE INTERVIEWS: CONTROL OR FEEDBACK?

The following statements, made by managers, supervisors, and employees in the three groups we interviewed, are representative of each group's views of computer-aided monitoring.

Managers: There is variation in the way that senior managers in the ACS offices conceive the use and consequences of computer-aided monitoring. For example, one manager stated:

> It has value inasmuch as it keeps employees on their toes. The more they are monitored, the more they realize there's a cop around the bend.

Almost as an afterthought, this manager added, "It's a positive tool also." Although others conceive the potential of monitoring more positively, they regard its use as less positive than it might be.

> Employees like to know how they're doing. The times when I see problems are when employees don't know what they're doing. The thing is how you use the information. Sometimes we fall down.

The view that monitoring is essential to conducting the work in these offices came up repeatedly in the interviews. The managers felt that computer-aided monitoring was the only way to assess whether employees were "doing their jobs properly":

> I think monitoring is absolutely vital. Documentation of monitoring is the only method to ensure that (1) you're telling the taxpayer the right information; (2) it's the only way that a manager can tell if an employee is using the techniques; and (3) it's important for the employee's positive and critical feedback, to develop the employee.

In each of the five offices visited, managers were fairly clear about why they felt computer-aided monitoring was important, but in different orders of magnitude they were just as clear that the monitoring process was not being managed as well as it might be. One manager lamented:

> We need an understanding of how to manage an automated environment. I don't think we understand the effects of certain things on employees. . . . There are unique problems and concerns here. You can take a hard line on everything, and you get a bad situation. Supervisors are almost forced to give negative feedback. At various times there is a lot of distrust between management and employees.

Supervisors: Some supervisors noted the potential for training employees that monitoring allows, viewing it as "a great way to give employees instant feedback on their progress." This was often mentioned, though the reality was noted to be far different, due in many cases to the tension between meeting the monitoring requirement and achieving this feedback potential. One supervisor stated:

> Supervisors may not use it as the really good tool that it is. It's a positive thing. We resent it because it takes so much time. Supervisors may not want to do it, so it turns out being negative.

Indeed, supervisors related that on average they spend 25 hours a week on monitoring-related activities.

Other supervisors viewed the control potential of the technology as a positive addition to accomplishing their work. One noted that it was "far easier to identify your weak and strong employees." Another supervisor, speaking for what she felt was the majority view, observed:

> Supervisors like it [computer-aided monitoring] better because they are now able to control the work environment—reward good people, sit on bad people.

Some supervisors, however, were clearly disenchanted with what they perceived over time as an exercise lacking value—on the whole more dysfunctional than functional.

> I don't see that much difference whether I monitor or not. Things that I would identify don't seem that significant.

> Since I have to do the monitoring, I say something one way or the other.

> Monitoring just ends up being negative management.

Employees: Surprisingly, the majority of employees we interviewed agreed with management's assessment of the general need for monitoring and some of its positive impacts.

> We have to have monitoring. I'm sure we don't like to have it done to us all the time, but it's necessary for quality control and as a check on new procedures. It increases performance. I know when I get comments that say you forgot to do something, I try to do it the next time.

> Monitoring reminds you not to get careless and to keep up with new procedures. . . . I think that when you're first learning it would be good if all your calls were monitored.

> You get good feedback from monitoring. Most of mine was positive.

> If we weren't monitored, you'd get all kinds of things going on.

However, another more negative side to monitoring was raised by employees.

> Some employees think it's being spied on.

> You can get a biased manager who is looking for the bad, rather than the good, in someone.

> They [supervisors] only tell you what you do wrong, not what was good.

> They [supervisors] give the feedback too late. By then you can't remember what happened in the call.

> Supervisors shouldn't be allowed to do any monitoring.

Employees also had mixed views of the objectivity of the monitoring process. One employee stated that she came to work in this setting because

> The performance evaluation is more objective. It doesn't depend on anyone's perception of what you're doing. You can argue on it, but it's right there for you to see and for them to see.

Other employees, however, disagreed that it was an objective process. Supervisory favoritism was often mentioned, as was the "central tendency" of performance ratings—"Everyone gets a 3"—on a five-point scale. Although the desired behaviors are made explicit in these offices, the actual criteria that the supervisors used to judge performance were often left unspecified.

Employees stressed that the approach taken by supervisors to computer-aided monitoring made all the difference. Some even suggested that supervisors "should do more telephone monitoring, but it should be used strictly as a quality control tool." They often felt that rather than a quality control tool it was frequently used as a "gotcha." Thus, most employees were not opposed to the use of computer-aided monitoring, but rather, they disliked the way that supervisors often used it as an approach characterized by negative feedback, delayed feedback, infrequent feedback, and subjective performance criteria.

On the whole, the interviews indicated, first, that computer-aided monitoring is a central activity that permeates the work in these automated offices; second, that the effective use of computer-aided monitoring and the employees' attitudinal responses depend largely on the characteristics of the performance-monitoring feedback process; and third, that there is the potential for control ("gotcha") or feedback ("employee development") to dominate the monitoring process. These interview results therefore led us to use the concepts of control and feedback as found in the performance appraisal literature to generate testable hypotheses for assessing the effects of computer monitoring on workplace outcomes.

CONCEPTUAL MODEL

Previous approaches to methods of control (Blau & Scott, 1962; Edwards, 1979; Eisenhardt, 1985; Ouchi, 1977; Ouchi & McGuire, 1975) treated control strategies as dependent variables to be explained by the nature of technology or the organization's task environment. In contrast, Chalykoff (1988) argued that there was need for a theoretical perspective capable of predicting individual responses to control strategies. Therefore, he place his study in a performance appraisal/feedback framework, as this offered a sharper analytical focus, recognizing, as does neither extreme in the debate over monitoring (Nussbaum & duRivage, 1986; Shaiken, 1987), that a monitoring and evaluation process has both control and feedback characteristics and that the employees' responses will differ depending on whether control or feedback dominates the monitoring process. Testing this required that the control process or activities take on the role of explanatory variables in predicting employees' affective responses to monitoring. In this chapter, the model is further developed, as shown in Figure 17.1.

Performance appraisal and feedback

The first stage of our model focuses on the factors derived from the interviews and rooted in the performance appraisal/feedback literature. These are (1) immediacy of feedback (U.S. Office of Technology Assessment, 1987), (2) the frequency of feedback (Taylor, Fisher, & Ilgen, 1984; Wexley, 1979), (3) the sign (positive or negative) of feedback (Halperin et al., 1976; Jacobs et al., 1973), (4) supervisory task knowledge (Halperin et al., 1976; Tuckman & Oliver, 1968), (5) supervisory consideration behavior (Halperin et al., 1976; Tuckman & Oliver, 1968), (6) tenure (Ilgen, Fisher, & Taylor, 1979), and (7) clarity of rating criteria (Berger, 1983). These studies found that performance feedback is useful for employee development when it is frequent, timely, and accurate; is based on objective criteria; and comes from a knowledgeable and trusted source.

Further, from interviews in automated offices, an additional variable emerged as a critical determinant. This variable is the absolute difference between the employees' actual percentage of remote monitoring and their percentage of desired remote monitoring.[1]

Taken together, these variables test the extent to which the employees' affective responses to monitoring are influenced by adherence to systematic feedback/ performance appraisal principles and practices. The results of the earlier study (Cha-

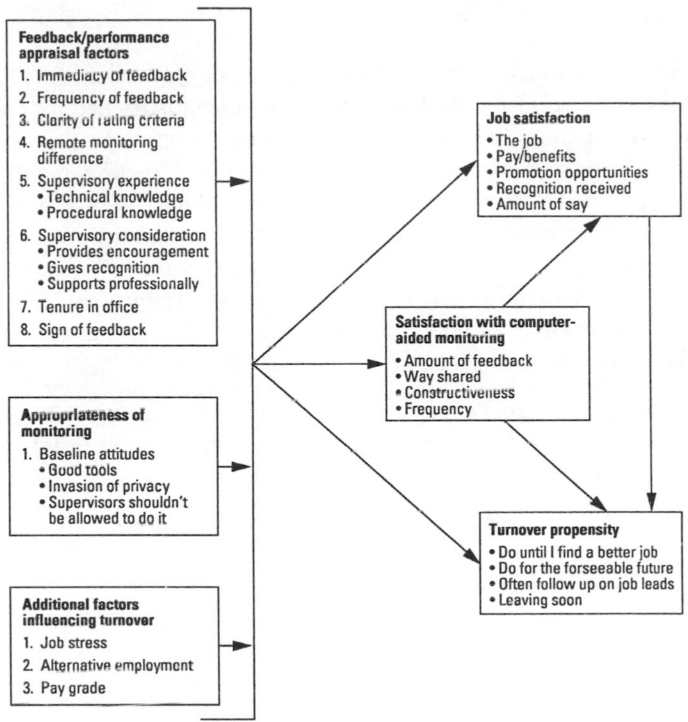

Figure 17.1. Conceptual model.

lykoff, 1988) showed that many of these variables (immediacy of feedback, sign of feedback, clarity of rating criteria, supervisory expertise, and supervisory consideration behavior) are significantly related to satisfaction with monitoring. By adding job satisfaction and turnover propensity as additional endogenous variables to the model, we can now test the extent to which the negative attitudinal consequences associated with monitoring can be avoided by adhering to these same principles.

Appropriateness of monitoring

Another exogenous variable was included in the model to capture the more generic effects of monitoring on satisfaction and turnover propensity that are not related significantly to specific perceptions of how well the monitoring process is managed (Chalykoff, 1988). This is an indication of employees' baseline beliefs about the appropriateness of monitoring employees. It is made up of three items assessing the extent to which employees agree or disagree that (1) monitoring is a good tool if it is used properly, (2) monitoring is an invasion of privacy, and (3) supervisors should not be allowed to do any monitoring.

The final set of control variables included in the model were added to reflect other important determinants of turnover that have been documented in previous research on this topic. These include job stress, alternative employment opportunities, and pay level (Cotton & Tuttle, 1986).

Hypotheses

As constructed, the model (Figure 17.1) is a mediational model. Its primary focus is on the indirect effects of the feedback process characteristics and the direct effects of satisfaction with monitoring on job satisfaction and turnover propensity. Put another way, this model tests for the centrality to the work situation of computer-aided monitoring, both as a direct determinant of job satisfaction and turnover propensity and as a mediator of other managerial practices that are expected to influence job satisfaction and turnover propensity through the employees' affective responses to monitoring. Significant indirect effects of the exogenous variables should be observed if monitoring is serving as an important mediating process or activity. The preceding discussion can be summarized as two formal hypotheses:

Hypothesis 1: *The indirect effects of the exogenous constructs, acting through satisfaction with computer-aided monitoring, have a significant influence on general work satisfaction and turnover propensity.*

Hypothesis 2: *Satisfaction with monitoring has a significant influence on job satisfaction and turnover propensity.*

METHOD

Data

A survey instrument based largely on our 91 interviews with employees, supervisors, and managers was developed and administered to 960 employees in the Automated Collection System. Seven hundred and forty completed questionnaires were returned for a response rate of 77 percent.

A list of all the indicators, together with questions from the questionnaire from which they were derived, is shown in Appendix 1. There are 30 indicators for the 12 exogenous constructs and three endogenous constructs in the model. The model (Figure 17.2) represents a structural equation system with observed variables and unobserved constructs. Six of the constructs—supervisory expertise, supervisory consideration behavior, employees' baseline attitudes toward computer-aided monitoring, satisfaction with computer-aided monitoring, general work satisfaction, and turnover propensity—are latent constructs derived from manifest (observed) variables.

The measure of turnover was propensity to leave and not actual leaving. Thus, we do not know the extent to which intentions to leave resulted in actual leaving. However, based on earlier empirical research, we can have some confidence that these two constructs are significantly related. In their meta-analysis of the turnover literature, Cotton and Tuttle (1986) found a positive and significant relationship in 15 of 16 studies that had used both constructs. Moreover, isolating the influence of monitoring on job satisfaction and intention to leave is by itself sufficient to assess the positive or negative impact of monitoring in these settings on employees' attitudinal responses, which is the principal focus of this chapter.

The model was tested using LISREL VI, with maximum-likelihood estimation (Joreskog & Sorbom, 1985). A principal strength of the LISREL program is its ca-

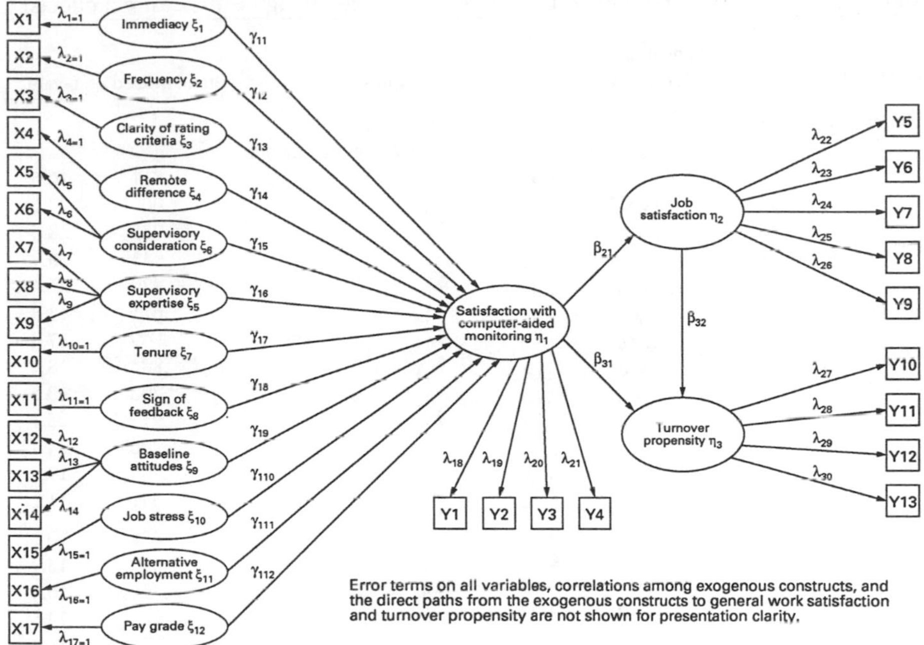

Figure 17.2. Structural equation path analytic model of satisfaction with computer-aided monitoring.

pability to estimate simultaneously the measurement model (loadings of observed variables on latent constructs) and the structural equation model (the causal relationship among latent constructs, and the unexplained variance). Missing observations on some of the variables reduced the sample size to 516 for the model tested.

Measurement tests

Reliability

All of the associated t-values for the measurement parameters (Table 17.1) are large and significant. This indicates that the variables explain a significant amount of the variation in the latent constructs they indicate. These parameter estimates can be used to calculate composite measure reliability (pc) of the constructs (Werts, Linn, & Joreskog, 1974), and these data can be seen in Table 17.2. The pc for supervisory expertise was 0.90; supervisory consideration behavior, 0.94; baseline attitudes, 0.76; satisfaction with monitoring, 0.91; job satisfaction, 0.78; and turnover propensity, 0.76.

These results indicate that the constructs have acceptable trait variance (Table 17.2). In addition, these results are the same as those derived from the more commonly used index, Cronbach's alpha.

Convergent and discriminant validity

We conducted a separate test of the convergent and discriminant validity of the endogenous constructs. This was necessary, as the satisfaction with monitoring construct was empirically, and not theoretically, derived. This construct validity test

Table 17.1. Maximum likelihood estimates for the model in Figure 17.1 (direct effects)

Causal paths	Standardized ML estimate	t-value
Endogenous constructs		
β_{21}	.269*	4.78
β_{32}	.125	1.88
β_{31}	–.662*	–6.75
Exogenous constructs		
γ_{11}	.292*	7.41
γ_{12}	.070	1.89
γ_{13}	.090*	2.41
γ_{14}	–.054	-1.50
γ_{15}	.114*	2.64
γ_{16}	.260*	5.04
γ_{17}	–.005	0.11
γ_{18}	.167*	4.12
γ_{19}	.056	1.38
γ_{110}	.029	0.79
γ_{111}	–.060	–1.72
γ_{112}	–.020	–0.48
γ_{21}	–.046	–1.07
γ_{22}	–.070	–1.77
γ_{23}	.157*	3.92
γ_{24}	–.005	–0.13
γ_{25}	.002	0 04
γ_{26}	.361*	6.12
γ_{27}	–.152*	–3 33
γ_{28}	.112*	2.59
γ_{29}	.161*	3.62
γ_{210}	–.113*	–2.96
γ_{211}	–.068	–1.83
γ_{212}	.106*	2.43
γ_{31}	–.195*	–3.85
γ_{32}	.045	1.00
γ_{33}	.092	1.94
γ_{34}	–.023	–0.53
γ_{35}	–.087	–1.66
γ_{36}	.138	1.94
γ_{37}	–.023	–0.60
γ_{38}	.049	0.98
γ_{39}	–.102*	–1.98
γ_{310}	.029	0.65
γ_{311}	.313*	6.94
γ_{312}	.001	0.01

Loadings	Standardized	t-value
Parameters for measurement model		
λ_5	.811	20.6
λ_6	1.00	27.6
λ_7	.935	28.6
λ_8	.943	28.9
λ_9	.870	25.1
λ_{12}	.611	13.3
λ_{13}	.769	17.4
λ_{14}	.801	18.1
λ_{18}	.792	20.5
λ_{19}	.916	25.1
λ_{20}	.906	24.7
λ_{21}	.769	19.6
λ_{22}	.551	11.7
λ_{23}	.485	10.3
λ_{24}	.650	13.7
λ_{25}	.794	16.4
λ_{26}	.692	14.6
λ_{27}	.722	14.1
λ_{28}	.616	12.2
λ_{29}	.646	12.8
λ_{30}	.739	14.3
Error term variance for endogenous constructs		
ψ_{11}	.553	
ψ_{22}	.418	
ψ_{33}	.491	

*Significant at $p \leq 0.05$

Summary statistics

$\chi 2$ (df:318) = 863, $p \leq .001$

GFI = .900

RMR = .044

$R^2 = .75$

$n = 516$

was done to rule out the rival explanation that the indicators of the three constructs together reflect a "super" construct and, therefore, should not be considered separate constructs.

Discriminant validity is achieved when the measures of each construct converge on their corresponding true sources, which are different from other constructs. Stated differently, it is the degree to which a theoretical construct in a theoretical system differs from other constructs in the same theoretical system.

A direct test of the discriminant validity of the endogenous constructs was

Table 17.2. Product-moment correlations, means, standard deviations, and reliabilities (pc) for path analytic model

Construct	Mean	S.D.	No. of variables	P_c	1	2	3	4	5	6	7	8	9	10	11	12	13	14	15
1. Immediacy of feedback	4.5	2.1	1	*	1.00														
2. Frequency of feedback	4.0	1.4	1	*	.26	1.00													
3. Clear rating criteria	3.2	2.0	1	*	.13	.02	1.00												
4. Remote mon, difference	24.5	33.6	1	*	–.11	.04	–.15	1.00											
5. Supervisor's expertise	9.4	2.7	2	.90	.26	.14	.25	–.15	1.00										
6. Supervisor's consideration	12.2	5.3	3	.94	.36	.18	.28	–.19	.58	1.00									
7. Employee tenure	4.6	1.7	1	*	–.13	–.25	–.11	–.06	–.18	–.14	1.00								
8. Sign of feedback	.62	.48	1	*	.19	.00	.23	–.18	.28	.43	.08	1.00							
9. Base-line attitudes	11.4	3.2	3	.76	.02	–.08	.12	–.07	.12	.15	.02	.13	1.00						
10. Job stress	4.5	1.8	1	*	–.05	.00	–.15	.04	–.03	–.08	.13	–.14	–.15	1.00					
11. Alternative employment	4.5	1.6	1	*	.00	.03	–.04	.04	.01	–.02	–.05	.02	.00	.02	1.00				
12. Pay grade	5.8	1.1	1	*	–.11	–.17	–.07	–.03	–.13	–.14	.53	–.02	.07	.10	–.08	1.00			
13. Satisfaction with computer–aided monitoring	10.9	4.0	4	.91	.48	.21	.28	–.19	.44	.56	–.12	.40	.14	–.06	–.06	–.11	1.00		
14. Job satisfaction	10 7	4.1	5	.78	.25	.04	.41	–.17	.41	.61	–17	.43	.31	–.23	–.10	–.04	.56	1.00	
15. Turnover propensity	10.2	4.3	4	.75	–.24	.04	–.16	.08	–.23	–.28	.06	–17	–.28	.17	.37	.03	–.29	–.59	1.00

*Not applicable

achieved by comparing the results of a model that hypothesized the three constructs to be distinct against a model in which the indicators of the three dimensions were hypothesized to represent one construct. A significantly lower χ^2 value for the first model in comparison with the second model supports the independence of the constructs. The χ^2 difference between the two models was $\chi^2 dif_3 = 1186$, $p < .001$. This provides strong support for rejecting the rival hypothesis of a composite model. Therefore, the three endogenous constructs in the model can be seen as distinct.

RESULTS

The coefficient of determination R^2 for all of the structural equations jointly was .750 (Table 17.1). The amount of variation explained for the equation predicting satisfaction with monitoring was $1-\psi$ equals .467, and for job satisfaction $1-\psi$ was .582, and for turnover propensity $1-\psi$ was .509. Thus the model explained a significant amount of total variation, as well as variation in the endogenous constructs individually. Large values for these coefficients are associated with good models (Joreskog & Sorbom, 1985).

The LISREL program provides several indicators for assessing the fit of the model. The estimation is one of essentially fitting the covariance matrix Σ implied by the model to the sample covariance matrix S. There is a perfect fit when the fitted Σ equals S. The extent to which Σ equals S can be assessed by a set of statistics, namely, chi-square statistic, the goodness-of-fit index, and the root mean square residual.[2] These results are discussed in Appendix 2.

Support For Hypotheses

Hypothesis 1: Assessment of indirect and direct effects on job satisfaction. Table 17.3 shows the results of this analysis. To test the hypothesis that satisfaction with monitoring plays a central role in job satisfaction we assessed the significance[3] of the performance appraisal/feedback variables that were expected to be mediated through monitoring. Table 17.3 shows that five of the indirect effects[4] on job satisfaction through monitoring were significant. These were for immediacy of feedback (indirect effect $\gamma_{11}*\beta_{21} = .078$, $t = 4.0$), clarity of rating criteria (indirect effect equals .025, $t = 2.1$), supervisory expertise (indirect effect equals .031, $t = 2.3$), supervisory consideration behavior (indirect effect equals .069, $t = 3.68$), and sign of the feedback (indirect effect equals .045, $t = 3.1$). Thus, satisfaction with monitoring does to a large extent play a central role in mediating the relationship between its antecedents and job satisfaction. Moreover, satisfaction with monitoring itself had a significant influence on job satisfaction, $\beta 21 = .269$; $t = 4.65$.

Hypothesis 2: Assessment of indirect and direct effects on turnover propensity
The results of this analysis are shown in Table 17.4.

None of the indirect effects through monitoring were significant (Table 17.4, column 4). However, seven of the indirect effects (examining all the exogenous con-

Table 17.3. Direct, indirect, and total effects on exogenous constructs on job satisfaction (standardized coefficients)

Construct	Direct effects	Indirect effects[a]	Ratio ind/dir	Total effects
Immediacy	–.048	.078*	1.7	.032
Frequency	–.070	.019	.27	–.051
Clear rating criteria	.157*	.025*	.16	.182
Remote monitoring difference	–.005	–.014	2.8	–.019
Supervisory expertise	.002	.031*	15.5	.033
Supervisory consideration	.381*	.089*	.19	.430
Tenure	–.152*	–.001	.01	.153
Sign	.112*	.045*	.40	.157
Base-line attitudes	.161*	.015	.09	.176
Job stress	–.113*	.007	.06	–.106
Employment alternative	–.068	–.016	.24	–.084
Pay grade	.106*	–.005	.05	.101

*Significant at $p \leq 0.05$

[a]Indirect effects were calculated from Table 1 as follows: γ_{11} to $\gamma_{112}\beta_{21}$.

structs) on turnover through job satisfaction were significant. Thus, the primary mediating construct for turnover propensity was job satisfaction, and not satisfaction with computer-aided monitoring. The major influence of satisfaction with computer-aided monitoring on turnover propensity was indirect, through job satisfaction. The indirect effect was $\beta_{21}*\beta_{32} = -.178$, $t = 3.9$.

Overall, there was support for Hypotheses 1 and 2. Five of the indirect effects

Table 17.4. Direct, indirect, and total effects on exogenous constructs on turnover propensity (standardized coefficients)

	Direct effects 1	Indirect effect[a] 2	3	4	Total indirect effect 5	Ratio indirect/ direct 6	Total effects 7
Immediacy	–.195*	.030	–.052	.036	.016	.08	–.179
Frequency	.045	.046	–.012	.009	.043	.96	.088
Clear rating criteria	.092	–.104*	–.016	.011	–.109	1.2	–.017
Remote monitoring difference	–.023	.003	.010	–.007	.006	.26	–.017
Supervisory expertise	–.087	.001	–.020	.014	–.007	.08	–.094
Supervisory consideration	.138*	–.239*	–.046	.032	–.252	1.8	–.114
Tenure	–.032	.100*	.000	.000	.100	3.1	.069
Sign	.049	–.074*	–.029	.021	–.083	1.7	–.034
Base-line attitudes	–.102*	–.107*	–.010	.007	–.109	1.1	–.211
Job stress	.029	.075*	–.005	.004	.073	2.5	.102
Alternative employment	.313*	.045	.010	–.008	.048	.15	.361
Pay grade	.001	–.070*	.004	.002	–.069	69.0	–.068

*Significant at $p \leq .05$

[a]Indirect effects were calculated from Table 1 as follows:

Column 2: γ_{21} to $\gamma_{212} \times \beta_{32}$

Column 3: γ_{11} to $\gamma_{112} \times \beta_{21} \times \beta_{32}$

Column 4: γ_{11} to $\beta_{112} \times \beta_{31}$

Column 5: columns 2 + 3 + 4

Column 6: column 5 divided by column 1

on job satisfaction through satisfaction with monitoring were statistically significant. Moreover, satisfaction with monitoring had a significant direct effect on general job satisfaction and a significant indirect effect on turnover propensity acting through job satisfaction.

These results, therefore, support the general argument that how computer monitoring is used in practice has significant effects on office workers' general attitudes and behaviors and that managers' attention to recognized standards for performance appraisal, feedback, and good supervision can significantly reduce the otherwise negative effects of monitoring.

Effects of earlier beliefs

We now examine the effects of employees' basic beliefs or views regarding the appropriateness or inappropriateness of computer monitoring. In this sample only a relatively small proportion of employees indicated that they were opposed to monitoring per se. For example, only 9 percent of the sample disagreed that "monitoring is a good tool if it is used properly" (Appendix 1). Of course we must be cautious in interpreting this percentage, as there is likely to be a certain, but unknown, amount of self-selection here. That is, because job applicants were informed of the monitoring policy during the recruitment process, those most opposed may have refused to take these jobs.

Recall that the expectation here is that earlier beliefs exert an independent effect on job satisfaction and turnover that is not mediated by satisfaction with monitoring or by how well or poorly the process is managed. The results provide strong support for this contention. There is no significant relationship between baseline beliefs and satisfaction with monitoring. Nor is there any substantive relationship between baseline beliefs and other exogenous variables (Table 17.2). On the other hand, baseline beliefs significantly affect job satisfaction directly [γ_{29} = .161 (t = 3.62)] and turnover propensity both directly [γ_{39} = –.109, (t = 1.98)] and indirectly through job satisfaction [$\gamma_{29}*\beta_{32}$ = –.107 (t = 4.02)].

Taken together, these results indicate that although in this organization only a relatively small minority was opposed to monitoring per se, their opposition was not ameliorated by positive approaches to monitoring, and their opposition was manifested in lower job satisfaction and a higher propensity to leave. Given the fact that some self-selection is likely here, causing a restriction of range effect, our results, if anything, could underestimate the true effects of this opposition among a random (non self-selected) sample of employees.

Effects of other variables on turnover

Support for the general model is enhanced by the fact that all the other variables (covariates) exhibited the traditional relationship with the propensity-to-leave construct (Cotton & Tuttle, 1986). The total effect on turnover of alternative employment was .361; job stress, .102; and pay, –.068.

DISCUSSION

To date, the public debate over methods of computer monitoring of employees has taken place largely in the absence of any empirical evidence of its actual use, the employees' feelings about monitoring, or their responses to monitoring. This study was a first step toward filling the empirical void. We used an intensive set of interviews, the control/feedback literature, and the performance appraisal literature to assess the effects of monitoring on job satisfaction and intention to quit.

Managerial implications

The first implication of these results is that variation in job satisfaction and turnover intention in automated offices, after controlling for traditional variables, can be largely attributed to two distinct factors: (1) the employees' affective responses to monitoring and (2) their previous beliefs about or dispositions toward monitoring. The first of these, affective response to monitoring, is one over which managers have substantial control. Attention to the principles of good performance appraisal and feedback can help mitigate the negative effects of monitoring and its influence on employees' job satisfaction and their desire to leave. This implies that there would be a significant payoff for supervisory training pertaining to characteristics of good performance feedback. Overall, the results of this study suggest that a majority of employees respond positively in these work settings, to the extent that a positive, developmental approach to the monitoring is fostered. However, we must again be cautious about generalizing this conclusion, given the likelihood of some unknown amount of self-selection.

The significance of employees' baseline attitudes toward monitoring implies that for at least some employees there is a poor match between their predispositions regarding privacy and the practice of monitoring. Like other critics of monitoring, these employees view it as inherently negative, irrespective of how it is conducted. These predispositions, as shown earlier, lower job satisfaction and increase the desire to leave this work setting. Moreover, for these employees the negative effects of monitoring are unlikely to be mitigated significantly by managerial actions.

Because managerial efforts are likely to have little or no effect on these employees, the alternatives are to (1) screen out job applicants who are opposed to monitoring, (2) transfer to nonmonitored jobs those incumbent employees who are opposed, or (3) find alternatives to the use of monitoring.

Public policy implications

The harshest critics of computer-aided monitoring believe that it should be banned from the workplace, whereas others have lobbied for legislation limiting its use ("Telephone Monitoring," 1987). At a minimum, the critics desire policies that will curtail the outright abuse of this technology.

The employees we sampled in this study were unionized. Moreover, in the offices we studied, many of the critics' policy prescriptions had been followed. First, telephones subject to monitoring had to be clearly marked. Second, employees had to be notified every six months, in writing, that their calls would be subject to monitoring. Third, machine statistics, such as the number of calls per hour, could not be used to set production quotas. Fourth, the information gathered through monitoring had to be shared with the employee, and the employee had the right to protest the assessment through the grievance procedure.

The employee's voice in negotiating the rules governing monitoring is desirable and possibly necessary. In a related part of this research Chalykoff (1987) found that managers as a group place a much higher value on monitoring as a mechanism for control than do employees as a group. This suggests that without the employee's voice, monitoring may not only be overused but may also be used for purposes (control) that employees find objectionable. Moreover, if the results of this study can be generalized to other settings, the use of monitoring for control purposes will have dysfunctional consequences for both the employees (lower job satisfaction) and the organization (higher turnover).

But the results of this study indicate that rules and policies alone cannot ensure either the effectiveness of monitoring or the minimization of negative outcomes for employees and the organization. For many employees, the negative impact of monitoring can be softened by management's attention to good principles of performance appraisal and feedback.

The finding that the employees in this sample have predispositions toward monitoring that are not influenced by its actual use implies that when information technology is introduced into existing work operations, there will be some employees who will be fundamentally opposed to the monitoring. Unless they are supported by a strong union, some other voice mechanisms, or clear government policies, their only recourse will be to select themselves out, thereby absorbing the economic and psychological costs associated with an involuntary job transfer or loss. At a minimum, therefore, policy initiatives should be focused on easing this potential outcome.

Extensions of research

The results of this study show that computer-aided monitoring plays a significant role in explaining job satisfaction and turnover intention in automated offices. Thus, this phenomenon cannot be easily dismissed as being neutral or of little consequence for understanding the nature of contemporary office work and the employees' responses to it.

Although employee-level outcomes in these settings can largely be captured in well-established theoretical frameworks (performance appraisal, turnover), this study shows that in future studies of job satisfaction or turnover in automated offices, an independent measure of employees' affective response to monitoring should be included. The construct derived from the interviews and used in this research—satisfaction with computer-aided monitoring—was found to be separate from employee job satisfaction and turnover propensity. At the same time, it exerted a substantial influence on both of these employee-level outcomes. Additional research is needed to identify additional antecedents and consequences of this variable for individuals and organizations.

A measure of employees' predispositions toward monitoring was found, in addition, to be important to explaining employee-level outcomes. This construct had no significant influence on satisfaction with monitoring, but it did have a substantial impact on both job satisfaction and turnover intention. Thus, like satisfaction with monitoring, this construct helps further explain employee-level outcomes in automated offices and therefore deserves attention in future studies. An important task would be to relate this construct to other employment outcomes, such as absenteeism, job performance, grievances, and labor–management conflict.

Finally, there are some broader research questions involving computer monitoring and privacy that this chapter does not address directly (Marx & Sherizen, 1986). Examples of these are (1) whether monitoring is necessary for these jobs, (2) what the alternatives to monitoring might be, and (3) whether monitoring contributes to improved performance and service quality. These are important topics for future research. A useful next step in this work would be to compare employee and organizational outcomes in automated office settings in which monitoring is used for some employees but not others.

CONCLUSION

Computer-aided monitoring is a phenomenon that is likely to become more prevalent in the workplace and thus is central to understanding employees' responses to work. This study provided a model for examining the impact of monitoring on employee-level job satisfaction and turnover. For some employees, the negative effects of monitoring are inherent, while for others its negative impact can be mitigated by attention to feedback processes. Although organizational-level rules and the employees' voice in the negotiation and application of those rules governing monitoring are important, so too are management's efforts aimed at improving the effectiveness of monitoring practices.

APPENDIX 1: QUESTIONS USED FOR ALL VARIABLES IN THE MODEL

EXOGENOUS CONSTRUCTS

Timeliness

X1 With regard to the feedback I receive from telephone monitoring, my supervisor presents it to me personally, on the same day. (1 = almost never; 7 = almost always)

Frequency

X2 How often are you given information pertaining to your performance on telephone monitoring? (1 = never; 7 = daily)

Rating criteria

X3 In this call site there are clear criteria regarding what is necessary to get an outstanding rating on telephone monitoring reviews. (1 = strongly disagree; 7 = strongly agree)

Remote difference

X4 There are different approaches to telephone monitoring. In some call sites, all of it is done on a remote basis (from supervisor's desk), and in other call sites it is done side by side (supervisor sits next to employee). Other sites use both methods. Please indicate in percentage terms the relative use of these methods by your supervisor. If only one method is used, please allocate all 100 percent to it.

Method	Percent
Remote monitoring	_____%
Side-by-side monitoring	_____%

The same question was asked for the percentage of either method that they desired.

Supervisory experience

X5 My supervisor knows a great deal about the technical side of my job.
X6 Has a good understanding of the procedures I use in my work.

Supervisor's consideration behavior

X7 Provides appreciation and encouragement.
X8 Gives recognition for a job well done.
X9 Is concerned that I grow and get ahead professionally.

Tenure

X10 Length of time in this call site. (1 = 0 to 3 months; 6 = over 24 months)

Sign

X11 Overall, the feedback I receive is mainly. (1 = positive; 2 = negative)

Baseline attitudes

X12 Telephone monitoring is a good tool if it is used properly.
X13 Telephone monitoring is an invasion of an employee's privacy. (Reversed scale)
X14 Supervisors should not be allowed to do any telephone monitoring. (Reversed scale)(1 = strongly disagree; 7 = strongly agree)

Job stress

How accurate is the following statement in describing your work?

X15 Stressful (1 = not at all accurate; 7 = extremely accurate)

Alternative employment

Please indicate the extent to which you agree or disagree with the following.

X16 It is possible for me to find a better job than the one I have. (1 = strongly disagree; 7 = strongly agree)

Pay grade

X17 What is your current grade?

ENDOGENOUS CONSTRUCTS

Satisfaction with computer monitoring

How satisfied are you with the following items pertaining to telephone monitoring?

Y1 The amount of feedback you receive.
Y2 The way in which feedback is shared.
Y3 The constructiveness of the feedback.
Y4 The frequency of the feedback. (1 = very dissatisfied; 7 = very satisfied)

Job satisfaction
All in all, how satisfied or dissatisfied are you with the following items pertaining to work in ACS?

Y5 Your job.
Y6 Your pay/benefits.
Y7 Promotion opportunities.
Y8 The recognition you receive for a job well done.
Y9 The amount of say you have in how the work is to be done. (1 = very dissatisfied; 7 = very satisfied)

Turnover propensity
Y10 I view this job as something to do until I can find a better job outside the IRS.
Y11 I often follow up on job leads I've heard about.
Y12 I view this job as something I would like to continue doing for the foreseeable future.
Y13 Before long I will be leaving ACS. (1 = strongly disagree; 7 = strongly agree)

APPENDIX 2

THE X^2 STATISTIC AND ASSOCIATED P VALUE

The chi-square statistic, χ^2 $dif_{318} = 863$; $p < .001$ (Table 17.1), suggests that the model does not fit the data well. The probability level of χ^2 is the probability of obtaining a χ^2 value larger than the value actually obtained, given that the model is supported. On the basis of the χ^2 statistic alone, the current model should be rejected. However, fit of the model should not be assessed on the basis of χ^2 alone when the distribution of the variables is not multivariate normal, and/or the sample size is large. Joreskog and Sorbom (1985) pointed out that either of these conditions inflates χ^2 above what results from specification error in the model. Because $n = 516$, the assessment of fit should rest on additional criteria, especially those that are insensitive to sample size.

GOODNESS-OF-FIT INDEX (GFI)

The goodness-of-fit index (GFI) is a measure of the relative amount of variances and covariances jointly accounted for by the model. The main advantage of GFI over χ^2 is that it is independent of sample size and relatively robust against nonnormality. But because its statistical distribution is unknown, there is no standard for comparison. A rule of thumb is that the GFI should be .90 or greater (Bentler & Bonett, 1980). For the present model the GFI is .90, suggesting an adequate fit.

This index does not prove, however, that this is the best fit that can be obtained with the data. A theoretically acceptable alternative model may fit the data equally well or better. Because there is no theoretically justified alternative model in this case, a base model was executed and compared with the theoretically specified model. This base model tests for the possibility that all the observed variables are indicators of one large construct. This is not an unreasonable assumption, as the data were collected at one point in time, and therefore it is possible that responses have a systematic method bias. The estimation of the base model yielded the following statistics:

$$\chi^2 dif_{405} = 4047, p < .0001, GFI = .597$$

The analysis of covariance structures provides a formal mechanism to compare directly these competing models. As Joreskog noted, it is possible

> to test the model (H_0) against an alternate model (H_1) by estimating each of them separately and comparing their χ^2 goodness-of-fit values. The difference in χ^2 is asymptomatically a χ^2 with degrees of freedom equal to the corresponding difference in degrees of freedom. . . . A large drop in χ^2, compared to the difference in degrees of freedom, indicates that the changes made in the model represent a real improvement. On the other hand, a drop in χ^2 close to the difference in number of degrees of freedom indicates that the improvement in fit is obtained by "capitalizing on chance," and the added parameters may not have real significance and meaning. (1979, p. 48)

The difference between the base model and the original specification was $\chi^2 dif_{87}$ = 3,184, $p < .0001$. Thus, the base model is strongly rejected in favor of the original specification (Figure 17.2).

THE ROOT MEAN SQUARE RESIDUAL (RMR)

The root mean square residual (RMR) is a measure of the average of the residuals (the difference between entries of Σ and S) and can be interpreted only in terms of the correlation matrix (Joreskog & Sorbom, 1985). For our model, the RMR is .044 and the average correlation of all variables is .17, which indicates that 76 percent of the variance in the indicators was accounted for by the model.

On the whole, the model provides an adequate fit to the data. As Joreskog and Sorbom noted, the test statistics are "measures of the overall fit of the model to the data and do not express the quality of the model judged by any other internal or external criteria" (1985, p.41). Above all, the reasonableness of the model rests on its theoretical justification.

ACKNOWLEDGMENT

This research was funded by the Management in the 1990s research program, Sloan School of Management, Massachusetts Institute of Technology. The authors wish to thank N. Venkatraman, Robert McKersie, John Carroll, Paul Osterman, and Jsun Wong for their comments on earlier drafts of this chapter, but the authors retain sole responsibility for its contents.

NOTES

1. This variable is included because the method of monitoring, side by side or remote, is decided by management in these offices. Thus, it was expected that the larger the discrepancy was between managerial practice and employee desires, with regard to the method of monitoring, the less positive would be the employees' perceptions of the monitoring process. *Note*: In side-by-side monitoring, the supervisor sits next to the employee while monitoring the calls. In remote monitoring, the supervisor monitors from his or her office, usually without the employee's being aware of it.

2. The clearest indication of a model's acceptability can be found by examining the results of the analysis. These are shown in Table 17.1, from which it can be seen that all the parameter results are reasonable. There was, however, a negative error variance of -.029 on indicator 6. This Heywood case can happen when two variables measuring a construct are highly correlated (Rindskopt, 1983). In our case the two variables measuring the supervisory expertise construct were correlated at $r = .82$. The model was reestimated fixing this error variance to zero. There was no change in any of the three assessment-of-fit indicators, or in any of the individual parameters.

3. A test for the significance of indirect effects in path analytic models was derived by Sobel (1982), and the general formula is

$$\frac{a \times b}{\sqrt{a^2 \times se_b^2 + b^2 \times se_a^2}}$$

4. The indirect effects (Tables 17.3 and 17.4) were calculated as a simple multiplicative measure of the relevant path coefficients using the Simon–Blalock technique, a commonly used procedure in path analysis (Duncan, 1972; Pedhazur, 1982;). With reference to Figure 17.2 as an illustration, the indirect effect of immediacy of feedback on general satisfaction through computer-aided monitoring is the value obtained by multiplying the path coefficient between immediacy of feedback and satisfaction with computer-aided monitoring, $\gamma 11 = .292$ (from Table 17.1), by the path coefficient between satisfaction with computer-aided monitoring and general work satisfaction, $\beta_{21} = .269$.

REFERENCES

Attewell, P. (1987). Big brother and the sweatshop: Computer surveillance in the automated office. *Sociological Theory* 5:87–99.

Bentler, P. M, & D. G. Bonett (1980). Significance tests and goodness of fit in the analysis of covariance structures. *Psychological Bulletin* 88:588–606.

Berger, L. (1983). The promise of criterion-referenced performance appraisal (CRPA). *Review of Public Personnel Administration* 3:21–32.

Blau, P. M., & W. R. Scott (1962). *Formal organizations*. San Francisco: Chandler.

Chalykoff, J. (1987). Computer-aided performance monitoring of employees in large-volume office operations. Ph. D. diss., Sloan School of Management, Massachusetts Institute of Technology.

——— (1988). Determinants of employees' affective response to the use of information technology in monitoring performance. Paper presented at the Academy of Management meeting, Anaheim, CA.

Cotton, J. L., & J. M. Tuttle (1986). Employee turnover: A meta-analysis and review with implications for research. *Academy of Management Review* 11:55–70.

Duncan, O. D. (1972). Path analysis: Sociological examples. In H. M. Blalock (Ed.), *Casual models in the social sciences* pp. 115–38, Chicago: Aldine-Atherson.

Edwards, R. C. (1979). *Contested terrain: The transformation of the workplace in the twentieth century*. New York: Basic Books.

Eisenhardt, K. M. (1985). Control: Organizational and economic approaches. *Management Science* 31:134–49.

Halperin, K. S., C. R. Snyder, R. J. Shenkal, & B. K. Houston (1976). Effects of source status and message favorability on acceptance of personality feedback. *Journal of Applied Psychology* 8:85–8.

Ilgen, D. R., C. D. Fisher, & M. S. Taylor (1979). Consequences of individual feedback on behavior in organizations. *Journal of Applied Psychology* 64:349–71.

Jacobs, M., A. Jacobs, G. Feldman, & N. Cavior (1973). Feedback II—the "credibility gap": Delivery of positive and negative emotional and behavioral feedback in groups. *Journal of Consulting and Clinical Psychology* 41:215–23.

Jacobson, B. (1984). When machines monitor work. *World of Work Report* 9 (May): 1–2.

Joreskog, K. G. (1979). Analyzing psychological data by structural analysis of covariance matrices. In K. G. Joreskog & D. Sorbom (Eds.), *Advances in factor analysis and structural equation models,* pp. 45–100. Cambridge, MA: Abt Books.

Joreskog, K. G & D. Sorbom (1985). *LISREL VI: Analysis of linear structural relationships by the method of maximum likelihood*. Mooresville, IN: Scientific Software.

Marx, G. T., & S. Sherizen (1986). Monitoring on the job: How to protect privacy as well as property. *Technology Review* 89 (November–December): 62–72.

9 to 5 (1986). *Computer monitoring and other dirty tricks*. Cleveland: National Association of Working Women.

Nussbaum, K., & V. duRivage (1986). Computer monitoring: Mismanagement by remote control. *Business and Society Review* 56:16–20.

Ouchi, W. G. (1977). The relationship between organizational structure and organizational control. *Administrative Science Quarterly* 22:95–113.

Ouchi, W.G., & M. A. Maguire (1975). Organizational control: Two functions. *Administrative Science Quarterly* 20:559–69.

Pedhazur, E. J. (1982). *Multiple regression in behavioral research*. New York: Holt, Rinehart and Winston.

Rindskopf, D. (1983). Parameterizing inequality constraints on unique variances in linear structural models. *Psychometrika* 48:73–83.

Shaiken, H. (1987). When the computer runs the office. (A threat to dignity?: Forum) *New York Times*, March 22, p. F3.

Sobel, M. E. (1982). Asymptotic confidence intervals for indirect effects in structural equation models. In S. Leinhardt (Ed.), *Sociological methodology*, pp. 290–312. San Francisco: Jossey-Bass.

Taylor, M. S., C. D. Fisher, & D. R. Ilgen (1984). Individuals' reactions to performance feedback in organizations: A control theory perspective. In K. M. Rowland & G. R. Ferris (Eds.), *Research in personnel and human resource management* Vol. 2, pp. 81–124. Greenwich, CT: JAI Press.

"Telephone monitoring examined at hearing." (1987). *Daily Labor Report*, July 16, p. 2

Tuckman, B.W., & W. F. Oliver (1968). Effectiveness of feedback to teachers as a function of source. *Journal of Educational Psychology* 59:297–301.

U. S. Congress Office of Technology Assessment. (1987). Electronic supervisor: New technology, new tensions. Publication no. OTA-CIT-333. Washington, DC: U.S. Government Printing Office.

Werts, C. E. , R. L. Linn, & K. G. Joreskog (1974). Interclass reliability estimates: Testing structural assumptions. *Educational and Psychological Measurement* 34:25–33.

Wexley, K. N. (1979). Performance appraisal and feedback. In S. Kerr (Ed.), *Organizational behavior*, pp. 241–59. Columbus, OH: Grid Publishing.

CHAPTER 18

Toward the Perfect Work Place? The Experience of Home-based Systems Developers

LOTTE BAILYN

Information technology makes it possible to free work from the constraints of location and time. No longer must employees commute daily to a central office place in order to perform their work. Telecommuting, estimates suggest, could save thousands of barrels of oil a day and significantly reduce the stress on individuals that stems from the current organization of work (Eder, 1983).

But what to some is the hope of the future and the solution to many social ills is to others the harbinger of a new era of exploitation in an electronic sweatshop (cf. the AFL–CIO Resolution on Computer Homework, 1985). The technology alone will not determine which of these these outcomes prevails (Elling, 1985, p. 28). Rather, that will depend on the people and tasks involved and on the structural, managerial, and cultural context in which the work gets done (Perin, 1991).

Using computers to work from home has been a topic of debate since the oil crisis of the 1970s, when the word *telecommute* was coined (Nilles et al., 1976), and since individual workstations have become inexpensive enough to allow their wide proliferation. Since that time, though researchers and journalists have focused much attention on this workplace innovation, the debate has been subject to a number of confusions.

First, it has not always been clear which segment of the work force and what types of tasks are being discussed. And it is important to make these distinctions. Routine clerical tasks and data entry, which are subject to repetitive measures of output and are primarily performed by women, hark back to the evils of cottage industry and are subject to similar kinds of exploitation (Risman & Tomaskovic-Devey, 1986). However, the situation is different at the upper end of the occupational scale, where technical and professional work is not routine (Olson & Primps, 1984) and people are paid for exercising their knowledge and judgment. The danger here is more likely to be workaholism than exploitation, and the constraints that these home workers face are more likely to be cultural than economic (Kraut, 1987; Olson, 1987a; Perin, 1991). It is this upper end of the work force that is the subject of this chapter.

Another area of confusion relates to the employee status of home-based workers. Currently, in the United States, an estimated 90 percent of home professionals are self-employed or work as free lancers on a contract basis (Castro, 1987). An earlier study of home-based computer workers by McClintock (1984) also found that only 15 percent were company employees. In the United Kingdom, Rank Xerox networkers and F-International programmers are examples of this independent contractor pattern (Handy, 1985; Judkins, West, & Drew, 1985; Kinsman, 1987). But the fastest-growing part of the home-based work force, at least in the United States, consists of telecommuters, those who are corporate employees (Center for Futures Research, as reported in Castro, 1987; ESU as reported in *TC Report*, 1987). Such an arrangement may be individually negotiated with an employer or may arise though a specific corporate unit of home-based workers. The Contract Program Services (CPS) business unit of ICL Ltd., is an example of the latter arrangement and served as the study site for this chapter.

Finally, even within the population of organizational employees who use computers to work from home, there is confusion because no distinction is made between those who work at home in addition to putting in a normal workweek at the office and those who work at home as a substitute for working at the office during regular hours. For example, in their survey of Pittsburgh firms, Hughson and Goodman (1986) found that most of those companies that reported any telecommuting stated that it all took place after hours: Only three firms allowed valuable employees—primarily women with children—to make part-time arrangements to telecommute during the regular workweek. Kraut (1987), reporting on a study in 1983–84 of employees of a high-tech corporation who worked at home, also found that most of them worked at home in addition to going to their office. And Olson (1985) discovered, on the basis of data from the readers of *Datamation* magazine, that only 10 percent of these computer users regularly substitute work at home for work at the office.

Telework, therefore, consists mainly of augmentation, not substitution. But it is the latter pattern, which combines work at home with work on site during the regular workweek, that has the potential for meeting new individual and organizational needs (Bailyn, 1988; Perin, 1991). CPS employees fit into this pattern, as they are based at home but spend anywhere from 20 to 70 percent of their working time at ICL or its customer clients. As their manager says, they are home based but not home bound. Nor are they the only ones who would like to work in this manner. When asked for preferences, many people express the desire to combine home-based with office-based work (e.g., Kraut, 1987; Olson, 1987a).

Thus, through CPS, we were able to study high-level company employees whose technical work is based at home but who are not confined to home, as they spend part of their working time face to face with the people directly involved in their projects. Further, there is in ICL a highly comparable group that does the same kind of work but in the traditional office-based manner. So ICL provides an unusual opportunity to investigate the differences between home-based and office-based work for employees working under the same corporate umbrella and performing essentially the same tasks.

PREVIOUS RESEARCH

Most previous attempts to investigate empirically the phenomenon of telecommuting were based on data from small groups of pioneers (McClintock, 1984; Pratt, 1984) or from pilot projects and other isolated informal and formal work-at-home arrangements (Olson, 1983, 1987b; Ramsower, 1985). These early studies confirmed the different issues faced by professional and clerical workers who wished to use computers to work at home. Pratt (1984) identified three types of telecommuters: clerical women, managerial and professional employees who were mothers of young children, and male managers and professionals. Olson (1987b) found that formal programs mostly involved women doing clerical work and so represented a trade-off for these employees. Their alternative was not being able to work at all, and hence these women were vulnerable to exploitation. In contrast, informal arrangements in hi-tech companies usually involved professional men with scarce skills, for whom working at home was based on free choice and so was a privilege. Ramsower (1985) identified one group of full-time telecommuters, mainly female, who had high productivity but were closely monitored and controlled and not very satisfied with their jobs. In contrast, a group of part-time telecommuters—men who worked at home two to three days a week—found the arrangement very satisfactory. Olson and Primps (1984) showed that in the clerical group they studied, autonomy decreased for those who worked at home, and autonomy increased for the professionals in their sample who worked at home.

This distinction between clerical and professional work blurs somewhat among the self-employed. Gerson and Kraut (as noted in *Telecommuting Review*, 1987) considered the results of a study based on a sample of 297 clerical workers from secretarial firms, 30 percent of whom worked at home. They concluded that the home-based workers benefited psychologically, but they could not determine whether it was the location of work or other factors—the number of hours worked (fewer for the home-based workers) and the nature of the relationship with the firm (more of the home-based workers owned their own businesses)—that accounted for these differences. Further, Christensen (1985) found that women who have home businesses for word processing no longer consider their work to be clerical but think of themselves as professionals. The main problems for these self-employed women are the lack of company-provided medical care, the isolation, the lack of separation between work and home, and the danger of workaholism. But their reaction is positive because they have high autonomy and flexibility. In contrast, the externally employed who work at home have different problems. They find that they do not fully control their own time, as it is subject to employer demands, and that they cannot combine their work with child care. They tend to be paid by the hour with no benefits and accept this situation only because it allows them to combine being at home with paid work. Compared with office-based employees, however, these workers are clearly at a disadvantage, and the danger of exploitation is very real (Risman & Tomaskovic-Devey, 1986).[1]

The role of telecommuting in the relation between work and family has interested researchers for a long time (Gordon, 1976; Risman & Tomaskovic-Devey, 1985). In an analysis of 1980 census data, Kraut and Grambsch (1985) showed that home workers earn less and have fewer options than do their counterparts working in offices and that home workers tend to have a smaller need for income and a greater need for flexibility—for example, white married women with children. But the consensus confirms the Christensen finding that telecommuting and child care can be combined only with difficulty.

Olson and Primps (1984) also found that telecommuting is not the answer to the problem of combining work with motherhood. The male professionals they studied, who entered a homework arrangement by choice, improved their relations with their children and had less stress and more leisure. For the women in their sample, who had replaceable skills, the arrangement was associated with more stress. Working at home, therefore, is not the ideal way to care for children, as explicitly stated in literature for new recruits at CPS:

> Although CPS provides the chance to combine a career and children, we do not recommend that they be mixed at the same time/in the same place for long periods. Everyone's views and arrangements are different but the rosy picture of a cherub playing at the feet of a mother happily keying in her program is what the press always asks for and most of us never experience for any useful period of time!

The picture therefore is complex, and it is unlikely that the electronic cottage will soon be with us. The pros and cons of the telecommuting phenomenon are summarized in Schlosberg (1985), Shamir and Salomon (1985), a BNA Special Report (1986), and Olson (1987a). Olson extended the discussion with data from three pilot projects comparing telecommuters to office-based controls. The pilot projects, which consisted of very small numbers of volunteers, were, in general, short-lived. The studies did indicate, however, that remote work requires a different form of supervision and thus represents a dramatic organizational change for companies (see also Bailyn, 1988; Handy, 1985; McClintock, 1984; Perin, 1991). Change of this magnitude comes only with difficulty, which may explain in part why the advantage of telecommuting cannot be easily translated into reality.

Because the data to be presented come from Britain, the question arises as to whether national differences are important to understanding home-based work. For example, there are more highly celebrated successes with this arrangement in Britain, including ICL, than exist in the United States (see Kinsman, 1987). And in Europe, a comparative survey by Empirica ("Trends and Prospects," 1985) indicated more interest in telework in England than in continental Europe. But there is also concern about exploitation in Britain (Deakin & Rubery, 1986), and the differences found in the United States between professional workers and those doing routine clerical work also pertain there to the same extent (Huws, 1984).

To sum up, research findings indicate that working at home with computers as an occasional but regular substitute for office-based work is more theoretically useful than actually available, despite the many champions of this workplace innovation (e.g., Gordon & Kelly, 1986). Researchers also agree that it is important to distinguish between professionals with scarce skills who make informal arrangements to spend some days at home for the sake of their work, and women performing routine clerical or data entry tasks who accept piece rates without benefits in order to be home with their families.

What is important about the sample in this study is that it combines elements from each of these categories. On the one hand, the home-based Contract Programming Service (CPS) unit of ICL consists principally of women who are working part time from home for family reasons; on the other hand, their work is professional and their skills are high and in great demand. Further, they are full employees of ICL with all benefits, and they have the option to move back into the regular ICL structure at any time. And within CPS itself, both a managerial and a technical hierarchy are available to them. Thus these people have benefits, career paths, and alternative options. They are, however, paid by the hour for the time they actually work, and although they receive a small amount of base pay for times between projects, they are subject to some irregularity of pay because of fluctuations in the availability of work. In some ways, pay by the hour is not as logical for this work force as a fee for output would be (Bailyn, 1988). But the compensation system does indicate the high level of trust between these workers and their managers. Many home-based employees are moved to piece rates because it seems too difficult to monitor how long they actually work when they are not visible to management. In the case of CPS, however, the employees' reports of hours worked are accepted because of the high level of trust within this unit.

STUDY SITE AND SAMPLE

CPS was started in 1969 to permit women with scarce computer skills to continue to serve the company part time and to maintain their skills and involvement with work while they raised their children (see also Handy, 1985; Kinsman, 1987). Initially, these women worked by the hour on small programming jobs and received no employee benefits. Now, these home-based workers constitute a separate, profitable business unit.

The unit is managed by a full-time home-based manager, has its own career structure with both a management and technical track, and is involved in a variety of projects developing systems for internal and external applications. Workers (but not managers) are still paid by the hour and many still work part time, but they are now eligible for all employee benefits. The unit employs approximately 180 people, including management, with about 35 technical authors.

From this unit we targeted 55 people who were clearly in systems development and could be compared with 51 office-based systems developers from the Group Information Systems (GIS) unit of ICL, who are office based.[2] The differences between these two groups—each with its own specific employment relationship to ICL—are the subject of this chapter.

In the spring of 1987, we sent everyone in both groups a detailed questionnaire based on intensive pretest interviews. The questionnaire asked the employees in each of these two groups to describe how they did their work and the meaning that it had for them. The response rate was good: Of the home-based group, 89 percent, and of the office-based group, 78 percent. It is the data from these 49 home-based and 40 office-based respondents that we analyzed (see Appendix 1).

Table 18.1 shows that factors other than membership in either the home-based or office-based unit differentiated these groups. The home-based unit (CPS) has more women, who are more likely to be married and to have children, a group that fitted the

Table 18.1. Characteristics of the sample

	CPS	GIS Total	GIS ICL	GIS Free-lance
Number of respondents	49	40	26	14
Sex				
Male	4	30	20	10
Female	45	10	6	4
Number currently married	42	24	15	9
Number with children	43	16	11	5
Number graduates	23	19	15	4
Mean age	36.8	32.0	32.5	30.9
Role				
Technical	42	25	13	12
Business /managerial	7	15	13	2
Mean years of computer experience	14.8	10.2	9.6	11.4
Average number of areas with high competence[a]	3.1	2.8	2.1	4.1
Relation to ICL[b]				
Company loyal (%)	65	39	56	8
Expect to go out on one's own (%)	6	31	17	54

[a]Based on a question asking respondents to indicate the extent of their knowledge of 11 different computer skills, from programming to UNIX and C.

[b]Based on an analysis of where the organization respondents realistically expect to be in 5 years from now, and where they would ideally most like to be.

vision of the unit when it was started. Thus gender also must be taken into account when exploring differences between the home-based and office-based systems developers. Similarly, because there were many fewer managers in the home-based group than there were among respondents from GIS, work role must also be considered. The design of the analysis, therefore, was based on an analysis of variance with three independent variables: the key factor of employing unit, gender, and work role.

The table also shows that the home-based group was somewhat more experienced, in both years of computer work and the number of areas of technical competence. The differences are not large, but they indicate that the home-based workers did not lag behind the office-based employees in technical proficiency, a concern frequently raised in discussions of telecommuting.

Another frequently voiced concern is the company loyalty of workers based at home, particularly for professional employees. Their commitment, the argument goes, is more to the work than to the company that provides it, with the frequent job jumping in Silicon Valley cited as evidence. In the case of ICL, however, loyalty does not seem to be an issue. On the contrary, more of the CPS workers than those in GIS expected and wanted to be working for ICL five years from now, even when the free-lancers were excluded. Fewer of the home-based employees expected to be in a business of their own at that time.

The factor that mainly accounted for this difference is gender, which leads one to wonder whether the home-based women are loyal to ICL only because they believe they have no other choices available to them. Such lack of choice is one of the aspects of exploitation that critics of telecommuting fear. Structurally, of course, these women do have a choice, as they are eligible at any time to return to the regular ICL hierarchy; moreover, they have skills that they could market elsewhere. But most seem to like the control over their time that the CPS arrangement permits:

> I don't think I would like to leave CPS; I don't think I would like to go back full time in an office. I would look to working full time if it were home-based. . . . I don't want to be tied to 9 till 5.

Though there may be some exceptions to this point of view, most of these women seem to be working from home out of choice and not because of unwelcome necessity, a choice constrained only by the practices of the working world as currently constituted.[3] The extent to which organizational, cultural, or national constraints affect this choice (Perin, 1991; Risman & Tomaskovic-Devey, 1985) is an important question that we touch on in the conclusion to this chapter.

In general, the control over time, rather than location, seems to be the key differentiating characteristic between home-based and office-based work. If given free rein, this autonomy leads to greater satisfaction and productivity (Bailyn, 1988; *BNA Special Report*, 1986). But it also represents the most serious barrier to the diffusion of this work option to the general professional work force, as being visibly at work between 9:00 A.M. and 5:00 P.M. on weekdays is such an integral part of our cultural assumptions about work (Perin, 1991). And yet, as Table 18.2 indicates, more than a quarter of the office-based systems developers in this study report that their most productive work times fall outside the traditional office day. Hence, individual control over the timing of work can significantly increase productivity. Further, the ability of the home-based to allocate work over all time periods, including weekends, seems to result in perceptions of greater work regularity with fewer problems about its distribution. Table 18.2 also shows the high proportion of both home-based and office-based employees who need quiet and privacy for their work, a condition not easily found in the open office plan of the GIS unit of ICL. Office-based workers also complained of too much smoke and too little ventilation, both conditions that can be adjusted at home.

Table 18.2 shows that differences in work location change the communication patterns of systems developers and indicates that the communication needs of home-based employees can be met. Thus both employer and employee can gain by allocat-

Table 18.2. Spatial and temporal characteristics of productive work (%)

	CPS ($n = 49$)	GIS ($n = 40$)
Percent who say their most productive time does NOT coincide with the traditional office day	17	26
Percent who work weekends	46	18
Of those with "off-time" productivity	62	20
Of those with "office day" productivity	45	18
Percent who say their workload is irregular	20	42
Percent for whom the distribution of work is a problem	15	27
Percent who mention home as a productive location of work	54	18
Percent who mention quiet and privacy as necessary conditions for productive work	91	74
Percent who say that almost all their work requires uninterrupted concentration	31	15
Percent who say that daily communication is necessary	18	88
Main communication is face-to-face	4	49
Main communication is by telephone	71	8

ing work according to individually optimal times. But the fact that ICL has a profit-making unit that has benefited from this arrangement has not prompted the company to make the option generally available. Indeed, one manager who tried several times to make individual arrangements for some of his most trusted employees to work at home a day or so a week was told by his personnel office that such arrangements violated ICL policy.

Technology has made it possible, therefore, to change the location of work, and the results to be presented point to potential advantages of using computers to work from home as an option for the independent and cognitively intensive tasks associated with high-level technical work. But the possibility of benefiting from these advantages depends less on the technology than on changes in management practices that must accompany the different way of working (Kochan, 1988).[4] Without managerial change, the CPS model is unlikely to diffuse more widely and may be unique. However, the systematic analysis of data—even from a unique case—may, one hopes, contribute to this process of change.

With that possibility in mind, this chapter addresses two questions: first, whether home-based and office-based workers differ in the way they develop their systems and, second, whether this workplace option changes the meaning and the satisfactions associated with the work.

RESULTS

Broadly speaking, the two groups do the same kind of work, as they were selected on that basis. But as is evident from Table 18.3, some differences nonetheless exist.

All respondents were asked to describe the last completed project on which they had worked. We assumed that the details for this project would be relatively easy to remember and that, in the aggregate, this information would provide a valid basis for comparison between the two groups. Table 18.3 shows that the home-based group was as likely to be working on applications for microcomputers as for mainframes,

Table 18.3. Nature of projects (based on information on last completed development)

	CPS	ICL[a]
System developed for		
Mainframe	19	20
Mini	9	2
Micro	19	1
Mainframe projects only		
Mean number of people[b]	4.2	12.9
Mean number of hours/week on project[b]	21.8	34.0
Mean length (in months)[b]	23.4	16.4
Mean number of project hours	8,570	28,772

[a]Because this information refers to the last completed project, the data in this table are based only on ICL employees, since the free-lancers might well be describing a project completed in another organization.

[b]The number of people on a project ranged from 1 to 35; the number of hours per week varied from 16 to 45; and the number of months from beginning to completion ranged from 2 to 72.

whereas the office-based systems developers were primarily assigned to mainframe projects. And even when we compared only developers working on mainframe systems, we found that the home-based group worked on assignments of shorter duration with fewer people.

Thus, there seems to be a bias toward allocating smaller, more self-contained projects to the home-based unit. Such biases are highly functional, as there should be a differential allocation based on the characteristics of the task. We have already indicated that home-based work is applicable mainly to cognitive rather than social tasks. And within cognitive tasks, there are further distinctions. Our data point to size as important. Previous work has also indicated that highly specific needs of interdependence and support (Bailyn, 1988) and the level of creativity required (Garden, 1987) are task characteristics that affect the advantage or disadvantage of doing technical work away from a central office.

We see a further distinction between the ways that the two groups perform their work, in their answers to a series of questions regarding the stages—from proposal through implementation—in systems development. The questionnaire asked who has the primary responsibility at each stage, how much involvement they themselves have in each stage, and the main location for each stage. Generally, few differences separated the two groups. The few that did exist may be summarized as follows:

1. Program managers at CPS (the home-based group) were more involved in system testing and in training than were those at GIS. More than a third of the CPS respondents reported that the project manager was most responsible for system testing and training, in contrast with fewer than one in six who gave this response at GIS.
2. At the same time, home-based respondents in clearly technical roles, in contrast with their office-based counterparts, reported more personal responsibility for certain aspects of the task, particularly estimating cost and time, link testing, and training. For example, nearly two-thirds of the technical CPS respondents claimed full responsibility for link testing, whereas fewer than one in three among the technical office-based employees reported this level of responsibility.
3. Finally, in regard to location, the CPS group, by definition, did most of its development tasks at home, whereas the GIS group performed these tasks at their offices. But members of the latter group were also usually at their offices for system testing, first-level support, and system maintenance, whereas almost half of the home-based workers performed these tasks at user sites.

These differences are small, but they seem to indicate that there is less differentiation in roles in the home-based group than in the office-based systems developers. And when we look at discretion and control over how the work is done, the difference between those in managerial and technical roles is much larger for the office-based group than at CPS. Further, the technical home-based employees perceive themselves to have more discretion and control than do their office-based counterparts, as is evident in Table 18.4. This mode of working, therefore, can result in increased control at the working level in organizations (Bailyn, 1988). But this same possibility is one of the key constraints to telecommuting's wide diffusion, as management's fears of losing control are a key barrier to the idea of allowing high-level employees to spend some of the regular workweek working out of their homes (Perin, 1990).

Table 18.4. Perceived discretion and control over work[a] (technical roles only)

	CPS	GIS Total	GIS ICL	GIS Free-lance
Mean score on control[b]	4.2	3.0	2.8	3.3[c]
Average of maximum length of time working on own without formally reporting progress to anyone—in weeks	2.4	1.5	1.4	1.6[C]

[a]By far the most significant effect on these variables is role: those in business/managerial roles report a great deal more control and discretion than do those in technical roles. This difference is much greater at GIS than it is in CPS. The table, however, presents the figures only for those in technical roles.

[b]This index ranges from 1 (minimal control) to 7 (full control) and consists of two parts: the first is based on the extent to which the respondent has control over setting deadlines, weighted by the perceived importance of deadlines, and the extent to which preset procedures are NOT used; the second part consists of the extent of control over the main stages of the development process in which one is engaged, weighted by the degree of one's involvement.

[c]Aspects of these variables depend on assessments based on the last development project in which one was involved. Hence free-lancers may be responding on the basis of a non-ICL project.

Thus we find that some differences do indeed separate the home-based and the office-based groups in the way the work of systems development is done. The differences are not large, but they indicate that even relatively minor aspects of tasks may be useful in allocating projects to their optimal location. We find much greater differences, however, when we look at the meaning and satisfactions of work for these two groups of systems developers. It is here that the most interesting results of the analysis emerge.

THE MEANING OF WORK

A number of items in the questionnaire relate to the meaning of work in the lives of these respondents. Based on a series of factor analyses of the total sample, we identified a set of items that differentiated between two clusters, each of which represents a different pattern of meaning. Table 18.5 lists the items and the results of analyses of variance based on three independent variables: employing unit, gender, and work role. As the table shows, being home based or office based has a statistically significant association with a number of items, even when gender and work role are controlled. In particular, the office-based group places a greater emphasis on income, on success as defined by pay and promotion, and on leisure. The home-based group, in contrast, is more concerned with interesting work, with keeping up their skills, and with flexibility. These differences are caught by the two patterns of meaning that emerged from an analysis of these items.

Table 18.6, which presents these two patterns as defined by the loadings of the items, shows that Pattern 1 is centered on interesting work, significance of the task, keeping up skills, and the importance of family and flexibility. It is also defined by the lack of concern with income and success and the low importance attributed to leisure activities. The meaning of work embodied in this pattern consists of an intrinsic involvement in the actual tasks, in the context of family.

Pattern 2, in contrast, is centered on work and career as the key aspect of one's life, on status and prestige as providing meaning to work, and on the importance of

Table 18.5. Items used in analysis of meaning of work[a]

A.[b] To help explain what working means to you, please assign a total of 100 points, in any combination you desire, to the following seven statements. The more a statement expresses your thinking, the more points you should assign to it. Please read all the statements before assigning points.
- Working gives me status and prestige
- Working provides me with an income that is needed [GIS][c]
- Working itself is basically interesting and satisfying to me [CPS; female]
- Working allows me to keep up my skills [CPS; technical]

B.[d] Please assign a total of 100 points to indicate how important the following areas are in your life at the present time. The more important a particular area is, the more points you should assign to it:
- My leisure (like hobbies, sports, recreation, and contacts with friends [GIS; male; technical])
- My work / career
- My family [female]

C.[e] When you think of your working life, which of the following aspects of working seem most significant and important to you?
Please rank the items from 1 = most significant, to 6 = least significant:
- The task I do while working [female]
- The money I receive from my work

D.[f] How important is it to you that your work life contains the following?
Please assign a number between 1 and 7 to each attribute, where 1 = not at all important, and 7 = extremely important.
- Success: good opportunity for upgrading or promotion; good pay [GIS]
- Flexibility: convenient work hours; convenient work location; flexible working arrangements (e.g. when and where to work) [CPS; female]

E.[g] In general how important and significant is working in your total life?
(from 1 = one of the least important things in my life, to 7 = one of the most important things in my life)

[a]Only those items that differentiated between the two emergent patterns of meaning are included. Response categories are in order in which they appeared on the questionnaire; categories that did not differentiate are briefly mentioned in the footnotes. I, and others, have used many similar items in previous research. Their present form, however, is based on Harpaz [13].

[b]Based on a question that fell into Harpaz's category of valued work outcomes. Based on pretest interviews, I added the item on skills to Harpaz's list, which also included that working keeps one occupied; permits one to have interesting contacts with other people; and is a useful way to serve society.

[c]Characteristics in brackets represent independent variables found to have statistically significant main effects on the item in question and the group that had the highest score on the item (e.g, in terms of income, employment relation had a significant main effect, and the GIS office-based group gave more points to this item than did the home-based CPS group).

[d]Based on a question that fell into Harpaz's category of centrality of work as a life role. Other items were community and religion. The leisure item is the only one that had a significant set of 2-way interactions: male technical employees were unusually high; female CPS employees were unusually low.

[e]Based on a question that fell into Harpaz's category of work role identification. Other items were my company or organization; the product or service I provide; the type of people with whom I work; the type of occupation or profession I am in.

[f]Based on a question that fell into Harpaz's category of importance of work goals. Based on the concerns in this paper I added convenient work location and flexible working arrangements. Items not mentioned: opportunity to learn new things; good interpersonal relations; interesting work; a lot of autonomy; good job security; good match between job requirements and abilities and experience; good physical working conditions; a lot of variety. A separate factor analysis of these 13 items yielded the flexibility and success factors that were used in the analysis of meanings.

[g]Based on a question that fell into Harpaz's category of centrality of work as a life role.

success as defined by promotion and pay. Pattern 2 is also defined by a low concern with family, flexibility, and maintaining skills. It embodies a meaning of work based on an instrumental involvement in the context of career.

Scores formed from these two patterns of meaning served as dependent variables in two separate analyses of variance, for which employing unit, gender, and work role were the independent variables. The analyses showed statistically significant main effects for both patterns, but the results were more dramatic for the first pattern

Table 18.6. Personal meaning of work (loadings on two emergent patterns of meaning[a])

	Pattern 1	Pattern 2
Meaning of work: income	−.80	
Meaning of work: interesting work	+.76	
Important life area: leisure	−.72	
Ranking on significance: money	−.43[b]	
Ranking on significance: task	+.36[b]	
Important life area: family	+.52	−.51
Meaning of work: keep up skills	+.50	−.33
Importance: success factor	−.38	+.33
Importance: flexibility factor	+.35	−.41
Meaning of work: status and prestige		+.46
Work's importance in total life		+.63
Important life area: work/career		+.83

[a]Based on a principal components analysis specifying two factors (as indicated by the screen test) which account for 41% of the total variance. Factors are rotated orthogonally with a varimax rotation since an oblique rotation yielded an insignificant correlation between the factors. Loadings < .25 are eliminated here.

[b]The signs on these loadings have been reversed so that a positive loading means an attribution of great significance, and a negative loading indicates little significance.

in which the multiple correlation coefficient is .65. Two of the independent variables account for this effect: employing unit (beta = .40) and gender (beta = .32).[5] CPS employees scored much higher on this pattern than did the office-based systems developers, with the free-lancers scoring lower than did office-based ICL personnel. Women scored higher than did men, independent of employing unit and work role.[6]

For the second pattern, the overall main effects were also statistically significant (p = .04), but the multiple correlation coefficient was less (r = .35), and no individual variable was independently significant. Gender was the most predictive (beta = .30), with men scoring higher than women, followed by work role (beta = .14), with managerial employees scoring higher than technical employees. The difference between ICL employees who were office based (mean = +.42) and those who were home based (mean = –.22) attentuated when gender and work role were controlled. Table 18.7 displays the means of scores on both these patterns of meaning for groups defined by employing unit, work role, and gender.

The table makes clear that CPS women are the embodiment of the first pattern. It is among these home-based ICL employees that one finds the meaning of work to be its intrinsic character in the context of family. Thus, almost 20 years later, CPS still seems to reflect the values on which it was founded. In contrast, the second pattern, which represents a career-centered instrumental approach to work, is most typical of the men employed by ICL in standard office-based positions, particularly when they are in managerial roles.

The table also indicates that CPS men and GIS women deviated from the expected picture of scoring high on one pattern of meaning and low on the other. Disaggregating the cluster scores into their components shows that these "deviant" groups combine elements of both patterns. In particular, GIS women shared with their male colleagues a concern with money, but they did not give work as important a place in their lives as

Table 18.7. Mean factor scores[a]

	CPS	GIS Total	GIS ICL	GIS Free-lance
Pattern 1: intrinsic involvement in the context of family	+ 0.54	− 0.67	− 0.56	− 0.87
Men	− 0.52	− 0.76	− 0.63	− 1.02
Women	+ 0.63	− 0.39	− 0.29	− 0.52
Technical men		− 0.91		
Managerial men		− 0.56		
Technical women	+ 0.66			
Managerial women	+ 0.46			
Pattern 2: instrumental involvement in the context of career	− 0.22	+ 0.27	+ 0.42	+ 0.01
Men	− 0.18	+ 0.34	+ 0.60	+ 0.18
Women	− 0.22	− 0.31	− 0.24	− 0.39
Technical men		+ 0.23		
Managerial men		+ 0.76		
Technical women	− 0.25			
Managerial women	− 0.04			

[a]Factor scores were computed by Bartlett's method. Across the total population, they have means of 0 and standard deviations of 1; the correlation between them is 0.0.

the men. They were somewhat younger, more likely to be childless, and less experienced than the GIS men were. Family was a more critical concern for the free-lance women; for those employed by ICL, the task itself had the greatest significance.

The CPS men, though very few in number, point to a pattern that also has been found among U.S. telecommuters. These men shared with their female colleagues a noninstrumental orientation—they were relatively little concerned with money, status, or success—and were equally interested in maintaining their skills and in flexibility. But they did not have the same interest as the women did in the task itself, and their emphasis was much more on leisure and considerably less on family. They tended to be single and older and more experienced than their female colleagues were. It appears as if they used their skills to forge a leisure-oriented life style for themselves. They may represent the forerunner of an emergent pattern of work, based at home or in an office as the task demands, centered on the development of skills and on autonomy, and concerned less with career and advancement than with balance and leisure. But these are speculative conclusions that depend on an analysis of the relation between the meaning of work and life satisfactions.

SATISFACTIONS

The final attitude question we asked was this:

> Most generally, at this time, how satisfied are you with the following aspects of your life? Please circle the number between 1 and 5 that best indicates your level of satisfaction with each of the following (1 = not very satisfied, 5 = very satisfied):
>
> - Your job
> - Your personal relations

- The balance between work and nonwork in your life
- The amount of time available for your family
- Your health/physical fitness
- Your sense of achievement
- The amount of fun and pleasure in your life
- Your success at work
- Your success in the nonwork parts of your life

Analyses of variance with the same three independent variables showed that the only statistically significant mean differences on satisfaction scores occurred for personal relations, balance, and the two success ratings. Women were more satisfied than men with their personal relations, especially the free-lance women; CPS men scored lowest on this measure. Managerial respondents were more satisfied with the balance in their lives than were technical employees; this difference was particularly evident among women. CPS respondents were least satisfied with the success they had achieved, in both their work and nonwork lives, and free-lancers were most satisfied with both; CPS men scored lowest on feelings of success with nonwork aspects of their lives. On success at work there were complicated interactions between sex and work role and between role and employing unit: In CPS and ICL, the managerial women were the most satisfied; among free-lancers, the most satisfied with their work were the managerial men and the technical women.

These first-order differences, however, are less interesting than the correlations between meaning of work and satisfactions. Overall, Pattern 1 and Pattern 2 scores are not correlated, by definition. Scores on the first pattern correlate significantly with job satisfaction ($r = .44$, $p < .01$), and scores on both patterns are significantly correlated with a sense of achievement ($r = .30$, $p < .01$ for Pattern 1; $r = .27$, $p < .05$ for Pattern 2). But these results hide a more interesting pattern of correlations when the sample is disaggregated, as Table 18.8 indicates.

It is the patterning of these results, rather than that of any of the individual figures, that is critical. The following points emerge from this table:

1. For the women and CPS employees as a whole, the two sets of scores are not correlated with each other. For the men, at GIS and mainly when they are technical, a fairly sizable positive correlation is evident. For these employees, the two patterns of meaning are by no means contradictory; rather, they go together. Their opposite, most likely, is a form of alienation from work in general.
2. Both sets of scores are correlated with satisfaction with job and with a sense of achievement. In other words, job and achievement are important and satisfactory whether one is involved with work through its intrinsic tasks in the context of family or instrumentally in the context of career.
3. Beyond that, clear differences between the two patterns of meaning are evident. An intrinsic involvement with work is positively correlated with a number of other satisfactions: personal relations, balance between work and nonwork, time for family, and fun and pleasure in life. Not so for the instrumentally involved, for whom there is a negative correlation with satisfaction with personal relations, time for family, and health and physical fitness.

Table 18.8. Satisfactions related to factor scores[a]

	Pattern 1 (intrinsic)	Correlation	Pattern 2 (instrumental)
CPS ($n = 49$)[b]	Job (.43)*** Success/work (.35)** Time for family (.31)**	[–.04][c]	
GIS ($n = 40$)	Achievement (.44)*** Job (.37)** Personal relations (.36)** Balance (.32)**	[+ .39]**	Achievement (.34)** Not health (–.32)** Job (.31)**
ICL ($n = 26$)	Personal relations (.49)**	[+ 29]	Job (.43) Achievement (.42)** Not health (–.39)** Not time for family (–.32)**
[freelance] ($n = 14$)	Achievement (.65)** Job (.49)* Balance (.35) Success /nonwork (.31)	[+ .49]*	Not personal relations (–.33)*
Women ($n = 55$)	Job (.49)***	[–.01]	
CPS women ($n = 45$)	Job (.49)*** Success/work(.41)*** Balance (.31)** Fun (.30)** Time for family (.30)**	[–.06]	
Men ($n = 34$)	Achievement (.38)**	[+ .50]***	Achievement (.48)*** Job (.43)** Not health (–.32)**
GIS men ($n = 30$)	Achievement (.40)** Personal relations (.34)*	[+ .54]***	Achievement (.49)*** Not health (–.46)** Job (.45)**
Technical ($n = 67$)	Job (.41)***	[+ .051	Achievement (.33)***
CPS technical ($n = 25$)	Job (.40)**	[–.06]	
GIS technical ($n = 25$)	Achievement (.48)** Personal relations (.42)** Job (.37)*	[+ .44]***	Achievement (.48)** Not health (–.40)** Job (.36)*
Technical women (n–45)	Job (.40)***	[–.07]	
CPS technical women ($n = 38$)	Job (.47)*** Success/work (.45)*** Fun (.40)**	[–.07]	
Technical men ($n = 22$)	Achievement (.44)** Personal relations (.33)	[+ .55]***	Achievement (.66)*** Job (.53)** Not health (–.38)*
Managerial ($n = 22$)	Job (.57)*** Achievement (.54)*** Balance (.48)***	[–.06]	Not personal relations(–.49)** Not success/work (–.41)*

*$p < 0.10$ **$p < 0.05$ ***$p < 0.01$

[a]Includes all satisfactions that correlate > |.3| with the factor scores, listed in order of the size of the correlation coefficient. With the exception of the initial free-lance listing, only groups with n > 20 are listed.

[b]Reduced, where necessary, by those not answering a particular item.

[c]Correlation between the scores for pattern 1 and pattern 2.

CONCLUSION

When combined with the findings from research in the United States, these results indicate that the CPS model represents what one might call a traditional home-based pattern. It is traditional because it is anchored in the traditional view that women's priorities center on their families and homes.[7] As such, it may represent an example of mutual exploitation. The home-based women, despite their level of skills, assess their situations as highly favorable compared with not working at all. However, they admitted that there were disadvantages in terms of position and pay when compared with an office-based mode of working:

> I would not want to go back to a 9-5 job, yet I am aware that my salary is considerably lower than it would have been had I stayed on. I am properly paid for the tasks I am doing, but not for my experience and career stage. . . . But of course that was my choice.

Nonetheless, these women valued this opportunity and, as already indicated, chose to stay with the arrangement even when the primary motivating circumstance of young children no longer existed. But women of comparable skills in the United States seem not to hold the same assumptions; hence the pattern is not prevalent there. American women with equivalent skills tend to be more career oriented and not likely to want to give up the visibility that an office presence provides. That may be one of the reasons, for example, that the experiment by F-International to start a home-based group in the United States did not succeed.

Thus, the fact that we can find in Britain more successful examples of work forces that use computers to work partially from home may depend on the more traditional sex-role expectations that still prevail there. The arrangement, therefore, may be seen as reinforcing the gender structure of society (Risman & Tomaskovic-Devey, 1986). This fact may also account for the observation that the principles underlying CPS are not filtering back into general ICL policies. In contrast, the presence of the independent home-based networkers at Rank Xerox, most of whom are male, was reported (Judkins, personal communication; Judkins, West, & Drew, 1985) to have greatly influenced, or at least to have been part of, a general change in managerial strategy throughout the company.

Yet when compared with the GIS pattern, primarily among men, who viewed work instrumentally in the context of career advancement up an organizational hierarchy (the modal office-based pattern of work), there were clear personal advantages in the home-based model. The GIS pattern, which is the prevalent one in the United States, is negatively associated with personal satisfactions. These results provide empirical corroboration of the personal costs associated with the way that high-level work is characteristically approached. They also highlight the potential value of allowing computers to free work from its traditional organizational constraints.

Even if the modal CPS model is constrained by national differences in gender roles, the few men in CPS pointed to an emergent pattern that is also evident among high-level telecommuters in the United States. Here are people with scarce skills, hired for their innovative potential, for whom life-style and balance are more important than a single-minded emphasis on career advancement. For them, the location and timing of work are important because they allow them to meet their personal needs. And for the organizations that need their services, providing this kind of autonomy is necessary to ensure their productive commitment. Thus working from home with computers for part of the regular workweek may, under the right conditions, provide the perfect work place for highly skilled employees whose skills and energies are needed for a productive society but who are unwilling to have their lives controlled by the organizations that employ them. However, companies must not manage these high-level employees in the traditional mode, or the advantages will be lost. Organizations must learn to value such employees' contributions and to trust their commitment and must resist the urge to dictate when and how they do their work.

APPENDIX: NOTE ON METHOD

This study began in 1986 with detailed, unstructured interviews with managers and employees of CPS and GIS. The goal of these interviews was, first, to specify as clearly as possible the tasks involved in systems development and, second, to identify those CPS and GIS employees whose work was most similar. The questionnaire was based on these interviews and was pretested and checked by managers in both groups. The target employees were selected by the managers involved, who knew both the employees and the purpose of this study.

Questionnaires were distributed in the spring of 1987. CPS questionnaires were mailed to respondents' homes and returned directly to me by mail, whereas the GIS questionnaires were distributed and collected by an administrative assistant and then mailed to me. The questionnaire was accompanied by a letter explaining the purpose of the study. All responses were anonymous, and questions, if any, were directed to me.

The questionnaire consisted of four parts. The first part dealt with the stages of systems development and asked respondents to answer a number of questions concerning each stage. This part was used to compare the actual way that the tasks in each of these stages were performed by the two groups. A second part consisted of another series of detailed questions about each group's work and working environment and the last completed development project. Part III dealt with the respondents' attitudes toward work and included all the questions used in the analysis of the meaning of work and the satisfactions that it provides. Finally, the fourth part asked for demographic information, including previous experience and extent of knowledge with various aspects of computing.

Table 18.1 is based on this last part of the questionnaire. Tables 18.2 through 18.4 use data from Part II, and the discussion on differences in dealing with the various stages of systems development stems from Part I. Though the main purpose of the study was to see whether there were differences between home-based and office-based systems developers, where possible, control was introduced for gender and for work role as well as for employing unit. The reported results, therefore, controlled for these possible alternative explanations of difference, unless otherwise stated in the text or in the footnotes to the tables.

A word should be added about recruitment into CPS. Most of its members had previously been full-time office-based ICL employees. No employees were hired by CPS who had not already had four years of work experience with computing. When they transferred from ICL to CPS, their current salary was translated into an hourly wage, which was the basis for their initial contract in CPS. Their rate of pay, therefore, remained the same, though their total wages were usually less, as most CPS workers started at less than full time. The income of the CPS workers, therefore, probably represents a smaller proportion of total family income than is true for the GIS employees, but no specific data were collected on this point.

ACKNOWLEDGMENT

This chapter is a slightly revised version of one published in *Communications of the ACM* 32 (1989):460–71. Permission has been granted by the ACM. The chapter is based on data collected in Britain as part of a larger project on the effect of information technology on the location and timing of work, done in collaboration with Dr. Constance Perin. The work was financed in part by the Management in the 1990s Research Program of the Sloan School of Management.

NOTES

1. A group of telecommuters sued Cal–West (California–Western States Life Insurance Company in Sacramento) because, they claimed, the company excessively increased quota requirements on piece work (*Telecommuting Review*, 1986). The legal issue rests on the definition of employee, as federal laws do not cover independent contractors. A U.S. House of Representatives Committee report (*Home-based Clerical Workers*) released on July 21, 1986, recommends that the laws be revised so that employers will no longer be able to treat their off-site workers as independent contractors and thus will have to provide the minimum wage, social security and unemployment, and other benefits such as health insurance, vacations, and pensions.
2. Both employees and contractors comprise this latter group, but all were working at company office sites.
3. Gerson and Kraut (*Telecommuting Review*, 1987) found that home-based workers perceived themselves as having considerable choice in work location. Nonetheless, besides business ownership, the best predictors they found of working at home were the presence of young children, age, and being married.
4. There is some evidence that remote work may itself be a catalyst in encouraging such organizational change (Bailyn, 1988).
5. These measures, adjusted for the effect of the other independent variables, are equivalent to standardized regression coefficients (see *SPSSX User's Manual*, 1986, pp. 461–62).
6. There is no statistically significant difference between technical and managerial employees in this pattern, once the other independent variables are controlled.
7. It is traditional, also, as it characteristically represents a "second" income, rather than the sole or primary family support.

REFERENCES

AFL–CIO Resolution on Computer Homework (1985). Adopted by the fifteenth Constitutional Convention of the AFL–CIO, Hollywood, FLA, October 3–6. Reprinted in *Office workstations in the home*, pp. 152–53. Washington, DC: National Academy Press.

Bailyn, L. (1988). Freeing work from the constraints of location and time. *New Technology, Work and Employment* 3:143–52.

BNA Special Report (1986). *The changing workplace: New directions in staffing and scheduling*. Washington, DC: Bureau of National Affairs.

Castro, J. (1987). Technology draws more workers home. *Boston Globe*, October 30, pp. 43, 50.

Christensen, K. E. (1985). Impacts of computer-mediated home-based work on women and their families. U. S. Congress, Office of Technology Assessment, June.

Deakin S.& J. Rubery (1986). Typology, dimensions and regulation of home work in the UK. Unpublished report, University of Cambridge.

Eder, P. F. (1983). Telecommuters: The stay-at-home work force of the future. *The Futurist*, June, pp. 30–35.

Elling, M. (1985). Remote work/telecommuting—A means of enhancing the quality of life, or just another method of making business more brisk? *Economic and Industrial Democracy* 6:239–49.

Garden, A-M. (1987). Behavioural and organizational factors involved in the motivation and satisfaction of high tech professionals: Or how to retain the spirit of excitement in growing companies. Unpublished working paper, London Business School.

Gordon, F. E. (1976). Telecommunications: Implications for women. *Telecommunications Policy,* December, pp. 68–74.

Gordon, G. E., & M. M. Kelly (1986). *Telecommuting: How to make it work for you and your company*. Englewood Cliffs, NJ: Prentice-Hall.

Handy, C. (1985). *The future of work: A guide to a changing society*. Oxford: Basil Blackwell.

Harpaz, I. (1986). The factorial structure of the meaning of working. *Human Relations* 39:595–614.

Home-based clerical workers open to exploitation (1986). News release from U. S. Congress, House of Representatives, Committee on Government Operations, Employment and Housing Subcommittee, July 21.

Hornby, D. (1986). Can we teach ourselves to change? *Royal Bank of Scotland Review*, September, pp. 14–21.

Hughson, T. L., & P. S. Goodman (1986). Telecommuting: Corporate practices and benefits. *National Productivity Review*, Autumn, pp. 315–24.

Huws, U. (1984). New technology homeworkers. *Employment Gazette*, January, pp. 13–17.

Judkins, P., D. West, & J. Drew (1985). *Networking in organisations: The Rank Xerox experiment*. Aldershot: Gower.

Kinsman, F. (1987). *The telecommuters*. Chichester: Wiley.

Kochan, T. K. (1988). Human resources and technology in the auto industry. Paper presented at a Management in the 1990s seminar, Sloan School of Management, Massachusetts Institute of Technology, February 11.

Kraut, R. E. (1987). Predicting the use of technology: The case of telework. In R. E. Kraut (Ed.), *Technology and the transformation of white-collar work*, pp. 113–33. Hillsdale, NJ: Erlbaum.

Kraut, R. E., & P. Grambsch (1985). *Prophecy by analogy: Potential causes for and consequences of electronic homework*. Morristown, NJ: Bell Communications Research.

McClintock, C. (1984). Expanding the boundaries of work: Research on telecommuting. Paper presented at the meeting of the American Association for the Advancement of Science, New York, May 29.

Nilles, J. M., F. R. Carlson, Jr., P. Gray, & G. J. Hanneman (1976). *The telecommunications–transportation tradeoff: Options for tomorrow*. New York: Wiley.

Olson, M. H. (1983). Remote office work: Changing work patterns in space and time. *Communications of the ACM* 26:182–87.

——— (1985). Do you telecommute? *Datamation*, October 15, pp. 129–32.

——— (1987a) An investigation of the impacts of remote work environments and supporting technology. Center for Research on Information Systems Working paper no. 161, New York University Graduate School of Business Administration, August.

——— (1987b). Telework: Practical experience and future prospects. In R. E. Kraut (Ed.), *Technology and the transformation of white-collar work*, pp. 135–52. Hillsdale, NJ: Erlbaum.

Olson, M. H., & S. B. Primps (1984). Working at home with computers: Work and nonwork issues. *Journal of Social Issues* 40:97–112.

Perin, C. (1990). The moral fabric of the office: Panopticon discourse and schedule flexibilities. In P. S. Tolbert & S. R. Barley (Eds.), *Research in the sociology of organizations* (special volume on organizations and professions), pp. 241–68. Greenwich, CT: JAI Press.

Pratt, J. H. (1984). Home teleworking: A study of its pioneers. *Technological Forecasting and Social Change* 25:1–14.

Ramsower, R. M. (1985). Telecommuting: The organizational and behavioral effects of working at home. Ph.D. diss., Ann Arbor, MI: University Microfilms International.

Risman, B. J., & D. Tomaskovic-Devey (1985). Technology as a social construct: The impact of telecommuting on family roles. *Family Perspective* 19:239–49.

——— (1986). The social construction of technology: Microcomputers and the organization of work. Paper presented at the meeting of the Society for the Study of Social Problems, New York, August 28.

Schlosberg, J. (1985). Computer commuters. *American Way*, March 19, pp. 41–47.

Shamir B., & I. Salomon (1985). Work-at-home and the quality of working life. *Academy of Management Review* 10:455–64.

SPSSX User's Manual, 2nd ed. (1986). New York: McGraw Hill.

TC Report: The monthly newsletter of trends and development in location-independent work (1987). New York: Electronic Services Unlimited, August, p. 1.

Telecommuting Review (1986). The Gordon report. Monmouth Jct., NJ: Gil Gordon Associates, February, pp. 10–14.

——— (1987). The Gordon report. Monmouth Jct., NJ: Gil Gordon Associates, January, pp. 15–16.

Trends and prospects of electronic home working—Results of a survey in the major European countries (1985). F.A.S.T. Telework Study Programme working paper no. 1, Empirica, Bonn, March.

CHAPTER 19

Building a Competitor Intelligence Organization: Adding Value in an Information Function

D. ELEANOR WESTNEY AND SUMANTRA GHOSHAL

Over a decade ago, Pfeffer and Salancik (1978) lamented that although organization theory had increasingly emphasized the importance of the environment in explaining the behavior of organizations, empirical studies of how organizations gathered and used information about their environment were surprisingly scarce. Since then, a small but growing body of work on environmental analysis units has emerged in the strategy field (Dieffenbach, 1983; Engledow & Lenz, 1985; Fahey & King, 1979; Fahey, King, & Narayan, 1981; Fuld, 1985; Ghoshal & Kim, 1986; Jain, 1984; Lenz & Engledow, 1986; Montgomery & Weinberg, 1979; Narchal, Kittapa, & Bhattacharya, 1987; Post et al., 1982; Prescott & Smith, 1987; Sammon, Kurland, & Spitalnic, 1984; Stubbart, 1982; Thomas, 1980). However, the findings have been contradictory and inconclusive. Despite the widespread assumption that business environments are becoming increasingly volatile and that therefore companies should want to set up formal systems to monitor and analyze those environments, studies to date have found no clear patterns of evolution and institutionalization. As one summary of the literature put it: "In practice, firms are experiencing difficulties in implementing and effectively conducting environmental analysis. . . . It is apparent that there is still considerable uncertainty about viable structures for environmental analysis units and significant administrative problems accompanying their use" (Lenz & Engledow, 1986, pp. 71, 83).

This uncertainty has marked the evolution of the most recent and most complex environmental analysis function: the analysis of competing companies (CI—competitor information or competitor intelligence). The complexity of the CI function stems from both its organizational structure and the range of its information tasks. Since the early 1980s, most multidivisional firms have moved to an organizational structure that pushes decision-making responsibility further down the corporation, into strategic business units (SBUs) and business groups. In the process, expert functions like CI have been widely dispersed and decentralized. CI has therefore emerged as both a corporate-level function and a business unit function, subject to considerable pressures to identify and exploit potential information synergies across organizational levels, lines of business, functions, and countries.

In addition, CI must cover a wide range of sources and kinds of information. Unlike economic analysis and political risk analysis, which draw almost exclusively on external information resources, CI is expected to develop networks for drawing information about the competitive environment from sources inside as well as outside the company. Moreover, the kind of information required ranges from published, externally validated, quantitative data to highly speculative interpretations of competitors' actions and strategic motivations. Finally, competitor information can have many uses within the company and therefore many potential users of the information.

CI, however, has emerged during a decade when the necessity of cutting staff and reducing overhead is rapidly becoming corporate gospel among large U.S. firms (see Drucker, 1988). The combination of the complexity of the information tasks and the pressure to carry out these tasks with a minimal number of personnel has made CI an arena in which the application of sophisticated information technology holds particular promise. Nevertheless, the actual applications of information technology (IT) have remained piecemeal and disappointing to both those in the CI function and those in the company that the function must serve. Understanding how IT is being used (and not being used) in the CI function requires a detailed study of the activities and problems in the CI organization.

Under the aegis of the Management in the 1990s Program, three of the world's largest multinationals served as research sites for a study of CI: how it carried out the tasks of delivering value-added information to potential users and how it was expanding its capacity to meet the evolving needs of those users. Since the early 1980s, all three companies have moved to formalize responsibility for competitor intelligence, as competitor information has been assuming greater importance and competitive pressures have increased. In all three companies, the formal CI function operates at three levels of the organization: strategic business unit, business group, and corporate unit. The size of the corporate-level units varied considerably across the three corporations: The smallest had four analysts, and the largest single corporate CI unit had 10. In addition, some corporate-level functions (especially research and development, R&D) had developed their own organization for analyzing competitors. At the business group and SBU levels, the responsibility for CI devolved on a single individual, sometimes on a part-time basis?

The location of CI as a staff function varies across firms, depending on how it evolved. In one of our three firms, competitor intelligence began in the corporate planning unit and has always been located there. In the second firm, CI evolved in two staff units, corporate planning and marketing support. Several years ago, in order to reduce the duplication of effort, the marketing support group was given the mandate to develop the CI function. In the third firm, three corporate staff units—corporate planning, marketing support, and economic analysis—have continued to share the responsibility for CI at the corporate level.

The core method of our study was the semistructured interview with individuals in three categories: those who had formal responsibility for competitor information, either full or part time (called *analysts* in the following discussion); staff managers, who were not themselves major users of the information, to whom the analysts reported; and those persons whom the analysts and managers at each level identified as the primary internal clients and users of competitor information. The clients included top corporate management (we interviewed at least one manager at the executive director level in each company), corporate planning managers, and general managers and planning managers at the business group and SBU level. We also interviewed specialists in information technology who supplied technical management information systems (MIS) support to the CI function. In total, we interviewed 73 analysts, 17 managers of analysts, 63 clients, and eight IT specialists. Among the analysts, 25 were at the corporate level, and among the clients, 13 were at the corporate level (three of them in planning and five in other staff functions).

ADDING VALUE TO AN INFORMATION FUNCTION

Two pieces of information land on a manager's desk one day. One is a message that Competitor X has just approached the chairman of a major event to inquire about sponsoring it. The second reports that Competitor Y's reported earnings have risen 40 percent over the previous year. In response to the first item, the manager picks up the phone and makes a preemptive offer on the event sponsorship. The second item he notes with some interest and perhaps with some irritation; he wants an explanation of the change in performance and a breakdown by product lines. The first piece of information has immediate action implications, without further processing: It is of high value but low value added. The second requires further information and analysis—value adding—before the manager can even begin to consider taking action.

The problem of defining *value added* in regard to information continues to plague those who study information processing. For example, one manager told us, "I don't want a data dump. If the information can't be summarized in a page, it's of no use to me." Another in the same company said, "I'd rather be inundated with information and not have time to read it than have it condensed and screened for me by staff people." For the first manager, screening and condensing information adds value, and for the second, it reduces it. Is there any way that a generic model of "value adding" can be constructed under such circumstances?

The first manager is assimilating CI into the dominant organizational model of information processing. That is, he thinks that adding value consists of standardizing information and using routinized procedures for summarizing it, so that the volume of data is diminished at each step of information processing. This is indeed a powerful way of adding value to information, but it is not the only way, as the second manager's comment recognizes. Information may well gain in value as it gathers additional interpretation and contextual information when it is transmitted within the organization. The processing systems and information technology for dealing with this type of information, however, are much less well developed than are the volume-reduction systems. Both organizational models of information processing and IT systems are usually based on the treatment of quantitative data, which is much easier to minimize. Clearly, any effort to develop concepts for information value adding processes must include "amplification" models as well as reduction models. In addition, it must also move away from the subjective, individual paradigm of value to a more organizational model.

DIMENSIONS OF VALUE ADDING

We began our study, as did others before us (e.g., Porter, 1980, pp. 71–74) with an explicitly sequential model of an information value-adding chain that we hoped to refine and test in the course of our investigation (derived from Ghoshal, 1985). But a different model formed from the scanners' descriptions of what they did and from the clients' perceptions of what made information more or less valuable. Instead of a "chain" of value-adding stages, we began to perceive three interrelated but distinct clusters of value-adding activities.

The following is just one example of the many comments that led us to the three-dimension model. When we asked one of the managers of the CI function about its development over time, he replied: "Some expansion has occurred in the amount of information on competitors, but the main change is the recognition that more information on competitors isn't what they need; it's information that is interpreted and tailored to their needs."

These remarks and similar comments from many others imply that there are three activity clusters: acquiring the information, analyzing it in order to interpret the competitors' behavior, and working on how the company might respond. Although much of the attention of clients and analysts alike was focused on "getting the information" as a distinct activity, it became clear during our interviews that acquisition is, in fact, only one of many activities that involve information handling.

We labeled this activity cluster *data management* because it goes well beyond acquiring information to include many aspects of the manipulation of information without transforming its basic content. Data management has 10 processes:

- Acquisition
- Classification
- Storage
- Retrieval
- Editing
- Verification and quality control
- Presentation (i.e., the choice of format)
- Aggregation (putting pieces of information in one place without making any explicit connections among them)
- Distribution
- Assessment (collecting information on clients' reactions to the output of CI)

The second dimension is *analysis*, which has three processes: synthesis (putting information together so as to assemble a complete picture that is more than the sum of the parts), hypothesis (creating scenarios and "what if" techniques of analysis), and assumption building and testing (continuing to explicate and test the underlying assumptions that guide synthesis and hypothesis). The third dimension is the elucidation of the possible responses to the competitors' behavior, the competitors' subsequent responses, and the consideration of future action alternatives; we labeled this dimension *implication*. Each dimension addresses a different question. Data management asks, "What do we know?"; analysis asks, "What does it mean?"; and implication asks, "How should we respond?" (Figure 19.1).[1]

The fact that an activity or a dimension adds value to information does not auto-

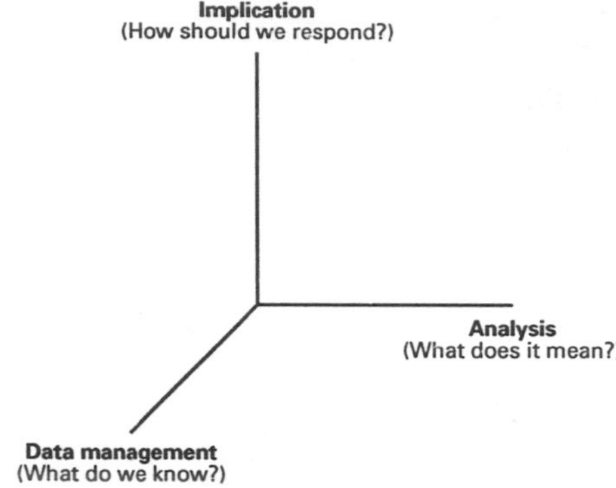

Figure 19.1. Dimensions of value adding.

matically mean that it is "valuable" to the firm. Just as it is possible for a product to be "overengineered"—that is, to have more value added than the market or the organization requires—so it is possible for information to be "overprocessed"—that is, to have value added unnecessarily. But understanding the ways in which value is added to information is a necessary first step to judging how much value needs to be added for a particular organization or use.

DATA MANAGEMENT

Data management encompasses the activities that are most routinized and most disliked by the analysts themselves. One of our questions to analysts was "What do you like most and least about your job?" The most frequent responses on the least-liked aspect concerned data management: for example, "reading all those journals, photocopying, and filing"; "the mechanics of number crunching"; "passing on information in multiple copies in set formats that haven't changed in years"; "getting people to put in information"; and "when information is too detailed and complex to categorize for the data base."

With few exceptions, CI analysts in all three companies are responsible for all of the value-adding processes in data management. As a result, they complain, they have too little time left for analyzing the data. One of the key issues in improving the performance of CI is to discover ways to minimize the time allocated to data management by CI analysts without reducing the level of value added—indeed, if possible, to raise the level of value added. In consequence, data management is where information technology can be expected to make the most significant contribution.

Acquisition

Acquisition is one of the most tedious parts of the analyst's job. As one respondent told us, "Just getting the information takes half my time; my productivity would be increased if the collection of the information could be farmed out. . . . Any well-trained secretary can gather information; interpreting it is what requires the skill."

Table 19.1 summarizes the answers given in the interviews to the question "What are your major sources of information about competitors?" It shows that analysts are indeed using both internal and external sources. Over 90 percent of them cited at least one source of internal information as important to them, and nearly 85 percent mentioned at least one external source.

Personal contacts are important as both external and internal sources, but they are more important internally, a further indication that CI is indeed tapping into internal sources. Note, however, the salience of "other CI people" among the internal personal sources. Fifteen of the analysts mentioned other CI specialists as significant elements of their internal information network, and this is worthy of mention because it indicates the importance of the formal CI network in moving information across SBUs, functions, geographic units, and levels.

Although we may have entered the age of IT, the most commonly cited external source was external publications and documents, with personal contacts remaining a more important external source (cited by 25 percent) than on-line data bases (17 percent), despite the more aggressive marketing efforts of data base companies and consultants. We asked those analysts who were not using on-line data bases what was preventing them from doing so. They indicated that the major impediments were inadequate information about the quality and relevance of the data bases, the lack of training in using such systems, the feeling that most external data bases contained information that was too general for their needs (this was especially common among SBU CI people), and the high cost. Several indicated that a corporate "center of expertise" that could provide up-to-date information and training and shared access to key external data bases would be extremely useful. However, none of the three companies was currently providing such services.

The use of IT in external information acquisition may well be greater than Table 19.1 indicates, although it may be indirect: That is, the external consultants and services cited by 30 percent of the analysts may be using external on-line data bases to produce their "product." Such services may be able to provide the benefits of such services at lower costs, because they can reap the advantages of scale and scope in a way that its client firms cannot. They may have additional advantages in acquisition,

Table 19.1. Acquisitions sources of competitor intelligence

	Degree of use by analysts	
	Number	Proportion
Internal	49	92.5%
Personal contacts	25	47.2
(Other CI people)	(15)	(28.3)
Internal reports and data	25	47.2
Overseas subsidiaries	13	24.5
Personal data base	3	5.7
External	45	84.9
Publications and documents	38	71.7
Consultants and contract services	16	30.2
Informal personal contacts	13	24.8
On-line databases	9	17.0
Trade shows	7	13.2

because for information they can approach the competitors' suppliers and customers and even in some cases the competitors themselves.

Why, then, is there not more extensive contracting out of the acquisition of external information? One manager of the function gave convincing reasons for keeping at least some of the process in-house. His company had decided to contract out external acquisition for certain competitors while keeping it in-house for a very few key "corporate" competitors (i.e., firms that compete with the dominant businesses and most major product lines). He believed that this system had two benefits. First, the understanding of those core competitors was so much higher within the firm than among outside consultants, even in a highly specialized contractor, that more value was added by keeping the process inside. Second, having in-house acquisition enabled him to benchmark the external contractors that he used for other competitor information, so that he could assess their costs and the quality and scope of the product. In turn, the external contractors provided a benchmark for the internal process. Only three analysts mentioned intracompany data bases as a major source. One of the three had created her own text data base of trade press clippings that an outside contractor, using an optical scanner, put on line. The other two cited preexisting market share or marketing data bases that contained competitor information.

We found only one example of an apparently successful application of IT to the routinized collection of internal information. In one SBU the CI analysts had created a "news hotline" using a voice-messaging system. The sales people in the field could call a dedicated number and leave a message about any competitor behavior that other sales people might find useful (primarily technical product information and pricing data). As the analyst described it, he received between 10 and 15 calls a day, often concerning the same trend. If he received no disconfirming reports within the next 24 hours, he put out a "news broadcast" over the voice-messaging system, summarizing the news received. It is worth noting that IT is not used to store this information; rather, the analyst took notes and then put them in a file.

There are several reasons for the apparent success of this system. The contributors are not required to add value to their information by classification, storage, or editing. Contribution is voluntary, and the contributors quickly receive back the value-added information (i.e., information that has been subjected to additional data management processes and, in most cases, to some analysis). Finally, the incentive to contribute is not recognition or reward, but receiving value-added information in return.

Those most concerned with CI continue to yearn for a more extensive use of information technology to acquire competitor information from internal sources. The most optimistic proponents of IT envision a huge electronic network linking every desk in the company. All employees would routinely feed in each piece of information about competitors picked up in the course of their daily activities. Such a system, however, would place an enormous burden on the other data management processes (not to mention the problems of analysis). The problems of classification, editing, and verification/quality control described in the following sections would be enormously magnified by such a system. Early efforts to induce people to contribute "hard copy" to a central CI data bank have usually foundered on the demand that those providing information do so in a standardized format to allow easy storage. CI analysts usually ascribe people's reluctance to contribute information to a companywide system to a reluctance to share information or to laziness. But a stronger disincentive may well be that such a system requires the provider of the information to classify it, format it, and verify at least some of it. Efforts to push off such value adding onto people whose jobs are not centered on CI lower their incentives for involvement.

Because Table 19.1 aggregates the data from all three companies, it does not capture an important dimension of variation across the three firms: how strongly the balance between internal and external sources is influenced by the richness of the external information environment. Industries vary considerably in the extent to which an external information market has developed to provide detailed competitor information. The automobile industry, for example, has received considerable attention in the general business press and sustains a great array of specialized trade publications. Moreover, a number of firms specialize in providing industry- and firm-level information to the major auto firms and their suppliers. In contrast, the photographic materials industry receives comparatively little attention in the general business press, and although consumer-oriented trade publications have proliferated, they focus on competing products and so contain relatively little information on competing firms.

Among the major factors determining the richness of the external information environment are the following: the number of competitors, the scale of the industry, the level of overlap with other industries (suppliers and customers, expanding the size of the potential market for external information suppliers), and the level of regulation (which influences the amount of public-sector information available).

In an information-rich external environment, clients are likely to feel that their own reading makes them generally well informed about their competitors. They look to CI to draw in more detailed and focused competitor information, especially the information from inside the company. In an information-lean environment, by contrast, managers can rely much less on their own surveillance of external published material to keep them abreast of their competitors' strategic behavior, and they are more likely to value external information that is sought out and supplied to them by CI. We do not have independent measures of the richness of the external information environment for the various businesses covered by our three companies, but our observations strongly supported our expectations about the effect of the external information markets on acquisition patterns. In information-rich environments, analysts relied more heavily on internal information, and in relatively information-lean environments, the resort to external sources of information was much greater.

Classification, storage, and retrieval

Classification, storage, and retrieval are three distinct processes with different activities and skills. Classification and retrieval are integrally linked to the storage mode. Currently, the filing cabinet is the dominant mode of storage in all three companies, a situation that creates serious problems in all three value-adding processes. Analysts complained of the "bulging file cabinet" and its associated inefficiencies: the problem of running out of storage space, the problem of deciding which file was suitable for a complex document (classification), the problem of retrieving information speedily when one's only guide was the certainty that "I knew I'd seen that information in an article only a week or so ago, but I couldn't remember where I'd put it."

Most CI specialists have no formal training as information handlers, and so they devise their own idiosyncratic methods of classification. Often their best guide to finding information in their files is their own memory of where they put it or of when they filed it. As a result, even though classification, filing, and retrieval are tedious and low-skill tasks, these people are reluctant to hand them over to clerical staff, fearing—rightly—that to do so would restrict their making efficient use of the information they are storing. But when another person takes over the position, the stored information is virtually unusable, given the impenetrability of the classification system. The situation is complicated by the fact that the more analysis a CI output contains, the more difficult it is to classify the information neatly and parsimoniously for subsequent retrieval. Therefore the most difficult classification, storage, and retrieval tasks are often associated with the analytical outputs of CI itself. These documents often have limited circulation, and yet the information and analysis they contain would be useful to another analyst working on a slightly different aspect of the same competitor. Yet those CI analysts not involved in its production may not even be aware that it exists.

The corporate CI unit in one company is trying to remedy this by creating an annotated bibliography of CI outputs. This effort at classification is laudable, but there is no central storage repository that would make it easy to retrieve a potentially useful document. The analyst must obtain it from whoever is listed as its producer, who may well be someone who has moved out of the CI function or who is away from his or her desk for the critical time period. As this example shows, a solution to a problem on one data management process may be excellent in itself, but if related problems in other processes are ignored, the solution may well fail to make a significant difference.

Classification systems that separate out "hard" (quantitative) and "soft" (qualitative) information may simplify problems of storage and retrieval of value-added information by creating at least two distinct kinds of files or data bases: quantitative "key indicators" files and descriptive, explanatory text files. This separation, however, can harden the resistance of SBUs and subunits to sharing CI with other units. One manager gave us a good example of this. In one product area, the SBU had collected information that showed that although the company's own sales had stayed virtually flat over a certain period of time, the principal competitor's had risen considerably. But during that period the company had shifted to a new production process that led to unforeseen quality problems, and in the eyes of the SBU the fact that the company had prevented its sales from falling represented a triumph of marketing. Subsequently, the sales figures had been taken out of that report and separated from this context. A corporate CI analyst then used them to show the superiority of the competitor's marketing. Thus, developing CI classification and storage systems that do not require uncoupling quantitative and contextual descriptive information is probably essential to the more open sharing of CI across units and to the accurate analysis of information.

Editing and verification/quality control

Editing and verification/quality control involve managing the stored data. Editing is primarily of weeding out information that is outdated or no longer relevant and either placing it in "dead storage" or discarding it altogether. Verification/quality control is checking to make sure that the stored information is accurate. Both these processes are fairly routine and because the value they add is often invisible to scanners and clients alike, they are apt to be neglected under the pressure of time. One of the reasons for the "bulging file cabinet" problem is that its keeper never has time to sit down and weed out information that has been made obsolete or to cross-check various sources to ensure that the stored information is the most accurate available.

Editing requires far less specialized knowledge than do verification and quality control. Someone with very little specialized training can assume this responsibility once the basic principles are established and an appropriate repository for "dead storage" is set up so that the information is not completely lost through an error of judgment.

Verification and quality control are far more demanding, especially for internally derived information. The formal CI system is caught in a dilemma: It is expected to use internal information, and yet managers view internal information as biased. For example, as one manager of CI said to us, "The primary source of information on competitor pricing is our sales people, but they are always wanting to lower prices and they will pass along any information that seems to justify that." The extra effort needed to verify internal information often means that it is collected but not used.

Aggregation and presentation/formatting

Aggregation is putting pieces of information together physically. It should be distinguished from synthesis, one of the analytical processes that makes the whole greater than the sum of the parts by defining a pattern from among the pieces of information. Aggregation is one of the value-adding processes in producing a newsletter, for example. In the absence of a shared on-line system, aggregation is an important value-adding process in sharing information across levels or functions. Newsletters and similar aggregations often are more highly valued outside the unit for which they are ostensibly produced. CI analysts often cited the newsletters produced by other CI units as important internal sources of information.

Presentation/formatting involves a different kind of aggregation than does the text aggregation just described. It means aggregating quantitative data and putting them into standardized summarizing formats such as bar graphs and pie charts. These techniques can also present qualitative information in an eye-catching and quickly comprehensible fashion, such as "headlines," executive summaries, and many of the techniques developed by newspapers and magazines to increase the visual appeal of information.

The value added by presenting and formatting in the CI function seems to be growing, with the proliferation of desktops with "user-friendly" graphics software and desktop publishing programs. Effective presentation and formatting can greatly enhance the impact of data; they can also, if not used carefully, induce misleading interpretations (Tufte, 1983). Indeed, statistical experts warn of the dangers inherent in the growing use of statistical graphics packages by people who have had little statistical training.

Dissemination

Dissemination asks three questions: What form should the CI outputs take; how should they be delivered; and to whom should they go? There are basically two types of CI outputs: regular (provided at set intervals) and irregular (or "as requested"). Outputs can be delivered in three ways: in "hard copy" (or written form), orally, or electronically. The kinds of CI outputs we encountered in the three firms are mapped onto these variables in Table 19.2.

The CI specialists in each company have considerable latitude in deciding on the frequency of outputs and the mode of delivery. Analysts strongly preferred oral presentations, either in tandem with written reports or instead of them. Many analysts feel more comfortable giving interpretations orally rather than in writing, in part because they can adjust quickly to additional information given by their listeners and in part because they are less likely to be cited later as incompetent if their interpretations turn out not to be accurate. Moreover, because oral presentations are interactive, they can serve to collect information as well as to disseminate it. They are more visible to the client community than are written documents, which can easily be overlooked. Finally, the opportunity for the analysts to interact with the clients is both personally gratifying and helpful in building learning curves in the function because of the opportunity to clarify what the clients want.

Of the three modes of dissemination, the electronic was the least frequently mentioned. The principal example of electronic dissemination of regular outputs was the "news broadcast." The voice-messaging system was also mentioned by other CI people in the same company as a way of disseminating "news flashes": urgent items of information about a competitor. Voice-messaging systems that allow one message to be distributed to a predefined list of recipients are well suited to such transmissions. Whether this mode is preferred to an on-line mode such as PROFS seems to be largely a function of internal information systems (IS) culture.

The use of electronic dissemination seems to be increasing, but it is not replac-

Table 19.2. The dissemination process

	Frequency	
Mode of delivery	Regular	"As needed"
Written	Newsletters Annual competitor profiles Quarterly reports Planning cycle support Documents	Strategic profiles of competitors Briefing notes Special project reports
Oral	Annual review of competitors	Briefings Informal hand-off Responses to queries Special project reports
Electronic	News broadcasts	"News flashes" Responses to electronic mail

ing either written or oral modes so much as it is adding a new mode for information that might otherwise not be passed on or might not be passed on so rapidly. For most outputs, the clients themselves strongly preferred hard copy or oral presentations to electronically delivered outputs. The reason that many of them gave was the superior portability of hard copy outputs and the fact that what they wanted from the CI function was value-added CI—analysis—that did not lend itself easily to electronic form.

In general, the richer the external information market is, the greater will be the need for the CI function to target its activities on specific managerial issues and problems and to produce "as needed" outputs rather than regular and routine outputs. The denser the internal information networks are, the more effective are oral as opposed to written outputs: Oral modes of dissemination add value to the information because it is shared, discussed, and debated. On this basis, we can begin to suggest what kinds of outputs might be most effective in which environments (Table 19.3).

There remains the issue of "dissemination to whom." Analysts themselves tend to prefer the widest possible distribution, in part because it is a way of enhancing the function's visibility and thereby possibly increasing the function's ability to draw in information about competitors from various parts of the company. Analysts were quite frustrated with the reluctance of senior management to encourage the wide circulation of CI outputs, especially those that contained analysis and interpretation or internally derived information. The higher the level of value-added information in the CI outputs is, the greater the resistance to broad circulation tends to become. This adds dissemination to the list of processes (the others are classification, storage, and retrieval) that are more difficult for high value-added CI.

Assessment

Assessment is an aspect of adding value to information that certainly exists in at least two of the three companies, but on a fairly irregular basis. It consists of collecting and analyzing data on how CI outputs are evaluated and used, and conducting "post-mortem" analyses of special CI projects. The distribution of evaluation sheets after major presentations and the inclusion of an evaluation sheet with major CI documents are the least intrusive measurement instruments, although their subsequent processing and analysis may take considerable time. And because time is one of the scarce resources in CI, assessment tends to be one of the most neglected process in data management. Yet assessment is an important contributor to learning curves in the function, if—and only if—the information so collected is used, that is, if it is used not simply as a signal to the clients that their opinions are valued.

Table 19.3. Dissemination in different information environments

External information environment	Internal information environment	
	Dense	Thin
Rich	As needed: oral or written	As needed: written or electronic
Lean	Regular: oral or written	Regular: written or electronic

ANALYSIS

Each of the three dimensions of CI is necessary and important, but if one dimension is critical to the success of the formal CI function, it is analysis. Yet in many companies, the focus of the formal function is on data management, especially acquisition. The approach often seems to be that described by one disgruntled client as "They're trying to pull in everything from everywhere, hoping someone will use it some day."

The basic processes in analysis are synthesis, hypothesis, and the specification and testing of the assumptions that undergird these two processes. Synthesis puts together different items of information to form a "map" of the competitor that is greater than the sum of the parts. For example, the analysts may combine data on a competitor's pricing behavior on several related product lines, its stated corporate goals, its patenting behavior, and its new product development and produce an interpretation that the competitor is moving toward the market in a new product area. Hypothesis is the construction of "what if?" scenarios and "if . . . then" analyses. For example, if Competitor X is planning to enter this product area, these are the indicators we would expect to see; or Competitor X has just done this, and here are the likely effects on its subsequent competitive behavior in these product lines.

Both synthesis and hypothesis are only as good as the assumptions on which they are built. Therefore an important part of the value-adding process in analysis is explicating and testing those assumptions. Indeed, the frequently heard statement that "analysis is only as good as the data on which it is based" is less accurate that the statement that "analysis is only as good as the assumptions on which it is based." If the data are wrong but the assumptions are right, exposing the errors in the data means that the analysis can quickly be corrected. But if the data are right and the assumptions are wrong, correction is much more time-consuming and difficult.

An important part of this process is drawing out and refining the clients' underlying assumptions about what drives competitor behavior. Managers and planners are continuously and necessarily making their own assumptions, some of which are well founded and some of which may lead to inappropriate competitive responses. By revealing its own assumptions in the course of presenting its analyses of competitors, CI can help elicit, refine, and improve the working assumptions of its clients—and of its own analysts.

Yet clients often complain that CI produces too little analysis. In our interviews, analysts discussed three major impediments to analysis in CI. The first was simply lack of time, which occurred for two reasons: Data management tasks simply ate up most of the time, and clients, not realizing how long it takes to produce a good analysis, set deadlines that could be met only with a very slight enhancement of a "data dump." The second impediment was the lack of an established discipline that provided well-tested assumptions and techniques for analyzing competitors. In contrast with economic analysis or political risk analysis, undergirded by the fields of economics and political science, respectively, competitor analysis is a complex, interdisciplinary field that is only beginning to develop as an academic and commercial specialty. Third, the corporate culture often makes it much more costly for individuals to make incorrect predictions or to offer analyses whose assumptions are later discredited than for them not to make analyses at all.

For CI as a whole and in the long run, however, the costs of providing no analyses are much higher than the costs of making incorrect analyses from which the function can learn. In other words, the reward and incentive structures for individuals run counter to the long-run interests of the function. As one CI person who chose analysis as what he most liked about his job put it: "I'd rather make 25 predictions and have 20 of them right than three and have them all right. But I'm not sure that attitude is shared in my company, and they make it very embarrassing for you if you're wrong."

One of the key problems in analysis is therefore unrealistic expectations by the client community, and all too frequently by the analysts themselves. As one manager put it, "Business is a poker game, and it sure helps to see the other guy's hand." Clients too often expect the CI function to provide the crystal ball that lets them see into the future in a way that eliminates uncertainty about the competitive environment.

As we saw in Table 19.3, CI can orient its analysis to producing regular profiles of competitors that may be either general or specific, for example, an annual general strategic review of key competitors, or regular profiles of how competitors are responding to certain environmental or internal changes, such as fluctuating exchange rates or changing commodity prices. In industries in which the external information markets are lean, in which there are significant new entrants or potential new entrants, or in which major competitors are undergoing drastic internal reorganizations and shifts in strategy, general profiles may be important, although how often they should be updated remains an open question. In industries with rich external information markets, few new entrants, and stable competitors, issue-targeted analyses are more highly valued.

We found only two cases in which IT was used in analysis. One was primarily useful for synthesis: It showed the distribution of a certain type of competitor assets in a way that allowed the analyst to assess quickly the impact of any competitor asset acquisition or divestment on the competitor's overall position vis-à-vis her own company. Another was used mainly for hypothesis: It showed the major competitors' manufacturing costs and those of the analyst's own company in a way that allowed the analyst to play out "what if" scenarios on changes in the costs of materials or labor. To date, the second system had been received with some skepticism by the client community, who had doubts about the accuracy of the profile of the competitors' costs.

IMPLICATION

In the client interviews we encountered an interesting paradox. Clients complained that CI specialists too often dumped on them information about competitors without telling them what it meant for their business. On the other hand, some clients—sometimes even the same clients—complained that analysts too often slanted the information toward a particular course of action. One manager put it succinctly: "I don't want some analyst telling me how to run my business."

Value adding in the implication dimension should resolve this paradox. Implication refers to explaining the possible responses to competitor behavior and the probable outcomes of those responses. Because competitor behavior is only a part of the estimation of those outcomes, albeit an important part, the implication dimension must include expertise from outside the CI function, especially from the managers and planners who are the CI's clients. As one client put it, "CI is at best two of the three pieces of the puzzle. . . . To build credible potential strategic options, you have to bring in people who really know the business and the market."

In other words, on this dimension the data and the analysis from the other dimensions of CI are combined with the data, analysis, and expertise on one's own company and with the data and analysis on other elements of the environment. The company's range of possible competitive responses are considered, and their potential consequences are assessed. For the implication dimension, much of the value is added by combining the data and analysis provided by the CI specialists with the experience and expertise of other information analysts, planners, and managers. Without value adding on this dimension, many of the data and much of analysis provided on the other two dimensions will remain unused.

To what extent should the CI analysts be involved in adding value to the implication dimension? Should their value-adding activities be restricted to data management and analysis, with the value-added information being handed over to planners and managers who will then use it for the implication dimension? In the three companies, there was considerable range even within each company on the level of involvement of CI specialists on the implication dimension. As one might expect, there was much less involvement of CI specialists in the implication dimension at the corporate level than at the SBU level.

One obstacle to involving the analysts is that value adding in the implication dimension must include detailed information on the company itself as well as on its competitors. Some CI groups have assumed the responsibility for gathering data on their own company; others have neither the resources nor the license to do so. A second impediment is the credibility of the CI analysts. Managers do not enjoy discussing the implications of whatever decisions they might make with subordinates who do not, in their view, understand the business. A third and related factor is time: When managers and planners are under time pressure—which is the usual state of affairs—they are reluctant to spend any of it educating the CI analysts. Finally, a management culture that strongly emphasizes the individual manager's mastery of decision making and action can seriously hamper a genuinely interactive process on the implication dimension.

The strongest argument for involving CI in value adding in the implication dimension, however, is that both clients and analysts expect that this should be part of CI's task, as we found when we asked both groups about their assessment of the current performance of CI.

PERCEIVED PROBLEMS IN DEVELOPING AN EFFECTIVE CI FUNCTION

In all three companies, an overwhelming majority of clients asserted that understanding their competitors was important and growing in importance. They frequently used expressions such as "absolutely vital" and "you can't imagine not using it." But most of the clients and the analysts perceived a significant gap between what the organization needed and what the CI system was currently supplying. Nevertheless, with few exceptions, they generally agreed that a formal system was necessary and that the company needed to improve the current system, not to abandon it.

Clients and analysts offered several reasons for the gap between expectations and performance. We first explicitly asked our interviewees to explain the gap; later in the interview we asked them what problems needed to be resolved. Table 19.4 summarizes their responses in two categories: those internal to the CI function and those external to it and largely beyond its control.

The obstacle that the analysts cited most frequently was external to the function itself: managerial culture, specifically, the reluctance of managers to use staff-generated analysis in general or competitor analysis in particular. Nearly a quarter of the clients shared this concern. Some attributed the problem to traditions of ignoring competitors,

Table 19.4. Impediments to effective competitor intelligence assessments of analysts and clients (%)

	Cited by	
	Proportion of clients ($n = 63$)	Proportion of analysts ($n = 73$)
External to competitor intelligence function		
Context: organizational		
Managerial culture	23.8[a]	34.2[a]
Lack of information synergy across levels	—	12.3[a]
Wide range of information needs	—	5.5[a]
CI driven from the top, not under driven	7.9[b]	2.7[c]
General information management problems	6.3[a]	16.4[a]
Client needs not specified	3.2[c]	10.9[a]
Resource constraint	1.6[c]	20.5[a]
Context: environmental		
Legal constraints	6.3[a]	3.5[c]
Availability of processed information from external sources	4.8[a]	—
Internal to competitor intelligence function		
Data management		
Inadequate systems (IT)	11.1[a]	19.2[a]
Need to improve acquisition from line	6.3[a]	1.4[c]
Redundancy of outputs	3.2[b]	5.5[c]
Inadequate quality check on sources	—	4.1[b]
Analysis		
Lack of appropriate methods	17.5[a]	6.8[b]
Need to be more predictive	15.9[a]	8.2[a]
Too much, too little analysis	15.9[a]	12.3[a]
Problems in reconciling hard and soft data	9.5[b]	9.6[b]
Noncumulative: output discontinuous	7.9[a]	11.0[b]
Own company template	7.9[a]	1.4[c]
Implications		
Lack of relevance of outputs to action	31.7[a]	9.6[c]
Credibility problems[d]	19.0[a]	15.1[a]

[a]Mentioned in all three companies.
[b]Mentioned in two companies.
[c]Mentioned in one company.
[d]The total for credibility problems consists of three factors: low level of line/product expertise (mentioned by 14.3% of clients and 5.5% of analysts), lack of self-checking postmortems (1.6% of clients and 1.4% of analysts), and high turnover in competitor analyst positions (3.2% of clients and 8.2% of analysts).

because of a historical legacy of market leadership. But other comments were more general: for example, a tradition of "management by instinct." As one manager described it, "Some of these guys will look at the data, but it makes them uncomfortable; they like to fly by the seat of their pants." And several clients and analysts said that although there was a growing willingness to pay attention to "hard data," many managers (particularly those with an engineering or finance background) had trouble with "soft" data, by which they meant any information without numbers attached.

Clients and analysts also recognized more specific information management problems that complicated the job of competitor analysis. One was the general information blockages in the organization. As one manager put it, "Information just doesn't move in this company." Information overload, a factor we expected to hear cited often, was mentioned by only one client and one analyst. For the analysts, an additional general information management problem was that corporate-level managers used information to control other parts of the organization, a pattern that made it difficult for a function like CI to persuade SBUs and subunits to share information with the corporate CI unit or even with one another. More clients than analysts suggested that the commitment of top corporate management to CI might actually be a drawback, as its development was not pulled by user needs but pushed by top management.

In general, analysts were more likely than clients were to emphasize factors external to the function as impeding its development; clients were more likely to be critical of the function itself. The problem cited by the most clients was with the implication dimension: CI's irrelevance to their immediate needs. Managers put this in a variety of ways: "It has to make a difference to your bottom line"; "It has to demonstrate a real payoff"; "It has to answer real questions." Although nearly a third of the clients saw this as a major problem, fewer than 10 percent of the analysts mentioned it—perhaps the most significant gap between the two groups.

The internal factor cited by the second largest number of clients was also on the implication dimension: the CI analysts' lack of credibility. The most frequently mentioned reason was that few of the analysts had any line or product management experience, so that some line managers doubted their ability to understand and interpret competitor information. This lack of credibility increased the analysts' reluctance to risk making an incorrect interpretation. In regard to analysis, three problems were cited by more than 15 percent of the clients. One was the need for more prediction and less description. As one manager put it, "I don't want to know what the other guy did to me yesterday; I want to know what he is going to do to me tomorrow." The second factor was similar: the tendency for CI to put out too much data and too little analysis. The third was the lack of appropriate methods. The most common example was the difficulty of generating data on production costs, productivity, and R&D efficiency that were broken down into product lines. Some clients recognized that "sometimes we do not know how to generate these figures for our own company, let alone competitors" but felt that this inability limited the utility of the CI function's analyses. Clients wanted numbers, but they also wanted to understand (or at least trust) the analytical methods that produced them and to be confident that these were consistent, systematic, and rigorous.

Other problems with analysis were the difficulty of combining "hard" and "soft" data in the corporation and a consequent tendency to uncouple the two; discontinuous and unrelated outputs; and too little ability to see the world from the competitor's point of view—a tendency to answer the question "What would we do if we were in their position?" rather than "What are they likely to do?"

But although implication and analysis problems were most important to the clients of the function, the analysts themselves were more likely to cite problems in data management. Both groups, but especially the analysts, cited the inadequacy of information systems. In particular, the analysts felt that the problem of the "bulging filing cabinet" full of clippings and notes, and the consequent difficulty of retrieving information, cried out for technological solutions in storage and retrieval. And both clients and analysts included better access to external information services and help in identifying the most useful and efficient services in their perceptions of what information technology could do to improve CI.

Although it is not surprising that analysts should be more concerned with data management issues than clients are, their focus on data management problems at the expense of analysis issues (compared with the clients' concerns) is disturbing, although understandable. Many analysts told us that they were frustrated by spending most of their time on gathering and retrieving information. They felt that freeing up more time for analysis by finding solutions to the data problems would solve many of the function's problems in meeting its clients' needs. But client distrust of CI methods suggests that the problems on analysis are more extensive than simply a misallocation of time. The most problematic aspect is the gap in the perception of the relevance of CI outputs to action and use. Managers want CI to provide "value-added" information that addresses current problems, is predictive, has greater credibility, and provides more systematic analysis. But this raises still another problem: If CI is to be more useful, its producers must understand how it is used.

In all our client interviews, we asked the following question: "Although clearly an increasing amount of competitor information is being gathered in this company, we are encountering some difficulty in finding out how it is actually used. Can you give us an example or two from your recent experience in which competitor analysis played a particularly important role?"

The skeptical tone of the question, designed to push respondents to think of concrete examples, was driven by a pervasive contradiction observed in an earlier study: Although managers often say that environmental intelligence is important to their firms and their own jobs, they have considerable difficulty identifying specific instances of their own use of such intelligence (see Ghoshal & Kim, 1986).

Responses to this question yielded 63 cases of how competitor analysis had been used. Our analysis of these suggested that although "useful" information about the external environment has customarily been defined by researchers as information that is used directly in operational and tactical decision making or in the strategic planning process, it was inappropriate to look only to these arenas for the use of CI (see, e.g., Prescott & Smith, 1987). In fact, we could identify four more ways in which CI can benefit the organization: sensitization, legitimation, benchmarking, and inspiration.

Sensitization is making people aware that the company faces significant and formidable competitors to whom it must respond and, in some cases, by changing the definition of the most significant competitor or of the most crucial dimensions of competition. One example was a competitor analysis presentation that addressed the perception that a particular company was in a vulnerable financial position and therefore was not a significant competitor, and demonstrated how in fact it continued to be a serious threat both in the home market and abroad. Sensitization was usually the focus of the CI's activities in its earliest years. Benchmarking provides specific measures comparing the firm with its competitors on a set of key variables, such as capital investment, productivity, and quality. Legitimation is using CI to justify certain proposals and to persuade members of the organization of the feasibility and desirability of a chosen course of action. Legitimation becomes particularly important when the company plans to take actions that conflict with the interests and beliefs of influential internal members or external constituencies. In such cases this opposition can be tempered by demonstrating that the action is necessary for meeting competitive challenges or by showing that a similar program worked effectively for a competitor. CI can also be used to give people new ideas about solving problems, by identifying what other firms have done in similar circumstances: that is, it can provide inspiration.

Sensitization, especially in the early stages of CI's development, can be carried out with relatively little value adding on the analysis and implication dimensions. The key activities are in data management, particularly acquiring and disseminating information. Benchmarking, legitimation, and inspiration all make much greater demands on analysis, and planning and decision making require higher levels of value adding for the implication dimension.

For two of the three companies we studied, CI's initial task was sensitization, or alerting the organization to the competitive threats posed in a changing business environment. The function's success in sensitization shifted the clients' demand to other uses that required more value adding. Indeed, this shifting of the clients' demand was a measure of the function's success. But the result for CI was a constant scramble to enhance its value-adding capacity.

As its clients' needs increasingly pull CI into higher levels of value adding, the interactions across the three dimensions—data management, analysis, and implication—become more important. The most obvious of the interactions is feedback across the dimensions. The needs of analysis and implication should help target the acquisition of information and improve the structure of classification, storage, and retrieval. However, at the present stage of CI's development, the needs for analysis are changing, and often are poorly defined. One of the complaints made by the IT support staff in two of the three companies was that every time they helped CI to work out a design for a data base, the CI people changed their minds about what they wanted.

The difficulties of institutionalizing a basic design for a CI data base are exacerbated by unrealistically high expectations of what it should do and potentially conflicting visions of its role. The most common ideal was of a system that would be a kind of internal vacuum cleaner that would continuously collect the information about competitors that was scattered around the company and therefore, as one MIS expert put it, "a central source of data from which people could do their own interpretation and analysis" and a repository of high value-added information that would allow managers to locate easily the competitor analysis they needed to support their decision making and planning. To date, however, the level of expertise in the analysis and implication dimensions of CI is not sufficient to generate an expert system that could make all managers their own analysts.

This points to a key problem in applying IT to CI: The often unstated assumption that solving the problems in data management by using IT is necessary for improving the function's analysis and implication capabilities. In fact, the contrary is true: Improving the level of expertise in analysis and implication is necessary for setting up IT systems to support these value-adding activities. Such an improvement is a matter of personnel development and organizational systems rather than information technology.

BUILDING LEARNING CURVES IN COMPETITOR INTELLIGENCE

Human resource development

There are two basic strategies for staffing an expert function like CI. One is to develop a cadre of specialists, at least some of whom are recruited from outside the company and most of whom spend much of their careers in the function. For convenience, we shall call this the *analyst strategy*. The other strategy is to bring in managers for whom the function is a development assignment, sensitizing them to certain skills and frameworks that will be added to their personal portfolio of management skills (the *fast-tracker strategy*).

At least in the short run, the analyst strategy—having people build up CI skills over time and keeping them in the function—has more advantages than does the fast-tracker strategy. The fast-tracker strategy not only creates rapid turnover in the function, but the incentive structure for the individual also may discourage building learning curves in CI. Fast-track managers achieve excellent evaluations and personal gratification from initiating new programs, but they tend to receive little recognition or satisfaction from institutionalizing and consolidating a program begun by someone else.

On the other hand, from the company's point of view, the fast-tracker strategy has its advantages. Most of the "fast-tracker" analysts we interviewed felt that the assignment had given them an invaluable strategic overview of their company and its competitive environment, and they believed that their way of thinking about the business had permanently changed. The production of managers with such an understanding may be one of the most important long-run contributions of CI. Moreover, although the analyst strategy may be best for building the function's capacities in data management and analysis, the background of the fast-trackers can provide invaluable inputs into the implication dimension.

The three companies that we studied resolved this dilemma by using both strategies: resorting to the fast-tracker strategy at the SBU level, the analyst strategy in functional positions (e.g., R&D), and a mixed strategy at the corporate level, at which the CI unit was large enough to accommodate some fast-trackers as well as a cadre of analysts. To be effective, such a strategy needs to make the training of recruits to the function a formal part of the corporate CI unit, and so persons given CI assignments anywhere in the corporation would spend the first two or three weeks in the corporate unit. This would reduce the time needed for each one to learn the basic requirements and techniques of the position; it would establish communications links with key individuals in the corporate unit and demonstrate where they could be most useful to the newcomer over time; and the newcomer's knowledge of the SBU or other function would perhaps contribute to the corporate unit's understanding of its needs at that level.

Building client learning curves

Two of the major challenges facing the evolving CI function are helping its clients and potential clients use CI more effectively and encouraging them to provide feedback on the function's performance. There are three major mechanisms for doing so:

1. CI training in in-house management education programs: One of the three companies arranged for the head of the corporate CI unit to teach a module on CI in each of six management development courses each year. The module includes both examples of the CI outputs provided by the formal function and an exercise in which the managers themselves analyzed materials regarding a specific competitor. Another company includes CI in its training on strategic planning, although this presentation is made not by the CI staff but by the corporate planning group. The advantage of participation by the CI staff is introducing managers to the function and its staff as well as to the material.
2. Interactive CI forums: As we noted earlier, interactive modes of disseminating CI outputs educate both clients and analysts.
3. Annual CI assessment: An annual review of the CI system can pose the following questions to clients in order to increase both their and the analysts' awareness of the perceived problems: Were there any decisions made over the past year that you think in retrospect would have been made differently if you had had certain information about your competitors? What were the most significant contributions of CI to your business and to you personally? Were there any businesses or parts of the business that suffered in the marketplace because of inadequate awareness of your competitors' intentions and actions? Has our understanding of the comparative efficiency and effectiveness of our operations improved?

Coordination within the CI function

The corporate CI unit is responsible for developing synergies in the entire dispersed CI system. The major coordinating mechanisms we observed were as follows:

1. Special project teams: In all three companies, projects focus on a particular issue or competitor aimed at producing a comprehensive report within a given time frame. The project team includes people drawn from all over the company who have relevant expertise, predominantly but not exclusively CI people.
2. Ongoing competitor teams: Whereas the project teams are "one-shot," single output structures, ongoing competitor teams regularly track a single competitor or group of competitors over time. Like the special project teams, they draw their members from all over the company, but they are much more likely to draw on CI specialists, because of the time commitment involved.
3. Joint presentations: One step removed from the sustained interactions fostered

by either type of team is the joint presentation organized around a specific theme or competitor. CI units from various parts of the company present their views of a competitor or competitive issue to an audience composed of corporate, group, and SBU managers and planners, with minimal advance coordination. The aim is to stimulate discussion across the presenting groups and with the audience.

4. CI support group: In contrast with the three preceding mechanisms, the CI support group does not produce any specific outputs. Instead, it brings together CI specialists from all over the company to exchange information and share problems. In one company, the CI support group is so large (from 30 to 50 people) that the regular meetings require a formal agenda and careful organization. In another, the group is fairly small and informal and is thus restricted to CI specialists in the corporate headquarters.

The special project teams have the advantage of concentrating on current issues and concerns and of being highly visible. However, the discontinuous outputs are likely to become an increasing problem as the function becomes more established. For the ongoing competitor teams, the situation is reversed: They provide continuity in outputs but risk becoming too routinized and thereby losing visibility. The joint presentation is best suited to a company in which there is relatively low information synergy across businesses.

Whatever the initial stimulus to the formation of these mechanisms, the responsibility for organizing them rests with the corporate CI unit. One of the key factors in recruiting people into that unit should therefore be team-building skills, perhaps coupled with further team-building training.

CONCLUSION

Virtually every function of the modern corporation adds value to information. Yet not every function is equally concerned with producing value-added information. Functions fall along a continuum that ranges from those whose activities are dominated by the production of value-added information (often called *expert functions*) to those for whom information is only a minor output, such as highly routinized manufacturing. CI is at the extreme end of this continuum, as an expert function whose sole output is value-added information. It shares this terrain with the other units that analyze aspects of the firm's business environment (political risk assessment, economic analysis, technology scanning, and public affairs) and with market research, quality control, and strategic planning.

The role of information value-adding functions in the firm has been changing. Their classic role was to feed a certain kind of information into the decision-making process at a predetermined stage. The main aspiration of those in expert functions was to persuade managers to incorporate the information at an earlier stage of the decision-making or planning process. Increasingly, however, practitioners are facing the challenge of relinquishing their exclusive claims to expertise in favor of raising the level of awareness and expertise among potential users of the information; working with users to add more value to information; and continuously improving its own practice. The economic analysis unit—a corporate-level group that provides projections of market size to be used in the annual strategic plan—epitomizes the classic role of the expert function. Although CI is, like economic analysis, an environmental analysis unit, it exemplifies the newer expert function. It has far more in common with quality control, which combines a widely dispersed quality control organization with a central expert staff whose mandate is to keep abreast of evolving techniques and to increase expertise throughout the corporation so that "quality is everyone's business."

The experience of building a successful CI function, then, is relevant not only to other environmental analysis units but also to a much broader range of knowledge-intensive functions. The problems of assessing the function, of thinking about how it adds value to the information that it brings into the corporation, and of expanding its capabilities to meet the changing needs of users have important implications for the expert function in the corporation of the 1990s.

NOTES

1. At first this definition of analysis may seem identical with the three categories of analysis used by Richard L. Daft and Karl E. Weick (1984), which consist of information acquisition, interpretation, and learning. But it is different on several counts: First, data management is much more than acquisition; second, we separate out analysis (interpretation of what the information means in terms of competitor behavior) and implication (what the information and analysis, combined with the knowledge of one's own company, together suggest about one's own behavior); and third, learning is not one of our value-adding processes. Rather, learning, in the sense that Daft and Weick use it, is a result of using value-added information, not an information value-adding process, although when learning about competitors' behavior is turned into information and is added to the company's information stock, it contributes to the value-adding process.

REFERENCES

Ball, R. (1987). Assessing your competitor's people and organization. *Long Range Planning* 20:32–41.

Daft, R. L., & K. E. Weick (1984). Toward a model of organizations as interpretation systems. *Academy of Management Review* 9:284–95.

Dieffenbach, J. (1983). Corporate environmental analysis in large U.S. corporations. *Long Range Planning* 16:107–16.

Drucker, P. F. (1988). The coming of the new organization. *Harvard Business Review* 66:45–53.

Engledow, J. L., & R. T. Lenz (1985). Whatever happened to environmental analysis? *Long Range Planning* 18:93–106.

Fahey, L., & W. King (1979). Environmental scanning in corporate planning. *Business Horizons,* August, pp. 61–71.

Fahey, L., W. King, & V. Narayan (1981). Environmental scanning and forecasting in strategic planning—the state of the art. *Long Range Planning* 14:32–39.

Fuld, L. (1985). *Competitor intelligence: How to get it, how to use it*. New York: Wiley.

Ghoshal, S. (1985). Environmental scanning: An individual and organizational level analysis. Ph.D. diss., Sloan School of Management, Massachusetts Institute of Technology.

Ghoshal, S., & S. K. Kim (1986). Building effective intelligence systems for competitive advantage. *Sloan Management Review* 28:49–58.

Jain, S. (1984). Environmental scanning in U.S. corporations. *Long Range Planning* 17:117–28.

Lenz, R. T., & J. L. Engledow (1986). Environmental analysis units and Strategic decision-making: A field survey of selected "leading edge" companies. *Strategic Management Journal* 7:69–89.

Montgomery, D. B., & C. Weinberg (1979). Towards strategic intelligence systems. *Journal of Marketing* 43:41–52.

Narchal, R. M., K. Kittapa, & P. Bhattacharya (1987). An environmental scanning system for business planning. *Long Range Planning* 20:96–105.

Pfeffer, J., & G. R. Salancik (1978). *The external control of organizations.* New York: Harper & Row.

Porter, M. E. (1980). *Competitive strategy: Techniques for analyzing industries and competitors.* New York: Free Press.

Post, J. E., E. A. Murray, R .B. Dickie, & J. F. Mahon (1982). The public affairs function in American corporations: Development and relations and corporate planning. *Long Range Planning* 15:12–21.

Prescott, J. E.& D. C. Smith (1987). A project-based approach to competitor analysis. S*trategic Management Journal* 8:411–23.

Sammon, W. L., M. A. Kurland, & R. Spitalnic (1984). *Business competitor intelligence: Methods for collecting, organizing, and using business information.* New York: Wiley.

Stubbart, C. (1982). Are environmental scanning units effective? *Long Range Planning* 15:139–45.

Thomas, P. (1980). Environmental scanning: The state of the art. *Long Range Planning* 13:20–28.

Tufte, E. (1983). *The visual display of quantitative information.* Cheshire, CT: Graphics Press.

CHAPTER 20

Information Technology in Marketing

JOHN D. C. LITTLE

INFORMATION TECHNOLOGY IS EVERYWHERE

Information technology pervades marketing

When you answer the telephone, a computer may be calling with a sales message. If you buy shares of Intel, Microsoft, or another company listed with NASDAQ, you trade on an electronic market. NASDAQ has no physical location where traders meet. Instead, a network of securities dealers set bid and ask prices through connections to a common computer (see Figure 20.1).

When I call Sears, Roebuck to place a catalog order, the Sears operator asks me my phone number. Then she tells me my name and address. Obviously she is sitting in front of a video terminal. Later, when I go to the store to pick up my order, I find another terminal. It too wants my phone number and tells me my name. Then it

NASDAQ NATIONAL MARKET ISSUES

365-day High	365-day Low	Stock	Yld	P-E	Sales (hds)	High	Low	Last	Net Chg.
25	15	Perceptn Tec	..	36	174	16¼	15½	16¼	+ ¾
11½	6½	Perceptnc Inc	..	27	115	7	6⅞	7	+ ⅛
20	10⅛	PerpetualSB s	..	12	268	15	14½	14⅝	+ ¼
14¾	10⅞	PerpSB pf.85d	6.7	..	23	12⅝	12½	12⅝	+ ⅛
2 9-16	1	Petrol Indus	..	..	44	1¼	1⅛	1⅛	...
2⅝	¾	PETCO Co	..	..	93	⅞	¾	¾	− ⅛
29	22¾	Petrolite 1.12	4.5	14	77	25	24½	25	+ ¾
5⅝	2¼	P&F Ind cl.A	..	5	29	2 15-16	2⅞	2 15-16	+ ⅛
27⅛	16½	Pharmcia .10d	.5	..	844	22¼	21¾	22¼	+ ⅜
19⅝	5¾	Pharmacntrl	..	..	124	9	8¾	9	+ ¼
3 5-16	1 5-16	Pharmkntc Lab	..	..	66	2⅛	2	2	...
1⅞	11-16	Pharmkntcs wt	..	..	125	11-16	11-16	11-16	....
19⅝	6	PhilipCrsby s	..	12	236	7½	7¼	7¼	...
25⅞	15⅝	PhilipG ADR	..	..	3936	20⅞	20½	20¾	− ¼
5¾	2⅞	Phoenix Amer	..	17	166	4⅝	4	4	− ⅜
(H)	1⅝	PhoneA Gram	..	..	136	3½	3¼	3½	+ ¼
7¼	2	Photronics Cp	..	14	21	6¾	6⅝	6⅝	− ⅛
13¾	2⅞	Physcnl Oh s	..	..	1	9	9	9	+ ½
30⅝	12½	Pic N Save s	..	22	2006	23⅜	22⅞	23	− ¼
26¼	11½	Piccadilly s.48	2.4	15	374	20¼	19¼	20	+1¼
24	13	PiedmtBk s.40	2.0	13	3	19½	19½	19½	...
18¼	10¼	PiedmtFed 5i	..	..	112	15¼	14¾	15⅛	+ ⅜
27½	13⅜	PiedmntM .36	2.4	..	10	15	15	15	...
11¼	5⅛	PionFed s.18d	2.6	4	937	7¼	6⅞	6⅞	− ⅜
13½	11¼	PioneerFn Sv	..	..	100	13¼	12½	12¾	...
24¾	16¼	SelectInsur .92	4.1	44	97	22¼	21¾	22¼	+ ½
11½	5	Selecterm Inc	..	10	65	5⅝	5½	5½	...
8⅛	5¾	Semicon Inc	..	..	5	6½	6½	6½	...
11¾	7⅛	Sensrm El .10	1.0	..	1822	10⅞	10⅝	10½	− ¼
5⅝	2	Svc Fracturng	..	..	3	2¼	2¼	2¼	− ¼
15⅛	8	SrvcMerch .08	.8	..	1796	10	9½	9¾	− ¼
27½	19¾	SrvcMastr .88	3.7	23	1136	23¾	23½	23¾	...
27	15¼	Servicolnc 10k	..	14	9	20	19¼	20	...
21⅛	9⅝	SevenOak s.16	1.1	15	473	14¾	14¼	14½	...
10	2⅝	SFE Tech .10e	2.6	..	304	4⅛	3⅞	3⅞	...
40½	26⅞	ShrMedSys .60	1.6	36	1692	38⅛	37½	37⅝	− ½
55½	30⅛	Shawmut 1.84	3.8	9	667	48⅞	48½	48⅝	...
28¼	9⅝	ShelbyWil s.16	.9	21	129	18⅝	18¼	18⅜	− ¼
11¼	6	Sheldhl Inc	..	40	44	9½	9¼	9¼	− ¼
12¾	11½	Shelton SvLn	..	..	17	12½	12	12½	...
22⅝	7⅞	SHL Systmhse	..	..	1333	22	21½	22	+ ½
11½	7¼	Shoe City	..	..	39	9	8¾	9	+ ¼
31	19⅛	Shoney's s.14	.5	24	511	26¾	26⅛	26¾	+ ⅜
18¾	10⅝	Shoneys South	..	14	99	14½	14¼	14½	+ ⅛
6¾	2¾	Shopsmith Inc	..	41	3	3¼	3¼	3¼	− ¼
11½	8¾	Shorewood Pk	..	..	31	10½	10¼	10¼	− ¼
9⅝	7½	SierraCap IV	..	152	1	9⅛	9⅛	9⅛	...
11	9	SierR83 .65d	6.7	81	17	9¾	9¾	9¾	...
10	8	Sier84 .62d	6.9	300	15	9¼	9	9	...
39½	17⅛	SigmaAld s.28	.8	21	539	36½	36	36¼	+ ¼

Figure 20.1. NASDAQ is an electronic market in which traders meet only by computer.

gives me a slip of paper indicating the storage bin that holds my order. The whole system works smoothly and efficiently, providing quick service with little hassle and, important to Sears, little clerical labor.

Telemarketing is more evidence of information technology at work. This is a big business, about which you may have mixed feelings if you are the recipient of many sales phone calls. But the technique reduces selling costs by screening prospects and saving travel. Unquestionably, it is a major success.

The phrase direct marketing applies to any activity in which individual prospects are pinpointed by name. Examples include mailed catalogs, other direct mail selling, and telemarketing. As you are well aware if you have a mailbox, direct marketing by catalog has exploded. Major catalog retailers like L.L. Bean and Lands' End are totally dependent on information technology. Here are the essential ingredients:

- Large, up-to-date, computerized mailing lists
- Toll-free 800 numbers
- Credit cards
- Rapid credit checks to computerized databases

Then deliveries can be authorized and made quickly, with fast service being a critical success factor in the rapid growth of direct marketing. Indeed, now it is easier and faster for me to buy computer equipment in New Hampshire or California by an 800 number than to find time to shop at a computer store in Boston (see Figure 20.2).

Figure 20.2 Catalog sales have exploded because of the convenient, fast service made possible by 800 numbers, credit cards, and computerized credit authorizations.

A friend of mine left a senior position in a consumer packaged goods company to become vice-president of marketing in a large U.S. bank. The CEO hired him to lead the bank's charge into new financial services under deregulation. His focus was retail banking, that is, services for individual customers. I saw him about a year later. He said, "I can design the new products. I can test them in the field and prove that they are good and that people will pay for them. But the bank can't deliver them. It doesn't have the required computer systems, and it cannot put them together in a reasonable length of time." Success in banking and other financial services has become dependent on good information technology.

In the 1960s, two management scientists working for an oil company discovered a fascinating marketing phenomenon that applies to gas stations. Most people thought that if you kept putting more Arco stations in the same city, they would soon start to cannibalize business from one another, with rapidly diminishing returns for Arco. But Hartung and Fisher (1965) discovered that on the contrary, as you add stations in the same market, the number of gallons sold per station will increase. The reasons are several. For example: (1) Each station is an outdoor advertisement for all stations of its brand; (2) people would rather have a credit card for a brand with many stations, rather than a few; and (3) local advertising is far more efficient if the company has many stations.

The same is true of most franchised outlets: Sales per outlet increase with the number of outlets in a city.

Now think about automatic teller machines.

In Massachusetts a few years ago, a holding company, BayBank, pulled together under a single umbrella many banks previously confined to individual counties by Massachusetts law. BayBank established a common name and logo across the state. It was not the first bank to have ATMs, but it was the first to have them everywhere. Now it owns retail banking in Massachusetts and is awash in consumer deposits, the envy of the big Boston commercial banks. Information technology strikes again. And in this case it follows well-known laws of marketing (see Figure 20.3).

More electronic markets

The Boston Computer Exchange runs an ad with a telephone number and a post office box. No physical address is given.

Video technology is big in marketing. Sales brochures on videotape are common; many schools send tapes to prospective students, for example. Buick will give you a diskette that you can run on a PC at home or in the showroom to view animated pictures of automobiles and examine models and options.

On the other hand, electronic home shopping has moved more slowly than expected. Several experimental systems have folded. The vision of people sitting at home and flipping through video catalogs has not yet materialized in a substantial way. Videotext services such as Prodigy, Delphi, and the Source, however, offer computer shopping, and usage may grow as the number of home computers equipped with modems increases. But it may take another generation of higher-resolution computer screens, greater communications bandwidth, and lower-cost graphics to make home shopping widespread. For example, the way to do grocery shopping at

Figure 20.3. Automatic teller machines not only enhance service and save labor, but also are robot soldiers in the battle for market share in retail banking.

home may be to push a video image of a shopping cart down store aisles on a screen, picking items off the shelves along the way by means of a mouse.

The sales force is an expensive and important part of any organization in which any leverage in effectiveness can have large payoffs. Here information technology is providing new efficiencies in lead tracking, field reporting, and, perhaps most important, new services such as the analysis of customer problems on laptop computers. Moriarty and Swartz (1989) found examples.

An oft-cited case of the impact of information technology on marketing is the airline reservation system. American and United gained significant competitive advantages by putting their systems in the hands of travel agents. But without as much publicity, something else is going on behind the scenes that uses information technology in combination with other activities, social and analytic, to place extra passengers on the planes. This is the overbooking system, known more politely in the industry as *yield management*. Overbooking sounds bad, but perhaps it should not, for there is a hidden marketing triumph here. Here's why:

The airlines subsist on business passengers, and business passengers need the service and pick up the tab. As queuing theory shows, however, if there are enough flights to make the business passengers happy, there will be empty seats. Therefore, why not sell the extra seats at a discount to people who are willing to stand by for last minute boarding? This is a good idea, but when the airlines try to do this, various not-too-scrupulous people call up and make reservation under false names. Then they show up at the airport as standbys, and surprise, there are no-shows and plenty of seats available.

The airlines' answer is overbooking. This also helps with the no-shows arising from road traffic delays, late business meetings, and the like. But overbooking raises other problems: If you want a fight, try to eject a passenger with a confirmed reservation from an airplane. Needed is one more good idea, and that is: buying people off the plane. Thus free market supply and demand are put to work. Every plane contains at least a few people who are not in a big hurry. So offer them something that is valuable to them but not quite so valuable to the airline. What is that something? It is airplane tickets. This creates a win–win situation. What makes it all possible is (1) the data provided by the reservation system, (2) some fine management science forecasting and seat inventory models, and (3) the basic strategic idea that you would be willing to do some marginal cost pricing. The whole system is a remarkably successful, if complex, informational and social operation that significantly increases capacity utilization.

A specialized workstation called DesignCenter, developed by a Weyerhaeuser subsidiary, Innovis, targets the do-it-yourself market. Home improvement stores install a kiosk containing DesignCenter in their display area. A customer, usually with modest help from a sales clerk, can easily design a home deck by himself or herself using the interactive system. The look and feel is somewhat analogous to a video game. The deck is visually displayed and easily manipulated to meet the customer's wishes concerning size, shape, type of wood, and the like. After the design is finished, a push of a button brings a complete bill of materials with dimensions, costs, and other specifications for all parts. The customer can walk away with a drawing of the finished product and a hard copy of the bill of materials. Using the DesignCenter, do-it-yourselfers created $150 million in projects during the first eight months of operation. Much of this represents a market expansion of projects that home owners would not otherwise have built.

DesignCenter typifies an important new class of applications of information technology in which the customer solves his or her own problem, thereby increasing the primary demand for the product. In presenting the workstation to retailers, Weyerhaeuser, emphasizes the involvement of store sales people in assisting the customer, thereby strengthening relations between manufacturer and retailer as well as ensuring that the customer can obtain any necessary information not contained in the computer program.

The first point is that information technology is pervasive in marketing. We use it at every turn to gain a little or a lot of competitive advantage, improve our services, save money, and generally do a better job. Successful applications create new benefits at one or more stages along the chain of added value in the product or service. A hierarchy of improvements is the following:

1. *Labor displacement.* This is a traditional computer role. Among the examples we cited, the Sears catalog order system clearly falls into this category. So does the automatic teller machine, and we can also include videotape presentations.
2. *Service enhancement.* Surprisingly, just about every example of labor displacement includes service enhancement, which, in fact, may be more important. Automatic tellers are open 24 hours a day and appear in more places than do branch banks. Machines lack the personal touch often associated with good service, but they bring timeliness, convenience, and the advantage of being impersonal: You can discover in privacy that your account is overdrawn. Some of the cited examples, for instance, catalog retailing, have blossomed because of service enhancements and then have maintained their competitiveness through labor efficiencies.
3. *Improved market intelligence.* An important source of value from information technology is better understanding and pinpointing your markets. Direct marketing benefits from computerized lists of names spun off from other activities. Screening lists by prespecified criteria is often possible; for example, you can restrict a mailing to people who have bought more than $100 worth of goods by mail in the last six months. Analyzing customer records reveals individual tastes and preferences so that people can be sent information only on goods that might interest them. One of the biggest new adventures is taking place with an explosion of marketing data in consumer package goods. We will probe this in depth later.
4. *Creation of new entities.* Some organizations and services could not have existed before an enabling information technology came into being. The electronic markets, like NASDAQ, are examples. DesignCenter is completely dependent on modern computer technology. Certain financial services also fall into this category. In principle they seem simple, but in practice they are remarkably difficult to implement and require sophisticated hardware, software, and communications.

CONSUMER PACKAGED GOODS: A DISCONTINUITY IN MARKETING INFORMATION

A striking example of the information age at work is taking place in the consumer packaged goods industry. Packaged goods consist primarily of the grocery business (i.e., food), along with health and beauty aids (e.g., aspirin and shampoo). The largest quantities of packaged products are sold through supermarkets, which therefore have become the main focus of the manufacturers' marketing attention. Supermarkets sell $280 billion of goods per year, or 20 percent of all retail sales.

The main information technology activity in packaged goods today is behind the scenes. There is a rush to use new information to understand better which marketing actions work and which do not, so as to improve marketing efficiency and effectiveness. The changes are taking place rapidly, which warrants calling them a discontinuity in marketing practice. There are lessons here, too, for other information-intensive industries.

Some of the forces at work are large quantities of new data, lower hardware costs, improved software, new marketing science models, and expert systems. As we shall see, these have led to the founding of new companies, organizational change within manufacturers, and power shifts in the distribution channels.

Early history of information use

Sixty years ago, in the 1930s, Arthur C. Nielsen invented a scorecard for packaged goods companies, called *market share*. He did this by collecting data on retail grocery sales in a national sample of stores. Teams of people called *auditors* were sent into the stores every two months. They counted inventory and went over invoices for hundreds of products in each store. The auditors adjusted the amounts on the invoices for the change in inventory and thereby determined bimonthly sales through the store. An acre of starched-collar clerks in Chicago added all this up with hand-cranked calculators. Another roomful drew bar chart reports, and presto, the Nielsen Food Index was born. Indeed, marketing stars at Procter & Gamble and General Foods rose and set based on Nielsen market shares.

By the 1960s, new sources of data had appeared, and a typical consumer packaged goods company ran its business with up to four kinds of numbers: its own factory shipments, Nielsen shares, warehouse withdrawal data provided by Selling Areas Marketing, Inc. (SAMI), and consumer purchase histories collected by national diary panels. As may be seen in Figure 20.4, these data sources represent different places to look at the distribution pipeline. Each source tells a story about a different actor in the system. Everything was in hard copy, but, we should note, the IBM 370 had arrived, and management information systems (MIS) departments were learning how to master the large systems that handled ordering, billing, and other high-volume jobs.

Decision support systems

In the 1970s came the initial flowering of decision support systems (DSSs). The original technological impetus was time-sharing. Then database management systems came in, along with fourth-generation languages. Most of the fourth-generation languages that found favor in financial analysis were not suitable for marketing, however, because they could not handle large databases. But the few that could became widely used, and marketing data slowly inched their way on-line.

The most significant accomplishment of information technology in this era was putting companies in control of their own shipments data. In the early 1970s I recall a sales crisis with one of Nabisco's flagship brands. As a result, the director of marketing wanted to compare the most recent six months' sales with the corresponding

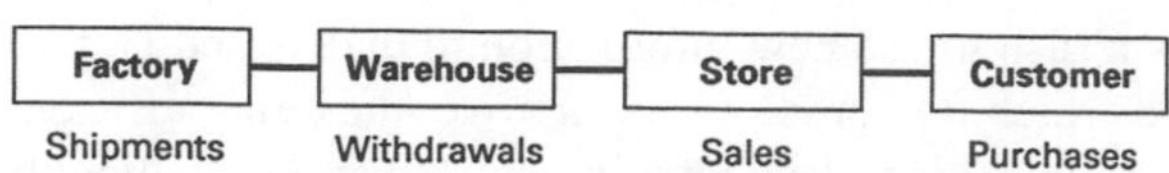

Figure 20.4. In the 1960s, data were available for measuring sales at each stage of the product pipeline, but all the reporting was in hard copy.

period a year ago in the midwest region. His chief lieutenant for doing this, the head of marketing research, was told by MIS that he would have to have, besides a budget—which was no problem—special priority and that even then it would take four to six weeks to do the programming and make the runs.

A colleague and I were visiting the company at the time. Contemplating the development of on-line systems, we asked the marketing research director whether he would be willing to pay $100 to have the answer in 10 minutes. He pulled out his wallet and said he would pay for it himself. The great irony of the story, however, occurred two months later when he received his report. He glanced at it for a few moments, and the numbers looked peculiar. Then he realized that he had forgotten that a teamsters' strike in Chicago had disrupted sales during a month of the previous year. The printout was meaningless. He immediately knew how to fix it, but that took another week.

Market response reporting

By the early 1980s the days of the MIS bottleneck were gone in most large companies as modern DSS databases and on-line systems for marketing information were put into place. Indeed, starting in the late 1970s people began to raise their sights and differentiate between *market status reporting* and *market response reporting*. Figure 20.5 makes the distinction. Before this time most marketing decision support systems had supplied what may be called *status information*: What are company and competitive sales volumes? Shares? Prices? And so forth. This is key information for running the business, but of equal and often greater importance are answers to market response questions: What is effect of price changes on sales? How profitable are promotions? What is the impact of advertising? With the data going into the on-line systems of the early 1980s, companies began to scratch at these questions and learn enough to whet their appetites.

All of this was good, but it was mostly doing what people had been doing laboriously in batch systems before DSS. It was quicker, better, and in greater quantity, but not a discontinuity.

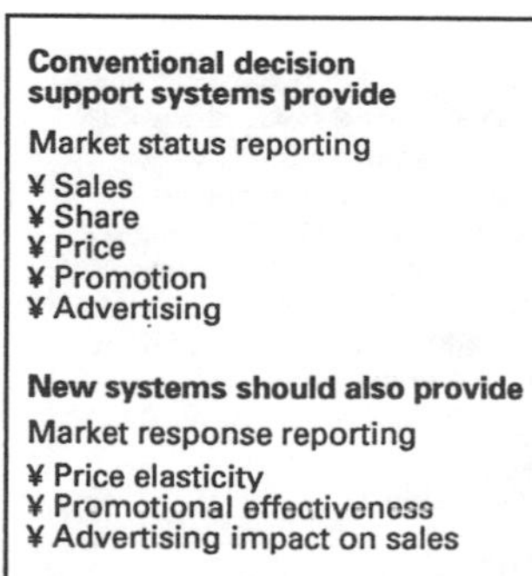

Figure 20.5. Improved data and analytic methods permit the measurement of market response and hold the promise of reporting it on a regular basis.

The Universal Product Code

Optical scanning of bar codes on grocery packages started in 1974 with the goal of saving labor by speeding up checkouts. Implementation of the Universal Product Code (UPC) represented a remarkable achievement of cooperation among manufacturers and retailers. The growth of installations was slow, however, and as late as 1980, less than 15 percent of national grocery sales were being scanned. Although there was much talk about using scanning information for "soft savings," that is, marketing purposes, nothing much happened because there were too few scanning stores? But in 1979 a pair of entrepreneurs in Chicago decided not to wait any longer. They simply bought and installed scanners themselves. The company, Information Resources, Inc. (IRI), developed what it calls BehaviorScan and may generically be called *laboratory markets*.

Figure 20.6 describes the idea. IRI initially put scanners in all the supermarkets in two small cities, Pittsfield, Massachusetts, and Marion, Indiana. This gave them sales and price data as a direct spin-off from the scanners. In addition, they started recording all the newspaper ads and all the special displays in the stores. In each market they recruited a panel of 3000 to 4000 households whose members identified themselves at checkouts so that their purchase records could be set aside in the store computer and accumulated. The two markets were chosen for high cable television usage, and the panelists on the cable had specially modified television sets so that different groups of people could be sent different commercials, in test and control fashion. Thus was introduced a powerful testing laboratory for new products, television advertising, and other marketing activities. The whole system was extremely successful and grew rapidly until now there are about eight such markets.

In instrumenting the markets, IRI made a look-ahead move. It extracted the data directly from the stores electronically, polling the stores at night by telephone from Chicago. Although this is more expensive than sending tapes by UPS, it is obviously faster and is also more reliable. (UPS does not lose the tape, but the stores may lose the data if they sit around too long.) As happens so often in information technology, there are unexpected fringe benefits from electronic delivery.

Here is an example of one such benefit: In late 1985 it became apparent that a drought in Brazil would very likely ruin the coffee crop and send world coffee prices skyward. A major food company contacted IRI and said, "How fast can you give us

Figure 20.6. Laboratory markets are ideal for testing new products, TV advertising, and other marketing activities.

coffee prices and sales movement at retail?" The answer was: "We can give them to you nine days after the close of the store week for the IRI laboratory markets." This compared with an average age of four to eight weeks for top-line reports from more conventional syndicated sources. The data arrived by diskette to run under flexible DSS software on a personal computer.

The drought did indeed devastate the coffee crop, and starting in late December, a coffee task force of senior managers in the food company met weekly to review the latest data on what the consumers and retailers were doing in the market. Out of these meetings came the company's pricing policy.

Figure 20.7 shows some of these data, which are fascinating. They show how your household was buying coffee that January. The top curve is the price. It is steady on the left, suddenly runs up in January, and then tapers down during 1986. The lower curve shows total coffee sales. We see some seasonality on the left; people switch to iced tea and soft drinks in summer. But notice the spike. When the price started to rise, people stocked up on coffee but stopped well before the price peak. Very smart. It also appears that during 1986, with coffee prices considerably higher than they were the previous year, overall coffee purchases were down. Such data permit easy calculation of price elasticity for the product category.

Note that this whole managerial scenario is a far cry from the frustrated marketing research director described earlier who had to wait a month to obtain an analysis of last year's data. The incident illustrates how advances in information technology speed up and improve the quality of marketing decision making. But it is just the start of the discontinuity that is taking place.

The data explosion

A new generation of tracking and status reporting services has been created. Scanner stores now represent most of the sales volume through supermarkets, and it is therefore possible to design a valid national sample of 2000 to 3000 scanner stores and develop a data service based on them. The two major players are Information Resources

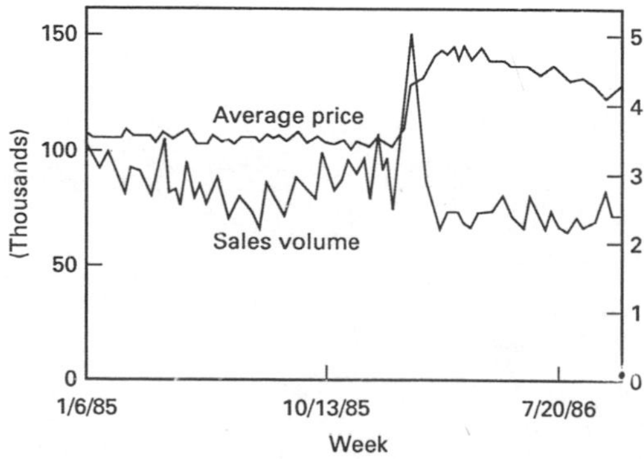

Figure 20.7. Weekly data, quickly reported, are valuable in fast-breaking marketing situations. A drought in Brazil caused a run-up of coffee prices and a rush by households to stock up. Then, because of high prices, sales fell below pre-drought levels.

and Nielsen Marketing Research. Their services cover individual major markets as well as the whole United States. Both companies include, besides basic sales and price data, specially collected information on store displays, newspaper advertising in the market, and coupon drops, all classified and broken out in a great variety of ways.

The distribution pipeline in Figure 20.8 shows the potential value of the new data for learning market response. Each actor in the system influences sales to the others by means of the marketing variable shown. Scanner data offer the possibility of measuring virtually all the response relationships along the pipeline.

All this sounds wonderful. But there is a hitch. The amount of data is overwhelming. Consider the new detail now available: weeks instead of four weeks or bimonths (this increases the data by a factor of 4 to 8), UPCs instead of aggregate brands (a factor of 3 to 5), the top 40 markets instead of broad geographic regions (a factor of 4 to 5), new tracking measures (a factor of 2 to 3), and chain breakouts (a factor of 1 to 3). Multiplying out these factors reveals that roughly 100 to 1000 times as many data are at hand than previously. Furthermore, any analysis that requires going to individual stores or to panel households brings in new, equally large databases. Let us take 100 as a conservative multiplicative factor for the data that many companies are now bringing in-house for everyday use.

This kind of change is not easy to comprehend. It means that if a report took an hour to look through before, the corresponding document with all the possible new breakouts would take 100 hours to look through. In other words, the new detail will not be looked at.

Solutions will come in stages

What should be done about this data explosion? Certainly there is value and competitive advantage to be found amid the detail, but how do we get at it? There is no single answer; solutions will come in stages:

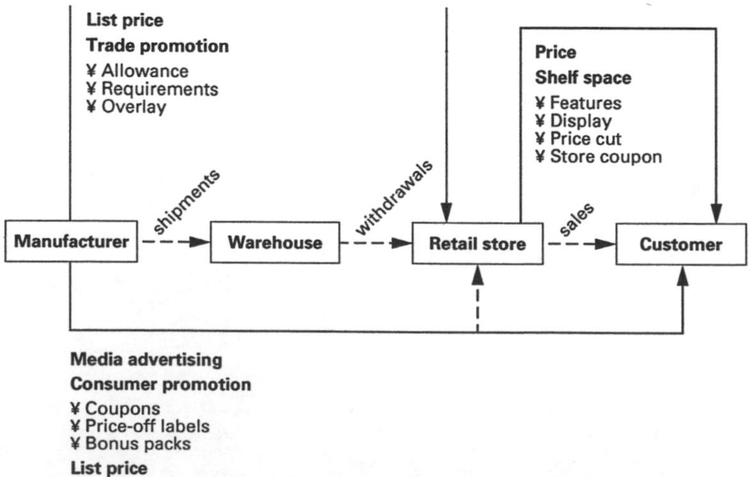

Figure 20.8. Each actor along the distribution pipeline influences other through its set of marketing activities. Each activity is a target for a measurement of effectiveness using the new data sources.

Stage 1: Get access. This is well under way. Manufacturers have set up systems that permit them to get their arms around the new databases. Because they must continue to run their businesses at the same time, they have given high priority to recreating aggregate numbers similar to those they have used before so as to make a smooth transition into new modes of operation.

Stage 2: Automate the analysis. Whatever people were doing to examine data previously is almost certainly inadequate now, at least for obtaining the new value. The old way consisted of an individual analyst, often an assistant product manager or management scientist, putting the data into a spread sheet or a statistical package and manipulating them to look for relationships and try to solve particular problems.

Although individual analysis continues, of course, no company is willing to hire 100 times its present staff in order to pour over the new data and find out what they contain. Some other solution must be found. Part of the answer lies in automation. Although the required software will have to be developed, market response analysis often follows identifiable rules and can be approached through expert systems techniques.

By analyzing market response, I mean going over historical events to determine the effectiveness of marketing activities. Trade promotions, coupons, price changes, store merchandising, and the like all are fair game for evaluation. There are thousands of such events when you break them out by brand, geographical area and time period. Much work is already under way to automate this type of analysis and obtain its benefits. The following are some examples:

Promotion evaluation

Packaged goods manufacturers run trade promotions. These are temporary wholesale discounts and usually include a contract with the retailers for merchandising activity, for example, putting the product on special display at the end of an aisle for a week. Or the retailer may agree to advertise the product in the local newspapers. Ordinarily the store temporarily reduces the shelf price, and the net result is often a big bump in retail sales. You can see an example in Figure 20.9, which shows the sales peaks for several successive promotions.

Now, how do you know whether a promotion was profitable for the manufacturer? Well, you would like to know what sales would have been without the promotion. The usual way to determine this is, essentially, to draw a line through the data points for which there were no promotions. Such a line is called a *baseline*. But as it turns out, drawing a baseline is difficult. Accordingly, Abraham and Lodish (1987) have developed a set of procedures and a computer program for drawing a baseline and determining the difference between the baseline and actual sales. This gives the incremental sales for the promotion, from which its profit can be calculated.

The baseline program extensively uses expert systems ideas. That is, it mimics the hands-on processes of the authors, a pair of skilled marketing scientists, and employs their heuristics for handling the many issues that come up when working with the data. To give you the flavor of this, we quote from the authors' flow diagram. They use such phrases as "contaminated points are removed from the data," "nonnormal points are diagnosed," and "corrective actions." Such words are more in the realm of human judgment than mathematical technique. The work thus is a good example of combining statistical methods and expert system ideas in an automated

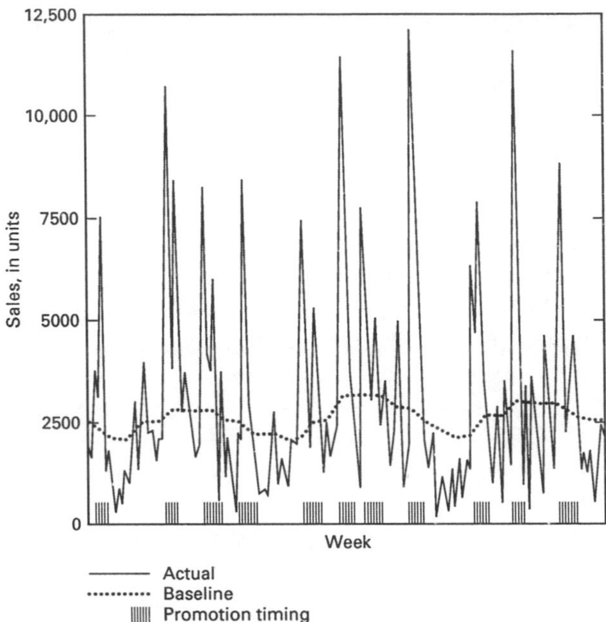

Figure 20.9. Weekly shipments to retailers show sharp peaks corresponding to manufacturers' promotions. The evaluation program constructs a baseline to represent what sales would have been without a promotion.

analysis. The methodology has since been hardwired into efficient code for high-volume commercial processing.

Coupon evaluation

Manufacturers in 1988 distributed about 220 billion cents-off coupons. Approximately 3.2 percent were redeemed at an average face value of about 42 cents. The cost of this, plus distribution and handling, produced a total bill of $ 4.7 billion. In the past people have had only the number of redemptions (cashed-in coupons) with which to evaluate their coupons. But this was inadequate because no one knew how many of the customers redeeming coupons would have bought the product anyway. The money at stake suggests a large payoff from a valid measurement of coupon profitability.

Today this can be routinely done using panel data—the purchase histories being collected from 60,000 households in 25 markets. These, and copious computer time, permit the building of a model that will predict the brand purchase probability for each household in the panel. The model is calibrated over some time period, say, a year, before a coupon drop. Then the model projects ahead to forecast what the households would have purchased without the coupon. An example is given in Figure 20.10. The difference between forecast and actual sales appears as the shaded area, which measures the extra sales attributable to the coupon and becomes the basis for a report card of coupon effectiveness for each coupon dropped.

The model underlying the evaluation comes from university research. The basic technique is the multinomial logit as adapted by Guadgni and Little (1983) for scanner panel data. In commercial practice, the process is partially automated. Full automation is needed, however, and will require building further intelligence into the program because real markets of real customers are full of unexpected (though understandable) events.

Derived data bases

Promotion and coupon evaluations themselves accumulate into valuable new databases. Some of these are big, not in the sense of megabytes, but in terms of people absorbing what they mean. Over a thousand coupons have already been evaluated, and hundreds of new ones are analyzed each year. Promotion response differs by event by market and by brand, adding up to tens of thousands of numbers.

These are *market response databases* and contain much valuable information. By analyzing them we can develop norms about what to expect and a detailed understanding of why certain marketing actions worked and others did not. For example, by looking at many different coupons, we can determine whether high face-values are more profitable than low ones, full-page ads better than half-page ones, and so on. There is a competitive advantage for the companies who understand these results first. It seems likely that except for day-to-day tracking purposes, internal analysts in companies will spend more time on market response databases than on the raw scanner data themselves.

Stage 3: Find the news. Suppose that a half-dozen new computer tapes have just come in with the latest four weeks of scanner data for our product category. What important has happened? Who has gained share? Where did it come from—what regions, what brands? Who has lost share? Perhaps there is a rumor that a major competitor was promoting heavily in Los Angeles. How heavy was it really? How much did it affect us?

These are typical events people want to know about early. In many companies, top-line reports of the latest results are distributed on a regular basis. They contain fairly detailed tables, breakouts and graphs, but almost always, they start with a cover memo that reports the major happenings. The memo is traditionally written by

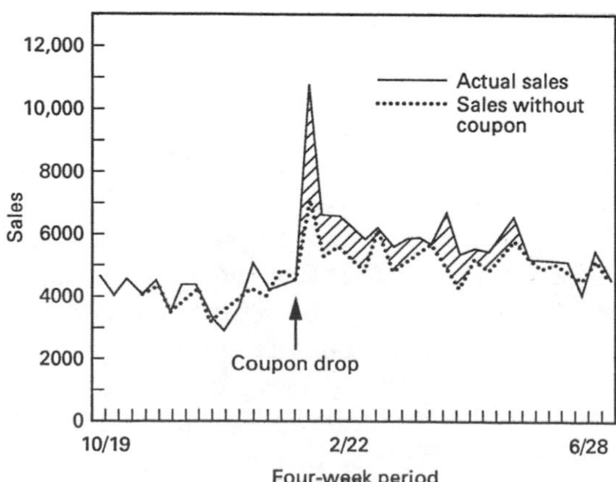

Figure 20.10. The difference between actual sales and predicted sales without the coupon measures the effect of the coupon and appears as the shaded area. Predicted sales are calculated from a product choice model based on 60,000 households.

the analyst who prepares the report. Significant changes in the market are noted—perhaps a substantial increase in category volume or a share loss for a key product in an important geographical area. The tables and charts provide details for the reader who wants to follow up.

A computer should write the cover memo.

In a project at MIT a few years ago, some students built a prototype that did this (Little, 1988; Stoyiannidis, 1987). Since then, the ideas have been picked up and further developed into a commercial product, CoverStory, by Information Resources (Schmitz, Armstrong, & Little, 1990). An example of the output appears in Figure 20.11.

Because the process is automated, you can easily generate the memo for any brand or category or segment of a category, depending on managerial interests. You can even look at the market through the eyes of your competitors, by running their brands. Or you can run the report for a district sales manager, in which instead of pulling out highlights by market, you can do it by key retail account.

This application also provides an important lesson for DSS architecture in the 1990s. Many companies have built DSSs that are basically retrieval systems. A file server holding the data is accessed over a local area network by a workstation that is essentially a PC. The design has focused on smooth user interfaces at the front end and standardized database management at the back. This was an ideal architecture for the marketing DSSs of the 1970s, when most applications involved people retrieving a few numbers to look at personally and analyze by hand.

But automated analyses and expert systems working against large databases require real processing power not available on a PC. They need what might be called MIPS, in the middle between a PC and a database. The computer architecture for this is not difficult to devise but probably will not happen unless marketing management makes known their need.

Knowledge delivery

Automated analysis is necessary for dealing with the data flood, but it is not enough. There is, I believe, too much response information. The issue is not what the computer can hold but, rather, how much a person can organize and assimilate just by looking at it. Needed are structures to turn the information into knowledge and techniques to deliver it. The former will come from people, and for the latter, technology will help.

Knowledge delivery will evolve through phases, typically: "What happened?" then, "Why did it happen?" and finally, "What do we do about it?"

Today people are focusing mostly on "What happened?" and the beginnings of "Why did it happen?" Prospects for rapid progress are good because many people inside and outside packaged goods companies are working with scanner data to solve day-to-day marketing problems. As successful applications emerge, they can be generalized and packaged for automatic on-line delivery. Expert systems technology is not the bottleneck but, rather, the development of marketing knowledge. Likely near-term applications are, for marketing, the diagnosis of brand performance and, for sales, the development of fact-based selling points for sales people's presentations to key accounts.

To: Director of Marketing
From: CoverStory
Date: 11/08/88
Subject: Ellios Brand Summary for four weeks ending June 26, 1988

Ellios' national share was 4.0% of the Total Frozen Pizza category for the four weeks ending 6/26/88. This is a decrease of .6 share points from a year earlier but up .7 points from last period. This share reflects volume sales of 1.2 million consumer units. The .6 point share loss may be partly attributed to 3.5 pts of ACV decrease in distribution vs yr ago.

Competitor Summary

Among Ellios' major competitors, the principal gainers are:

- Jenos: up 5.6 share points from last year to 13.1 (but down 1.3 since last period)
- Totinos +1.1 to 10.0 (but down 1.8 since last period)

and loser:

- Bernatellos -1.0 to .8

Ellios' share is 4.0 - down .6 points from the same period last year.

Jenos's share increase may be partly attributed to 6.0 pts of ACV increase in distribution versus a year ago.

Components of Ellios Volume

Within the Ellios line, share decreases have been sustained by:

- Ellios Frn Brd off .3 share points from last year to .1
- Ellios Trad -.3 to .5

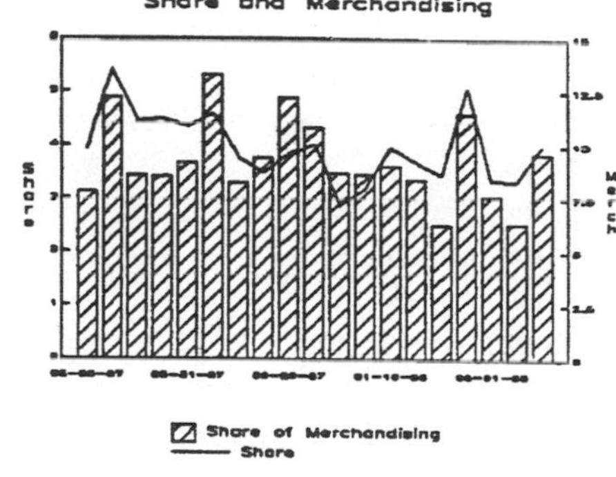

The brand components with relatively small changes since last year are:

- Ellios Snk / Slc unchanged from year ago but +.8 points since last period to 3.4

Ellios Frn Brd's share decrease may be partly attributed to 6.6 pts of ACV decrease in distribution vs yr ago.

Geographic Highlights

Ellios showed significant gains relative to a year ago in:

- Philadelphia, PA: up 2.6 share points from last year to 52.6. This may be partly attributed to 6.5 pts of ACV increase in distribution vs yr ago and 13.4 points increase in displays since last year.

but posted share losses in:

- Boston, MA -6.1 to 21.4. This may be partly attributed to 20.5 ACV points

Figure 20.11. Using expert systems techniques, a computer can scan a large database, identify important news, and report it in a natural-language memorandum.

The application of expert systems to scanner data is an active topic for a number of academic researchers. McCann and Gallagher (1988) have an ambitious program in progress, and Bayer and Harter (1989) reported on a PC-based system.

Looking ahead, I see a general problem and, out of it, a goal. Market response is analyzed today by internal staff groups, essentially internal consultants, and by external consultants. At the culmination of a study, they make a presentation to management. In the course of an hour's presentation the consultant summarizes the results of an effort that took perhaps three to six months of work. If the consultant is lucky, the audience will be interested, and the meeting will run over its allotted time by a half-hour or so. But no matter how well things work, a standard presentation provides a very narrow bottleneck through which to transmit information. Under these circumstances, there is great pressure to produce tight, top-line summaries and to uncover those implications that can be acted on immediately. This is all to the good, but much information is lost and never becomes available to product management because it does not happen to fit into the current need at the time the information was created.

One goal, therefore, is to find structures that will organize the market response information that will soon be generated and to devise methods for delivering relevant portions of that information to the decision maker at the time that he or she is thinking about the problem. I call this Stage 4 of the answer to the information glut.

As an example, consider a product management team that is planning its promotional program for the coming year. A brand has some set of current circumstances. It has a share and a rank in its product category. The category itself is characterized by an overall sales rate, a percentage of households using such products, a certain history of competitive activity, and the like. The brand may have specific current concerns, such as falling share, low distribution, or a new competitor. One would like a support system that could systematically bring to bear on the brand's problem at hand the distilled experience of hundreds of past marketing activities.

This could be done. Many companies have long had how-to-do-it handbooks on promotions, coupons, media, or whatever. These handbooks contain rules of thumb for what to do in various brand and market circumstances. Although the rules need extending and updating with the new knowledge being generated, they represent a worthwhile starting knowledge base. Based on such information, van Arsdell (1986) and Weise (1986) created a prototype promotion-advising system. It asks you questions about your product and then recommends actions. Although the system would require an order of magnitude more effort to become a practical tool, it suggests that with the output of automated market response analysis that is to come, we should be able to build a generation of electronic marketing advisers that would really be helpful.

Impact of information technology on the packaged goods industry

So far I have focused on behind-the-scenes data and their evolving utilization. Now let us stand back and assess the overall impact that this is having on the packaged goods industry, including its effect on organization and industry structure. Figure 20.12 provides an overview.

First of all, in the marketing function generally, we are seeing increased efficiency and effectiveness. This is what we have been discussing. Next, a major opportunity lies in using the new data to gain regional marketing advantage. Historically, the evolution of the grocery industry saw the emergence of giant companies like General Foods, Nabisco, and Procter & Gamble in the first half of this century. Such

INFORMATION TECHNOLOGY IMPACT ON PACKAGED GOODS INDUSTRY

In the marketing function
¥ Increased efficiency and effectiveness
¥ Shift to regional marketing

In the manufacturer's organization
¥ Sales and marketing move closer

In the grocery industry as a whole
¥ More power shifts to the retailer

Figure 20.12. New knowledge about marketing effectiveness is bringing changes at the company and industry levels.

companies invented national brands by producing uniform, high-quality goods, backed by national advertising budgets and reinforced with economies of scale in manufacturing, distribution, and marketing. Although national brands usually ended up being somewhat stronger in one part of the country than another and some of the marketing was tailored to the region, this was largely left to the sales force. The major elements of the marketing program—price, promotion, advertising, packaging—were determined at the home office.

Now with information costs dropping drastically, companies have data on a market-by-market basis for the top 40 or 50 markets and can act on the information. But they cannot reproduce the central staff in 50 regions. That is not the answer. They can, however, create small sales and marketing teams in their principal sales regions and give them strong DSS support. Several manufacturers are now implementing such an organizational change, a step that represents a major rethinking of the product management system that has been operating in the packaged goods industry for the last 50 years.

This is not likely to be the end of the changes, however. The new information is signaling a shift in power toward the retailers. Initially, retailers have not been as well situated as the manufacturers have been to gain value from the UPC data. They suffer from a lack of scale. A large food manufacturer deals with a few hundred or a thousand items that are clustered into brands, each of which might represent sales in the range of $10 million to $100 million. Therefore, a manufacturer deals with large entities and can afford to spend considerable money collecting and analyzing data for them. Consider, however, a retailer. A large supermarket may carry 20,000 items, whose sales might range from a few hundred to a few thousand dollars a year. Even when you multiply these figures by the number of stores in a chain, a retailer cannot afford to lavish as much attention on an individual item as a manufacturer can. However, the cost of processing information is plummeting, and already the retailers are beginning to find actionable content in their data, especially by analyzing them at the category level, which is the most meaningful unit for them. More and more retailers will certainly analyze such data. One implication of this is that strong brands will grow stronger, whereas weak ones will be in trouble. This is not a matter of market power but, rather, of increased efficiency in the marketplace. It also sounds like something that is, on net, a good outcome.

What we can conclude? A huge new database has arrived in consumer packaged goods and, lagging a little, the ability to extract useful information from it. The totality of the data has not been absorbed yet but soon will be. The data permit measurements and understanding that reveal inefficiencies in the system and opportunities for improvement. As a result, companies will stop doing a lot of things that do not work well and do some things better. By and large, the market will become more efficient: We are seeing changes in roles and in organization.

WILL INFORMATION TECHNOLOGY MAKE MARKETING OBSOLETE?

Paradoxically, although marketing is almost universally regarded as essential to modern organizations, marketing departments have come under increasing fire.

Charges of inadequacy and inefficiency are common. The U.S. automobile industry receives regular abuse, being accused of failing to provide the cars people want. Critics assert that the supermarket shelves are filled with products that differ from one another only in hype. Trade promotions in the packaged goods industry have created striking distribution inefficiencies by pushing products through distribution channels in big lumps—the promotional discounts offered by manufacturers cause retailers to "forward buy," that is, stock up at the low price to meet future needs. These large, lumpy orders not only require manufacturing plants to run in a stop-and-go manner but also lead the retailers to build new warehouses just to accommodate the promotional merchandise. A potentially smooth production and distribution process has been made inefficiently erratic.

One hears other criticisms: "Marketing is too important to be left to the marketers." A case in point is the "house of quality" methodology in manufacturing (Hauser & Clausing, 1988). In this planning and communication process, the "voice of the customer" permeates engineering design, parts specification, and manufacturing process planning, through to the production itself. Although the voice of the customer and the house of quality epitomize the fundamentals of marketing, the methodology originated in manufacturing at a Japanese shipyard and is sponsored in most U.S. companies by engineering, not by marketing.

One may reasonably ask: Will information technology alleviate or accentuate these difficulties? What is the role of marketing as business becomes increasingly information centered?

Before answering, we shall examine some of the forces that the information age is placing on the firm and thence marketing. As Glazer (1989) and Braddock (1989) pointed out, information technology blurs the classic strategies of cost leadership (seeking market share through low cost) and differentiation (targeting special market segments). Traditionally, low cost is achieved by standardization and economies of scale. Then broad markets can be approached competitively. Differentiation, on the other hand, focuses narrowly on meeting the needs of a specific customer group. But information technology offers the possibility of achieving both, because it facilitates not only rapid and flexible design but also targeted delivery of products and services.

Therefore, it is increasingly feasible to pursue a market niche strategy in many niches at once. As databases grow and supply more knowledge about customers, we can better determine their wishes and how to communicate with them. With the help of information technology we shall often be able to handle large groups of customers with remarkable individuality.

The opportunities for product flexibility have been widely recognized by the financial service industry with its proliferation of cash management accounts, different mutual funds, money market accounts with checking privileges, CDs, credit cards, debit cards, and so on. Citicorp, for example, sees itself as being in the information business. Braddock (1989) stressed the close connection between providing information-intensive services to customers (automatic tellers, automated voice interrogation of account data, varied kinds of accounts) and using the resulting databases to understand customers' wishes and cater to them.

The ability of information technology to permit large scale operations and yet provide individual attention is only just beginning to be tapped. As part of its information-oriented strategy, Citicorp plans to build a scanner database of grocery purchase histories for 20 million households. This is customer information on a grand scale. That many households is 100 times the number currently monitored by market research companies. The goal, of course, is different: It is operational—to provide new services to the household, such as "frequent buyer" programs that reward brand loyalty or store loyalty with a kind of electronic green stamps, or to deliver coupons to individual households based on their historical buying patterns.

Such an undertaking is but one example of a rapidly growing field of direct marketing to customers, sometimes known as *database marketing*. As Roscitt (1988) observed, there are dozens of commercial databases providing remarkable details about various characteristics of the American consumer, from demographics to product ownership and purchase habits. Many of these are broken out by small geographic areas, such as zip codes or neighborhoods, and even by household. Often the data can be combined with a firm's own customer transaction histories to understand better what products might be of interest. This process will lead to far more efficient and effective marketing programs than possible by means of indiscriminate mailings or broadcast media.

Yet such direct marketing, with its dependence on large systems of data collection, processing, and analysis, looks more like operations than marketing and calls into question the traditional marketing function.

To be competitive, companies will organize to get close to their customers. An example that we saw earlier was of packaged goods manufacturers moving to organize its marketing and sales teams regionally. Such teams know the local conditions, receive up-to-date tracking data via workstations, and, increasingly, can perform automated analyses such as generating potential selling points for use with key accounts. Certain kinds of activities have long been local—for example, community-oriented public relations—but one sees more and more television commercials for national products that show the local city in the background. This all fits with the concept of flat organizations and fast response to the customer, but it weakens the traditional national marketing planning at headquarters.

As one looks through the marketing mix in modern information-intensive customer relationships, one finds a blurring of lines once thought rather separate (Glazer, 1989). For example, when we buy from a catalog using an 800 number and a credit card and have the product sent directly to our home, the benefits of the product itself are almost swamped by the benefits we receive in the form of information and information processing. The fact that the catalog came to us in the first place, the presentation of the product in the catalog, the telecommunications by 800 number, the financial credit transaction, the prompt delivery by UPS of Federal Express (traceable at any point in time), all of these information-intensive operations are key service attributes that we see as benefits and help us make the purchase in this manner rather than at a store. One can call the catalog a communications medium, UPS a distribution channel, and the credit card a part of the price transaction, but we would be artificially disassembling the essential unity of the system.

Returning to our question: Will information technology make marketing obsolete? If we think of marketing in conventional, compartmentalized, planning-back-at-headquarters terms, separate from operations, sales, and R&D, the answer is likely to be yes. But the answer is no if we think of marketing as distributed throughout the organization, bringing in the voice of the customer through appropriately collected information and helping define and integrate a bundle of benefits with R&D, operations, and sales. Then information and information technology will help transform and strengthen marketing throughout the organization.

REFERENCES

Abraham, M., & L. Lodish (1987). PROMOTER: An automated promotion evaluation system. *Marketing Science* 6 (Spring): 101–23.

Bayer, J., & R. Harter (1989). SCAN*EXPERT: An expert system for analyzing and interpreting scanning data. Working paper, Carnegie-Mellon University, October.

Braddock, R. S. (1989). Keeping the customer at the fore. Paper presented to the 1989 Marketing Conference, Conference Board, New York, October.

Glazer, R. (1989). Marketing and the changing information environment: Implications for strategy, structure, and the marketing mix. Report no. 89–108. Marketing Science Institute, March.

Guadgni, P. M., & J. D. C. Little (1983). A logit model of brand choice calibrated on scanner data. *Marketing Science* 2 (Summer): 203–38.

Hartung, P. H., & J. L. Fisher (1965). Brand switching and mathematical programming in market expansion. *Management Science* 11 (August): 231–43.

Hauser, J. R., & D. Clausing (1988). The house of quality. *Harvard Business Review* 66:63–73.

Little, J. D. C. (1988). CoverStory: An expert system to find the news in scanner data. Working paper, Sloan School of Management, Massachusetts Institute of Technology, September.

McCann, J. M., & J. P. Gallagher (1988). The future of marketing systems: From information to knowledge systems. Report from the Marketing Workbench Laboratory, Duke University, September.

Moriarty, R. T., & G. S. Swartz (1989). Automation to boost sales and marketing. *Harvard Business Review* 67 (January–February): 100–109.

Roscitt, R. R. (1988). Direct marketing to consumers. *Journal of Consumer Marketing* 5 (Winter): 5–14.

Schmitz, J. D., G. D. Armstrong, & J. D. C. Little (1990). CoverStory—Automated news finding in marketing. *Interfaces* 20 (November–December): 29–38.

Stoyiannidis, D. (1987). A marketing research expert system. M.S. thesis, Sloan School of Management, Massachusetts Institute of Technology.

Van Arsdell, H. (1986). Expert systems in marketing: A promotion advisor. M.S. thesis, Sloan School of Management, Massachusetts Institute of Technology.

Weise, S. L. (1986). An expert system decision support system for marketing management. M.S. thesis, Sloan School of Management, Massachusetts Institute of Technology.

CHAPTER 21

The Influence of Communication Technologies on Organizational Structure: A Conceptual Model for Future Research

THOMAS J. ALLEN AND OSCAR HAUPTMAN

This chapter presents a conceptual model that hypothesizes how information technologies may help with two key functions of communication in research and development. The first function is to provide state-of-the-art information on the organizational technologies that are used. This function is typically carried out through a functional organization structure, which groups together individuals with similar technical specialties. The second function is to coordinate the technical specialties applied to the same task or project. This is typically accomplished by a project form of organization, which groups together individuals working on the same task. The cost of selecting one structure is the loss of the advantages of the other. Information technologies, such as electronic mail, computer conferencing, bulletin boards, and document search and retrieval systems, may be used to augment the chosen structure and to compensate to some degree for its limitations.

A very large body of research (Allen, 1984; Pelz & Andrews, 1966; Schilling & Bernard, 1964) shows communication among technical professionals in research and development (R & D) laboratories to be a significant determinant of technical performance and the productivity of R & D project teams. A major question today is what impact the explosive development in communication-related information technologies will have on communication in R & D. To what extent can these technologies show results at the "bottom line" and in what ways? Clearly, some organizational tasks are more amenable to productivity increase through information technologies than are others that might appear quite similar. The exploitation of these technologies thus must be administered with insight into communication-related issues and with organizational astuteness in implementing them.

Another question concerns the specific capabilities of communication-related information technologies. The extent to which the existing technological options such as electronic mail, computer conferencing, bulletin boards, and document search and retrieval systems differ from one another in accomplishing organizational objectives

Thomas J. Allen and Oscar Hauptman, *Communication Research,* Vol. 14, No. 5 (October 1987), pp. 575–87.

is still not known. Probably an equally important question concerns the task types for which they provide comparative advantages. The central question is to match taxonomies of task and communication-related information technologies.

A related issue is to determine just how much advantage can be gained from using new information technologies in R & D. Their new options are not panaceas for all communication problems. Their limits need to be explored, however, and developing models that can test those limits is a first step. In this chapter we present the initial formulation of a model for how new information technologies might be used to extend the range of options available for structuring organizational tasks. Although we know that communication technologies cannot substitute for other structural arrangements, they may be able to extend the reach of current options.

THE INFLUENCE OF STRUCTURE ON COMMUNICATION IN R & D

Communication plays a central role in achieving two goals that are critical to performance in an R & D organization. First, tasks must have state-of-the-art information in their technological base. One option is to build the organizational structure by clustering individuals who are in similar disciplines or technical specialties but who are working on different problems. This structure, the functional organization, will most effectively maintain current technological know-how. By grouping together people who share a common base of knowledge, functional structures enable them to keep one another informed on new developments in their area of knowledge.

Second, the activities across the various disciplines and specialties must be coordinated in order to accomplish the work of multidisciplinary tasks. When R & D professionals are put into project teams working toward a common output goal, activities can be coordinated more effectively. By gathering together people from different specialties who are working on related problems, the project organization enables those people to coordinate their efforts on those problems.

There is a clear trade-off between these two goals. Functional organizations promote communication to facilitate technological currency within specific disciplines or specialties, but at the cost of coordination across disciplines. Project organizations achieve this coordination by facilitating communication across disciplines, but at the cost of not maintaining state-of-the-art knowledge within specialties.

In the next section we present a conceptual model based on the communication needs of typical R & D tasks and show how functional and project structures help accomplish them. The model is closely linked to organizational information-processing theory (e.g., Daft & Macintosh, 1981; Tushman & Nadler, 1978) and its more recent articulation in studies of advanced information technologies (see Steinfield, 1985, for a review). The model addresses information processing on the task level, with implications for structural design on a departmental or functional basis.

ORGANIZATIONAL STRUCTURE SPACE: A CONCEPTUAL MODEL

The model defines a three-dimensional "organizational structure space" based on three factors that Allen (1984) showed to determine which of the two organizational forms will be preferred in any instance (Figure 21.1). The first dimension recognizes that technologies vary in their rate of development and in the rate at which new knowledge is generated. Some technologies, such as metal processing or oil refining, are currently mature and stable. Others, such as bioengineering or the development of superconducting materials, are more dynamic. The rate of change of technological know-how, defined as the first derivative of knowledge with respect to time, or dK/dt, serves as the first coordinate of the organizational structure space. The higher the value of dK/dt is, the stronger will be the need for an effective transfer of state-of-the-art technology. Consequently, there is a greater need for a specialty-oriented functional structure to do this. Although there is some similarity between the dK/dt dimension and Perrow's (1967) typology of technological "nonroutineness" (see also Whitey, Daft, & Cooper, 1983) or Tushman and Nadler's (1978) environmental uncertainty, these constructs lack the specific meaning of this dimension for technical activities on the task level. Thus the model states that if the technology is advancing rapidly, ceteris paribus, functional structures will be preferable to project teams.

The second dimension of the organizational structure space is also related to the need to acquire technical information—that is, the duration of the task. If the task duration (T) is comparatively short, a person working in even a rapidly advancing technology is unlikely to lose touch with its state of the art. On the other hand, in a long assignment of several years, being isolated from one's peers in one's specialty or discipline carries the danger of professional obsolescence. This suggests that if the scale of the task is such that the assigned personnel are expected to spend a long period of time on the task, ceteris paribus, functional structures will be preferable.

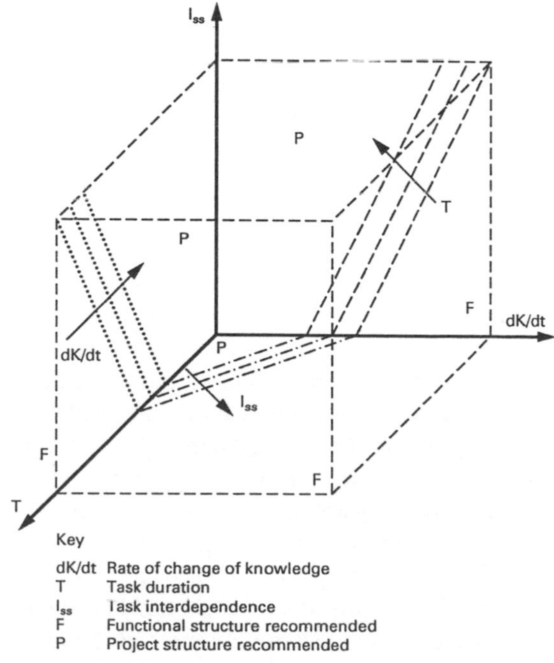

Figure 21.1. Organizational structure space.

The third dimension of the decision space is related to the requirement for organizational coordination, of bringing together the expertise of different professionals toward a single output goal. It is the interdependence among subsystems and components that the task comprises. The higher this interdependence (I_{ss}) is, and the more these subtasks join in the effort, the stronger the demand will be on the task team to coordinate its activities. This dimension cuts across Tushman and Nadler's (1978) intra- and interunit task interdependence, by looking at it as a task attribute rather than as a structural relationship. On the other hand, it is based to some extent on Thompson's (1967) typology of task interdependence and its articulation by Van de Ven and Delbecq (1974) and Van de Ven, Delbecq, and Koenig (1976).The following is proposed: If the subtasks of the joint effort seem to be highly interdependent, ceteris paribus, the project structure will be preferable, as it will effectively coordinate these subtasks.

A key question is how information technologies, such as electronic mail, computer bulletin boards, computer conferencing, and scientific information retrieval technologies, will influence this model. That is, how might new information technologies affect the prescribed division of the organizational structure space into "function" and "project" recommendations? Although there are still insufficient data to know whether or not communication-related information technologies are powerful enough to change individual and organizational behavior and performance, we can offer some tentative hypotheses for future investigation.

ALTERNATIVES FOR MEETING COMMUNICATION NEEDS

Our first hypothesis is that improvements in the information technologies make it easier for technical professionals to maintain up-to-date technological know-how. Document search and retrieval systems provide direct access to 3800 documentation files (Cuadra Associates, 1984). Although they have proved at best to be moderately successful for some disciplines or specialties, some can now be augmented by selective dissemination services based on artificial intelligence. These can find out a user's need and determine which journal articles or documents will be helpful. All of these systems unfortunately suffer from the same fatal flaw: They can provide the information, but it still must be read. And there is a substantial body of research to show that for the average engineer, this can be a problem (Allen, 1984).

Knowledge is best transferred to engineers by means of personal contact. The connection to literature and documentation is best made with the aid of intermediaries known as *technological gatekeepers* (Allen, 1984; Allen & Cohen, 1969). More recent developments in information technology may very well aid in connecting an engineer to an appropriate gatekeeper. Some companies, for example, have encouraged the creation of bulletin boards or forums that are organized around technical subjects. Anyone can send questions, or answers, or even dicta. Research (George, 1987) has shown that usually some people associated with these forums are experts on the particular subject and can supply most of the answers to the queries entered. In other words, the forum serves to connect people to the appropriate gatekeeper. This might help transfer knowledge in certain fields.

Table 21.1. Communication need, organizational solution, and technological contributions

Need	Organizational solution	Information-technology contribution
Coordination of subsystem or subelement work on a project	Project organization	Hierarchically organized, bulletin boards for project status reporting and configuration control
Knowledge transfer	Functional or departmental organization	Document search and retrieval systems
		Expert system-based selective dissemination of information
		Bulletin boards or forums for information search

Our second hypothesis is that the use of some information technologies can help coordinate a project team. This type of information system would work toward a goal currently provided by the project structure. For example, there are sophisticated forms of electronic mail in which forums are organized by topic (e.g., computer conferencing). These forums can be further organized hierarchically into subtopics or subsubtopics, and each of these topical subdivisions can be a subsystem, element, or component of a project (Stevens, 1981). Status reports are maintained and regularly updated, and they can also be used for queries and for managing interfaces among subsystems. Consequently, functional organizational structures might become feasible and effective for a somewhat broader range of interdependent technical tasks. Table 21.1 summarizes the potential points of influence of information technologies.

COMBINING STRUCTURE WITH TECHNOLOGY

The development of the new technologies affords an opportunity to use them to augment organizational structure. Despite their linking in the matrix form, the project and functional structures remain mutually exclusive. That is, in choosing one, the organization forgoes the benefits of the other. What cannot be done is to use either the project or the functional structure and enlarge it with the appropriate information technology to achieve some of the advantages of the alternative form. The potential effects of this are shown in Figure 21.2.

When using functional departments, work can be coordinated by using hierarchically organized computer bulletin boards for configuration control and subsystem status reporting. This allows team members to be dispersed among functional departments, thereby maintaining contact with their specialties and coordinating their joint effort electronically. In effect, this may shift the boundary for using functional structures to encompass a broader territory of high interdependence (I_{ss}) situations.

When using project organization, persons can be connected to their knowledge bases by means of computer forums organized around their technical specialties.

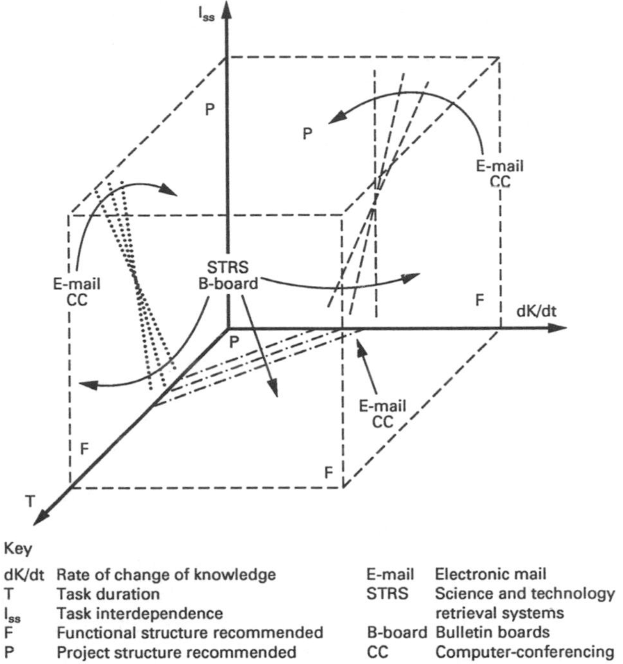

Key

dK/dt	Rate of change of knowledge	E-mail	Electronic mail
T	Task duration	STRS	Science and technology retrieval systems
I_{ss}	Task interdependence		
F	Functional structure recommended	B-board	Bulletin boards
P	Project structure recommended	CC	Computer-conferencing

Figure 21.2. Influence of communication-related information technologies on the organizational structure space in the 1990s.

They thereby gain more than the advantage of coordinating their work; they also are given some assistance in keeping abreast of the state of the art electronically, despite organizational and physical separation from colleagues in their own specialties. Thus the use of science and technology retrieval systems may shift the boundary to accommodate a greater use of project organizations when demand for technical updating remains high (i.e., higher rates of technological change, dK/dt, and longer duration tasks, T).

Note that in the dK/dt-T plane, there are two opposing forces. The more capable the knowledge-enhancing systems (i.e., forums and retrieval systems) are, the larger the region will be in which the project organization can be used. Conversely, the more capable the coordinating systems (e.g., hierarchical bulletin boards) are, the larger the area will be in which functional organization can be used. On the other hand, because the two variables dealing with know-how transfer (change in knowledge and task duration) are not differentially affected by information technology supplements, we do not expect significant changes in the slope of the function–project separating line in this plane.

In the dK/dt-I_{SS} plane, there also are two forces that operate in opposite directions. In this case, because one has more effect in dealing with subsystem interdependence, and the other with changes in knowledge, they result in a rotation of the project–function boundary. Because the task's coordination requirements may be more amenable to technological treatment, the dividing line will probably shift more toward the dK/dt coordinate, increasing the number of tasks for which the functional structure is recommended. The impact of document search and retrieval systems and of computer forums organized around specialties is expected to be somewhat less discernible, for the reasons cited earlier. Even though documents can be located and retrieved, they still must be read. Forums, at this point, have been shown to be effective for software developers, but it remains to be seen how well they will work in other specialties. As a result, the location of the dividing line in this plane will shift only slightly from the I_{ss} coordinate, somewhat increasing the number of tasks for which the project structure is recommended. Consequently, the more significant shift, that increasing the functional area, will occur for tasks of low interdependence and slow advancement of knowledge. On the other hand, the increase in the project area will be smaller and mostly for tasks of rapidly changing technologies and high interdependence. The net change in the number of tasks in the two structure areas will be a function of the power, effectiveness, and usability of the two information technologies.

This can be seen diagrammatically in Figure 21.3, which illustrates the trade-off between coordination and knowledge transfer. Moving along one of the curves, better coordination requires the sacrifice of some knowledge transfer, and vice versa. Improvements in the technology of communication may encourage a shift to a new curve. The new curve does not have to assume the same shape as its predecessor. Depending on whether the improvement is principally in the area of coordination or of knowledge, transfer tilts the curve in one direction or the other. In the figure, it is assumed that the advances in technology will affect coordination more than it will knowledge transfer.

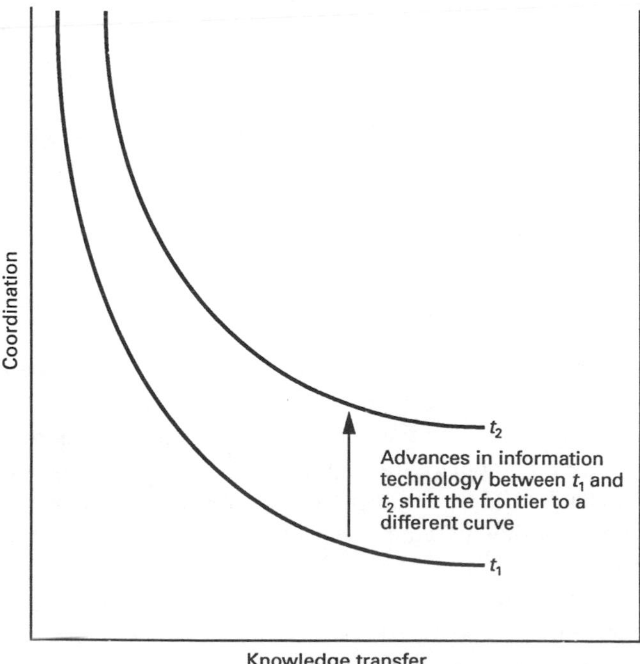

Figure 21.3. The trade-off between coordination and knowledge transfer in project management.

THEORETICAL IMPLICATIONS AND FUTURE RESEARCH

Theoretically, the proposed conceptual model is one of many that are useful in studying organizational behavior. It mainly applies to the task and departmental level, the operational and not the strategic organizational domain. The unit of analysis for a hypothetical study using this model should be a group of professionals performing an organizational task. Although the model was defined with R & D tasks in mind, it applies to any organizational tasks based on a changing field of knowledge or expertise. This expertise does not have to be technical in nature. Indeed, marketing or financial tasks, based on consumer behavior and economic knowledge, can benefit from coordination- or innovation-oriented analysis and from a better understanding of what communication-related information technologies can do for their effectiveness and efficiency.

Thus defining the general domain of the proposed model, the next question is how to use it for empirical research. Although the suggested model does not preclude qualitative, ethnographic, and case investigation, the final objective should be quantifying the model's dimensions. This will not be easy, but there certainly are possibilities.

In basic scientific fields, dK/dt can be estimated by measuring the half-life citations to journal articles (Kessler, n.d.). There are other possible measures such as the slope of technical progress curves (Fusfeld, 1970) that might be more appropriate to applied science and technology. These should be investigated in greater depth.

Subsystem interdependence can be estimated by project managers. Harris (1987) showed that valid estimates can be made and that project performance has a very strong inverse relationship to subsystem interdependence. Harris's research reinforces previous work in this field (e.g., Thompson, 1967; Van de Ven et al., 1976) that interdependencies and the resulting interface problems seriously affect performance. It also emphasizes the need for solving the problem of coordinating work in highly interdependent projects.

But this addresses only our understanding of the static model of Figure 21.1. Research also is needed on the dynamics of the process that results from introducing information-communication technology. We need to know much more about the magnitude of contributions that information technology can make to both coordination and technical currency. Information technology can provide some help in fulfilling these two key functions of communication in R & D. But it is not a cure-all, and its limits must be explored. At the same time, we must learn far more about the nature of the work itself, particularly in regard to white-collar work (see examples in Fleishman & Quaintance, 1984). Context-free typologies of communication-related information technologies should be quite useful for better matching of technologies and white-collar tasks.

Finally, even at the writing of this chapter the advances in information technologies offer new capabilities to organizations and raise new questions. For example, how can information technologies help meet R & D needs for creativity? This and other questions may be pursued through further conceptual development and research designed to investigate the hypotheses proposed here.

REFERENCES

Allen, T. J. (1984). *Managing the flow of technology*. Cambridge, MA: MIT Press.

Allen, T. J., & S. Cohen (1969). Information flow in R & D laboratories. *Administrative Science Quarterly* 14:12–19.

Cuadra Associates (1984). *Directory of online databases*. Santa Monica, CA: Cuadra Associates.

Daft, R. L., & N. B. Macintosh (1981). A tentative exploration into amount and equivocality of information processing in organizational work units. *Administrative Science Quarterly* 26:207–24.

Fleishman, E. A., & M. K. Quaintance (1984). *Taxonomies of human performance*. New York: Academic Press.

Fusfeld, A. (1970). The technological progress function: A new technique for forecasting. *Technological Forecasting* 1:301–12.

George, F. (1987). Usage and motivation of a large electronic bulletin board. M.S. thesis, Sloan School of Management, Massachusetts Institute of Technology.

Harris, M. S. (1987). Project performance as a function of subsystem interdependence for multi-site projects. M.S. thesis, Sloan School of Management, Massachusetts Institute of Technology.

Kessler, M. M. (n.d.). Technical information flow patterns. MIT Lincoln Laboratory report, Cambridge, MA.

Pelz, D. C., & F. M. Andrews (1966). *Scientists in organizations: Productivity climates for R & D*. New York: Wiley.

Perrow, C. (1967). A framework for the comparative analysis of organizations. *American Sociological Review* 32:194–208.

Shilling, C. W., & J. Bernard (1964). Informal communication among bioscientists. Report no. 16A. Washington, DC: George Washington University Biological Science Communication Project.

Steinfield, C. W. (1985). Explaining task-related and socio-emotional uses of computer-mediated communication in an organizational setting. Working paper, School of Communication, University of Houston.

Stevens, C. H. (1981). Many to many communication. Working paper no. 72. Sloan School of Management, Center for Information Systems Research, Massachusetts Institute of Technology.

Thompson, J. D. (1967). *Organizations in action*. New York: McGraw-Hill.

Tushman, M., & D. Nadler (1978). Information processing as an integrative concept in organizational design. *Academy of Management Review*, July, pp., 613–24.

Van de Ven, A. H., & A. L. Delbecq (1974). A task contingent model of work unit structure. *Administrative Science Quarterly* 19:183–97.

Van de Ven, A. H., A. L. Delbecq, & K. Koenig, Jr. (1976). Determinants of coordination modes within organizations. *American Sociological Review* 41:322–38.

Whitey, M., R. L. Daft, & W. H. Cooper (1983). Measures of Perrow's work unit technology: An empirical assessment and a new scale. *Academy of Management Journal* 26:45–63.

CHAPTER 22

Technological Innovation and Employment in Telecommunications

LISA M. LYNCH AND PAUL OSTERMAN

This chapter examines the impact of technological innovation on employment structures in a firm. It addresses two related questions: First, how does the diffusion of information technology influence employment levels across occupations within a firm? Second, how does a firm choose among alternative personnel mechanisms—layoffs, quits, retirements, early retirements, and transfers—to reach its target employment levels in each occupation?

Our study draws on two sets of literature; one analyzes how technology influences labor demand, and the other models internal labor market flows. Within the production function or cost function framework, it is customary to distinguish between educated (or high-skill) and uneducated (low-skill) labor and estimate elasticities of substitution or complementarity. One of the most recent efforts along these lines is Bartel and Lichtenberg's (1985) work, which builds on product cycle and learning curve ideas. The literature in this tradition typically provides few details about the impact of technological change on specific occupations because only very aggregated occupational data (e.g., blue collar versus white collar) are normally available. Another problem is that measures of technology are often crude (Bartel and Lichtenberg, e.g., have data only on the age of capital stock), and some occupational categories are often poor reflections of changes in the nature of job tasks. Two articles that address some of these problems are Denny and Fuss's (1983) study of the Canadian telephone industry and Osterman's (1986) analysis of the impact of computerization. Denny and Fuss examined the impact of a specific technology (direct long-distance dialing) on four occupational groups and found that the technology had the most adverse impact on the least-skilled workers. Osterman's work examined the impact of computerization on the employment of clerks and managers and found that the net effect of computerization had been to reduce the employment of these types of workers.

There have been few quantitative studies of internal labor market flows. The best work is in the context of the vacancy chain literature (Stewman & Konda, 1983;

White, 1970), which models flows using a Markov chain approach. However, these models are entirely descriptive and contain no behavioral relationships.

Our chapter focuses on the experience of the telecommunications industry, in which substantial technological and employment change occurred throughout the 1980s. Using a unique data set from one of the Bell Operating Companies, we estimate occupational labor demand curves that incorporate technology variables. This enables us to identify the varying impact of technology on specific occupations in much more detail than is typical in most research. We then extend this analysis to explore how the firm adjusts to change. The data permit us to identify several exit flows (quits, layoffs, retirements, early retirements, and transfers), and we try to show how these vary by the characteristics of the employees in the occupation.

THEORETICAL FRAMEWORK

To assess the effects of technological change on the demand for labor across occupations in a firm, we begin by using a simple model of labor demand. Assuming that the firm behaves as a cost minimizer for a given level of output, we can specify an equation for the determinants of the demand for labor for specific occupations. The determinants of current labor demand include past employment, output, technology, and relative factor prices, as shown in Equation 1:

$$\log L_t = f(\log L_{t-1}, \log Y_t, \log \text{Tech}, \log \text{RFP}_t) \qquad (1)$$

where L is the number employed in each occupation, Y is output, Tech is a measure of technological innovation, and RFP is relative factor prices. Because the local telephone operating companies' prices are regulated by their state public utility commissions, we assume that output is exogenously given. In addition, we assume that the technology variables we use are predetermined variables.

After using and estimating these occupational labor demand equations and identifying those occupations hardest hit by technological innovation, we examine how the firm used different adjustment mechanisms to reach its desired employment levels. To analyze the factors that determine the reasons and ways in which individuals enter and exit occupations, we have the following identity:

$$L_{t+1} = L_t - (\text{prTransferout} + \text{prQuit} + \text{prLayoff} + \text{prEarlyRetire} + \text{prRetire}) * L_t + H_t \qquad (2)$$

where L is employment in an occupation; prTransferout is the probability of transferring out of the occupation, prQuit is the probability of quitting, prLayoff is the probability of being laid off, prEarlyRetire is the probability of taking early retirement, prRetire is the probability of taking regular retirement, and H is the number of new hires and transfers into the occupation. Our analysis focuses on the determinants of exits from an occupation, as the hire rate over our sample period of time is very low.

Factors that influence the probability that an individual will exit by a particular way from an occupation include unionization, education, race, sex, age, and tenure on the job. The telephone industry pioneered job security provisions in collective bargaining contracts, so one might expect that unionized workers would be less likely to leave a firm in this industry because of technological displacement and would be more likely to be trained and transferred into another occupation. The Communication Workers of America have alleged, however, that phone companies have attempted to move work from bargaining unit positions into noncovered occupations. Bartel and Lichtenberg (1985) found evidence that highly educated workers had a comparative advantage with respect to the adjustments required by the introduction of new technologies. Consequently, telephone company workers with less education may be more likely to permanently exit the firm through layoffs or early retirements, as they may have more difficulty in adjusting to the new demands of the tasks created by new technology. The racial and sexual composition of an occupation also may affect the relative usage of one adjustment mechanism versus another. Older workers may be more likely to retire earlier as new technology is introduced, and younger workers may be more likely to quit the firm and explore other employment possibilities outside the firm. Finally, tenure on the job is critical to determining which workers are laid off first and which workers are eligible for early retirement.

THE DATA

We examine data from one of the seven Bell Operating Companies (BOC), and we refer to our sample BOC as Phone Company. Our data set is unique; it includes personnel files from one of the local operating companies within this BOC, detailed information on the number of access lines, and various measures of technological change. Although we have individual data on all employees in this company over time, our data on access lines and technology vary only by state and year. Our data cover the period 1980 through 1985. To protect the identity of Phone Company, we do not specify the number of states included in our analysis.

Two major organizational changes occurred in the telephone industry during the 1980–85 period. The first was Computer Inquiry II (initiated on January 1, 1983), which led to the creation in AT&T of a fully separate subsidiary composed of all people and assets associated with competitive services and products. The second structural change was the divestiture of AT&T (effective on January 1, 1984). This resulted in the creation of seven regional holding companies or BOCs to oversee the operations of the 22 local operating telephone companies that existed before the divestiture.[1]

The structure of the data allows us to identify whether and when an individual moved from the BOC to AT&T owing to divestiture or Computer Inquiry II. We removed from the data set all years any individual who, at any point in the period under study, moved to AT&T because of divestiture. Hence, no individual appears in our data set who was affected by divestiture. It is possible that the local operating companies used these two organizational changes to pass along to AT&T employees who were going to be displaced by technological innovation. Controlling for this possibility is beyond the scope of this chapter. Overall, however, we believe that we have controlled for divestiture sufficiently so that it should not contaminate our results.

Within Phone Company, there is virtually no movement of employees across state boundaries. Furthermore, technologies are introduced in the various states at different times and diffuse at different rates. For these reasons, we treat the states as distinct observations. In addition to the state groupings, we put all employees located in the central headquarters for the operating company into a separate category, as the role of central headquarters was distinct and hence the occupational distribution of these employees differed sharply from the distribution of workers in the state groupings.

Phone Company codes all employees into a job function matrix of approximately 47 functions. Working with the company's personnel staff, we grouped these 47 functions into the following ten functions/occupations: executive occupation (executive and general corporate services, finance, accounting, purchasing, and central administration); business, residence, and directory services occupation (general operations); operator services occupation; marketing occupation (general operations); network administration occupation (general operations); maintenance/engineering occupation (building and work equipment maintenance and land and buildings engineering); engineering services occupation; local operations occupation (local assignment, installation, dispatch, control, and maintenance operations [facilities and network services]); network distribution occupation (plant operations); and network installations occupation (installation, maintenance, assignment, and testing). These categories define broad job functions rather than specific tasks. By construction, any movement out of one of these occupations into another category requires a substantial change in the tasks performed by the employee.

Many technological innovations occurred in Phone Company over the sample period, but we concentrate on those with the largest potential employment effects. We use several different measures of the rate of diffusion of technology across the states in our sample and over time. These are the percentage of access lines covered by electronic switching systems (ESS), the percentage of access lines covered by multiple loop testing (MLT), and the average productivity of telephone directory operators (APT). In addition, we use data on expenditures for new capital (not including replacement capital) by state and by year, which also controls for shifts in the capital stock due to divestiture (Gross). These amounts varied substantially across the states and by year.

For some states, the percentage of access lines covered by ESS almost doubled, from 30 to 60 percent from 1980 to 1985. Because MLT allows computer-based diagnostics and repairs of faulty lines, it enhances the company's ability to provide a large amount of line maintenance and installation that are handled through a centralized office rather than through many substations. Indeed, one of the interesting aspects of the telephone industry's experience with information technology is that instead of decentralizing work and decision making, it has centralized these operations.

Lastly, the average productivity of telephone operators almost doubled over the sample time period, as a directory assistance computer system and an audio response system were installed to cut the average time that an operator spent on the line with a customer. This audio response system is the electronic "voice" that comes on the line giving the customer the number requested; the computer system puts access to all telephone numbers on a terminal screen in front of the operator. These systems were introduced at different rates across the various states and were completely implemented by 1985.

LABOR DEMAND CURVES BY OCCUPATION

To summarize the previous section, each data point is a year/state occupation cell, and for each cell we have data on the characteristics of all employees in that cell (e.g., employment level, percentage of females, percentage at specific educational levels, average wage, and percentage covered by collective bargaining). We also append to each cell the appropriate information on technology, capital stock, and output (which is measured by number of access lines). These three variables are available by state and year. The research strategy is to examine how employment changes in each occupation are affected by the average characteristics of the employees (information that is specific to each occupation, state, and year) and by technology and output variables (information that is state and year specific).

Distributions of employees over time and by occupational grouping are presented in Table 22.1, and sample characteristics are presented in Table 22.2. Across the states, the number of employees in each of the occupational groupings (excluding those working in central headquarters) declined between 1980 and 1985, and the number of employees in central headquarters rose. Within the states, the distribution of employees by occupational groupings changed over this period of time as well. The relative percentages of employees in executive and general corporate services, business, residence and directory services, and local and network installation and

Table 22.1. Distribution of employment, 1980–1985, in each occupation[a]

	1980		1985	
	Percent	Number	Percent	Number
Headquarters				
Executive	69.03	1,199	69.54	1,676
Business, residence, and directory services	7.25	126	6.64	160
Operator services	4.20	73	4.07	98
Marketing	1.78	31	3.73	90
Network administration	6.74	117	5.48	132
Maintenance/engineering	1.09	19	1.74	42
Engineering services	2.25	39	1.70	41
Local operations	1.84	32	2.24	54
Network distribution	1.27	22	0.33	8
Network installations	4.55	79	4.52	109
Total	100.00	1,737	100.00	2,410
All states (excluding headquarters)				
Executive	8.62	3,844	10.63	3,278
Business, residence, and directory service	11.81	5,260	15.22	4,694
Operator services	11.74	5,230	7.02	2,167
Marketing	1.67	742	1.44	444
Network administration	4.15	1,848	4.27	1,318
Maintenance/engineering	1.69	751	2.10	648
Engineering services	5.69	2,536	5.88	1,815
Local operations	17.65	7,866	20.45	6,310
Network distribution	23.10	10,609	17.06	5,262
Network installations	13.18	5,871	15.93	4,914
Total	100.00	44,557	100.00	30,850

[a]Descriptions of occupations are presented in the text.

Table 22.2. Variable definitions

Variables	Means[a]	
Race	.16	Percentage of the occupation which is black
Gender	.53	Percentage of the occupation which is female
Education 2	.31	Percentage of the occupation with a high school degree
Education 3	.38	Percentage of the occupation with more than a high school degree
Union	.60	Percentage of the occupation covered by a collective bargaining agreement
Age 1	.20	Percentage of the occupation aged 16–29
Age 2	.09	Percentage of the occupation aged 50–54
Age 3	.07	Percentage of the occupation aged 55–59
Age 4	.02	Percentage of the occupation aged 60–64
Tenure 1	.03	Percentage of the occupation with two years or less of tenure
Tenure 2	.13	Percentage of the occupation with 30 years or more of tenure
Wage	1.09	Weekly occupational wage (mean $424) deflated by average state manufacturing wage
ESS	6%	Annual change in percentage of access lines covered by electronic switching
MLT	20%	Annual change in percentage of access lines covered by multiple loop testing
APT	–2	Annual change in telephone operator seconds per call
Gross	768	Annual expenditures for new capital (in millions)

[a]Average over all years.

maintenance services increased. But the relative percentage of employees who were operators or were network and distribution plant operators (craft workers) declined. The distribution of employees across occupations in the central headquarters remained relatively stable over the sample period.

These data allow us to examine the impact of technology on the demand for labor within specific occupations. By including the number of access lines by state and year, we can control for changes in demand that have occurred over our sample period. We assume, however, that the coefficients for output and factor costs are the same for all occupations. To measure the impact of changing technologies on employment levels, we include the change in the four technology variables just described. All of these variables are interacted with occupation dummies, so that we do not impose the same coefficients on technology across all of the occupations.

The relative wage structure within the firm over the sample period did not change significantly. In addition, the user cost of capital, given the structure of the company, varied over time and not by state. Therefore, we summarize the effect of relative factor costs by including the average wage for each occupation and yearly time dummies to capture the variation over time of the user cost of capital. The wage variable is deflated by the state average wage. The time dummies also capture other factors, such as changes in business strategies in the company. In order to control for time in variant state and occupation effects, we estimate the following model of rates of change of employment:

$$\Delta 1nL_{jts} = a_0\, a_1 \Delta 1nY_{ts} + a_2 \Delta 1nWage_{tj}$$
$$= bj(Tech\Delta_{ts} * \text{occupation dummies}) + \text{time dummies} \qquad (3)$$

where L is employment, Y is number of access lines, Wage is the wage, Δ and Tech are the changes in the different technology variables, t = time, s = state, and j = occupation.

Estimates of the employment equation are presented in Table 22.3. Each equation represents the parameter estimates obtained by interacting the occupation dummies with a different measure of technology. Because these estimates are from a difference equation, state effects have been netted out, and time effects have been captured by the inclusion of time dummies. Therefore, our technology variables are picking up any additional effects of technology beyond the general time and state effects. We deleted observations from the central headquarters because we did not have appropriate measures for output and technology for these workers.[2]

Table 22.3. Determinants of labor demand[a] (t-statistics in parentheses)

Variables[b]	Eq. 1 (Gross tech)	Eq. 2 (ESS tech)	Eq. 3 (APT tech)	Eq. 4 (MLT tech)
Δ Log output	0.85	0.88	0.96	0.92
	(1.51)	(1.52)	(1.45)	(1.36)
Δ Log wage	− 0.87	− 1.00	− 1.11	− 1.08
	(− 3.58)	(− 4.26)	(− 4.38)	(− 4.28)
Executive occupation * tech Δ	0.03	0.05	3.60	0.06
	(1.49)	(1.99)	(0.99)	(0.85)
Business, residence, direction occupation * tech Δ	0.04	0.07	2.52	0.10
	(2.18)	(2.93)	(0.69)	(1.38)
Operator services occupation * tech Δ	− 0.06	− 0.13	− 6.84	− 0.16
	(− 3.15)	(− 4.83)	(− 1.87)	(− 2.07)
Marketing occupation * tech Δ	− 0.01	− 0.00	− 5.70	− 0.05
	(− 0.77)	(− 1.53)	(− 1.57)	(− 0.67)
Network administration occupation * tech Δ	− 0.00	− 0.01	− 3.13	− 0.01
	(− 0.25)	(− 0.43)	(− 0.86)	(− 0.14)
Maintenance/engineering occupation * tech Δ	0.03	0.05	0.95	0.05
	(1.82)	(2.04)	(0.26)	(0.75)
Engineering services occupation * tech Δ	− 0.00	− 0.04	− 4.26	− 0.01
	(− 0.35)	(− 1.46)	(− 1.16)	(− 0.14)
Local operations occupation * tech Δ	0.02	0.04	− 2.06	0.00
	(1.07)	(1.53)	(− 0.57)	(0.01)
Network distribution occupation * tech Δ	− 0.04	− 0.10	− 5.68	− 0.11
	(− 2.04)	(− 3.77)	(− 1.56)	(− 1.49)
Network installation occupation * tech Δ	0.02	0.05	1.51	0.02
	(1.34)	(1.83)	(0.42)	(0.27)
R^2	0.43	0.39	0.22	0.19

[a]Estimation includes time dummies and constant term; dependent variable = Log L_t − Log L_{t-1}

[b]Occupations are described in the text.

Estimation results

Overall, it appears that technological change increased the employment of workers in the business, residence, and directory services occupation, in the maintenance/engineering occupation, and in the network operations occupation. On the other hand, employees in operator services and network distribution were adversely affected by technology.[3] In 1980, these two occupations alone represented approximately 12 percent and 25 percent of the total work force, respectively.

In all of the equations, the most negatively affected occupation was operator services. The elasticity on this variable using the parameter estimates from the equation for the Gross measure of technology was –0.37. In other words, a 10 percent increase in the average productivity of operators resulted in a 4 percent decrease in their employment. The two major changes that affected the average productivity of telephone operators over our time period included the introduction of a directory assistance computer system and the audio response system. For some states, the combination of these two new systems represented a decrease of more than 15 seconds in the average time spent on a directory assistance call. According to Phone Company, a one-second decrease in the average time per call resulted in a $1.7 million savings for the company. The impact of these technological innovations on operator employment is clear from the equations presented in Table 22.3.

The other negatively impacted occupation was the network distribution function. As the operating company moved to electronic switching and multiple loop testing, the craft workers in this occupation, who had worked on the old electrical mechanical system, were displaced. Smaller substations were closed down, and the control and the repair of access lines became more and more centralized. The elasticity on this occupation was approximately –0.25. This means that a 10 percent increase in the percentage of access lines covered by electronic switching would result in a 2.5 percent decrease in the employment of workers in the network distribution occupation.

On the positive side, employment expanded somewhat for administrative staff and business and residence service workers, everything else being constant. With the introduction of ESS and MLT, new data bases were created that required more technical workers and managers to analyze these data and to use them in strategic planning. The introduction of an automated customer record system led to the relative expansion of employment in business and residence services. These relatively unskilled workers could now place requests for a telephone line and calling features (such as call forwarding) directly into the switching system.

TECHNOLOGICAL INNOVATION AND PATTERNS OF EMPLOYMENT

Reduction

In addition to assessing the differential impact of technology on occupations, we examine the methods that Phone Company used to reduce employment. The unique nature of our data makes it possible to investigate the magnitudes and determinants of five possible outflows from a job: quits, layoffs, retirements, early retirements, and transfers to other occupations. The first four of these flows are exits outside the organization; transfers represent an internal option. We begin by defining these categories and discussing the company rules that govern them.

Quits are resignations by the individual, and retirements may occur any time after the individual's retirement date. The layoff variable is a combination of several separate codes that Phone Company uses internally: dismissal, layoff, and technological displacement. Early retirements represent resignations before retirement age in return for a supplementary income package. For employees covered by the union contract, several different packages were available, depending on the age and seniority of the worker and the contract year. Nonunion employees were also eligible to receive incentive retirement schemes. We define transfers as movements across our 10 occupational categories. As already noted, these categories were constructed in order to represent relatively homogeneous work families, and so Phone Company's rules regarding transfers (which we describe later) apply to the movements that we capture.

One problem in interpreting our results is the extent to which the flows we study represent decisions by individuals, the firm, or some combination of the two. Clearly, simple perusal of contract language or rule books cannot always distinguish among these alternatives. For example, a quit may seem voluntary, but the firm can induce it by lowering wages. For workers covered by the CWA contract and for other employees, layoffs are at the firm's discretion, as is the volume of transfers and early retirements. In the contract, there are no restrictions on the volume of layoffs, only on steps (seniority, geographic transfers, and bumping) for implementing them. Because there is virtually no movement of employees across state boundaries, no ambiguity is introduced into our variables by geographic considerations. When faced with the necessity of reducing employment, however, the company has a wide range of choices. In addition to layoffs, it may choose to offer early retirement schemes, or it may force transfers across job titles.

In general, Phone Company can choose the job functions (or *occupations* in our terminology) and the number of positions within each function for which it offers various early retirement schemes. The programs are not entitlements for which any worker who meets the age and tenure criteria is eligible. Although the firm determines the upper bound of the number of people who accept such programs, it does not entirely set the lower bound, as the individuals eligible for the programs (by virtue of age and seniority) may not be the people at risk of being laid off and therefore may not accept the offer.

Transfers that are part of a layoff chain are clearly initiated by the firm. The contract also gives the firm the right to require other transfers should it need to fill positions. The transfers contain voluntary elements, however, such as the company's posting a vacancy for which individuals may then bid. Nevertheless, if an insufficient number of qualified persons bid, the firm can set and meet (via forced transfers) an employment target. The volume of transfers, therefore, appears to be a variable primarily determined by the firm.

With these conditions in mind, we assume for our analysis that quits and retirements are voluntary and that the firm retains a high degree of control over the volume of the remaining flows. The firm's choice of tools to use to reduce employment in an occupation is influenced by the characteristics of the workers in that occupation. For example, for an occupation composed primarily of high-seniority persons, the company may be more likely to use early retirements to lower employment, and for another occupation with low levels of seniority, it may use more layoffs.

Finally, Phone Company retains almost complete discretion in nonunion positions. Historically, the firm has been benevolent and hence relied largely on attrition and incentive resignations. Over the period represented in our data, the firm hardened its policies somewhat as the rate of technological innovation accelerated. There were several waves of layoffs in noncovered positions.

Table 22.4 presents the means of the various types of outflows for the entire period and for each year. It also shows the share of each type of outflow to all outflows. The transfers are the most significant adjustment mechanism, accounting for about 50 percent of all outflows. Each of the other outflows is significant, and there are clear timing patterns in the data. Early retirement grew in importance over the period, whereas layoffs peaked in 1982 and fell somewhat after that. The rise in layoffs and early retirements is mirrored by a fall in the quit and retirement rates.

At the heart of our analysis is the problem of explaining how outflow patterns differ by occupation. To see whether there was enough variation among occupations to make the problem interesting, we determined the distribution of exits by occupation and compared them. We found distinct differences. For example, the operator services and network distribution occupations, which the previous section showed to be the two occupations hardest hit, had quite different profiles. Layoffs and early retirements represented 36 percent of the departures in operator services, but only 19 percent of the departures in network distribution. In network distribution, however, transfers accounted for 70 percent of the outflows, whereas in operator services they represented only 36 percent of outflows. Differential patterns in outflows across occupations existed in quit rates and retirements as well. A quarter of the employees in marketing quit over the sample period, whereas only 3 percent of those in network distribution did so. Finally, a quarter of those in network installation retired over the sample period, and only 8 percent of those in network distribution did so.[4]

To provide some initial insight into the possibility that outflow shares are interrelated, Table 22.5 shows the correlations among the five outflow types. The correlations between transfers and the other flows are insignificant, but quits and retirements are significantly positively correlated. More interesting, the correlations indicate that early retirements appear to have more in common with layoffs than with regular retirements. In other words, early retirements look more like layoffs than like regular retirements.

In order to understand these issues better, we estimated a log odds model of the outflows. The dependent variable is the relative frequency of a given flow (such as

Table 22.4. Flow probabilities by year and average share of each type of flow

Outflow type	1980	1981	1982	1983	1984	All Years	Share
Quit	.024	.019	.016	.010	.008	.015	.112
Layoff	.008	.010	.024	.012	.017	.014	.095
Transfers out	.061	.092	.085	.059	.067	.073	.494
Retirement	.019	.035	.022	.010	.006	.018	.151
Early retirement	.013	.001	.023	.022	.038	.020	.146

Table 22.5. Correlation among flow probabilities

	Transfers out	Quit	Layoff	Retirement	Early retirement
Transfers out	1				
Quit	.045	1			
Layoff	−.090	.052	1		
Retirement	.025	.140**	.067	1	
Early retirement	−.085	−.028	.305**	−.280**	1

**Significant at .01 level.

layoff) relative to another flow (such as transfer), in which each data point is still a year, state, or occupation cell. The model estimates these relative probabilities as a function of average occupation characteristics. Given that there are five flows, there are 10 possible log odds equations (although only four are independent). The explanatory variables used in the equations include the percentage of the occupation unionized, the percentage with various levels of educational attainment, the percentage of nonwhites, the percentage of females, and finally, the percentage of the occupation in various age and tenure groups. Each equation also contains state and year dummy variables.

Whether or not it is appropriate to include dummy variables for the occupations is problematic. Certain characteristics, such as union status or sex composition, are highly correlated with occupation, and the inclusion of the dummy variables may obscure the effect of the variables of interest. This problem is analogous to one that has plagued much of the literature on wage differentials and gender. The values we report represent results obtained without occupational dummies; but we also indicate whether the variable retained (or attained) significance with the inclusion of occupational dummies (no variables change sign).

ESTIMATION RESULTS

Table 22.6 presents the results of the flow equations. Several conclusions emerge from this analysis. First, highly unionized occupations are more likely to adjust to falling demand by employees exiting the firm rather than by internal transfers. For the equations without the occupational dummies, the union coefficient is positive and significant in all of the exit flows compared with the internal transfers, whereas in the equations with the dummies, the union coefficient is positive and significant in the quit, early retirement, and retirement equations. Because transfers are largely at the discretion of management, this suggests that the firm's actions result in reducing the fraction of the labor force that is unionized. Although unionization seems to increase the probability of leaving the firm relative to being transferred, the overall impact is modest. Between 1980 and 1985, union employment fell by 29.1 percent, and nonunion employment fell by 25.8 percent.

Second, in many of the equations without occupational dummy variables, there is a strong gender effect. Those occupations with high proportions of women are more likely to have lower layoff rates relative to quits, retirements, and early retirements. This is consistent with an often-stated but rarely demonstrated observa-

Table 22.6. Flow equations[a] (t-statistics in absolute value in parentheses)

	Union	Educ.2	Educ.3	Race	Gender	W age	Age 1	Age 2	Age 3	Age 4	Tenure 1	Tenure 2	Constant	R^2
P(layoff/trans.)	3.94	– 1.14	1.54	2.70	– 0.81	1.01	5.52[b]	7.53[b]	8.82[b]	– 1.98	0.76	– 8.49[b]	– 10.18[b]	0.41
	(2.69)	(0.69)	(0.84)	(0.92)	(1.19)	(0.70)	(2.18)	(1.47)	(1.51)	(0.24)	(0.25)	(1.71)	(3.59)	
P(retire./trans.)	3.67[b]	– 3.12[b]	0.68	– 0.21	1.96	0.74	– 1.42	2.95	6.30[b]	19.82[b]	0.27	7.21	– 6.88[b]	0.44
	(3.26)	(2.46)	(0.48)	(0.09)	(3.76)	(0.67)	(0.73)	(0.75)	(1.40)	(3.08)	(0.11)	(1.89)	(3.16)	
P(early retire./trans.)	6.54[b]	– 0.03	5,02[b]	– 1.25	1.95	—1.80	– 2.75	1.74	15.22	2.63	448[b]	8.23[b]	– 8.91[b]	0.62
	(4.80)	(0.02)	(2.97)	(0.46)	(3.13)	(1.37)	(1.19)	(0.37)	(2.83)	(0.34)	(1.60)	(1.81)	(3.43)	
P(quit/trans.)	6.44[b]	– 1.95	6.92[b]	– 0.65	2.44	1.44	2.99	7.64	6.84	16.84	5.73[b]	– 1.41	– 13.53[b]	0.40
	(5.52)	(1.48)	(4.72)	(0.28)	(4.52)	(1.27)	(1.49)	(1.87)	(1.47)	(2.51)	(2.36)	(0.36)	(6.00)	
P(quit/layoff)	2.51	– 0.81	5.37	3.35[b]	3.25	0.44	– 2.53	0.12	– 1.98	18.76	4.97	7.08[b]	– 3.36	0.26
	(1.40)	(0.40)	(2.39)	(0.93)	(3.91)	(0.25)	(0.82)	(0.02)	(0.28)	(1.83)	(1.33)	(1.17)	(0.97)	
P(quit/retire.)	2.77	1.17	6.23	– 0.44	0.48	0.79	4.40	4.70	0.54	– 3.05	5.46	– 8.62	– 6.66	0.25
	(1.83)	(0.69)	(3.28)	(0.15)	(0.68)	(0.48)	(1.69)	(0.89)	(0.09)	(0.35)	(1.73)	(1.68)	(2.27)	
P(quit/early retire.)	– 0.10	– 1.92	1.90	0.60	0.49	3.24[b]	5 74	5.91	– 8.38	14.15	1.24	– 9.64	– 4.62	0.51
	(0.06)	(1.00)	(0.89)	(0.17)	(0.62)	(1.95)	(1.95)	(0.99)	(1.23)	(1.45)	(0.33)	(1.67)	(1.40)	
P(Layoff /retire.)	0.26	1.98	0.86	2.91	– 2.77	0.27	6.93	4.58	2.52	– 21.81[b]	0.49	– 15.70[b]	– 3.30	0.33
	(0.15)	(1.01)	(0.39)	(0.83)	(3.42)	(0.16)	(2.31)	(0.75)	(0.36)	(2.18)	(0.14)	(2.66)	(0.98)	
P(layoff/early retire.)	– 2.60	– 1.11	– 3.47	3.94	– 2.76	2.80	8.27[b]	5.79[b]	– 6.39	– 4.61	– 3.72	– 16.72[b]	1.27	0.42
	(1.41)	(0.53)	(1.50)	(1.07)	(3.23)	(1.56)	(2.60)	(0.90)	(0.87)	(0.44)	(0.97)	(2.68)	(0.35)	
P(retire./early retire.)	– 2.87	– 3.09	– 4.33	1.04	0.01	2.54[b]	1.34	1.21	– 8.91	17.20[b]	– 4.21	– 1.02	2.03	0.57
	(1.67)	(1.60)	(2.01)	(0.30)	(0.01)	(1.51)	(0.45)	(0.20)	(1.30)	(1.75)	(1.18)	(0.18)	(0.61)	

[a]The dependent variable is the log odds of the flows. All equations include time and area dummies.
[b]The variable is significant in an equation with occupation dummies.

tion that firms use high female turnover rates to help adjust to employment shifts. Even though women are heavily represented in the most seriously impacted occupation (operators), the company did not have to rely exclusively on layoffs. Furthermore, the adjustment did not occur by means of unusually high transfer rates, as the equations show that occupations with large fractions of women have lower transfer rates relative to exits than do other occupations. High female turnover, not layoffs or transfers, constituted the adjustment mechanism. What is striking about these results is that all of these effects disappear when occupational controls are introduced. This clearly reflects substantial sex segregation in the organization. (As we noted, it is an open question whether the inclusion of occupational controls is appropriate.)

Third, the age patterns are not surprising: The older groups are more likely to retire than they are to leave by other means. By the same token, occupations with a high concentration of young workers are more likely to experience high layoff rates (especially when occupation controls are included) and high quit rates. There is, however, an apparent anomaly in that the oldest group appears to have a higher probability of quitting relative to transfers or layoffs. It is important to remember, though, that these equations estimate relative probabilities. The number of older workers who quit, are transferred, or are laid off is extremely small. Therefore, this result is most likely due to small cell sizes.

Fourth, the tenure variables behave exactly as expected. They were designed to capture the relevant features of the collective bargaining contract (which was also applied to the nonunion group for purposes of retirement provisions). Before two years of tenure, workers are not eligible for even the least generous early retirement plan. Furthermore, for union workers, two or more years of tenure are required in order to exercise bumping rights with respect to transfers. Retirement provisions are complicated and difficult to summarize easily. However, the most significant "anniversary" is 30 years of tenure, after which an employee is automatically eligible for a full pension. We found that occupations with concentrations of employees with low tenure were more likely to experience quits, whereas retirement and early retirement rates rose with high tenure.

It is appropriate to raise an interpretive issue here before reaching any final conclusions. Although four of the flows are exits outside the firm, transfers are different, as for each transfer out of one occupation there must be a transfer into another occupation. In the extreme case, it could be conjectured that we are observing random movement with no net change in occupational distributions (i.e., all transfers balance out one another and the net change is zero). One way to check this is to look at the correlations between transfers in and other flows. The rate of transfers into an occupation is significantly positively correlated with the hire rate and significantly negatively correlated with layoff and early retirement rates. This suggests that we are not simply observing random movement or misclassification. At the same time, the rates of transfers out and transfers in are positively correlated, and this implies some random movement (although it also can be explained by the bumping provisions of the contract). These considerations suggest that a fruitful next step would be a complete modeling of all types of flows.

CONCLUSIONS

Over several decades the composition of employment in the telephone industry has shifted toward professional and technical employees, and our results suggest that these compositional changes will continue. We showed how the introduction of new technologies diminished the demand for labor in some occupations while it raised the demand in others, all else being constant. In particular, technological change in telecommunications is leading to more central office functions and the elimination of decentralized suboffices.

The telephone industry's long history of innovation includes not only pioneering efforts in physical technology but also an attempt to fashion new responses to change. In the 1970s the CWA bargained for issues such as termination pay in lieu of transfer to lower-rated jobs, reassignment pay, and various supplementary income protection plans in the event of technological displacement. These provisions were strengthened in later contracts. In modeling the magnitude and determinants of alternative adjustment mechanisms, we were able to distinguish between union and nonunion adjustment patterns. Although the CWA contract does place some constraints on management, it seems that all decisions regarding volumes of transfers, early retirements, and layoffs remain in management's hands. In other words, management and the union negotiate the rules determining which types of workers are the first to go in downsizing, but management maintains control over the number of workers affected.

Our dual strategy of estimating how technology affects labor demand and then investigating the firm's adjustment processes allowed us to demonstrate, for example, that occupations that are heavily unionized are more likely to adjust to falling demand through exits from the firm than through internal transfers. We also found that early retirements are quite unlike regular retirements and, in fact, seem to be complementary to layoffs. At the same time, our approach has generated many new questions. We did not model all the flows that occur in the firm, such as transfers into occupations and new hires. In addition, more light could be shed on the apparent importance of gender by working with individual data instead of the grouped occupational data that we used. We intend to address these issues in future research.

ACKNOWLEDGMENT

The research for this chapter was supported by the Massachusetts Institute of Technology, Sloan School of Management program, Management in the 1990s. Outstanding research support was provided by Karen Needels. We would like to thank participants in seminars at MIT and the University of California at Berkeley, and several anonymous referees for helpful comments on previous drafts of this paper.

NOTES

1. Divestiture should not be confused with deregulation, as the operating companies remained regulated by state public utility commissions.

2. We also estimated a labor demand equation in levels with lagged employment, output, wages, technology * occupational dummies, state dummies, year dummies, and occupation dummies. The results do not change with this specification, and none of the state dummies is significant.

3. We repeated this analysis, including in one equation all of the technology variables (except Gross) interacted with the occupation dummies, and found no difference in our results.

4. A detailed breakdown of shares of outflows by job occupation is available from the authors upon request.

REFERENCES

Bartel, A., & F. Lichtenberg (1985). The comparative advantage of educated workers in implementing new technology: Some empirical evidence. Working paper no. 1718, National Bureau of Economic Research, Cambridge, MA, October.

Denny, M., & M. Fuss (1983). The effect of factor prices and technological change on the occupational demand for labor: Evidence from Canadian telecommunications. *Journal of Human Resources* 18 (Spring):161–76.

Osterman, P. (1986). The impact of computers upon the employment of clerks and managers. *Industrial and Labor Relations Review* 29 (Spring):175–86.

Stewman, S., & S. L. Konda (1983). Careers and organizational labor markets: Demographic models of organizational behavior. *American Journal of Sociology* 88 (January): 637–85.

White, H. (1970). *Chains of opportunity*. Cambridge, MA: Harvard University Press.

CHAPTER 23

Employment Security at DEC: Sustaining Values amid Environmental Change

THOMAS A. KOCHAN, JOHN PAUL MACDUFFIE, AND PAUL OSTERMAN

In the 1960s and 1970s, a number of highly visible firms gained a reputation for innovative and progressive employment security policies by departing from the standard practice of reducing their work forces through layoffs in response to demand fluctuations. Instead these firms adopted an implicit or explicit commitment to employment security (Dyer, Foltman, & Milkovich, 1985; Foulkes & Whitman, 1985; McKersie, Greenhalgh, & Gilkey, 1985). Some attributed the choice of these policies to the strong values of their founders or chief executives (Foulkes, 1980). Others suggested that these policies were well matched to their firm's strategic needs, given their rapid growth (Dyer et al., 1985; Kochan & Barocci, 1985). Undoubtedly both values and strategic factors played important roles in sustaining commitments to employment continuity.

In recent years many firms are again reexamining their policies toward employment security in light of two conflicting sets of pressures. On the one hand, changing technologies, shortening product life cycles, and increased consumer sensitivity to product quality all are placing a premium on human resource policies that can achieve high levels of employee motivation, commitment, and flexibility attributes that are normally seen as by-products of an employment security policy. On the other hand, enhanced cost competition, changing skill requirements, and the maturing of markets that had been expanding rapidly all lead to pressures to cut staffing levels. It is not surprising, therefore, that in recent years a number of firms (e.g., Polaroid, Eastman Kodak, AT&T) have abandoned their employment security policies and resorted to layoffs. This suggests that commitments to maintaining employment security are more desirable in today's environment but also are more difficult to meet than in the past.

This chapter uses a case study of Digital Equipment Corporation (DEC) to explore strategies for responding to these conflicting pressures. Specifically, we describe the values and business strategies that supported DEC's commitment to

Thomas A. Kochan, John Paul MacDuffie, and Paul Osterman, *Human Resource Management*, 1988, Vol. 27, No. 2, pp. 121–43.

employment security during its years of rapid growth in the 1960s and 1970s. Then we show how DEC moved through a "transition process" in the early 1980s when its market environment had changed dramatically, by downsizing and redeploying its work force without laying off regular employees. Finally, we draw out the managerial and public policy implications of this experience. We highlight a set of human resource policy changes that will be needed if a commitment to employment security is to be successfully maintained in the more rapidly changing market and technological environments that characterize most firms today.

THEORETICAL PERSPECTIVES ON EMPLOYMENT SECURITY

An organization's employment security policies can be placed somewhere on a continuum. At one end of the continuum are organizations that guarantee no layoffs to some or all employees. At the other extreme are firms that hire and discharge workers immediately and in direct proportion to fluctuations in product or service demand. Most firms fall somewhere between these two extremes. Our interest here is in organizations that attempt to achieve employment security by avoiding layoffs of employees in response to cyclical or structural changes in product demand.

Although there is wide variation in practice, as yet there are no empirically grounded theories of what determines an organization's choice of an employment security or any other single human resource policy. Instead three different propositions for explaining why an organization might commit to an employment security policy have been put forward by researchers from different analytical perspectives.

Human resource management researchers who emphasize the importance of organizational culture focus on the personal values of founders and key executives (Deal & Kennedy, 1982; Schein, 1983). Clearly, such values serve as a necessary condition for initiating and maintaining employee commitment during organizational innovation. Dyer, Foltman, and Milkovich (1985) reinforced this interpretation in their examination of companies that follow employment security policies, by noting that in none of the organizations they studied could data or analysis be found that evaluated the costs versus the benefits of the policy. Instead, commitment to the policy could be traced to the values of the founder (or some other top executive), its perceived contribution to early organizational successes, and its gradual institutionalization in the organization's personnel policies. Yet a logical question arises: What other factors, besides personal values, lead some top executives to favor employment security policies?

Those who take a strategic perspective of the study of human resource policies answer this question by examining how employment security fits with the firm's competitive strategies. The basic proposition that emerges from this literature is that firms in rapidly growing market environments are more likely to emphasize employment security policies, as high commitment and low turnover are consistent with a business strategy that emphasizes the ability to get products to the market quickly and thereby to increase market share and enhance organizational growth. Thus, organizations in early stages of their organizational and/or product life cycles are more likely to initiate and maintain commitment to an employment security policy than are firms in more mature markets (Fombrun, Tichy, & Devanna, 1984; Kochan &

Barocci, 1985; Schuler & Jackson, 1987). Kochan and Barocci (1985) argued further that in rapidly growing organizations, the pressures to meet expanding market demands can lead to staffing practices that cannot be sustained if and when market conditions change and cost competition becomes a more important strategic concern to the firm. How, then, can employment security be sustained in mature markets?

A third perspective of employment security policies is derived from the growing literature on internal labor markets (Jacoby, 1985; Osterman, 1984, 1988). This perspective argues that employment security policies cannot be viewed in isolation but, rather, are part of a larger bundle of human resource policies that fit together to form a coherent package. Although these policies are to some extent constrained by their economic, technological, and political environments, firms are seen as having a range of discretion in choosing their strategy. It should be possible to adapt an employment security policy to different competitive environments if other human resource and related management strategies and policies are adapted as well. However, such adaptations are difficult and will require the sustaining power of organizational values if they are to succeed. Thus, it is only the combination of organizational values and strategic adjustments that can provide the impetus necessary to sustain employment security in a changing environment.

EMPLOYMENT SECURITY AT DEC

The evolution of employment security policies at DEC can be understood in the context of each of the three foregoing perspectives. Employees at DEC frequently refer to employment security as an important manifestation of "DEC values." It was apparent from our interviews that the firm's initial commitment to employment security derived from the values of its founder, Kenneth Olsen, and that the company's culture places a substantial premium on maintaining that commitment. Over the years, as the policy was reaffirmed whenever temporary volume swings raised the issue of reducing the work force, employment security became a fundamental decision premise at DEC, a starting point for deliberations rather than a policy whose merits were continually debated.

Although the policy had its roots in the founder's beliefs, other factors were clearly at work. Through the 1970s and early 1980s, DEC was a rapidly growing firm, and its manufacturing strategy stressed the imperative of high-volume production capable of meeting strong customer demand. Plant managers would staff for peak-volume periods, negotiating frequently with headquarters for production assignments that would maximize capacity utilization. The corporate manufacturing staff would, in turn, allow the production load to be moved to any plant temporarily short of work on its primary products.

Introductions of new products tended to accelerate staffing growth. About a year before launch, manufacturing would project its staffing needs based on peak-volume forecasts: first, the direct labor needed for that volume and, second, indirect labor based on past direct and indirect ratios. Design changes and higher volume estimates would boost these projections as the launch date approached. Widespread hiring would begin. New and existing products would be managed by separate groups to avoid the delays of coordinating the start-up of the former and the phaseout of the latter. To maintain the capacity to absorb surges in demand during start-up, plants would hire temporary and contract workers, generally constituting about 20 percent of the direct labor work force and sometimes reaching 50 percent.

If a plant did have surplus labor, there were a variety of ways to downsize for the short term. Besides releasing temporary and contract workers, these might include temporary assignments around the plant, temporary transfers to other plants in the area, and more efforts to get poor performers out of the work force. Indirect labor, in particular, might receive some not-so-subtle pressure to start looking for other jobs at DEC. The best people, with needed skills, often found jobs quickly. Others might have more trouble but would be kept on payroll until they found something, even if that took a year or more. This informal process generally worked well, particularly because the next surge in volume was usually right around the corner.

The internal labor market perspective also illuminates the company's policy. Employees at DEC appear to be highly committed to the firm and willing to respond in various ways to changing market demands. Interviews with both managers and workers indicate that the company enjoys substantial flexibility in the deployment of its human resources. This flexibility is reflected in a large training budget, loosely defined job boundaries, and an emphasis on rewarding individual initiative. It is fair to conclude that the firm's commitment to employment security is crucial to attaining a flexible set of internal labor market rules.

Changing circumstances

For each of these reasons, DEC has maintained its commitment to employment security. This commitment was made easier because the context in which it operated—with respect to products, markets, and technology—provided few challenges to the policy. Gradually, however, a number of factors began to affect staffing requirements long before a head-count problem became apparent.

Technological change

The miniaturization of components allowed new products to achieve the same price–performance ratio with up to 75 to 80 percent fewer parts than previous generations of equipment had. This dramatically reduced the need for direct labor; indeed, from one generation of VAX computers to the next, the direct labor hours dropped by 75 percent. Advances in chip technology and circuit board design required increased use of "clean room" equipment. robots, and vision systems. Skill mix requirements changed considerably as some jobs were completely automated and the content of many others were modified.

Outsourcing

At the time, DEC was trying to keep products at both the high and the low ends of the market, and so outsourcing was considered essential to the low-cost strategy. Managing these efforts required some additional indirect labor, but it clearly diminished the need for direct labor, particularly in the U.S. plants where the most cost sensitive products were produced.

Manufacturing policy

In an effort to reduce inventory costs, the policy of "build to inventory" that had been critical to "ability to ship" was eliminated, and much lower inventory targets were set. Plants were encouraged to meet their overall cost targets not with increased volume (which reduced unit costs) but by minimizing the use of all resources—space, energy, materials, and labor. In addition, the practice of moving load from plant to plant to balance production (and to keep each plant's work force busy) was largely discontinued because of its inefficiency. Product groups were consolidated so that most components for a product were produced in the same plant, thus further pinning the fortunes of a plant to a specific product.

The net result of these factors was an increasing pressure to cut the work force, without the buffering practices of "building to inventory" and "moving load" that were so important to supporting employment security during previous downturns. Still, the staffing problem was never addressed systematically until an event occurred that signaled the onset of a broader organizational crisis that galvanized the support needed to act.

The stock price crisis

On Tuesday, October 18, 1983, the news about DEC's worst quarter in its history hit the stock market, and its stock dropped 12 percent in one day and another 17 percent within three weeks. Coming after three bad quarters and amid signs of a pending industry slump, the plummeting stock was a symbolic watershed for DEC. Long accustomed to continual growth, in which falling volume for one product would be offset by increasing volume for another, DEC abruptly had to face the prospect of widespread volume declines hitting simultaneously. It was this crisis that triggered the response that eventually became the transition program.

MANAGING THE TRANSITION PROCESS

DEC's response to the overstaffing crisis—the "transition process"—reveals much about its commitment to employment security and the changes required to maintain that commitment. We will review it here in considerable detail, not only because it describes DEC's experience, but also because we believe that this experience highlights the key choices that most firms must make when confronted with similar downsizing requirements. As such, DEC's experience serves as a prototype for human resource decision making.

Eighteen months after the October 1983 stock price decline, the transition process was implemented at the first manufacturing plant. Table 23.1 provides a chronology of the key events during that period. There were several decisions that shaped the incipient transition process. For example, line managers rather than personnel staff were made responsible for managing the transition at the corporate level. Plant managers, who had considerable autonomy, were the focus of the corporate effort to convince the company that a transition was needed. A hiring freeze and the elimination of all contract and temporary positions were the first steps taken to avert layoffs.

Soon thereafter, a cross-functional transition task force was established to decide on the primary strategy—to manage transition as a decentralized, plant-level process

Table 23.1. Key events and decisions in the transition process

10/83	DEC's stock drops 29%.
12/83	Staffing needs for next two fiscal years projected, and problem defined as excess indirect labor. Contingency plan for overstaffing developed, involving sequential process for work-force reduction.
1/84	Responsibility for transition given to line management rather than human resources function.
5/84	Meetings with plant managers to convince them of need for transition.
6/84	Hiring freeze; manufacturing plants advised to release all temporary and contract employees.
8/84	Strategy of centralized guidelines and resources, with decentralized implementation developed. No required participation. Plants would "apply" for transition.
9/84	Transition task force established to develop guidelines for selection, training, and exit options, with representatives from manufacturing, engineering, sales and service, human resources.
11/84	Corporate-level financial incentives for participation in transition established.
12/84	Rapid volume reduction, and a shift of transition efforts to direct labor group First manufacturing plant signs up.
2/85	Special voluntary separation option for Southwest plants established.
4/85	First manufacturing plant begins transition process, 18 months after the stock market crisis.

following centralized, corporatewide guidelines. These guidelines were established to ensure that the transition would be implemented fairly, consistently, and in a way that allowed individual employees considerable choice. This approach was consistent with the autonomy that had always been accorded plant managers, while recognizing that the problem was companywide and that no individual plant was wholly responsible for the overstaffing predicament in which it found itself.

Plants were given the choice of whether or not to participate in the transition process and were given considerable flexibility to tailor the process to their needs. At the corporate level, financial incentives were used to encourage participation and to prevent the costs of the transition from weighing most heavily on the plants most needing it. These centralized resources were also used to counterbalance those forces at the plant level that supported overstaffing.

Stages of transition

The transition process had three stages: (1) selection and entry into the group of "available" employees, (2) counseling and training, and (3) exit from transition through transfer to another job at DEC or departure from the company. The corporate transition task force faced tough decisions regarding each stage.

Selection

Selection first required that each plant assess the staffing levels needed for ongoing operations, to determine the number of "available" people. If a whole work group or an entire production task were eliminated, all the affected employees would become "available." In the more common case, in which fewer people were needed to perform a particular task, selection was based on ranking employees, first by their most recent performance rating and, in the case of ties, by their seniority.

The decision to make performance rather than seniority the primary criterion was a controversial one. Although DEC is not unionized, many of its manufacturing employees had previous experience in unionized facilities. Indeed, many DEC plants used seniority as the basis for job transfer. Although the task force stuck to its position, in the end seniority played a significant role, as there were many ties in the merit ranking.

Training and counseling

The task force developed a two-week program of training and counseling for transition employees, to help them with the shock of being declared "available" and to teach them practical career development skills. The managers of "available" employees also were required to attend a week of training, focused on their responsibility in supporting employee job search efforts. A limited retraining program also accompanied the transition. Although the task force members believed that a broad reskilling effort would be crucial to sustain employment security in the new environment, they were reluctant to slow down the transition process by attempting to launch another complex, resource-intensive program. As a result, retraining was allowed only when a person had applied and been accepted for a new job at DEC that required additional skills.

Exit from the transition

The two main means of exit from the transition were reassignment to another job within DEC and outplacement to another company. For indirect employees, reassignment to "comparable jobs" at a different DEC location was the main emphasis. Direct employees were more likely to be reassigned within the plant or placed in a pool for temporary assignment to special projects in the plant and the community.

One tool used in the reassignment effort was a computerized job- and skill-matching system, containing the resumes of all "available" people and all open job requisitions. This had only limited use, because many managers were reluctant to put their "available" people on the system, preferring instead to work through their own informal channels to help them get jobs. Despite efforts by the task force to tie transition incentives to using the jobs system, this technological approach to reassignment continued to be bypassed in favor of the network of informal contacts among managers.

A "comparable job" could be any job requiring similar skills and responsibilities, whose salary was at least 80 percent of the midpoint salary level of the employee's old job. It could require relocation, a longer commute, new training, or a different shift. "Available" indirect employees could reject one "comparable job" offer that would relocate them, but a second rejection could result in their termination. Employees unwilling to relocate were required to take any "comparable job" within commuting distance. DEC also helped employees find outplacements at other companies, particularly those who were unwilling to relocate.

The special option of a voluntary separation program was offered to three plants in the Southwest hit heavily by volume reductions, because both relocation and outplacement were felt to be inadequate to deal with the surplus of direct labor employees. This separation program gave a large severance payment to any employee—not just to "available" employees—in these plants who left DEC before a certain date. In order to receive these payments, the employees were required to have found a job outside DEC.

THE RESULTS OF TRANSITION

Although this transition process was adopted in the manufacturing, engineering, and sales and service organizations, the efforts in manufacturing were by far the most substantial. Therefore, in the rest of this chapter, we shall focus exclusively on the impact of this transition on manufacturing.

AGGREGATE OUTCOMES

Table 23.2 shows the overall changes in employment levels for manufacturing worldwide and in the United States from just before the beginning of the transition, on June 30, 1984, to June 30, 1986. Worldwide, the number of employees at DEC was reduced substantially: A total of 5598 employees left DEC, both through the transition process and for other reasons. Of this total reduction, 1648 (or 29 percent) were temporary or contract employees, and 3950 (or 71 percent) were regular employees. Both the direct and indirect labor categories were reduced, but the ratio of indirect to direct employees did increase over this period, rising from 1.8:1 in 1984 to 2.0:1 in 1986.

Comparable figures for the United States are available for 1985–86. These data show substantial decreases in regular employment, both direct and indirect, but an increase in employment of temporary and contract employees. The ratio of indirect to direct employees remained identical in 1985 and 1986, standing at 2.40:1 in both years.

The foregoing discussion focuses on an overall cut in number of employees. Much of the activity recorded in these tables pertained to people who were not formally enrolled in the transition program, but the transition should receive a measure

Table 23.2. Employment levels for DEC manufacturing

	FY84		FY85		FY86	
	Worldwide	U.S.	Worldwide	U.S.	Worldwide	U.S.
Direct	10115	—	9563	5515	8219	4616
Indirect	18530	—	18039	13256	16476	11074
Contract /temp	3353	—	1154	791	1705	1428
Total	31998	—	28756	19562	26400	17118

Source: Aggregate data provided by DEC.

Table 23.3. Transition activities—worldwide manufacturing (FY84–FY86)

Left DEC	1986
Transfers in DEC	1020
Still "in transition" (as of June 30, 1986)	500
Total participants	2606

Source: Aggregate data provided by DEC.

of credit for the overall reduction, as it did minimize hiring throughout the organization and also affected the overall climate of the firm. There is some evidence that considerable informal activity in both outplacement and reassignment was triggered by the formal transition process. In addition, many people in the transition changed jobs without leaving DEC.

Table 23.3 provides some summary measures for the transition. Formal participants in the transition numbered 2606, and as of June 1986, 41 percent of this number had left the firm; 39 percent had transferred within the company; and 20 percent were still in the transition program, in either "available" status or some other phase of the effort.

With these summary data in hand, we now turn to a more textured analysis of the transition experience, using personnel data from several plants.

STATISTICAL PROFILE OF THE TRANSITION PROCESS

In this section, we ask about the people selected for the transition, the outcomes for them, and how effectively the transition restructured the firm's human resource profile. Our data are drawn from the DEC personnel data base for five plants. The data begin at the end of the fiscal year 1984 and continue through the end of the fiscal year 1986. When we speak of transition participants, we are referring to people who at some time during that period were selected for the transition; the nontransition participants are those who were never selected. This sample of five plants includes 1518 transition participants—well over half of the total transition population. Our analysis uses aggregate data for all five plants.

Selection

The selection process was heavily oriented toward direct labor. Nearly two-thirds of all the transition participants (63.8 percent) were drawn from direct labor, even though this group constituted less than half of all nontransition participants, or 42 percent. (For the sample as a whole, direct labor constituted 48.7 percent.) Because the characteristics of direct and indirect labor are likely to be quite different, throughout the rest of the analysis we will always look at the two groups separately.

We found no significant differences in the age and racial characteristics of the participants compared with those not selected. The data do suggest, however, that women were selected more frequently than men were, and the reasons for this remain unclear. It was also the case that tenure in the company was important, with the more recently hired selected more often than warranted by their distribution in the population. At the same time it is also apparent that tenure was not the only decision rule, as several employees with long tenure were selected for the transition despite the availability of large numbers of junior employees who were not selected.

Outcomes

What were the nature and consequences of the transition process? We are interested here in the degree to which certain company outcomes were achieved and in how the transition participants fared their career outcomes.

Table 23.4 classifies the outcomes into several categories. Transition participants left the firm, moved to a new location, or stayed at the same location. Whether or not they changed location, some participants exiting the transition program took new jobs, whereas others retained their old jobs. Finally, some participants were still involved in the transition process in June 1986, at the end of our data collection.

Leavers

Overall, 32.5 percent of those in the transition left the firm. Thirty-five percent of direct labor employees (DL) were "leavers," as were 28 percent of indirect labor employees (IL). The southwestern plants, for which the special voluntary separation programs were established, had the highest percentage of "leavers."

New location

Only 14.7 percent of the transition participants moved to new plants. Direct labor was less likely to move to a new plant than was indirect labor, as only 9 percent of DL shifted sites, compared with 24 percent of IL. It was not surprising, given the transition policy, that relocation was a more feasible and realistic option for IL than for DL. For both groups, however, moving to a new location was associated with getting a new job, with a far larger proportion of movers changing jobs than remaining in the same one.

Table 23.4. Transition outcomes (transition participants only)

	Direct	Indirect
Same site		
Same job	20.0%	12.2%
New job	14.3	7.4
New site		
Same job	2.9	7.1
New job	6.2	17.3
Left company	35.2	27.7
Still in transition	20.7	27.5
	100.0%	100.0%
	$n = 969$	$n = 549$

Source: Personnel files for five manufacturing plants.

Same location

Twenty-nine percent of the transition participants stayed at the same site—34.3 percent of DL and 19.6 percent of IL. Of this group, nearly 60 percent, a surprisingly large fraction, returned to the same job code that they had had before the transition. This was presumably due to either the restoration of production volume in their old work area or a move to another part of the plant but in the same job category as before.

Still in transition

Of those still in the transition program, 20 percent were direct labor and 27.5 percent were indirect labor. Although some were selected for the transition just before the close of our sampling period, most had been in the process for some time, unable or unwilling to find another job inside or outside the company. Sixty-three percent of those still in the transition in June 1986 had held that status for six to 12 months, and another 31 percent had been in the transition for over 12 months. This is in contrast with those participants who had left the transition. Table 23.5 shows that for the bulk of employees who completed the transition, it was a relatively short process, with nearly two-thirds finishing in six months and only 7.7 percent in the process for more than a year.

Indirect and direct labor status

The mobility patterns for IL and DL were strikingly different. Although 55 percent of both direct labor and indirect labor groups either left the company or remained in the transition program, a larger fraction of DL left and a larger fraction of IL remained in the transition. Normally, one would expect that indirect labor workers would have better opportunities in the external labor market and hence would be more likely to leave the firm. Our data suggest, however, that either this expectation is wrong or the indirect labor group felt less pressure to leave than did the direct labor workers.

Comparing transition and nontransition participants

In Table 23.6, the top panel shows quite dramatically that those people who were in the transition program were far more likely to leave the company than were those who were not. This suggests that the transition did in fact help achieve one of the firm's goals, redeploying its employees without laying them off. We still want to know, however, the results of transition's efforts to reskill and redeploy employees within the firm.

Table 23.5. Distribution of time in transition (%)

	Completers only	Still in transition only
0–6 months	63.2	6.3
6–12 months	28.9	62.8
12–24 months	7.5	31.0
24+ months	0.2	0.0
	$n = 1167$	$n = 351$

Source: Personnel files for five manufacturing plants.

Table 23.6. Outcomes for transition and nontransition employees

	Direct labor (%)		Indirect labor (%)	
	Transition	Nontransition	Transition	Nontransition
Stayers and Leavers				
Left	44.7	17.3	38.6	11.6
Same site				
New job	18.2	27.2	10.4	33.8
Same job	25.4	45.0	17.0	40.9
Off site				
New job	7.8	8.0	24.1	10.9
Same job	3.6	2.3	9.9	2.9
	100.0	100.0	100.0	100.0
	$n = 769$	$n = 1453$	$n = 398$	$n = 2004$
Stayers only				
Same site				
New job	32.9	32.8	16.9	38.2
Same job	45.9	54.4	27.6	46.2
New site				
New job	14.1	9.6	39.2	12.3
Same job	6.5	2.7	16.1	3.2
	100.0	100.0	100.0	100.0
	$n = 428$	$n = 1221$	$n = 246$	$n = 1754$

"Still in transition" category excluded from sample.

Source: Personnel files for five manufacturing plants.

In the second panel, we examine the experience of those transition participants who stayed at DEC, using the nontransition group for comparison. We see that for direct labor employees, the transition group was slightly more mobile. A somewhat higher fraction of the transition's DL workers moved to a new site and/or changed jobs, regardless of site, than nontransition DL workers. In contrast, a substantial majority of IL transition employees changed location, whereas only 15 percent of the nontransition IL workers made such a change. But there is much less difference between the two IL groups with respect to job change, with 56 percent of the transition employees changing jobs, compared with 50 percent of the nontransition group. The point is not that IL workers did not change jobs—over half of both groups did so over just a two-year period—but, rather, that the transition only marginally affected that process. For those individuals who did change their job, what was the nature of the shift? In order to answer this question, we developed three measures. The first, called *labor change*, indicates whether a person switched between the DL and IL categories. The second, *occupational change*, measures whether a person moved among the aggregate government occupational categories (these are nine categories such as managerial, technician, craft, and operative). The third measure, *job level*, is based on the salary midpoints of the DEC job classification and characterizes a person as remaining at the same level if the salary of his or her new job was within 10 percent of that of the prior job, as moving up if the salary midpoint were 10 percent or higher, and as moving down if the salary midpoint were 10 percent or less. The relevant data are provided in Table 23.7.

Among direct labor employees, these data suggest that with respect to the labor

Table 23.7. Outcomes of job change (job changes only).

	Direct labor (%)		Indirect labor (%)	
	Transition	Nontransition	Transition	Nontransition
Status Change				
None	60.5	57.7	93.3	98.4
DL to IL	39.5	42.3	—	—
IL to DL	—	—	6.7	1.6
Occupation change				
None	61	63.5	52.3	71.5
Change	39	36.5	47.7	28.5
Job level/skill compensation				
Equivalent (+ 10%)	66.8	51.5	49.6	35.3
Up	20.3	35.8	37.6	60.2
Down	12 9	12.7	12 .8	4.5
	n = 205	n = 537	n = 149	n = 927

Source: Personnel files for five manufacturing plants.

change and occupational change, there was essentially no difference between the transition and the nontransition group. In both cases, about two-thirds of the groups remained in the previous status. However, a portion of the transition people appear to have paid a price with respect to the salary (and hence presumably the skill level) of their job. This shows up not, as one might expect, as a larger fraction of employees actually moving down—the percentages are the same for the two groups—but, rather, as a smaller fraction moving up than was true for the nontransition group. However, keeping in mind that those selected for the transition were frequently the poorer performers, the gap is not especially large and may indicate that the transition workers were protected more than one might have expected.

The difference between the transition and nontransition participants is quite a bit more dramatic for the indirect labor employees. Here, for both the first and the third variable, there is strong evidence that the indirect employees who changed jobs (and, remember, this is a minority of IL workers) were considerably more downward mobile than were the nonparticipants.

This raises again the question noted earlier: Did the transition process tend to select relatively less able IL than DL employees? The smaller differential between transition and nontransition employees in rates of change as well as the worse outcomes for IL employees suggest that this may be the case. Additional evidence is that the relationship between selection and company tenure is weaker for indirect than direct labor, and this implies that (poor) performance was more of a factor in their selection than it was for direct labor.

Restructuring

The final step is to determine how the occupational profiles of the plants changed as a result of the transition process.[1]

Table 23.8 compares the plants before and after the transition. There was a shift in proportion away from direct and toward indirect labor, which is also reflected in

Table 23.8. Plant employment structure before and after transition (%)

	1984	1986[a]
Occupation		
Managers	11.0	12.5
Professionals	16.9	18.2
Technicians	13.5	15.6
Clerical	9.0	9.6
Craft	5.9	5.4
Operative	39.8	33.4
Laborer	2.7	2.8
Service	1.1	2.4
Status		
Direct	48.7	40.9
Indirect	51.3	59.1
Company tenure		
1 year	9.3	0.2
1–2 years	5.2	0.5
2–5 years	25.3	12.2
5–7.5 years	25.8	31.8
7.5–10 years	22.6	26.4
10+ years	11.9	28.8
	$n = 4975$	$n = 3430$

[a]Excludes those who transferred to another plant or left the company and includes those who were hired or transferred during the period.

Source: Personnel tapes for 5 manufacturing plants.

the occupational distribution of the two samples. In the period before the transition, managers and professionals accounted for 28 percent of employment, and after the transition they held 31 percent of all jobs. By the same token, blue-collar labor (craft, operative, and laborer) employment declined from 48 to 42 percent. Technicians, whose status is somewhat ambiguous, recorded a gain in employment shares.

The other striking change is the shift in the tenure profile as a result of the transition. Whereas before the transition there were many recent recruits, after the transition virtually no one in 1986 was employed who had been with the firm less than two years, and the total distribution had shifted well toward the most senior members. This kind of shift brings both opportunities and problems. A long-tenured work force is more skilled and more committed to the firm, but it may be less flexible in its willingness to be retrained or relocated.

DISCUSSION AND IMPLICATIONS

The transition process

The task force balanced centralized principles with decentralized implementation, thus guaranteeing a fair and equitable treatment of "available" employees while honoring the tradition of plant-level autonomy. Although not requiring plant participation, it provided incentives for plants to "buy in" to the process and then gave them the resources for their plant-level efforts and the flexibility to adapt the process. It gained credibility and commitment by assigning primary responsibility for the process to line management, but it also provided a clear support role for corporate and plant-level personnel staff.

One dilemma not completely resolved by the transition experience was how "hard" or "soft" to make the treatment of "available" employees. The task force opted for maximizing the available options and offering training and counseling to help employees make informed choices. But many employees chose to stay "in the transition" for long periods of time, unwilling to accept job opportunities involving redeployment or relocation. Although a person's right to turn down job offers was limited somewhat, the transition participants faced little formal pressure to exit from the process. But although some people may have taken advantage of this policy, it would have been difficult to eliminate such behavior without changing the character of the transition for all those involved in it, thus imperiling the intangible benefits of the process.

Retraining was another problem in the transaction process. The retraining program was offered only to "available" employees who had applied and been accepted for a new job requiring additional skills. Expecting this program to be oversubscribed, the task force established only a few retraining slots. But to their surprise, even these few slots proved difficult to fill. Many employees were unwilling to take the risk of training for a new occupation, even in the face of evidence that their former jobs might be permanently eliminated. For many, past experiences had convinced them that downturns would be brief. Ultimately only 600 employees (23 percent of the transition participants) agreed to be retrained.

On the whole, however, the transition process can be considered a success. Its guidelines were carefully crafted to preserve the respect and dignity of the people participating in it and to maintain a company culture in which local initiative is encouraged. Difficult "turf" issues across functions and divisions were negotiated and resolved. The employment security policy was not challenged, even under pressure to reduce employment.

Transition outcomes

The outcome goals for the transition were to reduce staffing without any layoffs; to move employees internally within DEC by means of transfers and job changes; to assist "available" employees with internal and external job searches and to train them in new skills; to restructure staffing patterns in order to lower the ratio of indirect to direct employees; and to change managerial behaviors and policies that had encouraged overstaffing in the past.

The transition program thus must be judged a mixed success. Among its accomplishments were a substantial reduction of the work force and a significant number of job changes and transfers. Because the transition participants were selected in part because of their low performance ratings, the number of occupational changes and job level increases is impressive, though consistently lower than that for the nontransition group. Some employees were retrained, and this retraining appears to have contributed to some positive job outcomes, particularly for the direct labor group. In areas such as engineering, DEC retained valued employees who might otherwise have left the company.

On the other hand, a high percentage of the staffing left through the voluntary separation program for regular employees and contract terminations for temporary and contract employees. Of those participants who stayed at DEC, a high percentage returned to their former jobs or remained in transition status. A relatively small percentage was retrained, and many retraining slots were left unfilled. There was very little evidence of restructuring, and the ratio of indirect to direct employees actually worsened. Finally, the effort was undoubtedly very costly in staff time, training, and relocation expenses and in the voluntary separation payments.

Measuring the success of the transition program is complicated. If the primary goal is seen as lowering employment levels, it must be judged as peripheral to those efforts that brought about the greatest reduction. Even the contribution of the transition to the flexible redeployment of the work force during a critical adjustment period was perhaps less than the company might have expected. It does, however, seem likely that the effort to preserve the values underlying DEC's commitment to employment security substantially boosted the employees' motivation and loyalty during a difficult period, although these benefits are intangible and difficult to substantiate.

What occurred at DEC was, in the broadest sense, a transition from one set of policies supporting employment security to another set, necessitated by a more competitive and uncertain environment. Sustaining the credibility of the employment security policy, during its most severe challenge, was perhaps the foremost goal of the transition planners. To succeed meant, first and foremost, preserving DEC's values. This explains the strong emphasis of the transition task force on those aspects of the process concerning individual dignity and choice.

One discovery that DEC made was that offering employment security did not automatically motivate employees to learn new skills, change jobs, or relocate to the extent demanded by the crisis. In the past, the company had always shown its readiness to move work, build inventory, or sustain short-term inefficiencies in order to maintain employment security. Now that these policies have changed, one challenge for DEC is persuading employees that sustaining employment security requires from them a greater readiness to engage in ongoing training and accept new job assignments. The transition program marks the first step in that process, but a vital step, for its reaffirmation of company values will allow the process to continue.

Ultimately, the most significant question is whether DEC will learn from its experiences and avoid the need for another transition effort in the future. It is clear that "veterans" of transition—those managers who directly experienced the process—have learned a great deal and are motivated to change the policies that lead to overstaffing. But at a time when DEC's fortunes have rebounded and employment levels are rising again, it is not clear whether managers without this direct experience have any inclination to change.

The following quotations illustrate both the power and the limited diffusion of the learning that resulted from the transition process. One plant manager described the transition as a powerful learning experience:

> We used to hire contract people to use our space to capacity, even though we were less productive with more people. Now we don't let the departments use all their floor space. We don't automatically equate "bigness" with "goodness" anymore. And we don't automatically replace people. We look for ways to combine functions. I don't ever want to hire another direct labor person again. That's probably too strong, but before I hire another person, I'd better be convinced that I have a job for that person as long as I'm working here. I don't want to have to go through this process again.

When asked to describe what changed during the transition, an engineering product manager had these thoughts:

> I sign all requisitions for new people, and I sign them differently now than I used to. I know that we need to have a long-term plan for using each person. The mind-set has changed about human resource planning. Before, the first thought when people were needed was to go out and hire them or transfer them in from somewhere. Only then would we think of training. Now we reverse this—train first, transfer if necessary, and as a last resort hire from the outside if the skills aren't available.

A personnel manager from the same manufacturing group, responding to these remarks, countered with the following:

> What the engineering product manager does now does not reflect management in general. He has gone through managing the transition and learned from it. He's the leading positive example of what we need to do here, but he's not the norm. In fact, in general, reassignment was an "event." It will be out of the organization's memory in six months. Most senior managers here avoided it, saw themselves victimized by it, and therefore won't learn from it.

Human resource strategy

What does the DEC experience tell us about what is required to maintain a commitment to employment security in today's market and technological environment? For the purposes of our discussion we assume that the environment facing most firms will be characterized by (1) variable or uncertain growth prospects—that is, some product lines will be growing rapidly while others are stabilizing or declining; (2) product and process technologies are changing rapidly; (3) cost competition is increasing for both mature and new products; and (4) product life cycles are shortening. The experiences of DEC suggest the following:

1. Human resource policies that are driven by management pressures to "ship at all costs" are not compatible with employment security, as they lead to overstaffing and underinvestment in training.
2. Transition processes such as the one reviewed here are likely to be recurring phenomena in employment security firms. If DEC's experience can be generalized, it would imply that firms must be prepared to absorb the costs of reducing their work force slowly, invest in various financial incentives for voluntary sev-

erance and early retirement, and absorb the costs associated with this transition strategy as an investment in the commitment and flexibility that this policy is expected to achieve. In the long run this will require an agreement among management decision makers on the broader concept of organizational effectiveness that goes beyond traditional short-term cost considerations.

3. In this environment, human resource professionals will need to participate more in new product planning and other strategic decision-making processes. The life cycle of the product, its marketing strategy, and the timing of replacement products all are crucial determinants of human resource requirements and not only must be coordinated but also must be influenced by the organization's long-term human resource strategies and capabilities.
4. Training will need to take on a higher priority as an ongoing investment activity. The DEC experience demonstrated clearly the work force's limited ability and/or willingness to be retrained in a crisis (i.e., as part of the transition process). Yet DEC's earlier strategy of hiring first and training only as a last resort must be reversed. What some managers have learned about retraining first and only hiring as a last resort will have to be adopted everywhere. A corporate-level commitment to ongoing training will be needed to support an employment security policy in this type of environment.

Public policy implications

This case raises several salient questions with respect to public policy. On a positive note, it is apparent that DEC succeeded in maintaining employment levels higher than those that would have been characteristic of a hire–fire firm faced with comparable product market difficulties. This strongly indicates that firm-level employment security policies have desirable macroeconomic consequences and therefore warrant the support of national policymakers. The question, then, is how to encourage and diffuse these practices. It is apparent from this case that the costs of undertaking the policy are substantial and that the gains, although significant, are difficult to identify and quantify. Furthermore, those in most corporations who focus on cost controls are not the same people who receive the benefits. Without some support and encouragement, firms that lack the strong commitment to employment security that is characteristic of DEC's culture are unlikely to undertake these efforts. The question then is whether public training subsidies can help tip the balance in the firm's calculations. Considerable thought would need to be given to the design of such subsidies. Certainly these programs would need to be ongoing and not simply emergency responses to crises.

By the same token, the case of DEC also makes clear that private efforts to provide employment security cannot suffice as a national policy. Even at DEC, many temporary workers were released into the labor market, as were those who accepted its incentive retirement schemes. If these groups have difficulty finding new employment, and especially if they are composed disproportionately of women and minority groups, then it seems that a strengthened training and employment exchange will be appropriate.

What these considerations imply is that employment security efforts by private firms represent useful and powerful tools in more general efforts to reduce insecurity in the labor market. Employment security programs in firms need to be encouraged and supported; the difficult issue is how to diffuse these practices. An important task for future research is to design models that permit public policy to encourage such private action. At the same time, even if these policies were widely adopted, they would not be sufficient, and hence continued public programs would be necessary.

ACKNOWLEDGMENT

Funds for this research were provided by the Management in the 1990s research program of the Sloan School of Management, Massachusetts Institute of Technology. The authors are grateful to the Digital Equipment Corporation for its assistance and cooperation with this project and to Ed Schein and Robert McKersie for their comments on an earlier draft. The authors remain solely responsible for the contents of the article.

NOTE

1. We already examined this issue partially in the previous section, when considering the occupational and job-level changes for transition versus nontransition participants. To get a comprehensive "before" and "after" profile of each plant, however, we added data on new hires and transfers in during the two-year period

REFERENCES

Deal, T. E., & A. A. Kennedy (1982). *Corporate culture*. Reading, MA: Addison Wesley.

Dyer, L., F. Foltman, & G. Milkovich (1985). Contemporary employment stabilization practices. In T. A. Kochan, and T. A. Barocci (Eds.), *Human resource management and industrial relations*, pp. 203–14. Boston: Little, Brown.

Fombrun, C. J., N. M. Tichy, & M. A. Devanna (1984). *Strategic human resource management*. New York: Wiley.

Foulkes, F. K. (1980). *Personnel practices of large non-union companies*. Englewood Cliffs, NJ: Prentice-Hall.

Foulkes, F. K., & A. Whitman (1985). Marketing strategies to maintain full employment. *Harvard Business Review*, July-August, pp. 30–35.

Jacoby, S. (1985). *Employing bureaucracy: Managers, unions, and the transformation of work in American industry*. New York: Columbia University Press .

Kochan, T. A., & T. A. Barocci (Eds.) (1985). *Human resource management and industrial relations.* Boston: Little, Brown.

McKersie, R., L. Greenhalgh, & R. Gilkey (1985). Rebalancing the workforce at IBM: A case study of redeployment and revitalization. Working paper no. 1718–85, Sloan School of Management, Massachusetts Institute of Technology.

Osterman, P. (1984). *Internal labor markets*. Cambridge, MA: MIT Press.

——— (1988). *Employment futures: Reorganization, dislocation, and public policy*. Oxford: Oxford University Press.

Schein, E. (1983). The role of the founder in creating organizational culture. *Organizational Dynamics*, Summer, pp. 13–28.

Schuler, R. S., & S. E. Jackson (1987). Linking competitive strategies with human resource practices. *Academy of Management Executives*, August, pp. 207–20.

Contributors

THOMAS J. ALLEN is the Gordon Y. Billard Fund Professor of Management at the Sloan School of Management, Massachusetts Institute of Technology. He served as research director of the Management in the 1990s Program.

LOTTE BAILYN is professor of organizational psychology and management at the Sloan School of Management, Massachusetts Institute of Technology.

ROBERT I. BENJAMIN is visiting research associate at the Center for Information Systems Research, Massachusetts Institute of Technology, and is a consultant on information technology and its effects on organizational strategy.

STANLEY M. BESEN is senior economist at the RAND Corporation.

JOHN S. CARROLL is professor of behavioral and policy sciences at the Sloan School of Management, Massachusetts Institute of Technology.

JOHN CHALYKOFF is associate professor of industrial relations and human resource management at the University of New Brunswick.

JAY C. COOPRIDER is assistant professor of information systems at the Graduate School of Business, University of Texas at Austin.

KEVIN CROWSTON is assistant professor of computer and information systems at the School of Business Administration, University of Michigan.

SUMANTRA GHOSHAL is associate professor of business policy at the European Institute of Business Administration (INSEAD).

OSCAR HAUPTMAN is assistant professor in the Production Operations Management Group, Graduate School of Business, Harvard University.

JOHN C. HENDERSON is professor of management information systems and director of the Systems Research Center, Boston University School of Management.

CHARLES JONSCHER is chief executive of the Central Europe Trust Company.

THOMAS A. KOCHAN is George Maverick Bunker Professor of Management at the Sloan School of Management, Massachusetts Institute of Technology.

JEONGSUK KOH is an associate with McKinsey & Co.

JOHN D. C. LITTLE is Institute Professor at the Massachusetts Institute of Technology.

GARY W. LOVEMAN is assistant professor of business administration at the Graduate School of Business, Harvard University.

LISA M. LYNCH is I. R. I. Career Development Associate Professor of Management at the Sloan School of Management, Massachusetts Institute of Technology.

JOHN PAUL MACDUFFIE holds the Roger Stone Term Chair at the Wharton School of the University of Pennsylvania, where he is assistant professor of management.

THOMAS W. MALONE is Patrick J. McGovern Professor of Information Systems at the Sloan School of Management, Massachusetts Institute of Technology.

PAUL OSTERMAN is professor of management at the Sloan School of Management, Massachusetts Institute of Technology.

BRIAN T. PENTLAND is assistant professor of organizational behavior and human resource management at the School of Business Administration, University of Michigan.

CONSTANCE PERIN is research scientist with the International Program for Enhanced Nuclear Power Plant Safety, Massachusetts Institute of Technology.

MICHAEL J. PIORE is professor of economics and management at the Massachusetts Institute of Technology.

LAURA POPPO is assistant professor of organization and strategy at the Olin School of Business, Washington University.

GARTH SALONER is professor of strategic management and economics at the Graduate School of Business, Stanford University.

EDGAR H. SCHEIN is professor of management at the Sloan School of Management, Massachusetts Institute of Technology.

MICHAEL S. SCOTT MORTON is the Jay W. Forrester Professor of Management at the Sloan School of Management, Massachusetts Institute of Technology. He served as director of the Management in the 1990s Program.

N. VENKATRAMAN is Richard S. Leghorn (1939) Management of Technological Innovation Career Development Associate Professor of Management at the Sloan School of Management, Massachusetts Institute of Technology.

ERIC VON HIPPEL is professor of management at the Sloan School of Management, Massachusetts Institute of Technology.

GORDON WALKER is adjunct associate professor at the School of Organization and Management, Yale University.

D. ELEANOR WESTNEY is associate professor in international management at the Sloan School of Management, Massachusetts Institute of Technology.

JOANNE YATES is associate professor of management at the Sloan School of Management, Massachusetts Institute of Technology.

AKBAR ZAHEER is assistant professor of management at the Curtis Carlson School of Management, University of Minnesota.

Index